Barbara S. Arnold

German Grammar and Usage

German Grammar and Usage

A E Hammer

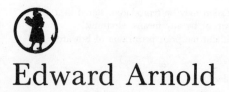

Edward Arnold

First published in Great Britain 1971
by Edward Arnold (Publishers) Ltd.
41 Bedford Square
London WC1B 3DQ

Edward Arnold (Australia) Pty Ltd.
80 Waverley Road
Caulfield East 3145
PO Box 234
Melbourne

First published in United States of America 1983
by Edward Arnold
3 East Read Street
Baltimore
Maryland 21202

First published as a paperback 1973
Reprinted with corrections 1974
Reprinted with corrections 1976
Reprinted with extensive corrections 1977
Reprinted with corrections 1978
Reprinted with corrections 1980
Reprinted with corrections and Supplement 1983
Reprinted with corrections 1984
Reprinted 1985, 1986, 1987

ISBN: 0 7131 5699 6

Text set in 9/10 pt. 'Monotype' Baskerville
Printed in Hong Kong by
Wing King Tong Co Ltd

PREFACE

This book is intended as a reference grammar for sixth form and university use, while teachers may also find it helpful. I have sought to test traditional rules and forms by current German practice, to avoid smoothing over the complications and vagaries of a living language and at the same time to present its complexities in as handy a form as possible. I hope the user may find that the book answers a good many of the questions.

No one writing a book on German grammar at this point of time starts from scratch or can avoid indebtedness to earlier workers in the field. My own great and principal debt is to the Dudenverlag in Mannheim and to the grey volumes of 'Der große Duden'. Volume 4, *Grammatik* (1966), has been invaluable as a sheer guide for the ground to be covered, as a reminder of many details which might have escaped inclusion (the paragraphs on the uses of the subjunctive may serve as an example) and for its exhaustive lists (e.g. of nouns with double genders, of adjectives used with the dative and of verbs with prepositional constructions). In the case of particularly helpful and perceptive sections of Duden, I have given specific references; factually, my chapter on word formation owes most to the *Grammatik*. Where I have used examples from Duden, I have frequently mentioned the fact, and always where the example is a quotation. I should, however, say that I have never accepted Duden as infallible, have frequently checked his rulings by reference to the layman and sometimes reached different conclusions. Exceptions to this are the chapters on orthography and punctuation, which are based more or less unquestioningly on the *Duden-Taschenbücher* listed in the Bibliography and especially on vol. 3, from which my examples are largely taken. Finally, I cannot forbear mentioning a magic week's work, in August 1967, at the 'Sprachberatungsstelle' of the Dudenverlag in Mannheim, with Dr. Wolfgang Mentrup as my untiring guide, philosopher and friend; he has been equally untiring in answering queries by letter.

My book owes much, too, to the Anglo-German dictionary of Muret-Sanders and to *Cassell's New German Dictionary* by Dr. H. T. Betteridge, who very kindly gave me permission to draw on his admirable examples without individual acknowledgement, which, in the event, I have only sometimes presumed to do.

My indebtedness to the other items of the Bibliography has everywhere been specifically indicated. Beyond that, I owe something to the sound competence of F. R. H. McLellan's book and to J. A. Corbett's very full treatment of prepositions, while my section on the rendering of English prepositions in further contexts goes back to paragraph 296 in H. S. Beresford-Webb's *Practical German Grammar*; I also owe something to the treatment of prefixes in that book.

Some of my illustrative quotations are taken from papers set at Advanced Level by the Oxford and Cambridge Schools Examination Board and for Cambridge Scholarship Examinations; some of these come from works that I have not read.

I acknowledge with pleasure and sincere gratitude my debt to countless Germans of every age and calling, some of them complete strangers, who have willingly submitted to linguistic interrogations and have furthered my attempt to make this book at least an approximate reflection of current German usage. (As the late Professor Boyanus once observed, 'the native is always right'.) Even those who have, in addition, meticulously answered many pages of queries by letter are too numerous to mention by name. I must, however, make an exception in the case of my friend Dr. Günther Deitenbeck, of the Zeppelin-Gymnasium, Lüdenscheid, and his family, who have helped me indefatigably over so many years.

Among those on this side of the North Sea who have kindly helped me in various ways, I would particularly like to thank Dr. C. H. Good, of the University of East Anglia, who read the manuscript, correcting many points of detail and suggesting numerous, in some cases far-reaching improvements; Mr. C. W. Oakley, Head of the Modern Languages Department, Selhurst Grammar School for Boys, Croydon, who checked the proofs and suggested various clarifications; and Mr. J. A. Towers, sometime Senior Mathematics Master at Sedbergh School, who supplied the material from which 'some contemporary mathematical terms' (paragraph 259) were selected.

Finally, I gratefully remember the late Dr. S. H. Steinberg and his ever ready collaboration in the production of a privately printed booklet of German Grammar Notes that formed the nucleus of the present volume.

A. E. H.

London
June, 1971

POINTS FOR THE USER

1. Lists of words are in general alphabetical, though occasionally a deviation from this has seemed more helpful.
2. Where required, a noun is followed by a bracket containing its nominative plural in abbreviated form, e.g. das Lager (–) = die Lager; der Hut (–e) = die Hüte; (–en, –en) and (–n, –n) indicate that the noun has those endings except in the nominative singular, e.g. der Affe (–n, –n).
3. A separable prefix is indicated by a hyphen, but where this factor is of no immediate relevance, the hyphen is often omitted in the interests of clarity.
4. Where required, a stressed word is indicated by italics, a stressed syllable by a grave accent, e.g. Ich habe die Birne *ihr* gegeben; der Dòktor, die Doktòren.
5. All numbers refer to paragraphs, unless preceded by p. or pp., when they refer to pages.
6. For time phrases, the user should go to Chapter X; they have been kept to a minimum in the chapter on prepositions.
7. North German, rather than South German, has been taken as standard.
8. The symbol (**S**) indicates that additional matter will be found in the Supplement (pp. 421ff.). There is one new paragraph, 286A, treating 'da' as a particle. The Index does not include references to the Supplement.

CONTENTS[1]

---

[1] The numbers following the sections of each chapter refer to paragraphs, not pages.

1*

[1] For Subordinating Conjunctions not included in E—I, see D.

BIBLIOGRAPHY

Agricola, Erhard, *Wörter und Wendungen*, Leipzig, 1968
Bech, Gunnar, *Studien über das deutsche Verbum Infinitum*, Copenhagen, 1955 and 1957
Beresford-Webb, H. S., *A Practical German Grammar*, Longmans, 1914
Betteridge, H. T., *Cassell's New German Dictionary*, 1957
Carstensen, Broder, *Englische Einflüsse auf die deutsche Sprache nach 1945*, Heidelberg, 1965
Collinson, W. E., *The German Language Today*, Hutchinson's University Library, 1968
Corbett, J. A., *Essentials of Modern German Grammar*, Harrap, 1948
Der Große Duden, Dudenverlag, Mannheim
   1 *Rechtschreibung*, 1967
   2 *Stilwörterbuch*, 1963
   4 *Grammatik*, 1966
   8 *Synonymwörterbuch*, 1964
   9 *Hauptschwierigkeiten*, 1965
Duden-Taschenbücher
   1 *Komma, Punkt und alle anderen Satzzeichen*, 1968, by Dieter Berger
   3 *Die Regeln der deutschen Rechtschreibung*, 1968, by Wolfgang Mentrup
   6 *Wann schreibt man groß, wann schreibt man klein?* 1969, by Wolfgang Mentrup and others
Eggeling, H. F., *A Dictionary of Modern German Prose Usage*, Oxford, Clarendon Press, 1961
Erben, Johannes, *Abriß der deutschen Grammatik*, Darmstadt, 1963
Es geht weiter, Everyday German by Radio, B.B.C., 1965
Fleischer, Wolfgang, *Wortbildung der deutschen Gegenwartssprache*, Leipzig, 1969
Grubačić, Emilija, *Untersuchungen zur Frage der Wortstellung in der deutschen Prosadichtung der letzten Jahrzehnte*, Zagreb, 1965
Mater, Erich, *Rückläufiges Wörterbuch der deutschen Gegenwartssprache*, Leipzig, 1965
McLellan, F. R. H., *A School Grammar of Modern German*, Cambridge University Press, 1938
Möller, Georg, *Deutsch von Heute*, Leipzig, 1962
Muret-Sanders, *Enzyklopädisches englisch-deutsches und deutsch-englisches Wörterbuch*, Berlin, 1910
Schulz-Griesbach, *Grammatik der deutschen Sprache*, Longmans-Hueber, 1965
Stopp, F. J., *A Manual of Modern German*, University Tutorial Press, 1960
Wahrig, Gerhard, *Deutsches Wörterbuch*, Gütersloh, 1968

Articles from periodicals are mentioned at the relevant place in the text.

List of main authors and journals quoted

Vicki Baum	Gerd Gaiser	Thomas Mann
Heinrich Böll	Albrecht Goes	Theodor Plievier
Hermann Broch	Michael Horbach	Thomas Valentin
Hans Fallada	Annette Kolb	Ingeborg Wendt
Max Frisch	Elisabeth Langgässer	Carl Zuckmayer

Also numerous authors included in the anthology *Erfundene Wahrheit, Deutsche Geschichten seit 1945*, herausgegeben von Marcel Reich-Ranicki, München, 1965

Frankfurter Allgemeine Zeitung   *Der Spiegel*
Hamburger Abendblatt   *Süddeutsche Zeitung*
                                          Die Zeit

ABBREVIATIONS

A., acc.	accusative	m., masc.	masculine
adj.	adjective(s)	MHG	Middle High German
adv.	adverb	misc.	miscellaneous
attrib.	attributive	N.	Note; Nominative
ch., chap.	chapter	n., neut.	neuter
cl.	clause	neg.	negative
coll.	colloquial	nom.	nominative
compar.	comparative	obj.	object
condit.	conditional	obs.	obsolete
conj.	conjunction	OHG	Old High German
D., dat.	dative	o.s.	oneself
decl.	declension, declined	part.	participle
def. art.	definite article	perf.	perfect
demonstr.	demonstrative	pers.	person
dimin.	diminutive	phr.	phrase(s)
dir.	direct	pl., plur.	plural
elev.	elevated style	pluperf.	pluperfect
exc.	except, exception(s)	possess.	possessive
f., fem.	feminine	prep.	preposition, prepositional
fig.	figurative(ly)	pres.	present
Fr.	French	pron.	pronoun; pronounced
fut.	future	refl.	reflexive
G., gen.	genitive	rel.	relative
Gn.	German	(s)	conjugated with 'sein'
Gr.	Group	s.o.	someone
(h)	conjugated with 'haben'	s.th.	something
imperf.	imperfect	sep.	separable
impers.	impersonal	sing.	singular
indecl.	indeclinable	sl.	slang
indef. (art.)	indefinite (article)	str.	strong
indic.	indicative	sub. cl.	subordinate clause
indir.	indirect	subj.	subjunctive
inf., infin.	infinitive	subst.	substantive, substantival
insep.	inseparable	superl.	superlative
interrog.	interrogative	tr.	transitive
intr.	intransitive	uninfl.	uninflected
lit.	literal(ly)	wk.	weak

The five volumes of *Der große Duden* listed in the Bibliography are respectively referred to as:

Du. Rechtschreibung

Du. Stil.

Du. Gram.

Du. Synonymwörterbuch

Du. Haupt.

Newspapers:

FAZ = Frankfurter Allgemeine Zeitung

Hbg. Abendblatt = Hamburger Abendblatt

Spiegel = Der Spiegel

SZ = Süddeutsche Zeitung

Zeit = Die Zeit

I NOUNS

A. GENDER RULES

1. **German nouns are masculine, feminine or neuter,** e.g. der Tisch *table*, die Blume *flower*, das Buch *book*.
There are a certain number of useful gender rules, but it is all-important to learn all nouns with their definite article. With growing familiarity with the language, the ear becomes increasingly helpful for determining the gender of a noun not covered by rules, e.g. 'der Schrank' sounds right; 'die Schrank' and 'das Schrank' sound wrong. The Plural Lists (20 ff.) are also a mine of gender information.
Only those gender rules are here given, which, in the author's view and experience, are of practical use.

2. **Masculine by meaning are:**

   (a) **Names of male persons and animals** (but see 8):
   der Vater, der Arzt, der Tischler *carpenter*, der Löwe, der Hengst *stallion*.

   Note:
   i The species may be masc., fem. or neut., e.g. der Fisch, die Ratte, das Pferd.
   ii In the absence of a current specific term, the male or female of any species of animal or bird, irrespective of size, may be indicated by 'das Männchen' or 'das Weibchen', e.g. das Zebramännchen, das Weibchen des Elefanten.
   iii The terms for the young (human and animal) are neuter (see 6(a)).

   (b) **A picture by such-and-such an artist:** Er will seinen Rembrandt verkaufen.

   (c) **Most instruments or inanimate agents in -er:** der Computer, der Wagenheber *jack*, der Wecker *alarm-clock*.
   They are masculine by analogy with animate agents (der Bäcker, der Maler); in other words, they are personified. In some cases the same word may denote an animate and an inanimate agent: der Anhänger 1. *adherent* 2. *trailer*; der Hörer 1. *listener* 2. *receiver, headphone*.

(d) **Makes of cars** ('der Wagen' being understood): der Mercedes, der Opel, der Rolls-Royce.

(e) **Seasons, months, days of week, points of compass:** der Frühling, der Januar, der Montag, der Norden.

3. Masculine by form are:

(a) **Nouns in -ich, -ig, -ing, -ling:** der Teppich, der Honig, der Hering, der Liebling.

(b) **Foreign nouns in -ant, -ast, -ismus, -or:** der Konsonant, der Kontrast, der Idealismus, der Regulator.

Some further foreign suffixes mainly denote male persons: der Ingenieur, der Offizier, der Optimist (male or female), der Student.

(c) **Most nouns 'formed from strong verb stems to which nothing has been added'**[1] (cf. 714): der Biß *bite,* der Fall *fall; case,* der Wurf *throw* (BUT: die Falle *trap,* die Flucht *flight*).
Common exceptions are: das Band *bond; ribbon,* das Grab *grave,* das Leid *harm; sorrow, care,* das Maß *measurement,* das Schloß *lock; castle,* das Verbot *prohibition.*

4. Feminine by meaning are:

(a) **Names of female persons and animals** (but see 8): die Mutter, die Ärztin, die Löwin, die Stute *mare.*

Note:
i The commonest way of forming nouns denoting females is to add -in to the masculine form, often with Umlaut (cf. 715(c)).
ii All diminutives in -chen, -lein etc. are neuter (see 7(b)); therefore: das Mädchen, das Fräulein.

(b) **Most makes of aeroplanes** ('die Maschine' being understood): eine Boeing 727, die Comet, eine Junker (eine Ju) 52, BUT: der PAN-AM Clipper, der Starfighter.

(c) **Ships named after countries or towns** (die Deutschland, die Bremen) **and many others** (e.g. die Bismarck, die Graf Spee).

(d) **German rivers:** die Donau, die Mosel, die Ruhr. Exc. der Rhein, der Main, der Neckar, der Inn, der Lech.
Non-German rivers are mainly masculine, e.g. der Ganges, der Nil, der Severn, but those ending in -a or -e are feminine, e.g. die Wolga, die Loire, die Themse.

(e) **Cardinal numbers:** eine Null (0), eine Fünf; ich habe für den Aufsatz eine Eins[2] bekommen.
Hundert and Tausend are feminine when they denote 'the numerical symbol, but neuter when used substantivally as a unit of quantity (cf. 245(b)). Thus: Unter die Tausend schrieb er eine Hundert. BUT: das erste Tausend Soldaten.

---

[1] from Corbett, op. cit., 62(c).
[2] the best of the six grades (Noten) used in German schools.

5. Feminine by form are:

(a) **Most nouns in -e:** die Blume, die Garage, die Wärme.

EXCEPTIONS:

i Names of male persons and animals: der Junge, der Lotse *pilot* (of ship), der Riese, der Löwe.

ii 7 masculines in Group 1, usually without -n in nom. sing., e.g. der Name (see 20).

iii der Käse (see 50).

iv Most nouns with prefix Ge- (see 27), these being mainly neuter: das Gebäude, das Gelaufe *running about, bustle*.

v das Auge, das Ende, das Erbe *inheritance*, das Interesse.

(b) **Nouns with the suffixes -ei, -heit, -keit, -schaft, -ung:** die Schmeichelei, die Kindheit, die Ehrlichkeit, die Freundschaft, die Landung.

Exc. das Petschaft *seal, signet*.[1]

(c) **Foreign nouns in -a[2], -anz, -enz, -ie, -ik, -ion, -tät, -ur:** die Kamera, die Eleganz, die Existenz, die Biologie, die Musik, die Explosion, die Qualität, die Natur.

Exc. der Atlantik, der Pazifik, der Spion; das Genie *genius*, das Stadion *stadium*.

6. Neuter by meaning are:

(a) **Most terms for the young (human and animal):** das Baby, das Kind, das Mündel *ward, minor*; das Ferkel *young pig*, das Füllen *foal*, das Kalb, das Küken *chick*, das Lamm.

Note: In the absence of a specific term, the substantival adjective das Junge (ein Junges) is used, e.g. das Junge des Leoparden.

(b) **Continents, countries, towns:** das gärende Afrika *Africa in ferment*; das schöne Italien; Paris—ich liebe es!

EXCEPTIONS:

MASCULINE, generally used with definite article: (der) Irak, (der) Iran, der Jemen, der Kongo, der Libanon, der Sudan; der Haag *The Hague*.

FEMININE, always used with definite article:
i die Schweiz ii countries in -ei: die Tschechoslowakei iii die Bundesrepublik Deutschland (die BRD), die Deutsche Demokratische Republik (die DDR), die Sowjetunion (die UdSSR).

N.B. UdSSR = Union der Sozialistischen Sowjetrepubliken.
USSR = Ukrainische Sozialistische Sowjetrepublik.

PLURAL: die Niederlande, die Vereinigten Staaten (von Amerika), die US(A). While officially die USA is plural, in conversation it is generally treated as fem. sing.: die USA hat (haben) noch nicht geantwortet; in der (den) USA.

For the gender of names of regions (der Balkan, die Arktis, das Elsaß)

---

[1] of Czech origin; MHG petschat; the f crept in by analogy.
[2] but not in -ma (see 31(b)ii).

consult a dictionary. The 11 Länder of the German Federal Republic are all neuter, e.g. das eigenwillige Bayern.

(c) **Metals:** das Eisen, das Kupfer.
Exc. der Stahl, die Bronze.

(d) **Other parts of speech used as nouns:** das Schwimmen, ein zartes Blau, das vertraute Du, sein ewiges Nein, das Für und Wider, das Jenseits *the next world*, das Ach (cf. 639).
Exc. der Rechtsaußen *outside right*, der Linksinnen, and Cardinals (see 4(e)).

(e) **Onomatopoeic words:** das Kikeriki *cock-a-doodle-doo*, das Tucktuck-tuck des Motors.
The numerous masculine exceptions are generally well established words, some of which have further, derived meanings:
der Klaps (–e) *smack, slap*; '*screw loose*' (sl.)
der Klatsch (–e) *smack, crack* (of whip); *gossip*
der Krach (–e) *crash*; *noise, din*; *quarrel*; *bankruptcy*
der Puff (–e) *puff, bang*; *blow, nudge*
Also e.g. der Bums, der Plumps, der Schwaps.

(f) **Letters of the alphabet:** ein großes M, das hohe C.

(g) **Fractions:** das Fünftel. Exc. die Hälfte.

7. Neuter by form are:

(a) **Most nouns with the prefix Ge-;** see 27.

(b) **Diminutives in -chen, -el, -erl, -le, -lein and -li:** das Bäumchen, das Mädel, das Fräulein (cf. 715(b), but see also 672(b)iii).

(c) **Nouns in -nis:** das Ereignis, das Gefängnis, das Geheimnis.
The five commonest fem. exceptions are: die Erlaubnis, die Ersparnis *saving*, die Finsternis, die Kenntnis, die Wildnis.

(d) **Nouns in -tum:** das Christentum *Christianity*. das Eigentum *property*.
Exc. der Irrtum *error*, der Reichtum *wealth*.

(e) **Foreign nouns in -at, -ett, -fon (older: -phon), -ma, -ment, -um, -ium:** das Internat *boarding-school*, das Ballett, das Telefon, das Klima *climate*, das Experiment, das Album, das Stadium *stage, phase*.
Exc. die Firma, der Zement.

B. MISCELLANEOUS GENDER POINTS

8. Some anomalous genders of names of human beings

die Memme *coward* (commoner: der Feigling)
die Ordonnanz *orderly*
die Person *person*
die Wache *guard, sentry*
die Waise *orphan* (m. or f.)
   (BUT: zum Waisen machen *to orphan*)

das Genie *genius* (creative power + person)
das Haupt *head* (e.g. of family, the state) cf. das Staatsoberhaupt
das Individuum *individual*
das Mitglied *member*
das Weib *woman, wife* (archaic, elev. or pejorative)

9. Teil *part, share* is generally masc. in modern German: dieser Teil von Deutschland; er behielt den größeren Teil. It is neut. in certain fixed phrases, e.g. du hast dein Teil getan, ich für mein Teil; see dictionary. Compounds of 'Teil' (they all add -e to form plural):

DER Anteil, Hinterteil *back part*; *stern.*

DAS Abteil, Erbteil, Gegenteil, Hinterteil *buttocks, crupper*, Oberteil, Vorderteil.

10. Meter and its compounds:
Meter, Millimeter and Zentimeter are officially neuter, but colloquially they are often masculine; in Switzerland they are officially masc.
Kilometer and Gasometer are masculine.
Barometer and Thermometer are neuter.

11. Fußball is masculine, both for the ball and the game.

12. Compound nouns have the gender of the last component: der Pflaumenbaum, die Bushaltestelle, das Seebad.

EXCEPTIONS:
i Compounds of 'der Mut': about half are feminine:
DER Edelmut, Freimut, Gleichmut, Hochmut, Kleinmut, Mißmut, Übermut, Unmut, Wankelmut.
DIE Anmut, Demut, Großmut, Langmut, Sanftmut, Schwermut, Wehmut.
(die Armut *poverty* is not a compound of 'Mut'.)
ii die Scheu *timidity* BUT: der Abscheu *abhorrence.*
iii das Wort *word* BUT: die Antwort *answer.*

13. The gender of abbreviations is determined by the basic word, e.g. die CDU (die Christlich-Demokratische Union), die NATO (die Organisation). (See also 6(b): Exceptions) Cf. colloquial abbreviations: der Krimi (der Kriminalroman), die Kripo (die Kriminalpolizei), die Uni (die Universität), das Labor (das Laboratorium).

14. The gender of foreign loan-words in German[1] (See also 3(b), 5(c), 7(e).)

(a) **Greek and Latin loan-words** normally retain their original gender: der Planet, der Zirkus; die Dosis, die Kamera; das Symptom, das Album.

(b) **(S) French masc. nouns:**
i all animates are masc. in German: der Ingenieur, der Kadett.
ii nouns in -ant are masc. in German: der Konsonant ['nant]
iii nouns in -age are fem. in German: die Etage (pron. as 3 syllables).
iv nouns in -et and -ment are neut. in German: das Ballett, das Instrument, das Abonnement; exc. der Zement.
v the remainder are partly masc. and partly neut. in German: der Karton, der Likör; das Bonbon, das Café, das Restaurant [rã:]

Words derived from French fem. nouns are fem. in German; -tät corresponds to French -té: die Existenz, die Fassade, die Nation, die Qualität.

[1] cf. Corbett, op. cit., 65.

(c) **English (and American) words** are mainly masc. (der Boom, der Job, der Slogan, der Streik, der Trend) or neut. (das Hobby, das Image, das Make-up, das Quiz, das Understatement).[1]

Sometimes an analogous German or French word decides the gender; where the English word is fem. in German, this is almost always the case. Thus:

der Container (cf. 2(c))	die Story (die Historie)
der Hit (der Schlager)	das Dumping (corresponds to a
die City (la cité)	Germ. infin. used as a noun)
die Party (die Partie)	das Festival (das Fest)

15. **Nouns with varying genders:** there are very many of these; the following list is selected from Du. Gram. 1385, with the gender most commonly used:

der Abscheu *abhorrence*	das Match *match, game*
der Barock *Baroque*	der Meteor *meteor*
der Chor *choir; chancel*	das Pendel *pendulum*
der Dschungel *jungle*	das Radar *radar*
das Gelee *jelly*	das Radio *radio*
der Kehricht *sweepings, refuse*	das Taxi *taxi* (commoner: die Taxe)
der Keks *biscuit*	das (Vogel)bauer *bird-cage*
der Knäuel *skein, tangle*	das Willkommen *welcome*
der Kompromiß *compromise*	das Zepter *sceptre*
der Liter *litre*	das Zubehör *accessories*

16. For lists of **double genders with different meanings,** see 39.

C. PLURAL FORMATION

17. **Note on the Plural Groups in 18:**

i In the way in which they form the plural, German nouns fall into 7 main groups.

ii The plural groups supersede the older terminology of strong, weak and mixed declensions; a scheme similar to that given in 18 is used in Schulz-Griesbach, op. cit., C 101.

iii The following vowels can have Umlaut (modification): a, o, u, au; in the case of Groups 4 and 5, (⸚e) and (⸚er) imply 'with Umlaut where possible'.

iv (-(e)n), in Groups 6 and 7, means that -n is added to nouns ending in -e, in unstressed vowel + l or in unstressed vowel + r; otherwise -en is added. E.g.

Nom. Sing.	Nom. Plur.	Nom. Sing.	Nom. Plur.
die Schule	die Schulen	die Uhr	die Uhren
die Tafel	die Tafeln	der Pfau	die Pfauen
der Nachbar	die Nachbarn		

v Where two examples are followed by 'etc.', this means that they are the first two nouns of the corresponding list; these lists follow in 20–26.

[1] Regarding the spread and influence of English and American words, see articles by D.V. White, Estelle Morgan and David Heard in *Modern Languages*, June 1959, June 1965 and December 1970 respectively; Du. Haupt.: Amerikanismen/Anglizismen; and Carstensen, op. cit. in Bibliography.

vi For the plural of Ge- nouns, see 27.
vii For the plural of foreign nouns, see 28–31.

18. Plural Groups

1 (–) Most masc. and all but one neut. in $\begin{cases} \text{-el: der Onkel} \\ \text{-en: der Schatten} \\ \text{-er: das Ufer} \end{cases}$
(see Group 2)
Neut. in -chen and -lein: Mädchen, Fräulein

2 (ÿ) 22 masc. in -el, -en, -er: Acker, Apfel etc.
2 fem.: Mutter, Tochter
1 neut.: Kloster

3 (–e) 57 masc.: Aal, Abend etc.
56 neut. monosyllabics: Beet, Beil etc.
nouns in -nis (–nisse): das Ereignis, die Ersparnis

4 (ÿe) **Most masc.:** Stuhl, Vorhang
33 fem. monosyllabics: Angst, Axt etc.
1 neut.: Floß

5 (ÿer) **Most neut.:** Buch, Eigentum
12 masc.: Geist, Gott etc.

6 (–(e)n) **Most fem.:** Schule, Uhr, Lehrerin (–innen)
18 masc.: Ahn, Dorn etc.
5 neut.: Auge, Bett etc.

7 (–(e)n) (thus in plur. and also in acc., gen. and dat. sing.)
Masc. in -e: Affe, Russe
33 masc. not in -e: Asiat, Bär etc.

19. Survey of plural formation according to gender

MASCULINE
MOSTLY Group 4: der Stuhl (ÿe)
Those in -el, -en, -er:
    mainly Gr. 1 (–): der Onkel, der Schatten, der Lehrer
    22 in Gr. 2 (ÿ): Acker, Apfel etc.
57 in Gr. 3 (–e): Aal, Abend etc.
12 in Gr. 5 (ÿer): Geist, Gott etc.
18 in Gr. 6 (–(e)n): Ahn, Dorn etc.
Those in -e $\big\}$ Gr. 7 (–(e)n $\qquad \begin{cases} \text{der Affe} \\ \text{Asiat, Bär etc.} \end{cases}$
33 not in -e $\big\}$ except in nom. sing.)

FEMININE
MOSTLY Group 6: die Schule (–n)
2 in Gr. 2 (ÿ): Mutter, Tochter
Those in -nis: Gr. 3 (–e): die Ersparnis (–se)
33 monosyllabics in Gr. 4 (ÿe): Angst, Axt etc.

NEUTER
MOSTLY Group 5: das Buch (⸚er)
Those in -el, -en, -er, -chen, -lein: Gr. 1 (–):
     das Segel, das Kissen, das Ufer, das Mädchen, das Fräulein
     One exception: das Kloster (⸚)
56 monosyllabics }   { Beet, Beil etc.
Those in -nis   }: Gr. 3 (–e) { das Ereignis (–se)
1 in Gr. 4 (⸚e): das Floß
5 in Gr. 6 (–(e)n): Auge, Bett etc.

D. PLURAL LISTS

(These lists are not 100% complete, but include all nouns normally required and
which are used in the plural.)

20. Group 1 (–): 7 masc. are usually without -n in nom. sing.

Buchstabe[1] *letter of alphabet*   Example:
Friede *peace*   N. der Name
Funke *spark*   A. den Namen
Gedanke *thought*   G. des Namens
Glaube *belief*   D. dem Namen
Name *name*   Plur. die Namen etc.
Wille *will*

21. Group 2 (⸚): 22 masc. in -el, -en, -er

Acker *ploughed field*   Laden *shop; shutter*
Apfel *apple*   Magen *stomach*
Boden *floor; attic*   Mangel *lack, deficiency*
Bogen[2] *arch, curve, arc*   Mantel *overcoat*
Bruder *brother*   Nagel *nail*
Faden *thread*   Ofen *oven, stove*
Garten *garden*   Sattel *saddle*
Graben *ditch*   Schnabel *beak*
Hafen *harbour*   Schwager *brother-in-law*
Hammer *hammer*   Vater *father*
Kasten *(wooden) box*   Vogel *bird*

Note: das Lager (–) *camp; couch* sometimes has plur. die Läger, especially when
used in the sense of supplies in store (commercialese).

22. (S) Group 3 (–e): 57 masc.

Aal *eel*   Erfolg *success*
Abend *evening*   Forst *forest* (as part of afforestation)
Ahorn *maple*   Fund *find*
Akt *act* (of play); *nude* (art)   Gau *district* (elev., obs.)
Amboß *anvil*   Grad *degree*
Arm *arm*   Gurt *girth, belt*
Besuch *visit*   Halm *blade, stalk*
Dachs *badger*   Horst *eyrie; air-station; shrubbery*
Dolch *dagger*   Huf *hoof*
Dom *cathedral*   Hund *dog*

---

[1] never: der Buchstaben in nom. sing.
[2] BUT: der Rundbogen (–), der Spitzbogen (–).

Knall *bang, report*
Kobold *goblin*
Kork *cork*
Kuckuck *cuckoo*
Lachs *salmon*
Laut *sound*
Leichnam *corpse*
Luchs *lynx*
Molch *salamander*
Monat *month*
Mond *moon; month* (elev.)
Mord *murder*
Ort *place; town, village*
Pfad *path*
Pol *pole* (astronomy, magnetism); *terminal* (electricity)
Puls *pulse*
Punkt *point, dot*
Raufbold *rowdy*

Ruck *jolt, jerk*
Ruf *call, cry; reputation*
Salm *salmon*
Schalk *rogue*
Schlot *factory chimney*
Schuft *scoundrel*
Schuh *shoe*
Spalt *crack, cleft*
Sproß *shoot; offspring*
Star *starling*
Stoff *material*
Strand *shore*
Tag *day*
Takt *tact; beat, bar* (music)
Thron *throne*
Trunkenbold *drunkard*
Verlag *(firm of) publishers*
Verlust *loss*
Versuch *attempt*

Group 3 (–e): 56 neut. monosyllabics

Beet *flower-bed*
Beil *hatchet*
Bein *leg*
Bier *beer*
Boot *boat*
Bord *shelf*
Brot *bread, loaf*
Bund *bundle*
Ding[1] *thing*
Erz *ore*
Fell *hide, skin*
Fest *festival*
Garn *yarn*
Gas *gas*
Gift *poison*
Gleis *rails, track*
Haar *hair*
Heer *army*
Heft *exercise book*
Heim *home*
Jahr *year*
Kinn *chin*
Knie[2] *knee*
Kreuz *cross*
Los *lot, fate; lottery ticket*
Mal *time[3]; sign, mark*[4]
Maß *measure(ment)*
Meer *sea*

Moor *moor, bog*
Moos *moss*
Netz *net*
Öl *oil*
Paar *pair*
Pferd *horse*
Pfund *pound*
Pult *desk*
Recht *right*
Reh *roe*
Reich *realm, empire*
Rohr *reed, cane; pipe, tube; barrel* (of gun)
Roß *steed*
Salz *salt*
Schaf *sheep*
Schiff *ship*
Schwein *pig*
Seil *rope*
Spiel *game*
Stück *piece*
Tau *rope, cable*
Tier *animal*
Tor *gate; goal* (in games)
Vlies *fleece*
Werk *work* (of art)
Zelt *tent*
Zeug *stuff*
Ziel *aim, goal*

---

[1] plur. also die Dinger (coll. and pejorative).
[2] Plur. is written 'die Knie, auf den Knien', and pronounced either as one or as two syllables.
[3] e.g. die ersten paar Male (see 255).
[4] Commoner in compounds, where plur. varies, e.g. die Merkmale *characteristic features*, die Denkmäler *monuments*.

23. Group 4 (⸚e): 33 fem. monosyllabics

Angst *fear, anxiety*

Axt *axe*

Bank *bench*

Braut *fiancée; bride*

Brust *breast, chest*

Faust *fist*

Frucht *fruit*[1]

Gans *goose*

Gruft *vault, tomb*

Hand *hand*

Haut *skin*

Kluft *cleft*

Kraft *strength*

Kuh *cow*

Kunst *art*

Laus *louse*

Luft *air*; Pl. *air* (elev.), *breezes*

Lust *pleasure; desire*[2]

Macht *might*

Magd *maid*

Maus *mouse*

Nacht *night*

Naht *seam, join*

Not *need, distress, difficulty*[3]; *necessity*

Nuß *nut*

Sau *sow*

Schnur *string*

Stadt[4] *town, city*

Wand *wall* (of room, of rock)

Wurst *sausage*

Zunft *guild*

compounds of -flucht, e.g.
   Ausflucht *excuse*
compounds of -kunft, e.g.
   Auskunft *information*

24. Group 5 (⸚er): 12 masc.

Geist *spirit*

Gott *God*

Irrtum *error*

Leib *body*[5]

Mann *man*

Mund[6] *mouth*

Rand *edge*

Reichtum *wealth*

Strauch[7] *shrub*

Vormund[8] *guardian*

Wald *forest*

Wurm *worm*[9]

25. Group 6 (-(e)n): 18 masc.

Ahn *ancestor*

Dorn *thorn*

Fasan *pheasant*

Lorbeer *laurel*

Mast *mast*

Muskel *muscle*

Pantoffel *slipper*

Papagei *parrot*

Pfau *peacock*

Schmerz *pain; grief*

See[10] *lake*

Sporn (Pl. Sporen) *spur*

Staat *state* (country)

Stachel *prickle*

Strahl *ray*

Untertan *subject* (of ruler)

Vetter *cousin* (m.)

Zeh[11] *toe*

5 neut.

Auge *eye*

Bett *bed*

Ende *end*[12]

Hemd *shirt*

Ohr *ear*

---

[1] das Obst (sing. only) = fruit (collective).

[2] plur. e.g. die Lüste des Fleisches.

[3] plur. e.g. in Nöten sein (commoner: in Not sein).

[4] plur. often pronounced with long ä.

[5] more serviceable: der Körper.

[6] plur. also: Munde.

[7] plur. also: Sträuche.

[8] plur. also: Vormunde.

[9] BUT: das arme Wurm (the poor little mite).

[10] Plur. is written 'Seen', but pronounced 'See-en'; see also 39(a).

[11] or: die Zehe(-n).

[12] BUT: das Westend.

26. Group 7: (–(e)n) in all cases except nom. sing.

33 masc. not in -e

Asiàt (–en, –en) *Asian*
Bär (–en, –en) *bear*
Bauer (–n, –n) *peasant, farmer*
Bayer (–n, –n) *Bavarian*
Bub (–en, –en) *boy* (S. Gn., Austr.)
Bursch (–en, –en) *lad*[1]
Christ (–en, –en) *Christian*
Elf (–en, –en) *elf*
Fels (–en, –en)[2] *rock*
Fink (–en, –en) *finch*
Fürst (–en, –en) *sovereign*
Geck (–en, –en) *fop*
Graf (–en, –en) *count*
Held (–en, –en) *hero*
Herr (**–n, –en**)[3] *gentleman*
Hirt (–en, –en) *herdsman*
Kosàk (–en, –en) *Cossack*

Lump (–en, –en) *scamp*
Mensch (–en, –en) *human being*
Mohr (–en, –en) *Moor*
Nachbar (–n, –n) *neighbour*
Narr (–en, –en) *fool*
Nerv (–en, –en) *nerve*
Oberst (–en, –en) *colonel*
Ochs (–en, –en) *ox*
Pommer (–n, –n) *Pomeranian*[4]
Prinz (–en, –en) *prince*
Spatz (–en, –en) *sparrow*
Steinmetz (–en, –en) *stone-mason*
Ta(r)tàr (–en, –en) *Ta(r)tar*
Tor (–en, –en) *fool*
Ùngar (–n, –n) *Hungarian*
Vorfahr (–en, –en) *ancestor*

Note: There is a fairly strong tendency to treat some masc. Group 7 nouns as Group 6 nouns, either (a) in acc., gen. and dat. sing. or (b) in acc. and dat. sing. Of the nouns in the above list, der Bär and der Narr are prone to deviation (a): den Bär, des Bärs, dem Bär, and the following to deviation (b): der Bub, der Fink, der Kurfürst *Elector*, der Nerv, der Oberst, der Spatz: ich sprach mit dem Bub; ich sah den Oberst. (See also 57(a) and 63(d).)

E. Ge- NOUNS: GENDER AND PLURAL

27. It is convenient to treat **nouns beginning with Ge-** separately. The following lists classify them as regards gender and plural. Some have no plural by meaning. (Cf. Word Formation 716(a).)

Masculine

Names of male persons, e.g.

der Gehilfe (–n, –n) *assistant*
der Gemahl (–e) *husband*
der Genosse (–n, –n) *companion, comrade*
der Gevatter (–n)[5] *godfather*

11 others: Group 4 (-̈e), unless indicated.

der Gebrauch *use*
der Gedanke[6] *thought*

Feminine

Names of female persons, e.g.

die Gehilfin (–nen) *assistant*
die Gemahlin (–nen) *wife*

11 others: Group 6 (–(e)n), unless indicated.

die Gebärde *gesture*
die Gebühr *fee*

---

[1] 'der Bursch' is a regional form of 'der Bursche', which also means 'fellow'.
[2] or: der Felsen (Group 1).
[3] Plur. is often pronounced 'Herrn'.
[4] Pomeranian dog: der Spitz (–e).
[5] old-fashioned; current usage: der (Tauf)pate.
[6] see 20.

der Gefallen (–) *favour*[1]
der Gehalt (–e) *content, capacity*[2]
der Gehorsam *obedience*
der Genuß *enjoyment*
der Geruch *smell*
der Gesang *singing*
der Geschmack *taste*
der Gestank *stink*
der Gewinn *profit*

die Geburt *birth*
die Geduld *patience*
die Gefahr *danger*
die Gemeinde *congregation*
die Geschichte *history, story*
die Geschwulst (–̈e) *swelling, tumour*
die Gestalt *figure*
die Gewähr *security, guarantee*
die Gewalt *force*

NEUTER: all others

Group 1 (–): those in -e, -el, -er

das Gebäude[3] *building*
das Gebirge[3] *mountain-chain*
das Gemurmel *murmuring*
das Geländer *railing*

Group 3 (–e): MOST

das Gebot *commandment*
das Gebüsch *shrubbery*
das Gedicht *poem*
das Gespräch *conversation*

Group 5 (–̈er): 7

das Gehalt *salary*
das Gemach *room* (elev.)
das Gemüt *temperament*;[4] *heart, mind*;[5]
    soulfulness, feeling[6]
das Geschlecht *family, stock, line; sex,*
    gender; generation
das Gesicht *face*
das Gespenst *ghost*
das Gewand *robe*

F. PLURAL OF FOREIGN NOUNS

Note: Most foreign nouns are stressed on the last syllable; in what follows, the stressed syllable is indicated when it is not the last.

28. Masculine foreign nouns

Group 1: those in -er: der Minìster (–), der Revòlver.
Exc. der Charàkter, die Charaktère.

Group 3: MOST: der Boß (Bosse), der Frisör, der General, der Roman, der Triumph.

Group 4, e.g. der Abt (–̈e), der Altar, der Baß (Bässe), der Bìschof, der Choral, der Kanal, der Kardinal, der Palast, der Tenor.

Group 5: der Ski (–er) only; also spelt and always pronounced 'Schi'.

Group 6
i Nouns in -or with the stress on the penultimate syllable; note the shift of stress in the plural: der Dòktor, die Doktòren; der Profèssor, die Professòren.

---

[1] e.g. jemandem einen Gefallen tun.
[2] The normal word for 'contents' is 'der Inhalt'.
[3] declined like 'der Käse' in 50.
[4] Er hat ein heiteres Gemüt.
[5] Die Nachricht verwirrte die Gemüter (men's minds).
[6] Er ist ganz ohne Gemüt. 'Gemüt' is a German monopoly: 'cette vie intime, cette poésie de l'âme', as Madame de Staël called it.

der Mòtor conforms to the above type, with an alternative: der Motòr, die Motòre (Group 3).

der Pastor may be stressed on either syllable in the sing.; the plur. is die Pastòren, but regionally also Pastòre and Pastòre

ii A few others: der Kònsul (–n), der Dàmon (Dämònen), der Partisan (–en), der Psalm[1], der Typ.[2]

Group 7

i Nouns in -e: der Sklàve (–n, –n), der Stratège *strategist.*

ii Nouns in -t denoting persons: der Fabrikant (–en, –en), der Komponist, der Rekrut, der Student.

iii Nouns in: -ant   der Diamant (–en, –en)
          -aph   der Paragraph (–en, –en)
          -oph   der Philosoph (–en, –en)
          -arch   der Monarch (–en, –en)
          -nom   der Astronom (–en, –en)
          -og(e)   der Psychologe[1] (–n, –n)

Note on foreign nouns in -og(e): The form with -e is preferred; cf. der Biologe, der Demagoge, der Theologe. Foreign nouns in -og denoting inanimates have no alternative form in -oge and belong to Group 3: der Katalog (–e), der Monolog (–e).

iv Many others, e.g.:

der Barbar (–en, –en)	der Kamerad	der Lakai	der Planet
der Chirurg	der Katholik	der Leopard[4]	der Tyrann
der Elefant[3]	der Komet	der Magnet	der Zar

29. Feminine foreign nouns

Group 6: ALL: die Armee,[5] die Krìse, die Nation, die Tour.
Exc.: die Ànanas *pineapple* has plur. Ànanas or Ànanasse.

30. Neuter foreign nouns

Group 1: those in -en, -er: das Exàmen (–), das Theàter.

Group 3: MOST: das Grammophon (–e), das Ideal, das Konzert, das Produkt, das Symptom, das Telegramm.

Note:
i das As *ace* (1. at cards 2. champion) doubles the s before an ending.
ii das Regime (–) is pronounced as a bisyllabic in the sing. and as a trisyllabic in the plur.; it may therefore be assigned to Gr. 3.

Group 5: Two nouns only: das Hospital (⸚er), das Regiment.

Group 6: a few, e.g. das Insekt (–en), das Interèsse, das Juwel, das Statut, das Verb (–en) BUT: das Adverb (–ien).

[1] pronounced p + s.
[2] or: der Typus (gen. sing.: des Typus, nom. plur.: die Typen).
[3] also: den Elefant, dem Elefant.
[4] also Group 6.   [5] plur. written 'Armeen', pronounced: Armee-en.

31. Some special types of foreign nouns

(a) **Foreign nouns in -us (all masc.)**

i The commoner and more concrete have plur. in -usse: die (Àuto)-busse, Bònusse, Zìrkusse.

ii The more abstract and all those in -ismus have plur. in -en: der Gènius, die Gènien *guardian-angel*; der Rhỳthmus, die Rhỳthmen; der Organìsmus, die Organìsmen.

iii Note the following analogies and deviations:
der Àtlas, die Atlànten   der Kàsus, die Kàsus
der Kàktus, die Kaktèen[1]   der Kùrsus, die Kùrse

(b) **The following neuter foreign nouns have plur. in -en or -ien:**

i Those in -um, e.g. das Àlbum, die Àlben[2]; das Indivìduum, die Indivìduen; das Ministèrium, die Ministèrien; das Musèum, die Musèen[3]; das Zèntrum, die Zèntren.

ii Those in -ma, e.g. das Dògma (die Dògmen), das Dràma, das Thèma. Cf. one fem.: die Fìrma.
Exc. das Kòmma, die Kòmmas; das Schèma, die Schèmata.[4]

iii Some in -al and -il, e.g. das Material, die Materialien; das Reptil, die Reptilien; BUT: die Minerale (commoner than 'Mineralien'), die Portale, die Ventile *air-valves, vents*.

iv das Èpos, die Èpen   das Rìsiko, die Rìsiken[6]
das Mỳthos, die Mỳthen   das Prinzip, die Prinzipien
das Kònto *account* (financial),
die Kònten[5]

(c) **A large number of foreign nouns have not been assimilated to German and end in -s throughout the plural.** They have a normal singular, e.g. der Klub, den Klub, des Klubs, dem Klub. They include all foreign nouns in -o. Examples:

der Balkon (–s)	der Israèli	der Park	der Waggon *railway-*
der Bankier	der Jòckei[7]	der Scheck	*carriage; goods truck*
der Chef	der Klub	der Streik	
der Èskimo	der Lèutnant[8]	der Tee[9]	

die Couch (–es), die Pàrty (die Pàrtys, Pàrties)

---

[1] pronounced: Kaktèe-en.
[2] also: die Àlbums.
[3] pronounced: Musèe-en.
[4] also: die Schèmas.
[5] also: die Kòntos.
[6] also: die Rìsikos.
[7] pron. as in Engl., but also [jɔkɪ] or [jɔkaɪ].
[8] plur. also: die Lèutnante.
[9] die Tees = tea-parties; die Tees or die Teesorten = types of tea; cf. die Kaffeesorten, die Obstsorten, die Fleischarten.

das Arrangement	das Detail	das Hòbby	das Niveau *level, standard*
das Aùto	das Ècho	das Hotel	das Pendant *counterpart*
das Bonbon	das Èxtra	das Klischee	das Restaurant
das Café	das Genie	das Lèxikon[1]	das Tèmpo[2]

Note: Where the sing. of an unassimilated noun ends in a mute s, the form of the noun remains unchanged throughout, but the final s is pronounced in the gen. sing. and throughout the plur., e.g. der Kommis, *clerk,* der Korps *army corps.*

G. NOTES ON PLURALS

32. Nouns in -sal, fem. or neut., are mainly Group 3; few are in common use, e.g.

> die Mühsal (–e) *toil, trouble* das Scheusal (–e) *monster*
> die Trübsal (–e) *sorrow*   das Schicksal (–e) *fate*

33. A few Germanic 'Nordseewörter' and German abbreviated words generally have -s throughout the plural: der Kai *quay,* das Deck, das Dock, das Wrack *wreck* (pron. Vrack); der Krimi, der Vati, die Mutti. (For foreign nouns with plur. in -s, see 31(c).)

34. The following have a colloquial plural in -s in addition to the orthodox form: der Bengel *rascal,* der Junge (die Jungens, die Jungs), der Kerl, der Onkel, das Fräulein, das Mädel.

35. Other parts of speech used as nouns (see 6(d)): most of these, if used in the plural, remain unchanged: diese vielen Wenn und Aber; er schreibt sich mit zwei M (he spells his name with double M).

EXCEPTIONS:

i Some infinitives: see 713.

ii The cardinals have plural in -en: drei Nullen, Einsen; die Fünfen sind schlecht geschrieben. (See also 4(e), 244, 245(b).)

iii Plural of colours: colloquial usage: add -s: die verschiedenen Blaus, Rots; literary usage generally prefers a circumlocution: die verschiedenen blauen/roten Töne.

iv Interjections ending in a vowel or vowel+h add s: die Bravos, die Pfuis, die Ohs; the rest remain unchanged: die Ach, die Pst.

v Masc. onomatopoeic words add e in plur.; der Puff also modifies (see 6(e)).

36. Plural of 'Mann' and its compounds

i Normal: der Mann, die Männer *man, husband.*

ii Archaic and poetic (or facetious): die Mannen *vassals.*

iii After cardinals, generally with reference to troops: dreitausend Mann (stark); cf. Alle Mann an Deck! Unser Chor ist 70 Mann stark (may be used of a mixed choir).

---

[1] plur. better: die Lèxika.
[2] plur. 'die Tèmpi' is common in discussing music.

iv Compounds of 'Mann' generally form plur. with 'Leute,' e.g.

der Hauptmann	die Hauptleute	*captain* (army)
der Kaufmann	die Kaufleute	*merchant*
der Landsmann	die Landsleute	*fellow-countryman*

Exc. Ehemänner *husbands* (BUT: Eheleute *married couples*), Ehrenmänner, Ersatzmänner *substitutes*, Feuerwehrmänner, Lebemänner *men of the world*, Milchmänner, Schneemänner, Seemänner (individual) *sailors* (BUT: Seeleute *sailors* (in general)), Staatsmänner, Steuermänner *helmsmen*, Strohmänner *figure-heads, dummies* (also at cards).

37. Leute and Menschen

Frequently either may be used, but while 'Menschen' suggests individuals, however numerous, 'Leute' suggests a vague or impersonal mass or group:

Was werden die Leute dazu sagen?	*What will people say?*
Vier Leute (or: Vier Menschen) kamen ins Wirtshaus	*Four people entered the inn*
Die Stadt wimmelte von Menschen (more vivid than: von Leuten)	*The town was swarming with people*
Alle Menschen müssen sterben	*All men must die*

'Herr und Frau Müller sind sehr nette Leute' is a colourless compliment; 'Herr und Frau Müller sind sehr liebe Menschen' is warmer, more personal.

38. Some nouns have two plurals with different meanings

das Band *bond; ribbon*	die Bande *bonds*
	die Bänder *ribbons*
die Bank *bench; bank* (financial)	die Bänke *benches*
	die Banken *banks*
der Bau *building; burrow, earth*[1]	die Bauten[2] *buildings*
	die Baue *burrows, earths*
der Block i *block, bulky piece*	der Felsblock, die Felsblöcke
ii *group, alliance*	der Militärblock, die Militärblöcke
iii *pad of paper*	der Notizblock, die Notizblocks
iv *block of houses, flats*, etc.	der Wohnblock, die Wohnblocks

der Druck (–e)[3] *print* (cf. drucken); cf. Neudrucke *reprints*, Sonderabdrucke *off-prints*
der Druck (–̈e)[3] *pressure* (cf. drücken); cf. Dampfdrücke *steam-pressures*, Fingerabdrücke *finger-prints*

das Gesicht *apparition; face*	die Gesichte *apparitions*
	die Gesichter *faces*
das Land *land, country*	die Lande *lands, regions* (elev.)
	die Niederlande *Netherlands*
	die Länder *lands, countries*
die Mutter *mother; (screw-)nut*	die Mütter *mothers*
	die Muttern *nuts*

[1] cf. der Fuchsbau (–e) *foxes' hole*.
[2] rare except in a few compounds e.g. die Neubauten; otherwise use 'die Gebäude' (plur. of 'das Gebäude').
[3] cf. Du. Haupt.: Druck.

der Rat *council*; *councillor*;   die Räte *councils*; *councillors*
     counsel, advice   die Ratschläge *counsels*

der Strauß *ostrich; bunch of*   die Strauße *ostriches*
     flowers; fight (elev.)   die Sträuße *bunches; fights* (elev.)

das Tuch *cloth*: die Tuche: *cloths, kinds of cloth*
     die Tücher: *cloths, tea-cloths*, and in all compounds:
         Handtücher, Taschentücher etc.

das Wort *word*: die Worte: connected words, cf. geflügelte Worte *familiar quotations*
     die Wörter: unconnected words, cf. Hauptwörter *nouns*, Zeitwörter
     verbs, but also Sprichwörter *proverbs*

der Zoll *customs (duty)*; *inch*   die Zölle *customs duties*
     drei Zoll *three inches*

39. Double genders with different meanings (cf. Du. Gram. 1390 ff.).

(a) Related words

der Band (–̈e) *volume, book*	das Band (–e) *bond*[1]
	das Band (–̈er) *ribbon*
der Bund (–̈e) *waistband; union*	das Bund (–e) *bundle* (e.g. of hay)
der Erbe (–n, –n) *heir*	das Erbe[2] *inheritance*
der Flur (–e) *entrance-hall, passage*	die Flur (–en) *fields, plain* (elev.)
der Gehalt (–e) *content, capacity*	das Gehalt (–̈er) *salary*
der Gummi (–s) *india-rubber eraser*	das Gummi *rubber*
der Hut (–̈e) *hat*	die Hut *protection, guard*[3]
der Kunde (–n, –n) *customer*	die Kunde *news, tidings*
der Militär (–s) (coll.) *military man, professional officer*	das Militär *the military, soldiery, army*
der Moment (–e) *moment*	das Moment (–e) (determining) *factor*[4]
der Pack (–̈e) *package, bundle*	das Pack *mob, rabble*
der Schild (–e) *shield*	das Schild (–er) *signboard*
der See (–n) *lake*	die See (–n) *sea*
die Steuer (–n) *tax*	das Steuer (–) *rudder, helm*
der Stift (–e) i *peg*	das Stift (–e) *foundation, home* (for old
ii *stripling* (coll.)	people)
der Verdienst *earnings*	das Verdienst (–e) *service, merit*

(b) Unrelated words

der Heide (–n, –n) *heathen*	die Heide (–n) *heath*
der Kiefer (–) *jaw*	die Kiefer (–n) *pine*
der Laster (–) (coll.) *motor-lorry*	das Laster (–) *vice, depravity*
der Leiter (–) *manager*	die Leiter (–n) *ladder*
der Mangel (–̈) *lack, deficiency*	die Mangel (–n) *mangle*
die Mark i *mark* (coin)	das Mark *marrow* (of bone)
ii *border-country*[5]	
der Messer (–) *surveyor; gauge*[6]	das Messer (–) *knife*
der Tau (–e) *dew*	das Tau (–e) *rope, cable*
der Tor (–en, –en) *fool*	das Tor (–e) *gate; goal* (in games)

[1] also distinguish: die Bande *band, gang* (die Räuberbande).
[2] gen.: des Erbes; for plur. use 'die Erbschaften'.
[3] e.g. auf der Hut sein *to be on one's guard*.
[4] e.g. Dies ist ein wichtiges Moment in unsrer Außenpolitik.
[5] e.g. die Mark (Brandenburg): the Brandenburg Marches.
[6] cf. der Landmesser *surveyor*, der Höhenmesser *altimeter*, der Durchmesser *diameter*.

40. Nouns with special plurals

SINGULAR	PLURAL	MEANING
der Saal	die Säle[1]	*large room, hall*
der Streit	die Streite	*dispute*
	die Streitigkeiten	
der Betrug	die Betrügereien	*deception, fraud*
der Zank	die Zänkereien	*quarrel*
das Bestreben	die Bestrebungen	*effort, endeavour*
die Furcht	die Befürchtungen	*fear*
das Unternehmen	die Unternehmungen[2]	*enterprise*
das Versprechen	die Versprechungen[2]	*promise*
der Atem	die Atemzüge	*breath*
der Glaube	die Glaubensartikel	*belief*[3]
	die Glaubenssätze	
der Kohl	die Kohlköpfe	*cabbage*[4]
das Lob	die Lobsprüche	*praise*
der Luxus	die Luxusartikel	*luxury*
der Schmuck	die Schmucksachen[5]	*jewellery*; pl.: *pieces of jewellery*
das Spielzeug	die Spielsachen	*toy*
der Raub	die Raubfälle	*robbery*
der Tod	die Todesfälle	*death*
das Unglück	die Unglücksfälle	*misfortune* (in sing. only[6]), *accident*

41. **Some nouns are plural only and take a plural verb;** most of these correspond to plural nouns in English, e.g. die Eltern *parents*, die Ferien *holidays*,[7] die Lebensmittel *provisions*, die Leute *people*, die Trümmer *ruins*. To be noted are die Händel[8] *quarrel(s)* and die Noten[9] (*books of*) *music*.

The following nouns are mainly used in the plural:

(der Gewissensbiß)	die Gewissensbisse	*pangs of conscience*
(das Möbel)[10]	die Möbel	*furniture*
(die Vergnügung)	die Vergnügungen	*pleasures, amusements*[11]
(der Zeitlauf)	die Zeitläufte	*times* (as in *better times*)
(der Zins)	die Zinsen	*interest* (e.g. 5%)

42. Weihnachten, Ostern, Pfingsten

These are generally treated as plurals, e.g. Fröhliche (but also: Fröhliches) Weihnachten! Haben Sie schöne Weihnachten gehabt? Er besuchte uns letzte Ostern; but as subjects they are followed by a singular verb, e.g. Weihnachten steht vor der Tür.

---

[1] cf. 727(d).   [2] cf. 713.   [3] What are your beliefs? Woran glauben Sie?
[4] BUT: der Blumenkohl (–e) *cauliflower*.
[5] also, less common, die Schmuckstücke.
[6] after all these misfortunes: nach all diesen Mißgeschicken.
[7] a short holiday = kurze Ferien or ein kurzer Urlaub.
[8] der Handel (sing.) = trade.
[9] die Note (sing.) = i note (musical or diplomatic) ii grade, mark (at school); 'die Noten' also denotes the plur. of these.
[10] for 'piece of furniture,' 'das Möbelstück' is commoner than 'das Möbel'.
[11] pleasure (sing.) = das Vergnügen.

43. The following nouns are singular in German and plural in English:

die Asche *ashes*
der Bodensatz *dregs, lees*
die Brille (*pair of*) *glasses*
der Dank *thanks*
   Vielen Dank! *Many thanks!*
die Dynamik *dynamics*
das Feuerwerk *fireworks*
der Hafer *oats*
das Hauptquartier *headquarters*
der Hopfen *hops*
die Hose (*pair of*) *trousers*[1]
der Inhalt *contents*
die Kaserne *barracks*
der Lohn *wages*
die Mathematik *mathematics*
das Mittelalter *the Middle Ages*
   im Mittelalter *in the Middle Ages*

der Mohn *poppies*[2]
die Nachricht (*piece of*) *news*
die Physik *physics*
das Quartier *quarters*
im Rückstand (m.) *in arrears*
der Schadenersatz *damages, compensation*
die Schere (*pair of*) *scissors*
die Statistik *statistics* (science of)
die Treppe (*flight of*) *stairs*
die Umgebung *surroundings*
die Umgegend *surroundings, neighbourhood*
das Unkraut *weed, weeds*
das Werk *works, factory*
das Stahlwerk *steel-works*
die Zange (*pair of*) *tongs*

Note:

i Clearly, many of the above German nouns may also be used in the plural, e.g.

Die meisten Löhne sind erhöht worden   *Most wages have been raised*
Er erhielt von beiden gute Nachrichten   *He received good news from both of them*
Er wohnt zwei Treppen hoch   *He lives on the second floor*

ii The following nouns are virtually singular only:
   der Kummer *care, sorrow*   der Verdacht *suspicion*
   die Sehnsucht *longing*   der Verdienst *earnings*

H. DECLENSION OF NOUNS

44. Paradigms of declensions

Note:

i Allowing for the differences in the formation of the plural between the various groups, the first three paradigms respectively stand for any masculine, feminine and neuter noun in Groups 1–6.

ii The fourth paradigm represents the exceptional Group 7, whose nouns end in -(e)n in all cases except the nom. sing.

		MASC.		FEM.		NEUT.	
SING.	N.	der	Onkel	die	Schule	das	Buch
	A.	den	——	die	——	das	——
	G.	des	——s	der	——	des	——es
	D.	dem	——	der	——	dem	——(e)
PLUR.	N.	die	Onkel	die	Schulen	die	Bücher
	A.	die	——	die	——	die	——
	G.	der	——	der	——	der	——
	D.	den	——n	den	——	den	——n

[1] plur. also possible: Er trug eine graue Hose *or* graue Hosen.
[2] a poppy=eine Mohnblume.

Group 7

SING.			PLUR.		
N.	der	Affe	N.	die	Affen
A.	den	——n	A.	die	——
G.	des	——n	G.	der	——
D.	dem	——n	D.	den	——

I. NOTES ON THE DECLENSION OF NOUNS

45. Masc. and neut. gen. sing.: -es or -s?

-es must be added:

i   to nouns ending in a sibilant: des Krebses, des Busches;

ii   to the word 'Gott': die Wege Gottes;

iii   to German (not to foreign) monosyllabics, or polysyllabics ending in a stressed syllable, if used as a preceding attributive genitive (the Saxon Genitive): des Tages Hitze, des Geschenkes Wert, BUT: des Chefs Tochter.

-s is added:

i   generally to nouns ending in a vowel (des Baus) or in vowel + h (des Viehs);

ii   generally to polysyllabics ending in an unstressed syllable: des Bahnhofs, des Christentums; where the last syllable is el, em, en, er, chen, lein, only s can be added: des Atems, des Vaters, des Mädchens;

iii   to proper names: J. S. Bachs Kantaten;

iv   to most foreign nouns: des Klubs, des Hotels.

Otherwise, it is a question of style, rhythm and ease of pronunciation, the ending -s being favoured, especially in conversation.

46. Neut. nouns in -nis have gen. sing. -nisses, e.g. das Ereignis, des Ereignisses.

Foreign nouns in -as, -os, -us have no ending in the gen. sing., e.g. der Atlas (des Atlas), das Epos, der Zirkus.
Exc. das As, des Asses; der (Auto)bus, des (Auto)busses.

47. Masc. and neut. dat. sing.: add e?

This again is a question of style and rhythm. Except in certain fixed phrases, the e is never essential and is, in fact, dying out.

It is mainly added to monosyllabics: auf dem Pulte.

It is rarely added to polysyllabics ending in an unstressed syllable: am Bahnhof.

It is **not** added in the following cases:

i   to nouns ending in -el, -em, -en, -er, -chen, -lein: auf dem Boden, mit dem Kätzchen;

ii   to nouns ending in a vowel (mit einem Ei) or in vowel + h (mit dem Schuh);

iii   to a noun used immediately after a preposition or a genitive: aus Holz; in dessen Haus; dies hat Bismarcks Ruf geschadet;

iv in phrases denoting quantity: mit einem Glas Wein, mit einem Stück
   Seife;
v to geographical names (am Main) and names of months and days (im
   März, am Montag);
vi to foreign nouns: in dem Klub.

The -e is generally added in certain fixed phrases, e.g.: bei Hofe, unter
Tage arbeiten *to work below ground*, hierzulande *in this country*, jemanden
zu Rate ziehen *to consult s.o.*, sich zu Tode arbeiten. (In spoken German, nach/zu Haus are at least as common as nach/zu Hause.)

48. Feminine nouns remain unchanged throughout the singular

EXCEPTIONS:
i Sui generis is 'boredom': die Langweile or, more commonly, die
   Langeweile; mainly in literary language, the first part of the latter
   form is declined as an adjective, e.g. wegen der Langenweile, aus
   Langerweile.
ii Mutters Kleid, Tantes Hut: see 51(f).

49. All German nouns end in -(e)n in the dative plural

EXCEPTIONS:
i a few German nouns with -s throughout plur.: see 33–4.
ii unassimilated foreign nouns with -s throughout plur.: see 31(c).
iii proper names, e.g. bei Müllers: see 54.

50. Two special cases:

der Käse, den Käse, des Käses, dem Käse; die Käse, der Käse, den
Käsen.

das Herz, des Herzens, dem Herzen; die Herzen etc.

J. DECLENSION OF PROPER NAMES AND TITLES

51. Genitive singular of proper names without titles and of geo-graphical names

(a) Proper names (other than those ending in a sibilant: see 51(g)) take -s
   in the gen. sing.: **Heinrichs Mantel,** Annas Kind, Goethes Werke,
   die Werke Goethes, die Ermordung Cäsars, Johann Sebastian Bachs
   Werke, die Werke Johann Sebastian Bachs, die Werke Heinrich von
   Kleists, der Tod Friedrichs des Großen, der Tod Friedrich Wilhelms
   III. (des Dritten), **Deutschlands Städte,** die Städte Deutschlands,
   Nürnbergs Kirchen, die Kirchen Nürnbergs.

Note: 'die Kirchen von Nürnberg' is also common usage, but not 'die
   Städte von Deutschland'. In the majority of the examples in 51(a) (d)
   (e), 'von' could be used; it is colloquial, but frequently sounds ineffec-
   tive, e.g. die Siege von dem großen Napoleon.

(b) A colloquial variant for the gen. of proper names is illustrated by the
   following (bad German): Dem Wenter sein Krecht (H. Broch);

Huck Finn (dat.) sein Vater (A. Andersch), the speaker being a ship's boy; Else (dat.) ihr Bruder ist krank (cf. end of 61).

(c) After some prepositions taking the genitive, proper names drop the -s, e.g. statt Müller, trotz Wagner, unweit Frankfurt, wegen Heinrich, BUT: hinsichtlich Berlins, um Hermanns willen, von seiten Karls, zugunsten Roberts.
With außerhalb, oberhalb, diesseits and their opposites, von + dat. is colloquially more usual than the gen.: innerhalb von Frankreich (innerhalb Frankreichs), diesseits von Nürnberg.

(d) If they are preceded by a def. art.,[1] demonstrative or possessive, proper names of persons have no -s in the gen.: die Rolle des Egmont, die Werke des Johann Sebastian Bach, die Siege des großen Napoleon, die Briefe dieses Schmidt, die Krankheit unsres Peter. (N.B. Goethe's title 'Die Leiden des jungen Werthers' is archaic.)

(e) Geographical names 1. used after the def. art. (i.e. when limited by an attributive adjective, cf. 84(c)) or 2. of which the def. art. forms a part (e.g. der Nil, der Balkan) frequently drop the -s of the genitive; in the second category, German names tend to retain the s. E.g.
    1. die Probleme des heutigen Deutschland, die Einwohner des geteilten Berlin.
    2. des Kreml, das Problem des Kongo, an den Ufern des Nil, auf dem Gipfel des Brocken, BUT: an den Ufern des Rheins.

Note: Compounds formed with -berg, -gebirge, -wald etc. always have the -s of the genitive (cf. Du. Gram. 1940): auf dem Gipfel des Feldbergs, die Täler des Schwarzwalds.

(f) The generic names of members of the family are colloquially treated like proper names: Vaters Anzug, Mutters Kleid, Tantes Hut (cf. Annas Kind).

(g) **Gen. sing. of proper names ending in a sibilant: s, ß, x, z, tz.**

    i Fem. Christian names: use 'von' or an apostrophe: die Schwester von Agnes, Agnes' Schwester.

    ii Masc. Christian names, surnames and classical names: four possibilities:
       1. an apostrophe (mainly confined to writing, where the apostrophe is perceptible): Fritz' Handschuhe, bei Klaus' Hochzeit, Marx' Einfluß, Sophokles' Tragödien.
       2. von (the commonest): die Handschuhe von Fritz, der Einfluß von Marx, die Operetten von Johann Strauß.
       3. add the ending -ens (old-fashioned): Fritzens Handschuhe, Vossens Homerübersetzungen.
       4. def. art., with classical names only: die Tragödien des Sophokles.

    iii Geographical names: use 'von' (or an adjective, if available): die Straßen von Paris or die Pariser Straßen.
Where the def. art. forms part of a geographical name, the gen. is used

---

[1] normally when limited by an attributive adjective (cf. 84(c)); the first two examples in 51(d) are less common variants of 'die Rolle Egmonts' and 'die Werke Johann Sebastian Bachs'. (Never: die Werke des Bach, des Goethe.)

with -es or, more frequently, uninflected: die Gipfel des Harzes, die Dörfer des Elsaß, die Städte des Peloponnes.

52. **Proper names do not change in the dative,** but, of course: nach Friedrich dem Großen; see also 81 N.

53. **Declension of proper names with titles**

   (a) **Title + name:** only the name is declined, the combination being regarded as a unit: König Heinrichs Politik, die Politik König Heinrichs, Onkel Roberts Haus, die Gründung Kloster Beurons, die Regierungszeit König Ludwigs XIV. (des Vierzehnten), ich hörte gestern Präsident Heinemann (not: Präsidenten), ich ging zu Kollege Müller (not: Kollegen).

Two exceptions:
    i 'Herr' is always declined: Herrn Müllers Söhne; (Herrn) Professor (Doktor) Kramers Vortrag (*lecture*).
    ii After some prepositions taking the gen., neither title nor name is declined, e.g. statt, trotz, wegen König Heinrich, BUT: um König Heinrichs willen; hinsichtlich, von seiten, zugunsten Professor Naumanns.

   (b) **Article (demonstrative, possessive) (+ adj.) + title + name**

    i Official usage is to decline the title: die Siege des (mächtigen) Kaisers Karl, die Rede des Präsidenten Heinemann, die Söhne dieses Herrn Müller; cf. die Werke des (berühmten) Philosophen Kant, die Hauptstadt des Landes Niedersachsen.

    ii Provided the title is not a Group 7 noun, it is now commoner to decline neither title nor name: der Vortrag des Professor Klein, das Haus unseres (alten) Onkel Robert, die Schwester des Leutnant(s) Schmidt.

    iii 'Doktor' and 'Fräulein' are not declined: die Erfolge unseres Doktor Meyer, die Mutter dieses Fräulein Lehmann.

54. **Proper names in the plural**

   (a) **Masc. Christian names**
    i names with Group 1 endings: same in plur.
      die zwei Peter, die zwei Hänschen.
    ii names ending in a sibilant: same in plur. or add -e
      die zwei Fritz/Fritze.
    iii names ending in other consonants: add -e or, more colloquially, add -s: die zwei Heinriche/Heinrichs.
    iv names ending in a vowel: add -s: die zwei Ottos.

   (b) **Fem. Christian names**
    i diminutives in -chen and -el: same in plur.
      die zwei Gretchen, die zwei Bärbel.
    ii names ending in a sibilant: same in plur.
      die zwei Agnes.

2*

   iii names ending in other consonants: add -s
      die zwei Gertruds.
   iv names ending in -e: add -n: die zwei Luisen.
   v names ending in other vowels: add -s
      die zwei Klaras.

(c) **Surnames**
   i They mostly add -s:
      Müllers sind heute bei Schlegels; Müllers' neues Haus.
   ii Those ending in a sibilant add -ens and are sometimes used with the
      def. art.: (Die) Benzens und (die) Straußens kommen heute.

(d) **Names of countries and towns:** no ending or add -s: die zwei
    Deutschland, die beiden Berlin (U. Johnson), die zwei Chinas.

**55. Titles of poems, plays etc. and names of journals, hotels etc.
are declined:** in der letzten Strophe des ,,Erlkönigs''; ein Zitat aus
Schillers ,,Räubern''; haben Sie ,,Nathan den Weisen'' gelesen?; ich
wohne im ,,Goldenen Anker''; in der neusten Nummer des ,,Spiegels'',
BUT: in der Zeitschrift ,,Der Spiegel''.
Note: short titles preceded by the def. art. sometimes drop the -s of the
masc. gen.: der Dichter des ,,Faust''.

K. NOUNS OF WEIGHT, MEASURE AND VALUE

56. Nouns of weight, measure and value

(a) Nouns denoting weight, measure or value, preceded by a cardinal or
    by an adjective indicating number, do not take the form of the plural;
    the noun denoting the thing measured is in apposition to the noun
    of measurement and not in the genitive:

    Ich kaufte zwei Pfund[1] Kirschen und zwei Sack Kartoffeln; er trank ein Glas
    Bier; er trank zwei Glas (Bier); er trank mehrere Glas Bier; mit zwei Glas
    Bier; ich bestellte drei Dutzend Eier; zwei Paar Schuhe.

ein paar Schluck (Kaffee)	*a few mouthfuls (of coffee)*
Wir hatten fünf Grad Kälte	*We had five degrees of frost*
zehn Schritt	*ten paces*
3 Schuß—50 Pfennig!	*3 shots for 50 Pfennig!*
Mit zwanzig Mark komm'	*I can't make do with twenty marks*
ich nicht aus	

Note:
   i Particularly when shopping, the word 'Stück' is much used to indicate
    the number of articles required, from writing-pads to electric bulbs
    and from peaches to handkerchiefs: Diese hier sind gerade das
    richtige; geben Sie mir bitte drei Stück!

   ii Time units take the form of the plural, but a noun following them is
    generally in apposition: sechs Jahre Krieg; die ersten Monate
    Parlamentserfahrung (*Zeit*); nach einer Stunde Warten (*Zeit*).

---

[1] an English pound=450 grams; a German pound=500 grams; butter, cheese, sausage,
meat, fruit and vegetables are usually bought by the 'Pfund'.

iii Feminine nouns of measurement etc., other than 'die Mark', take the plural form: zehn Flaschen Wein, zwei Ladungen Holz.

iv After 'viele', practice varies: Er trank viele Glas/Gläser Bier.

(b) Beyond the recognized nouns of measurement illustrated in 56(a), there are numerous words denoting quantity which are followed by a noun in apposition, e.g. zwei Gruppen Schulkinder, eine Menge Schallplatten, zwei Pakete Lebensmittel, eine Schar Schulkinder, mehrere Sträuße Nelken.

Used in the plural without a preceding cardinal or adjective denoting number, they are followed by 'von': große Mengen von Schallplatten, Pakete von Lebensmitteln (or: Lebensmittelpakete), Schwärme von Bremsen *swarms of horseflies* (E. Jünger).

The following are almost always followed by 'von': eine Sammlung, eine Ansammlung *accumulation*, eine Versammlung *gathering*, eine Serie; after eine Reihe, 'von' is safer.

(c) kind, type, make of

i die Sorte and die Art are generally followed by a noun in apposition: zwei Sorten Äpfel; eine neue Art (von) Religion; es ist eine Art (von) Museum.

ii der Typ either forms a compound noun (Er schildert einen neuen Menschentyp) or is followed by a genitive (ein neuer Typ des Mercedes) or by von (see 555(c)ii).

iii die Marke forms a compound noun: diese Automarke.

(d) When a masc. or neut. noun of measurement is in the gen. sing. and is followed by a masc. or neut. noun denoting the thing measured, normal usage is to inflect the latter, but not the former; ('von' is commoner when practicable):

der Preis eines Pfund Fleisches/von einem Pfund Fleisch	*the price of a pound of meat*
der Geschmack dieses Stück Kuchens/ von diesem Stück Kuchen	*the taste of this piece of cake*
jenes Blättchen Papiers (A. Goes)	*of that slip of paper*
anstatt eines Glas Weins	*instead of a glass of wine*

Where the thing measured is fem.:

der Preis eines Pfundes Butter (or: von einem Pfund Butter)	*the price of a pound of butter*
anstatt eines Glases Milch	*instead of a glass of milk*

Where the noun of measurement is fem.:

der Preis (von) einer Flasche Wein/Milch	*the price of a bottle of wine/milk*
statt einer Tasse Kaffee/Milch	*instead of a cup of coffee/milk*

(e) When the noun of measurement is in the dative (sing. or plur.), the noun denoting the thing measured, if plur., is often given the inflection of the dat. plur., though practice varies:

mit einem Haufen Butterbrote(n)	*with a pile of sandwiches*
mit vielen Haufen Butterbrote(n)	*with many piles of sandwiches*
mit einem Dutzend Kühe(n)	*with a dozen cows*

(f) Nouns of measurement have the plural inflection if they are viewed as concrete individual objects. (Only 'Mark' never changes.) E.g.

| Auf dem Hof lagen zehn Fässer | *In the yard there were ten barrels* |
| Ich gab ihm meine letzten zehn Pfennige | *I gave him my last ten pfennigs* |

(g) Note the following restaurant usage:

| Drei Erdbeereis, bitte! | *Three strawberry-ices, please* |
| Noch zwei Bier, bitte! | *Two more beers, please* |

(h) For normal usage if the noun denoting the thing measured is preceded by an adjective, see 99 ff., e.g. Ich trank zwei Tassen starken Kaffee (Apposition).

(i) If the noun denoting the thing measured is preceded by the def. art., a demonstrative or a possessive, it goes into the genitive, with 'von' as a common alternative: zwei Glas des besten Weins (vom besten Wein), von diesem Wein, von unserm Wein.

L. SOME FURTHER INSTANCES OF NON-INFLECTION[1]

57. There are a number of instances, apart from nouns of measurement, in which nouns are not inflected:

(a) A Group 7 noun has no -en in acc. or dat. sing.:

  i (S) when used, without a qualifying word, after a preposition (the inflected -en form might be sing. or plur.):

| das Verhältnis zwischen Fürst und Volk | *the relationship between sovereign and people* |
| Er war ohne Kamerad[2] | *He was without a comrade* |

  ii when it is, as it were, quoted: Was ist die Bedeutung von 'Astronom'?

(b) The genitive of nouns denoting languages: der Stil des modernen Englisch.

(c) The genitive of the names of months frequently drops the -s, by analogy with proper names; the months in -er tend to retain it: am Morgen des zehnten Juni; in den ersten Tagen des Oktobers.
None of the months are inflected when in apposition to 'des Monats' (in den letzten Tagen des Monats Oktober) nor after Anfang, Mitte, Ende (Anfang Dezember) (see 329).

(d) In the genitive of the names of the days of the week, practice varies: am Morgen des folgenden Mittwoch(s); mit Ausnahme des (kommenden) Donnerstag(s).

(e) 1. Certain foreign nouns (especially modern loan words) and 2. certain German nouns frequently drop the -s of the gen. sing. Duden (Gram. 2020) cites for instance:
der Barock (des Barock), der Dativ, der Dynamo, das Establishment, der Gulasch, das Interesse, der Islam, das Parlament, das Parterre *back stalls* (theatre), das Radar, der Test.

---

[1] cf. Du. Gram. 1980 (2), 1990 f., 2005 f., 2020.
[2] Regarding the omission of 'einen', see 563.

der Heilige Abend (des Heiligen Abend), der Gründonnerstag, der Karfreitag, der Ostersonntag, der Biedermeier (Early Victorian Style), der Hanswurst *clown.* der Holunder *elder,* der Löwenzahn *dandelion.* (These are all in the nature of proper names.)

(f) In the genitive of some other parts of speech used as nouns practice varies: ein Stück des eignen Ich(s); eines klaren Entweder-Oder; meines Gegenüber(s); seines ewigen Nein(s); des grauen Einerlei(s); anstatt eines A.

(g) **The declension of abbreviations,** e.g.

der LKW: der Lastkraftwagen *motor lorry*
die GmbH: die Gesellschaft mit beschränkter Haftung *limited liability company*

gen. sing.:   des LKW(s)   der GmbH
(nom.) plur.: die LKW(s)   die GmbH(s)
   In conversation, the form with -s is commoner.

(h) See also 51(c)(d)(e)(g), 53(b), 63(d) and 581.

M. THE MAIN USES OF THE CASES

Note: Only those uses which seem to demand it and which are not dealt with elsewhere are here treated at any length.

58. **The nominative case** is used for the subject, for the person or thing addressed and for the complement of sein, werden, bleiben, heißen, scheinen, sich betrachten als *to regard o.s. as,* sich dünken *to imagine o.s. to be* (archaic or facetious), sich erweisen als *to prove to be,* sich fühlen als *to feel o.s. to be* and of nennen *to name, call* used in the passive. E.g.
Karl bleibt mein bester Freund; er dünkt sich ein großer Künstler; er erwies sich als der Mörder; er wird immer der Faulenzer genannt.

59. **The accusative case** is used for the direct object, after certain preposi-tions (558 ff., 566 ff.), in certain time-phases (315 f., 319 f.) and:

(a) for the complement of nennen, heißen *to call,* schelten *to call* (chidingly), ansehen als *to look upon as,* bezeichnen als *to designate as* etc.: Er nennt sich einen Optimisten; er schalt mich einen Taugenichts; ich sehe Sie als meinen Freund an.

(b) as an **adverbial accusative,** to denote weight, measure, value, space traversed: Der Sack wog einen Zentner *a hundredweight* (or: war einen Zentner schwer); der Tisch ist ein Meter breit; einen Schilling wert; wir gingen noch einen Kilometer; ich bin den ganzen Weg zu Fuß gegangen; wir sind den Berg hinaufgestiegen.

(c) for **absolute phrases,** where these may be regarded as the object of a suppressed transitive present participle, e.g. haltend or habend:
Den Hut in der Hand [haltend],   *Hat in hand, he entered the room*
  kam er ins Zimmer
und sagte, gemäßigten Vorwurf in der   *and said, with mild reproach in his voice:* ...
Stimme [habend]: ... (A. Goes)

(Genuine absolute accusatives are rare, e.g.

Seinen üblichen Eifer vorausgesetzt, wird er sicher Erfolg haben	*Assuming his usual keenness, he's sure to succeed)*

Otherwise, absolute phrases go into the nominative, being regarded as the subject of intr. pres. participles, e.g. liegend or seiend:

Er saß am Feuer, der Hund zu seinen Füßen [liegend]	*He sat by the fire, the dog at his feet*
Holmes saß schweigend und gefaßt, . . . aber jeder Nerv gespannt [seiend]	*Holmes sat silent and composed, . . . but every sense on the alert* (Conan Doyle)

Both the acc. and the nom. construction are frequently replaced by mit + dat.: Mit dem Hut in der Hand, . . .; mit dem Hund zu seinen Füßen.

60. (S) The genitive case is, in conversation, felt to be somewhat stilted and there is a strong tendency to avoid it, mainly by using von + dat. This tendency is referred to in 51(a) N.(c), 56(d) (i), 63(a), 101, 113 (b)N, 152, 172, 181, 207(e) ii 2, 212(b), 227 ff., 498, 555(c) v 2 and vi, 578, 715(b) N.i.

In line with this tendency is the dropping of the -s of the masc. and neut. gen. sing. by proper names in certain circumstances (see 51(c)(d)(e) (g), 53(b)) and by some other nouns (see 57(b)–(g))[1]

With the above proviso, the genitive is used to express possession, partitively (die Hälfte des Kuchens, manche meiner Freunde, but see 555(c)i, 56, 99 ff.), as a subjective or objective genitive (die Abfahrt des Zuges, der Umbau des Hauses), to define a preceding generic word (die seltene Tugend der Bescheidenheit *the rare virtue of modesty*), after certain prepositions (574 ff.), after certain verbs (498 ff.), with certain adjectives (118), to denote indefinite or habitual time (317) and as an adverbial genitive.

Only the first and last of these uses need further comment here:

(a) to express possession:

Das ist das Haus meines Bruders	*That is the house of my brother*
Das ist meines Bruders Haus	*That is my brother's house*

The latter order, the so-called **Saxon genitive,** is normal with proper names: Goethes Gedichte, Karls Handschuhe; apart from this, it is mainly literary and is not much used in conversation, especially not with fem., plur. and Group 7 nouns; thus always: die Wohnung meiner Schwester, die Eltern des Studenten. Examples of Saxon Genitive:

seiner Vorfahren großes altes Haus (Th. Mann)	*the large old house of his ancestors*
Nicht ohne Schauder greift des Menschen Hand In des Geschicks geheimnisvolle Urne (Schiller)	*Not without awe does the hand of man plunge into the dark urn of Fate*

(b) examples of **adverbial genitive:**

meines Erachtens (m. E.)	*in my view*
leichten/schweren Herzens	*with a light/heavy heart*
Er fährt erster Klasse	*He travels first class*
schlimmstenfalls	*if the worst comes to the worst*

[1] For a full treatment of the decline of the genitive in modern German, see Winfried Weser: Der Genitiv im neuesten Deutsch (*Muttersprache*, Juli/August and September 1968).

61. The dative case is used for the indirect object (654), as a dative of advantage or disadvantage (83, 489 f.), instead of a possess. adj. with parts of the body (82(b)-(f)), after certain prepositions (547 ff., 566 ff., 576 ff.), after many verbs (486 ff.), in various impersonal expressions (373 ff.) and with certain adjectives (117).

Two further uses require illustration here:

(a) **The ethic dative** (of the person indirectly interested, emotionally involved) (cf. Erben, op. cit., 221):

Du bist mir ein schöner Schwindler!	*You're a nice fraud*
Falle mir ja nicht hin!	*Now be sure you don't fall*
Karl, rühr' mir den Bub nicht an!	*Karl, don't you touch the boy*
(H. Weis)	

(b) a colloquial use, with a possess. adj., to indicate possession (bad German) (cf. 51(b)):

Das ist meiner Mutter ihr Hut	*That's my mother's hat*
Unserm Onkel sein Garten ist ganz groß	*Our uncle's garden is quite big*

N. APPOSITION

62. Basic rule for apposition: a noun in apposition has the same case as the noun or pronoun to which it refers:

Ich sah meinen Freund, den Pfarrer	*I saw my friend, the parson*
	I knew him as a boy
Ich kannte ihn als Junge[1]	= *when I was a boy*
Ich kannte ihn als Jungen[1]	= *when he was a boy*
Es gibt nichts Schlimmeres als einen Betrunkenen (cf. Du. Haupt.: Apposition II)	*There is nothing worse than a drunken man*
in Michelstadt, einem Städtchen im Odenwald	*in Michelstadt, a little town in the Odenwald*

cf. der Fall Hamlets, des Dänen, dieses typischen Literaten (Th. Mann).

63. Main deviations from the apposition rule given in 62:

(a) Especially in conversation, there is a strong **tendency to avoid an appositional genitive singular,** using instead one of the following: 1. von + dat. 2. a relative clause 3. the nominative (Weser, loc. cit., p. 227, draws attention to the clearer, more emphatic effect of the nominative, as opposed to the appositional genitive.)

1. der Sohn von meinem Freund, dem Pfarrer.
2. or 3. nach dem Tod meines Onkels, der früher der Bürgermeister unsrer Stadt war/der frühere Bürgermeister unsrer Stadt.
3. mit der Hilfe meines Freundes, Professor Kretschmar; die Verantwortung meines Bruders, als ältester Sohn.

(b) **Appositional phrases with 'als' *as* referring to a noun or pronoun in the dative.** Orthodox version:

Er sprach mit ihr als ältester Tochter   *He spoke with her as the eldest daughter*

Colloquially, three alternatives occur:

---

[1] Regarding the absence of an article, see 85(h).

1. Provided there is no ambiguity, the appositional phrase is put in the nominative: Er sprach mit ihr als älteste Tochter.
2. The dative is used, but the adj. is given the weak ending -en (cf. Du. Gram. 2185): Er sprach mit ihr als ältesten Tochter.
3. The rather cramped sentence is loosened up: Er sprach mit ihr, weil sie die älteste Tochter ist.

(c) For **comparative phrases introduced by 'wie'** *like* normal usage is the nominative, here justified as the subject of a truncated clause, e.g., in Zeiten wie die heutigen [es sind]; in einem Fall wie dieser (or: diesem) (Du. Gram. 5825); zwischen zwei Männern wie du und ich (Du. Haupt.: Apposition II); ich fühlte mich wie ein Fremder.

(d) **Group 7 nouns** used in apposition often remain uninflected: Ich schrieb an Herrn Schulze, Präsident (not: Präsidenten) des Gesangvereins; mir als Tourist war dies einerlei.

64. Miscellaneous types and uses of apposition

(a) die Ära Adenauer, der Fall Lehmann *the Lehmann case*, im Monat Mai, die Stadt Bremen, die Universität Heidelberg, BUT: die Schlacht bei Leipzig (see also 84(f)).

(b) in der Zeitschrift „Der Spiegel"; in dem Drama „Die Raüber"; im Hotel „Deutscher Hof".

(c) See also 51(a), 53, 56, 99 ff., 109, 115, 313(b).

II SOME SPECIAL USES AND OMISSIONS OF THE ARTICLES

A. DECLENSION OF THE ARTICLES

65. Declension of the definite article ('the')

	MASC.	FEM.	NEUT.	PLURAL (all genders)
N.	der	die	das	die
A.	den	die	das	die
G.	des	der	des	der
D.	dem	der	dem	den

66. Declension of the indefinite article ('a')

	MASC.	FEM.	NEUT.	
N.	ein	eine	ein	No
A.	einen	eine	ein	Plural
G.	eines	einer	eines	
D.	einem	einer	einem	

B. USE OF THE DEFINITE ARTICLE WITH ABSTRACT NOUNS

67. Note: The use of the def. art. with abstract nouns is one of the most elusive parts of German grammar and usage and some 'Sprachgefühl' is essential. Brackets indicate that the article may be used or omitted, for German practice varies considerably. If in doubt, it is on the whole safer to put in the def. art.

68. Abstract nouns may here be divided into two groups. (Purists may query whether some of the nouns in Group A are abstract.)

Group A: the names of features and forms of human life and thought

EXAMPLES:

das Alter *old age*
das Altertum *antiquity*

die Arbeit *work*[1]
das Christentum *Christianity*

[1] Included here in the general sense: 'application of effort to some purpose' (C.O.D.).

die Dämmerung *dawn; dusk*
die Ehe *marriage, married life*
die Einsamkeit *solitude*
das Elend *misery*
die Forschung *research*
die Freiheit *freedom*
die Gesellschaft *society*
das Glück *fortune, fate; luck; happiness*
der Handel *trade*
die Industrie *industry* (manufacture)
die Jugend *youth*
der Kommunismus *Communism*
der Krieg *war*

das Leben *life*
die Menschheit *humanity*
die Nacht *night*
die Nachwelt *posterity*
die Natur *nature*
die Not *need, want, distress*
die Politik *politics*
das Schicksal *fate*
der Schlaf *sleep*
die Sklaverei *slavery*
der Tod *death*
die Wahrheit *truth*
die Zeit *time*

Group B: human qualities and emotions

EXAMPLES:

die Angst *fear*
die Beliebtheit *popularity*
der Ehrgeiz *ambition*
die Eifersucht *jealousy*
die Eitelkeit *vanity*
die Faulheit *laziness*
die Geduld *patience*
die Gerechtigkeit *justice*
die Gesundheit *health*
die Größe *greatness*
der Haß *hatred*
die Liebe *love*
die Menschlichkeit *humaneness*
das Mißtrauen *distrust, suspicion*

die Müdigkeit *tiredness*
der Mut *courage*
die Schönheit *beauty*
die Sehnsucht *longing*
der Stolz *pride*
das Talent *talent*
die Treue *faithfulness*
die Tugend *virtue*
die Vernunft *reason, good sense*
der Verrat *treason, treachery*
die Verschwendung *wastefulness, extravagance*
das Vertrauen *confidence*

69. Nouns in Group A are distinctive and familiar phenomena and are almost always used with the def. art.:

Er fürchtet das Alter
Er liebte die Demokratie (Kl. Mann)
... daß die Ehe ein Wagestück sei (C. Zuckmayer)
Wir hängen von der Industrie ab
Der Krieg brach aus[1]
Ich interessiere mich für (die) Politik
Der Schlaf kam über ihn
Die Zeit vergeht

He is afraid of old age
He loved democracy
... that marriage is a risk

We depend on industry
War broke out
I'm interested in politics
Sleep came upon him
Time passes

In the same way, numerous non-abstract nouns, used in the plural in a general sense, have the def. art. where there is, or need be, none in English. E.g.

Die Beschwerden vermehren sich
Die Geschmäcke sind verschieden
Die Maßstäbe sind heutzutage strenger
Die Preise sind gestiegen
Die Steuern waren drückend (B. Brecht)

Complaints are increasing
Tastes differ
Standards are higher nowadays
Prices have gone up
Taxes were oppressive

---

[1] All the more arresting is Heinrich Böll's unorthodox: Krieg kam.

70. Nouns in Group B are generally used with the def. art. when the quality as a whole, as an individualized and familiar concept, is referred to or envisaged; they are then the equivalent of Group A nouns:

Ich bewundere den Ehrgeiz	*I admire ambition*
eine Schwäche wie die Eitelkeit	*a weakness such as vanity*
Die Erfahrung lehrte ihn, daß dies die Liebe sei. Aber obgleich er genau wußte, daß die Liebe ihm viel Schmerz . . . bringen müsse, . . . (Th. Mann)	*Experience taught him that this was love. But although he knew very well that love must cause him much suffering, . . .*
Er war die Liebenswürdigkeit selbst	*He was amiability personified*
Die Vernunft gebietet, daß du das tust	*Reason demands that you should do this*

Group B nouns may similarly be used with the def. art. in a more circumscribed context, especially when the presence of the quality in question is already known to the reader or listener, e.g.

Im Heer sinkt der Mut	*Courage is sinking in the army*
Das Mißtrauen wächst unter seinen Anhängern	*Distrust is increasing among his adherents*

To appreciate that the courage is sinking and the distrust increasing we must know, or be expected to assume, that they already existed. In the second example 'the distrust' would be possible in English.

Contrast with these two examples the sentence:

Unter seinen Anhängern entstand Mißtrauen	*Distrust arose among his followers*

Here distrust comes as something new and 'das Mißtrauen' would be impossible.

In some contexts the def. art. is used with Group B nouns with the sense of a possessive adjective:

Du mußt versuchen, die Angst (=deine Angst) zu überwinden	*You must try to overcome your fear*
Ich werde ihm die Faulheit austreiben (from Du. Stil.)	*I'll rid him of his laziness*
Er verlor den Mut	*He lost his courage*

71. Nouns in Group B are generally used without the def. art. when the quality is referred to, not as an entity, but in an indefinite and often partial sense. This is almost always the case where the quality or emotion, as the object, is the essential completion of the sense of the verb, e.g. Angst haben, Geduld lernen, Mut fassen, Vertrauen erwecken.

Das klingt wie Eitelkeit	*That sounds like vanity*
Er fühlte Liebe für sie	*He felt love for her*
Zu dieser Aufgabe gehört Mut	*This task demands courage*
Unentschlossenheit wäre jetzt verhängnisvoll	*Indecision would now be fatal*
Er versucht es mit Untertänigkeit (H. Fallada)	*He [a salesman] tries humility*
Ich habe ihm Vernunft gepredigt (from Du. Stil.)	*I urged him to be reasonable*

Es war nicht das erstemal, daß Verrat   *It was not the first time that treachery had*
seinen Lebensweg gekreuzt hatte   *crossed his path*
(S. Hermlin)

72. Similarly, **some group A nouns** may be used in an indefinite or partial
sense or as the essential completion of the sense of the verb; they are
then used without the def. art.

Er hat mir Arbeit gegeben   *He took me on*
Dieses Gemälde hat Leben   *This painting has life*
Gibt es Leben auf anderen Planeten?   *Is there life on other planets?*
Ich brauche (nichts als) Schlaf   *I need (nothing but) sleep*
Hast du heute Zeit für mich?   *Have you any time for me today?*

Arbeit suchen *to look for work*   Not haben *to have difficulty*
Glück haben *to be lucky*   Ich hatte Not, ein Zimmer zu
Handel treiben *to trade*   finden
Deutschland treibt mit vielen   Not leiden *to suffer want*
  Ländern Handel   Zeit sparen *to save time*
Krieg führen *to wage war*

73. **Infinitives used as nouns and denoting an activity are in general
treated like Group B nouns:**

(a) with def. art. when the activity as a whole is referred to:
Das Kaffeetrinken kam im 17. Jht.   *Coffee-drinking came to Europe in the 17th*
  nach Europa   *century*
  (*Der Volksbrockhaus* (1956))
Vermeide das Spekulieren!   *Avoid speculating*

(b) without def. art. when they are used in an indefinite and partial sense:
Spekulieren war sein Verhängnis   *Speculating was his undoing*
Diese Sache verlangt Nachdenken   *This matter demands reflection*
Sein Hobby ist (das) Schreinern   *His hobby is carpentry*

74. **Some modifications of the guide-lines for Group A and Group B
nouns**

(a) **after some prepositions** (see also 78):

außer *except*: Group B nouns are better used with def. art.:
Er hat keine Schwächen außer dem   *He has no weaknesses except pride*
  Stolz[1]

durch: some Group A nouns may be used without def. art.:
durch Arbeit, Forschung, Handel,   *through/by means of work, research, trade,*
  Krieg   *war*

    Group B nouns almost always without def. art.:
Durch Feigheit kann man alles   *Through cowardice one can lose everything*
  verlieren

---

[1] Without 'dem', 'Stolz' is accusative: cf. 549(b)N.

gegen: Group B nouns tend to be used without the def. art. even when the quality as a whole is referred to:

Ich bin nicht gegen (die) Freiheit	*I'm not against freedom*
Ich bin gegen (das) Spekulieren	*I'm against speculating*

in + dat. always has the def. art. except in certain types of phrase (see (b) below and 78) and in pairs of words (see 79):

im Krieg	*in wartime*
im Vertrauen	*in confidence*
Mein Haß gegen ihn wurzelte in der Furcht	*My hatred towards him was rooted in fear*
Die Gefahr liegt im Zögern	*The danger lies in hesitating*

in + acc.: generally without def. art. with Group B nouns and occasionally with certain Group A nouns:

Er geriet in Wut	*He flew into a rage*
Sein Glück verwandelte sich in Elend	*His happiness was transformed into misery*
Die Dämmerung ging allmählich in Nacht über	*Dusk gradually passed over into night*

ohne is preponderantly used without the def. art., even with many Group A nouns:

Es schien eine Stadt ohne Jugend und ohne Leben zu sein	*It seemed to be a town without youth and without life*
Ohne (den) Kommunismus sähe die Welt anders aus	*Without Communism the world would look different*
ohne Arbeit, Glück, Handel, Not, Schlaf, Wahrheit	*without work, happiness, trade, want, sleep, truth*

über *about, concerning*: Group B nouns tend to be used without the def. art. even when the quality as a whole is referred to:

Seine Ansichten über (die) Freiheit	*his views on freedom*
Wir sprachen über (die) Gesundheit	*We spoke about health*
ein Aufsatz über den Ehrgeiz	BUT: *an essay on ambition*

zu is almost always used with the def. art.:

Ich brachte ihn zur Vernunft	*I brought him to reason*
Er neigt zur Verschwendung	*He is prone to extravagance*
der Weg zum Erfolg	*the road to success*
Ich komme wenig zum Lesen	*I have little time for reading*

(b) **Set phrases,** mainly with prepositions, in which nouns from both groups are used without an article:

bei Nacht	*by night*
Ist er in Arbeit?	*Is he in a job?*
sich in Geduld üben	*to practise patience*
in Not sein	*to be in distress*
in Wahrheit	*in fact*
in Wirklichkeit	*in reality*
Da können Sie von Glück sagen	*You can count yourself lucky*
von Jugend auf	*from (his) youth upward*
Er ist von Natur aus bescheiden	*He is by nature modest*
Er hat sich zu Tode gearbeitet	*He has worked himself to death*
wenn Not an den Mann geht	*when help is needed*

(c) **When Group B nouns are preceded by an adjective,** the def. art. tends to drop away or to be replaced by the indef. art.:

Ich verachte kleinliche Eifersucht	*I scorn petty jealousy*
Im Heere wuchs (ein) neuer Mut	*In the army a new courage was growing*
Er neigt zu unnötiger Ver- schwendung	*He is prone to unnecessary extravagance*

The same applies to a number of Group A nouns, e.g. Arbeit, Elend, Forschung, Freiheit, Glück *happiness*, Not, Wahrheit:

anstrengende Arbeit	*strenuous work*
politische Freiheit	*political liberty*
ungetrübtes Glück	*unclouded happiness*
Sie bekämpfen schwere Not	*They are combating great distress*
wissenschaftliche Wahrheit	*scientific truth*

(d) **Straightforward necessity for def. art.** when an abstract noun is particularized by a gen. sing., a relative clause or by some other means: Er zeigte den Mut eines Helden; das ist die Tugend, die ich am meisten bewundere; er hatte die Unverschämtheit, das zu behaupten.

(e) **No article in many recognized proverbs or comparable statements:**

Alter schützt vor Torheit nicht	*Age is not proof against folly*
Not kennt kein Gebot	*Necessity knows no law*
Stolz ist keine Tugend	*Pride is no virtue*

(f) For the omission of an article in pairs of words and enumerations, which applies to abstract as to other nouns, see 79.

(g) For the use of the def. art. to indicate the genitive or dative case, with abstract as with other nouns, see 80 f.

C. USE OF THE DEFINITE ARTICLE WITH NOUNS DENOTING ARTS, SCIENCES AND SPORTS

75. **With nouns denoting arts, sciences and sports the def. art. is, for the most part, used or omitted as with abstract nouns.** The following examples will serve as guide-lines and ear-training:

Die Literatur ist etwas Wunderbares	*Literature is something wonderful*
Ich erwartete von der Literatur mehr Anregung als vom Leben (Günter Grass)	*I expected more stimulus from literature than from life*
Es wird großes Interesse für Literatur gezeigt	*There is great interest in literature*
Die deutsche Literatur ist im ganzen ernst	*German literature is on the whole serious*
Gute Literatur ist heutzutage selten	*Good literature is rare today*
Wir sprachen über (deutsche) Literatur	*We talked about (German) literature*
Darüber schweigt die Geschichte (from Du. Stil.)	*History is silent about that*
Geschichte ist sein Hauptfach	*History is his main subject*

Er studiert (deutsche) Geschichte	*He is studying (German) history*
die Kunst fördern	*to promote art*
Ich interessiere mich für Kunst	*I am interested in art*
In der Kunst ist der Stil alles	*In art style is everything*
(die) abstrakte Kunst	*abstract art*
Es klang wie Musik	*It sounded like music*
Musik treiben	*to go in for music*
Die Physik wird immer schwerer	*Physics is becoming more and more difficult*
Ich kann Physik nicht verstehen	*I can't understand physics*
Ich kann die moderne Physik nicht verstehen	*I can't understand modern physics*
(Der) Sport ist gesund	*Sport is healthy*
Er hat sich beim Fußball verletzt	*He got hurt at football*

D. USE OF THE DEFINITE ARTICLE WITH NAMES OF SPECIES AND SUBSTANCES

76. The use of the def. art. with the names of species

(a) The def. art. is always used with 'Mensch', and any other species, in the singular:

Der Mensch ist ein seltsames Geschöpf	*Man is a strange creature*
Der Tiger ist ein Raubtier	*The tiger is a beast of prey*

(b) Before a species in the plural, the def. art. is generally omitted; the fourth is a counter-example; the last example is a fixed usage:

(Die) Menschen sind seltsame Geschöpfe	*Men are strange creatures*
Hunde sind mir sympathischer als Katzen	*I prefer dogs to cats*
Ich interessiere mich für Flugzeuge	*I am interested in aeroplanes*
Woran man sieht, daß es auch bei den Schiedsrichtern Charakterunterschiede gibt (*Zeit*)	*From which one can see that referees too differ in character*
N.B. Die Leute meinten, er sei verrückt	*People thought he was mad*

(c) No def. art. when a species in the plural is used partitively:

Menschen haben dies getan, nicht Tiere	*Men did this, not animals*
In dem Wildpark kann man Hirsche und Bisamtiere sehen	*In the game-preserve one can see stags and musk-deer*

77. The use of the def. art. with the names of substances

(a) The def. art. is generally omitted, e.g. some quotations from *Der Volksbrockhaus* (1956):

Gold hat hohe Politurfähigkeit; Kaffee wird in fast allen tropischen Ländern angebaut; Elektrizität wurde früher als ein unwägbares Etwas (*an imponderable something*) angesehen; Seife entsteht, wenn ... cf. Bier ist erfrischender als Wein.

(b) No def. art. when the name of the substance is used partitively:

Wir aßen Brot mit Käse	*We ate bread and cheese*
Wir importieren Kaffee aus Afrika	*We import coffee from Africa*
Holz hacken	*to chop wood*

(c) The def. art. is used before the names of substances in the following cases (in addition to those where it would likewise be used in English):

i Especially in conversation, it brings out the familiar character of the substance in question:

Die Butter kostet drei Mark das Pfund	*Butter costs three marks a pound*
Der Wein war sein Verderben	*Wine was his undoing*
Die Steuern waren drückend, und das Brot hatte erst kürzlich wieder aufgeschlagen (B. Brecht)	*Taxes were heavy and only recently the price of bread had gone up again*

cf. the book-title *Du und die Elektrizität*

Similarly, in an encyclopaedia article, after the name of the substance has been introduced without the def. art., at a later mention it often has the def. art.

ii Occasionally the def. art. has demonstrative force (as in English):

Trinkst du noch ein Glas?—Nein, ich mag den Wein nicht	*Are you having another glass?—No, I don't care for the wine*

iii The def. art. is often used before the name of a substance in the accusative where it is used in a general and not in a partitive sense:

Wer hat den Kaffee in Europa eingeführt?	*Who introduced coffee into Europe?*
Faraday hat die Elektrizität erforscht	*Faraday investigated electricity*

iv to indicate case (cf. 80 f.):

der Alkoholgehalt des Weines	*the alcoholic content of wine*

v a few special cases:

im Wasser leben	*to live in water*
beim Bier sitzen	*to sit over a glass of beer*
Das steht nur auf dem Papier	*That is only on paper*
Am Bahnhof trank ich einen Kaffee	*At the station I had a cup of coffee*

E. PREPOSITIONAL PHRASES WITHOUT AN ARTICLE

78. Prepositional phrases without an article[1]

(a) **Set phrases,** e.g. auf Wache *on guard*, auf Wunsch *on request*, bei Tisch *at table*, nach Kriegsende *after the end of the war*, nach Wunsch *as desired*, von Beruf *by profession*, über Erwarten *beyond expectation*.

See also 74(b), 79 and 620 ff.; for phrases of the type 'seit Anfang Januar', see 329 N.ii.

(b) **Preposition + a noun formed from a verb + a genitive** (often officialese):

bei Ausbruch des Ersten Weltkriegs	*at the outbreak of the First World War*
in Anerkennung seiner Verdienste	*in recognition of his services*
nach Empfang Ihres Briefes	*after receiving your letter*
zwei Monate vor Ablauf seiner Amtszeit (*FAZ*)	*two months before the expiration of his term of office*

---

[1] See also the examples of some figurative uses of: an+dat., 597(a); auf+acc., 600(c); aus, 601 (a); nach, 604(a)(b); vor+dat., 612(a).

(c) **Preposition + adjective/participle + noun**

This is a crisp and effective combination; English will generally have the indef. art.; Duden frowns on the insertion of the indef. art. in German (Du. Haupt., p. 185: ein (Artikel): 1).

i adjectival

... einen Virtuosen mit italienischem Namen (Th. Mann)	*a virtuoso with an Italian name*
ein Anzug von altmodischem Schnitt	*a suit of old-fashioned cut*

ii adverbial

in endloser Kette	*in an endless chain*
mit letzter Anstrengung (G. Gaiser)	*with a final effort*
nach kurzer Pause	*after a short pause*
auf eigne Kosten	*at my (his etc.) own expense*
auch bei bester Organisation	*even with the best organization*
nach bestandener Prüfung	*after passing his exam*

F. OMISSION OF ARTICLE IN PAIRS OF WORDS AND ENUMERATIONS

79. **The article is frequently omitted in pairs of words, with or without a preposition, and in enumerations.** The first group of examples are set phrases.

(in) Form und Inhalt	*(in) form and content*
in Hülle und Fülle	*in plenty*
in Krieg und Frieden	*in war and peace*
(BUT: im Krieg	*in wartime)*
mit Müh und Not	*with great difficulty, only just*
mit Rat und Tat	*by word and deed*
Es geht um Leben und Tod	*It's a matter of life and death*
der Unterschied zwischen Stolz und Hochmut	*the difference between pride and arrogance*
Er haßt Lesen und Schreiben	*He hates reading and writing*

Sie biß in eine von den Bananen und ließ Schale und Rest im Eßzimmer liegen (V. Baum)
Eine mehrstündige Militärparade auf dem Roten Platz demonstrierte ... Geschichte und heutige Stärke der Roten Armee (*Zeit.*)

Example of an enumeration:
... die alten menschlichen Werte (*values*)—ich möchte hier nur Pflicht, Gehorsam, Anstand (*good manners*), Autorität, Ordnung nennen (Th. Valentin)

G. USE OF THE DEFINITE ARTICLE TO INDICATE CASE

80. **The def. art. may be used to indicate a genitive**

(a) With the exceptions noted below, no German noun can be given a genitive inflection without a preceding article or a possessive, demonstrative or ordinary adjective. Thus 'the smell of seaweed' is 'der

Geruch des Seetangs' (or 'der Geruch von Seetang'); 'an expression of astonishment' is 'ein Ausdruck des Erstaunens'.

EXCEPTIONS:

i proper names: Peters Buch, Nürnbergs Kirchen.
ii generic names of members of the family: Vaters Anzug.
iii after some prepositions + gen.: wegen Menschenraubs.
iv sometimes after a word of quantity: voll Hasses; hinter Stürzen Wassers (H. Mann).

(b) For the use of 'von' in place of the genitive, see 555(c) and (c) below.

(c) With abstract nouns and infinitives used as nouns, the use of 'von', with or without the def. art., instead of the gen. sing., is not to be recommended; it is generally poor style and frequently wrong. Therefore: die Bande der Freundschaft, ein Gefühl der Verzweiflung, die Wichtigkeit des Stils, die Kunst des Fechtens *the art of fencing*.

EXCEPTIONS:

i ein Mann von Erfahrung *a man of experience*, eine Frau von Geschmack *a woman of taste* and the like.
ii 'von' is used before two or more abstract nouns of different genders, to avoid repeating the article, e.g.

der Abgrund von Ironie, Unglaube, Opposition, Erkenntnis, Gefühl, der Sie von den Menschen trennt . . . (Th. Mann)	*the gulf of irony, scepticism, opposition, perception and feeling that separates you from others*

81. The def. art. may be used to indicate a dative

Ich ziehe Kaffee dem Tee vor	*I prefer coffee to tea*
Dieses Metall gleicht dem Gold	*This metal resembles gold*
Er hat sich der Physik gewidmet	*He has devoted himself to physics*
(BUT: Er studiert Physik	*He is studying physics*)

Note: With proper names and generic names of members of the family, the insertion of a clarifying def. art. is possible but not usual: (Dem) Karl scheint es zu riskiert zu sein. Wir müssen (dem) Lehmann mal wieder was schicken. Das will ich (der) Mutter sagen.

H. USE OF DEFINITE ARTICLE WITH PARTS OF BODY AND ARTICLES OF CLOTHING

82. The def. art. is generally used instead of the possess. adj. when speaking of parts of the body and articles of clothing

(a) Where there is no contrary indication, the def. art. refers back to the subject:

Er machte die Augen auf	*He opened his eyes*
Er hob den Arm	*He raised his arm*
Er steckte die Hand in die Tasche	*He put his hand in his pocket*
Er zog den Mantel aus	*He took off his coat*
Er hielt den Hut in der Hand	*He held his hat in his hand*

Das Mädchen . . . zog den rötlichen Kamm aus dem Haar, nahm ihn in den Mund und fing an, mit den Fingern die Frisur zurechtzuzupfen (H. Böll) (. . . *and began to put her hair right by plucking it with her fingers.*)

(b) With actions which are slightly more complex, the def. art., even though it obviously refers back to the subject, is reinforced by a reflexive pronoun in the dative (a kind of dative of advantage or disadvantage). 'Sprachgefühl' may have to decide whether the addition of the reflexive sounds convincing or not, for it is rarely optional.

Ich wusch mir die Hände	*I washed my hands*
Er wischte sich den Schweiß von der Stirn	*He wiped the sweat from his forehead*
Er kratzte sich den Kopf	*He scratched his head*
Ich habe mir die Haare schneiden lassen	*I had my hair cut*
Ich habe mir den Fuß verstaucht	*I've sprained my ankle*
Ich habe mir in den Finger geschnitten	*I've cut my finger*

(c) Where the def. art. does not refer back to the subject, a dative is essential to show who is involved:

Er trat mir auf den Fuß	*He trod on my foot*
Das Blut schoß ihm ins Gesicht	*The blood rushed to his face*

(d) Even where the question of avoiding the possess. adj. does not arise, the dative of advantage is generally preferred to a genitive:

Die Mutter wusch dem Kind die Hände	*The mother washed the child's hands*
Wir zogen dem Verletzten die Jacke aus	*We took off the injured man's jacket*
BUT, significantly:	
Sie wuschen die Beine des Toten[1]	*They washed the dead man's legs*

(e) The def. art. cannot be used when the part of the body or the article of clothing is the subject and the sentence is purely descriptive (cf. Kolisko and Yuill: *Practice in German Prose*, p. 31):

Ein Fremder erschien; seine Stirn glänzte; sein Anzug war altmodisch	*A stranger appeared; his forehead glistened; his suit was old-fashioned*
Die Augen taten ihr weh	BUT: *Her eyes hurt*
Der Finger juckt mich (or: Mein Finger juckt)	*My finger itches*

(f) Apart from the exception noted in 82(e), the use of the def. art. instead of the possess. adj. with parts of the body and articles of clothing is usual, but not sacrosanct; the first two examples are taken from modern novels:

Sie legte ihre Hand auf seine Hand (I. Wendt)	*She laid her hand on his hand*
Groenewold nahm die Brille ab, preßte die Lider zusammen und rieb seine Schläfen (Th. Valentin)	*Groenewold took off his glasses, pressed his eyelids together and rubbed his temples*
Zieh lieber deinen Mantel an!	*You'd better put on your coat*

In some instances, the use of the possess. adj. is inevitable:

Er blickte hinab; dicht bei seinen Füßen lag ein Ring	*He glanced down; close to his feet lay a ring*

[1] From Weser, loc. cit. in 60(footnote), p. 223.

('dicht bei den Füßen lag ihm ein Ring' would be impossible, while 'bei den Füßen' alone would not refer back to 'Er'.)

Ich sah eine Wespe auf meinem Ärmel   *I saw a wasp on my sleeve*
(On *whose* sleeve must be specified, and 'mir auf dem Ärmel' would be impossible; contrast 'Ich hatte eine Wespe auf dem Ärmel', which is unambiguous.)

83. The use of the def. art., coupled with a dative of advantage or disadvantage, is found in other contexts, e.g.

Er füllte meinem Vater das Glas	*He filled my father's glass*
Er ebnete mir den Weg	*He smoothed my path*
Er trug ihr den Koffer zur Bahn	*He carried her bag to the station*
Der Appetit ist mir vergangen	*I've lost my appetite*
Er versauert mir das Leben	*He spoils my whole life*
Wir kamen ihm auf die Spur	*We got onto his track*
Dem Alten ist gerade die Frau gestorben (J. Ziem)	*The old man's wife has just died*

I. USE OF DEFINITE ARTICLE BEFORE GEOGRAPHICAL AND PROPER NAMES

84. Before geographical and proper names, the def. art. is used in German as in English with the following main exceptions. (A few further cases will be found in 51(d)(g), 55) It is used:

(a) before masc. and fem. countries and regions (see 6(b)): der Libanon, die Normandie, die Schweiz. But no article in addresses: Hotel X., Kandersteg, Schweiz.

(b) before a few neuter regions, e.g. das Elsaß *Alsace*.

(c) before all geographical and proper names if preceded by an adjective: das schöne Italien, das betriebsame Frankfurt (*busy Frankfurt*), der junge Heinrich, der alte (Doktor) Schulze.

(d) in the following and analogous cases:

der Bodensee *Lake Constance*	der Jupiter *Jupiter* (planet)
der Montblanc *Mont Blanc*	Er spielt den Brutus *He plays Brutus*
die Königstraße *the Königstrasse*	

(e) before the names of persons:
  i occasionally to clarify case; see 81N.
  ii before the surnames of women where nothing else indicates the sex: Ich habe eben mit der Rupp (BUT: mit Anna Rupp) gesprochen.
  iii (S) familiarly, in Central and South Germany: Ich habe den Rudolf gesehen. Ich bin bei der Frau Schmidt gewesen.
  iv to individualize the person concerned more strongly: Ich hätte den Klaus sofort wiedererkannt. Der Lehmann hat vorzüglich geredet.
  v in the rural formula 'die Sabest Minna' (H. Broch) = Minna Sabest.

(f) No def. art. in German for Emperors (Kaiser Karl V., the Emperor Charles V) nor in names of the following type (where German has apposition): Schloß Sanssouci *the Palace of Sanssouci*, Kloster Beuron *the Monastery of Beuron*.

J. MISCELLANEOUS USES AND OMISSIONS OF THE ARTICLES

85. (a) **The def. art. is generally used before the names of seasons, months and meals**

Der Sommer ist zu Ende; der Juli war sehr warm; im Sommer, im Juli; BUT: Es war Sommer/Juli; das Wetter war kühl für Juli; vor, nach, seit Juli

Das Frühstück war reichlich (*plentiful*); vor dem/zum/beim Frühstück; BUT: Ich habe (das) Frühstück bestellt; wann bekommen wir Frühstück?

(b) **Further common nouns and phrases where English has no article and German has the def. art.**

im Bett *in bed*	das Parlament *parliament*
(BUT: Ich ging zu Bett)	im Parlament *in parliament*
beim Fußball *at football*	mit der Post *by post*
im Gefängnis *in prison*	Die Schule ist gut für ihn *School is*
der Himmel *heaven*	*good for him*
die Hölle *hell*	vor der Schule *before school*
in der Kirche *at church*	in der Stadt *in town*
zum Markt *to market*	mit dem Zug (Schiff etc.) *by train*
das Paradies *paradise*	(*boat etc.*)

(c) **The def. art. is always used before 'meist'**

Er hat das meiste Geld	*He has most money*
das meiste davon	*most of it*
die meisten Jungen	*most boys; most of the boys*
die meisten meiner Freunde	*most of my friends*
der größere Teil unserer Triebkraft/	N.B. *most of our industrial energy/of the*
des Kuchens	*cake*

(d) **The def. art. is used with the sense of 'each' as an alternative to 'pro':** Die Butter kostet drei Mark das Pfund; wir fuhren 80 Kilometer die Stunde; sie kommt zweimal die Woche (or: in der Woche); er verdient 1000 Mark im Monat (also: den Monat (coll.)).

(e) **No article before professions and other broad classes, used as the complement of sein, werden or bleiben:** Er ist Arzt; er wurde Arzt; ihr Mann ist Franzose/Deutscher; er ist Katholik, Oberleutnant; er blieb Junggeselle *a bachelor*.

BUT: Er ist ein bekannter Arzt, ein Schwindler, ein Narr, (ein) Fanatiker.

(f) **Omission of article in officialese** (cf. Du. Gram. 1490), as in: Beklagter hat zugegeben . . . *The accused has admitted* . . . Überbringer *the bearer*, Unterzeichneter *the undersigned*.

(g) **Other idiomatic instances of complement or real subject without an article:**

Das ist Geschmacksache	*That is a matter of taste*
Es ist Mode (geworden)	*It is (has become) the fashion*
Das ist hier Sitte	*That is the custom here*
Donnerstags ist Sitzung[1]	*On Thursdays there is (always) a meeting*

[1] From Erben, op. cit., p. 93.

Es ist Tatsache, daß ...	*It is a fact that* ...
Tatsache ist, daß ...	
Es ist Sache der Soziologie, diesem Konflikt nachzuspüren (*Hbg. Abendblatt*)	*It is the business of sociology to investigate this conflict*
Grund meines Schreibens ist der Artikel 'Unser Garten' (Letter in *Hbg. Abendblatt*)	*The reason for my writing is the article 'Our Garden'*

(h) No article after 'als' meaning 'as' (in the capacity of, by way of, as being)

Er sprach als Franzose	*He spoke as a Frenchman*
Er sprach wie ein Franzose	BUT: *He spoke like a Frenchman*
Er gab mir dies als Belohnung	*He gave me this as a reward*
Als (überzeugter) Demokrat, kann ich das nicht gutheißen	*As a (convinced) democrat, I can't approve of that*
Als erstes kaufte ich mir eine Zeitung	*The first thing I did was to buy a paper*
Er gilt als guter Chirurg	*He is considered [as being] a good surgeon*
Er gilt als der beste Chirurg	BUT: *He is considered the best surgeon*

(i) The article is often omitted, in literary and journalistic German, before a substantival phrase in apposition to the subject

Westfale von Geburt, lebte er jetzt in Bayern	*A Westphalian by birth, he was now living in Bavaria*
Bei aller Geschäftigkeit hat dieses Zürich, Treffpunkt der Kaufleute, etwas Kurorthaftes (M. Frisch)	*For all its bustle, this Zürich, the meeting-place of businessmen, has something of a spa about it*
Neil Armstrong, amerikanischer Astronaut, betrat als erster Mensch den Mond (*Zeit*)	*Neil Armstrong, the American astronaut, was the first man to set foot on the moon.*

(j) The article (mainly the def. art.) is sometimes omitted before an attributive adjective. This can be an effective and often arresting literary device, demanding a good deal of 'Sprachgefühl', though the first three examples represent almost fixed usage:

Beigefügter Zeitungsausschnitt dürfte Sie interessieren	*The enclosed cutting might interest you*
folgendes Beispiel	*the following example*
Das ist beschlossene Sache	*That's definitely arranged*
Jüngstes Mitglied der Regierung ist X.	*The youngest member of the government is X*
Gleicher Doppelsinn ... lauert im Titel (from a book review in *FAZ*)	*A similar ambiguity lurks in the title*
Im Straßengraben grünte erstes Unkraut (H. Broch)	*The first weeds sprouted in the roadside ditch*

Sie erschrak oft, wenn ihr klar wurde, wie vernünftig er war: genauer Rechner, scharfer Kalkulator, ... : kühles Hirn, scheues Gesicht ... (H. Böll)

(k) No article in the adverbial genitive, e.g. schweren Herzens *with a heavy heart*: see end of 60.

(l) i The names of indispositions and illnesses are generally used without an article: Er hat Kopfschmerzen, Husten, Grippe, (eine) Lungenentzündung *pneumonia*, (die) Gelbsucht *jaundice*
EXCEPTIONS: Er hat eine Erkältung, einen Schnupfen *a cold in the head*,

den Schluckauf *hiccups*

ii With actual illnesses denoted by a plural noun, the def. art. is frequently used and is never wrong: Er hat (die) Masern *measles*, (die) Röteln *German measles*

iii Examples of indispositions and illnesses limited by adjectives:

Er hat schlimme Masern	*He's got measles badly*
Ich habe ekligen Rheumatismus	*I've got nasty rheumatism*
Er hat einen schlimmen Husten	*He has a bad cough*
Ich hatte eine langwierige Grippe	*I had a lengthy bout of flu*
Er hat eine leichte Lungenentzündung	*He has slight pneumonia*

(m) **Articles are often omitted in newspaper headlines and advertisements**

Verbrechen gestanden. Münchner Kaufmann von Geschäftspartner erschlagen (*Hbg. Abendblatt*)	*Crime admitted. Munich business-man killed by partner*
Möglichst nahe Stadtmitte (*Hbg. Abendblatt*)	(accommodation required) *as near as possible to town-centre*

III ADJECTIVES

A. UNINFLECTED AND INFLECTED USE OF ADJECTIVES

86. Uninflected use of adjectives: used non-attributively, German adjectives are not inflected: Sie waren fleißig. Vor dem Haus stand ein Mann, kahl, blaß und mager.[1] Optimistisch wie immer, ließ sie sich von ihrem Vorhaben nicht abhalten.

The exceptional instances of attributive adjectives being uninflected are treated in 116.

87. Inflected use of adjectives: used attributively, i.e. when they limit a following noun, German adjectives are inflected, being declined in three different ways: the weak declension, the mixed declension and the strong declension. (Logically, the strong declension should be treated first, but in view of its more protracted commentary, it has seemed preferable to place it last.)

The adjective endings are presented schematically at the beginning of each of the three declensions.

B. WEAK DECLENSION

88. Weak declension: der (dieser etc.) + adj. + noun

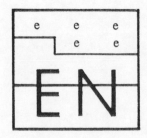

---

[1] Only where there are two or more adjectives can they be placed after the noun; the effect is rather literary.

SING.

N.	der gute Wein	die gute Suppe	das gute Brot
A.	den guten Wein	die gute Suppe	das gute Brot
G.	des guten Weines	der guten Suppe	des guten Brotes
D.	dem guten Wein	der guten Suppe	dem guten Brot

PLUR.	N.	die guten Suppen
	A.	die guten Suppen
	G.	der guten Suppen
	D.	den guten Suppen

SING.

N.	dieser gute Wein	diese gute Suppe	dieses gute Brot
A.	diesen guten Wein	diese gute Suppe	dieses gute Brot
G.	dieses guten Weines	dieser guten Suppe	dieses guten Brotes
D.	diesem guten Wein	dieser guten Suppe	diesem guten Brot

PLUR.	N.	diese guten Suppen
	A.	diese guten Suppen
	G.	dieser guten Suppen
	D.	diesen guten Suppen

89. The weak declension is used after the def. art. and after the following:

aller *all*
beide *both, two* (plur. only)
dieser *this*
irgendwelcher *some (or other), any (whatsoever)*
jeder *each, every*
jedweder (archaic) *each, every*

jeglicher (obsolescent) *each, every*
jener *that*
mancher sing.: *many a*
    plur.: *some, many*
sämtlicher *all, complete*
solcher *such*
welcher? *which?*

These words are all declined like 'dieser' (with the deviation given in N.i below); the paradigms in 88 show that the endings of 'dieser' are identical with those of 'der' except in the nom. and acc. fem., neut. and plur., where they are similar: the weak declension is therefore used after 'der' and words declined like it. (One deviation from this is given in N.ii below and a few others are noted in Chap. VI Sect. B where the words listed above are treated in detail; see Index.)

NOTE:

i Masc. and neut. gen. sing.: a variation: the declension of der, dieser and jener is fixed, but all the other words listed above, apart from beide, may have the ending -en before the gen. sing. of a masc. or neut. noun other than a Group 7 noun or a substantival adjective (see 106 ff.); the ending of the attributive adjective is not affected:

Das war der Ursprung alles/allen späteren Fortschritts	*That was the origin of all later progress*
ein Beweis solchen starken Glaubens	*a proof of such strong faith*
	BUT:
jedes guten Christen (Gr. 7)	*of every good Christian*
der Genuß manches Schönen (subst. adj.)	*the enjoyment of many things of beauty*

3+

This masc. and neut. gen. in -en, as circumscribed above, is found:

occasionally in the case of jeder and welcher.
frequently in the case of aller, mancher, solcher.
always in the case of irgendwelcher, jedweder, jeglicher, sämtlicher.

The above variation is largely determined by ear; if in doubt, it is safer to use the gen. in -es.

ii dieser + mein (dein etc.) + adj. + noun: the declension of 'mein' is fixed and the adjective has the mixed declension (see 90): dieser mein jüngster Sohn; mit diesem meinem jüngsten Sohn.

C. MIXED DECLENSION

90. Mixed declension:[1] **ein (kein, mein etc.) + adj + noun**

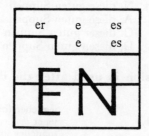

SING.

N. ein guter Wein	eine gute Suppe	ein gutes Brot
A. einen guten Wein	eine gute Suppe	ein gutes Brot
G. eines guten Weines	einer guten Suppe	eines guten Brotes
D. einem guten Wein	einer guten Suppe	einem guten Brot

N. ihr guter Wein	ihre gute Suppe	ihr gutes Brot
A. ihren guten Wein	ihre gute Suppe	ihr gutes Brot
G. ihres guten Weines	ihrer guten Suppe	ihres guten Brotes
D. ihrem guten Wein	ihrer guten Suppe	ihrem guten Brot

PLUR. N. ihre guten Suppen
A. ihre guten Suppen
G. ihrer guten Suppen
D. ihren guten Suppen

Here the adjective indicates the case in the masc. nom. and the neut. nom. and acc., where ein (kein, mein etc.) have no ending and, incidentally, in the fem. nom. and acc.

91. The mixed declension is used after the indef. art. and after the words which, in the sing., are declined like it, viz.

---

[1] The convenient term 'mixed declension' is used in some German grammars written in English, but German grammarians do not normally use an equivalent term.

irgendein *some* (*or other*), *any* (*whatsoever*), kein *no* and the possessive adjectives:

mein *my*	unser *our*
dein *your* (familiar sing.)	euer *your* (familiar plur.)
sein *his, its*	ihr *their*
ihr *her, its*	Ihr *your* (polite)

In the plural:

i ein drops away, leaving adj. + noun (strong declension).

ii kein, mein etc. are declined like dieser and the adjective ends in -en throughout; the plural of irgendein is irgendwelche (see 207(e)i).

92. Note:

(a) **A warning:** through their ending in -(e)r, a common error is to bring the masc. nom. and the neut. nom. and acc. of unser, euer and ihr into line with those of dieser and to write or say 'ihrer Vater' instead of 'ihr Vater', 'unseres Haus' instead of 'unser Haus'. The thing to remember is that all the possessive adjectives are declined like ein; therefore where ein has no ending, unser, euer and ihr have no ending.

(b) **Spelling of inflected unser and euer:** wherever unser and euer have an ending, the unstressed e of the stem is frequently dropped, especially in spoken German. In the masc. acc., the masc. and neut. dat. and the dat. plur. the alternative possibility of dropping the e of the ending is commoner. (It is not wrong to retain both e's.) E.g. das Dach unsres Hauses, in unsrer Stadt, die Namen eurer Kinder, in unserm/unsrem Garten, mit unsern/unsren Eltern.

(c) **The titular Euer:** an uninflected Euer is an alternative in the four singular cases of feminine titular words, e.g. Euer (commoner: Eure) Majestät, mit Euer (commoner: Eurer) Exzellenz; the written abbreviation of any of these is Ew. A declined Ihr will also be accepted.

D. STRONG DECLENSION

93. Strong declension: adj. + noun

er	e	es
en	e	es
en	er	**en**
em	er	em

e
e
er
en

SING.

N. guter Wein	gute Suppe	gutes Brot
A. guten Wein	gute Suppe	gutes Brot
G. guten Weines	guter Suppe	guten Brotes
D. gutem Wein	guter Suppe	gutem Brot

Plur. N. gute Suppen
     A. gute Suppen
     G. guter Suppen
     D. guten Suppen

94. Here the adjective does the work of indicating the case (thence, no doubt, the 'strong' declension), having the endings of dieser, except in the masc. and neut. gen. where the -(e)s ending of the noun indicates the case and the adjective ends in -en.

In two instances, however, the adjective must end in -es in the masc. and neut. gen., viz. before a Group 7 noun and before a substantival adjective (see 106ff.), neither of which has a distinctive genitive ending. As most Group 7 nouns denote persons, the combination adj. + Group 7 in the gen. sing. is negligibly rare. In a pseudo-Schillerian drama, the following stirring iambic might conceivably occur:

    Das nenn' ich edles Helden kühnen Mut.

Quite normal, of course, is the combination miscellaneous adj. + Group 7 (sing.); miscellaneous adjectives with a tendency to end in -en in the masc. and neut. gen. must end in -es before Group 7 (cf. 89 N.i), e.g. Er kannte den Namen jedes/jeden neuen Schülers BUT: jedes Studenten.

Note: The terms 'strong declension' and 'strong endings' as used in this book imply -en in the masc. and neut. gen. sing., while 'the endings of dieser' is used to indicate -es in masc. and neut. gen. sing.

95. The simplest form of the strong declension is adj. + noun (mit neuem Mut, das hohe Niveau französischer Filme); **it is also used when adj. + noun** are immediately preceded by, and **form a unit with, a word or phrase that does not indicate their case.** Such are:

(a) the following uninflected forms:
    manch *many a, many*: manch reichen Landes.
    solch *such*: bei solch gutem Wetter.
    viel *much, many*: viel indischer Tee.
    welch! *what (a)!*: Welch herrliches Wetter!
    wenig *little, few*: wenig deutsche Bücher.
    (See Chap. VI for the detailed treatment of these words.)

(b) indeclinable words and phrases denoting quantity or range, e.g.

ein bißchen *a little*	derlei *suchlike*
ein wenig *a little*	keinerlei *of no sort, not any*
ein paar *a few*	mancherlei *various*
etwas *some, any* (sing. only)	mehrerlei *various*
lauter *nothing but, a whole lot of*	solcherlei *suchlike*
mehr *more*	vielerlei *many kinds of*
weniger *less, fewer*	welcherlei *what kind of; whatever*
was für . . .?[1] *what (kind of)?*	wievielerlei? *how many kinds of?*
was für . . .![1] *what!*	zweierlei *two kinds of*
	dreierlei etc. *three kinds of*
allerhand⎫ *all kinds of, various*	
allerlei ⎭	

---

[1] plur. of was für ein, but also used in sing. without ein (see 175(a)ii).

etwas frisches Obst	*some fresh fruit*
lauter wertvolle Bilder	*a whole lot of valuable pictures*
Er trank noch mehr starken Kaffee mit ein bißchen braunem Zucker	*He drank some more strong coffee with a little brown sugar*
Er redete allerlei dummes Zeug	*He talked a lot of nonsense*
Er nannte mir die Namen zweierlei englischer Äpfel	*He gave me the names of two kinds of English apples*

(c) cardinal numbers (other than 'one'):

zwei schöne Pfirsiche	*two fine peaches*
Da standen an siebenhundert deutsche Kriegsgefangene (Th. Plievier)	*Getting on for seven hundred German prisoners of war were standing there*
	BUT:
die zwei schönen Pfirsiche	*the two fine peaches*
seine zwei jungen Söhne	*his two young sons*

See also 242(a)

(d) genitives denoting possession:

Karls unermüdlicher Eifer	*Karl's indefatigable zeal*
in meines Vaters kleinem Arbeitszimmer	*in my father's little study*
Mein Freund, dessen ältester Sohn krank ist, ...	*My friend, whose eldest son is ill, ...*

in den ... Gartensalon hinab, hinter dessen hoher Glastür die Terrasse lag (Th. Mann).

96. The adjective is still used attributively, and inflected, if the following noun is understood, being represented by 'one' in English:

Welcher Junge ist das? Es ist der dumme	*Which boy is that? It's the stupid one*
Ich habe mein Taschenmesser verloren; ich muß mir ein neues kaufen	*I've lost my penknife; I must buy a new one*
Englische Äpfel sind besser als deutsche	*English apples are better than German ones*

E. ADJECTIVAL USE OF PARTICIPLES

97. The following types of participle may be used as attributive adjectives, being declined exactly as adjectives are:

(a) all present participles, though 'seiend' and 'habend' may be excluded.

ein lachendes Kind	*a laughing child*
lachende Kinder	*laughing children*

(b) the past participle of transitive verbs:

mein verlorener Schirm	*my lost umbrella*

(c) the past participle of intransitive verbs conjugated with sein and signifying a completed action:

die angekommenen Gäste	*the guests who had arrived*
nach der geglückten Generalprobe gegen Frankreich (*Die Zeit* on football)	*after the successful dress-rehearsal against France*

der hereingelaufene Junge   *the boy who had run in*
der Junge, der gelaufen war,   BUT: *the boy who had been running*
     (stress on duration, not on comple-
     tion)

98. Adjectival participles: many present participles, and many past participles (when they are not being used to form compound tenses), have come to be felt as adjectives rather than participles, e.g.

angreifend *tiring, trying*	angegriffen *worn, ill*
auffallend *striking, conspicuous*	aufgeregt *excited*
aufregend *exciting*	erfahren *experienced*
empörend *shocking*	gelehrt *learned*
reizend *charming*	verrückt *deranged, insane*

F. NOUN OF MEASUREMENT + ADJECTIVE + NOUN

99. (S) Noun of measurement + adj. + noun denoting the thing measured: the noun denoting the thing measured may be put in the genitive, but, since the gen. of adj. + noun—and especially the gen. sing.—has a somewhat stilted ring, the case in apposition is generally preferred, especially in conversation:[1]

Eine Tasse starker Kaffee würde mir   *A cup of strong coffee would do me good*
gut tun
. . . und beschloß, mir noch zwei   *. . . and decided, before going ahead, to*
Tassen echten Kaffee zu bereiten   *make myself two cups of real coffee*
(A. Goes)
Er kam mit einer Tasse starkem   *He came with a cup of strong coffee*
Kaffee
Ich aß ein Stück frisches Brot   *I ate a piece of fresh bread*

NOTE: As Duden rightly observes (Gram. 2185), in the dative the adjective preceding the second noun is frequently given the weak ending -en:

mit einem Stück brüchigen Eisen   *with a piece of cracked iron*
(W. Raabe) (Duden's example)
Ich bestrafe Sie mit drei Wochen   *I'm giving you three weeks' close arrest*
geschärften Arrest (A. Goes)

Examples of literary usage; genitive instead of apposition:
eine bedeutende Fläche sumpfigen   *a considerable area of marshy meadow-land*
Wiesenlandes (Storm)
ein Stück frostigen Winterhimmels   *a piece of frosty winter sky*
(Th. Plievier)

100. When the noun denoting the thing measured, preceded by an adjective, is plural, the following is the commonest practice:

(a) **(S)** After a specific noun of weight or quantity, use the case in apposition:
zwei Dutzend frische Eier   *two dozen fresh eggs*
Er kam mit einem Paar braunen   *He came with a pair of brown shoes*
Schuhen

---

[1] For usage where there is no adj., see 56.

(b) After a vaguer, more general word of quantity, use gen. or von:

Er saß hinter einem Berg neuer Bücher (or: von neuen Büchern)	*He was sitting behind a pile of new books*
eine Menge nützlicher Anregungen (*SZ*)	*a number of useful suggestions*
eine Gruppe müder Reisender	*a group of tired travellers*

(c) After ein Korb, ein Kasten and analogous words, use mit: ein Korb mit süßen Äpfeln.

101. If both nouns are in the gen. sing. and the second is preceded by an adjective, official usage is to put both into the genitive. Normal usage conforms to this if one of the two nouns is fem., but, if both are masc. or neut., uses von instead of the first gen.; whereupon the second becomes dative, in apposition, its adjective possibly having the weak ending -en (cf. 99 N.):

der Preis	*the price*
eines Liters frischer Milch	*of a litre of fresh milk*
eines Pfundes gekochten Schinkens/von einem Pfund gekochtem (or: gekochten) Schinken	*of a pound of boiled ham*

102. After 'die Sorte' the genitive is used, after 'die Art' the case in apposition: diese Sorte englischer Äpfel; diese Art englische Rose; mit einer Art zornigen Unschuld (E. Langgässer).[1]

G. SPELLING OF CERTAIN ADJECTIVES

103. Spelling of adjectives in -el, -en, -er and of 'hoch', when inflected

(a) Those in -el always drop the e of the stem, e.g. ein dunkler Wald, eine respektable Leistung (Duden's example: Haupt: Adjektiv 10).

(b) Those in -en sometimes do so: Er hat einen seltenen (seltnen) Schmetterling gefangen.
This may also apply, in speech but hardly in writing, to the past participle of strong verbs: in der gegebnen Situation; zerrißnes Papier (But only 'die Geschworenen' *the jury*).

(c) Those in -er: foreign adjectives in -er (e.g. makaber) always drop the e of the stem: eine makabre Geschichte (Du. Haupt. Adjektiv 10); others sometimes do so, especially where the e of the stem is preceded by a diphthong (e.g. teuer): mit teuren Weinen; mit munteren (or: muntren) Studenten.

(d) Note:
  i The -er of comparatives is usually retained: see 121 N.B.
  ii ander: see 190(c).
  iii The e of an internal -el or -er is also frequently dropped: neb(e)lig, wäss(e)rig.

[1] see 99 N.

(e) hoch drops the c when inflected: Dieser Berg ist hoch, BUT: ein hoher Berg.

104. Adjectives spelt with or without a final e

e.g. Er ist feig or feige *cowardly*; both have the same inflected forms: der feige Junge, ein feiger Junge etc.

The following list of these adjectives gives what is probably the commoner of the two forms: blöd, böse, fade *insipid; dull, trite*, feige, irre *confused*, leise, mild, müde, öde, träge *indolent, sluggish*, trübe, vage, zäh.

Note:

i Adverbially, only the forms böse, fade, leise, öde, vage are usual, but either form of the remaining words may be used.

ii Colloquially, the adj. and adv. allein often adds an e.

iii dick and dünn add an e in two slang phrases:

Du mußt es ja sehr dicke haben	*You must be rolling in money*
Ich habe mich dünne gemacht	*I made myself scarce*

H. INFLECTION OF A SERIES OF ADJECTIVES[1]

105. In all three declensions, two or more adjectives have the same ending: dieser schöne, große Garten; mein lieber alter Vater; gutes bayrisches Bier; die Lösung wichtiger politischer Probleme.

Note: There is **one occasional deviation** in the strong declension: in the masc. and neut. dat. there is a tendency to give the second (and subsequent) adjectives the weak ending -en, especially where the second adjective forms a conceptual unit with the noun, such that the two adjectives are not separated by commas and could not be joined by 'und', as in the second and third examples below:

Nach langem, beunruhigenden Schweigen ließ er wieder von sich hören	*After a long disquieting silence he wrote again*[2]
mit dunklem bayrischen Bier	*with dark Bavarian beer*
mit hohem steifen Kragen (Arno Schmidt)	*with a high stiff collar*[2]

I. SUBSTANTIVAL ADJECTIVES AND PARTICIPLES

106. All adjectives and all those participles which may be used as attributive adjectives (see 97) can be used as nouns. In the masc., fem. and plur. they mainly denote persons; in the neut. they mainly denote abstract or collective concepts. They are written with a capital letter (with the exceptions noted in 110 and 732) and are inflected as if they were followed by Mann, Frau, Menschen and e.g. Element (neut.) respectively, e.g.

MASC.: der Fremde *the stranger*, ein Fremder, ich fragte einen Deutschen.

FEM.: eine Angestellte *employee*, die Antwort der Angestellten.

---

[1] for punctuation see 743(i).

[2] Regarding the absence of the indef. art. in the German, see 78(c).

PLUR.: Fremde, die Angestellten.

NEUT.: Das Wahre ist wichtiger als das Schöne; das Hervorragende (*the outstanding thing*) an diesem Film; Schöneres habe ich nie gesehen.

N.B. Hereafter the term 'substantival adjective' will be used to include both adjectives and participles used substantivally, unless specifically stated.

107. Notes on substantival adjectives

(a) **They are rarely used alone in the gen. plur.**; thus in the phrase 'mit der Hilfe Verwandter' normal usage would substitute 'von Verwandten'.

(b) **der Beamte** *the official* was formed from an old participle 'beam(p)t' *entrusted with an office* (Du. Haupt. p. 103), which, in the form 'beamtet', is little used today.

(c) **der Junge** *boy* is declined as a Group 7 noun, **die Brünette** and **die Kokette** *coquette* as Group 6 nouns, and not according to the adj. declensions: Er ist ein netter Junge; ich sprach mit der Brünette.

(d) **(S) Some substantival adjectives have special meanings,** e.g.
die Rechte 1. *right hand* 2. *the Right* (in politics) (cf. die Linke)
die Gerade 1. *straight line* (geom.) 2. *the straight* (on a racecourse) 3. eine rechte Gerade *a straight right* (boxing)
die Elektrische *tram* (from 'die elektrische Bahn')
das Junge *young* (of animals), *cub* etc.
Wir gingen ins Freie *We went into the open*
Wir schliefen im Freien *We slept in the open*
die Schwarzen 1. *negroes* 2. *Roman Catholics* (as a political force, a clerical party)

(e) **A substantival adjective may be limited by an adverb:**
das typisch Deutsche an seiner Rede   *the typically German thing about his speech*

108. Declension of substantival adjectives when preceded by an attributive adjective

In the weak and mixed declensions regularity prevails: with the one exception noted below, the attrib. adj. and the subst. adj. are inflected identically throughout: der arme Fremde, ein armer Fremder

EXCEPTION: In the neut. nom. and acc. of the mixed declension, Äußere, Innere, Ganze are generally given the weak ending (cf. Du. Gram. 2260). E.g.
sein schlichtes Äußere   *his plain outward appearance*
ein einheitliches Ganze(s)   *a uniform whole*

In the strong declension:

(a) Attrib. adj. and subst. adj. have the same endings (e.g. Karls alter Bekannter; arme Alte!) except:
i in the dat. sing.: here the subst. adj. ends in -en:
Ich sprach mit Karls altem   *I spoke to Karl's old acquaintance*
    Bekannten

3*

ii in the nom. and acc. plur. after a gen. expressing possession: here the
subst. adj. ends in -en:

Vaters alte Bekannten[1]   *father's old acquaintances*
                               BUT:
lauter alte Bekannte   *a whole lot of old acquaintances*

(b) The gen. sing. is not used, 'von' being substituted.

(c) The gen. plur. is somewhat stilted:[2] die Erlebnisse mancherlei armer
Heimatloser/vier junger Deutscher.

Normal usage is 'von': die Erlebnisse von vier jungen Deutschen/von
ein paar jungen Deutschen.

Coupled with a gen. expressing possession, 'von' **must** be used:

die Erlebnisse von Karls alten   *the experiences of Karl's old acquain-*
Bekannten   *tances*

(d) The neut. nom., acc. and dat. are in practice rare, e.g.

Neues Aufregendes ist geschehen   *New exciting events have occurred*

109. The substantival adjective in apposition: Herr Müller, der neue
Angestellte; Heinrich Schulze, Geschäftsreisender, 35 Jahre alt; das
hat uns, als junge Deutsche, interessiert.

There are two deviations from orthodoxy:

i Where the noun to which the subst. adj. refers is in the gen. sing.; see
63(a).

ii In the dat. sing. of the strong declension, the commonest practice is to
give the substantival adjective the weak ending (–en), but a preceding
attributive adjective the strong ending (–em or –er) (see also 115):

Der Chef sprach mit ihm, als   *The director spoke to him as the oldest*
ältestem Angestellten   *employee*

**110. Substantival adjectives are written with a small letter in many
set phrases,** e.g.

auf dem laufenden bleiben   *to be acquainted with what is going on*
Es bleibt beim alten   *Things remain as they were; we carry on*
                            as before
bei weitem   *by far*
Er ging bis ins kleinste   *He went into the smallest details*
Ich fragte den ersten besten   *I asked the first person I met*
den kürzeren ziehen   *to get the worst of it*
im allgemeinen   *in general*
im (großen und) ganzen   *on the whole*
im stillen   *on the quiet*
im trüben fischen   *to fish in troubled waters*
jemanden zum besten haben   *to make a fool of someone*
(BUT: zum Besten der Armen   *for the benefit of the poor*)

Note:

i See also 116(h) and 732, Exc. (b).

---

[1] It is thus distinguished from the fem. sing. Vaters alte Bekannte.
[2] To be sure, a letter recently received contained: Ich komme zum Besuch guter Bekannter
für ein paar Tage nach London.

ii With few deviations, the indefinite adjectives (see 112(b)) have a small
   letter when used substantivally (cf. 732, Exc. (c)):

Ich habe noch verschiedenes zu tun   *I've still got various things to do*
Jetzt sind viele dagegen   *Now many people are against it*

iii Von allen Tieren ist der Hund das treueste: here 'das treueste', standing
    for 'das treueste Tier', is not a substantival adjective in the true
    sense; thence the small letter. Contrast: Alice könnte überall die
    Schönste, die Erste und Einzige sein (H. Mann); here there is no
    noun, elsewhere in the sentence, that is understood after the three
    adjectives.

J. NICHTS NEUES and ALLES NEUE

111. (a) When linked up with a preceding indeclinable or uninflected word,
   the neuter adjective has the strong endings,[1] but the genitive case is
   generally avoided.

(b) When linked up with a preceding inflected word, the neuter adjective
    has the weak endings.

In both cases it often has a collective connotation, that can only be
rendered by a plural in English.

The neuter adjective has a capital letter, except for most of the indefinite adjectives (see 732, Exc. (c)).

This gives the following two types:

(a)	(b)
N.A. **nichts Neues** *nothing new*	**alles Neue** *everything new*
G. (nichts Neuen)	alles[2] Neuen
D. nichts Neuem	allem Neuen

Further instances of type (a):
allerhand/allerlei Neues   *all kinds of new things, various new*
                                        things
etwas ganz Neues   *something quite new*
ganz was Neues (coll.)
genug Neues   *enough new things*
lauter Neues   *nothing but new things; a whole lot of*
                                        new things
eine Liste von mancherlei Neuem   *a list of various new things*
   (avoiding gen.)
was für Neues?   *what new things?*

Further instances of type (b):
folgendes Neue   *the following new matter*
der Einkauf verschiedenes Unnötigen   *the purchase of various unnecessary things*
weiteres Neue   *further new things*

N.B. Distinguish:
alles Mögliche   *everything possible*
alles mögliche   *all kinds of things* (idiomatic)

---

[1] Historically, Neues was a gen. sing. ('nothing of the new'): cf. Weser loc. cit. in 60 (footnote), p. 226.
[2] Miscellaneous adjectives with a tendency to end in -en in the masc. and neut. gen. sing.
(cf. 89, N.i) must end in -es in this context.

K. DECLENSION OF ADJECTIVES AFTER AN INDEFINITE ADJECTIVE

112. Indefinite adjectives

(a) The declension of adjectives after a number of words to which the term 'indefinite adjective' would be applicable has been treated in 89 (irgendwelcher, mancher) and 95(b) (e.g. allerhand, allerlei, mancherlei etc., ein bißchen, etwas *some, any*, lauter, mehr, weniger); , this will not be repeated here.

After irgendein *some (or other)*, any *(whatsoever)* the mixed declension is used.

(b) The term 'indefinite adjective' is traditionally and conveniently applied to the following. (An asterisk denotes that the word is fully treated in Chap. VI B.):

ähnlich *similar*
ander* *other*
besagt *aforesaid*
bestimmt *certain*
derartig *suchlike, such*
einige* *some, a few*
einzeln *single, individual*
etliche[1] *some, several, a few*
etwaig *possible, potential*
folgend *the following*
genannt *aforenamed*
gewiß *certain*
mehrere *several*

obig *above-mentioned*
sogenannt *so-called*
sonstig *other, remaining*
übrig *other, remaining*
unzählbar *innumerable*
unzählig *innumerable*
verschiedene *various, several*
vieler,[2] viele* *much, many*
weiter *further, additional*
weniger,[2] wenige* *little, few*
zahllos *innumerable*
zahlreich *numerous*

(c) These indefinite adjectives have strong, weak or mixed endings like any other adjective: ähnlicher Wein; die Wirkung derartigen Mutes; dieser ähnliche Wein; sein übriges Leben.

113. The declension of attributive and substantival adjectives in the following combinations:

indef. adj. + attrib. adj. + noun

indef. adj. (+ attrib. adj.) + subst. adj.

(a) **in the singular:**

i For ander, einige, viel and wenig, see 190(b)ii, 205(a), 228, 230.

ii After folgend, weak endings predominate:

folgender neue Plan   *the following new plan*
folgendes unglaubliche Ergebnis   *the following incredible result*
mit folgender nachdrücklichen Warnung   *with the following emphatic warning*

iii With most of the remainder, the above combinations rarely occur in the singular; where they do, the attrib. adj. normally has the strong

---

[1] has a somewhat archaic flavour, but is by no means rare.
[2] After the uninflected forms viel and wenig, an attrib. adj. has the strong endings (see 228).

endings, though the weak ending is often used in the masc. and neut. dat.:

obiger griechischer Philosoph	*the above-mentioned Greek philosopher*
weiteres dummes Gerede	*further foolish talk*
nach weiterem dummem (or: dummen) Gerede	*after further foolish talk*

iv In neuter collective phrases of the type alles Neue *everything new*, mehreres Neue *several new things*, the second component has the weak endings: see 111, type (b).

(b) **in the plural**:

Commonest usage: strong endings for all the adjectival components in all cases.

EXAMPLES: *many big rooms*   *several (young) Germans*

N.	viele große Zimmer	mehrere (junge) Deutsche
A.	viele große Zimmer	mehrere (junge) Deutsche
G.	vieler großer Zimmer	mehrerer (junger) Deutscher
D.	vielen großen Zimmern	mehreren (jungen) Deutschen

Note: In the gen., some Germans give the attrib. and subst. adjectives the weak ending -en, e.g. vieler großen Zimmer, vieler Reisenden, mehrerer (jungen) Deutschen. Colloquially, von + dat. is preferred.

114. **If the indefinite adjective is preceded by one of the words after which the weak or mixed declension is regularly used** (e.g. der, dieser, aller etc. or ein, kein, mein etc.), then the indef. adj., the attrib. adj. (and a subst. adj.) all and always have the weak or mixed endings as the case may be. E.g.

aller ähnliche französische Wein	*all similar French wine*
kein weiteres wichtiges Problem	*no further important problem*
unsere vielen neuen Angestellten	*our many new employees*

L. INFLECTION OF ATTRIBUTIVE AND SUBSTANTIVAL ADJECTIVES IN APPOSITION TO A PERSONAL PRONOUN

115. On the whole, **this construction is not much used**; instead of 'Ich gab ihm armem Kranken die Hand', the German will normally say: 'Ich gab ihm die Hand, als er krank dalag'.

The following should cover all practical needs. The little used gen. of the personal pron. is never followed by a phrase in apposition. (Str. and wk. refer to the inflection of the attrib. and subst. adj.)

N. SING.: str.: ich einsamer Fremder, du dummer Kerl, Sie Ärmster!
A. SING.: str.: für ihn als einsamen Fremden.
D. SING.: masc.: generally str.: Er hat sein Geld mir, als Ältestem, vermacht; fem.: wk.: mir alten Frau.
N. PLUR.: generally wk.: wir früheren Kollegen, wir (jungen) Deutschen (also: wir (junge) Deutsche).
A. PLUR.: str.: uns frühere Kollegen, uns (junge) Deutsche.
D. PLUR.: uns (jungen) Deutschen.

M. INSTANCES OF UNINFLECTED ATTRIBUTIVE ADJECTIVES

116. Attributive adjectives are uninflected in the following instances:

(a) before a nom. or acc. neut. noun (cf. Du. Gram. 2200 and 2210)
  i in certain set phrases and uses:

Ich bekam ein gut Teil[1] vom Geld	*I got a good part of the money*
ein gut Stück	*a good amount* (e.g. of work), *a good way* (distance)
ein gehörig (or: tüchtig) Stück Kuchen	*a substantial piece of cake*
etwas auf gut Glück tun	*to take a chance*
ruhig Blut bewahren	*to keep calm*
Er will sich lieb Kind bei mir machen	*He is trying to ingratiate himself with me*
groß A	*capital A*

N.B. one masc. and one fem. instance:

Wir sind wieder gut Freund	*We're friends again*
römisch III	*Roman figure III*

ii in some proverbs and in archaic and poetic style, e.g. Gut Ding will Weile haben (Du. Gram. 2210) *Nothing good is done in a hurry.*

iii sometimes, in conversation, outside the set phrases given in 116(a)i: ein einzig Wort, ihr eigen Kind, wir haben unser ander Haus verkauft, ein wunderbar Glas Bier. (In none of these would the inflected form be wrong.)

(b) einzig is often left uninflected before adj.+noun, where it refers primarily to the adjective, e.g.: Er war der einzig zufriedene Mensch *He was the only contented person*; die einzig mögliche Lösung; mein einzig anständiges Paar Schuhe.

cf. einzig before a substantival adjective: das einzig Gute *the one good thing*; das einzig Wahre an der Geschichte; er als einzig Überlebender.

(c) halb and ganz before the names of continents, countries (other than those used with the def. art.)[2] and towns, e.g.: halb Europa, in ganz München BUT: die ganze Schweiz, im ganzen Kongo.

(d) (S) the names of the inhabitants of towns, used adjectivally, but retaining their capital letter: Frankfurter Würstchen, des Kölner Doms, auf den Londoner Straßen.

Note:
i The origin of e.g. 'Frankfurter Würstchen' was 'die Würstchen der Frankfurter'.
ii For deviations from the type Frankfurt: Frankfurter, see 715(a)-er:1; the adjective of Hannover is hannoversch (declined).
iii der Kölner Dom, Hauptbahnhof etc., BUT: Kölnisch Wasser *eau-de-cologne*; Die Kölnische Zeitung.
iv Uninflected adjectives of the above type are also formed from die Schweiz and from the names of a number of provinces and regions,

---

[1] 'Teil' is here neut.; see 9.
[2] see 84(a) and (b) and 6(b).

where they are again identical with the name of the inhabitants.
E.g.

Kärntener *Carinthian* (Kärnten is an Austrian Bundesland.)
Pfälzer *of the Palatinate*
Rheingauer *of the Rheingau* (a wine-growing district west of Wiesbaden)
v Less common than the forms in -er are the inflected forms with the
suffix -isch, which are used attributively or predicatively and mainly
in contexts conveying the ethos of the place:
Er hat einen echt frankfurterischen (or: Frankfurter) Humor.
Sein Humor ist echt frankfurterisch (münchnerisch, düsseldorferisch etc.,
BUT: kölnisch).

(e) a number of adjectives of colour, foreign loan-words, of which the
commonest are rosa *pink* and lila *lilac* (cf. prima *first-rate*). Colloquially, 'rosan' and 'lilan' (inflected) are used attributively. Thus:
mit rosa (or: rosanen) Bändern *with pink ribbons*.
For 'orange' normal usage is e.g. ein orangenes Halstuch.

(f) the first of two adjectives of colour.
Duden (Gram. 2195) distinguishes between:

ein blau-grünes Kleid   *a blue and green dress*
ein blaugrünes Kleid   *a bluey-green dress*

In spoken German, the former is normally 'ein blau und grünes Kleid'.

(g) Certain miscellaneous adjectives have alternative uninflected forms:
all (see 187(b)), manch (217(c)), solch (222(b)), viel (226 ff.), welch
(174(e)), wenig (226 ff.).

(h) Substantival adjectives are uninflected in set phrases often involving
opposites (Du. Gram. 2275): Alt und jung, arm und reich,[1] strömten
aus der Stadt; bei arm und reich; jenseits von Gut und Böse *beyond
good and evil*.

N. ADJECTIVES USED WITH THE DATIVE CASE

**117. Many adjectives are used with the dative case, mostly cor-
responding to 'to' in English**

Note:
i These adjectives normally follow the dative noun or pronoun dependent
on them, but the following may also precede it: ähnlich, gleich, nahe,
treu, ungleich, untreu, e.g. Treu seinen Grundsätzen, hat er sein
Amt sofort niedergelegt.
ii Where indicated, the adjective may alternatively be used with 'für' (but
never with 'zu', a not uncommon error). The 'für' construction is
slightly more colloquial. The 'für' phrase generally precedes, but may
follow, the adjective. Thus:
Dieses Instrument ist mir sehr nützlich.
Dieses Instrument ist für mich sehr nützlich.
Dieses Instrument ist sehr nützlich für mich.

---

[1] These phrases have small letters, being the equivalent of jedermann (cf. Du. Taschen-
bücher 3: R 286).

iii Those marked with an asterisk are only used predicatively, e.g.

Das Glück war ihm hold   *Fortune favoured him*

The common ones are the following (mainly selected from Du. Gram. 5425):

ähnlich	*similar to*
Er ist (sieht) seinem Bruder sehr ähnlich	*He is (looks) very much like his brother*
angenehm (or für)	*agreeable to*
begreiflich	*comprehensible to*
behilflich	*helpful to*
Er war mir beim Umzug behilflich	*He helped me when I was moving*
bekannt	*known, familiar to*
dankbar	*grateful to*
eigen, eigentümlich	*peculiar to*
Er hatte das mit der ihm eigenen griesgrämigen Fröhlichkeit gesagt (H. Broch)	*He had said that with the surly cheerfulness that was peculiar to him*
ergeben	*devoted, attached to*
feind*	*hostile to*
fremd	*unknown to; alien to*
gehorsam (or with gegenüber)	*obedient to*
gemeinsam	*common to*
gesinnt	*disposed towards*
Er ist mir gutgesinnt, übelgesinnt, freundlich (feindlich) gesinnt.	
gewogen (rather literary)	*well disposed towards*
gleich	*a matter of indifference to, all the same to*
Es ist mir ganz gleich (gleichgültig, einerlei, egal, piepe (sl.), Wurst (sl.), Wurscht (sl.), Schnuppe (sl.)), ob er kommt oder nicht	*It's all the same to me whether he comes or not*
gram*	*angry with, bearing a grudge against*
hold* (elev.)	*favourably disposed towards*
lästig (or für)	*troublesome, a nuisance to*
leicht (or für)	*easy for*
nah, nahe	*near to*
Sie war dem Weinen/dem Tode nahe	*She was near to tears/to death*[1]
nützlich (or für)	*useful to*
peinlich (or für)	*embarrassing for*
schädlich (or für)	*injurious to*
schuldig	*owing*
Du bist mir 3 Mark schuldig	*You owe me 3 marks*
schwer (or für)	*difficult for*
treu	*faithful, loyal to*
überlegen	*superior to*
Er ist mir an Schlagfertigkeit überlegen	*He surpasses me at repartee*
unangenehm (or für)	*disagreeable for*
unbegreiflich (or für)	*incomprehensible to*
unbekannt	*unknown, unfamiliar to*
unentbehrlich (or für)	*indispensable to*
unmöglich (or für)	*impossible for*

---

[1] In literal, spatial contexts, 'near to' is usually nah(e) bei or in der Nähe von; nahe forms the sep. prefix of a number of verbs taking the dat., e.g. Sein Tod ist mir nahegegangen *I felt his death keenly.*

unterlegen	*inferior to*
untreu	*unfaithful, disloyal to*
unzugänglich (or für)	*inaccessible to*
verhaßt	*hateful to*
wichtig (or für)	*important to*
willkommen	*welcome to (someone)*
zugänglich (or für)	*accessible to*
zugetan*	*well-disposed towards, attached to*
zuwider*	1. *contrary to* (e.g. the law)
	2. *repugnant to*

Note:

iv An adjective or adverb limited by 'zu' or 'genug' is used with a preceding dative of the person interested. This construction is neater than the use of für; with the latter, the adjective may precede or follow the für phrase.

Diese Uhr ist mir zu teuer/ist zu teuer für mich	*This watch is too expensive for me*
... eines Mörders, dem keine Lüge zu frech ist (*Zeit*)	*of a murderer for whom no lie is too brazen*
Du gehst mir zu schnell	*You walk too fast for me*
Dieser Mantel ist mir nicht warm genug	*This coat is not warm enough for me*

O. ADJECTIVES USED WITH THE GENITIVE CASE

118. A certain number of adjectives are used with the genitive case, mostly corresponding to 'of' in English. Except for 'bar', they follow the genitive noun or pronoun dependent on them. The resultant phrases tend to have a somewhat stilted or literary ring and are not much used in ordinary conversation. **The commoner ones are the following** (selected from Du. Gram. 5445):

bar	*devoid of*
Seine Handlungsweise war bar aller Vernunft	*His mode of action was devoid of all reason*
bedürftig	*in need of*
bewußt	*conscious of*
Ich war mir meines Irrtums bewußt	*I was conscious of my error*
fähig (also: zu)	*capable of*
Er ist einer solchen Tat (or: zu einer solchen Tat) nicht fähig	*He is not capable of such a deed*
Er ist zu allem fähig	*He's capable of anything*
gewiß	*certain of*
Ich bin seiner Zustimmung gewiß	*I am certain of his consent*
kundig (elev.)	*versed in*
ledig	*free from* (e.g. an anxiety, a duty)
mächtig	*master of*
Sie ist des Deutschen absolut mächtig	*She has a complete command of German*
schuldig	*guilty of*
sicher	*sure of*
Du kannst seiner Freundschaft sicher sein	*You can be sure of his friendship*
überdrüssig (coll. also with acc.)	*tired of, sick of*
wert 1. with gen.	*worth (worthy of)*

Es ist nicht der Mühe wert	*It's not worth the trouble*
2. with acc.	*worth* (in value), also fig., e.g.
Er ist keinen Schuß Pulver wert	*He's not worth a cent*
würdig	*worthy of*

An example from officialese:

Er ist der Bürgerrechte für verlustig erklärt worden	*He has been deprived of his civic rights*

P. FULL OF

119. full of: the alternatives in normal use are covered by the following examples:

i *He brought a basket full of fruit*
   Er brachte einen Korb voll Obst, voller Obst

ii *He brought a basket full of apples*
   Er brachte einen Korb voll Äpfel, voller Äpfel

iii *He brought a basket full of lovely fruit*
   Er brachte einen Korb voll herrlichen Obstes (elev.)
   Er brachte einen Korb voll herrlichem Obst
   Er brachte einen Korb voll von (or: voll mit) herrlichem Obst

iv *He brought a basket full of lovely apples*
   Er brachte einen Korb voll herrlicher Äpfel
   Er brachte einen Korb voll von (or: voll mit) herrlichen Äpfeln
   Er brachte einen Korb voller herrlicher Äpfel

Note:

1. The indeclinable 'voller' cannot be used attributively and is never used with von or mit.
2. full of it: voll davon (voll damit)
   full of them (persons): voll von ihnen.
          (things): voll von ihnen, voll davon (voll damit)

Some literary examples:

Augen voll Ernst und Schwärmerei (Th. Mann)	*eyes full of seriousness and rapture*
Er erhielt ein Eßgeschirr voll heißen Wassers (Th. Plievier)	*He was given a mess-tin full of hot water*
Die Luft war voller Vogellaut, voll zierlich-innigem und süßem Flöten, Zwitschern . . . und Schluchzen (Th. Mann)	*The air was full of the sound of birds, full of a sweet, a delicate and moving fluting, twittering and sobbing*
aus Bunkern voller Sterbender (Th. Plievier)	*from pill-boxes full of dying men*

N.B. Adjectives used with prepositions are treated in Chap. XIII.

IV COMPARISON OF ADJECTIVES AND ADVERBS

A. FORMATION AND DECLENSION OF COMPARATIVE AND SUPERLATIVE

120. The normal rule for the formation of the comparative and superlative is as follows:

(a) **Adjectives**: the comparative and superlative are formed by adding -er and -st to the simple form:

voll	voller	der vollste[1]
langsam	langsamer	der langsamste[1]

The same rule is followed for polysyllabics (in contrast to English usage):

unwiderstehlich	unwiderstehlicher	der unwiderstehlichste

(b) **Adverbs**: the comparative is the same as that of the adjective; the main superlative is formed with 'am':

Hans läuft schneller als ich	*Hans runs quicker than I*
Heinrich läuft am schnellsten	*Heinrich runs quickest*
die am schlechtesten bezahlten Arbeiter	*the worst paid workers*
Das hasse ich an den Schulmeistern am meisten (Th. Valentin)	*That's what I hate most about schoolmasters*
Er war am leichtesten zu überreden	*He was the easiest to persuade*

121. Comparative of adjectives in -el, -en, -er (their superl. is normal)

Those in -el regularly drop the e of the stem:
dunkel, dunkler, der dunkelste.

Those in -en and -er may drop the e of the stem when inflected (to avoid three consecutive unstressed e's):
selten *rare*: die seltneren (or selteneren) Schmetterlinge.
bitter: ein bittrerer (or bittererer) Geschmack.
BUT:
Diese Schmetterlinge sind seltener; diese Orangen sind bitterer.

---

[1] As the use of the uninflected superl. is limited to one type of adverbial superlative (see 137), der vollste, der langsamste etc. has been chosen as the stock superlative form, ready for use in e.g. Der vollste Korb stand auf dem Boden; von allen Zügen nach Köln ist dies der langsamste.

Those ending in diphthong + er generally drop the e even when uninflected: teuer: Die Butter ist teurer geworden.

N.B. In the comparative of all adjectives, the e of the -er with which the comparative is formed and the e of the flexional endings -e, -em, -en, -es are both retained in written German and, preponderantly, in spoken German:

Wärmere Tage werden kommen	*Warmer days will come*
Er hat ein netteres Zimmer	*He's got a nicer room*

122. The superlative is formed by adding -est after the following:

(a) s, ß, x, z.

hilflos, der hilfloseste	fix (*quick, nimble*), der fixeste
süß, der süßeste	stolz, der stolzeste

Occasional deviations may be heard, determined by individual ease of pronunciation: der fixte Schüler, der stolzte Kerl.

(b) after sch, d and t: 1. in monosyllabics 2. if the last syllable of the simple form is accented and 3. with the suffix -haft:

rasch, der rascheste	verhaßt, der verhaßteste
gesund, der gesündeste	boshaft *malicious*, der boshafteste
sanft, der sanfteste	

BUT:

kòmisch, der komischste	gefùrchtet, der gefürchtetste
pàssend, der passendste	

Occasional deviations may be heard, e.g. die frischsten Brötchen, der aufgeregteste Junge.

(c) generally after a diphthong or a diphthong + h, sometimes after a vowel + h: Er ist mein treuester Freund; der früh(e)ste Zug.

(d) Individual taste occasionally adds -est to endings other than those listed above, e.g. die dumpfesten Töne *the most muffled sounds*.

123. Eighteen common monosyllabics modify in the compar. and superl. (e.g. alt, älter, der älteste), as do three of the irregulars in 124 (groß, hoch, nah):

alt	stark	warm	arg *bad*[1]	krank
jung	schwach	kalt	arm	oft[2]
lang	klug	grob *coarse, rude*	scharf	
kurz	dumm	hart	schwarz	

Among those that fluctuate between modifying and not modifying the following are the commonest, the modified form being preferred in conversation, except for 'blaß': blaß, fromm, gesund, glatt, naß, rot, schmal.

---

[1] e.g. Es war die ärgste Enttäuschung; es könnte nichts Ärgeres geschehen.

[2] häufiger *more frequently* is often used instead of öfter, while am häufigsten is commoner than am öftesten.

124. Nine irregulars

bald	eher	am ehesten	*soon*
gern[1]	lieber[1]	am liebsten[1]	*willingly, gladly*
groß	größer	der größte	*big*
gut	besser	der beste	*good*
hoch	höher	der höchste	*high*
nah	näher	der nächste	*near*[2]
ungern,[1]	noch weniger gern, am wenigsten gern *unwillingly*		
viel	mehr[3]	der meiste	*much, many*
wenig	weniger[3]	der wenigste	*little, few*

Colloquially one may occasionally hear 'bälder' and 'am ungernsten'.

125. The following 8 adjectives, only used attributively, are comparative in form; they form a superlative:

der äußere *outer, external*	der äußerste *outermost, utmost*
der innere *inner, internal*	der innerste *innermost*
der obere *upper*	der oberste *uppermost, top(most)*
der untere *lower*	der unterste *lowest, bottom*
der vordere *front*	der vorderste *foremost, front*
der hintere *back*	der hinterste *back(most)*
der mittlere *central, middle; medium*	der mittlerste *central, middle*
der niedere *low, inferior* (mainly of social rank)	der niederste *lowest*

EXAMPLES:

seine äußere Erscheinung	*his external appearance*
mit der äußersten Höflichkeit	*with the utmost politeness*
seine innersten Gedanken	*his innermost thoughts*
die untere Schicht	*the lower layer*
Wir saßen in der vorderen (or vordersten) Reihe	*We sat in the front row*

Note: When 'external' and 'internal' are used predicatively or adverbially, 'äußerlich' and 'innerlich' are available:

Seine Verletzungen sind nicht äußerlich, sondern innerlich	*His injuries are not external, but internal*
Äußerlich blieb er ganz ruhig	*Externally he remained quite calm*

126. The comparison of compound adjectives and participles.
Duden (Gram. 2470) gives the following guide-lines:

(a) If, in the simple form, both components have retained their original meaning, the first should be compared:

schwerverständlich	*difficult to understand, abstruse*
schwerer verständlich	-comparative
am schwersten verständlich	-superlative
dichtbevölkert	*densely populated*
tiefblickend[4]	*perceptive*
tiefgehend[4]	1. *profound, far-reaching* (e.g. difference)
eine viel tiefer gehende Skepsis (*Zeit*)	*a much deeper scepticism*
	2. *profound, penetrating* (e.g. investigation)*

---

[1] for the use of these, see 277 ff.
[3] not declined; see also 234.
[2] see also 550.
[4] absolute superlative: tiefstblickend, tiefstgehend

(b) If, in the simple form, the combination forms a single concept, especially with a new and figurative meaning, the second component is compared; in other words, the compound is regarded as an indissoluble single word and is compared as such:

hochfliegend	*lofty, ambitious* (e.g. plans)
hochfliegender	-comparative
der hochfliegendste	-superlative
vielversprechend	*promising, full of promise*
weittragend	*far-reaching* (e.g. consequences)
zartfühlend	*sensitive, tactful*

Note:

i Some compounds fluctuate between (a) and (b), e.g. schwerwiegend *weighty* (e.g. reasons), weitgehend *extensive* (e.g. support). In such cases, and if in doubt, method (b) is recommended as the neater and more convincing.

ii naheliegend *obvious* (e.g. reasons) rather surprisingly belongs to type (a): näherliegend, nächstliegend.

127. Declension of the compar. and superl. of the adjective used attributively: they are declined like the simple form (cf. 88, 90, 93):

der alte/ältere/älteste Lehrer; ich sah den ältesten Lehrer; mein junger/jüngerer/jüngster Bruder; meine jüngeren Brüder; jüngere Brüder.

B. LESS, FEWER, LESSER AND LEAST

128. The rendering of less, fewer, lesser and least (In what follows, alternative versions are deliberately limited.)

(a) less and fewer are rendered by weniger (indeclinable).[1]

Er war weniger optimistisch als sein Bruder	*He was less optimistic than his brother*
Er hat weniger Geld (weniger Freunde) als ich	*He has less money (fewer friends) than I*
Er kann das Rauchen nicht reduzieren, viel weniger aufgeben	*He can't reduce his smoking, much less give it up*
Er war mehr oder weniger (or: mehr oder minder) zufrieden	*He was more or less satisfied*

In three instances 'less' is not rendered by 'weniger':

Seine Chancen sind geringer als meine	*His chances are less* (predic. adj.) *than mine*
kein Geringerer als	*no less a person than*
Es ist schon fast ein Wunder	*It's little less than a miracle*

(b) lesser.

das kleinere (or: geringere) Übel	*the lesser evil*
ihre geringeren Forderungen	*their lesser demands*

(c) least (adjectival) = slightest: mindest or geringst.

Er hat nicht die mindeste/geringste Chance	*He hasn't the least chance*

[1] see also 234.

least (adjectival) = smallest amount of: wenigst or am wenigsten.

Von allen Anwesenden zeigte er das wenigste/am wenigsten Interesse	*Of all those present, he showed least interest*
Er machte die wenigsten/am wenigsten Fehler	*He made the least (or fewest) mistakes*
N.B. Das wissen die wenigsten Hausfrauen	*Very few housewives know that*

the least (substantival).

Das ist das mindeste (das Geringste, das wenigste), was man erwarten kann	*That is the least one can expect*
gelinde gesagt	*to say the least of it (putting it mildly)*

least (adverbial): am wenigsten.

Von allen Gästen sprach er am wenigsten	*Of all the guests he spoke least*
am allerwenigsten	*least of all*
Seine Rede war am wenigsten interessant (or: die wenigst interessante)	*His speech was the least interesting*
Er arbeitet am wenigsten gut	*He works least well*

(d) at least: wenigstens is always correct; there are varying alternatives:

Das Buch kostet wenigstens (or: mindestens) 20 Mark	*The book costs at least 20 marks*
Er wird mir das Geld leihen, wenigstens (or: zumindest) hoffe ich es	*He will lend me the money, at least I hope so*
Wenn er wenigstens angerufen hätte!	*If at least he had rung up!*

(e) not least: nicht am wenigsten, nicht zum mindesten.

Alles interessierte sie, nicht zum mindesten die Frisuren	*Everything interested her, not least the hair-styles*

(f) not in the least: nicht im mindesten, nicht im geringsten.

Er war nicht im mindesten beleidigt	*He wasn't in the least offended*

C. THE ABSOLUTE COMPARATIVE

129. The absolute comparative does not imply comparison with other persons or things, but merely a fair degree of the quality in question: ein älterer Herr *an elderly gentleman*.

Only a limited number of comparatives can be used thus, e.g.

alt	groß	lang	dick	hell	neu
jung	klein	kurz	dünn	dunkel	bekannt

EXAMPLES:

in jeder größeren Stadt	*in every town of any size*
seit längerer Zeit	*for quite a time now*
irgendein hellerer Stoff	*some fairly light material*
ein bekannterer Schriftsteller	*quite a well-known author*

A predicative comparative and the comparative of an adverb may have this same meaning:

Mein Onkel ist schon älter	*My uncle is elderly*
Er hat uns öfter (or: öfters)[1] besucht	*He visited us quite often*

[1] a colloquial alternative, peculiar to oft; a more literary alternative is des öfteren.

D. TYPES OF PREDICATIVE AND ADVERBIAL COMPARISON

130. Equality

(a) main type: as old as: so alt wie.
Er ist so alt wie ich; er arbeitet so fleißig wie ich; er besucht uns so gut wie nie.

Note: In certain set phrases, the 'so' may be omitted (cf. Du. Gram. 2315): Er ist (so) hart wie Stahl; er ist (so) schlau wie ein Fuchs.

(b) In spoken German, a faulty 'als' is frequently used instead of 'wie'; it has become an accepted alternative in the following cases:
  i as well as (=and also): sowohl Karl wie (auch)/als (auch) Hans.
  ii as little as: Fritz wollte so wenig wie/als ich Tennis spielen.
  iii before 'möglich': so bald wie/als möglich.

(c) just as

Er ist ebenso (geradeso, genauso) alt wie ich	*He is just as old as I am*

(d) (just) as much (indicating degree)

Die Brücke ist ebensosehr ein Teil der Landschaft wie der Fluß	*The bridge is as much a part of the landscape as the river*
Ich habe dich ebensosehr beneidet wie bewundert	*I envied you just as much as I admired you*

(e) To convey two attributes possessed in equal measure by the same or, respectively, by two different persons: ebenso . . . wie.

Er ist ebenso fleißig wie geschickt	*He is as industrious as he is skilful*
Cf. Er arbeitet ebenso fleißig wie geschickt	*He works as industriously as he does skilfully*
Er ist ebenso faul, wie sein Bruder fleißig ist	*He is as lazy as his brother is industrious*

131. Superiority

(a) main type: older than: älter als.
Er ist älter als ich; er arbeitet fleißiger als ich; er arbeitet fleißiger, als du glaubst.

(b) Mainly colloquially, 'wie' is so frequently used instead of 'als' that it can barely be called wrong. ('als wie' is also to be heard but should not be imitated.)

(c) Note the sequence of cases in the following:

Ich kenne faulere Jungen als ihn	*I know lazier boys than him*
Ich habe nie einem besseren Spieler zugesehen als ihm	*I have never watched a better player than him*

(d) The use of 'denn' for 'than':
  i to avoid 'als als' for 1. *than as* 2. *than when*; the far commoner solution is to use 'wie' for 'than' in 1. and for 'when' in 2., e.g.

Er ist als Kritiker bekannter denn als (or: wie als) Dichter	1. *He is better known as a critic than as a poet*
Er sieht besser aus, denn als (or: als wie) ich ihn zuletzt sah	2. *He's looking better than when I saw him last*

  ii in the set phrase 'denn je' *than ever*, though 'als je' is perfectly idiomatic.

iii not infrequently in literary style, e.g.

der eher einem Bäcker denn einem Landwirt ähnelt (H. Broch)	*who looks like a baker rather than a farmer*

(e) Degree of difference is expressed by um + acc. or, more commonly, simply by the acc.:

Er ist (um) drei Jahre älter als ich	*He is three years older than I am*

(f) Comparing two qualities of the same person or thing, or two adverbs: this is done with 'mehr' or, more delicately, with 'eher' (cf. 292(b)):

Er ist mehr faul als dumm	*He is more lazy than stupid*
Er sprach eher geistreich als überzeugend	*He spoke wittily rather than convincingly*

(g) twice as, three times as etc.

Er ist zweimal (or: doppelt) so alt wie ich	*He is twice as old as I am*

132. Inferiority (less than)

Er ist weniger optimistisch als ich; er ist nicht so optimistisch wie ich; er arbeitet weniger fleißig als ich; er ist nicht so sehr dumm wie faul *He is not so much stupid as lazy*

133. Progression (faster and faster)

Er lief immer schneller (or: schneller und schneller)	*He ran faster and faster*
Meine Arbeit wird immer schwerer (or: schwerer und schwerer)	*My work is getting harder and harder*

Note:

i The bracketed alternative is rather less common and is virtually limited to monosyllabics.

ii A further alternative is to place 'mehr und mehr' before the simple adj. or adv.: Er arbeitet mehr und mehr intensiv. This is rare with monosyllabics.

134. Proportion (the more . . ., the more . . .)

Je länger man Deutsch lernt, um so/ desto/je leichter wird es (The second 'je' is uncommon in modern usage.)	*The longer you learn German, the easier it becomes*
Je älter er wird, desto witzigere Reden hält er	*The older he gets, the wittier are the speeches he gives*

The reverse order of clauses is possible, though less usual; 'um so' could then be omitted or replaced by 'desto', but not by 'je':

Er hält (um so) witzigere Reden, je älter er wird	*He gives wittier speeches the older he gets*

Further examples and applications:

Je besser das Wetter, um so mehr können wir wandern	*The better the weather, the more we can go hiking*
je eher, desto besser	*the sooner, the better*
je länger, je lieber	*the longer, the better* (set phrase)

Dies machte meine Lage um so schwieriger	*This made my situation all the more difficult*
um so/desto besser	*all the better (for that)*
um so mehr, als/da/weil	*all the more because*
um so weniger, als/da/weil	*even less as*

E. THE PREDICATIVE SUPERLATIVE

135. (a) **When a person or thing is compared with other persons or things:**

> i if their common denominator, their distinctive group, is stated, or implied (3rd example), either the form with 'am' or the form with the def. art. may be used, but with 'best' only the latter (4th example):

Von den drei Brüdern ist Karl am gescheitesten/der gescheiteste	*Of the three brothers, Karl is the most intelligent (one)*
Diese Blume ist am schönsten/die schönste	*This flower is the most beautiful*
Wer (von euch) ist am stärksten/der stärkste?	*Which of you is the strongest?*
Von all seinen Werken ist dieses das beste	*Of all his works this is the best*

> ii if their common denominator, the group to which they belong, is not stated, the form with 'am' is used:

Für meinen Geschmack ist eine Nelke schöner als eine Tulpe, aber eine Rose ist am schönsten	*For my taste a carnation is more beautiful than a tulip, but a rose is the most beautiful*
Ein Mercedes ist am teuersten	*A Mercedes is the dearest*

(b) **When a person or thing is compared with himself or itself in different circumstances,** the form with 'am' is used:

Ich bin montags am faulsten	*I'm (at my) laziest on Mondays*
Der Rhein ist hier am romantischsten	*The Rhine is (at its) most romantic here*

(c) **Where the subject is, or refers to, not a specific person or thing, but a course of action,** the form with 'am' is generally used (cf. Erben, op. cit., 169):

Es würde am einfachsten sein, seinen Brief unbeantwortet zu lassen (or: wenn du es ihm sagtest)	*It would be simplest to leave his letter unanswered (or: if you were to tell him)*

F. THE ABSOLUTE SUPERLATIVE

136. (a) **The absolute superlative does not imply comparison with other persons or things, but merely a high degree of the quality in question:**

Ich schließe immer sehr vorsichtig ab	*I always lock up most (= very) carefully*
Er war äußerst dankbar	*He was most (= extremely) grateful*

(b) Further adverbs available to form the absolute superlative:
außerordentlich *extraordinarily,* höchst *extremely, in the highest degree,* überaus *exceedingly.*

(c) 'höchst' is **not** used before most monosyllabic adjectives and adverbs, nor before numerous others, e.g. billig, dunkel, durstig, fröhlich, glänzend, glücklich, großartig, herrlich, hungrig, langsam, plötzlich, schrecklich, teuer, traurig, wenig, wunderbar.

Some examples of the use of 'höchst':
höchst anständig *respectable*, bemerkenswert *noteworthy*, erstaunt, günstig, leichtsinnig *thoughtless*, notwendig *necessary*, sonderbar *strange*, unangenehm, ungern, ungesund, ungünstig, unwillkommen

The following are written as one word: höchstwahrscheinlich, höchstpersönlich *in his own person* (generally facetious), der Höchstbietende *the highest bidder*.

(d) (**S**) An attributive superlative frequently has absolute and not comparative force:

Meine liebste Mutter!	*My dearest mother*, . . . (letter)
Ich habe den ehrlichsten Respekt vor ihm	*I have the most genuine respect for him*
Es herrschte das rauheste Wetter	*The weather was extremely raw*
Modernste Kureinrichtungen stehen zu Ihrer Verfügung (Advert. for Baden-Baden in *FAZ*)	*You have the use of the most up-to-date curative equipment*

137. **Two somewhat stilted types of adverbial absolute superlative:** Ich danke dir (a) **herzlichst** (b) **aufs herzlichste.** *I thank you most cordially.*

Type (a) is mainly found with a number of adverbs formed from adjectives in -ig and -lich and is characteristically used in commercialese. Thus:

Sie werden höflichst gebeten, diesen Irrtum zu berichtigen	*You are politely requested to rectify this error*

cf.: baldigst *as soon as possible*, freundlichst *kindly*, gefälligst, gütigst *obligingly*, kindly, schleunigst *as promptly as possible*, sorgfältigst *most carefully*

gefälligst may have a sharper edge (cf. Betteridge op. cit.), e.g. Sie werden gefälligst davon schweigen *You will kindly not speak about it.*

Type (b): Examples:

Ich war aufs angenehmste überrascht	*I was most pleasantly surprised* (set phrase)
man versteht sich aufs beste (Th. Mann)	(at a social gathering:) *everyone is getting on very well together*
aufs genaueste	*most exactly, accurately*
Der Vorfall hat mich aufs peinlichste berührt	*The incident made a most painful impression on me*

G. MISCELLANEOUS POINTS CONNECTED WITH COMPARATIVE AND SUPERLATIVE

138. (a) **Adjectives which are only used predicatively** (e.g. those marked with an asterisk in 117) **and participles that are not felt as adjectives** (contrast those exemplified in 98) **are compared by placing 'mehr' and 'am meisten' in front of them** Used

attributively, passive past participles may alternatively form a superlative with a prefixed 'meist-'.

Er ist mir noch mehr zuwider als sein Bruder	*He is still more repugnant to me than his brother*
Von den beiden ist dies das mehr gelesene Buch	*Of the two, this book is read more*
der meistgekaufte Geschirr- spülautomat Deutschlands (advert. in *Die Zeit*)	*The most popular washing-up machine in Germany*

(b) **ersterer ... letzterer *the former ... the latter***, with strong
endings: Da sind Karl und Wilhelm; ich habe mit ersterem Tennis
und mit letzterem Federball gespielt.

Note:
i For the gen. sing. use des (or der) ersteren/letzteren.
ii An alternative rendering is jener *the former* ... dieser *the latter*, not used in
gen. sing.: see 166(a).

(c) **The adverbial superlative 'am meisten' is used colloquially
in the sense of 'most, the greatest amount or number of',
applied to the object**: Mein ältester Bruder hat am meisten/das
meiste Geld; er hat am meisten/die meisten Fehler gemacht.

(d) **A group of frequently needed adverbial superlatives in -ens**:

höchstens *at the most*	spätestens *at the latest*
wenigstens *at least*	nächstens *shortly, soon*
frühstens *at the earliest*	

Further instances shown in a context:

Ich danke (Ihnen) bestens	*Thank you very much*
Ich stehe meistens[1] früh auf	*I mostly get up early*
Die Einwohner sind meistens[1] Katholiken	*The inhabitants are mostly Catholics*
Grüßen Sie ihn schönstens von mir	*Give him my kindest regards*
strengstens verboten	*strictly prohibited*
Ich kann das Buch wärmstens empfehlen	*I can recommend the book most warmly*

(e) **'möglichst' is used as follows** (never after the def. art.):

Du mußt einen möglichst guten Eindruck machen	*You must make the best possible impression*
Komme möglichst früh (so früh wie möglich)	*come as early as possible*
Gib ihm möglichst viel Geld (so viel Geld wie möglich)	*Give him as much money as possible*
Er hat sein möglichstes getan	*He has done his utmost*

(f) **'möglich' may be adjoined to the superlative forms best,
größt, höchst, kleinst, kürzest** (little used in conversation):

die bestmögliche Lösung	*the best possible solution*
der größtmögliche Schaden (*Spiegel*)	*the greatest possible damage*

---

[1] also meist (more literary)

V THE PERSONAL PRONOUN

A. DECLENSION

139.

	I	*you* (familiar sing.)	*he*	*she*	*it*
N.	ich	du	er	sie	es
A.	mich	dich	ihn	sie	es
D.	mir	dir	ihm	ihr	ihm

	we	*you* (familiar plur.)	*they*	*you* (polite: sing. & plur.)
N.	wir	ihr	sie	Sie
A.	uns	euch	sie	Sie
D.	uns	euch	ihnen	Ihnen

For the genitive case, see 151.

B. THE USE OF 'DU' AND 'IHR'

140. The familiar 2nd person du (plur. ihr) is used as follows:

i in addressing relatives, intimate friends, children (up to about 16 years of age), animals and inanimate objects (du, mein treuer Regenschirm!).

ii among all schoolchildren; their teachers call boys Sie in the top three forms of secondary schools, girls in the top four forms.

iii among workmen, privates, N.C.O.'s of the same rank, students and athletes.

iv to address the reader: Lies Goethes, . . . Rilkes Briefe—und du begreifst . . . (A. Goes). Vermeide Mißverständnisse! (Duden). But also: Lesen Sie weiter auf Seite 30 (*Zeit-Magazin*).

v in poetry and proverbs.   vi the Deity is always Du.

Note:

i In a letter Du (Dein), Ihr (Euer) etc. are written with a capital (cf. 731(b)).

ii Note the verbs duzen (Fr. tutoyer) and, less used, siezen.

iii For a short sketch of the history of the pronouns used as forms of address, see Corbett, op. cit., 45 (c), 46.

C. THE 3RD PERSON

141. The personal pronoun of the 3rd pers. sing. agrees in gender with the noun for which it stands

Leih mir deinen Bleistift!	*Lend me your pencil*
Ach, ich hab' ihn verloren; eben lag er auf dem Tisch; er ist rot	*—Oh. I've lost it; just now it was lying on the table; it's red*
Er hörte meine Meinung und stimmte ihr bei	*He heard my opinion and expressed agreement with it*

Regarding personal pronouns standing for neuter diminutives referring to persons (e.g. das Mädchen, das Söhnchen), see 672 (b).

142. The personal pronoun of the 3rd pers. is used in comparative clauses introduced by wie *such as* **to repeat, in the grammatical context of the clause, the person or thing to which the clause refers:**

Hier gibt es keine Wälder, wie man sie in Deutschland findet	*Here there are no forests such as you find in Germany*
Ein Kuchen, wie ihn Ihre Mutter backt, ist etwas Besonderes	*A cake such as your mother makes is something special*
Es war ein Auto, wie ich es noch nie (or: wie ich noch keins) gesehen hatte	*It was a car such as I had never seen before*

In a comparative clause introduced by 'as (good) as', 'ein' or 'kein' is used with the same function as the personal pron. above:

Sie hatte eine so leckere Torte gebacken, wie ich noch nie eine gegessen habe	*She had made as delicious a flan as I have ever eaten*
Der Film war so spannend, wie ich noch keinen gesehen habe	*The film was as exciting a one as I have ever seen*

In an 'als' clause (*than*), 'es' is sometimes introduced to represent the preceding main clause:

Er arbeitet viel besser, als ich (es) erwartet hatte	*He works much better than I had expected*

D. SOME SPECIAL USES OF 'ES'[1]

143. (a) (S) 'es' is used as complement and demonstrative with the verb 'sein':

Wer ist es? Wer ist's?	*Who is it?*
Bist du es? Bist du's? Sind Sie es?	*Is it you?*
Ich bin es. Ich bin's	*It's me*
Wir sind es. Wir sind's	*It's us*
Es ist meine Mutter	*It's my mother*
Es sind meine Brüder	*It's my brothers*
Was sind es?	*What are they?*
Sind es Ihre Handschuhe?	*Are they your gloves?*

Note: Was ist es? Was sind es? but only: Wer ist es?

---

[1] See also 372 ff., 382 ff. and 512 ff.

(b) **It was he who ..., It was then that ... etc.**

i In German 'he' comes first:

Er war es, der es mir sagte	*It was he who told me*
Du warst es also, der es getan hat	*So it was you who did it*

ii With a noun, either order is possible:

Es war mein Vetter (Mein Vetter war es), der es mir erzählte	*It was my cousin who told me*

iii Except with relative clauses this formula is less common in German, where the item to be emphasized is placed first followed by inversion:

In diesem Augenblick trat mein Vater ins Zimmer	*It was at this moment that my father entered the room*
Aus diesem Grunde habe ich nichts gesagt	*It was for this reason that I said nothing*

(c) **It is used to avoid repeating the complement of 'sein'** where in English nothing equivalent is required:

Er soll zuverlässig sein, und ich bin sicher, daß er es ist	*He is said to be reliable and I am sure he is*
Er ist immer so argwöhnisch.—Und warum ist er's?	*He is always so suspicious.—And why is he?*
Wir sind nie so erfolgreich, wie wir (es) sein möchten	*We are never as successful as we would like to be*

In the same type of context 'es' may correspond to English 'so':

Wer jetzt allein ist, wird es lange bleiben (Rilke: *Herbsttag*)	*He who is now alone will long remain so*

(d) **It corresponds to English 'so' used as the object of to say and to do:**

Er hat es gesagt	*He said so*
Warum hast du es getan?	*Why did you do so?*

With to think and to hope, 'es' is not generally used:

Kommt er heute?	*Is he coming today?*
—Ja, ich glaube (Ja, ich hoffe)	*—Yes, I think so/hope so*
Das will ich meinen!	N.B. *I should think so!*

(e) **It is used as an introductory subject,** only in normal order and when the real subject is a noun; its most usual effect, apart from purely rhythmical considerations, is to give greater emphasis to the real subject. This construction is widely used in German; in English, it may sometimes be rendered by 'there':

Es saß eine alte Frau am Fenster	*There was an old woman sitting at the window*
Es erhoben sich die Anwesenden	*Those present rose to their feet*
Es stieg ein kalter Nebel	*There was a cold mist rising*

cf. Es zeigte sich ein großer Unterschied; es wird dies nicht das letzte Mal sein.

(f) **It is used to denote a subject that is vague,** often conveying the feeling of an impersonal force at work:

bar jeglicher Ordnung, wie von einem Trichterwirbel erfaßt, strudelte es zähflüssig dieser Toreinfahrt zu (H. Broch)	*without a semblance of order, as though seized by a whirlpool, the crowd swirled in a thick mass towards this gateway*

Es drängte mich, ihm alles zu sagen	*I felt an urge to tell him everything*
Plötzlich schüttelt es ihn in einem wilden Krampf (A. Goes)	*Suddenly a fierce spasm shakes him*

(g) **(S) It is used as an indeterminate object in certain set phrases,** e.g.

es gut haben	*to be fortunate*
es besser haben (als)	*to be luckier, to be better off (than)*
es gut meinen	*to mean well*
es sich (dat.) bequem machen	*to make oneself comfortable*
es weit bringen	*to go far* (fig.)
Er hat es zum Generaldirektor gebracht	*He has attained the post of Director General*
Er hat es mit mir zu tun	*He has me to deal with*

(h) **The 'es' which appears to be used as the object of a number of adjectival phrases with the verb 'sein' is really an old genitive,** e.g. Ich bin es los *I'm rid of it*; ich bin es satt *I'm sick of it.*[1]

E. THE USE OF DAMIT, DARAUF ETC.

144. After the following prepositions, the personal pronouns of the 3rd person acc. and dat. are normally used only with reference to persons; if they refer to things, the usual form is da + preposition, e.g. damit *with it*; if the preposition begins with a vowel, an 'r' is inserted, e.g. darauf *on it*, darüber *above it, about (concerning) it*; colloquially these often become drauf, drüber etc.

preps. + dat.: aus, bei, mit, nach, von, zu
preps. + acc.: durch, für, gegen, um
the 9 preps. + dat. or acc.: an, auf, hinter, in, neben, über, unter, vor, zwischen

(The above list comprises all the common prepositions except außer, gegenüber, seit; bis, ohne; and those taking the genitive.)

Leih mir dein Messer. Ich will das Paket damit öffnen	*Lend me your knife; I want to open the parcel with it*
Ich erkannte das Haus mit der großen Eiche daneben	*I recognized the house with the big oak next to it*

Colloquially, these forms are sometimes divided: Da hab' ich (nichts) von gewußt. Da will ich nichts mit zu tun haben (G. Gaiser).

145. Compounded with da, some prepositions are restricted in sense

(a) **aus, durch, nach and zu** do not usually have their literal sense of motion from, through or to a place, but connotations such as the following:

Er kaufte sich Holz und machte einen Schrank daraus	*He bought some wood and made a cupboard out of it*
Dadurch ist alles so schwierig geworden	*Through that, everything has become so difficult*
danach	1. *after that* 2. *according to that*

For dazu, see 288.

---

[1] cf. Eggeling, op. cit., es 1 and 2

Note: dàraus (stressed thus) may have its literal sense:

Ich habe das Geld dàraus genommen	*I took the money from there* (i.e. out of that drawer)

(b) **darin** means 'in it', but not 'into it'

(c) **daran** may mean 'on it' or 'on to it' (the wall) but not 'by it' or 'up to it' (the door, the blackboard):

Diese kahle Wand!	*This bare wall:*
Früher hingen Bilder daran	*there used to be pictures on it*
Ich will ein paar Bilder daran hängen	*I'll hang a few pictures on it*

(d) To express motion, the da- compounds of an, aus, durch, in, nach and zu are best replaced by separable prefixes:

hin *to it*	hinein, herein *into it*
hinaus, heraus *out of it*	durch, hindurch *through it*

Endlich fand ich den Schalter und ging hin	*At last I found the booking office and went to it*
Der Hund kam zur Hütte und lief hinein	*The dog came to the hut and ran into it*
Wir kamen an einen langen Gang und eilten hindurch	*We came to a long passage and hurried through it*

146. Usage with prepositions that are not compounded with da

(a) For the main prepositions + gen., see 153(a)ii.

(b) With gegenüber and ohne, the ordinary personal pronoun may be used or, more commonly, omitted:

Dies ist ein vorzügliches Wörterbuch; ohne (es) kann ich nicht fertig werden	*This is an excellent dictionary; I can't get on without it*

(c) außer: use one of the adverbs außerdem or sonst.

(d) When in doubt, use derselbe (see 168), which, though cumbersome, is generally possible:

Seine Ankunft verursachte eine gewisse Unruhe; dank derselben (better: infolgedessen) konnte ich mich wegstehlen	*His arrival caused a certain restlessness; thanks to it I was able to steal away*

147. da + prep. is the more usual and the safer form with reference to things, but, as the following examples show, it is by no means sacrosanct, particularly when referring to a plural noun:

In der Nähe standen drei Eichen; ein Weg führte um sie herum.

Man spürt es an der Luft ganzer Städte, ob der Schmied oder der Weber in ihnen regiert (E. Jünger).

Er hatte ihn [den Wagen] erst seit einigen Wochen und war sehr zufrieden mit ihm (I. Wendt) (here 'mit ihm' harmonizes better with 'ihn' than would 'damit').

N.B.: darunter, in the sense of 'among them', is frequently used with reference to persons, e.g. Ich erwarte zehn Gäste, darunter meine zwei ältesten Freunde.

148. with it, with that, with this

with it, in it etc. = damit, darin etc., with a slight stress on the preposition.

with that, in that etc. = dàmit, dàrin etc., with a strong stress on da.

with this, in this etc. = hiermit, hierin etc., with a slight stress on the prep. unless 'this' is to be emphasized.

Dàmit kann ich die Büchse nicht öffnen	*I can't open the tin with that*
Dàrüber sprechen wir nie	*We never talk about that*
ein Beispiel hiervon	*an example of this*
Kann man etwas hiergegen machen?	*Can one do anything against this?*

149. The form da + prep. is never used as the antecedent of a relative clause:

Ich richtete meine ganze Aufmerksamkeit auf das (*not*: darauf), was er erklärte	*I focused my whole attention on what he was explaining*

150. The many idiomatic uses of these compounds are not included in this chapter,[1] e.g.

Ich kann nichts dafür	*I can't help it*
Es liegt mir viel daran	*I attach great importance to it*

F. THE GENITIVE OF THE PERSONAL PRONOUN

151. The forms of the genitive

NOM.	GEN.	NOM.	GEN.
ich	meiner (mein)	wir	unser
du	deiner (dein)	ihr	euer
er	seiner (sein)	sie *they*	ihrer (ihr)
sie *she*	ihrer	Sie	Ihrer
es	seiner (sein)		

The bracketed forms are archaic and poetic, e.g.
> So oft der Mond mag scheinen,
> Gedenk ich dein allein, ... (Brentano: *Der Spinnerin Lied*)

152. Outside a few contexts, the gen. of the personal pronoun sounds stilted and literary and its use is very limited in modern colloquial German. It is used:

(a) after a few verbs + gen. which have no alternative construction:

Er hat sich meiner angenommen	*He befriended me*

(b) with a few adjectives used with the genitive:

Ich bin seiner nicht sicher	*I'm not sure of him* (i.e. if I can count on him)
Er ist ihrer nicht würdig	*He's not worthy of her*

(c) in the phrases:

Das ist unser aller Wunsch	*That is the wish of all of us*
Das ist unser beider Wunsch	*That is the wish of both of us*

---

[1] for dabei and dazu see 287 f.

153. How the use of the gen. of the personal pronoun is avoided

(a) preps. + gen.

i referring to persons:

1. the prepositions wegen, um ... willen and ... halber have special forms: meinetwegen etc., (um) meinetwillen, meinethalben (see 582(b), 586(b)(d)).

2. the prepositions wegen, statt and trotz are colloquially often used with the dative: wegen mir, statt ihm (or: an seiner Stelle).

3. in the case of the remaining relevant prepositions + gen. there is always an alternative possibility. E.g.
   with regard to him: was ihn betrifft, or: in bezug auf ihn (not: hinsichtlich seiner).
   including you: Wir sind alle eingeladen, du mit eingeschlossen, or: auch du (not: einschließlich deiner).

ii referring to things:

1. adverbs or adverb phrases may be used: deswegen *because of it*, trotzdem *in spite of it*, außerhalb, draußen *outside (it)*, diesseits, auf dieser Seite *on this side (of it)*, statt dessen *instead (of it)*.

2. in the case of preps. + gen. which are often used with von (see 576(b)), davon may be used, e.g. auf Grund davon *on the strength of it*.

(b) verbs + gen.: the alternative construction or a different verb is used, e.g.

Erinnern Sie sich an mich? Ich schämte mich für ihn (though not all Germans would eschew: Erinnern Sie sich meiner? Ich schämte mich seiner).

Gib mir jetzt deinen Rat; ich brauche ihn (not: ich bedarf seiner).

(c) adjectives used with gen. (referring to things): use dessen *of that, of it*; for fem. and plur. use derselben:

Ich war mir dessen bewußt	*I was conscious of it*
Eine solche Ehre? Er ist derselben (but also: ihrer) nicht würdig	*Such an honour? He's not worthy of it*

VI MISCELLANEOUS ADJECTIVES AND PRONOUNS

SECTION A: REFLEXIVE AND RECIPROCAL, POSSESSIVE, DEMONSTRATIVE, INTERROGATIVE, RELATIVE

A. REFLEXIVE AND RECIPROCAL PRONOUNS

154. Forms of the reflexive pronoun

(a) The personal pronouns are used as reflexive pronouns except for the acc. and dat. of the 3rd person and of the polite 2nd person, which are 'sich'. The refl. pron. is sometimes strengthened with 'selbst' (cf. 159); this is especially so in the genitive[1] (cf. 155).

(b) Present tense of sich setzen *to sit down*

REFL. PRON.: ACCUSATIVE
ich setze mich
du setzt dich
er setzt sich
wir setzen uns
ihr setzt euch
sie setzen sich
Sie setzen sich

Pres. of sich erlauben (etwas zu tun) *to allow oneself (to do something)*

REFL. PRON.: DATIVE
ich erlaube mir
du erlaubst dir
er erlaubt sich
wir erlauben uns
ihr erlaubt euch
sie erlauben sich
Sie erlauben sich

155. The genitive of the refl. pron. is barely used except in conjunction with one or two adjectives:

Er ist seiner selbst sicher
Er war seiner selbst nicht mehr mächtig

He is sure of himself
He had lost control of himself

156. Care must be taken to use the reflexive form for a pronoun following a preposition, when the pronoun refers back to the subject:

Er hatte kein Geld bei sich
Sie schlossen die Tür hinter sich

He had no money on him
They closed the door behind them

An exception must be made in certain contexts, to avoid producing ambiguity or the wrong sense. E.g.

Karl fand Walter mit einem Bericht über sich

Karl found Walter with a report about himself (i.e. about Walter)

Karl fand Walter mit einem Bericht über ihn

Karl found Walter with a report about him (i.e. about Karl)

---

[1] cf. Schulz-Griesbach, op. cit., D 108.

157. (S) After verbs followed by a plain infinitive without 'zu', especially sehen, hören, lassen, the refl. pron. normally refers to the object and the personal pron. is used to refer to the subject:

Er sah seinen Sohn ihm entgegenkommen	*He saw his son coming to meet him*
Er hörte seinen Freund sich tadeln	*He heard his friend blaming himself*
Er hörte seinen Freund ihn tadeln	*He heard his friend blaming him*

But after a preposition, the refl. pron. refers to the subject:

Er sah seinen Freund vor sich hergehen	*He saw his friend walking along in front of him*
Er ließ den Tiger auf sich zukommen	*He let the tiger come towards him*
Er fühlte Mariannes Blick auf sich ruhen (V. Baum)	*He felt Marianne's gaze resting on him*

158. The dative of the refl. pron. is used idiomatically in a good many contexts as a kind of dative of advantage (or disadvantage)

Ich muß (mir) einen neuen Füller kaufen	*I must buy (myself) a new fountain-pen*
Er will sich das Haus ansehen	*He's going to have a look at the house*
Mein Versuch ist mir mißglückt	*My attempt has failed*
Er steckte sich eine Zigarette an	*He lit a cigarette*
Ich will mir bald Urlaub nehmen	*I'm soon going to take a holiday*
Ich habe es mir notiert	*I've made a note of it*
Ich habe (mir) oft gedacht, daß . . .	*I often thought (to myself) that . . .*

159. (a) The emphatic 'myself', 'yourself' etc. is rendered by 'selbst' or 'selber' (invariable)

Note:

i selbst and selber follow the noun or pronoun to which they refer, though not always immediately;

ii they are always stressed;

iii selber is the more colloquial of the two.

Ich habe selbst mit dem Minister darüber gesprochen	*I have spoken to the minister about it myself*
Ich habe mit dem Minister selbst darüber gesprochen	*I have spoken to the minister himself about it*
Ich habe selber den Brief gelesen	*I have read the letter myself*
Ich habe den Brief selber gelesen	

In the last example, both positions of 'selber' are equally idiomatic; the second version clearly could convey 'the letter itself', but in practice the context generally obviates such theoretical ambiguities.

(b) **selbst (unstressed) can also mean 'even' (cf. sogar).**

Selbst mein alter *Vater* ist dafür; man wußte selbst in *Berlin* nichts davon.

160. The reciprocal pronoun (*each other*) is rendered either by the plural forms of the reflexive pronoun or by 'einander' (invariable); the former are preferred in conversation, except after a preposition, where only 'einander' can be used; prep. + einander is written as one word.

Sie sahen sich (or einander) oft	*They often saw each other*
Wir gehen uns aus dem Wege	*We evade each other*
Wir verlassen uns aufeinander	*We rely on each other*
Fünf Autos standen hintereinander	*Five cars were standing behind one another*

Where the refl. pron. might be ambiguous, 'selbst' may be added to give the reflexive sense and 'gegenseitig' *mutually* to give the reciprocal sense:

Sie bewunderten sich selbst   *They admired themselves*

Sie bewunderten sich gegenseitig   *They admired each other*
  (or: Sie bewunderten einander)

B. THE POSSESSIVE PRONOUN[1]

161. The possessive pronoun has three forms:

(a) **meiner** – meine – mein(e)s *mine*   uns(e)rer *ours*
    deiner *yours*   eu(e)rer *yours*
    seiner *his, its*   ihrer *theirs*
    ihrer *hers, its*   Ihrer *yours*

Note:

i This form has the endings of dieser; it is therefore identical with the possess. adj. (see declension of 'ihr' in 90) except in the masc. nom. and the neut. nom. and acc.

ii In the neut. nom. and acc., the forms meins, deins, seins, ihrs and Ihrs are generally used, especially in conversation; 'unseres' and 'eueres' are fairly common alongside 'unsers' and 'euers'.

iii In the remaining cases, unserer and euerer frequently drop the unstressed e of the stem, especially in spoken German. In the masc. acc., the masc. and neut. dat. and the dat. plur. there is the alternative possibility of dropping the e of the ending. It is not wrong to retain both e's. E.g. Wir sprachen mit seinem Vater und er sprach mit unsrem (unserm, unserem).

(b) **der meinige** – die meinige – das meinige *mine*, der deinige *yours* etc.

Note:

i meinige, deinige etc. have the weak endings (cf. 88).

ii der uns(e)rige, der eu(e)rige: the bracketed e is generally dropped in spoken German, but frequently retained in writing.

(c) **der meine** – die meine – das meine *mine*, der deine *yours* etc.

Note:

i meine, deine etc. have the weak endings (cf. 88).

ii der uns(e)re, der eu(e)re: the bracketed e is frequently dropped, especially in spoken German; alternatively, in all cases other than the nom. sing. and the fem. and neut. acc. sing., the e of the ending may be dropped, e.g. den unsren or den unsern.

Of the three forms, (a), (b) and (c):

  (a) is the neatest and the most used, except in the gen. sing. and gen. plur.;

  (b) is cumbersome but not uncommon;

  (c) is somewhat literary.

Unser Garten ist größer als ihrer (der ihrige, der ihre).

Er sprach mit meinen Eltern, ich sprach mit seinen (den seinigen, den seinen).

Das ist die Unterschrift deines Lehrers, und dies ist die Unterschrift des meinigen (des meinen) (commoner: von meinem).

---

[1] for the possessive adjective, see 90–92 and 165 v.

162. **mein, dein, sein, unser, euer** (but not 'ihr' or 'Ihr') **are used predicatively, uninflected, to express possession,** but never after 'es ist' or 'das ist'. Historically, these forms are genitives of the personal pron. This usage is archaic and literary. E.g.

> Mein ist der Helm, und mir gehört er zu (Schiller)
> Die Stadt ist unser (normal version: ist in unseren Händen)

163. Note the following:

die Meinigen, die Meinen	*my people, my family*
Grüße auch die Deinigen (die Deinen)!	*And give my kind regards to your people*
Ich habe das Meinige getan	*I have done my part*
ein Freund von mir	*a friend of mine*
einer meiner Freunde	
einer von meinen Freunden	
Freunde von mir	*friends of mine*
verschiedene meiner Freunde (von meinen Freunden)	*several friends of mine*

C. DEMONSTRATIVE ADJECTIVES AND PRONOUNS

164. The form der – die – das

(a) **As a demonstrative adj., it is declined like the def. art.**, but it is stressed and is sometimes italicized; if strengthened with 'da' or 'hier', it can, but need not, be stressed. It is not used in the genitive.

Mit *dem* Lehrer habe ich wenig zu tun	*I don't have much to do with that master*
just in *dem* Moment (Th. Plievier)	*just at that moment*
Das Bild da gefällt mir gut	*I like that picture*

(b) **As a demonstrative pronoun it is declined as follows:**

	MASC.	FEM.	NEUT.	PLUR.
N.	der	die	das	die
A.	den	die	das	die
G.	dessen	deren	dessen	deren
		(derer)		(derer)
	(des)	(der)	(des)	(der)
D.	dem	der	dem	denen

For the use of bracketed forms of the gen., see Notes vi and vii in 165.

165. Notes on the demonstrative pronoun der – die – das

i Except as used in Notes iii, v, and ix, it is always stressed, even when strengthened with 'da' or 'hier'.

ii **Typical uses:**

mein Wagen und der meines Bruders	*my car and my brother's*
Die Sache ist nämlich die: er ist schon verheiratet	*You see the thing is this: he's married already*
Diesen Schulze, den kann ich nicht leiden	*This chap Schulze, I can't stand him*
Den (da) kann ich nicht leiden	*I can't stand that chap*

Diese Seife ist besser als die, die ich gebrauche	*This soap is better than the one I use*
Wohl dem, der . . .	*Happy is he who . . .*
Die im Wartezimmer reden. Denen wird die Zeit auch lang (H. Fallada)	*The people in the waiting-room are talking. They too find time hanging heavily*

iii It is frequently used, unstressed, with virtually no demonstrative force:

Müllers? Ich glaub', die sind verreist	*The Müllers? I think they're away*
Von den Töchtern—es sind deren fünf—hat die älteste . . . (A. Kolb)	*Of the daughters—there are five of them— the eldest . . .*

iv A 't' is added to dessen and deren when they are compounded with halben, wegen, willen:

Derentwegen hat er keinen Finger gerührt	*He didn't raise a finger to help that lot (or: to help her)*

v A particular use of the genitive is to replace the possessive adj. when the latter might be ambiguous

Karl sprach zuerst mit Heinrich, dann mit seiner Schwester(= with his (Karl's) sister)/dann mit dessen Schwester(= with his (Heinrich's) sister)

Sie [unsere Partei] hat den Menschen nichts als deren eigene objektive Interessen verständlich gemacht (*Neues Deutschland*)	*Our Party has made clear to people nothing but their own objective interests*

vi As antecedent to a relative clause, the fem. and plur. genitives are derer. (The fem. gen. is rarely used thus):

auf der Seite derer, die unter die Räder gekommen sind (A. Goes)	*on the side of those who have been crushed by life*

vii The short forms of the genitive (des, der, des, der) are archaic and poetic, except before a genitive; here only they can be used (3rd and 4th examples):

Des freuet sich der Engel Schar (Martin Luther)	*Thereat rejoices the angelic host*
Wes Brot ich ess', des Lied ich sing' (Proverb)	*Never quarrel with your bread and butter*[1]
Infolge meiner Rede und der meines Kollegen wurde der Antrag angenommen	*As the result of my speech and that of my colleague the motion was carried*
Die Interessen meiner Kinder und der meines Bruders sind sehr verschieden	*The interests of my children and of my brother's (children) are very different*

viii Before ist and sind (war, waren etc.), 'das' is used irrespective of the gender and number of the person or thing indicated:

Das ist mein Bleistift, meine Mutter, ihr Kind; das sind die jungen Deutschen; das waren glückliche Tage

ix das is used, mainly pejoratively, meaning 'they' or 'such people':

Das hat an allem etwas auszusetzen	*Such people find fault with everything*

x such-and-such (a one)

Er nannte mir die und die Adresse	*He gave me such-and-such an address*
Er sagte, der und der hätte es getan	*He said such-and-such a one had done it*

[1] Betteridge's rendering: op. cit. Lied.

166. dieser *this* **and jener** *that* **are used adjectivally and pronominally**

(a) **Declension**: see 88; the masc. and neut. gen. sing. dieses and jenes are rarely used pronominally.

EXAMPLES:

Dieser Stuhl ist bequemer als jener (commoner: als der da)	*This chair is more comfortable than that one*
Karl und Hans sind beide auf Urlaub; jener ist in Frankreich, dieser in der Schweiz	*Karl and Hans are both on holiday; the former is in France, the latter in Switzerland*[1]
Ich habe mit diesem und jenem gesprochen	*I talked with one or another*

(b) **The form dies** is often used in place of the neut. nom. or acc. dieses, mainly pronominally; cf. 166(c). E.g. Dies geschieht nicht oft; gerade dies hatte ich vergessen; hast du dieses/dies Buch gelesen?

(c) Before 'ist' and 'sind', **dies** is used irrespective of the gender and number of the person or thing indicated (cf. 165 viii): Dies sind meine Schwestern *These are my sisters.*

(d) **jener** is mainly used:
 i when contrasted with dieser, as in the examples in (a) above.
 ii when speaking of something remote in time or space:[2]
In jenen glücklichen Tagen hatte er nie gedacht, daß ihm so etwas passieren könnte.

Otherwise jener has something stilted and is relatively little used. Thus:

Dieser Junge (or: Der Junge da) arbeitet gut	*That boy works well*

N.B. dieser can never be used, in place of jener, adjectivally in 'that/those . . . who, which' or pronominally in 'those who':

Er zeigte wiederum jene Aggressivität, die ihm so oft geschadet hatte	*Once again he displayed that aggressiveness which had so often done him harm*
Er sprach von jenen/denen/denjenigen, die ihm geholfen hatten	*He spoke of those who had helped him*

(e) **Preposition + pronominal 'this' or 'that'** is most commonly rendered by stressed hier or da + prep. (cf. 144 and 148):

Stelle den Topf hìerauf, nicht dàrauf!	*Put the saucepan on this, not on that*

167. derjenige *that*

(a) Declension (cf. 88)

	MASC.	FEM.	NEUT.	PLUR.
N.	derjenige	diejenige	dasjenige	diejenigen
A.	denjenigen	diejenige	dasjenige	diejenigen
G.	desjenigen	derjenigen	desjenigen	derjenigen
D.	demjenigen	derjenigen	demjenigen	denjenigen

---

[1] It is logical that dieser (this one) refers to the second or closer noun (i.e. Hans). See also 138(b).
[2] cf. Schulz-Griesbach, op. cit., D 450.

4*

(b) A cumbersome and ugly form, derjenige should be used sparingly.

i Used pronominally, it is followed by a relative clause, a genitive or a prepositional phrase:

Er sprach oft von denjenigen (better: von denen or jenen), die ihm geholfen hatten.

Mein Haus ist größer als dasjenige meines Bruders. (Commoner and better: als das von meinem Bruder or als meines Bruders).

Diejenigen (better: Die) in den hinteren Reihen konnten nichts sehen.

ii Used adjectivally, it is followed by noun + relative clause:

Er gab mir diejenigen Bücher, die er selber gelesen hatte.

N.B. It is *not* used thus: Ich habe dieses Buch lieber als dasjenige; this should be: als das da or als jenes.

(c) Note the facetious 'derjenige, welcher':

Sie sind wohl derjenige, welcher!　　　　　*I suppose you're the one (who did it)*

168. derselbe – dieselbe – dasselbe *the same*[1]

(a) Declension: like 'derjenige' (see 167(a)), but with 'derselbe' a contraction of preposition + def. art. is possible.

EXAMPLES:

Er gab mir dieselbe Antwort	*He gave me the same answer*
Er gab mir diese selbe Antwort	*He gave me this same answer*
Es läuft auf (eins und) dasselbe hinaus	*It comes to (one and) the same thing*
Sind das dieselben?	*Are those the same ones?*
Ich wohne im selben Haus wie mein Chef	*I live in the same house as my boss*
Er geht aufs selbe Gymnasium wie sein Bruder	*He goes to the same grammar school as his brother*

Note:

i it may be strengthened by prefixing 'eben':

an ebendemselben Tag　　　　　*on the very same day*

ii the forms 'derselbige' and 'selbiger' are archaic.

(b) 'derselbe' is sometimes used pronominally in place of a personal pronoun or a possessive adjective, but this use is cumbersome and should be avoided:

Ich erhielt seinen Brief mit der ersten Post; erst später las ich denselben (say: ihn); der Inhalt desselben (say: sein Inhalt) erstaunte mich.

169. For solcher *such*, see 222.

D. THE INTERROGATIVE PRONOUN

170. Declension of the interrogative pronoun

N.	wer? *who?*	was? *what?*	
A.	wen?	was?	
G.	wessen? (archaic: wes)	wessen? (archaic: wes)	
D.	wem?	—	

---

[1] Purists distinguish between derselbe *the same* and der gleiche *the same, a similar*; e.g. Er trug den gleichen (not: denselben) Hut wie ich.

The above are singular in form, but may be singular or plural in meaning. As subject, 'wer' and 'was' take a singular verb, but they can be the complement of a plural verb; where the subject is the demonstrative 'es' or 'das', this applies only to 'was' (cf. 143(a)N.).

Wer hat diesen Brief geschrieben?	*Who wrote this letter?*
Wer sind diese Leute?	*Who are these people?*
Wessen Mäntel sind diese?	*Whose coats are these?*
(commoner: Wem gehören diese Mäntel?)[1]	
Was sind diese Dinge?	*What are these things?*
Was sind das?	

Note:

i For a colloquial means of indicating that 'wer' and 'was' are plural in meaning, see 173(b).

ii The archaic genitive 'wes' still occurs in the compounds weshalb? and weswegen? *why? wherefore?* and in the set phrase 'Wes Geistes Kind ist er?' *What kind of a fellow is he?*

171. When the interrog. pron., referring to a thing, is used with one of the following prepositions, the usual form is wo + prep., e.g. womit? *with what?*; if the preposition begins with a vowel, an r is inserted, e.g. worauf? *on what?*

an, auf, aus, bei, durch, für, gegen, hinter, in, mit, nach, über, um, unter, von, vor, zu

Womit schreibst du?	*What are you writing with?*
Ich wußte nicht, worauf ich mich setzen sollte	*I didn't know what to sit down on*

Note:

i Compounded with 'wo', durch, nach, von and zu do not generally express motion:

Wodurch weißt du das?	*How is it that you know that?*
Wonach sehnst du dich?	*What are you longing for?*
Wonach soll man die Lage beurteilen?	*By what is one to judge the situation?*
Wovon sprachen wir?	*What were we talking about?*
Wozu gebrauchst du dieses Instrument?	*What do you use this instrument for?*

To express motion, the following renderings may be used: durch: durch was? von: von wo? woher? *from where?* nach and zu: wohin? *where to?*

ii Colloquially, prep. + was is also used, even with prepositions taking the dative:

Von was lebt er?	*What does he live on?*
„Biste fertig oder machste weiter?"	'*Have you finished or are you going on?*'
„Mit was?" „Schreiben." (J. Rehn)	'*With what?*' '*Writing.*'

iii In practice, prepositions not compounded with 'wo' are rarely required before the neut. interrog. pron.; because of what? = weswegen? or, coll. and emphatic, wegen was?

[1] cf. Collinson, op. cit., p. 49.

172. The genitive and dative of 'was'

(a) The neut. gen. 'wessen' sounds stilted and is avoided. Thus normal usage is: Worauf lautet die Anklage? (Not: Wessen ist er angeklagt?) Warum (not: Wessen) schämst du dich?

In other contexts 'of what?' may be rendered by 'wovon?' or turned more freely, e.g.

Wozu gehört diese Schraube?   *Of what is this screw a part?*

(b) For the non-existent dative of 'was', a serviceable substitute is 'welcher' followed by a suitable noun:

Welcher Konstruktion ähnelt Ihre   *What does your invention resemble?*
Erfindung?

Welcher Ursache kann man seinen   *To what can one ascribe his success?*
Erfolg zuschreiben?

173. Miscellaneous points connected with the interrogative pronoun

(a) **wer and was may be used exclamatorily:**

Wer hätte so was erwartet!   *Who would have expected such a thing!*
(a rhetorical question)

Was *haben* wir gelacht!   *How we laughed!*

Compare some of the examples in 173(b)

(b) **Colloquially an uninflected 'alles' may be added to (though generally separated from) wer, was, etc. (and also to wo, wohin, woher) to show that more than one person, thing or place is referred to:**

Wer kommt denn alles?   *What people are coming?*
Was hat er alles gefragt?   *What were the things that he asked?*
Du weißt ja, was sie alles   *Of course you know everything that she's*
durchgemacht hat (H. Böll)   *been through*
Wofür ist diese Salbe alles gut?   *What are the things that this ointment is*
     good for?
Wem *hat* er nicht alles geholfen!   *Whom hasn't he helped!*
Was er nicht alles tut!   *The things he does!*
Wo bist du in den Ferien alles   *What places have you been to in the*
gewesen?[1]   *holidays?*

(c) **Neuter collective substantival adjectives are used in apposition to the interrogative was,** but are separated from it:

Was haben sie Wichtiges besprochen?[2]   *What important matter (or matters) did*
     they discuss?
Was ist Komisches daran?   *What is there funny about it?*
Was gibt es Neues?   *What's the news?*
Was könnt ihr hier anderes erwarten?   *What else can you expect here?*
(H. Fallada)

(d) **The regional use of wer in the sense of someone, anyone** (not used in gen.) should be recognized but not imitated, e.g. Es ist wer an der Tür. Hast du wen gesehen? Er wird schon wen finden, den er mit seinem Geschwätz glücklich machen kann (H. Broch).

---

[1] from Eggeling op. cit.: all (German) 6(b).
[2] Historically, Wichtiges was a partitive gen.: 'What of the important did they discuss?' The same applies to the other examples. Cf. Eggeling op. cit.: was (interrogative) 4(a).

(e) (S) Some phrases and idioms

Was stößt du mich immer? (coll.)	*Why do you keep nudging me?*
Wie ist der Name, bitte?	*What is your name?*
Wie ist das Buch?	*What's the book like?*
Wie (bitte)?	*What did you say? I beg your pardon?*
Du kommst doch, was? (or wie?) (coll.)	*You are coming, aren't you?*

E. THE INTERROGATIVE ADJECTIVE

174. The interrogative adjective welcher? welche? welches? plur. welche? *which? what?*

(a) Declension
It is declined like dieser, except for a fluctuation in the masc. and neut. gen. sing.: see 89 N.i; in practice the genitive is rare, 'von' being preferred.

(b) It may be used pronominally:

Hier sind zwei gute Romane: welchen willst du lesen?	*Here are two good novels: which one do you want to read?*

(c) Before ist, sind (war, waren), the neuter welches may be used irrespective of the gender and number of the person or thing to which it refers: Welches ist die jüngere Schwester? Welches sind die besten Zeitungen? ('Welche', respectively fem. and plur., would also be correct.)

(d) welcher may be used exclamatorily, though was für (ein) is commoner (see 175(d)): Welcher Unterschied! *What a difference!* Welche Überraschung! *What a surprise!*

(e) An **undeclined welch** is used, mainly exclamatorily, before ein or before an attributive adjective, which has the strong endings: Welch ein Pedant! Welch herrliches Wetter! (Was für (ein) is commoner)

(f) For the use of welcher as an indefinite pronoun (some, any), see 237.

175. The interrogative adjective was für ein *what kind of (a)? what (a)?*

(a) Declension
i was für is invariable and does not affect the case.

ii ein is declined like the indef. art.; it is, of course, absent in the plural and generally in the singular before nouns denoting materials and substances. Where there is no ein, an attributive adjective has the strong endings.

Aus was für einer Familie stammt er?	*From what kind of family does he come?*
Sie können sich denken, in was für einer schwierigen Lage ich mich befand	*You can imagine in what an awkward situation I found myself*
Was für ausländische Marken haben Sie?	*What kinds of foreign stamps have you got?*
Was für Käse soll ich kaufen?	*What kind of cheese shall I buy?*

(b) Colloquially, was für ein is sometimes used instead of welcher, without any ingredient of 'what kind of?':

Was für deutsche Dramen haben Sie gelesen?   *What German plays have you read?*

(c) **(S)** 'was für ein' may be used pronominally: masc. nom.: was für einer? neut. nom. and acc.: was für eins? plur.: was für welche?

Er hat sich ein Auto gekauft.—Was für eins? *What kind of one?*
Ich habe ihr Blumen gebracht.—Was für welche? *What kind?*

(d) It may be used exclamatorily:

Was für eine Chance!   *What a chance!*
Was für herrliche Blumen!   *What lovely flowers!*
Er ist ein Schauspieler und was für   *He's an actor and what an actor!*
einer!

(e) In the nom. and acc. was is frequently, though never necessarily, separated from für (ein): Was hast du denn für ein Buch gekauft? Was sind das für herrliche Blumen!

F. THE RELATIVE PRONOUN

176. The relative pronoun has two forms:

(a) **(S)**

	MASC.	FEM.	NEUT.	PLUR.
N.	der	die	das	die
A.	den	die	das	die
G.	dessen (des)	deren	dessen (des)	deren
D.	dem	der	dem	denen

Note:
i The two bracketed forms are archaic and poetic.
ii When 'dessen' and 'deren' are compounded with 'halben', 'wegen', and 'willen', a 't' is inserted: dessenthalben, dessentwegen, (um) dessentwillen *for whose sake, because of which.*

(b)

	MASC.	FEM.	NEUT.	PLUR.
N.	welcher	welche	welches	welche
A.	welchen	welche	welches	welche
G.	—	—	—	—
D.	welchem	welcher	welchem	welchen

It will be noted that form (a) is identical with the def. art. except for the four genitives and the dat. plur. and that form (b) is identical with the interrog. adj. welcher? but is not used in the genitive.

177. The use of the two forms

i 'der' is used far more than 'welcher' and **must** be used when the antecedent is a personal pronoun (see 184) or a non-neuter indefinite pronoun (e.g. jemand, niemand, jedermann).
ii 'welcher' is sometimes preferred for reasons of rhythm and style.
iii 'welcher' can be used adjectivally before a noun referring to part or the whole of the main clause:

Er wurde zum Stadtdirektor ernannt, welches Amt er gewissenhaft verwaltete	*He was appointed town-clerk, which office he conscientiously administered*
Er will sich zunächst an seinen Onkel um Geld wenden, mit welchem Plan ich einverstanden bin (better: ein Plan, mit dem ich einverstanden bin)	*He intends in the first place applying to his uncle for money, of which plan I approve*

178. Agreement of relative pronoun: as in Latin, the rel. pron. agrees with its antecedent in gender and number, but takes its case from its function in the relative clause:

Ich kannte den Rechtsanwalt, der gestern gestorben ist	*I knew the barrister who died yesterday*

179. The relative pronoun is never omitted in German

Das Buch, das ich lese, ist recht interessant	*The book I'm reading is very interesting*

180. whose eldest son etc.: see 95(d).

whose one son: 'ein' here has the endings of dieser; colloquial usage would favour 'von': Mein Freund, dessen einer Sohn (von dem der eine Sohn) krank ist, . . .

181. Where 'of which' would be used in English, the normal genitive of the relative pronoun is used in German:

Wir kamen an die Straße, an deren anderem Ende er wohnt	*We came to the street, at the other end of which he lives*
die . . . Dialekte . . ., deren Studium ich mich einmal . . . gewidmet hatte (G. Hartlaub) ('Studium' is dat.)	*the dialects, to the study of which I had once devoted myself*

This does not apply to phrases of the type 'one of whom', 'some of which', 'most of whom'; here 'von denen einer', 'von denen manche', 'von denen die meisten' are normal usage (e.g. Seine Bücher, von denen ich drei gelesen habe), while 'deren einer' etc. is distinctly literary.

Note:

i Dieser Schriftsteller, drei von dessen Büchern ich gelesen habe, . . . (smoother: von dem ich drei Bücher gelesen habe)	*This author, three of whose books I have read, . . .*

ii For the translation of 'all of which' etc., see 189.

182. 'was' is used as a rel. pron. with the following antecedents:

(a) **neuter indefinites,** e.g. allerhand, allerlei, alles, das (demonstrative), das bißchen, dasjenige, einiges, etwas, folgendes, mancherlei, manches, nichts, vieles, weniges.

Nichts, was er sagte, war mir neu	*Nothing that he said was new to me*
Ich bin mit allem, was er tut, zufrieden	*I am satisfied with everything that he does*

... ein eifriger Leser dessen, was neu   ... *a keen reader of what is new on the*
auf den Markt kommt (*Zeit*)   *market*

Note:

i In the genitive, 'dessen' (and not 'wessen') is normal usage:

Ich dachte an so manches, dessen ich   *I thought of many things of which I am*
mich schäme   *ashamed*

ii After 'etwas' (and occasionally after some of the others) there is a
tendency to use 'das' where 'etwas' represents something sharply
specific:

Gerade in diesem Moment fiel ihr   *Just then she remembered something that*
etwas ein, das sie erstarren ließ. Die   *paralysed her; the gas bill*
Gasrechnung (V. Baum)
irgend etwas, was ich nicht verstand   BUT: *something or other that I did not*
(H. Böll)   *understand*

iii When these indefinites are coupled with an adjective used substantivally, a following rel. pron. is generally 'was'; 'das' is sometimes
used, bringing out the individual nature of what is referred to.

Der alte Seemann lehrte mich   *The old seaman taught me many useful*
manches Nützliche, was ich seitdem   *things that I have since forgotten*
vergessen habe
vieles Interessante, was (or das) er   *many interesting things that he related*
erzählte
Ich erinnere mich an etwas   *I remember something strange that he said*
Merkwürdiges, das er sagte

(b) a neuter substantival adjective

After this type of antecedent, there is some fluctuation between 'das'
and 'was'; 'was' is more usual, especially when the adjective is a
superlative or a superlative equivalent (das erste, das letzte, das
einzige); 'das' is used if the thing in question is envisaged as, or associated with, something definite and specific (last example):

Das Richtige, was man sich ansehen   *The right things* [in museums], *that one*
müßte, finden wir nie (H. Fallada)   *ought to look at, we never find*
Das Beste, was du tun kannst, ist nach   *The best thing that you can do is to go*
Hause zu gehen   *home*
Das erste, was Evelyn sah, waren   *The first thing that Evelyn saw was*
Mariannes Augen (V. Baum)   *Marianne's eyes*
Das Gute, das er getan hat, wird ihn   *The good that he has done will outlive him*
überdauern

(c) a clause

Er hat sein Examen bestanden, was   *He has passed his examination, which*
mich sehr erstaunt   *very much surprises me*
Seine Frau kann das Klima nicht   *His wife can't stand the climate, for*
ertragen, weswegen sie umziehen   *which reason they are going to move*
werden

Note: The relative 'was' is not used after a preposition; after most
common prepositions, other than those taking the genitive, wo +
preposition is used; if the preposition begins with a vowel, an 'r' is
inserted (e.g. woraus):

das, wozu er berechtigt ist   *what he is entitled to*

Es ist das einzige, wofür es sich lohnt, Richter zu sein (V. Baum)	*It is the only thing for which it is worth while being a judge*
Er hat sein Examen bestanden, worüber ich mich sehr freue	*He has passed his examination about which I am very pleased*

183. wo + preposition (cf. note at end of 182) **is frequently used with ordinary substantival antecedents if they are things,** though rarely if they are plural; but prep. + rel. pron. is both better style and more commonly used: Der Füller, mit dem (womit) ich gewöhnlich schreibe, war ganz billig.

Note:

i Distinguish 'wovon' *about which, concerning which* and 'von wo' *from where, from which.*

ii da + prep. is used as an alternative to wo + prep. with ordinary substantival antecedents, but is not recommended for imitation. E.g.

... Masken oder Faschingsnasen, dahinter sich der Genius verbirgt (E. Penzoldt)	*... masks or carnival noses, behind which genius hides*

184. If the antecedent is one of the personal pronouns ich, du, wir, ihr, Sie, the pers. pron. is generally repeated after the relative, but this rather stilted construction is avoided in conversation:

Du, der du so viel erlebt hast, wirst mich verstehen	*You, who have experienced so much, will understand me*
Sie, der Sie so viel erlebt haben, werden mich verstehen	
Doch nicht nur ich, der ich mich schließlich irren kann, ... (H. Broch)	*But not only I, who after all may be wrong, ...*

Note: This construction is not used where the pers. pron. antecedent is introduced by the verb 'sein' + 'es'; here the verb in the rel. clause goes into the 3rd person: ihr wart es also, die es getan haben; warst du es, der es getan hat?

185. wer and was may be used as compound relatives, combining antecedent and relative: *who* or *he who*; *what* or *that which*:

Wer viele Freunde hat, ist glücklich	*He who has many friends is happy*
Und was noch schlimmer ist, er realisiert es selber nicht	*And what is worse, he doesn't realize it himself*
Woran die Menge glaubt, ist leicht zu glauben (Goethe, quoted in Du. Gram. 6210)	*What the mob believes in is easy to believe in*

Note:

i The comprehensiveness of wer and was may be strengthened by the addition of auch, nur or immer:

Jeder Vater, jede Mutter und wer immer der wachsenden Generation gegenübersteht (*FAZ*)	*Every father, every mother and whoever has to deal with the younger generation*

ii Where the suppressed antecedent and the relative are in different cases, the former is generally represented by a demonstrative, in the case required, at the beginning of the main clause:

Wem du traust, der wird auch dir trauen	*He whom you trust will also trust you*
Wen die Götter lieben, der stirbt jung	*Whom the gods love, die young*

iii wer and was cannot be used as compound relatives where the antecedent is preceded by a preposition, even if antecedent and relative are in the same case:

Wir lachten über das, was er getan hat	*We laughed about what he had done*

iv Referring to specific persons, or to restricted groups, the demonstrative 'der' is used in the same way, i.e. for 'he who':

Der da sitzt, ist mein Onkel	*The man sitting there is my uncle*
Die da arbeiten, waren aber nicht eben heiter (*Zeit*)	*Those who work there were, however, not exactly cheerful*

186. Some other forms of the relative

weshalb	*for which reason*
der Grund, weshalb (or warum) . . .	*the reason why . . .*
die Art, wie . . .	*the way in which . . .*
die Stadt, wo er wohnt,	*the town where he lives*
die Stadt, wohin wir fahren,	*the town to which we are driving*
die Stadt, woher ich komme,	*the town from which I've come*
Er beantwortete all unsere Fragen, wobei er sich oft räusperte	*He answered all our questions, often clearing his throat*

Note: For the translation of 'when' introducing relative clauses (e.g. the day when . . .) see 534(f).

N.B. All the miscellaneous adjectives and pronouns treated in 187–239 always have a small letter with the following exceptions: Er hat ein gewisses Etwas an sich; ein gewisser Jemand; das Nichts *nothingness, void; a trifle*; viele Wenig machen ein Viel.

187. **aller**, alle, alles *all*; uninflected: all (also alle and alles)

(a) **The inflected aller is declined like dieser** (with the exception given in i N. 1 below).

  i **used adjectivally**

aller Wein	*all wine*
Alles Zögern wäre verhängnisvoll	*Any hesitation would be fatal*
in aller Heimlichkeit	*in all secrecy*

Note:

1. The masc. and neut. gen. sing. are frequently allen; see 89 N.i:

trotz allen Spottes, den sie im Herzen . . . trug (H. Böll)	*in spite of all the feelings of derision that she harboured in her heart*
allen Ernstes	*in all seriousness* (set phrase)

2. The plur. alle is generally used to convey both 'all' and 'all the':

Alle Frauen sind neugierig	*All women are inquisitive*
Ich habe alle Fehler korrigiert	*I've corrected all the mistakes*

3. An attrib. or subst. adj. following the inflected aller has the weak endings (with occasional variations): aller gute Wein; alle Deutschen.

  ii **used pronominally**

Alles ist bereit	*Everything is ready*
Alle waren anwesend	*Everyone was present*
Alles lachte	*Everyone laughed* (idiomatic)
Er ist die Hoffnung aller	*He is the hope of all*
Sind das alle?	*Is that the lot?*

Note: The gen. sing. alles is not used alone; the gen. of das (demonstrative) must be added:

Ich erinnere mich alles dessen, was er sagte[2]	*I remember everything that he said*

(b) **all (uninflected)** is used before the def. art. and before a demonstr. or possess. adj. or pron.; only in the fem. nom. and acc. and in the nom. and acc. plur. is the inflected alternative at all common (cf. Du. Gram. 2880):

all das schlechte Wetter; all das Schöne, was ich gesehen habe; nach all diesem Regen; mit all diesem; wir sehen uns kaum—ich mit all meiner Arbeit und sie mit all ihrer; all/alle unsre Freunde.

Note: Thorolf Hansen (*Deutschunterricht für Ausländer*, 13. Jahrgang 5/6,

---

[2] from Eggeling, op. cit., p. 24.

p. 139) suggests, with some corroborating quotations, that 'alle unsre Freunde' implies 'without exception' more strongly than 'all unsre Freunde'.

(c) **alle** (**uninflected**)

i It is very occasionally found as an alternative to the uninflected 'all'; cf. two fixed phrases:

Bei alledem bin ich hoffnungsvoll	*For all that, I'm hopeful*
trotz alledem	*despite all this*

ii Regionally and colloquially, it has the sense of 'finished, used up':

Der Wein ist alle	*The wine's finished*
Die Kataloge sind leider alle	*I'm afraid there are no more catalogues*
Meine Geduld ist alle[1]	*My patience is exhausted*
Es muß alle werden[2]	*It's got to be eaten up*

(d) **alles** (**uninflected**) (coll.) has two uses:

i See interrog. pron. 173(b)

Wer kommt denn alles?	*What people are coming?*

ii It may precede a plural complement of the verb sein with the sense of lauter (all, nothing but):

Es sind alles Lügen	*It's all lies*
Seine Freunde waren alles Geschäftsleute	*His friends were all business men*

(e) **alls, generally spelt als**, is used adverbially with the sense of 'continually' or 'occasionally'. It is regional and colloquial, but should be recognized:

Er hat als geflucht	*He kept on cursing*
Er kommt als (einmal) am Sonntag	*He sometimes comes on a Sunday*
Sie tut als weinen	*She keeps crying*

(f) **Some order points**

i alle follows a personal pronoun:

Ich habe mit ihnen allen gesprochen	*I have spoken to all of them*
wenn sie ihn alle gern haben	*if they all like him*
cf. sing.: Ich habe es alles getan	*I have done it all*

ii The demonstr. pronouns das, dies(es) and diese (plur.) are preceded by the uninflected all (the commonest usage), but may be preceded or followed by inflected alles etc.:

all das/alles das/das alles	*all that*
Mit all diesem werde ich nicht fertig	*I can't cope with all this*
Aus diesem allen[3] sieht man, daß ...	*From all this one can see that ...*

Both forms precede the gen. dessen

Ich war mir all/alles dessen unbewußt	*I was unconscious of all that*

alles is less emphatic if separated from the demonstrative by the verb:

Dies muß alles getan werden	*This must all be done*
Dies alles muß getan werden	*All this must be done*

---

[1] from Collinson op. cit., p. 60.
[2] from Corbett op. cit. 49(h)(v).
[3] the weak form allen is here more usual.

    iii A declined 'all' may follow its noun in the fem. and neut. nom. and
       acc. and in the nom., acc. and dat. plur.

Note: 1. Where it limits the subject, 'all' follows the verb.

      2. This usage is colloquial except in the nom. and acc. plur.

Das Brot ist alles trocken; ich habe die Hoffnung alle aufgegeben; die Kindei
spielten alle im Garten; ich habe mit den Kindern allen gesprochen.

188. The rendering of all by 'ganz'

(a) all + the/demonstr./possess. (+ adj.) + sing. noun may usually be rendered by ganz *whole*. It has a more unifying effect than 'all' and is,
in general, the preferred usage. (Clearly, all the English equivalents
that follow could alternatively be expressed with 'whole' or 'the whole
of'.)

Die ganze Butter ist schlecht	*All the butter is bad*
diese ganze Unsicherheit	*all this uncertainty*
Er hat sein ganzes Geld (or: all sein Geld) verloren	*He has lost all his money*
mit seiner ganzen jugendlichen Energie	*with all his youthful energy*

With a plural noun, this use of 'ganz' is purely colloquial, e.g.

Die ganzen Straßen waren voll Menschen	*All the streets were full of people*

(b) 'ganz' is essential before collective nouns such as the following: das
ganze Regiment *all the regiment*, die ganze Familie, in der ganzen
Schule.

(c) 'ganz' is essential in time phrases of the type 'all the morning', 'all
day' (see 315); cf. der ganze Januar war kalt *all January it was cold*.

(d) Before the names of continents, countries and towns, 'all' is rendered
by 'ganz'; see 116(c).

189. 'all' with the relative pronoun

Sometimes a free rendering is necessary; the relevance of 187(f)iii will be
noticed; otherwise the following examples must speak for themselves.

REL. PRON. IN NOM. SING.

Der Wein, der ohne Ausnahme (without exception) gut ist, . . .	*the wine, which is all good, . . .*
Die Butter, die alle schlecht ist,	*The butter, that is all bad*

REL. PRON. IN ACC. SING.

Der Park, den Sie jetzt ganz (completely) gesehen haben,	*The park, all of which you've now seen*
Das Brot, das er alles gegessen hat,	*The bread, all of which he's eaten*

REL. PRON. IN GEN. SING.

Mein Freund, dessen ganzes Geld gut angelegt ist,	*My friend, all of whose money is well invested*
Diese Stadt, deren Kirchen ich alle kenne,	*This town, all of whose churches I know*
Das Schloß, in allen dessen Zimmern ich gewesen bin (or: in dem ich in allen Zimmern gewesen bin),	*The palace, in all of whose rooms I have been*

REL. PRON. IN DAT. SING.

Der Garten, in dem überall Unkraut wächst,	*The garden, in all parts of which weeds are growing*
Seine Arbeit, mit der ich ohne Ausnahme zufrieden bin,	*His work, with all of which I'm satisfied*

REL. PRON. IN THE FOUR CASES OF THE PLURAL

Die Bücher, die alle interessant sind,	*The books, which are all interesting*
Die Bücher, die ich alle gelesen habe,	*The books, all of which I've read*
Die Kinder, deren Eltern ich alle kenne,	*The children, all of whose parents I know*
Die Kinder, mit denen ich allen gesprochen habe,	*The children, with all of whom I've spoken*

190. ander *other*

(a) **ander is declined like an ordinary adjective or subst. adj.:**

der andere Student	*the other student*
der andere	*the other one*
irgendein anderer	*some (or any) other one*
kein anderer (als Müller)	*none other, no one else (but Müller)*
die drei anderen, die anderen drei	*the three others, the other three*
alle anderen	*all the others*
Er war anderer Meinung (als ich)	*He was of a different opinion (from me)*
etwas (or was) anderes	*something different, something else*
irgend etwas anderes	*something (or anything) else*
ganz was anderes	*something quite different, quite another matter*
alles andere	*everything else*

Note:

i Regionally and colloquially ander is frequently used without an ending in the neut. acc. after ein, kein or a possess. adj., e.g. Wir haben ein ander Haus gekauft; wir haben unser ander Haus verkauft.

ii we others = wir anderen; you others = ihr anderen. ('Sie anderen' is not used.)

(b) **The inflection of an attrib. adj. following ander**

i if ander is preceded by an article, a demonstr. or a possess. adj., ander and the other adjective have the same orthodox ending: der andere deutsche Student.

Note: After a possessive, and especially after unser and ihr, the second adjective is sometimes given a weak ending in conversation, e.g. unser anderer neue Sekretär (not to be imitated).

ii ander + adj. + noun: the predominant literary practice is to give the adjective the strong endings, i.e. the same endings as ander (cf. Hansen, pp. 129–37 of loc. cit. in 187(b)N.), except in the masc. and neut. dat. sing., where the weak ending preponderates (Du. Gram. 2110).

anderes dummes Gerede	*other stupid talk*
mit anderer moderner Musik	*with other modern music*
anderer italienischer Maler	*of other Italian painters*

cf. ander + subst. adj. or participle:

die Erfahrungen anderer Reisender	*the experiences of other travellers*

While the above would not sound stilted in conversation, there is a collo-quial tendency to give the second adjective weak endings, except in the nom. and acc. plur., e.g. anderes dumme Gerede, mit anderer modernen Musik, anderer italienischen Maler.

(c) **Orthography:** wherever ander has an ending, one of the e's is fre-quently dropped, especially in spoken German, though it is not wrong, or even particularly unusual, to retain them both.

With -e and -er, only the e of the stem can be dropped.
With -en, it is commoner to drop the e of the ending.
With -em, it is much commoner to drop the e of the ending.
With -es, it is much commoner to drop the e of the stem, in contrast with the special (adverbial) form anders, treated in 191.

Therefore:
der andre Student, ein andrer, die andern (or andren) Studenten, mit etwas anderm, ein andres Buch.

191. The invariable anders *else, different, differently*

It is an (adverbial) genitive (see Eggeling, op. cit., pp. 32 and 205: jemand, niemand: 2). It is used in three ways:

(a) meaning 'else' after jemand, niemand and wer.

Note:
i Here it is sometimes written and pronounced 'anderes'.
ii It is not used with the genitive.
iii In the dative, the forms 'jemand anderm' and 'niemand anderm' are not uncommon, especially where there is no preposition to indicate the case, as in: Dieser Schirm gehört jemand anderm (or anders) (coll.: Dies ist jemand anders sein Schirm: see end of 61)
iv Other South German variants cause no difficulty of comprehension.

EXAMPLES:
(irgend) jemand anders; mit jemand anders; niemand anders (als) *no one else (but)*; wer anders kann es getan haben? (commoner: wer kann es sonst getan haben? cf. 194).
die Ansichten von jemand anders (or: eines anderen) *someone else's views*

(b) meaning 'else' in conjunction with wo, wohin, woher, nirgendwo:

woanders, anderswo	*somewhere else*
Wo anders könnte es sein?	*Where else could it be?*
irgendwo anders	*somewhere/anywhere else*
Ich gehe irgendwo anders hin	*I'm going somewhere else*
Ich gehe woandershin	
Ich gehe anderswohin	
Er kommt anderswoher, nicht aus Hamburg	*He comes from somewhere else, not from Hamburg*
nirgendwo anders	*nowhere else*
Ich gehe nirgendwo anders hin	*I'm not going anywhere else*

(c) it is used independently, meaning 'different' or 'differently'.

Er ist ganz anders (als sein Bruder)	*He is quite different (from his brother)*
Es ist etwas anders[1]	*It's a bit different*
Es ist nicht viel anders	*It's not very different*
Wie anders das klingt!	*How different that sounds!*
Er hat es anders getan	*He did it differently*

Note:

i wenn anders *provided that* is archaic.

ii else, otherwise, if not = sonst (see 194(f)), e.g. sonst muß ich es selber tun; the use of anders in this sense is rare.

192. Some miscellaneous instances of the use of 'ander' and the rendering of 'other'

alles andere als	*anything but*
Er hat uns ganz andere Dinge erzählt	*He told us far worse/stranger things*
cf. e.g. ganz andere Szenen	*cf. far worse scenes*
ganz andere Schnitzer	*far worse howlers*
Es geht nicht anders	*It's got to be done, there's no other way*
Es war nicht anders zu erwarten	*One could expect nothing else*
Eins kommt zum andern	*It's not just one thing*
Ein Wort gab das andere	*One word led to another*
Er sagte kein Wort mehr	*He didn't say another word*
jeder außer dir	*anyone other than yourself*
Diese Männer sind Verbrecher wie andere auch	*These men are criminals like any others*

193. other, different, various, varied; distinguish the following:

Dies ist ein anderes Buch	*This is another (a different) book*
Er trank noch eine Tasse Kaffee	*He drank another cup of coffee*
Gibt es noch weitere Fragen?	*Are there any other questions?*
Er ist anders als sein Bruder	*He is different from his brother*
(less common: Er ist verschieden von seinem Bruder)	
Die zwei Brüder sind sehr verschieden	*The two brothers are very different*
Er reagierte anders	*He reacted differently*
Die zwei Brüder reagierten verschieden	*The two brothers reacted differently*
Der Lehrer gebrauchte verschiedene Methoden	*The teacher used various methods*
Die zwei Lehrer gebrauchten verschiedenartige Methoden	*The two teachers used different methods*
Wir besuchten die verschiedenen Museen	*We visited the different (various) museums*
ein abwechslungsreiches Programm	*a varied programme*

194. 'sonst' is a common variant for 'anders' in the sense of 'else' and for some other uses of 'ander'; this and the other uses of 'sonst' may conveniently be treated here.

(a) with etwas, alles, nichts, jemand and niemand, either word can be used, except where 'else' has a strong sense of 'different', when only 'ander(e)s' is used, as in the last two examples:

Kannst du etwas anderes/sonst etwas vorschlagen?	*Can you suggest anything else?*

---

[1] contrast: Es ist etwas and(e)res *It's something else.*

War noch jemand anders/sonst (noch) jemand da?	*Was anyone else there?*
Niemand anders/Niemand sonst hat mir geholfen (or: Sonst hat mir niemand geholfen)[1]	*No one else helped me*
Mir hat er etwas anderes gesagt	*He told me something else*
Das ist Professor Neumann und niemand anders	*That's Professor Neumann and no one else*

(b) with 'wer?' either word can be used to denote 'what other person(s)', but only 'sonst' to denote 'what further person(s)':

Wer anders kann es getan haben?/ Wer kann es sonst getan haben? (commoner)	*Who else can have done it?*
Wer kommt sonst noch?	*Who else is coming?*
Mit wem hast du sonst (noch) gesprochen?	*With whom else did you speak?*

(c) with 'was?', only 'sonst' is used:

Was soll ich denn sonst tun?	*What else am I to do?*
Was hat er sonst (noch) gesagt?	*What else did he say?*

(d) in conjunction with wo, wohin, woher, nirgendwo, either word can be used; compare 191(b) with the following:

sonstwo, sonst irgendwo, irgendwo sonst	*somewhere else, anywhere else, elsewhere*
Wo könnte es sonst sein?	*Where else could it be?*
wo auch (immer) sonst noch	*wherever else*
Ich muß noch sonstwohin	*I still have to go somewhere else*
Ich gehe sonst nirgendwo hin	*I'm not going anywhere else*

(e) in conjunction with a noun, either word can be used, meaning 'any other':

Brauchst du noch (irgend)ein anderes Buch/sonst noch (irgend)ein Buch?	*Do you need any other book?*
Wenn noch andere Probleme/sonst noch Probleme auftauchen, ...	*If any other problems arise, ...*

(f) (S) Some further uses of 'sonst':

sonst irgendwann	*at some (or any) other time*
und sonst noch allerhand	*and all kinds of other things*
Gibt es sonst noch Neues?	*Is there any other news?*
Sonst geht alles gut	*Otherwise all is well*
Wir müssen uns eilen, sonst verpassen wir den Zug	*We must hurry up, otherwise we shall miss the train*
länger als sonst	*longer than usual*
Er ist sonst viel lebhafter	*He's usually much more lively*

(g) 'ansonsten' is an archaic variant of 'sonst', in the sense of otherwise, else, in other respects, and is a current journalistic 'Modewort'.

Ansonsten aber war das Gemini-Experiment ein voller Erfolg (*Die Zeit* on American astronauts)	*But in other respects the gemini experiment was a complete success*

[1] 'sonst' never immediately precedes 'niemand' or 'nichts' at the beginning of a sentence.

195. beide *both, two.*

(a) beide is frequently the equivalent of two, but only when it is preceded by the def. art., a demonstr. or possess. adj. or a personal pronoun: die beiden Brüder.

(b) Used after the def. art., a demonstr. or a possess. adj., beide has the weak endings: diese beiden (Männer), meiner beiden Brüder.

Otherwise, it is declined like dieser (apart from the exceptions noted in (c) below): beide Schwestern; sie sind beide krank; die Bewohner beider Stadtteile.

An attrib. or subst. adj. following beide has weak endings: beide neuen Lehrer; die Beschwerden (*complaints*) beider Angestellten.

(c) After a personal pron., beide has the weak endings:
i generally after the nominative ihr:

Ihr beiden/beide müßt mitkommen	*You two must come too*

ii always when placed between the nominatives wir, ihr and a noun:

wir beiden (alten) Freunde	*we two (old) friends*
wir beiden Heimatlosen	*we two homeless ones*

Otherwise, following a personal pron., it has strong endings:

wir beide	*we two*
für euch beide alten Freunde	*for you two old friends*
Ich habe sie beide gesehen	*I saw them both*

196. The use of the neut. sing. beides *both, either*

(a) Referring to persons, it is used colloquially as the subject of sind or waren + plural noun:

Ich habe mit den Brüdern Schmidt zu Mittag gegessen; beides (better: beide) sind Vegetarier	*I had lunch with the Schmidt brothers— they're both vegetarians*

(b) Referring to two different things, it may be more widely used; as subject it is followed by a singular verb, except before sind or waren + plural noun:

Das Hotel und die Landschaft:	*The hotel and the scenery:*
beides enttäuscht mich	*they both disappoint me*
beides ist wunderbar	*they are both wonderful*
beides sind Enttäuschungen	*they are both disappointments*

(c) Referring to two different small specific things, beides is only used as object, or as subject of sind or waren + plural noun:

Sie hatte einen Ring und eine Uhr und hat beides verloren	*She had a ring and a watch and she's lost them both*
Ihr Ring und ihre Uhr, beides waren (or: es waren beides) Wertgegenstände	*Her ring and her watch, both were valuables*

BUT:

Ihre zwei Ringe, sie hat beide verloren	*Her two rings—she's lost them both*
Der Ring und die Uhr, beide gefielen ihr	*The ring and the watch—she liked them both*

(d) Further examples of beides:

Ich will beides tun	*I'm going to do both things*
Beides ist möglich	*Either is possible*

(e) The neut. dat. beidem is only used referring to verbal nouns:

Kochen und Putzen, ich kann mit beidem nicht fertig werden	*Cooking and cleaning—I can't cope with either*
Der Ort und das Hotel, ich bin mit beiden zufrieden	BUT: *The place and the hotel—I'm satisfied with both*

197. (S) Miscellaneous instances of the use of 'beide' and the rendering of 'both'

Wir waren alle beide enttäuscht[1]	*We were both of us disappointed*
Ich will alles beide(s) tun[1]	*I'm going to do both things*
Einer von beiden könnte uns helfen	*One/Either of the two could help us*
An beiden Enden des Ganges hängt ein Bild	*There's a picture at either end of the corridor*
in beiden Fällen	*in either case*
Keiner von beiden ist gekommen	*Neither of them has come*
Sowohl seine Frau als (auch) seine Tochter sind krank[2]	*Both his wife and his daughter are ill*

198. dergleichen, desgleichen

(a) dergleichen *of such a kind, suchlike*: indeclinable adjective and pronoun, e.g. dergleichen Behauptungen *suchlike assertions*, nichts dergleichen *no such thing*, und dergleichen (mehr) (u. dgl. (m.)) *and so forth*.

(b) desgleichen:
   i *similar, suchlike*: indecl. adj. (less serviceable than 'dergleichen').
   ii *in like manner, likewise*: adverb.
Ould wurde abgelöst (*was relieved*), der schläfrige Matrose auf dem Achterdeck (*quarter-deck*) desgleichen (E. Schnabel).

199. ein, einer *a, one, someone*

(a) For the declension of **ein** (*a* or *one*) + **adj.** + **noun**, see 90.

(b) (S) **Used after the def. art., a demonstr. or possess. adj.:**
   i ein *one* is declined like an ordinary adjective, whether followed by a noun or used pronominally.
   ii ein is stressed.
   iii a following attrib. or subst. adj. has the same endings as ein.

Der eine deutsche Tourist beschwerte sich	*The one German tourist complained*
Das eine Gute ist, daß er Mut hat	*The one good thing is that he has courage*
das eine, das ich brauche	*the one thing that I need*
Die Mutter des einen ist französisch	*The mother of the one is French*
die einen . . ., die andern	*some . . ., others*
Mit dieser einen Hand konnte er Wunder tun	*With this one hand he could do wonders*
Ihr eines neues Kleid ist blau	*Her one new dress is blue*

---

[1] colloquial and emphatic.
[2] cf. 523 ff.

(c) **Used as a pronoun, with no preceding def. art., demonstr. or possess.**, ein is declined like dieser, i.e. like the indef. art. except for masc. nom. einer and neut. nom. and acc. eines, usually pronounced and written 'eins'.

Einer (commoner: Irgendeiner) muß es getan haben	*Someone must have done it*
Ist einer (commoner: irgendeiner) bereit, mir zu helfen?	*Is anyone ready to help me?*

einer der Männer; einer von uns; einer, der ihn kannte, hat ihn mir beschrieben; ein Fenster war offen, und eins war zu; eins von Karls Büchern; ich sprach mit einer der Damen; ich besorge das alles in einem.

Note:

i The gen. 'eines' is literary and is little used except before a gen. plur.:

Dies war der Eindruck eines Menschen, der ihn kannte/eines seiner Freunde	*This was the impression of one who knew him/of one of his friends*

ii The neut. 'eins' may be used where an alternative male or female reference is required:

Die beiden alten Geschwister lebten zusammen; eins half dem andern	*The old brother and sister lived together; one helped the other*

200. Some idiomatic uses of 'einer' and 'eins' and renderings of 'one'

Das ist einer!	*He's quite a lad*
Du bist mir einer!	*You're a nice one!*
Er ist belesen wie selten einer (from Du. Stil.)	*He's uncommonly well read*
Eins wollt' ich noch sagen	*There's one more thing I wanted to say*
Trinken wir noch eins!	*Let's have another one (i.e. glass)*
einen heben	*to drink (lit. raise) a glass of beer, etc.*
Ich hab' ihm eins/eine [Ohrfeige] gegeben	*I gave him one (a blow/a box on the ears)*
Es ist mir alles eins	*It's all the same to me*
Es läuft auf eins hinaus	*It comes to one and the same thing*
Er redet in einem fort	*He talks without stopping*
ein gewisser Pinneberg	*one Pinneberg*
Ich bin keiner, der sich leicht beklagt	*I'm not one to complain easily*
Sie waren alle miteinander zufrieden	*One and all were satisfied*
Das Kind ist ihr ein und alles	*The child is her one and all*
Er ist mein einziger Freund	*He's my one (i.e. only) friend*

201. Note:

i For further information on the numeral eins, see 241.

ii For man *one, you, they, people* (cf. Fr. on), see 216.

202. (a) **ein und derselbe** *one and the same*
    (b) **ein oder der andere** *one or another*

In both, 'ein' is generally uninflected:

An ein und demselben Tag machten drei Firmen Pleite	*On one and the same day three firms went bankrupt*

Ein (or: Einer) oder der andere machte   *One or another made a short remark*
eine kurze Bemerkung
Ich kaufte noch ein oder das andere   *I bought one or two things more*

203. ein bißchen (dialectally ein bissel, ein bisserl) *a little*; generally uninflected, a following adjective having the strong endings: Ich hatte noch
ein bißchen deutsches Geld, mit ein bißchen Geld, BUT: die Wirkung
eines bißchen gesunden Humors (commoner: von).

Note:

i The 'ein' may be replaced by das, a demonstr. or possess. adj., which
are duly declined: mit ihrem bißchen Talent.

ii its common adverbial use: *a bit, somewhat, rather*: ein (klein) bißchen
schneller, ein bißchen spät, ich will ein bißchen lesen.

204. ein paar *a few* (often pronounced 'n paar)[1]

(a) It is indeclinable; a following adjective, whether attributive or substantival, has strong endings: ein paar hundert Pfund, mit ein paar
Freunden, ein paar gute Bücher, ein paar Vorübergehende *a few
passers-by.*
There is a tendency to avoid using it in the gen.: mit der Hilfe von ein
paar alten Freunden.

(b) If 'paar' is preceded not by 'ein', but by the def. art., a demonstr. or
possess. adj., these are declined and the gen. is freely used:
Was soll ich mit den paar Mark   *What am I to do with these few marks?*
anfangen?
der Wert meiner paar Möbel   *the value of my few bits of furniture*

(c) the translation of 'few' and 'a few':
Er hat ein paar/einige Freunde   *He has a few friends*
Er hat wenige Freunde   *He has few friends*
Ich habe ganz viele Bücher   *I've got a good few books*
alle paar Stunden   *every few hours*

205. einige

(a) **In the singular** (**einiger, einige, einiges**):
i it means *some, a certain amount* (*of*).
ii it is declined like dieser, except in the masc. and neut. gen., which are
einigen.
iii a following attrib. or subst. adj. usually has the weak endings.
iv it is used as follows, 1–4 being common uses, 5–7 relatively restricted:

1. before Entfernung and Zeit, e.g. in einiger Entfernung (von), vor
einiger Zeit.

2. before a neuter substantival adjective:
Er hat einiges Interessante erzählt   *He related a few interesting things*
Er hat einiges Nützliche getan   *He did some useful things*

3. as a neuter collective:
Ich habe noch einiges zu tun   *I've still got a certain amount to do*
einiges davon   *some of it*

[1] Collinson, op. cit., p. 61.

4. before a good many abstract nouns, e.g.

Seine Rede hat einigen Eindruck gemacht	*His speech made a certain amount of impression*
Er zeigte einige Energie	*He showed a certain amount of energy*
Hierin habe ich einige Erfahrung	*I have some experience of this*
mit einiger Sicherheit	*with some certainty*
mit einiger Ungeduld (V. Baum)	*with some impatience*
bei einigem guten Willen (Th. Mann, quoted in Du. Gram. 2120)	*with a certain amount of good will*

> 5. before a few collectives:

Er hatte einiges Gepäck bei sich	*He had a certain amount of luggage with him*
Ich hatte noch einiges Geld	*I still had a certain amount of money*

6. occasionally, before an infinitive used as a noun:

nach einigem mühsamen Graben	*after some hard digging*
nach einigem Überlegen	*after some reflection*

7. before some nouns with the prefix Ge-, formed from verbs and denoting a protracted activity:

Immerhin erregte es doch einiges Gemurmel (H. Fallada)	*Nevertheless it caused a certain amount of muttering*
cf. einiges Geschwätz/einiges Geflüster	*a certain amount of gossip/of whispering*

(b) **In the plural (einige):**
 i it means *some, a few* and is widely used, both pronominally and adjectivally.
 ii it is declined like dieser and a following attrib. or subst. adj. usually has the strong endings (cf. 113(b)).

Einige mußten stehen	*Some had to stand*
einige tausend Bücher	*a few thousand books*
einige fünfzig Bücher	*some fifty books or more*
Es ist das Streben einiger weniger, aber doch vorhandener Zeitgenossen, ihren Pkw zum 'Statussymbol' zu erheben (*Wochenpost*, Ostberlin)	*It is the aim of some few of our contemporaries, who nevertheless do exist, to make their car a status symbol*

206. etwas (indeclinable)

(a) **something, anything**

Etwas störte mich	*Something disturbed me*
Hat er etwas gesagt?	*Did he say anything?*

For etwas Neues *something new*, see 111: type (a).

(b) **some, any, a little**; a following attrib. adj. has the strong endings:

Ich brauche etwas (frisches) Fleisch	*I need some (fresh) meat*
Hast du etwas Butter?	*Have you any butter?*
etwas von seinem Geld	*some of his money*
etwas davon	*some of it*

(c) etwas is not used in the genitive; even when it is followed by an adjective, which would show the case, 'von' is more usual:

der Genuß von etwas frischem Obst	*the eating of some fresh fruit*

(d) **etwas and was**

i In conversation, etwas meaning *something, anything* is more often than not shortened to was:

Hat er was (Interessantes) gesagt?   *Did he say anything (interesting)?*

ii In the nom. was can be used only if preceded by 'so' or followed by a subst. adj.:

So was interessiert mich   *Anything like that interests me*
Was Erfrischendes (commoner: etwas   *Something refreshing would do us good*
Erfrischendes) würde uns gut tun

(e) For irgend etwas, irgendwas *something (or other)*, *anything (at all)*, see 207(c); for so etwas, so was *something like this*, see 304(d).

(f) not . . . anything = nichts; not . . . any = kein.

Ich habe heute nichts getan   *I haven't done anything today*
Ich brauche kein Fleisch   *I don't need any meat*

(g) etwas is much used adverbially meaning **somewhat, a bit**: Er ist etwas nervös; es geht ihm etwas besser; er zögerte etwas *he hesitated slightly*.

(h) etwas must not be confused with the adverb and particle etwa (see 295).

207. irgend: adverb, signifying or emphasizing indefiniteness

(a) **Used as an independent adverb,** it has the sense of irgendwie *somehow, anyhow, in any way*:[1]

Wenn es irgend geht, wäre ich froh   *If it's somehow possible, I should be glad*
wenn irgend möglich   *if at all possible*
Die Gelegenheit war so günstig wie nur   *The opportunity was as favourable as it*
irgend möglich (Ompteda)[2]   *could possibly have been*

(b) When **prefixed to the interrog. adverbs wann, wie, wo, wohin, woher,** it converts them into indef. adverbs:

irgendwann   *some time or other; any time*
irgendwie   *somehow; anyhow*
Du mußt es irgendwie machen   *You must do it somehow*
Du kannst es irgendwie machen   *You can do it any way you like*
irgendwo   *somewhere; anywhere*
Er geht heute nachmittag irgendwohin   *He's going somewhere or other this afternoon*
irgendwoher   *from somwhere; from anywhere*
N.B. Ich gehe nirgendwohin   *I'm not going anywhere*
(or nirgendswohin)

(c) **It increases the indefiniteness of jemand** *someone, anyone*, **etwas and was** *something, anything*; irgendeiner (see (f) below) and irgendwer *someone, anyone* are commoner than einer and wer used in this sense (see 199(c) and 173(d)):

Irgend jemand muß dich gesehen   *Someone (or other) must have seen you*
haben
Hier ist irgend jemands Schirm   *Here is someone or other's umbrella*

---

[1] noted by Stopp, op. cit., 62(c).
[2] example quoted by Eggeling, op. cit., p. 202.

Irgendwann wurden von irgendwem diese . . . Briefe aus dem Kasten genommen (H. Böll)	*At some time or other these letters were taken out of the letter-box by someone or other*
Versteht er irgend etwas/irgendwas vom Wein?	*Does he know anything (at all) about wine?*
irgend so etwas	*something/anything like this*

Note:

i For practical purposes:

jemand *someone*; irgend jemand *someone (or other)*, anyone *(at all)*
etwas *something*; irgend etwas (irgendwas) *something (or other)*, any-thing *(at all)*

ii an irgend etwas and irgendworan:

With a number of common prepositions, the second alternative is some-times found and heard, but its use is very limited and it is not to be recommended:

Ich habe mich an irgend etwas (irgendworan) gestoßen	*I knocked against something or other*
Ist das zu irgend etwas (irgendwozu) zu gebrauchen?	*Can that be used for anything?*

(d) **irgendein** is an indefinite adjective meaning *some (or other)*, *any (whatsoever)*; it is declined like ein and a following adjective is declined as after ein (cf. 90); its plural is irgendwelche (see (e) below).

Er zeigte mir irgendein (neues) Buch	*He showed me some (new) book or other*
Machte er irgendeine Bemerkung?	*Did he make any remark?*
Irgendein anderer antwortete	*Someone else answered*

(e) **irgendwelcher -e -es** *some (or other)*, *any (whatsoever)* has the endings of dieser and a following attrib. or subst. adj. has the weak endings, with some fluctuation in the gen. plur. It is used in the following instances:

i as the plural of irgendein (cf. (d) above):

Er zeigte mir irgendwelche (neuen) Bücher	*He showed me some (new) books (or other)*
der Besuch irgendwelcher Verwandten	*the visit of some relatives*

ii instead of irgendein (sing.):

1. before collective nouns which are not used after the indef. art.:

irgendwelches magere Vieh	*some lean cattle (or other)*

2. before the names of substances and abstract nouns, unless they are individualized, when 'irgendein' is more usual:

Haben wir irgendwelchen Käse im Haus?	*Have we some cheese of any sort in the house?*
Er hat mir irgendeinen neuen Käse empfohlen	BUT: *He recommended some new cheese or other*
Wenn ich irgendwelche Angst hätte, . . .	*If I felt any fear, . . .*
ohne irgendwelche Schwierigkeit	*without any difficulty*
Es gab irgendeine unerwartete Schwierigkeit	BUT: *There was some unexpected difficulty or other*

'von' is preferred to the genitive:

die Folge von irgendwelchem unnötigen Zögern	*the consequence of any unnecessary hesitation*

3. colloquially, before the names of concrete objects, where irgendein is the correct German:

Er hat mir irgendwelche Broschüre gegeben	*He gave me some brochure or other*

(f) **irgendein may be used pronominally**: irgendeiner, -eine, -eines; plur.: irgendwelche; the gen. sing. is only used before a gen. plur., as in the last example:

Irgendeiner muß dich gesehen haben	*Someone (or other) must have seen you*
Ich habe mehrere Bücher über München; Sie können irgendeins/ irgendwelche haben	*I've got several books about Munich; you can have any one/any (ones) you like*
Nennen Sie mir den Titel irgendeines seiner Romane	*Give me the title of any (one) of his novels*

(g) **irgend so ein** (plur. irgend solche) *one/some of those, any/some such* (frequently pejorative):

Wer war es?—Es war irgend so ein Vertreter für Waschmittel (Du. Stil.)	*Who was it?—It was one of those men selling washing powders*
Er machte irgend solche komischen Bemerkungen	*He made some such strange remarks*

Pronominally (sing. only): irgend so einer *some fellow of that sort*.

(h) **Orthography**: irgend and the word with which it is used are written as one word (e.g. irgendwie, irgendein, irgendwelche) with four exceptions: 1. when irgend is used as an independent adverb (see (a) above) 2. irgend jemand 3. irgend etwas (BUT: irgendwas) 4. irgend so ein, irgend solche.

208. jeder *each, every*;[1] *everyone, everybody*

(a) Used adjectivally, it is declined like dieser; exc.: masc. and neut. gen. sing. are occasionally jeden (see 89 N.i). An attrib. adj. following jeder has the weak endings.

das Törchen jedes (kleinen) Gartens	*the gate of every (little) garden*
Funktionäre jeden Ranges (*Spiegel*, quoted in Du. Gram. 2955)	*civil servants of every grade*

(b) Used pronominally, it is declined like dieser, but is not used in the gen.; the masc. jeder and the neut. jedes may have common gender:

Jeder muß um ein Uhr bereit sein	*Everyone must be ready at one o'clock*
Seine Eltern waren sehr tüchtig, jedes auf seine Weise	*His parents were very able, each in their own way*

Note the appositional use:[2]

Meine Brüder schenkten mir jeder ein Buch	*My brothers each gave me a book*

(c) Used after the indef. art., mainly pronominally, jeder has the mixed declension. 'Ein jeder' is a slightly emphatic variant for jeder and

---

[1] see also 239(b).
[2] cf. Schulz-Griesbach, op. cit., D 848.

5+

usefully supplies the missing gen. of the pronominal jeder (cf. (b) above):

Ein jeder wollte was sagen	*Everyone wanted to say something*
Die Wünsche eines jeden (or: jedes einzelnen) wurden berücksichtigt	*The wishes of every individual were taken into account*

(d) While correctly jeder can only be used in the sing., colloquially it is often used instead of 'alle' in phrases of this type: jede fünf Minuten, jede paar Jahre, jede zehn Schritte; also: in jeden Ferien[1] (*in*) *every holiday*

209. jedermann *everyone, everybody* takes a singular verb and inflects only in the gen. (jedermanns). It is less used than 'jeder'.

Jedermann/Jeder hatte die Nachricht gehört	*Everyone had heard the news*
Er zeigt jedermann/jedem seine neue Uhr	*He shows everyone his new watch*
Das ist nicht jedermanns Sache	*That's not everyone's line*

210. jedweder *each, every; everyone*: (a) it is declined and used like 'jeder' with two exceptions: 1. its gen. sing. before a masc. or neut. noun of Groups 1–6 can only be 'jedweden' 2. it is not used after the indef. art. (b) it is archaic, emphatic and confined to elevated style, e.g.

Nutznießer . . . jedweden Luxus (Th. Mann, quoted in Du. Gram. 2965)	*beneficiaries of every luxury*

211. jeglicher *each, every, any; everyone*: (a) it is declined and used like 'jeder', but its gen. sing. before a masc. or neut. noun of Groups 1–6 can only be 'jeglichen'. (b) it is obsolescent, rarely heard in modern conversation, but still used in literary language as an effective and emphatic variant:

. . . Verständlichkeitsstörungen, die jegliche Deutung nahezu jeglicher Szene zulassen (from a film review in the *Hbg. Abendblatt*)	*. . . lapses in intelligibility which allow any interpretation of almost every scene*

212. jemand *someone, somebody*; **niemand** *no one, nobody, not . . . anyone*

(a) Declension

N. jemand	niemand
A. jemand, jemanden	niemand, niemanden
G. jemand(e)s	niemand(e)s
D. jemand, jemandem	niemand, niemandem

In the acc. and dat., both forms are used in conversation, but the inflected form predominates in literary German.

Ich habe heute niemand (or niemanden) gesehen; ich habe jemand (or jemandem) das Paket gegeben.

Examples of genitive:

Ist das nicht jemandes Aktentasche? (Commoner: Hat nicht jemand diese Aktentasche liegenlassen?)

[1] mentioned by Stopp, op. cit., 83(b)(2)

Es scheint niemandes Sache zu sein, hierfür zu sorgen (Commoner: Es scheint niemanden anzugehen, hierfür zu sorgen.)

(b) jemand/niemand + adj.: the following is the commonest usage, both colloquial and literary; deviations will cause no difficulty of comprehension.

      N.A. jemand/niemand Intelligentes
      G.   (avoid)
      D.   jemand/niemand Intelligentem

Das ist der Brief von jemand Intelligentem	*That's the letter of someone intelligent*

Note: someone/anyone/no one else: here 'anders' is rather more common than 'anderem' in the dat.: mit jemand/niemand anders; see 191(a) and 194(a).

(c) Miscellaneous

so jemand	*someone like that*
Das tut/sagt/weiß kein Mensch	*Nobody does/says/knows that* (idiomatic)
niemand als mein Bruder	*no one but my brother*
Er ist eine Null	*He's a nobody* (*a mere cipher*)

(d) For irgend jemand *someone (or other)*, *anyone (at all)*, see 207(c).

213. kein, keiner *not a, no, not any; no one, none*

(a) Used adjectivally, kein is declined like ein in the sing. and like dieser in the plur.; a following attrib. or subst. adj. has the mixed declension:

Es war kein angenehmer Anblick	*It wasn't a pleasant sight*
Kein Erwachsener war zugegen	*No adult was present*
Kennst du keine Deutschen?	*Don't you know any Germans?*

(b) Used pronominally, it is declined like dieser, but 1. it is not used in the gen. and 2. in the neut. nom. and acc. 'keins' is commoner than 'keines' in conversation.

Keiner im Dorf wollte was sagen; keiner von uns (euch etc.); haben Sie ein Radio? Nein, wir haben keins; keins der neuen Häuser (or: von den neuen Häusern); keiner von beiden *neither of them*.

Note: The neut. keins (von beiden) is used to refer to a small group, or a pair, of different sexes, e.g. Ich fragte meine Geschwister/meine Eltern, aber keins (von beiden) hatte davon gehört.

214. kein and nicht

(a) kein is used even where the corresponding affirmative statement does not contain an indef. art.: Er hat (kein) Geld; er ist (kein) Arzt; er hat (keine) Arbeit gefunden;[1] wir hatten (keine) Schwierigkeiten;[2] haben wir keine frischen Brötchen?[3]

(b) Where an object is so closely connected with the verb that it is felt as the equivalent of a sep. prefix, nicht is used in the negative version:

---

[1] cf. Schulz-Griesbach, op. cit., J 261.
[2] cf. Schulz-Griesbach, op. cit., H 735.
[3] cf. N. A. Bulach: Zum Wesen und Gebrauch der Negation 'kein' (*Deutsch als Fremdsprache*, 6/1968).

Er spielt nicht Klavier; er läuft nicht Schi; er hat in Berlin nicht Wurzel gefaßt. Sometimes either nicht or kein may be used: Er spricht nicht/kein Deutsch; wir haben heute nicht/kein Tennis gespielt; er hat nicht/keinen Abschied von mir genommen. Sometimes only kein is idiomatic: Ich habe keine Lust, es zu tun; er hat sich keine Mühe gegeben.

(c) The idiomatic penchant for kein is illustrated by the following examples, in the first three of which nicht instead of kein would be perfectly correct:

Er ist noch keine zehn Jahre alt	*He's not yet ten*
Es ist noch keine acht Uhr	*It's not yet eight o'clock*
Er ist noch keine fünf Minuten hier	*He hasn't been here five minutes*
keine zwei Stunden vor meiner Abreise	*within two hours of my departure*
Er ist kein Kind mehr	*He's no longer a child*

(d) When the sentence opens with an emphatically placed complement or object and this is to be negatived, it may be done either by means of nicht or by means of keiner, placed later in the sentence; keiner is regional and colloquial (cf. Du. Gram. 2980):

Ein Diplomat ist er nicht	*He's no diplomat*
Ein Diplomat ist er keiner	
Geld habe ich nicht	*I haven't got any money*
Geld habe ich keins	

215. kein and nicht ein

(a) After wenn *if*, nicht ein is more usual than kein: Man hätte ihn kaum bemerkt, wenn ihm nicht ein Schnurrbart etwas Distinguiertes verliehen hätte.

(b) nicht ein is sometimes used before sondern: Dieses Buch ist nicht ein Roman, sondern eine Biographie.

(c) nicht ein may be used to render 'not one', ein being stressed:

Nicht *ein* Junge wußte die Antwort	*Not one boy knew the answer*
Einer kann das nicht zustandebringen	cf. *No one man can achieve that*

216. man *one, you, they, people etc.* (cf. French 'on')

(a) Forms N. man   (derived from 'ein Mann')
     A. einen   (borrowed from 'einer')
     G. (none)
     D. einem   (borrowed from 'einer')
     REFLEXIVE: sich
     POSSESSIVE: sein *one's* (not used in nom.)

(b) Examples

NOM.

Man sollte nichts riskieren	*One shouldn't risk anything*
Als man sich zum Abendessen setzte, fehlte der alte Herr	*When they (or we) sat down for supper, the old gentleman was missing*

ACC.

Man weiß nie, ob er einen erkannt hat	*You never know if he's recognized you*

DAT.

So leid es einem tut, man muß manchmal hart sein	*However much you regret it, you sometimes have to be hard*

REFLEXIVE

| Man hat sich nach dir erkundigt | *People have been inquiring about you* |

POSSESSIVE

Verwandte können lästig sein	*One's relatives can be a nuisance*
Die Ansichten, die man hat, sind selten originell	*One's opinions are rarely original*
Man sollte seinen Freunden helfen	*One should help one's friends*

(c) Note:

i Not infrequently, the object 'einen' is omitted:

| durch einen . . . Nebel, der [einen] nur ein paar Schritte weit sehen ließ (G. Gaiser) | *through a fog that only let one see a few steps ahead* |

ii It is well to be aware of the North German colloquial adverb 'man' *only, just*; a sometimes untranslatable expletive, it is often close to 'einmal, mal':

Das ist man en bißchen wenig	*That's (only) rather little*
Geh du man vor!	*You just go ahead*
Der hat's man eilig	*He's in a hurry, isn't he?*

217. mancher; uninflected: manch

(a) **Meanings**

SING.: *many a (man, one)*; *quite a lot of things*
PLUR.: *some* (frequently: some as opposed to others)
many, quite a number of (slightly poetic and fewer than 'viele')

(b) **The inflected mancher -e -es**

i Used as a pronoun, it is declined like dieser, but is not used in the genitive:

Mancher hat es nicht geglaubt	*Many a man did not believe it*
Das ist schon manchem passiert	*That has happened to many a man*
Ich habe noch manches zu tun	*I still have quite a lot of things to do*
Manche (Leute) trinken Tee, manche (or andere) trinken Kaffee	*Some (people) drink tea, some (or others) drink coffee*
Manche meiner Bekannten (or: von meinen Bekannten)	*some of my acquaintances*

ii Used adjectivally, it is declined like dieser; one exception: masc. and neut. gen. sing. are frequently manchen (see 89 N.i). An attrib. or subst. adj. following mancher has the weak endings, though strong endings are also found and heard in the plural:

manches Reich	*many an empire*
die Geschichte manchen Reiches	*the history of many an empire*
manches Studenten (Group 7 Noun)	*of many a student*
An manchen Tagen bleibt er im Bett	*On some days he stays in bed*
die Schwierigkeiten manchen/manches jungen Lehrers	*the difficulties of many a young teacher*
Ich habe manche schönen/schöne Tage in Deutschland verlebt	*I have spent many happy days in Germany*
manche Arbeiter und Angestellte (*Die Welt*)	*some workers and employees*

iii mancher is frequently preceded by gar or so (cf. Du. Gram. 2990):

gar strengthens it quantitatively and is rather literary; so is expletive and normal:

Gar mancher erinnert sich daran	*Many a man (indeed) remembers it*
so mancher junge Lehrer	*many a young teacher*
so manches Mal	*many a time*

(c) **The uninflected manch** may be used before the following; in the
case of iii, iv and v manch is archaic or poetic in flavour:

i einer (pronominal); not used in the gen.:

Manch einer (commoner: Mancher) hat es nicht geglaubt	*Many a man did not believe it*

ii ein (+adj.)+noun:

manch ein (erfahrener) Arzt (commoner: mancher (erfahrene) Arzt)	*many an (experienced) doctor*

iii adj.+noun; the adjective has strong endings:

manch reiches Land	*many a rich land*
manch reiche Länder	*many rich lands*

iv a subst. adj., which has the strong endings; not used in the gen. sing.:

Manch anderer hätte uns nicht geholfen	*Many another would not have helped us*
Er hat manch Gutes getan	*He has done many good things*

v certain neut. nouns in the nom. and acc. sing., e.g.:
manch Abenteuer (from Du. Gram. 2995), manch Fest, manch Mädchen

218. meinesgleichen *people like me, the likes of me, my equal(s)*: indeclinable
pronoun, e.g.
Ich und meinesgleichen interessieren uns für so was nicht.
Mit mir und meinesgleichen spricht er nie.

cf. deinesgleichen, seinesgleichen, unseresgleichen, euresgleichen, ihresgleichen, Ihresgleichen.

219. nichts *nothing, not anything*[1] (coll. also nix; S. German: nit)

(a) It is invariable and may be used in the nom. and acc. and, after a
preposition, in the dat.

Aus nichts wird nichts	*Nothing produces nothing* (proverb)
nichts als Schwierigkeiten	*nothing but difficulties*

(b) For nichts Neues *nothing new*, see 111; cf. nichts Besseres; ich kann
mit nichts anderem schreiben.

220. niemand: see 212.

221. sämtlich *all (without exception), complete*

(a) Use and endings:
i When not preceded by a def. art., demonstr. or possess. adj., it has the
strong declension and a following adjective then commonly has the
weak endings with some fluctuation in the gen. plur.

[1] For an account of the historical origins of nichts and of the true nature of a following
subst. adj., see Eggeling, op. cit., nichts.

ii It is not much used in the singular.

iii The last example in (b) below illustrates its uninflected use.

(b) Examples:

Sämtliche neuen Häuser sind verkauft.	*All the new houses are sold*
Goethes sämtliche Werke	*Goethe's complete works*
Meine sämtlichen Verwandten haben mir geschrieben	*All my relatives (without exception) wrote to me*
sämtliche politische Propaganda	*all political propaganda*
Sie haben es sämtlich bestätigt	*They confirmed it, one and all*

222. solcher *such*; uninflected: solch

(a) **The inflected solcher -e -es**

i Except after jeder, mancher, ein and kein, solcher is declined like dieser (though the masc. and neut. gen. is frequently solchen: cf. 89 N.i) and a following attrib. or subst. adj. has the weak endings:

solches (gute) Wetter	*such (good) weather*
Ich habe solchen Durst	*I'm so thirsty*
Der Stoff als solcher gefällt mir	*I like the material as such*
Bist du mit deinen neuen Schuhen zufrieden? Ich habe auch solche	*Are you satisfied with your new shoes? I've got some like that too*

ii After jeder and mancher, solcher has weak endings, except that after manche (nom. and acc. plur.) the strong form solche is commoner; a following adjective has weak endings throughout:

jeder solche (kühne) Gedanke	*every such (bold) idea*
manche solche deutschen Bücher	*some such German books*

iii After ein and kein, solcher and a following adjective have the mixed endings:

ein solches dummes Spiel; mit keiner solchen (persönlichen) Freiheit; ein solcher ist für die Stellung nicht geeignet

(b) **The uninflected solch**

i A following attrib. adj. has mixed endings if the phrase contains ein or kein; otherwise strong endings.

ii It may be used in the following cases:

1. before the indef. art. (commoner: so ein): solch ein Wetter, solch ein großes Haus.
2. before an attrib. adj. (somewhat literary; commoner: so): solch gutes Wetter, ein solch großes Haus, mit solch unermüdlichem Eifer.
3. colloquially, before certain neut. nouns in the nom. and acc. sing.: Solch Wetter ist wirklich furchtbar; ein solch Gespräch; ein solch Gefühl.

223. 'so' is much used to render 'such', particularly in conversation

(cf. the commoner alternatives given in 222(b)ii). It may be used:

(a) before ein + noun or + subst. adj. and before einer (pronominal):

so ein Geschenk	*such a present*
in so einer Stadt	*in such a town*

so ein Armer	*such a poor man*
(Commonest plur.: solche armen Leute	*such poor people*)
so einer (or: ein solcher)	*such a man, a man like that*
(Commonest plur.: solche Männer	*such men*)

Note: 'so ein' is often pronounced 'so'n', e.g. in so'ner Stadt (cf. Collinson op. cit. p. 53).

(b) before adj.+noun, with or without ein, or before a subst. adj.:

ein so großes Haus	*such a big house*
so ein großes Haus	
so große Häuser	*such big houses*
bei so gutem Wetter	*in such good weather*
Er sagt immer so Komisches	*He always says such funny things*

Note: In the first example, the order 'so ein großes Haus' is more colloquial than 'ein so großes Haus'; further, it may convey 'a big house like that', e.g.: So ein großes Haus macht viel Arbeit; cf. So ein kleines Kind (not: ein so kleines Kind) sagt die drolligsten Dinge.

(c) between kein and adj.+noun:

Es ist keine so wichtige Sache	*It's not such an important matter*

(d) so etwas, so was: *such a thing, something like that.*

224. Note:

i For such-and-such (a one), see 165 x.
ii such as=wie zum Beispiel; see also 142.
iii travelling as such (or in itself): das Reisen an (und für) sich.

225. unsereiner (fem. unsereine) *people like us, people of our social class,*[1] *the likes of us* is sing. only, with the endings of dieser, but is not used in the gen. The neut. nom. and acc. unsereins is used colloquially for either sex.

Unsereiner (Unsereins) kann das nicht wissen	*People like us can't know that*
Er würde unsereine (unsereins) nie heiraten	*He would never marry the likes of us*
Mit unsereinem spricht er nie	*He never speaks to people like us*

226. viel, viele *much, many;* **wenig, wenige** *little, few*

Used substantivally in the neut. sing. they have the following forms:

N.A. viel or vieles	wenig or weniges
G. (not used)	
D. viel or vielem	wenig or wenigem

The uninflected forms are more general and collective in their connotation, the inflected forms more particular and distributive.

This distinction is succinctly made by Betteridge (op. cit.: viel) with the tag 'nicht vieles, sondern viel': non multa, sed multum. Further examples:

Er ist mit wenig zufrieden	*He is content with little*
Mit vielem bin ich nicht ein-verstanden	*There's much that I don't agree with*

---

[1] Eggeling's apposite rendering (op. cit., p. 126).

Used substantivally in the plur. they are declined like dieser: wenige dieser Bücher; die Hoffnungen vieler wurden enttäuscht.

227. viel (wenig) + noun: commonest usage:

SINGULAR

MASC. AND NEUT.		FEM.
N.	viel, wenig	viel, wenig
A.	viel, wenig	viel, wenig
	(Exc. Vielen Dank!)	
G.	vielen; commoner: von vielem	vieler
	von wenig	weniger (or: von wenig)
D.	i after a preposition:	
	viel, wenig	viel, wenig
	ii without a preposition:	
	vielem, wenigem	vieler, (weniger) (if 'weniger' might mean 'less', it must be circumvented)

PLURAL

N.	viele (viel)	wenige, wenig
A.	viele (viel)	wenige, wenig
G.	vieler	weniger
D.	vielen (viel)	wenigen (wenig)

Note on the plural forms:
i The uninflected forms are more general and collective, stressing sheer quantity, the inflected forms more particular and distributive (cf. Du. Gram. 3030); this distinction is not, however, consistently observed.
ii In time phrases the inflected forms are used, e.g. Die Firma bestand nur wenige Jahre; vor vielen Jahren.

EXAMPLES:

NOM. SING.
Dazu ist viel Mut nötig — *Much courage is needed for that*

ACC. SING.
Ich trinke wenig Milch — *I drink little milk*

GEN. SING.
der Genuß vielen Obstes — *the eating of much fruit*
der Genuß von vielem Obst
das Ergebnis vielen Nachdenkens — *the result of much reflection*
die Wirkung von bloß wenig Wein — *the effect of only a little wine*
infolge vieler/weniger Opposition — *as a result of much/little opposition*

DAT. SING.
Er handelte mit viel Geschick — *He acted with much skill*
mit wenig Zucker — *with little sugar*
Er hat vielem Übel vorgebeugt — *He forestalled much evil*
Er begegnete vieler Opposition — *He met with much opposition*
Er widerspricht jetzt in geringem Maße der Kritik[1] — *He now rebuffs little criticism*

---

[1] 'weniger' could mean 'less' and is therefore circumvented.

5*

Nom. Plur.
Viele Probleme wurden besprochen   *Many problems were discussed*

Acc. Plur.
Er hat viel (or viele) Freunde   *He has many friends*

Gen. Plur.
die Reden vieler Politiker   *the speeches of many politicians*

Dat. Plur.
mit vielen Ausnahmen   *with many exceptions*
mit ganz wenig Ausnahmen[1]   *with very few exceptions*

228. viel (wenig) + adj. + noun: commonest usage:

Singular

viel (wenig) uninflected; adj. has the strong endings (von + dat. is more used than the gen.; see Variations below).

Examples:

Nom.
Viel indischer Tee wird in England   *Much Indian tea is drunk in England*
  getrunken

Acc.
Ich habe wenig moderne Kunst   *I have seen little modern art*
  gesehen

Gen.
der Genuß viel frischen Obstes   *the eating of much fresh fruit*
infolge viel unerwarteter Opposition   *as a result of much unexpected opposition*

Dat.
mit viel kaltem Wasser   *with a lot of cold water*
nach viel unnötigem Zögern   *after much unnecessary hesitation*
Ich mißtraue so viel abstrakter   *I distrust so much abstract theory*
  Theorie

Variations

In the gen. some Germans give viel (wenig) the strong endings and the adjective -en, but -er before fem. abstract nouns: die Wirkung vielen frischen Obstes, vieler guten Milch, vieler scharfer Kritik. **Far commoner than the gen. is von + dat.**: die Wirkung von viel frischem Obst, von viel scharfer Kritik.

In the dat., before abstract nouns, some Germans give viel (wenig) the strong endings and the adjective -en in the masc. and neut., -er in the fem.: nach vielem unnötigen Zögern; ich mißtraue so vieler abstrakter Theorie.

Plural

viele (wenige) and the adjective have the strong endings.

In the gen., some Germans give the adjective the weak ending -en; colloquially, von + dat. is again preferred. For example, see 113(b).

229. viele (wenige) + attrib. adj. + subst. adj. in the plur.: see 113(b), substituting viele (wenige) for mehrere.

---

[1] from Du. Gram. 3030.

230. Declension of viel (wenig) + neut. subst. adj. in the sing.:

N.A. viel Gutes (vieles Gute), wenig Nützliches

G.   der Eindruck vieles Guten (commoner: von viel Gutem), von wenig
      Nützlichem

D.   außer viel Gutem (vielem Guten), wenig Nützlichem

**231. viel and wenig may be used substantivally or adjectivally after
the def. art., a demonstrative or a possessive;** they then have the
ordinary adjective endings:

Ich staunte über das viele, was er erledigt hatte	*I was amazed at the large number of matters that he had seen to*
Ich staunte über das viele Geld, das er ausgab	*I was amazed at the large amount of money that he spent*
die wenigen, die ihn erkannten	*the few who recognized him*
Er war mit diesem wenigen zufrieden	*He was satisfied with this small amount*
Sie hat ihr weniges Geld verloren	*She has lost her small amount of money*
(Commoner: ihr bißchen Geld)	

232. ein wenig *a little* is invariable; it is not used before a genitive; a following attributive adjective has strong endings. E.g.

Ich habe mich ein wenig ausgeruht; die Sehnsucht . . . nach ein wenig Freundschaft (Th. Mann); mit ein wenig weiblicher Eitelkeit; ich bin ein ganz klein
wenig eifersüchtig *I'm a tiny bit jealous*

233. An ambiguity: Wir bekamen wenig gutes Fleisch

This sentence could mean one of two things:
i We got not very good meat ('wenig' being an adverb limiting 'gutes').
ii We got little meat that was good ('wenig' being an uninflected adjective).

One solution is to stress, underline or italicize 'wenig' to produce the
first sense and 'gutes' to produce the second.

Alternatively, 'wenig' may be replaced by 'nicht sehr' to produce the
first sense and by 'nicht viel' to produce the second.

In the plural, a clear distinction is made:

Wir bekamen wenig gute Brötchen	*We got not very good rolls*
Wir bekamen wenige gute Brötchen	*We got few good rolls*

Distinguish similarly 'viel' and 'viele' before a comparative adj.:

Später schrieb er	*Later he wrote*
viel bessere Bücher	*much better books*
viele bessere Bücher	*many better books*

For the ambiguity inherent in weniger *less*, see 234(d).

234. The comparative of viel and wenig: mehr: (*some*) *more*
                                              weniger: *less, fewer*

(a) These are undeclined and a following adjective has strong endings:
Er hat weniger Geld als ich; er kam mit mehr nutzlosem Plunder (*rubbish*); er
kaufte noch mehr deutsche Bücher; wir haben keine Butter mehr.

(b) 'von' is used in place of the genitive:

die Wirkung von mehr (starkem) Kaffee   *the effect of more (strong) coffee*

der Verlust von weniger Stunden   *the loss of fewer hours*

(c) weiter *further* is frequently used instead of mehr, where 'further' could be substituted for 'more' in English:

nach weiterem (unnötigem) Zögern   *after more (unnecessary) hesitation*

Er schickte mir die Titel weiterer deutscher Romane   *He sent me the titles of more German novels*

(d) An ambiguity: Sie trinken jetzt weniger guten Wein. This sentence could mean one of two things:

i They now drink inferior wine.

ii They now drink less wine of good quality.

To ensure the first sense, replace 'weniger' by 'nicht so'; to ensure the second sense, replace 'weniger' by 'nicht so viel'.

235. soviel, zuviel, wieviel (sowenig etc.): one word or two?

Note: I am here accepting the ruling given in *Duden: Rechtschreibung* and *Hauptschwierigkeiten* and using some of their examples.

(a) With 'so':

They are written as one word when the stress is on viel or wenig, e.g.

as conjunctions: soviel ich weiß; sowenig du auch gelernt hast (*however little you've learnt*), du wirst die Antwort wissen.

as adverbs: ich bin sowenig schuldig wie du; ich kann es ebensowenig wie du (*I can do it just as little as you can*).

miscellaneous: soviel wie möglich; soviel du kannst; das ist soviel wie eine Absage (*that is the equivalent of a refusal*).

EXCEPTION: Soviel ist gewiß, (nämlich) daß ... N.B. soundso viel.

They are written as two words when 'so' and 'viel/wenig' are both stressed, 'so' being a straightforward adverb of degree:

Er muß immer so viel arbeiten; ich habe so viele Freunde; ich habe so viel (Geld) wie du; du hast so wenig gelernt, daß ...

(b) With 'zu':

They are written as one word if the stress falls on viel or wenig and they are uninflected:

Er gab mir viel zuviel; das ist zuviel des Guten (*too much of a good thing*); Sie haben zuwenig Erfahrung.

They are written as two words:

i if they are inflected: Ich habe zu viele Eier gekauft.

ii if the stress falls on 'zu': Sie haben für diese Stellung zu wenig Erfahrung.

(c) With 'wie': wieviel: one word, unless inflected.
             wie wenig: always two words.

Wieviel Birnen haben wir dieses Jahr! Wie viele Pfirsiche hast du gekauft?

236. Renderings of miscellaneous phrases with little, few, less[1]

Ich habe mich nicht wenig geärgert	*I was not a little annoyed*
in nicht viel weniger als einem Jahr	*in little less than a year*
Er machte einige wenige (ironische) Bemerkungen	*He made some few (ironical) remarks*
Es ist geradezu skandalös	*It's nothing less than monstrous*

237. welcher -e -es used as an indefinite pronoun some, any

It has the following characteristics:

    i it refers back to a preceding noun, except occasionally in the plural when it may mean 'some people' (see the last example).

    ii in the singular it generally refers to a substance.

    iii it has the strong endings.

    iv it is not used in the genitive, nor after 'nicht'.

    v it is primarily colloquial, but is widely used by German authors and not merely in conversational contexts (cf. Eggeling, op. cit., pp. 383 f.).

Hast du (etwas) Käse?	*Have you got some cheese?*
—Ja, ich habe welchen (or etwas)	*—Yes, I've got some*
—Nein, ich habe keinen	*—No, I haven't got any*
Es gab ja nur wenig Tabak, aber das Mädchen beschaffte mir immer welchen (J. Federspiel)	*As you know, there wasn't much tobacco going, but the girl always got hold of some for me*
Ich brauche Marken—kannst du mir welche geben?	*I need some stamps—can you give me any (or some)?*
Von seinen Zeitgenossen waren kaum noch welche am Leben	*Of his contemporaries hardly any were still alive*
Es gibt welche, die sind froh, der Wirklichkeit ins Auge zu sehen (I. Wendt)	*There are some who are glad to look reality in the face*

238. wenig, wenige: see 226 ff.

239. The main equivalents of any (some), anyone, anything

(a) any (some): miscellaneous uses:

Hast du (etwas) Geld bei dir?	*Have you any/some money on you?*
Hast du (ein paar) Bananen gekauft?	*Did you buy any/some bananas?*
Nein, sie hatten keine	*No, they hadn't any*
Kannst du mir irgendein Buch hierüber leihen?	*Can you lend me any/some book about this?*
Ich brauche Marken—kannst du mir welche geben?[2]	*I need some stamps—can you give me any/some?*
Hast du noch mehr (noch ein bißchen, noch ein paar, noch welche)?	*Have you any more/some more?*
Ich ging nicht mehr (more emphatic: nie wieder) hin	*I did not go there any more*
(noch) länger	*any longer*
Ist noch etwas übrig?	*Is there any/some left?*
Wenn ich (etwas) Geld hätte, ...	*If I had any/some money, ...*
Wenn du (irgendwelche) Schwierigkeiten hast, ...	*If you have any difficulties, ...*

[1] see also 128.
[2] see 237.

Wenn (irgend)einer/irgendwelche von meinen Freunden es wüßte/ wüßten, . . .	*If any of my friends knew, . . .*

(b) When its basic meaning is every or all, any = jeder (or sometimes 'aller'):

Das weiß jeder Schuljunge	*Any schoolboy knows that*
Jeder Aufschub wäre verhängnisvoll	*Any delay would be fatal*
Er kann jeden Augenblick aufwachen	*He may wake up at any moment*
Er ist ohne jede (or alle) Erfahrung	*He is without any experience*
Es war ein Tag wie jeder andere	*It was a day like any other*

(c) anyone

Hast du irgend jemand gesehen?	*Did you see anyone?*
Jeder wird dir das gleiche sagen	*Anyone will tell you the same thing*

(d) anything

Hast du (irgend)was gekauft?	*Did you buy anything?*
Er ist für irgend etwas/für alles dankbar	*He's grateful for anything*
Er ist alles andere als faul	*He's anything but lazy*
Er tut alles eher als arbeiten	*He does anything rather than work*
Er hat nichts gesagt	*He didn't say anything*

VII NUMERALS[1]

A. CARDINALS

240. Cardinals (die Kardinalzahlen or Grundzahlen)

0 null	18 achtzehn	101 hunderteins	
1 eins	19 neunzehn	102 hundertzwei	
2 zwei	20 zwanzig	151 hunderteinundfünfzig	
3 drei	**21 einund-**	200 zweihundert	
4 vier	**zwanzig**	1000 tausend *a thousand*	
5 fünf	22 zweiund-	eintausend *one thousand*	
6 sechs	zwanzig	1001 tausendundeins	
7 sieben	**30 dreißig**	1099 tausendundneunundneunzig	
8 acht	40 vierzig	1100 tausendeinhundert	
9 neun	50 fünfzig[3]	2000 zweitausend	
10 zehn	**60 sechzig**	1,000,000 eine Million	
11 elf	**70 siebzig**	2,000,000 zwei Millionen	
12 zwölf	80 achtzig	5,200,789 fünf Millionen zweihundert-	
13 dreizehn	90 neunzig	tausendsiebenhundertneunundachtzig	
14 vierzehn	100 hundert		
15 fünfzehn[2]	*a hundred*	1,000,000,000 eine Milliarde	
16 sechzehn	einhundert	1,000,000,000,000	
17 siebzehn	*one hundred*	eine Billion	

241. eins (ein, einer) (see also 199 and 216)

(a) in counting and calculating: eins, cf. hunderteins, BUT: einundzwanzig, einunddreißig etc.

(b) used before a noun and not preceded by the def. art., a demonstr. or possess. adj.: ein, declined like the indef. art. To indicate that it means 'one' (and not 'a') it is vocally stressed and often italicized:

Er brachte nur *ein* Buch	*He brought only one book*
aus mehr als *einem* Grunde	*for more than one reason*

Note:
i In 'ein oder zwei' and 'ein bis zwei', ein is generally uninflected: Ich

---

[1] for punctuation see 745.
[2] illiterate pronunciation: fuffzehn.
[3] illiterate pronunciation: fuffzig.

pflückte ein oder zwei Rosen; ich sprach mit ein oder zwei anderen; in ein bis zwei Jahren.[1]

ii Before Uhr, ein is uninflected: kurz nach ein Uhr.

iii 101, 1001 etc. used before a noun: normal usage is an uninflected hunderteins, tausendundeins etc., e.g. ein Buch mit dreihunderteins Seiten. Exc. hundertundeine Mark; Tausendundeine Nacht *The Arabian Nights*

(c) used as a pronoun, ein is declined like dieser: einer der Männer, eines/eins der Bilder.

242. zwei and drei

(a) These have the slightly literary genitive forms zweier and dreier; a following attrib. or subst. adj. usually has the strong endings. These forms are used only if the case is not indicated by a preceding def. art., demonstr. or possess. adj.; in conversation 'von' is more usual. E.g.

Mutter zweier Kinder (V. Baum); die Garantie zweier alter Herren (= Adenauer and de Gaulle) (*Zeit*); die Ansichten zweier Deutscher, zweier Experten/von zwei Deutschen, von zwei Experten, BUT: die Ansichten dieser zwei Experten; während dreier Tage (normally: während drei Tagen).[2]

(b) In stating telephone numbers, in military parlance and often in other contexts, the old feminine form 'zwo' is used instead of 'zwei', to avoid phonetic confusion with 'drei'. This is frequently extended to the ordinal 'der zwote', although there can be no confusion of 'der zweite' and 'der dritte'.

243. The cardinals 2–6 and 8–12

(a) These can have -en in the dative plural (though not when used attributively):

nur einer von zweien (or zwei) ist als gesund zu bezeichnen (*Zeit*)	*only one out of two can be called physically fit*

The commonest uses of this form are in the phrase 'auf allen vieren' *on all fours* and in the formula 'zu zweien, zu dreien' etc. *in twos, in threes*, where, however, the alternative 'zu zweit, zu dritt, zu viert' is commoner. (This form in -t may be used up to 10.)

diesen Spaziergang zu zweien (Th. Mann)	*this walk together (à deux)*
Wir waren zu dritt	*There were three of us*
Die Tänzer traten zu fünft auf	*The dancers came on to the stage in fives*

(b) 2–6 and 8–12 have a form in -e, in poetry, archaic style, popular speech and certain set phrases:

Bei Nacht im Dorf der Wächter rief: Elfe! (Mörike: *Elfenlied*); ich habe alle fünfe gesehen; ich muß um fünfe aufstehen; alle viere von sich strecken 1. *to stretch oneself out* 2. *to give up the ghost.*

244. (S) Cardinals have a form in -er (indeclinable except for -n in the dat. plur. when used substantivally) to denote value (generally in)

---

[1] The case of Jahren is determined by 'in'.
[2] während is also used with the dative.

Pfennig and decades:

zwei zwanziger Marken, bitte	*two 20 pfennig stamps, please*
zwei Zwanziger, bitte	
Er gab mir eine Zehner (Marke)	*He gave me a 10 pfennig stamp*
Er gab mir einen Zehner	*He gave me a 10 pfennig piece*
Er gab mir einen Zehner (Schein)[1]	*He gave me a 10 mark note*
in den siebziger Jahren des neunzehnten Jahrhunderts	*in the seventies of the nineteenth century*
Er ist (hoch) in den Sechzigern	*He's in his (late) sixties*
ein Sechziger (or Sechzigjähriger)	*a sexagenarian*
ein Vierundsechziger	*a 1964 wine*
Er ist Anfang/Mitte/Ende (der) Dreißig	BUT: *He's at the beginning/in the middle/ at the end of his thirties*

245. hundert, tausend and Dutzend

(a) Only hundert and tausend are used adjectivally (uninflected and written with a small letter):

hundert/zweihundert Häuser	*100/200 houses*
viele hundert Häuser	*many hundreds of houses*
mit mehreren hundert Häusern	*with several hundred houses*

(b) (S) All three are used substantivally (always with a capital): das Hundert (-e), das Tausend (-e), das Dutzend (-e).

das zweite Dutzend	*the second dozen*
Hunderttausende von Häusern	*hundreds of thousands of houses*
Es geht in die Hunderte	*It runs into hundreds*
Die Menschen verhungerten zu Hunderten und Tausenden[2]	*People starved in hundreds and thousands*

Note:

i If they are in the gen. plur. and this is not shown by an accompanying word, they take the adjectival gen. plur. ending -er:

die Beschwerden Dutzender von Touristen	*The complaints of dozens of tourists*
Die Ersparnisse Tausender gingen verloren	*The savings of thousands were lost*
die Ersparnisse vieler Tausende	BUT: *the savings of many thousands*

ii Dutzend does not take the form of the plural in combinations such as drei Dutzend (Eier): see 56(a).

246. eine Million, eine Milliarde and eine Billion are only used substantivally and are always inflected in the plural: fünf Millionen Bücher; viele Millionen sind ihm dankbar.

247. Substantival numeral (+adj.)+noun (or subst. adj.)
There are three ways in which a following noun may be linked to a substantival numeral: (a) is the safest (b) is also common (c) is rather literary:

---

[1] Schein is omissible if it is clear from the context that a 10 mark note and not a 10 pfennig piece is meant.
[2] Duden's example: Gram. 3110.

(a) with 'von':

Dutzende von Anfragen	*dozens of inquiries*
Tausende von jungen Arbeitslosen	*thousands of young unemployed*
in Hunderten von deutschen Dörfern	*in hundreds of German villages*

(b) The following noun may be in apposition. (Here the substantival numeral is often written with a small letter.)

Hunderte neue Häuser	*hundreds of new houses*
Tausende junge Arbeitslose	*thousands of young unemployed*
Sie wurden von tausenden West- Berlinern freudig begrüßt (*FAZ*)	*They were cheered by thousands of West Berliners*

(c) If preceded by an attrib. adj., the following noun may be in the genitive:

ein Dutzend südamerikanischer Radioreporter (*Zeit*)	*a dozen South American radio-reporters*
Millionen grauer Stäubchen (H. Fallada)	*millions of tiny grey particles*

Note: Where Millionen is preceded by a cardinal and/or a def. art., demonstr. or possess., the first preceding word determines the inflection of a following attrib. or subst. adj.:

drei Millionen Weiße	*three million whites*
die drei Millionen Weißen	*the three million whites*
unsrer Millionen jungen Arbeiter	*of our millions of young workers*

248. (S) Qualification of cardinals

E.g. Er besitzt über (*over*), rund, ungefähr (*approximately*), knapp (*barely*) 10 000 Briefmarken.

Note:

i an + acc. signifies 'getting on for, almost': Da standen an siebenhundert deutsche Kriegsgefangene (Th. Plievier).

ii an and um are frequently followed by die + cardinal, but a following attrib. or subst. adj. has the strong ending: Im Hotel waren zur Zeit um die vierzig deutsche Gäste.

iii (a) an, bis zu, gegen, über, um, unter and zwischen used adverbially before cardinals have no effect on the case of a following noun. (But see (b) below.)

Bis zu zehn Kinder können mitfahren	*Up to ten children can come with us*
Sie ist zwischen 30 und 40 Jahre alt	*She is between 30 and 40 years old*

(b) When they introduce an attributive phrase, an, bis zu, unter and zwischen take the dative; gegen, über and um take the accusative: Kinder unter sieben Jahren zahlen die Hälfte; Kinder über sechs Jahre zahlen voll, BUT: Kinder von über sechs Jahren (dat. after 'von').

B. ORDINALS

249. Ordinals (die Ordinalzahlen or Ordnungszahlen)

(a) Apart from the deviations given below, **the ordinals are formed by adding -te to the cardinals 2–19 and -ste from 20 upwards**

(This gives the ending required after der, die, das, the ordinals always being inflected):

der zweite Tag, die zwanzigste Sitzung, das tausendste Flugzeug

(b) Deviations:

der erste *the first*	der siebte[1] *the seventh*
der dritte *the third*	der achte (one 't') *the eighth*

(c) In compound ordinals, only the last component has the ordinal suffix: auf der, man muß es ausschreiben, dreihundertneununddreißigsten Sitzung [of a Geneva conference] *(FAZ)*; der hunderterste[2] Tag.

(d) Ordinals are always inflected and are declined like ordinary adjectives:

Das ist sein viertes Buch	*That is his fourth book*
eine Leistung ersten Ranges	*a first-rate achievement*

(e) **to be the first to**: the following quotation from *Die Zeit* (25.11.66) illustrates the two possibilities:

Die Russen waren die ersten, die einen künstlichen Erdsatelliten um den Globus schickten; sie brachten als erste einen Menschen in den Weltraum	*The Russians were the first to send an artificial satellite round the earth; they were the first to put a man into space*
Ich war als erster an Ort und Stelle	*I was the first to be on the spot*
cf. Ich hatte ihn als einziger gesehen	*I was the only one to have seen him*

(f) Three idiomatic uses of ordinals:

mein x-ter (pronounce ikster) Versuch	*my nth/umpteenth attempt*
Er war im siebten Himmel	*He was in the seventh heaven*
Er kam vom Hundertsten ins Tausendste	*He kept digressing*

(g) **erstens** (*firstly*), zweitens, drittens, siebtens etc.; a regional alternative: zum ersten, zum zweiten etc. (See also 642(c)vi).

(h) die zweitbeste (*second best*) Arbeit, die drittgrößte Stadt.

C. FRACTIONS

250. Fractions (die Bruchzahlen)

(a) Except for half (see 251), **fractions are formed by replacing the final -te of the ordinals by -tel** (= Teil *part*). They are neuter and are declined like a Group 1 noun, except that they have no -n in the dat. plur.

In general, decimals take the place of fractions and only a few of the latter, with low numbers, are used. E.g.

ein Drittel ($\frac{1}{3}$), ein (und) zwei Drittel[3] ($1\frac{2}{3}$), dreiviertel[4] ($\frac{3}{4}$), dreieinviertel[4] ($3\frac{1}{4}$).

Zwei Drittel des Materials ist gut	*Two thirds of the stuff is good*
die Bezahlung eines Drittels des Betrags/von zwei Drittel des Betrags	*the payment of a third of the sum/of two thirds of the sum*

---

[1] commoner than the older form 'der siebente'.
[2] more usual than 'der hundertunderste'.
[3] after 'ein', 'und' is generally omitted.
[4] almost always written as one word.

(b) Examples of fractional compounds: eine Viertelstunde, ein Vierteljahr, ein Viertelpfund Leberwurst, ein Viertel(liter) Weißwein, Dreiviertelkilo Bohnen.

251. half: 1. halb (noun, adjective or adverb)
          2. die Hälfte (noun)

(a) half (noun)

(Ein) Halb ist mehr als ein Drittel	*Half is more than a third*
Er gab mir nur die Hälfte (or: nur halb) (davon)	*He gave me only half (of it)*
halb soviel (wie)	*half as much (as)*
die eine (die größere) Hälfte	*the one (the bigger) half*

(b) half a and half the (this, my)

A serviceable working rule is to use 'halb' for 'half a' and 'die Hälfte' for 'half the (this, my, your etc.)', though for the latter 'halb' may also be possible:

Ich aß einen halben Apfel	*I ate half an apple*
ein halbes Dutzend	*half a dozen*
die Hälfte der Jungen	*half the boys*
Die Hälfte der Butter (or: die halbe Butter) ist schlecht	*Half the butter is bad*
Er aß die Hälfte des Kuchens (or: den halben Kuchen)	*He ate half the cake*
die Hälfte des/dieses Geldes	*half the/this money*
die Hälfte meines Geldes	*half my money*

(c) half (adverb)

halb angezogen	*half dressed*
Er weiß alles nur halb	*He only half knows things*

(d) Phrases and idioms[1]

zum halben Preis	*at half the price*
mit halber Geschwindigkeit	*at half speed*
nach der ersten Halbzeit, bei Halbzeit	*at half-time* (football)
Er ist mir auf halbem Wege entgegengekommen	*He met me half way* (lit. and fig.)
Das ist nichts Halbes und nichts Ganzes	*That's neither fish nor flesh*
Ich nehm' noch ein Halbes	*I'll have another small glass*
seine bessere Hälfte	*his better half* (his wife)
Die Besucher waren zur Hälfte Deutsche	*Half the visitors were Germans*

(e) For equivalents of the many idiomatic uses and compounds of 'half', a dictionary must be consulted. E.g.

Das ist lange nicht gut genug	*That's not good enough by half*
Ich hätte beinah Lust, schwimmen zu gehen	*I've half a mind to go swimming*

(f) 1½, 2½ etc.

1½: anderthalb, einundeinhalb, eineinhalb Stunden.[2]
2½: zwei(und)einhalb.   7½: sieben(und)einhalb.

---

[1] I am particularly indebted to Du. Stil. for the examples in this section.
[2] anderthalb (i.e. das zweite (andre) nur halb) is more used than the other two, of which einundeinhalb is the commoner.

Note:

i In normal usage, these forms are not declined: Er ist vor zweiundeinhalb
   Stunden angekommen.

ii For comprehension purposes, the archaic forms dritt(e)halb (2½),
   viert(e)halb (3½) etc. may be mentioned.

D. EQUAL DISTRIBUTION (5 MARKS EACH ETC.)

252. Numerically equal distribution is expressed by 'je' (from
MHG ie = always):

Ich gab den Jungen je 5 Mark	*I gave the boys 5 marks each*
A. und B. wurden zu je drei Jahren Haft verurteilt (*SZ*)	*A and B were sentenced to three years' imprisonment each*

Three less common uses of this 'je':

Je zwei von ihnen kamen herein (normal usage: Sie kamen zu zweit herein)	*They came in in twos*
nach je sechs Monaten (normal usage: alle sechs Monate)	*(after) every six months*
Je der (= Jeder) zehnte Baum war ein Kirschbaum	*Every tenth tree was a cherry-tree*

E. SINGLE, TWOFOLD

253. single, twofold etc.: einfach, zweifach etc.

eine einfache Karte	*a single ticket*
ein dreifacher Sieg	*a treble victory*
. . . stiegen die Grundstückspreise zunächst aufs Zehnfache (H. Böll)	*. . . the price of land in the first instance went up tenfold*

cf. **vielfach** or **mehrfach** *manifold, frequent(ly), repeated(ly),* **mannigfach**[1]
manifold, varied.

ein vielfacher Millionär	*a multi-millionaire*
Er wird vielfach kritisiert	*He is frequently criticized*
Die Preise sind aufs Mehrfache gestiegen	*Prices have multiplied several times*

Parallel to the above are the forms **zwiefältig, dreifältig** etc., vielfältig,
mannigfaltig, e.g. ein dreifältiger Sieg, seine mannigfaltigen Gaben.

Note:

i double = doppelt.

ii zweifach has the literary variant zwiefach.

iii einfältig generally means simple-minded.

iv the Trinity = die Dreifaltigkeit (or die Dreieinigkeit, die Trinität).

v mehrfältig does not exist.

vi single, individual, separate = einzeln, e.g. Er betrachtete die einzelnen
   Fotos (or: jedes Foto einzeln).

vii Er hat keinen einzigen Freund *He hasn't a single friend.*

---

[1] less used than mannigfaltig.

F. ONCE, TWICE AND THE USES OF 'MAL'

254. Once, twice, three times etc.: einmal, zweimal, dreimal etc.

Ich habe es hundertmal bereut	*I've regretted it a hundred times*
anderthalbmal so groß (wie)	*one and a half times as big (as)*
Also, Herr Ober, zweimal Gulasch	*Well now, waiter, goulash for two*
See also 258: multiplication.	

einmal, zweimal etc. form adjectives in -ig:

eine einmalige Gelegenheit	*a unique opportunity*
Kleists *Penthesilea* ist etwas Einmaliges	*Kleists* Penthesilea *is something unique*
nach dreimaligem Durchlesen seines Briefes	*after reading his letter through three times*
mehrmalig	*repeated, reiterated*

255. (S) A selection of the uses of Mal *time, occasion*

In the sing. Mal is written as a separate word, with a capital: Ich habe ihn oft besucht; das eine Mal zeigte er mir seine Markensammlung. Das letzte Mal war das schönste; das erste Mal, daß ich ihn sah; dieses *eine* Mal *this once*; kein einziges Mal *not once*; ein ums andere Mal *every other time*; nächstes Mal.[1]

Exc. 1. where a combination of def. art. + adj. + mal, often with zu (or bei), is regarded simply as an adverb phrase: Als er das letztemal hier war; heute kam er zum drittenmal (hintereinander)/zum erstenmal (seit langem); das nächstemal, das übernächstemal, das vorletztemal, zum wievieltenmal? beim erstenmal.

Exc. 2. a few common adverbs and adverb phrases, e.g. diesmal, jedesmal, ein andermal. (For einmal, see 294(a)(b)).

In the plur. Mal is written as a separate word with a capital when it is inflected: Die letzten paar Male war er nicht zu Hause; beide Male; viele (hundert) Male.

BUT: hundertemal, ein (halbes) dutzendmal, ein paar dutzendmal, dutzendemal, ein paarmal; x-mal, zigmal *umpteen times*.

vielmals is much used in three contexts only:
Ich danke Ihnen vielmals/Danke vielmals! *Many thanks.*
Ich bitte vielmals um Entschuldigung. *Many apologies.*
Er läßt Sie vielmals grüßen. *He sends you his kind regards.*

G. TWO KINDS OF ETC.

256. two, three etc., many kinds of: zweierlei, dreierlei, vielerlei

Note:
i These forms consist of a gen. of the cardinal or indefinite + MHG lei(e) *kind, sort* (see also 95(b)).
ii They are used attributively and substantively.
iii They are indeclinable and a following adjective has the strong endings.

---

[1] nächstes Mal cannot be used with a verb in the past; therefore: Das nächstemal war er nicht zu Hause.

EXAMPLES:

Ich ziehe zweierlei Bohnen	*I grow two kinds of beans*
Er hat hunderterlei Pläne	*He's got hundreds of different plans*
Ich habe ihm dreierlei vorgeschlagen	*I suggested three different things to him*

Uses of einerlei:

Die Schwestern trugen einerlei Kleider	*The sisters wore identical dresses*
Die Stühle sind alle einerlei	*The chairs are all the same*
Es ist mir ganz einerlei	*It's all the same to me*
Ich ziehe nur eine Art Bohnen	BUT: *I only grow one kind of beans*

H. MISCELLANEOUS NUMERICAL USAGES AND FORMULAE

257. Miscellaneous usages[1]

3 525 400 DM/Einwohner/Bücher	*3,525,400 marks/inhabitants/books*
71 83 22 (einundsiebzig dreiundachtzig zwoundzwanzig)	*718322* (telephone number)
3 21 (drei einundzwanzig)	*321* (telephone number)
einmal erster Bremen einfach	*first single Bremen*
zweimal zweiter Bremen Rückfahrkarte (or: hin und zurück)	*two second returns Bremen*
3,75 (dreikommasiebenfünf)	*3·75* (decimal)
0,5 (nullkommafünf)	*0·5* (decimal)
Das Zimmer ist 5,50 m (Meter) lang und 4,20 m breit	*The room is 5·5 metres long and 4·2 metres wide*
Das Zimmer ist 5,50 mal 4,20 (fünfkommafünfnull mal vierkommazweinull)	*The room is 5·5 by 4·2 metres*
10,75 DM (zehn Mark fünfundsiebzig)	*10 marks 75 pfennig*
ein Motor von 1700 cm³ (ein Motor von 1700 Kubikzentimeter)	*an engine of 1700 c.c.*
ein 60-PS-Motor (PS = Pferdestärke)	*a 60 b.h.p. engine*
Er hat einen Ford 1500	*He's got a Ford 1500*
Er hat einen fünfzehnhunderter	*He's got a 1500*
Er hat einen 3,2 l (Liter) BMW	*He's got a 3·2 litre BMW*
Das Thermometer steht auf null Grad (0°C)	*The thermometer is at zero* (Celsius, i.e. centigrade)
ein Winkel von neunzig Grad (90°)	*an angle of 90°*
ein rechter Winkel	*a right angle*
Die zwei Mauern stehen in einem Winkel von 70° zueinander	*The two walls form an angle of 70°*

Note: 7 is often written 7̸, to distinguish it from 1.

258. Some mathematical processes and equations

Note: In all the following except the last two, 'ist' may be used in place of 'gleich'; for multiplication 'macht' is also used.

addieren	*to add*
vier plus (or und) fünf gleich neun	$4+5=9$ (footnote[2])
abziehen or subtrahieren (von)	*to subtract (from)*

---

[1] See also 565(e).   [2] same symbols in German.

zwölf minus (or weniger) zwei gleich zehn	$12 - 2 = 10$ (footnote [1])
multiplizieren (mit)	*to multiply (by)*
sieben mal drei gleich einundzwanzig	$7 \times 3 = 21$ (footnote [2])
das Einmaleins	*multiplication table(s)*
dividieren (durch or mit)	*to divide (by)*
zwanzig (geteilt) durch fünf gleich vier	$20 \div 5 = 4$ (footnote [3])
vier hoch zwei (or: vier Quadrat) gleich sechzehn	$4^2 = 16$ (footnote [1])
zwei hoch minus fünf gleich eins durch zwei hoch fünf	$2^{-5} = \frac{I}{2^5}$ (footnote [1])
n-te Wurzel aus b gleich a	$\sqrt[n]{b} = a$ (footnote [1])
a verhält sich zu b, wie 9 zu 7	*a is to b as 9 is to 7*

259. Some contemporary mathematical terms

die Mengenlehre	*theory of sets*
x ist Element der Menge A	$x \in A$
die Untermenge or Teilmenge	*subset*
Vereinigung von zwei Mengen	*union of 2 sets*
Durchschnitt von zwei Mengen	*intersection of 2 sets*
die Allmenge	*the universal set*
gleichmächtige Mengen (mit derselben Kardinalzahl)	*equivalent sets (with the same number of elements)*
eineindeutige Entsprechung	*one-to-one correspondence*
Abbildung *mapping*	Drehung *rotation*
Kongruenz *isometry*	Verschiebung *translation*
Spiegelung *reflection*	Identität *identity*
fünf größer drei	$5 > 3$
a größer oder gleich b	$a \geqslant b$
a kleiner oder gleich b	$a \leqslant b$

260. A typical German address

> Herrn
> Dr. Friedrich Lehmann
>
> Lindenstraße 16
>
> 2800 Bremen 5

16 is the number of the house; where a house contains numbered flats or individual letter-boxes, write e.g. W18 (=Wohnung 18) after the house-number.

The sender's name and address should be written on the back of the envelope; cf. the provision made for this on postcards obtained at a German post-office.

---

[1] same symbols in German.
[2] The German alternative symbol is $7 \cdot 3$ (not: $7 . 3$).
[3] German symbol: $20 : 5 = 4$.

If the above letter were for Dr. Lehmann's wife, it would be addressed e.g.:
>Frau
>Else Lehmann

if it were for both of them:
>Herrn
>Dr. Friedrich Lehmann und Frau

VIII ADVERBS

A. INTRODUCTORY

261. All adjectives and participles with suitable meanings can be used as adverbs; they are then, of course, uninflected. E.g.

Er hat die Sache überraschend schnell erledigt	*He has settled the matter surprisingly quickly*
ein Dokument . . . zeigt doch, daß er mäßigend und bremsend zu wirken versuchte (*Zeit*)	*one document nevertheless shows that he tried to exercise a moderating and retarding influence*

Note:

i Sometimes what appears to be adverb + adjective is really two adjectives, the first one being uninflected, e.g.

Nicht, was lebendig, kraftvoll sich verkündigt, Ist das gefährlich Furchtbare (Schiller)	*Not that which proclaims itself in vital power is that which is dangerous and terrible*

ii For the comparative and superlative of adverbs, see Chap. IV.

262. There are also a considerable number of words which are exclusively adverbs, some of them corresponding to an adverb phrase in English, e.g. außerdem *besides, in addition*, gleichsam *so to speak, as it were*, notfalls *in case of need*, oben *up above, upstairs*, (cf. 726).

B. SOME ADVERBS OF DEGREE

263. sehr

i *very*: sehr schwer; er weiß es sehr gut; das ist sehr nett von dir.

ii *very much, greatly*, limiting a verb or phrase and denoting degree: Das interessiert mich sehr; ich bewundere ihn sehr; er ist sehr dafür; das ist sehr nach meinem Geschmack.

iii *much* denoting degree after so, wie, zu: Nicht so sehr die Handlung (*plot*) wie der Stil hat mich gefesselt. Wie sehr ich es bedaure! Er hat es sich zu sehr zu Herzen genommen.

264. lange and längst, generally preceded by noch, are used interchangeably before a negative to denote a substantial difference in degree.[1]

Das ist noch lange nicht gut genug	*That's not nearly good enough*
Dieses Buch ist lange nicht so gut wie sein letztes	*This book is not nearly as good as his last one*
Das ist noch längst kein Grund	*That is far from being a reason*
Er hat's lange gut	N.B. Idiom: *He's extremely fortunate*

265. Miscellaneous idiomatic adverbs of degree

Er arbeitet recht gut	*He works very well*
Er ist noch arg jung für diese Stellung	*He's still awfully young for this post*
Er ist ausgesprochen begabt	*He's distinctly gifted*
Er ist durchaus zuverlässig	*He is thoroughly reliable*
Wenn ich gegen etwas bin, so tut er's erst recht	*If I'm against anything, he does it all the more*
Das hatte ich glatt vergessen (coll.)	*I had completely forgotten that*
Er ist richtig faul (coll.)	*He's downright lazy*
Sie hat tüchtig geweint (coll.)	*She had a good cry*

C. ADVERBS AND ADVERB PHRASES OF PLACE: SOME SPECIAL POINTS OF USAGE

266. Wo? Wohin? etc. In contrast with English usage, German consistently differentiates between rest and motion in the following cases:

Wo ist er? *Where is he?*	Er geht dahin *He is going there*
Wohin geht er? *Where is he going?*	Er ist hier *He is here*
Er ist da *He is there*	Er kommt hierher *He is coming here*

In den Ferien fahren wir dahin, wo ihr letztes Jahr wart[2]	*In the holidays we're going where you were last year*
Komm hierher, wo ich stehe[2]	*Come where I'm standing*
Er geht heute nachmittag irgendwohin (coll. wohin)	*He's going somewhere or other this afternoon*
Er geht überallhin	*He goes everywhere*

Note:

i As is apparent from the examples above and below (with a few idiomatic exceptions), 'hin' denotes motion away from the speaker or his original situation, whereas 'her' denotes motion towards the speaker or his present situation. (For 'the speaker' it may be necessary to substitute 'the person concerned'.)

ii Especially in conversation, the two elements of wohin and dahin are often separated, hin going to the end in the manner of a separable prefix:

Wo gehört dieses Buch hin?	*Where does this book belong?*
Da geh' ich nie hin	*I never go there*
ein kleines, gutes Restaurant . . ., wo keine Amerikaner hinkamen (V. Baum)	*a small, good restaurant, to which no Americans came*

---

[1] coll. (As adverbs of time, lange=*for a long time*, längst=*long since*; see 315 and 330).
[2] cf. Schulz-Griesbach, op. cit., J 170.

iii hierher is always treated as a sep. prefix, dahin only when it has a meaning other than 'to that place': Er ist heute hierhergekommen; wir
sind gestern dahin gegangen; die Tage sind schnell dahingegangen
(cf. 706).

iv dahin and hierher are often replaced by the prefixes hin and her:[1]

Ja, ich werde hingehen	*Yes, I shall go there*
Wenn er das nächstemal her- kommt, . . .	*When he next comes here, . . .*

267. from where? whence? from there, thence

Von wo kommt er? Woher kommt er? Wo kommt er her?	*Where does he come from?*
Weißt du, wo er herkommt?	*Do you know where he comes from?*
Ja, er kommt von da	*Yes, he comes from there*
Ja, da kommt er her	*Yes, that's where he comes from*
Wo ist er her?—Er ist aus Berlin	*Where is he from?—He's from Berlin* *(a Berliner)*
Wo hast du das her?	*Where have you got that from?*
Wo soll ich das Geld hernehmen?	*From where shall I take the money?*

268. da and dort, dahin and dorthin etc.

(a) dort is more definite and incisive and is rather less used.
(b) dort only has local force; thus: Die letzte Hoffnung ist dahin (not
dorthin) (Du. Stil.) *The last hope has vanished.*

269. hin and her are frequently used to strengthen or complete a preceding place phrase (cf. 594(b)N.iii):

Wir wanderten bis zu den Bergen (hin); der Hof ist zur Straße hin offen.
Die Stimmen kamen von oben her, von innen her, von überall(her); von rechts
(her), von Süden (her); von weit her; ringsum(her) *all around*, rings um mich
(her). Cf. Ich kenne ihn von früher (her).

270. hin und her *to and fro*, **hierhin und dorthin** *hither and thither*.

Note:

Ich habe hin und her überlegt	*I've considered the matter from every point* *of view*
Freund hin, Freund her, er hat mich beleidigt (Du. Stil.)	*Friend or no friend, he's offended me*

271. worein *into which* and darein *into it, into them* are virtually obsolete,
apart from the use of darein (often drein) as a separable prefix (see 706)
and in the compounds obendrein *in addition, into the bargain* and hinterdrein 1. *subsequently, later* (Hinterdrein habe ich es bereut) 2. (less common) *following after, bringing up the tail.*

Eggeling (op. cit.: wo(r)) gives an example in which worein does not sound
antiquated:

Das sind Sachen, worein (or: in die) ich mich niemals mische	*Those are matters in which I never meddle*

---

[1] for the treatment of hin and her as sep. prefixes, see 695 ff.

272. at the top of, at the bottom of

oben auf dem Turm	*at the top of the tower*
oben im Haus	*at the top of the house*[1]
oben im Baum	*at the top of the tree*
oben auf dem Schrank	*on top of the cupboard*
Er lehnte den Arm oben auf die Mauer	*He leant his arm on top of the wall*
am oberen Ende der Treppe, oben	*at the top of the stairs*
zuoberst	*on top (of everything else)*
unten im Kasten	*at the bottom of the box*
unten am Bein	*at the bottom of my leg*
auf der nächsten Seite unten	*at the bottom of the next page*
zuunterst	*at the bottom, under everything else*
von oben bis unten	*from top to bottom*

For figurative uses, consult a dictionary, e.g.

aus voller Kehle	*at the top of one's voice*

273. (da) drüben – hier drüben *over there – over here*

hüben und drüben, hüben wie drüben	*here and over there* (e.g. in Europe and America, in the Bundesrepublik and the DDR)

Note: Instead of by hier drüben, 'over here' is often rendered by hier followed by a specific indication of place: hier im Schatten *over here (in the shade)*, hier in England *over here (in England)*.

274. mitten

(a) mitten is an adverb meaning *in the middle* and is generally followed by a preposition. It is very freely used, as shown by the following examples:

Mitten im Garten ist ein Teich	*In the middle of the garden there is a pond*
Sie stellte die Vase mitten auf den Tisch	*She put the vase in the middle of the table*
mitten auf der Leiter	*halfway up the ladder*
mitten in der Nacht	*in the middle of the night*
mitten in der Aufregung	*in the midst of the excitement*
Er war mitten aus seinem Urlaub zu der Konferenz gekommen	*He had come to the conference in the middle of his leave*
Ich war . . . mitten unter den Leuten auf der Straße (C. Zuckmayer)	*I was in the midst of the people in the street*
Er bahnte sich mitten durch die Menge einen Weg	*He forced his way through the middle of the crowd*

(b) Many of the above examples could be rendered with **die Mitte**, e.g. in der Mitte des Gartens, auf die Mitte des Tisches, in der Mitte der Nacht.

'Mitte' is essential in the following: Er ging in der Mitte des Weges *He walked in the middle of the path.*

Note the set phrase: Wir freuen uns, dich in unserer Mitte zu sehen (Du. Stil.)

---

[1] cf. ein Zimmer hinten im Haus *a room at the back of the house.*

(c) mitten is also used:

i in conjunction with the sep. prefix entzwei:

Der Stock brach mitten entzwei	*The stick broke in two in the middle*

ii before adverbs of place formed with da(r)-:

mitten darin, mittendrin (coll.)	*in the middle of it, in the centre*
Er sortierte seine Papiere; mitten darunter/mittendrunter fand er eine Fotografie	*He sorted his papers; in the midst of them he found a photo*

D. ADVERBS IN -WEISE

275. Adverbs formed from noun + weise (= *way, manner*)

i
beispielsweise	*by way of example*
beziehungsweise (bzw.)	*respectively, as the case may be*
dutzendweise	*by the dozen*
gruppenweise	*in groups*
pfundweise	*by the pound*
stellenweise	*in places*

ii
ausnahmsweise	*by way of exception, exceptionally*
paarweise	*in pairs*
probeweise	*on approval, on probation*
ruckweise	*by jerks*
schrittweise	*step by step*
stückweise	*piece by piece, piecemeal*
stundenweise	*by the hour*
teilweise	*partly*
versuchsweise	*by way of experiment, tentatively*
zeitweise	*intermittently; temporarily*
zwangsweise	*compulsorily*

Originally and organically, both groups were exclusively adverbs:

Sein Sohn und seine Tochter sind 10 bzw. 14 Jahre alt (from Du. Haupt.)	*His son and daughter are 10 and 14 years old respectively*
Übergeben Sie den Brief dem Chef beziehungsweise seinem Stellvertreter	*Hand the letter to the manager or his deputy, as the case may be*
Sein neues Buch ist stellenweise ganz gut	*His new book is quite good in parts*
Er wird stundenweise bezahlt	*He is paid by the hour*

The words in group ii above have also come to be used as attrib. adjectives, and others may go the same way:

eine probeweise Anstellung	*a probationary appointment*
eine schrittweise . . . Verminderung der Streitkräfte in Europa (*SZ*)	*a gradual . . . reduction of armed forces in Europe*
die stundenweise Bezahlung	*payment by the hour*
ein teilweiser Erfolg	*a partial success*

276. Adverbs formed from adj. + weise (being a one-word adverbial gen.)

merkwürdigerweise	*strange to say*
vernünftigerweise	*sensibly enough*

(a) Instead of having the direct, qualifying function of an adverb, these adverbs convey the speaker's or writer's view of the occurrence in question.
Contrast:

i Er war merkwürdig müde	*He was strangely tired*
ii Er war merkwürdigerweise müde	*Strange to say, he was tired*

i Er hat vernünftig geantwortet	*He replied sensibly*
ii Vernünftigerweise hat er geantwortet	*Sensibly enough, he replied*

Similarly:

bedauerlicherweise	*regrettably (enough)*
begreiflicherweise	*understandably*
dummerweise	*foolishly (enough)*
erstaunlicherweise	*astonishingly (enough)*
glücklicherweise	*fortunately*
interessanterweise	*interestingly (enough)*
komischerweise	*funnily (enough)*
liebenswürdigerweise	*obligingly (enough)*
möglicherweise	*possibly, perhaps*
überflüssigerweise	*superfluously*
unglücklicherweise[1]	*unfortunately*

(b) The following, all much used, deviate from the typical connotation of these adverbs:

falscherweise	*wrongly*
Ich hatte falscherweise angenommen, daß . . .	*I had wrongly assumed that . . .*
natürlicherweise	*in the natural course of events*
normalerweise	*in the normal course of events*
notwendigerweise	*of necessity*
unnötigerweise	*unnecessarily*
unvermuteterweise	*unexpectedly*

E. GERN

277. gern (or gerne) *gladly, willingly* is used to form the commonest German equivalent of 'to like, to be fond of'.

etwas/jemanden gern haben	*to like something/someone*
etwas gern tun	*to like doing something*

E.g. Ich habe dieses Bild/seine Schwester gern; ich radle gern; ich gehe gern ins Kino; ich bin gern in London.

Regarding the form gerne: In MHG -e was the regular ending of adverbs; in New High German this -e survives in a few alternative forms, cf. lang(e), fern(e), nah(e). As Duden rightly observes (Du. Haupt. Adverb 6), 'gerne' sounds warmer than 'gern'.

278. Synonyms of 'gern haben'

i **lieben** *to love* implies greater intensity and depth of feeling than gern haben.

---

[1] or leider.

ii **lieb-haben** *to be fond of, to love* is warmer and more intimate than gern haben; it is only applied to persons, particularly when speaking of the affection felt for parents, sons, daughters, brothers and sisters: Sie hat ihren jüngsten Sohn besonders lieb.

iii **gefallen + Dat.** *to please* and gern haben are often interchangeable, but while 'gefallen' is used to convey a first impression, 'gern haben' expresses an established and lasting fondness. E.g.

Ja, dieses Bild gefällt mir	*Yes, I like this picture*
Ich habe dieses Bild gern	*I'm fond of this picture*

iv **mögen** *to like* and gern haben are virtually synonymous; gern haben is the commoner of the two; mögen is mainly used negatively: Ich mag ihn nicht.

gern is frequently used in conjunction with mögen:

Ich mag ihn gern	*I like him*
Ich möchte gern mit ihm sprechen	*I should like to speak to him*

279. Miscellaneous points connected with 'gern'

(a) Of **intensifying words and phrases used with gern** (sehr, recht, so etc.) two may be illustrated:

Ich habe das Kindchen *zu gern/gar zu gern* (coll.)	*I just adore the little child*
Ich gehe für mein Leben gern in die Oper	*I adore going to the opera*

(b) For **to like food and drink**, etwas gern essen/trinken is more usual than etwas gern haben, e.g. Ich trinke Kaffee gern.

(c) The negative form **ungern** gives a sharper edge to an aversion than nicht gern; it may also express reluctance (see also 124):

Ich gehe ungern ins Kino	*I dislike going to the cinema*
Ich habe ihn ungern unterbrochen	*I was reluctant to interrupt him*

(d) **Colloquially gern haben is used for to like doing something** (though not in a brief remark e.g. I like cycling): it is used with 'es' to anticipate an infinitive phrase with 'zu' (cf. 512); the same construction may be used with a passive infin. (2nd example):

Ich habe es gern, nach dem Mittagessen einen Spaziergang zu machen (better: Ich mache gern nach dem Mittagessen einen Spaziergang).
Er hat es gern, gelobt zu werden (Commoner: Er liebt es, gelobt zu werden).[1]

(e) In complicated contexts **es gern haben, wenn** may be used, e.g.

Ich habe es gern, wenn er uns sonntags besucht	*I like to have him visiting us on Sundays*

Compare the idiomatic formula:

Ich würde es gern sehen, wenn du eine bessere Stellung bekämst	*I should very much like you to get a better job*

280. The comparative and superlative of gern

(a) The forms are lieber and am liebsten, the comparative and superlative of lieb.[2] They are used in the same way as gern. Thus:

---

[1] 'Er wird gern gelobt' would be slightly ambiguous; it could idiomatically mean: *People are fond of praising him.*

[2] cf. Es wäre mir lieb/lieber/am liebsten, wenn Sie nichts darüber sagten *I'd be glad/I'd prefer if you said nothing about it.*

Ich habe München gern; ich habe Hamburg lieber (als München); ich habe Frankfurt am liebsten.
Ich radle gern; ich reite lieber; ich schwimme am liebsten.

(b) Intensifications: viel, weit, bei weitem lieber; am allerliebsten.

(c) preference of one activity or course of action to another:

| Ich habe Reiten lieber als Radeln | *I prefer riding to cycling* |
| Ich stehe lieber früh auf als hetzen zu müssen | *I prefer getting up early to having a rush* |

With a change of subject, 'als daß' must be used:

| Ich möchte es lieber selber tun, als daß er sich einmischt | *I would rather do it myself than that he should interfere* |

(d) Both 'lieber' and 'am liebsten' may be used in place of 'gern' in the constructions discussed in 279(d) and (e).

(e) 'lieber' is frequently used to convey a wiser course of action, corresponding to English 'better'; 'besser' is also possible, but not in conjunction with 'wollen'. Thus:

| Sie behalten das lieber (or: besser) für sich | *You had better keep that to yourself* |
| Ich will es lieber selber tun | *I had better do it myself* |

(f) The use of lieber indicated in (e) above does not apply to am liebsten:

| Sie behalten das am besten für sich | *You had best keep that to yourself* |
| Es wird am besten sein, ich tue es selber | *I had best do it myself* |

281. Position of gern/lieber/am liebsten in the sentence

(a) With gern haben, gern generally stands at the end of the sentence, like a sep. prefix:

| Ich habe meinen Onkel trotz all seinen Schwächen gern | *I like my uncle despite all his weaknesses* |

The same applies to lieber and am liebsten

(b) Otherwise:
i gern normally has the position of an unemphatic adverbial limitation of manner (cf. 658):

| Er hilft seinem Onkel samstags gern im Garten | *He likes helping his uncle in the garden on Saturdays* |

If gern bears on some particular word or phrase, this is placed at the beginning of the sentence, but gern is not moved:

| Seinem Onkel hilft er samstags gern im Garten | *It's his uncle he likes helping in the garden on Saturdays* |

ii lieber, am liebsten normally precede the word or phrase on which they bear:

| Ich möchte es meinem Vater am liebsten erst nächsteWoche zeigen | *I'd rather not show it to my father till next week* |

cf. the examples in 280(e).

(c) gern, lieber and am liebsten can themselves be emphasized by being placed at the beginning of the sentence, followed by inversion.

6+

282. Some idiomatic uses of gern and lieber

Ich will dir gern helfen	*I'll gladly help you*
Das glaub' ich gern	*I'm quite ready to believe it*
Du kannst das gern tun	*You can certainly do that as far as I'm concerned*
Gern geschehen!	*Don't mention it*
Er ist überall gern gesehen	*He is welcome everywhere*
Diese Zigarre wird gern geraucht	*This cigar is very popular (commercialese)*
Er verdient gut und gern 2000 Mark im Monat	*He may very well earn 2000 marks a month*
Lieber aushalten als nachgeben!	*Better hold out than give in*
je länger, je lieber	*the longer, the better*
Ich ginge lieber nach Hause	*I'd rather go home*
Ich wüßte nicht, was ich lieber täte	*There's nothing I'd rather do*

IX PARTICLES[1]

283. Introductory

Colloquial German stands or falls by an ample scattering of denn, doch, ja, mal, schon, so etc., without which it sounds bleak and impersonal; their correct use is a considerable test for the foreigner.

For the sake of completeness, the purely adverbial use of the particles has been briefly included, e.g. eben *just (now)*, einmal *once*, etwa *about, approximately*; *perhaps, by chance*, nämlich *namely*, nun *now*, nur *only*, schon *already*; this, too, frequently offers points of interest.

For a list of the particles treated, with paragraph numbers, see CONTENTS.

284. aber[2]

(a) **It gives emphasis**:
   i to an expression of satisfaction or admiration:

Der Film war aber gut	*The film really was good*

   ii to an expression of reproach:

Du kommst aber spät heute	*You are late today*

   iii to ja, nein, sicher and the like:

Hast du was dagegen?—Aber nein!	*Have you any objection?—Of course not*

(b) **aber auch** gives strong emphasis, often to a repeated word:

Er hat (alles,) aber auch alles vergessen	*He's forgotten absolutely everything*

(c) **oder aber** *or on the other hand*:

Seine Befürwortung könnte der Sache helfen oder aber schaden	*His support might help the cause or on the other hand it might harm it*

(d) **aber can mean 'again'** (cf. abermals *once more*) (elev.):

tausend und aber tausend	*thousands and thousands*

(e) **Its substantival use may here be noted**:

Die Sache hat ein Aber	*There's one difficulty* (or *objection*)

---

[1] I am here occasionally indebted to articles by Gisela Schröder and Siegfried Colditz in *Deutsch als Fremdsprache* (1/1965 and 1/1966 respectively) and to W. E. Collinson: 'Some German Particles and their English Equivalents' in *German Studies presented to H. G. Fiedler* (Oxford, Clarendon Press, 1938).

[2] For the use of aber as an orthodox conjunction 'but' and as 'however', see 517 ff.

285. allerdings, freilich, zwar

Note: 'freilich' never means 'freely', which is primarily 'frei' (e.g. Du kannst ganz frei entscheiden), with many alternatives according to the context.

(a) **Their commonest meaning is concessive: admittedly, to be sure, certainly, indeed, it is true**

　i Where they have the force of the conjunction 'although', either allerdings or freilich is used:

Ich will mein Bestes tun, allerdings /freilich kann ich nichts garantieren	*I'll do my best, though certainly I can't guarantee anything*

　ii Otherwise all three may be used, but, whereas 'zwar' must be balanced by 'aber', 'doch' or 'jedoch', 'allerdings' and 'freilich' need not be:

Es ist zwar/allerdings/freilich ein gutes Buch, aber seine anderen gefallen mir besser	*It is certainly a good book, but I prefer his other ones*
Es ist allerdings/freilich ein gutes Buch	*It is certainly a good book*

(b) **allerdings and freilich are used to express agreement or to give an affirmative reply**; both may contain a hint of indignation:

Er hat sich wirklich angestrengt.— Allerdings!	*He really exerted himself.—Indeed he did*
Kannst du es auch alles besorgen? —(Ja,) freilich!	*Can you see to it all?—Certainly I can (or: Obviously I can)*

(c) **Less commonly, allerdings and freilich may serve to correct a previous negative statement:**[1]

Die Lage ist nicht ernst.—Freilich ist sie ernst	*The situation isn't serious.—Of course it's serious*

(d) **und zwar introduces a phrase giving greater precision to what precedes: and moreover, and what is more, and in fact, namely:**

Ich habe ihn für heute abend eingeladen und zwar für 7 Uhr	*I've invited him for this evening, (namely) for 7 o'clock*
Mein Freund ist Schauspieler, und zwar ein ganz bekannter	*My friend is an actor and in fact quite a well-known one*

286. auch

(a) **(S) also, too, and, duly, what's more**

Mein Bruder ist auch krank	*My brother is also ill*
Ich habe ihn gestern gesehen.—Ich auch	*I saw him yesterday.—So did I*
Er bat mich, den Brief zu beantworten, was ich (dann) auch tat	*He asked me to answer the letter, which I duly did*
Ich habe ihn eingeladen, und er kommt auch	*I've invited him and what's more he's coming*

(b) **even**

Auch[2] die besten Schüler machen Fehler	*Even the best pupils make mistakes*

---

[1] cf. Eggeling, op. cit.: allerdings 1(a) and freilich 1.　　　　[2] or sogar or selbst.

Auch nicht sein bester Freund kann
ihn beeinflussen[1]
Not even his best friend can influence him

Er ist auch noch stolz darauf
He's even proud of it

und wenn auch
even so, no matter

(c) **auch nur** *even* (= *as few as, as little as*)[2]

wenn ich auch nur zwei Freunde
hätte
if I had even two friends

ohne auch nur zu fragen[3]
without as much as asking

Ich war außerstande, die Szene
auch nur annähernd zu schildern
*I was incapable of giving even an
approximate description of the scene*

(d) **oder auch** *or else; or even*

Du kannst Birnen kaufen oder auch
Pflaumen
You can buy some pears or else some plums

(e) **nor, neither, either** (**with negative**) (cf. 527)

Ich wußte nichts davon.—Ich auch
nicht
*I knew nothing about it.—Nor (did) I/
Neither did I*

Das wird ihm auch nichts helfen
(from Du. Stil.)
That won't help him either

(f) **confirmatory**

Er scheint intelligent zu sein.—Das
ist er auch
He seems to be intelligent.—So he is

(g) **correcting a false impression**

Das hättest du nicht tun sollen.—
Ich hab' es auch gar nicht getan
*You shouldn't have done that.—But I
never did it*

Er ist aber nicht sehr intelligent.—
Das hab' ich auch gar nicht gesagt
*But he's not very intelligent.—Well, I
never said he was*

(h) **reinforcing a request or admonition**

Kauf mir eine Zeitung und vergiß es
auch nicht![4]
*Buy me a paper and be sure you don't
forget*

Hörst du auch zu?
Are you sure you're listening?

(i) **giving emphasis to a comment on the remark of another speaker**

Was *hast* du auch für seltsame
Ideen!
*What strange ideas you have, upon my
word!*

Das will ich (aber) auch tun
I'll certainly do that

Wer *gibt* auch so ein Versprechen?
What fool would make such a promise?

cf. in a question:

Bist du auch glücklich?
And are you really happy?

(j) **compliant**

Du bist anscheinend dagegen; wir
können es auch lassen
*You seem to be against it; if you prefer,
we'll leave it*

(k) **explanatory**

Er hat die Stellung bekommen; sein
Vater hat auch viel Einfluß
*He's got the job, but then his father has a
lot of influence*

Ich konnte es nicht tun; was hätten
die andern auch gedacht?
*I couldn't do it, for what would the
others have thought?*

---

[1] or: Nicht einmal sein bester Freund . . ..
[2] cf. Kolisko and Yuill: *Practice in German Prose*, p. 89.
[3] from Betteridge, op. cit.
[4] from Muret-Sanders, op. cit.: auch.

Wie trocken ist der Rasen!—Es hat auch nur wenig geregnet[1]	How dry the lawn is!—Don't forget, we haven't had much rain

(l) concessive[2]

Wer es auch sein mag, ich kann nichts für ihn tun	Whoever it may be, I can do nothing for him

(S) See 286A. da

287. dabei (see also 353(b) ii)

(a) proximity and inclusion

die Dabeistehenden	the bystanders
Waren Sie auch dabei?	Were you there too? (Were you at the meeting, in the army etc., too?)
Er war nur halb dabei	He was only half taking part/attending
Einige haben Ferngläser dabei (*Zeit*)	Some have brought binoculars

(b) at the same time, yet

Sie erzählte mir davon und strickte dabei	She told me about it and knitted as she did so
Er ist gescheit und dabei fleißig	He is clever and industrious besides
Er suchte nach dem Brief, und dabei hatte er ihn in der Hand	He looked for the letter, yet he had it in his hand
Er lebt sehr einfach, dabei ist er ganz wohlhabend	He lives very simply, yet he's quite well off

(c) idiomatic (basically often 'in the matter')

Das Merkwürdige dabei ist . . .	The strange thing about it is . . .
Was ist denn da dabei?	Whatever is there to object to? What does it matter?
Es ist nichts dabei	There's no objection, it's quite all right
Ich finde nichts dabei	I see no objection
Es kam nichts dabei heraus	It led to nothing
Da kann man nichts bei machen (H. Fallada) (dabei divided)	One can do nothing in such a matter (coll.)
Er denkt sich nichts dabei	He thinks nothing of it (i.e. sees no harm in it)
Wir wollen es dabei lassen	We'll leave it at that
Es bleibt dabei	We are not changing our decision

288. dazu (see also 511 i)

(a) purpose (stress as indicated)

Dàzu braucht man ein scharfes Messer	For this you need a sharp knife
Dàzu ist er nicht intelligent genug	He's not intelligent enough for that
Ich hatte keine Gelegenheit/keinen Grund dazù	I had no opportunity/no reason to do it
Ich bin nicht dàzù da, um deine Arbeit zu tun	I'm not there in order to do your work
Ich kann nichts dàzù tun	I can't do anything about it

(b) addition (stress on 'zu') (cf. 706)

Es wäre das eine Ungerechtigkeit und ein Fehler dazu (*FAZ*)	This would be an injustice and in addition a mistake
Dazu kommt noch das Porto	To this must be added the postage
Er schenkte mir ein Hemd und einen Schlips dazu	He gave me a shirt and a tie to go with it

---

[1] from Muret-Sanders, op. cit.: auch.   [2] see 471-4.

289. denn

(a) **conjunction 'for'**: see 521

(b) **used for 'than'**: see 131(d)

(c) **Inserted in a question**, 'denn' implies a lively interest or impatience on the part of the questioner, or makes the question less abrupt:[1]

Wie geht es dir denn?	*Tell me, how are you?*
Was ist denn los?	*Whatever's the matter?*
Wer redet denn von nachgeben?	*Come now, who is talking of giving in?*
Der Bus hält ja. Sind wir denn schon da?[2]	*Why, the bus is stopping. Have we arrived?*
Wieso denn?	*How so?*

It may also convey doubt or perplexity:[3]

Ist das denn so wichtig?	*Is that really so important?*
Was soll ich denn machen?	*Whatever am I to do?*

(d) **denn noch** is used when trying to recall a fact:[4]

Wie *heißt* er denn noch?	*What is his name now?*

(e) **denn auch** indicates the result of a previous fact:

Es war schwül im Zimmer; er nickte denn auch bald ein	*It was sultry in the room and so he soon dozed off*

(f) Often preceded by 'so', denn is used **in an exclamation expressing surprise** at some piece of news:

So hat er denn die Stellung erhalten!	*So he has got the job!*

(g) **denn doch** (unstressed) expresses indignation or protest:

Das ist denn doch unerhört!	*But that really is scandalous!*
Das ist denn doch zuviel verlangt!	*I must say, that's asking too much*

(h) **es sei denn, (daß)** is a common conjunctional phrase meaning *unless*, mainly used in Open Conditions (cf. 462):

Ich komme also gegen ein Uhr, es sei denn, daß ich aufgehalten werde (or: es sei denn, ich werde aufgehalten)	*So I'll come about one o'clock unless I'm delayed*
Das kann dir niemand sagen, es sei denn ein Fachmann	*No one can tell you that except, perhaps, an expert*

The idea of 'unless' can be conveyed by 'denn' alone (archaic and literary) or by 'denn' coupled with the imperfective subjunctive of 'müssen' (rather literary):

„Ich lasse dich nicht fort", rief sie, „du sagst mir denn, was du im Sinn hast." (E. Wiechert)[5]	*'I shan't let you go', she cried, 'unless you tell me what you have in mind'.*
Er kommt noch, er müßte denn krank sein[6]	*He is sure to come unless he is ill*

(i) **geschweige denn** *not to mention, let alone, much less* (The phrase stands

---

[1] Eggeling's admirable formulation, op. cit.: denn (adverb).
[2] Es geht weiter (B.B.C.), p. 95.
[3] cf. Schröder loc. cit. (see p. 145, footnote 1).
[4] cf. Collinson, loc. cit., p. 119.
[5] quoted by Eggeling, op. cit.: denn (adverb).
[6] from Betteridge, op. cit.: müssen.

for 'ich geschweige' *I am silent about, I do not mention.*)[1] Occasionally the 'denn' is omitted.

Er wollte mir kein Geld leihen, geschweige denn schenken	*He wouldn't lend me any money, let alone give it me*
Ich glaube nicht, daß er sich für Tennis interessiert, geschweige denn, daß er selber spielt	*I don't think he's interested in tennis, much less that he plays himself*
Er kann kein Französisch, geschweige denn Deutsch	*He doesn't know French, not to mention German*

(j) In North Germany, 'denn' is often used colloquially for 'dann'; this should not be imitated (cf. Du. Gram. 3630):

Na, denn geht es eben nicht	*Well, then it just can't be done*

290. doch

(a) yet, but, nevertheless

Ich sehe ihn oft, doch kennen wir uns kaum	*I often see him, yet we hardly know each other*

Note: 'doch wir kennen uns kaum' would be possible, if slightly less usual; after 'und doch' only the inverted order is possible.

(b) Vocally stressed, it has the sense of **after all, all the same, despite everything**:

Ich hab' ihm abgeraten, aber er hat es (nun) *doch* getan	*I advised him against, but he has done it all the same*
Zwingen kann ich ihn ja *doch* nicht	*Why* (ja), *in any case I can't compel him*
Also *doch!*[2]	*What did I tell you?/There you are!*
Lieber nicht drüber nachdenken. Oder *doch?* (Arno Schmidt)	*Better not think about it. Or should one after all?*
lieber *doch* nicht	*better not after all*

(c) intensifying an imperative, often with a pleading or impatient note;[3] 'doch mal' often conveys encouragement, as in the last example:[4]

Lassen Sie mich doch mal das Foto sehen!	*Do let me have a look at the photo*
Reg dich doch nicht so auf!	*For heaven's sake, don't get so excited*
Gehen Sie doch mal nach Italien!	*Why don't you go to Italy?*

(d) turning a statement into a question that hopes for, or expects, a favourable or corroborative reply; often the equivalent of 'nicht wahr':

Du kannst mir doch helfen?	*Surely you can help me? You can help me, can't you?*
Er kommt doch heute? Er kommt heute, nicht wahr?	*He is coming today, isn't he?*

With a negative, the remark may convey incredulity or surprise:

Du glaubst doch nicht, daß ich es getan habe?	*Surely you don't think that I did it?*

---

[1] cf. Eggeling, op. cit.: denn: adverb.
[2] from Betteridge, op. cit.: doch.
[3] Eggeling amusingly illustrates its nuances: op. cit.: doch (adverb) 2(b).
[4] cf. Collinson, loc. cit., p. 112.

(e) **In the following reactions to a statement or question of another speaker**:

i contradicting another speaker's negative statement:

Er hat nie etwas für uns getan.— Doch, er hat mir einmal 100 Mark geliehen	*He's never done anything for us.—Yes he has: he once lent me 100 marks*

ii expressing agreement with an affirmative statement:

Er ist eigentlich ganz intelligent.— Doch, (doch)	*He's really quite intelligent.—Indeed he is*

iii lending emphasis to a statement by protesting against an imaginary remark to the contrary:

Und die Anzeigen, doch, das interessiert mich immer (I. Seidel)	*And the announcements* (on the radio), *oh yes, that always interests me*

iv giving an affirmative reply to a question expecting a negative one (cf. Fr. 'si'):

Bist du nicht zufrieden?—Doch!	*Aren't you satisfied?—Yes, I am*

v used alone, or mildly emphasizing e.g. ich glaube, ich denke, ich dächte, in an affirmative reply:

Kommt er bald?—Doch!	*Is he coming soon?—Oh, yes*
Haben Sie eine [Antwort]?—Ich dächte doch (Th. Mann)	*Have you got an answer?—Yes, I think I have*

vi strengthening 'nein' or 'nicht' in a negative reply:

Mutti, kann ich ein Stück Schokolade haben?—Nein doch, du hast jetzt genug gegessen	*Mummy, can I have a piece of chocolate? —Certainly not, you've had enough to eat now*

(f) **intensifying an exclamatory remark**:

Wie *haben* wir doch gelacht!	*How we did laugh!*
Wie *winzig* doch alles von hier oben aussieht!	*But how tiny everything looks from up here!*

(g) **in exclamations expressing a wish** (cf. 476(b)):

Wenn er doch jetzt käme!	*If only he would come now!*

(h) **straining one's powers of memory or comprehension**:

Wie *hieß* er doch (or noch)?	*What was his name?*
Was *hat* er doch gesagt?	*What was it he said?*
Wie *konnte* er doch so was tun?	*However could he do such a thing?*

(i) **oder doch** *or at least, or at any rate*:

Es geht ihm wieder gut, oder doch viel besser	*He's well again, or at any rate much better*

See also 298: a common analogous use of ja and doch

291. eben

N.B. Used adverbially, eben never means 'even', which is sogar or selbst; as an adjective, it means 'even, level'.

6*

(a) **When accented, it is the equivalent of just (just now) in two different senses:**

i **(S) temporal,** referring to past, present or future:

Er ist eben[1] (erst) angekommen	*He has (only) just arrived*
Wovon sprachen wir eben?	*What were we talking about just now?*
Das wollte ich eben sagen	*I was just going to say that*
Eben geht mir ein Licht auf	*It's just dawning on me*
Ich komme eben	*I'm coming in a moment*

ii **denoting 'by a narrow margin'** (often followed by 'noch'):

Mit 500 Mark im Monat komme ich eben (noch) aus	*I can just manage on 500 marks a month*

(b) **When unaccented:**

i **(S) it means 'just, exactly, precisely':**[2]

Eben dieses Haus hatte mir zugesagt	*It was just this house that attracted me*
Das wäre mir eben[3] recht	*That would be just what I should like*
Eben dàran hatte ich nicht gedacht	*That's the one thing I hadn't thought of*
Die Lage ist nicht eben ernst	*The situation is not exactly serious*

Compare the colloquial rejoinders:

Er müßte eine andere Stelle suchen.— (Ja) eben![3]	*He ought to look for another job.—* *Exactly*
Der Chef war eigentlich ganz verständnisvoll.—Na eben![3]	*The director was really quite under-* *standing.—Of course he was (That's* *just what I said he'd be)*

Compare with the last example the reminding function of 'eben' in a context such as this: enumerating the main nationalities to visit Baden-Baden, the speaker might conclude: 'und dann eben Amerikaner' *and then, as I said before, Americans.*

Compare the compounds of 'eben' (in all of which it is accented) e.g. ebensoviel, ebensosehr *just as much,* ebenderselbe *the very same.*

ii **it suggests an explanation:**

Ich kann ihn nicht überreden; er ist eben hartnäckig	*I can't persuade him; the thing is that (or: you see,) he's obstinate*
Peter hat das Examen *doch* bestanden.—Er hat eben Glück gehabt	*Peter has passed the exam after all.—* *It's just that he was lucky*

iii **it expresses the resigned acceptance of a situation or the necessity for such an attitude:**

Aber so ist es eben!	*But there, that's how it is*
Nun ja, alles ist eben anders	*Ah well, everything's different and it can't be helped*
Karl hat angerufen, er hätte den Zug verpaßt; wir essen eben eine halbe Stunde später	*Karl has rung up to say he's missed the train; we'll just have to have dinner half an hour later*
Gut, dann eben nicht	*Well, then we won't (petulantly)*
Ich tue es, so gut ich eben kann	*I'll do it as well as I can in the circumstances*

---

[1] or, more emphatic: soeben.
[2] cf. 298(a), 2nd pair of examples. accented.

Note: The widely used South German dialectal **halt** could be substituted for eben in any of the examples in (b)ii and iii.

292. eher

(a) **sooner, earlier** (comparative of 'bald')[1]

Ich konnte nicht eher kommen	*I couldn't come any sooner*
je eher, desto besser	*the sooner, the better*

(b) **rather** (=more, to a greater extent)

Er sah eher wie ein Geschäftsmann als wie ein Schriftsteller aus	*He looked more like a businessman than like an author*
Das Gerücht seines Mißgeschicks hatte sie eher gereizt als abgeschreckt (A. Seghers)	*The rumour of his misfortune had attracted rather than deterred them*
Das ist eher möglich	*That is more likely*
Das geht schon eher	*That's rather more feasible*

eher must here be distinguished from **vielmehr**, which is strongly corrective; contrast i and ii:

i Es ist eine Ehre eher als eine Schande	*It's an honour rather than a disgrace*
ii Es ist keine Schande, (sondern) vielmehr eine Ehre	*It's no disgrace; rather it's an honour*
Ich achte ihn, vielmehr ich bewundere ihn[2]	*I respect, nay I admire him*

(c) **rather** (=in preference to)

Ich tue alles andere eher als nachgeben	*I'll do anything rather than give in*
Eher als daß ich ihn belästige, will ich es selber tun	*Rather than trouble him I'll do it myself*

(d) **if anything** (one thing rather than the opposite)

Es geht ihm eher besser	*He's if anything better*
Ich hatte eher bedauert, daß das Hotel so leer war	*I had been sorry rather than glad that the hotel was so empty*

(e) **um so eher** *all the more probably* (or *all the sooner*)

Er wird um so eher kommen, als er weiß, daß du da bist	*He's the more likely to come as he knows that you're here*

(f) **am ehesten**

i In the temporal sense (*soonest*), this is not much used:
Wer ist am ehesten angekommen? (normal usage: zuerst.) Rather commoner is the form **ehestens** *at the earliest*: Er kann ehestens morgen früh hier sein (normal usage: frühstens) (Du. Stil.)

ii By a figurative extension of 'soonest', it may mean *with greatest probability, most readily, most easily*:

Du wirst es am ehesten in der Mansarde finden	*You're most likely to find it in the attic*
Man könnte ihn am ehesten mit Gottfried Keller vergleichen	*One could most nearly compare him to Gottfried Keller*

---

[1] Colloquially one may occasionally hear 'bälder'.
[2] Normal order is more incisive than inversion after vielmehr.

293. eigentlich: see 307.

294. einmal, mal

  (a) **once (as opposed to twice etc.**) is 'einmal', with the first syllable stressed:

Ich habe ihn nur einmal getroffen	*I've met him only once*

    Compare some idiomatic uses:

Dieses Paket ist noch einmal[1] so schwer wie das da	*This parcel is as heavy again as that one*
einmal (or erstens) . . ., sodann . . .[2]	*in the first place . . ., in the second place*
Ich kann nicht alles auf einmal tun	*I can't do everything at once*
Alle antworteten auf einmal	*Everyone answered at the same time*
Auf einmal erschien er	*All at once he appeared*

Note: In all the following uses either 'einmal' or the colloquial 'mal' can be used. The form selected in the examples is, on balance, the more convincing in the particular case. Only in the last example of (b) the alternative could not be used.

  (b) **once, some time, one day, for once in a way**

Es war einmal eine alte Hexe	*Once upon a time there was an old witch*
Ich hab' ihn mal besucht	*I once visited him*
Ich werd' ihn mal besuchen	*I'll visit him one day*
irgend einmal	*some time or other*
Er wird es (noch) einmal bereuen (Du. Stil.)	*He'll regret it yet*
Da ich einmal im Zuge war, erzählte ich weiter	*Having once got going, I went on with my story*
Hier konnte er sich einmal richtig satt essen	*Here for once he was really able to eat his fill*
mal zur Abwechslung	*for once in a way*
Na ja, so mal	*Well, for once in a way*

  (c) **With an imperative or its equivalent, it corresponds to 'just'**:

Komm (eben) mal her!	*Just come here*
Denken Sie mal, er hat hundert Pfund gewonnen!	*Just think, he's won £100*
Überleg dir's mal!	*Just think about it*
Moment mal!	*Just [wait] a minute*
Das muß man sich mal vorstellen	*I ask you, just picture that*

    With suitable intonation, it may express protest or indignation:

Erlauben Sie mal!/Hören Sie mal! So was hab' ich nie gesagt	*Pardon me/Look here, I never said that*

    Sometimes, while it is essential in German, it is better left untranslated:

Laß mal sehen!	*Let's have a look*
Sieh mal, ich habe es mir *so* gedacht	*Look, this is what I thought (we'd do)*
Sag mal, *wo* wohnst du jetzt?	*(Just) tell me, where do you live now?*

  (d) **After 'wollen', it frequently corresponds to 'just'**:

Ich will (doch) mal sehen, wer es ist	*I'll just (or: I'll go and) have a look who it is*

---

[1] or, colloquially, noch mal.
[2] from Eggeling, op. cit.: einmal 1.

Ich will ihn (schnell) mal anrufen	*I'll just give him a ring*
Jetzt will ich dir mal was sagen	*Now I'll (just) tell you something*

(e) **noch einmal** (also 'nochmals') **and wieder**: noch einmal *once again*, *once more* is limited to the repetition of a clearly defined action; wieder *again* is more general:

Er öffnete noch einmal die Tür und rief „Auf Wiedersehen!"	*He opened the door once more and called 'Good-bye'*
Im folgenden Jahr war er wieder krank[1]	*In the following year he was ill again*
Nach zwei Jahren kam er wieder nach Hause	*After two years he came home again*

(f) **nicht einmal (nicht mal)** *not even*

Nicht einmal der Bürgermeister war dagegen	*Not even the mayor was against it*

(g) **nun einmal** expresses resigned acceptance of a fact:

Es ist nun einmal so	*There you are, that's how things are (implying: and there's nothing to be done about it)*
Er will nun mal nicht—da ist nichts zu machen	*He just doesn't want to—there's nothing to be done about it*
Er braucht nun einmal viel Schlaf	*He happens to need a lot of sleep*
So was verkauft sich nun einmal	*Surprisingly or not, that kind of thing sells*

(h) **(S) Examples of further idiomatic uses and nuances of 'mal'**

Du sollst mal sehen, wie das Geld geflitzt kommt (H. Fallada)	*You'll be surprised how the money comes pouring in*
Sie haben ja erst mal die Arbeitslosenunterstützung (H. Fallada)	*To start with, of course (ja), you'll have the unemployment benefit*
Da du (schon) einmal hier bist, könnten wir die Sache besprechen	*Seeing that you are here, we could discuss the matter*
Mal sehen	*We'll see*
Das sollte mal einer tun!	*Do that and see what happens!*
Gestern hab' ich mir's mal angesehen ('mal' is purely expletive)	*I had a look at it yesterday*

295. etwa

(a) about, approximately: Es kostet etwa dreißig Mark.

(b) perhaps, by chance (in a question or condition): Ist er etwa verreist? *Can he be away?* Wenn er etwa verreist ist, . . .

(c) After nicht, etwa often implies that a certain conclusion has been, or might be, drawn:[2]

Sie wollen doch nicht etwa nach London ziehen?	*You don't mean to say that you intend moving to London?*
Sie müssen nicht etwa denken, daß ich ihn verteidigen will	*Now don't go and think that I'm trying to defend him*

296. freilich: see 285.

---

[1] noch einmal would give an almost impatient emphasis.
[2] well analysed by Eggeling, op. cit., p.140.

297. ja.

Note: ja is moderately accented as used in (a), (b) and some items of (g); heavily accented in (f); otherwise unaccented.

(a) **yes.** The following example illustrates the effect of some idiomatic additions:

Bist du zufrieden?	—Ach ja! *Oh yes, I think so*
—Ja, ja! *Oh yes*	(also: *Yes, of course (I remember)*)
—Jawohl[1] *Yes/Yes, indeed*	—Nun ja! *Yes, I suppose so*
—Ja, freilich! *Certainly/Of course*	—Na ja! *Yes, I suppose so*

N.B.: As S. Colditz points out (loc. cit. p. 145, footnote 1), Ja, ja! may convey nostalgia:

Ja, ja! Das waren schöne Zeiten　　　*Yes, those were happy days*

(b) Placed before the second and more intense of two analogous words, it corresponds to English **nay** or **indeed**:

Es war ein Erfolg, ja ein Triumph	*It was a success, indeed a triumph*
Es war ein unerwarteter, ja ein sensationeller Erfolg	*It was an unexpected, indeed a sensational success*

(c) **It underlines the inevitable consequence of a fact stated by another speaker**:

Ich habe den Brief gelesen.—So? Dann weißt du ja alles	*I've read the letter.—Have you? Then, of course, you know everything*

(d) **of course, certainly, to be sure, indeed, before 'aber' or in a conditional clause**:

Ich will ihm ja helfen, aber leicht wird es nicht sein	*Certainly I'll help him, but it won't be easy*
Wenn er ja kommt, kann er das Paket mitbringen	*If, of course, he's coming, he can bring the parcel with him*

(e) **It conveys a wide range of feelings**, according to the context and intonation (see also 298):

Surprise:

Da ist ja Onkel Fritz!	*Why, there's Uncle Fritz!*
Er hat ja ein neues Auto!	*Why, he's got a new car!*

Indignation:

Das ist ja unerhört!	*That really is a scandal*

Agreement (concessive):

Es ist ja wahr	*It's true, to be sure*

Satisfaction:

Da kommt ja der Arzt	*Good—here comes the doctor*

(f) A stressed 'ja' emphasizes the importance of an action, or of avoiding it, and appears most frequently **in conjunction with an imperative (Be sure to . . .)**:

Bleibe *ja* hier!	*Be sure to stay here*
Tu das *ja* nicht!	*Be sure not to do that*
Er soll *ja* nichts sagen	*On no account must he say anything*
Ich tat mein Bestes, damit er *ja* zufrieden wäre	*I did my best to ensure his being satisfied*

---

[1] regulation affirmative reply in the Bundeswehr; coll. pron. jawoll.

(g) Miscellaneous

Ja, wissen Sie, so was ist nie leicht	*Well, you know, that kind of thing is never easy*
Ja, was will er denn?	*Well, and what does he want?*
Ja und?	*1 And what then? 2 Well then?*
Ja (often stressed and prolonged), wenn das der Fall ist	*Well, of course, if that's the case*
Ja so, das ist etwas anderes[1]	*Ah, that's another matter*
Ja, was ich sagen wollte[2]	*Oh, by the way I was going to tell you*
Du hattest ja herrliches Flugwetter	*You had grand weather for flying, didn't you?*
ja sagen	*to give one's consent*
Er antwortete mit einem eindeutigen Ja	*He replied with an unequivocal affirmative*

298. A common analogous use of 'ja' and 'doch'

They are both used to enlist the understanding of the person addressed or of the reader, often protesting at the simplicity of a question (3rd pair of examples) or recalling a circumstance which justifies a preceding statement (4th pair of examples). The difference between 'ja' and 'doch' lies in the fact that 'doch' often conveys a stronger note of protest[3] or impatience. The main English equivalents are: *why, surely, don't you see, after all, you know, of course.*

(a) parallel examples:

Du könntest dir ja Karls Rad leihen	*You could borrow Karl's bike, couldn't you?*
Du könntest dir doch Karls Rad leihen	*Surely you could borrow Karl's bike?*
Das ist es ja eben	*Why, that's just the point* (or: *the difficulty*)
Das ist es doch eben	*Don't you see, that's just the point*
Warum gehst du nie ins Kino?	*Why do you never go to the cinema?*
—Du weißt ja, daß ich Filme nicht leiden kann	*—Why, you know that I can't stand films*
—Du weißt doch, daß ich Filme nicht leiden kann	*—You know very well that I can't stand films*
Er kann unmöglich kommen; er ist ja krank er ist doch krank	*He can't possibly come; he's ill, you know don't you see, he's ill*
Ich habe ihn ja/doch noch gestern gesehen!	*You know, I saw him only yesterday*

(b) further examples of 'ja':

Es ist nicht meine Schuld, wenn du dich langweilst; du hättest ja zu Hause bleiben können	*It's not my fault if you're bored; after all, you could have stayed at home*
Niemand drängte ihn, es eilte ja auch nicht (H. E. Nossack)	*No one pressed him, nor, after all, was there any hurry*

---

[1] from Eggeling op. cit.: ja 2(b).
[2] from Betteridge op. cit.
[3] cf. *Es geht weiter* (B.B.C.), p. 15.

(c) further examples of 'doch':

Das hätte ich doch nie gedacht	*You know, I should never have thought that*
Sie wissen doch, was ich meine?	*You know what I mean, don't you?*
Der Clown fiel wieder hin; die Kinder lachten; es war doch unendlich komisch, wie er immer hinfiel	*The clown fell down again; the children laughed; it was, after all, extraordinarily funny, the way he always fell down*

(d) example of **ja doch**:

Ich zählte die Kratzer an der Wand; ich mußte mich ja doch mit etwas beschäftigen	*I counted the scratches on the wall; after all, I had to occupy myself with something*

(e) a slightly literary usage, peculiar to 'doch'; here the 'doch' sentence has the inverted word-order, without being a question:

Natürlich leihe ich ihm das Geld; ist er doch mein Freund	*Of course I'll lend him the money; after all, he's my friend*

Analogous to this, is the use of 'doch' to express surprise and indignation:

Ist doch der Junge wieder am Zucker gewesen! (from Erben, op cit., 81)	*I'm blowed if that boy hasn't been at the sugar again!*

Plötzlich guckte ich aus dem Fenster, schleppten doch zwei Polizisten meinen Wagen ab—er war ja nicht abgeschlossen und außerdem falsch geparkt (*Zeit*)

299. nämlich

(a) **namely**

diese zwei Städte, nämlich Hamburg und Bremen	*these two cities, namely Hamburg and Bremen*

(b) **explanatory: you know, you see, for . . .**

Du mußt etwas lauter sprechen, er ist nämlich taub	*You must speak a bit louder; he's deaf, you know*
Sonst hätte ich es nämlich selber getan	*Otherwise, you see, I would have done it myself*

300. noch[1]

(a) **temporal**

i *still, yet*; often 'immer noch' or 'noch immer', where continuation is denoted; Er war (immer) noch krank.

ii some idiomatic applications of this meaning:

Ich werde das Problem noch lösen	*I'll solve the problem yet*
Ich habe nur noch zwei Mark	*I've only got two marks left*
Mein alter Vater kann nur noch wenig tun	*My old father can do very little now*
Weißt du noch?	*D'you remember?*
Du hast seinen Brief gelesen und da fragst du noch?	*You've read his letter and yet you ask?*
Diese Aufgabe ist so schwer.—Nun, das ist noch die einfachste	*This problem is so hard.—Well, it's the simplest compared with the rest*

iii **noch nicht** *not yet*, **noch nie** *never (yet), never before*

---

[1] see also 290(h), 472, 523 ff.

(b) **still, yet, more, further,** with a comparative and, analogously, in other combinations (cf. Fr. encore): noch schneller; noch drei Tage; ich nehme noch ein Bier (*another glass of beer*); was willst du denn noch? *what else do you want?* noch etwas.

301. nun

(a) **now (temporal)**: less incisive than 'jetzt':

Nun (or jetzt) wollen wir umkehren	*Now we'll turn back*
Geht es dir nun (or jetzt) besser?	*Are you better now?*
nun endlich	*now at last*
cf. Als es nun Winter wurde, . . .	*Now when it turned to winter,* . . .

(b) **well (often 'na') and some further colloquial equivalents**:

Nun?	*Well?*
Nun und?	*And then what?*
Na und?	1. *Well, what's the outcome?* 2. *So what?*
Nun ja (or: Na ja), klassisches Deutsch ist es gerade nicht (Th. Valentin)	*Well (to be sure), it's not exactly classical German*
Nun, meinetwegen	*All right then, as far as I'm concerned*
Nun/Na, wir werden ja sehen	*Well, we shall see*
Haben Sie nu was retten können?[1]	*Now were you able to save anything?*
weil ich die ja nun sehr gut kenne,[1] (nun is purely expletive)	*because, of course, I know her very well*

(c) **nun einmal**: see 294(g).

302. nur

(a) **only**

Man kann ihn nur bewundern	*One can only admire him*

(b) **It may have intensifying force**:

Das macht es nur noch schlimmer	*That makes it even worse*
Wie kann er nur so taktlos sein?	*However can he be so tactless?*
Was können wir nur tun, um ihm zu helfen?	*Whatever can we do to help him?*
so schnell wie nur möglich	*as quickly as ever you can*

(c) **Used with an imperative or an imperative equivalent it expresses an exhortation or a warning**:[2]

Sehen Sie nur, was Sie gemacht haben!	*Just look what you've done*
Denken Sie sich nur!	*Just imagine*
Geh nur!	*Go along*
Treten Sie nur ein!	*Come right in*
Er soll nur kommen	*By all means let him come*
Nur weiter!	*Carry on* (often implying: *It's all right so far*)
Nur her damit!	*Come on, hand it over*
Nur nicht ängstlich!	*Don't be afraid*
Nur Mut!	*Be brave*

---

[1] taken from an article by Ulrich Engel in *Forschungsberichte des Instituts für deutsche Sprache*, Jan. 1968, pp. 85 ff.; 'nu' for 'nun'.

[2] cf. Schulz-Griesbach, op. cit., H 623 and H 626, Betteridge, op. cit., Collinson, loc. cit., and Du. Stil.

Nimm dich nur in acht!	*You be careful!*
Geh *nur* nicht in diesen Laden!	*Whatever you do, don't go into this shop*
Nur nicht!	*For heaven's sake, don't!*

(d) **nur so**: see 304(l)

(e) For the use of nur **in concessive clauses**, see 471(c)iii, e.g.

Wo er sich nur zeigte, . . .	*Wherever he showed himself, . . .*

303. schon

(a) **already**. With this basic meaning it will often require a different
   rendering in English or can barely be translated:

Er war schon angekommen	*He had already arrived*
schon am nächsten Tag	*the very next day*
Da bist du ja schon wieder!	*Why, there you are back again*
Sind Sie schon in Köln gewesen?	*Have you been to Cologne yet?*
Sind Sie schon einmal in Köln gewesen? (slight stress on 'schon')	*Have you been to Cologne before?*
Sind Sie (schon) einmal in Köln gewesen? (slight stress on 'Köln')	*Have you ever been to Cologne?*
Ich hab' ihn auch schon in der Bibliothek gesehen	*I've sometimes seen him in the library*
Nicht alles, was nicht demokratisch ist, ist auch schon faschistisch (W. Alff)	*Not everything that is not democratic is necessarily fascist*

(b) **even, no more than, (if) only**:

Schon dieses 'good morning' war unvorsichtig genug (A. Goes)	*Even this 'good morning' was imprudent enough*
Schon der Gedanke (allein) ist mir unsympathisch	*The mere thought is repugnant to me*
Wenn ich ihn schon sehe, ärgere ich mich	*I've only to see him and I feel annoyed*
schon ihrer Kinder wegen	*if only because of their children*
Das geht schon daher nicht, weil . . .	*That's impossible if only because . . .*

(c) **expressing confidence or reassurance**:

Er wird uns schon helfen	*He'll help us all right*
Es wird schon gehen	*Don't worry, we'll manage*
Sie verstehen schon, nicht wahr?[1]	*I'm sure you understand, don't you?*

(d) **(S) certainly, undoubtedly, generally with a concessive slant**
   and often accepting the view of another speaker:

Das ist schon möglich	*That's quite possible*
Das stimmt schon, aber es könnte auch anders kommen	*I admit that that is so, but things might turn out differently*
Ja, ich glaube schon, aber . . .	*Yes, I think so, but . . .*
Es ist schon besser du gehst (H. Böll)	*I think it would be better if you went*

(e) **giving persuasive force to what is usually a rhetorical question: but then, after all**:

Wer kann schon dem Angebot widerstehen, für die Hälfte des normalen Preises bis Ostafrika und Bangkok zu fliegen. (*Zeit*)	*After all, who can resist the offer of a flight to East Africa and Bangkok for half the normal fare?*

[1] *Es geht weiter* (B.B.C.) p. 18.

Was sagt die Regierung zu Ungarn? — *What does the government say to*
—Nichts. Was sollen sie schon *events in Hungary?—Nothing, but then*
sagen? (M. Horbach) *what are they to say?*

(f) giving a note of preference or encouragement to an imperative or its equivalent:

Ein Achtel. Nein, bring schon ein *An eighth of a pound. No, you'd better*
Viertel. Wenn wir doch einmal *bring a quarter, as we're being so*
so üppig sind (H. Fallada) *extravagant*
„Nun machen Sie schon, daß Sie *'Come on, now, let's get a move on',*
weiterkommen!" sagte er zu *he said to his driver*
seinem Fahrer (Th. Plievier)

(g) (S) Used in an Open Condition and sometimes strengthened by 'einmal', it has the force of überhaupt *at all*:

Wenn ich ihm schon (einmal) *If I've got to write to him at all, I'd*
schreiben muß, so mach' ich es *rather do it today*
lieber heute

(h) Some fixed phrases

Schon gut! 1. *All right. Very well*
2. *That will do (You've said enough)*
und wenn schon! *even so; what about it?*
Wenn schon, denn schon *What is worth doing at all is worth doing well*

Das will schon etwas sagen (or *That is saying a good deal*
bedeuten or heißen)
schon gar nicht *less than ever, even less*

304. so

(a) so (to such a degree)
Er ist so alt, daß er alles vergißt *He is so old that he forgets everything*
soundso oft *ever so often*

(b) as . . . as
Er ist so alt wie ich *He is as old as I am*

(c) so (ein): such (a); a/that kind of; one of those etc.
so ein großes Haus *such a big house*[1]
So ist das Leben *Such is life*
Ich habe so ein Gefühl[2] *I have a kind of feeling*
Er trug so eine Baskenmütze *He was wearing one of those berets*
  Sometimes pejorative:
Das ist auch so eine Firma *That's another of those shady firms*
So ein Wetter! *What weather!*
Das sind so Fragen (idiomatic) *Those are difficult questions*
Das sind so Sachen (idiomatic) *Those are strange things*

(d) so etwas, so was[3]
Haben Sie so etwas/so was? *Have you got something like this (or: that)?*

irgend so etwas *anything like this*

---

[1] see also 223.
[2] cf. Collinson, op. cit., p. 53; 'Gefühl' is stressed.
[3] cf. so jemand *someone like that.*

So etwas Dummes hab' ich noch nie gelesen	*I've never read anything so stupid*
So was von Frechheit hab' ich noch nie erlebt (from Du. Stil.)	*I've never met with such impertinence*
Er ist so etwas wie ein Dichter	*He's something of a poet*
Er hat so ein gewisses Etwas	*There's something about him*

With omission of 'etwas':

Jedenfalls hatte das Mädchen eine Stelle in einem Kino. An der Kasse oder so [etwas] (J. Federspiel) (*in the box-office or something like that*).

(e) thus, like this, like that, in this way, in such a way; as things are, as it is ('so' is stressed in all but the 4th and 5th examples):

Du mußt es *so* tun	*You must do it like this*
Er handelte *so*, daß wir alle erstaunt waren	*He acted in such a way that we were all surprised*
So oder *so*, die Frage muß erledigt werden	*One way or another, the question has got to be settled*
Es kann Ihnen auch so gehen	*The same thing may happen to you*
Sieh mich nicht so an!	*Don't look at me like that*
So wirst du nie damit fertig	*Like this you'll never get it done*
So brauchte er es nicht zu erwähnen	*In this way he didn't have to mention it*
Auch *so* können wir nur eben auskommen	*Even as it is we can only just make both ends meet*
Ich bin *so* schon müde	*I'm tired anyhow/as it is*

(f) (S) 'just' and other renderings underlining the casualness of the remark, the ordinariness of the action or situation referred to:

Ich will dir keine Vorwürfe machen, ich meinte nur so . . . ,(from Du. Stil.)	*I'm not trying to reproach you; I just thought . . .*
Die Schiffe beobachten, die da so vorbeikommen (W. Kempowski)	*To watch the ships that just happen to pass*
Was halten Sie eigentlich so von Picasso? (Th. Valentin)	*What do you think offhand of Picasso?*
Können Sie uns nicht 'nen Tip geben? So als Klassenlehrer (Th. Valentin)	*Can't you give us a hint? You know, as our form master*
Wie kommst du darauf?—Nur so (F. Dürrenmatt)	*What makes you ask?—Oh, nothing special*
Was machen Sie denn so abends?	*What do you generally do in the evening?*
was Manager so verdienen (*Zeit*)	*the kind of salaries that managers (usually) get*
Der Posten: ,, Ja, um sechs ist hier Essensausgabe, dann ist Schluß. Nur noch so Streifenzug." (A. Goes)	*The sentry: 'Yes, at six there's supper; that's the last thing. Only the usual patrolling.'*
Das weiß niemand so recht zu sagen	*No one can really say* (expletive)

(g) about (giving vagueness to numerals)

,,Seit wann sitzt ihr hier?" . . . ,,So seit neun." (Th. Valentin)	*Since when have you been sitting here?— Since about nine*

(h) so, thus

Und damit, so möchte man meinen, war es eigentlich erledigt	*And with that, so one would think, the matter was really settled*

(i) so, therefore

Es war schon elf Uhr, so mußten wir uns eilen	*It was already eleven o'clock, so we had to hurry*

(j) **if, when** (archaic and literary)

so Gott will	*if it please God*
und auch dann nur, so es ganz still ist, dann hört man es [das Meer] singen und brausen (H. Broch)	*and moreover only then, when it's quite still, can one hear the sea singing and roaring*

(k) **used as a relative pronoun** (archaic, biblical and poetic):
Die Wanduhr pickt, im Zimmer singet leise
Waldvöglein noch, so du im Herbst gefangen (*which you caught*)
(Eichendorff: *Das Alter*)

(l) **nur so** has intensifying force, generally corresponding to the idiomatic 'fairly'. (The context will distinguish this sense of 'nur so' from that of 'nur so' as it figures in several examples of (f) above.)

Der Wagen sauste nur so dahin (from Du. Stil.)	*The car fairly whizzed along*
Es strömt nur so	*It's simply pelting down*
Er hat ihn heruntergemacht, daß es nur so eine Art hatte	*He told him off with a vengeance* (idiom)

(m) **Further colloquial and idiomatic uses** (see also 639, 641)

So?	*Really? Is that so?*
So! (often clipped short)	*Well, that's that*
soso	*so so, tolerably well*
So, du hast es vergessen	*I see; you've forgotten*
Wie geht's Ihnen heute?—So ziemlich	*How are you today?—Not too bad*
Das ist so recht nach meinem Geschmack (suggested by Du. Stil.)	*That's exactly according to my taste*
Er hat nicht so ganz unrecht	*He's not so far wrong*
Er tut nur so	*He's only pretending*
Er schlägt sich so durch	*He just manages to make a living*
. . ., so Brandt, . . .	*. . ., so says/according to Brandt, . . .*

(n) For the use of 'so':
to introduce subordinate clauses: see 467(c), 471, 542(f), 545–6
(e.g. so daß er alles wußte; so schnell er auch lief, . . .)
to follow subordinate clauses: see 462(c), 470(c), 473(c)N., 542(d) (f), 544(a) (e.g. Wenn ich ihm heute schreibe, so bekommt er den Brief morgen.) (Analogous to this: 464(a).)

305. überhaupt (accented on the last syllable)

(a) Only dialectally 'überhaupt' sometimes means 'above all, especially'; this use is best ignored; above all = vor allem, vor allen Dingen.

(b) **The basic meaning of überhaupt is 'considered as a whole, in a general way'**; this generalizing function requires the presence, or implication, of a particular case, a point well made by Eggeling (op. cit.: überhaupt).
The main English equivalents are: in general, altogether, at all; in certain types of question: really, in fact; a few of the following illustrations require other renderings.

(c) **used affirmatively:**

Er liebte die italienische Sprache, die Sprachen überhaupt (A. Goes)	*He loved the Italian language and languages in general*
Er ist flüchtig, faul und uninteressiert; überhaupt ist er ein schlechter Schüler	*He is careless, lazy and uninterested; altogether, he's a bad pupil*
Seinen Mut müßte man haben, dachte ich. Oder überhaupt Mut. (M. Walser)	*One ought to have his courage, I thought. Any sort of courage*
Ich komme morgen auf diesen Punkt zurück; überhaupt habe ich noch einiges zu erklären	*I'll come back to this point tomorrow; for that matter, I've still got a number of things to explain*
Wir müssen uns eilen, damit wir ihn überhaupt noch sehen.	*We must hurry up in order to see him at all*
Und überhaupt! (coll.)	*and really, you know!* (or: *if you think about it*)

(d) **in conditional clauses:**

Wenn ich überhaupt komme, wird es nicht für lange sein	*If I come at all, it won't be for long*

(e) **in questions:**

Er singt nicht besonders gut.—Kann er überhaupt singen?	*He doesn't sing particularly well.—Can he sing at all?*
Wie konntest du überhaupt so was tun?	*How could you do such a thing at all? (i.e. under any circumstances)*
Hier ist der Brief nicht; wo kann er überhaupt sein?	*The letter isn't here; wherever can it be?*
Was will er überhaupt?	*What does he really want?* (or, with aggressive intonation: *What the dickens does he want?*)
Weißt du überhaupt, was dieses Wort bedeutet?	*Do you in fact know what this word means?*

(f) **used with a negative:**

Du hättest es überhaupt nicht tun sollen, und besonders jetzt nicht	*You shouldn't have done it at all, and particularly not now*
Er ist überhaupt kein Dichter	*He isn't a poet at all*
Ich kann dir nicht sagen, ob er in die Schweiz will; ich weiß überhaupt nichts von seinen Plänen	*I can't tell you if he intends going to Switzerland; indeed I know nothing whatever of his plans[1]*

306. weiter

(a) **main meanings: further** (Er ging weiter als ich; weiter hinten), **else** (Wer war weiter da? weiter niemand, weiter nichts), **continuation** (Wir spielten weiter; immer weiter *on and on*).

(b) **coupled with a negative: not particularly, no particular:**

Es sah weiter nicht schlimm aus (Th. Plievier)	*Things didn't look particularly bad*
Es machte weiter keinen Eindruck auf ihn	*It made no particular impression on him*
Das hat weiter nichts zu sagen	*That has no particular significance*

---

[1] Without the preceding sentence, 'nothing whatever' would be 'gar nichts', merely an emphatic negative. Cf. Eggeling, op. cit.: überhaupt: 2.

307. (a) 'wirklich' must be distinguished from 'eigentlich'

wirklich can always, and eigentlich can generally, be rendered by 'really',
yet the two German adverbs are never interchangeable:
wirklich means: in truth, positively, I assure you;
eigentlich means: at bottom, in actual fact, actually, in reality, generally
implying 'contrary to appearances, expectations or later developments';
colloquially it may mean no more than 'tell me'.
Some pairs of examples may illustrate this difference:

Er ist wirklich sehr fleißig	He really is (I can assure you) very hard-working
Er scheint manchmal faul zu sein, aber er ist eigentlich sehr fleißig	He sometimes appears to be lazy, but he's really (in actual fact) very hard-working
Das geht wirklich nicht	That really (positively) can't be done
Eigentlich geht das nicht, aber . . .	Really (strictly speaking) that can't be done, but . . .
Es ist wirklich schade, daß er nicht hier ist	It really is a pity that he isn't here
Es ist eigentlich schade, daß er nicht hier ist	Come to think of it, it's a pity that he isn't here
Ist er wirklich krank?	Is he really ill?
Ist er eigentlich krank?	Tell me, is he ill?

N.B. Wirklich? So? Tatsächlich? Wahrhaftig? *Really?*

(b) As adjectives, the two words have the same basic difference

Es war ein wirklicher Triumph	It was a real (positive) triumph
im wirklichen Leben	in real life
Was ist die eigentliche Ursache?	What is the real (fundamental) cause?

(c) (S) Some further examples of eigentlich

Was willst du eigentlich?	What exactly do you want?
Eigentlich könntest du mir helfen	Really (in actual fact) you could help me
Wir wollten eigentlich nach München (from Du. Stil.)	We really (originally) intended going to Munich
Wo ist eigentlich der Büchsenöffner?	Tell me, where is the tin-opener?

308. wohl

(a) **As an adjective** (never used attributively) it means well (in health);
also: happy, at ease:

Er ist wieder wohl	He's well again
Mir ist heute nicht sehr wohl	I'm not very well today
Wohler habe ich mich nie gefühlt	I've never felt better
In Italien fühl' ich mich am wohlsten	I am happiest (or: It suits me best) in Italy
Ich fühle mich immer sehr wohl bei Ihnen	I always feel very much at my ease when staying with you

(b) **As an adverb, it does *not* mean 'well, excellently'**; thus: Er
singt gut (not: wohl); exceptions are some idiomatic phrases (cf. v

below) and some compounds (e.g. wohlschmeckend *tasty*). **The following are its main uses as adverb and particle:**

i Stressed, **it may mean 'well' in the sense of 'fully, full well, carefully':**

Er weiß sehr wohl, daß er unrecht getan hat	*He knows very well that he has done wrong*
Du hättest wohl kommen können[1]	*You might very well have come*
und er war so geartet, daß er solche Erfahrungen wohl vermerkte (Th. Mann)	*and he was so constituted that he took careful note of such experiences*

ii **wohl aber** (with stress on wohl): **but certainly, but (on the other hand):**

Herr Gérade, der mitnichten ein Tor, wohl aber ein Träumer war (A. Kolb)	*Herr Gérade, who was by no means a fool, but certainly a dreamer*
Ich habe ihn nie gesprochen, wohl aber oft gesehen	*I've never spoken to him, but (on the other hand) I've often seen him*

iii Unstressed, and sometimes preceded by 'ja', it expresses uncertainty or probability: **I suppose, probably etc.:**

Er ist noch nicht hier; er hat wohl den Zug verpaßt	*He's not here yet; I suppose he's missed the train*
heute nicht, wohl aber morgen	*not today, but probably tomorrow*
Das weißt du ja wohl	*No doubt you know that*
Ob er wohl alles verstanden hat?	*Do you think/I wonder if he's understood everything?*
Würden Sie wohl so liebenswürdig sein und den Brief mitnehmen?[2]	*I wonder if you'd be so good as to take the letter with you?*

By an extension of the meaning 'probably', **wohl auch** may mean 'sometimes': Er besuchte uns oft und brachte wohl auch ein kleines Geschenk mit.

iv Moderately stressed, it may have concessive force: **admittedly, indeed, certainly** (cf. 285):

Er ist wohl mein Freund, aber ich kann ihm nicht helfen	*He is indeed my friend, but I can't help him*
Er besuchte uns wohl manchmal	*Certainly he occasionally visited us*
Das ist wohl möglich	*That may be so (I admit)*

v **Some idiomatic phrases**, with 'wohl' stressed where indicated:

Das kann man wohl sagen	*You're right there*
Ich möchte wohl wissen, warum . . .	*I'd really like to know why . . .*
Kinder, wollt ihr wohl endlich still sein!	*Children, now at last will you be quiet!*
Siehst du nun wohl, daß ich recht habe? (from Du. Stil.)	*Now do you at last see that I'm right?*
Wohl bekomm's!	*I trust it may do you good (or, ironically: Much good may it do you!)*
Leb *wohl!*	*Farewell, good-bye*
Schlaf *wohl!*	*Sleep well*
wohl oder *übel*	*willy-nilly, come what may*

[1] with unstressed 'wohl': You could probably have come (cf. iii)).
[2] from Collinson, loc. cit., p. 116.

309. zwar: see 285.

310. Some examples of multiple particles

Ich will eben mal nachgucken	*I'll just go and have a look*
Du wirst doch wohl nicht meinen, daß ich es war?	*Surely you don't think it was me?*
Und das heißt ja schon eigentlich, daß dieser Jüngling ein Sinnierer war (H. von Doderer)	(a young man's hobby was bee-keeping): *and, you know, that in itself really means that this young man was a dreamer*
Das hatte ich während meiner literarischen Laufbahn ja nun doch auch immerhin gelernt (Arno Schmidt)	*Now that, after all, was something I had learnt during my literary career*
Ja, aber ich bin doch nun mal mit Marek und Jan befreundet und nicht mit einem Österreicher (Th. Valentin)	*Yes, but don't you see I happen to be friends with Marek and Jan and not with an Austrian*
Es ist doch nun mal so	*After all, that's how it is*
So schlecht wie ihr Ruf ist die Stadt nun auch wieder nicht	*On the other hand the town is not as bad as its reputation*

X TIME PHRASES

(S)

A. TIMES OF THE CLOCK

311. Wieviel Uhr ist es?

What time is it?

Wie spät ist es?	*What time is it?*
Es ist ein Uhr/eins	*It's one o'clock/one*
Wieviel Uhr haben Sie?	*What time do you make it?*
(Es ist) drei Uhr	*I make it three o'clock*
Es ist zehn (Minuten) vor eins	*It's ten (minutes) to one*
Es ist zehn (Minuten) nach eins	*It's ten (minutes) past one*
Es ist Viertel nach (elf)	*It's quarter past (eleven)*
Es ist Viertel (auf) zwölf[1]	
Es ist fünfundzwanzig nach (elf)	*It's twenty-five past (eleven)*
Es ist fünf vor halb (zwölf)	
Es ist halb zwölf	*It's half past eleven*
Es ist zwanzig vor zwölf	*It's twenty to twelve*
(Es ist fünf Minuten vor dreiviertel zwölf)	
Es ist Viertel vor zwölf	*It's quarter to twelve*
Es ist dreiviertel (auf) zwölf[1]	
Um wieviel Uhr kommt er?[2]	*What time is he coming?*
Er kommt um halb sechs	*He's coming at half past five*
um drei Uhr nachts	*at 3 a.m.*
um neun Uhr vormittags (vorm.)	*at 9 a.m.*
um zwölf Uhr mittags	*at twelve o'clock noon*
um sechs Uhr nachmittags (nachm.)	*at 6 p.m.*
um sieben Uhr abends	*at 7 p.m.*
um Mitternacht	*at midnight*
Es ist Punkt/genau/gerade[3] neun Uhr	*It's exactly nine o'clock*
Es ist gerade[3] halb	*It's just half past*
Schlag neun (Uhr)	*on the stroke of nine*
Es ist ungefähr/gegen neun Uhr	*It's about nine o'clock*
Es ist neun Uhr vorbei	*It's past nine o'clock*
Er kommt ungefähr um neun Uhr (not: um ungefähr)	*He's coming about nine o'clock*
Er kommt gegen neun Uhr (see Note i below)	

[1] This alternative is often used in Central and South Germany; the auf (upon, i.e. towards) explains its logic but is normally omitted.

[2] The 'Um' is often omitted in rapid speech. (This does not apply to the examples that follow.)

[3] pron. grade.

Er will um neun Uhr herum da sein (coll.)	*He intends being here round about nine o'clock*

Note:

i **'gegen' before a time of the clock** (e.g. Er kam gegen zwei Uhr an) signifies for some Germans 'towards, getting on for', for others 'about, approximately'. To convey the first sense without ambiguity, the sentence would run: Er kam kurz vor zwei Uhr an; for the second sense: Er kam ungefähr um zwei Uhr an.

ii **Some further less common variants**

Es ist vier ein Viertel	*It's quarter past four*
Es ist viereinhalb	*It's half past four*
Es ist vier dreiviertel	*It's quarter to five*
Es ist sechzehn ein Viertel/ein halb/ dreiviertel	*It's 16.15/16.30/16.45*

312. The 24-hour clock

(a) This is exclusively used in time-tables, television and radio programmes, in all official announcements of theatrical performances, meetings, hours of business etc. and on printed invitations.

In conversation and letters German practice varies a good deal. Most Germans use it in connection with the times of a journey; beyond that, and where there is no ambiguity, the tendency is to use the 12-hour clock; it would be slightly unusual to say: Die Tante hat uns für fünfzehn Uhr dreißig zum Kaffee eingeladen.

(b) In time-table parlance, 'Uhr' is omissible in spoken German only in giving the full hours 1–12:

Mein Zug fährt um neun	*My train goes at 9.00*
Mein Zug fährt (um) neun Uhr fünfzehn	*My train goes at 9.15*
Wir kommen (um) siebzehn Uhr in Hamburg an	*We arrive in Hamburg at 17.00*

(c) In connection with '13–23 Uhr' and with 'null Uhr', only time-table parlance is used, e.g. Die Vorstellung beginnt um neunzehn Uhr dreißig (19.30 Uhr) (not: um halb zwanzig Uhr); similarly: um neunzehn Uhr fünfundvierzig (not: um Viertel vor zwanzig Uhr). One possible exception is given in 311 N.ii.

(d) **vierundzwanzig Uhr or null Uhr?**
A performance is scheduled to finish 'gegen 24.00 Uhr', but a train leaves at 0.23 (null Uhr dreiundzwanzig).

B. DATES

313. (a) **Der wievielte ist heute?**   *What's the date today?*

Den wievielten haben wir heute?	*What's the date today?*
Welches Datum ist heute?	
Heute/Es ist der erste März	*It's the first of March*
Wir haben den ersten März	
Es ist der Zwanzigste	*It's the 20th.*

Am wievielten kommt er zurück?	*What's the date of his return?*
Er kommt am zehnten Juni (am 10. Juni) zurück	*He's returning on the tenth of June*
Er kommt am Zehnten zurück	*He's returning on the tenth*
Er kommt am zehnten sechsten zurück	*He's returning on the tenth of the sixth*
am ersten Oktober nächsten Jahres (commoner: nächstes Jahr)	*on the first of October (of) next year*

(b) **Where the day of the week precedes the date**, there are three alternatives; the third is the most formal:

Er kommt Montag, den zehnten Juni, am Montag, den zehnten Juni, am Montag, dem zehnten Juni, zurück	*He's returning on Monday, the tenth of June*
Die Premiere findet Freitag, den 3. Januar (1971), statt	*The first night is on Friday, 3 January (1971)*

(c) **At the head of a letter**:

Köln, 20.10. (or x.) 69 or Köln, (den/d.) 20. Oktober 1969; spoken:
Köln, den zwanzigsten Oktober neunzehnhundertneunundsechzig

C. LAST NIGHT ETC.

314. gestern abend

gestern abend	*last night* (**before bedtime**)
heute nacht	*last night, in the night*
heute morgen, heute vormittag	*this morning*
heute früh	*(early) this morning*
heute nachmittag, heute mittag	*this afternoon*
heute abend	*this evening, tonight* (before bedtime)
heute nacht	*tonight* (after bedtime)
morgen früh	*tomorrow morning*
morgen ganz früh	*early tomorrow morning*
morgen in aller Frühe	

D. DURATION

315. Duration: adverbial accusative (+lang). Wherever, in the following examples, 'lang' is bracketed, it is an optional addition which has no effect on the meaning and is purely a matter of personal choice:

Ich war einen Monat (lang) in Berlin	*I was in Berlin for a month*
drei Monate (lang)	*for three months*
viele Jahre (lang)	*for many years*
monatelang	*for months*
ganze Stunden lang	*for hours on end*
eine Weile, ein Weilchen	*for a while, for a little while*
eine Zeitlang	*for a time*
einige Zeit (lang)	*for some time*
lang(e)[1], eine lange Zeit	*for a long time*
wie lang(e)?[1]	*how long?*
kurz, eine kurze Zeit (lang)	*for a short time*

[1] The e of lange (see 277) is frequently dropped (cf. Du. Gram. 4445).

Ich bin jede Woche einen Tag (zwei Tage) in Frankfurt	*I'm in Frankfurt one day (two days) every week*
den ganzen Morgen (lang)	*all the morning*
den ganzen Tag (lang)	*all day*
den ganzen Winter (lang)	*all the winter*
die ganze Zeit (lang)	*all the time, all this time*
die ganze letzte Zeit	*throughout these last few weeks (or months)*
sein ganzes Leben (lang)	*all his life*

E. DEFINITE TIME (e.g. next week)

316. Definite time: adverbial accusative. This applies to time units, parts of the day, days of the week, months, preceded by **this, next, last, every;** often a prepositional phrase is a common alternative:

Wir werden dieses Jahr (in diesem Jahr) nicht verreisen	*We are not going away **this** year*
Er kommt nächste Woche	*He's coming **next** week*
Er kommt nächsten/kommenden/ am nächsten Dienstag	*He's coming next Tuesday*
Den nächsten Morgen (am nächsten Morgen) starb er	*The next morning he died*
Das nächste/im folgenden Jahr war er wieder krank	*The next/the following year he was ill again*
Kommende Woche (in der kommenden Woche) will ich ihn besuchen	*In the coming week I'm going to visit him*
Er kommt nächsten Mai (commoner: im Mai)	*He's coming next May*
Ich sah ihn (am) letzten/(am) vorigen/am vergangenen Freitag	*I saw him **last** Friday*
Wir waren die letzten drei Jahre in der Schweiz	*The last three years we've been to Switzerland*
Er kam jeden Tag	*He came **every** day*
Er kam alle zwei Tage	*He came every other day*
Er kam alle drei Wochen	*He came every three weeks*
alle paar Jahre	*every few years*
jede halbe Stunde	*every half hour*

Note:

i In the case of **'the'** and **'that'**, a prepositional phrase is normal usage:

Am Tag nach seinem Tode starb auch seine Frau	*The day after his death, his wife died too*
An diesem Morgen war er schlechtgelaunt	*That morning he was in a bad mood*
Wir waren in jenem Jahr in Italien gewesen	*We had been in Italy that year*

ii A common rendering of **'the next'** or 'the following' is **'ander'**, but its use is confined to: am andern Tag, Morgen, Nachmittag, Abend and (less common) in der andern Nacht and it is not used of the future; thus: Am nächsten/folgenden Morgen werden wir weiterfahren.

iii **this morning**, this evening etc. = heute morgen, heute abend (see 314).

F. INDEFINITE AND HABITUAL TIME

317. Indefinite and habitual time: adverbial genitive

eines Tages	*one day*
eines schönen Tages	*one fine day* (lit. and idiomatic)
eines schönen Sommers (M. Frisch)	*one fine summer*
eines Sonntags	*one Sunday*
eines Morgens	*one morning*
eines Sonntagmorgens	*one Sunday morning*
eines nebligen Morgens (A. Kolb)	*one misty morning*
eines Nachts (by analogy, although fem.)	*one night*
donnerstags	*on Thursdays*
wochentags, werktags	*on weekdays*
morgens (rather less common: des Morgens), vormittags	*in the mornings*
nachts; tags	*at night; by day*
donnerstagabends	*on Thursday evenings*

Note:

i morgens, abends etc. are also frequently used with reference to one occasion, e.g. Nachmittags machten wir einen Spaziergang *In the afternoon we went for a walk*. The same applies to frühmorgens *early in the morning* and spätabends (or abends spät).

ii Ich habe ihn letzte Woche (einmal) gesehen   *I saw him one day last week*

iii In einer Woche (in einem Monat, in einem Jahr) war er schwer krank   *One week (one month, one year) he was seriously ill*

G. AGO, BEFORE, AFTER

318. ago: main construction: vor + dative.

vor einem Jahr, vor zwei Jahren, vor Jahren *years ago*, vor langer Zeit, vor einiger Zeit, vor kurzem (less common: vor kurzer Zeit), unlängst *not long ago*.

gestern vor acht Tagen	*a week ago yesterday*
Wie lange ist es her?	*How long ago is it?*
Es ist schon lange her	*It's a long time ago*
Es ist schon einen Monat her	*It's a month ago*

319. before: main construction: accusative + vorher.

Ich war ein Jahr vorher dagewesen	*I had been there a year before*
zwei Jahre vorher	*two years before*
am Tag (or: den Tag) vorher, am vorhergehenden Tag, tags zuvor	*(on) the day before*

cf. lange vorher, einige Zeit vorher, kurz vorher

Distinguish 'vorher' and 'vorhin'

vorher *previously, beforehand* can refer to past or future:

Ich hatte ihn vorher gesprochen	*I had spoken to him previously (or: before that)*
Ich muß ihn vorher sprechen	*I must speak to him beforehand*

vorhin *a short time ago, just now* refers to the past only:

Ich habe vorhin mit ihm gesprochen	*I spoke to him just now*

320. after, later

Einen Monat nach seiner Verhaftung wurde er freigelassen	*A month after his arrest he was released*
Ich habe ihn einen Monat danach/ später gesehen	*I saw him a month after*
lange danach, lange nachher, nach langer Zeit, lange Zeit danach	*a long time after*
einige Zeit danach	*some time after*
nach einiger Zeit	
kurz danach, kurz nachher, nach kurzer Zeit	*a short time after*
nach einer Weile	*after a while*
nach Wochen, Jahren etc.	*weeks, years etc. later*
tags darauf	*the day after*

H. ERST

321. erst: i *at first, first of all* (cf. zuerst)
ii **(S)** *only, not until, (so far) not more than:*

Er kommt erst am Montag	*He is only coming on Monday*
	He is not coming till Monday
Es ist erst acht Uhr	*It's only eight o'clock*
erst heute	*not till today*
Ich kam erst letzten Sommer nach Heidelberg	*I never got to Heidelberg till last summer*
Er ist erst sieben Jahre alt	*He is only seven years old*
Ich habe erst zwei deutsche Romane gelesen	*I have only read two German novels so far*
Es hatte eben erst zu schneien aufgehört (E. Jünger)	*It had only just stopped snowing*
Wäre er doch erst zu Hause! (H. Fallada)	*If only he were home!*
Wenn er erst zu Hause ist, . . .	*Once he is home, . . .*
Dieser Garten ist ganz schön, aber du solltest erst mal unsern sehen!	*This garden is quite nice, but wait till you see ours*
erst wenn (erst als)	*only when, not until*

I. GUIDE TO THE USE OF PREPOSITIONS BEFORE NOUNS DENOTING TIME

322. an+dat.: before days and parts of the day: am Montag, an einem Wochentag, am ersten Mai, an besonderen Tagen (BUT: in diesen kritischen Tagen); am Tag *in the daytime, by day,* am Abend, am Montagabend; **Exc.** in der Nacht.
Idiomatic variants: Er kommt Montag (Montagabend) zurück; bei Tag, tags; bei Nacht, nachts; abends etc. (see 317 N.i).

323. in+dat.

(a) before Augenblick, Minute, Woche, Monat, Jahr, Jahrhundert,

Zeitalter *period, age*, Epoche, the months and the seasons (see also 326):

im Augenblick	*at the moment*
im letzten Augenblick	*at the last moment*
in letzter Minute	
in der Woche vor Weihnachten	*in the week before Christmas*
in den letzten paar Jahren	*in the last few years*
im Jahre neunzehnhundertfünfzig	*in 1950*
(or merely: neunzehnhundert-	
fünfzig)[1]	
im Januar	*in January*
im Sommer	*in summer*
im Sommer 1963	*in the summer of 1963*
in dieser Jahreszeit	*in this season*
zu dieser Jahreszeit	BUT: *at this time of the year*

Idiomatic variants: Er kam Juli/Sommer 1963 zurück.

(b) to denote a period within or after which something is done or occurs:

Ich habe die Arbeit in zwei Stunden gemacht	*I did the work in two hours*
Er kommt in einer halben Stunde	*He's coming in half an hour*
heute in acht Tagen	*in a week's time, a week today*
heute über acht Tage	

Note:

Man kann dies an einem Morgen/ an (or: in) einem Tag/in zwei Tagen schaffen	*One can get this done in one morning/ in one day/in two days*

324. um: 'at' before times of the clock: um zehn Uhr.

325. zu: usually before Weihnachten, Neujahr, Ostern, Pfingsten: zu Weihnachten (S. Germ. also 'an') *at/for Christmas*

Idiomatic variant:

Er kommt Weihnachten (Ostern, Pfingsten)	*He's coming at Christmas (Easter, Whitsun)*

N.B. an Silvester *on New Year's Eve*, BUT: Wir fahren zu Silvester (*for New Year's Eve*) nach Mannheim.

326. zu or in + dat. before 'Zeit'?

(a) 'zu' is used in contexts denoting one or more specific points or limited periods of time:

zur Zeit (or: dèrzeit)	*at present, at the moment, at the time*
zur Zeit der letzten Wahlen	*at the time of the last election*
zur Zeit Shakespeares	*in Shakespeare's day*
Zu *einer* Zeit (or: Eìnmal) hatte ich gehofft, Arzt zu werden	*At one time I had hoped to become a doctor*
zu *der* Zeit, zu dieser Zeit ('damals' is rather less precise)	*at that time*

---

[1] But: im Jahre tausendsechsundsechzig *in 1066*.
Duden condemns 'in 1950', which is sometimes found, as an Anglicism (Du. Haupt.p. 47).

zu der Zeit, als du hier warst	*at the time when you were here*
zu einer anderen Zeit	*at some other time*
zu jeder Zeit (jederzeit)	*at all times, at any time*
zu keiner Zeit (nie, niemals)	*at no time*
zu gewissen Zeiten	*at (certain) times*
zur gewohnten Zeit	*at the usual time*
gerade noch zur rechten Zeit	*in the nick of time*
zu gleicher Zeit (zugleich, gleichzeitig)	*at the same time, simultaneously*
Zu meiner Zeit war alles anders	*In my time (in my day) everything was different*
Ich habe in meinem Leben viele Veränderungen mitgemacht	BUT: *I've seen many changes in my time (in my day)* (cf. (b) i below)

(b) in + dat. is used:

i to denote a period within or after which something is done or occurs:

In all der Zeit (in der ganzen Zeit) haben wir ihn nicht gesehen	*In all that time we didn't see him*
In kurzer Zeit war er wieder da	*In a short time he was back again*

ii in phrases which are felt to denote duration and not merely a point or limited period of time:

In unserer Zeit tut man das nicht mehr	*In our times that is no longer done*
in einer Zeit, in der die Städte wachsen	*at a time when towns are growing*
in einer solchen Zeit wie heute	*at a time like the present*
in früheren Zeiten	*in days past*
in künftigen Zeiten	*in days to come*
in der ersten Zeit	*at first (in the first few weeks or months)*

327. Phrases with 'Stunde'

zur Stunde (elev.)	*at the present moment; so far; now, at once*
zu dieser Stunde	*at this hour*
zu jeder Stunde	*at any time*
zur selben Stunde	*at the same hour*
zu später Stunde (elev.)	*at a late hour*
in ruhigen Stunden	*in peaceful hours*
in elfter (or zwölfter) Stunde	*at the eleventh hour*

328. The translation of 'for'

(a) for a period of time lying completely in the past or the future:

Wir waren drei Wochen (lang) in Deutschland	*We were in Germany for three weeks*
Wir werden drei Wochen (lang) in Deutschland sein	*We shall be in Germany for three weeks*

Note: 'für' is also used in this type of context, e.g. Sie ging zurück ins Schlafzimmer ... und ... saß für zehn Minuten ganz reglos auf ihrem Bett (V. Baum). Wir waren für drei Wochen in Italien.

(b) for a period of time beginning in the past and still continuing in the present or at a more recent point in the past:

Er ist seit drei Wochen hier (or: Er ist jetzt schon drei Wochen (lang) hier)[1]	*He has been here for three weeks*
Er war schon seit drei Wochen krank, als ich ankam[1]	*He had been ill for three weeks when I arrived*

(c) for a period of time beginning in the present (or at some indicated point of time) and extending thence into the future:

Ich gehe für drei Wochen nach Deutschland (or, somewhat stilted: auf drei Wochen (acc.))	*I'm going to Germany for three weeks*
Am nächsten Tag fuhren wir für einen Monat in den Schwarzwald	*The next day we went to the Black Forest for a month's stay*

Colloquial variant:

Ich gehe eine halbe Stunde (lang) ins Café	*I'm going to the café for half an hour*

329. No preposition before Anfang, Mitte and Ende in a number of time phrases. (The examples apply to all three words):

Anfang Januar (Februar etc.)	*at the beginning of January (February etc.)*
Mitte des/dieses Monats	*in the middle of the/this month*
Ende nächster Woche	*at the end of next week*
Ende letzten Jahres	*at the end of last year*
Anfang 1960	*at the beginning of 1960*
Anfang der zwanziger Jahre	*at the beginning of the 1920s*
Er ist Mitte (der) Dreißig	*He is in his middle thirties* (between 30 and 40 years of age)

With Anfang and Ende only:

Anfang des Winters	*at the beginning of the winter*
Ende der Ferien	*at the end of the holidays*

Note:

i The above usage is essential in the types: Anfang Januar, Anfang 1960, er ist Mitte Dreißig; in the others, am Anfang, in der Mitte, am Ende are possible, but less idiomatic.

ii Note the absence of an article in analogous phrases with prepositions, e.g. seit Ende Januar, bis Mitte des Monats, vor Anfang 1960, seit Anfang des Winters.

J. FURTHER SELECTED TIME PHRASES AND TIME WORDS

330. Selected time phrases and time words not covered in 311–29, arranged in alphabetical order of the English equivalents.

Note:

For the use of Mal ('time', as in 'three times, next time') see 254 f.

For noch *still*, noch nicht *not yet* etc., see 300(a).

For 'in the twenties' etc., see 244.

---

[1] Regarding the tenses used, see 554.

For the difference between e.g. 'my three weeks' holiday' and 'our three-weekly conference', see 720, -lich, N.3.

(ungefähr) um diese Zeit	about this time
A.D. (=Anno Domini) (little used)	A.D.
n. Chr. (=nach Christus)	
n. Chr. G. (=nach Christi Geburt)	(Christi=gen. of Christus)
Er ist im richtigen Alter	He's the right age (see also 'at')
Jahrgang 1950	of the 1950 age-group; also used to denote the vintage of a wine
die ganze Zeit	all along
(noch) länger	any longer
Ich konnte keine Zeitung mehr bekommen	I couldn't get a paper any more
	around: see round about
zu jeder Tageszeit	at any hour
bei Tagesanbruch	at daybreak
bei Einbruch der Nacht	at nightfall
bei Sonnenaufgang	at sunrise
im Alter von 15 (Jahren)	at the age of 15
mit 15 (Jahren)	
in aller Herrgottsfrühe	at the crack of dawn
seinerzeit	at the time, e.g.
Ich habe sie seinerzeit besucht	I visited them at the time
gleich am Anfang	at the very beginning
zu diesem Zeitpunkt	at this point of time
zu dieser (or: um diese) Tageszeit	at this time of day
um diese Zeit	at this time of day/of night
v. Chr. (=vor Christus)	B.C.
v. Chr. G. (=vor Christi Geburt)	
Ich bin bis Montag zurück	I'll be back by Monday
rückwirkend vom 1. März	back-dated to 1st. March
bis dahin	by that time, cf.
Bis dahin bin ich längst zurück	I'll be back well before that
bis zum dritten Januar	by the third of January
morgen um diese Zeit	(by) this time tomorrow
bis wann?	by when?
bis in unsere Tage	down to our own day
bis auf den heutigen Tag	down to the present day
den Tag über, tagsüber	during the day
Hast du ihn je gesehen?	Have you ever seen him?
Es ist der beste Film, den ich je gesehen habe	It's the best film I've ever seen
bis tief in die Nacht hinein	far into the night
zu guter Letzt	finally, to finish up, to cap everything
Ich habe ihn ewig nicht gesehen	I haven't seen him for ages
für alle Zeiten	for all time
Wenn Sie länger da sind, . . . (cf. 129)	If you are there for any length of time, . . .
auf ewig	for ever
ganze drei Wochen	for a full three weeks
Ich habe ihn seit langem/lange/seit Jahr und Tag (idiomatic) nicht gesehen	I haven't seen him for a long time
für immer, auf immer	for good
auf Monate hinaus	for months to come
seit einiger Zeit	for some time past

augenblicklich	*for the moment*
bis auf weiteres, vorderhand	*for the present*
einstweilen, vorderhand, vorerst	*for the time being, meanwhile*
vorläufig	*for the time being, provisionally*
von Anfang bis Ende	*from beginning to end*
von Kindesbeinen an	*from early childhood*
von morgens bis abends	*from morning till evening*
von neun Uhr an	*from nine o'clock onwards*
von heute auf morgen	*from one day to the next, overnight*
von Anfang an	*from the beginning, from the start*
von vornherein	*from the first, from the outset*
von da an	*from then onward*
von der Zeit an ('der' is stressed)	
seit Menschengedenken	*from time immemorial*
seit undenklicher Zeit	
von jeher	*from time immemorial, always*
von Jugend auf	*from his (my etc.) youth upwards*
Er war eine gute Stunde bei mir	*He was with me a good hour*
vor einer guten Woche	*a good week ago (see also quite)*
stundenlang	*hour after hour, for hours*
Er wohnt stundenweit (drei Stunden weit) von hier	*He lives hours (three hours) from here*
Wie lange sind Sie noch da?	*How much longer will you be here?*
im voraus	*in advance, beforehand*
in alter Zeit, anno dazumal (coll.)	*in days of yore*
in künftigen Zeiten	*in days to come*
zur rechten Zeit	*in due course*
Schließlich kam auch Herr G.	*In due course Herr G. also arrived (coll. use)*
rechtzeitig	*in good time*
in seinem Alter	*in his old age*
auf seine alten Tage	
im Handumdrehen	*in no time*
im Lauf der Zeit, mit der Zeit	*in the course of time*
im Lauf von vier Jahren	*in the course of four years*
in absehbarer Zeit	*in the foreseeable future*
auf die Dauer	*in the long run*
inzwischen, mittlerweile, indessen, währenddessen, solange	*in the meantime, meanwhile:* = during this period of time
inzwischen, mittlerweile	= since then
in der Nacht von Sonntag auf Montag	*in the night from Sunday to Monday*
rechtzeitig, beizeiten	*in (good) time*
vor alten Zeiten	*in times of old, in days gone by*
auf unabsehbare Zeit	*indefinitely*
Ich kam noch eben zurecht	*I was just in time*
Es ist gleich halb fünf	*It's just on half past four*
zu allerletzt	*last of all*
der vorletzte Tag	*the last day but one*
der zweitletzte Tag	
der drittletzte Tag	*the last day but two*
längst	*long since (long ago, for a long time)*
Ich weiß es schon längst	*e.g. I have known it for a long time*
Es ist noch lange hin	*It's a long time to come*
mittelalterlich	**medieval**
in mittlerem Alter	**middle-aged**
die meiste Zeit	*most of the time*
den größten Teil der Zeit	

dann, sodann	*next, then*
nicht mehr	*no longer*
nicht mehr lange	*not much longer*
bald . . ., bald . . .	*now . . ., now . . .*
ab und zu	*on and off*
an diesem Datum	*on that date*
auf die Minute	*on the dot*
einmal (zweimal etc.)	*once (twice etc.) a week*
in der Woche pro Woche	
die Woche wöchentlich	
jede Woche	
dieser Tage	*one of these days, shortly; recently*
	(see 331)
übers (or: am) Wochenende	*over the weekend*
über Nacht	*overnight, during the night*
am vorhergehenden Dienstag	*(on) the previous Tuesday*
Er war gut zwei Stunden bei mir	*He was with me quite two hours*
vor gut drei Wochen	*quite three weeks ago*
	recent, recently: see 331
bis in den Herbst hinein	*right into autumn*
um Weihnachten herum	*round about Christmas*
um/ungefähr 1930	*round about 1930*
nach wie vor	*the same as before, the same as ever*
von alters her	*since ancient times*
seitdem, seit damals	*since that time, since then*
seit Mittwoch voriger Woche	*since Wednesday of last week*
früher oder später	*sooner or later*
über kurz oder lang	
vom ersten Oktober an	*starting on October the first*
heutzutage	*these days*
gestern um diese Zeit	*this time yesterday*
heuer	*(in) this year* (Austrian dialect)
sein ganzes Leben hindurch	*throughout his life*
zeit seines Lebens	
den ganzen Winter hindurch	*throughout the winter*
den ganzen Winter über	
verschieben auf + acc.	*to postpone till*
bis spät in die Nacht	*till late at night*
bis dann, bis dahin	*till then*
Ist es Zeit?	*Is it time?*
Ist es schon soweit? (idiomatic)	
anfangs	*to begin with, at first*
zuerst, zunächst	*to begin with, first of all*
bis auf den heutigen Tag	*to this day*
die heutige Sitzung	*today's meeting*
die Sitzung heute	
bis zu eineinviertel Stunden	*up to an hour and a quarter*
gleich am nächsten Tag	*the very next day*
Woche um Woche	*week after week*
übernächste Woche	*the week after next*
vorletzte Woche	*the week before last*
am Freitag vorletzter Woche	*on Friday of the week before last*
nach Feierabend	*when the day's work is done*
heute über ein Jahr	*a year today, a year hence*
heute übers Jahr	
die Stunde Null	*zero-hour*

331. recently

kürzlich, vor kurzem, unlängst	1. *a short time ago, a short time previously*
neulich	2. *the other day*
neulich morgens	*the other morning*
dieser Tage,[1] in diesen Tagen	3. *the other day, on one of the last few days*
letzthin, in letzter Zeit, seit kurzem, (neuerdings)	4. *latterly, during the last few weeks or months, e.g.*
Ich habe ihn letzthin nicht gesehen	*I haven't seen him recently*
bis vor kurzem	*until recently*
Ich habe ihn noch später gesehen als du	*I have seen him **more recently** than you*
Karl hat ihn zuletzt gesehen	*Karl has seen him **most recently***

recent: There is no satisfactory German adjective; 'kürzlich' is an adverb and is unconvincing as an adjective, while 'neuerlich' also means 'renewed, fresh' (cf. Eggeling op. cit., p. 284):

beim kürzlichen Staatsbesuch von Bundespräsident Lübke (*SZ*)	*during the recent state-visit of Federal President Lübke*
die neuerliche Verletzung des vereinbarten Viermächtestatus (*FAZ*)	*the recent (or renewed?) violation of the agreed four-power status* [of Berlin]

One is therefore driven to circumlocutions and substitutions such as the following:

bei der kürzlich stattgefundenen Konferenz	*at the recent conference*
bei unserer Begegnung (von) neulich	*at our recent meeting*
als er vor kurzem krank war	*during his recent illness*
die jüngsten Zwischenfälle auf Zypern (*Zeit*)	*the (most) recent incidents in Cyprus*
eine neuere Verordnung	*a **more recent** regulation*
eine erst kürzlich eingeführte Neuerung	*a more recent innovation*
bei unserer letzten Begegnung	*at our **most recent** meeting*
die neuesten Verordnungen	*the most recent regulations*
sein neuestes/jüngstes/letztes Buch	*his most recent book*

332. der Termin *date, fixed day; appointment; court summons*

Er zahlte zu dem vereinbarten Termin	*He paid on the day agreed upon*
den Termin ein-halten/ versäumen	*to keep to/miss the date*
der (äußerste) Termin	*the deadline*
die Ferientermine	*the dates of the holidays*
Nennen Sie mir bitte einen Termin!	*When could I have an appointment?*
der Terminkalender	*engagement-diary*

---

[1] 'dieser Tage' may also mean 'on one of these coming days, shortly'.

XI VERBS

A. CONJUGATION

333. Conjugation of verbs: introductory

German verbs are of two main types, weak and strong.

Weak verbs form their imperfect by adding -te to the stem and their past participle by prefixing ge- and adding -t to the stem; the stem is obtained by cutting off the -en (or -n)[1] of the infinitive. E.g.

holen *to fetch* – holte – geholt

Strong verbs change the vowel of their stem in the imperfect; in the past participle the vowel of the stem may again change or it may be the same as that of the infinitive or of the imperfect. In the 1st and 3rd pers. sing. of the imperfect, strong verbs have no ending; in the past participle they prefix ge- and add -en to the stem. E.g.

singen *to sing* – sang – gesungen
tragen *to carry* – trug – getragen
schreiben *to write* – schrieb – geschrieben

(For verbs with no ge- in the past part., see 343).

Most strong verbs with the stem-vowels e, a, au and o have a vowel change or modification in the 2nd and 3rd pers. sing. of the present indicative, where e becomes ie or i, while a, au and o modify (see 341).

There follow below:

i the full conjugation of haben *to have*, sein *to be* and werden *to become*. In their simple tenses, these are not typical of either a weak or a strong verb; as auxiliaries they help to form the compound tenses of all other German verbs.

ii the full conjugation of a typical weak and of a typical strong verb (holen and tragen respectively) in the active voice.

iii the full conjugation of the passive of loben.

iv variations in verb forms.

Note on the paradigms that follow:

1. The polite form of the 2nd pers., sing. or plur., is, except in the imperative, not given separately. It is the same as the 3rd pers. plur., except

---

[1] -n where the infinitive ends in -eln or -ern: see 340(g).

that Sie *you* has a capital letter: sie haben = *they have*; Sie haben = *you have*.[1]

2. In the compound tenses, the past part. and infin. go to the end of the sentence, except in a subordinate clause (see 649).
   Perfect: Ich habe das Buch geholt
   Pluperfect: Ich hatte das Buch geholt
   Future: Ich werde das Buch holen
   Future Perfect: Ich werde das Buch geholt haben

In the following paradigms, dots are inserted in the fut. perf. and condit. perf. to divide off the part that goes to the end (i.e. the perfect infinitive). The same device has been used in all tenses of the passive paradigm.

3. The compound tenses of 'haben' typify the compound tenses of all verbs conjugated with haben.

4. The compound tenses of 'sein' typify the compound tenses of all verbs conjugated with sein.

334. haben *to have*

Indicative	Subjunctive

PRESENT

Indicative	Subjunctive
ich habe	ich habe
du hast	du habest
er hat	er habe
wir haben	wir haben
ihr habt	ihr habet
sie haben	sie haben

IMPERFECT

Indicative	Subjunctive
ich hatte	ich hätte
du hattest	du hättest
er hatte	er hätte
wir hatten	wir hätten
ihr hattet	ihr hättet
sie hatten	sie hätten

PERFECT

Indicative	Subjunctive
ich habe gehabt	ich habe gehabt
du hast gehabt etc.	du habest gehabt etc.

PLUPERFECT

Indicative	Subjunctive
ich hatte gehabt	ich hätte gehabt
du hattest gehabt etc.	du hättest gehabt etc.

FUTURE

Indicative	Subjunctive
ich werde haben	ich werde haben
du wirst haben	du werdest haben
er wird haben	er werde haben
wir werden haben	wir werden haben
ihr werdet haben	ihr werdet haben
sie werden haben	sie werden haben

FUTURE PERFECT

Indicative	Subjunctive
ich werde . . . gehabt haben	ich werde . . . gehabt haben
du wirst . . . gehabt haben etc.	du werdest . . . gehabt haben etc.

---

[1] For the use of the familiar, as opposed to the polite 2nd pers., see 140.

Conditional

ich würde haben
du würdest haben
er würde haben
wir würden haben
ihr würdet haben
sie würden haben

Conditional Perfect

ich würde . . . gehabt haben
du würdest . . . gehabt haben
er würde . . . gehabt haben
wir würden . . . gehabt haben
ihr würdet . . . gehabt haben
sie würden . . . gehabt haben

Imperative		**Infinitives**		**Participles**	
2nd sing.	hab(e)!	Pres.	haben	Pres.	habend
2nd plur.	habt!	Perf.	gehabt haben	Past	gehabt
2nd polite	haben Sie!				

335. sein *to be*

Indicative	**Subjunctive**

Present

ich bin	ich sei
du bist	du sei(e)st
er ist	er sei
wir sind	wir seien
ihr seid	ihr seiet
sie sind	sie seien

Imperfect

ich war	ich wäre
du warst	du wär(e)st
er war	er wäre
wir waren	wir wären
ihr wart	ihr wär(e)t
sie waren	sie wären

Perfect

ich bin gewesen	ich sei gewesen
du bist gewesen etc.	du sei(e)st gewesen etc.

Pluperfect

ich war gewesen	ich wäre gewesen
du warst gewesen etc.	du wär(e)st gewesen etc.

Future

ich werde sein	ich werde sein
du wirst sein etc.	du werdest sein etc.

Future Perfect

ich werde . . . gewesen sein	ich werde . . . gewesen sein
du wirst . . . gewesen sein etc.	du werdest . . . gewesen sein etc.

Conditional

ich würde sein
du würdest sein etc.

Conditional Perfect

ich würde . . . gewesen sein
du würdest . . . gewesen sein etc.

Imperative		**Infinitives**		**Participles**	
2nd sing.	sei!	Pres.	sein	Pres.	(seiend)[1]
2nd plur.	seid!	Perf.	gewesen sein	Past	gewesen
2nd polite	seien Sie!				

[1] barely used.

7*

336. werden *to become*

Indicative		Subjunctive
	PRESENT	

Indicative	Subjunctive
ich werde	ich werde
du wirst	du werdest
er wird	er werde
wir werden	wir werden
ihr werdet	ihr werdet
sie werden	sie werden

IMPERFECT

Indicative	Subjunctive
ich wurde[1]	ich würde
du wurdest	du würdest
er wurde	er würde
wir wurden	wir würden
ihr wurdet	ihr würdet
sie wurden	sie würden

For compound tenses (ich bin geworden, ich sei geworden etc.) see 335.

Imperative		Infinitives		Participles	
2nd sing.	werde!	PRES.	werden	PRES.	werdend
2nd plur.	werdet!	PERF.	geworden sein	PAST	geworden
2nd polite	werden Sie!				

337. Weak Verb: holen *to fetch*

Indicative		Subjunctive
	PRESENT	

Indicative	Subjunctive
ich hole	ich hole
du holst	du holest
er holt	er hole
wir holen	wir holen
ihr holt	ihr holet
sie holen	sie holen

IMPERFECT

Indicative	Subjunctive
ich holte	ich holte
du holtest	du holtest
er holte	er holte
wir holten	wir holten
ihr holtet	ihr holtet
sie holten	sie holten

For compound tenses (ich habe geholt, ich hatte geholt etc.) see 334.

Imperative		Infinitives		Participles	
2nd sing.	hol(e)!	PRES.	holen	PRES.	holend
2nd plur.	holt!	PERF.	geholt haben	PAST	geholt
2nd polite	holen Sie!				

---

[1] The singular forms ich ward, du wardst, er ward are archaic and literary.

338. Strong Verb: tragen *to carry*

Indicative		Subjunctive
	PRESENT	

Indicative	Subjunctive
ich trage	ich trage
du trägst	du tragest
er trägt	er trage
wir tragen	wir tragen
ihr tragt	ihr traget
sie tragen	sie tragen

IMPERFECT

Indicative	Subjunctive
ich trug	ich trüge
du trugst	du trüg(e)st
er trug	er trüge
wir trugen	wir trügen
ihr trugt	ihr trüg(e)t
sie trugen	sie trügen

For compound tenses (ich habe getragen, ich hatte getragen etc.) see 334.

Imperative		**Infinitives**		**Participles**	
2nd sing.	trag(e)!	PRES.	tragen	PRES.	tragend
2nd plur.	tragt!	PERF.	getragen haben	PAST	getragen
2nd polite	tragen Sie!				

339. Passive of loben *to praise* (Weak)

Indicative	Subjunctive

PRESENT

Indicative	Subjunctive
ich werde . . . gelobt	ich werde . . . gelobt
du wirst . . . gelobt	du werdest . . . gelobt
er wird . . . gelobt	er werde . . . gelobt
wir werden . . . gelobt	wir werden . . . gelobt
ihr werdet . . . gelobt	ihr werdet . . . gelobt
sie werden . . . gelobt	sie werden . . . gelobt

IMPERFECT

Indicative	Subjunctive
ich wurde . . . gelobt	ich würde . . . gelobt
du wurdest . . . gelobt etc.	du würdest . . . gelobt etc.

PERFECT

Indicative	Subjunctive
ich bin . . . gelobt worden	ich sei . . . gelobt worden
du bist . . . gelobt worden etc.	du sei(e)st . . . gelobt worden etc.

PLUPERFECT

Indicative	Subjunctive
ich war . . . gelobt worden	ich wäre . . . gelobt worden
du warst . . . gelobt worden etc.	du wär(e)st . . . gelobt worden etc.

FUTURE

Indicative	Subjunctive
ich werde . . . gelobt werden	ich werde . . . gelobt werden
du wirst . . . gelobt werden etc.	du werdest . . . gelobt werden etc.

FUTURE PERFECT

Indicative	Subjunctive
ich werde . . . gelobt worden sein	ich werde . . . gelobt worden sein
du wirst . . . gelobt worden sein etc.	du werdest . . . gelobt worden sein etc.

etc.

Conditional
ich würde . . . gelobt werden
du würdest . . . gelobt werden etc.

Conditional Perfect
ich würde . . . gelobt worden sein
du würdest . . . gelobt worden sein
etc.

Imperative
2nd sing.	sei (werde) gelobt!
2nd plur.	seid (werdet) gelobt!
2nd polite	seien Sie (werden Sie) gelobt!

Infinitives
PRES.	gelobt werden
PERF.	gelobt worden sein

Participles:　PRES. gelobt werdend　　PAST (gelobt worden)

Note:

i The future perf. passive is virtually never used; see 362.

ii The imperative passive with 'werden' is rare; thus, from the end of a letter: Seien Sie herzlich von uns beiden gegrüßt.

iii The passive present participle is very rarely used.

iv The passive past part.: except when forming part of an active compound tense, the active past part. of all transitive verbs is passive in meaning, e.g. mein verlorener Schirm *my lost umbrella*; cf. 435 ff.

B. VARIATIONS IN VERB FORMS

340. Miscellaneous variations

(a) **1st sing. pres. indic.**: the ending -e normally drops away in spoken German (and often, for rhythmic reasons, in literary German), e.g. Ich kauf' noch was; ich les' ganz gern. (But see (f) and (g) below).

(b) **1st sing. imperf. indic. of weak verbs**: the -e of the -te ending often drops away in spoken German (and, for rhythmic reasons, in literary German), especially before a vowel, e.g. Ich sucht' ihn überall, BUT: ich suchte meinen Bruder.

(c) **When the stem ends in a vowel or in h**, the -e of the -en ending generally drops away in spoken German (and often, for rhythmic reasons, in literary German) in the following forms:
Pres. Infin.: schaun, sehn.
1st and 3rd plur. Pres. Indic. and Subj.: wir/sie schaun, sehn; e.g. (Pres. Subj.): Gehn wir jetzt in den Garten!
Polite form of Imperative: schaun Sie! sehn Sie!
　　With strong verbs only:
1st and 3rd plur. Imperf. Indic. and Subj.: wir/sie sahn, sähn.
Past Part.: gesehn.

N.B. Pres. Indic. and Imperative of 'tun':
　　ich tu(e), du tust, er tut, wir tun, ihr tut, sie tun.
　　tu(e)! tut! tun Sie!

(d) **When the stem ends in a sibilant**:

i In the 2nd sing. pres. indic. the s of the ending drops away: lesen: du liest; schließen: du schließt; heizen: du heizt. Exc.: when the sibilant is sch: waschen: du wäschst.

ii In the 2nd sing. imperf. indic. of strong verbs the s of the ending is retained and an e is inserted: lesen: du lasest; schließen: du schlossest; waschen: du wuschest. (colloquially also: du last, du schloßt, du wuschst).

(e) **When the stem ends in d or t:**

i The stem of a weak verb ending in d or t is always followed by an e, e.g.

Pres. Indic.: du redest, er redet, ihr redet.
Imperfect: ich antwortete, du antwortetest etc.
Past Part.: geredet, geantwortet.
Imperative plur.: redet! antwortet!

Note: The ending e of the 1st sing. pres. indic. and of the imperative sing. is frequently dropped in spoken German, e.g. Ich antwort' nicht; antwort doch! See also ii N. below.

ii The stem of a strong verb ending in d or t adds -est (instead of -st) in the 2nd sing. pres. indic. (but not in the imperfect) and -et (instead of -t) in 3rd sing. pres. indic. and 2nd plur. pres. indic., imperf. indic. and imperative. (For strong verbs with a vowel change in pres. indic., see 341(c)).

e.g. du findest, du bittest (BUT: du fandst, du batst)
    er findet, ihr findet, ihr fandet, findet!

Note: In rapid speech frequently no e is inserted in the 2nd sing. pres. indic. (whether weak or strong) e.g. Du redst zu viel; findst du es komisch?

(f) **The stem of a weak verb ending in -m or -n preceded by a consonant** is followed by an e if without it the word would be awkward or impossible to pronounce, e.g. atmen *to breathe*, segnen *to bless*. In this case, moreover, the e is never dropped in the 1st sing. pres. indic. or in the imperative sing. (There are no strong verbs in this category).

Pres. Indic.: ich atme, du atmest, er atmet, ihr atmet.
Imperf.: ich atmete, du atmetest etc.
Past Part.: geatmet.
Imperative: atme! atmet! atmen Sie!

Contrast e.g., filmen *to film*, lernen *to learn*: no necessity to insert an e.

(g) **Weak verbs with infinitives in -eln and -ern:** the stem is obtained by cutting off the -n, giving principal parts e.g. segeln, segelte, gesegelt; rudern, ruderte, gerudert.

Pres. Indic.:

ich seg(e)le	wir segeln	ich rud(e)re
du segelst	ihr segelt	du ruderst
er segelt	sie segeln	er rudert etc.

Imperative:

seg(e)le! segelt! segeln Sie!   rud(e)re! rudert! rudern Sie!

Note:

i The bracketed e of the 1st sing. pres. indic. and of the imperative sing. is generally omitted with verbs in -eln, but is often retained with those in -ern.

ii The pres. subj. is identical with the pres. indic., except for the 3rd sing.: er seg(e)le, er rud(e)re.

(h) **In shops, restaurants and hotels,** the 3rd person is often used as a polite form of address, e.g. Was wünscht der Herr? Wollen die Herrschaften zu Mittag essen?

341. Vowel changes and modification in Pres. Indic. of Strong Verbs

(a) Rule: In the 2nd and 3rd sing. of the pres. indic. of strong verbs, the following changes occur:

long e	becomes	ie:	lesen:	ich lese	du liest	er liest
short e	,,	i:	helfen:	ich helfe	du hilfst	er hilft
a	,,	ä:	fangen:	ich fange	du fängst	er fängt
au	,,	äu:	laufen:	ich laufe	du läufst	er läuft
o	,,	ö:	stoßen:	ich stoße	du stößt	er stößt

N.B. e is long before a single consonant or before h + consonant.
e is short before two or more consonants, other than h + consonant.

(b) Exceptions:

i The following strong verbs, with the above stem-vowels, have no vowel change in the pres. indic.:

bewegen *to induce*[1]   heben *to lift*   schaffen *to create*
erschallen *to resound*   kommen *to come*   scheren *to shear*
gehen *to go*   melken *to milk*   stehen *to stand*
genesen *to recover*   saugen *to suck*   weben *to weave*[2]
hauen *to hew, cut*

ii geben and nehmen change long e to i: du gibst, er gibt; du nimmst, er nimmt.

iii erlöschen *to go out* (of light or fire): du erlischst, er erlischt.

(c) Strong verbs with a vowel change or modification in 2nd and 3rd sing. pres. indic. and whose stem ends in a t, add -st in 2nd sing. and nothing in 3rd sing.:

schelten *to scold*: ich schelte, du schiltst, er schilt.
cf. fechten *to fight*, flechten *to twine, plait*, gelten *to be valid, carry weight, be considered (as)*
N.B. du fichtst, flichtst are often pronounced du fichst, flichst.

raten *to advise; to guess*: ich rate, du rätst, er rät.
cf. braten *to roast, fry*, halten *to hold; to stop*

The following (with stems in -t and -d) show individual variations of the above rule:

bersten	*to burst*	ich berste	du birst	er birst
treten	*to step, go*	ich trete	du trittst	er tritt
werden	*to become*	ich werde	du wirst	er wird
laden	*to load; to summon*	ich lade	du lädst	er lädt

---

[1] strong with this meaning; see principal parts in 351.
[2] generally weak in current usage.

342. The forms of the Imperative

(a) The orthodox forms of the imperative may be summed up thus:

2nd sing. (du)	hole!	lies!	sprich!
2nd plur. (ihr)	holt!	lest!	sprecht!
polite (sing. or plur.)	holen Sie!	lesen Sie!	sprechen Sie!

Three further imperatives may be added:

sein:	sich setzen (Refl.):	auf-stehen (sep. prefix):
sei!	setze dich!	stehe . . . auf!
seid!	setzt euch!	steht . . . auf!
seien Sie!	setzen Sie sich!	stehen Sie . . . auf!

Regarding the use of the exclamation mark after imperatives, see 744(d)ii.

(b) 2nd sing.: add e to the stem.
Note:

i Strong verbs that change e to ie or i in the 2nd and 3rd sing. of the pres. indic. (cf. 341(a)(b)) have the same vowel change in the imperative sing. and do not add an e; the same applies to erlöschen: erlisch. (In regional colloquial German this vowel change is (incorrectly) frequently not made in the imperative sing. (cf. Du. Gram. 1025), e.g. Nehm doch meinen Schirm! Vergeß es *ja* nicht!)

ii sehen has siehe in certain exclamations (e.g. Siehe da! *behold*) and in giving references in books: s. S. 90 = siehe Seite 90!

iii nehmen and treten have nimm! and tritt!

iv werden has werde! wissen has wisse!

v Strong verbs that modify the stem vowels a, au, o in the pres. indic. (cf. 341(a)) do not modify in the imperative: fange, laufe, stoße!

vi The e ending is generally dropped in spoken German (and sometimes, for rhythmic reasons, in literary German): Komm in den Garten! Stör mich nicht! Setz dich! Schlaf gut! It is never dropped in verbs such as atmen and segnen and rarely in verbs with infinitives in -eln and -ern. (See 340(f)(g)).

vii Occasionally a stressed 'du' is used after the imperative sing. for the sake of emphasis, e.g. Bestell *du* inzwischen das Frühstück (I. Wendt) *Meanwhile, you order breakfast.*

(c) 2nd plur.: as in the pres. indic., omitting ihr.
Note:

i In verse this imperative sometimes ends in -et, where it is not phonetically necessary: Nun danket alle Gott (Martin Rinkart).

ii Occasionally a stressed ihr is used after this imperative for the sake of emphasis: Kinder, wir kommen gleich; geht ihr schon vor!

(d) Polite form: as in the pres. indic., but verb and pronoun are reversed.

343. Verbs with no ge- in the Past Part. (These are verbs that are not stressed on the first syllable, except for type iii below and verbs of types iv and v when used with a separable prefix):

i verbs with inseparable prefixes (cf. 368)
e.g. besuchen: besucht; erfinden: erfunden.

ii verbs with variable prefixes, when the prefix is inseparable
e.g. second pair of examples in 371.

iii verbs with double prefixes (cf. 370)
e.g. ànvertrauen *to entrust*: ànvertraut.

iv foreign verbs in -ieren (cf. 675(c))
e.g. arrangieren: arrangiert; àufforcieren: àufforciert.

v a few others:

aùs-posaunen *to trumpet forth*	rumòren *to rummage noisily*
miaùen *to mew*	schmaròtzen bei *to sponge on*
offenbàren *to reveal*	trompèten *to blow (on the trumpet)*,
prophezèien *to prophesy*	*to trumpet forth*

e.g. Er hat sein eignes Lob ausposaunt   *He blew his own trumpet*

Note:

1. werden has no ge- in the past part. when used as an auxiliary to form the passive (cf. 339); thus: Er ist gelobt worden, BUT: Er ist Schauspieler geworden.

2. For the use of the infinitive form as past part., see 389(c)ii, 420.

344. The auxiliary of the perfect and particularly of the pluperfect tense is sometimes elegantly omitted in a subordinate clause, mainly in literary German:

Nachdem er dem Minister alles gesagt [hatte], stand er auf	*After he had told the minister everything, he stood up*
. . . daß die Gruppe den Verband, gegen den sie angesetzt worden [war], nicht entdeckt hatte (G. Gaiser)	*. . . that the wing had not found the formation, against which it had been brought into action*

Note:

(a) This omission should not be made where the past part. is identical with the 3rd sing. pres. indic. and a temporal ambiguity might result:

Da er nichts entdeckt hat, geht er nach Hause	*As he has discovered nothing, he's going home*

(b) A comparable omission is that of 'sein' as a copulative verb in a subordinate clause (elev.) (cf. Du. Haupt: Hilfsverb):

Ich weiß, wie schwer die Aufgabe (ist)	*I know how hard (is) the task*

345. The forms of the Subjunctive (cf. paradigms in 334ff.)

(a) Rules:

i The subjunctive is always regular. (No vowel changes in pres. subj.).

ii 2nd sing. always ends in -est.
  2nd plur. always ends in -et.

iii 3rd sing. is always the same as 1st sing.

iv imperf. subj. weak: same as imperf. indic.[1]
  imperf. subj. strong: start it by adding -e to imperf. indic. and modifying if possible.

(b) Exceptions to (a)ii:

i sein: du sei(e)st, du wär(e)st, ihr wär(e)t. The bracketed e is generally omitted in spoken German.

---

[1] In South German, brauchen frequently has imperf. subj. bräuchte.

ii Weak verbs in -eln and -ern: see 340(g)N.ii.

iii In the imperf. subj. of strong verbs, the e of the 2nd sing. and 2nd plur. endings (-est and -et) is generally omitted in spoken German provided that modification distinguishes subjunctive from indicative: du trüg(e)st, ihr trüg(e)t, BUT: du schriebest, ihr schriebet.

If the stem ends in a sibilant, the 2nd sing. *must* end in -est: du schlössest, ihr schlösset (schlößt); du läsest, ihr läset ('ihr läst' would be too similar to pres. indic. 'ihr lest').

If the stem ends in d or t, the 2nd plur. *must* end in -et: du fänd(e)st, ihr fändet.

(c) The following strong verbs have an irregular imperf. subj.:[1]

INFIN.	IMPERF. INDIC.	IMPERF. SUBJ.
beginnen	begann	begönne
gewinnen	gewann	gewönne
helfen	half	hülfe
schelten	schalt	schölte
schwimmen	schwamm	schwömme
schwören	schwor	schwüre
spinnen	spann	spönne
stehen	stand	stünde
sterben	starb ·	stürbe
verderben	verdarb	verdürbe
werben	warb	würbe
werfen	warf	würfe

Most of these irregular imperfect subjunctives sound stilted and are generally avoided in conversation, e.g.

Wenn das Konzert früher beginnen sollte, . . . (not: begönne)

Wenn er mich schelten sollte/würde, . . . (not: schölte)

346. The 9 mixed verbs

In the imperf. and past part. these verbs have (a) the weak endings -te and -t (b) a vowel change and, in the case of 'bringen' and 'denken', a consonant change. The form of their imperf. subj. must also be noticed:

INFIN.	3rd sing. PRES. INDIC.	IMPERF. INDIC	IMPERF. SUBJ.	PAST PARTICIPLE
brennen	brennt	brannte	brennte	gebrannt
bringen	bringt	brachte	brächte	gebracht
denken	denkt	dachte	dächte	gedacht
kennen	kennt	kannte	kennte	gekannt
nennen	nennt	nannte	nennte	genannt
rennen	rennt	rannte	rennte	gerannt
senden	sendet	sandte	sendete	gesandt
		sendete		gesendet
wenden	wendet	wandte	wendete	gewandt
		wendete		gewendet
wissen	weiß	wußte	wüßte	gewußt

Note:

i For their meanings and for the use of the alternative forms of senden and wenden, see 351.

[1] With a few others, an irregular form is less common than the regular.

ii Pres. indic. of wissen: ich weiß, du weißt, er weiß, wir wissen, ihr wißt, sie wissen; imperative sing.: wisse!

347. The 6 modal verbs: dürfen, können, mögen, müssen, sollen, wollen. For the forms of these verbs see 389; they are also included in 351.

C. THE AUXILIARIES HABEN AND SEIN[1]

348. The following verbs are conjugated with 'haben':

(a) **all transitive verbs**: Ich habe ihn gesehen; ich habe mein neues Auto gefahren.

EXCEPTIONS:
i a few compounds of gehen, e.g.

Er ist die Strecke abgegangen	*He paced the distance*
Er ist die Arbeit mit dem Schüler durchgegangen[2]	*He went through the work with the pupil*
Er ist die Wette eingegangen[3]	*He made the bet*

ii Gefahr laufen *to run a risk*: Er ist Gefahr gelaufen, sein ganzes Vermögen zu verlieren.

iii los-werden *to get rid of someone or something*: Ich bin ihn endlich losgeworden.

(b) **all reflexive verbs**:

Ich habe mich erholt	*I have recovered*
Ich hatte mich aus dem Zimmer gestohlen	*I had stolen out of the room*
Ich habe mich müde gelaufen	*I have run* (or: *walked*) *till I'm tired out*
Ich hatte mir alles nur eingebildet	*I had only imagined everything*

EXCEPTIONS:
i Du bist dir gleichgeblieben   *You haven't changed*
ii Where the reflexive pron. is used reciprocally (=each other) with a verb conjugated with 'sein', the auxiliary remains 'sein':

Sie sind sich ausgewichen	*They evaded each other*
Wir sind uns in der Stadt begegnet	*We met in town*

(c) **impersonal verbs and expressions**:
Es hat geregnet; es hat geklopft; es hat mir vor ihm gegraut *I shuddered to look at him.*

EXCEPTIONS:
i gelingen, mißlingen, glücken, mißglücken.
ii impersonal expressions based on verbs normally conjugated with 'sein', e.g. Es ist mir kalt geworden *I began to feel cold.* Wie ist es Ihnen in Berlin gegangen? *How did you fare in Berlin?*

(d) **intransitive verbs other than those mentioned in 349**, e.g. Ich habe gearbeitet; ich habe gepfiffen; ich habe gut geschlafen.

---

[1] see also 351 N.iii.
[2] cf. Du. Haupt. durchgehen.
[3] Among other objects of 'eingehen' are: ein Bündnis *an alliance*, eine Ehe *a marriage*, ein Risiko *a risk*, einen Vergleich *a compromise*, Verpflichtungen *obligations*.

Note: liegen, sitzen and stehen are conjugated with 'sein' in South German, but the North German 'ich habe gelegen, gesessen, gestanden' is normal usage.

349. Four groups of intransitive verbs are conjugated with 'sein':

(a) **(S) verbs denoting change of place**, e.g.

an-kommen *to arrive*, aufstehen *to get up*, entkommen *to escape*, erscheinen *to appear*, fahren, fallen, fliegen, gehen, klettern, kommen, paddeln *to canoe*, radeln, reiten, rudern, Schi fahren or Schi laufen, schwimmen, segeln, stürzen *to rush; to fall, plunge*, tanzen, treten *to step, tread, go*, verschwinden.

Note: Some such verbs of motion are sometimes conjugated with 'haben' if the activity as such is referred to, without mention of direction or destination:

Ich habe als junger Mensch viel getanzt	*I did a lot of dancing when I was young*
Sie ist aus dem Zimmer getanzt	BUT: *She danced out of the room*
Ich habe den ganzen Morgen gesegelt	*I've been sailing the whole morning*
Ich bin nach der Insel gesegelt	BUT: *I sailed to the island*

This practice is on the decline and, of the verbs in the above list, it is normal only with paddeln, rudern, segeln and tanzen. Thus current usage favours:

Ich bin den ganzen Morgen geklettert, geritten, geschwommen.
Ich bin in der Schweiz Schi gelaufen.
Er ist gut gesprungen.
Ich bin auch im Krieg etwas geflogen (V. Baum).

(b) **verbs denoting change of state**, e.g.

altern *to age*	platzen *to burst*
auf-wachen *to wake up*	reifen *to ripen, mature*
ein-schlafen *to go to sleep*	schmelzen *to melt* (intr.)
entstehen *to come into being, begin, arise*	verbluten *to bleed to death*
erblassen *to turn pale*	vergehen *to pass* (of time)
erklingen *to ring out, resound*	verhallen *to die away* (of sound)
erschrecken (str.) *to get a fright*	wachsen *to grow* (intr.)
ertrinken *to drown* (intr.)	welken *to fade*
heilen *to heal* (intr.)	

Er ist schon eingeschlafen; die Glocken sind erklungen; der Junge war gewachsen.

(c) **5 verbs denoting 'to happen'**: geschehen, passieren (coll.), vor-gehen, vor-kommen, zu-stoßen + Dat. *to happen to someone* (only of misfortune). E.g. Was ist (ihm) denn passiert? (stattfinden *to take place* is conjugated with haben).

(d) **8 others**

begegnen *to meet* (by chance)	glücken *to succeed*
bleiben *to remain*	mißglücken *to fail*
fehl-schlagen *to fail, come to nothing*	mißlingen *to fail*
gelingen *to succeed*	sein *to be*

Er ist zu Hause geblieben; es ist mir gelungen, ihn zu überzeugen; der Plan ist mißglückt.

350. Selected instances of the use of 'haben' and 'sein' with the same verb

i bekommen

Ich habe einen Brief bekommen	*I have received a letter*
Das Essen ist mir gut bekommen	*The dinner agreed with me*

ii fahren

Ich habe meinen neuen Wagen gefahren	*I drove my new car*
Ich bin nach Stuttgart gefahren	*I drove to Stuttgart*
Ich bin zu schnell gefahren	*I drove too quickly*
Ich bin diese Strecke öfters gefahren	*I have often driven along this stretch of road*

('diese Strecke' is an adverbial extension, not the object, of 'fahren'. Cf. Er war einen Baum hinaufgeklettert.)

iii folgen

Er hat mir gefolgt	*He obeyed me*
Er ist mir gefolgt	*He followed me*

iv frieren

Es hat heute nacht gefroren	*There was a frost last night*
Ich habe (or: Es hat mich) bei dem eisigen Wetter gefroren	*I felt frozen in the icy weather*
Das Wasser ist gefroren	*The water has frozen*
Der See ist gefroren (or: zugefroren)	*The lake has frozen*

v gären

Der Wein hat gegoren	*The wine has been fermenting* (process)
Der Wein ist gegoren (or: ausgegoren)	*The wine has fermented* (completed process, resultant state)

vi treten *to kick, tread, step, come etc.* It is conjugated with 'haben':

1. when transitive: Er hat mich mit dem Fuß getreten *He kicked me*; sie hat das Spinnrad getreten.
2. when intransitive, but denoting sheer activity, e.g. *to pedal* (cycle): Ich habe sehr schnell getreten.

    It is conjugated with 'sein' when it denotes change of place: Er ist ins Zimmer getreten.

    A further distinction:

Er hat/ist mir auf den Fuß getreten: 'hat' denotes deliberately; 'ist' denotes by mistake.

Note: The following are conjugated with 'haben':
zu-nehmen *to increase* (intr.), *to put on weight*
ab-nehmen *to decrease* (intr.), *to lose weight*
kochen *to boil, come to the boil.*

D. PRINCIPAL PARTS OF STRONG, MIXED AND IRREGULAR VERBS

351. Note on, and list of, principal parts

i A very few verbs, rarely used in current German, are not included in the list that follows.

ii Alternative forms are avoided as far as possible in favour of the one most commonly used in current German.

iii 'ist' before the past part. indicates that the verb is conjugated with 'sein'; all others are conjugated with 'haben'; where a verb is conjugated with either auxiliary, according to sense, this is shown.

iv Two past participles are given for the 6 modal verbs (see 389(c)ii and (d) and 392) and for heißen, helfen, lassen, sehen (see 420 f.).

INFINITIVE	3rd SING. PRES. INDIC.	2nd SING. IMPERATIVE	IMPERF. INDIC.	IMPERF. SUBJ.	PAST PART.	MEANING
backen	backt	back(e)!	backte	backte	gebacken	to bake
bedürfen	bedarf		bedurfte	bedürfte	bedurft	to need
befehlen	befiehlt	befiehl!	befahl	befähle	befohlen	to command
beginnen	beginnt	beginn(e)!	begann	begönne	begonnen	to begin~
beißen	beißt	beiß(e)!	biß	bisse	gebissen	to bite
bergen	birgt	birg!	barg	bärge	geborgen	to salvage, bring to safety
bersten	birst	birst!	barst	bärste	ist geborsten	to burst (intr.)
betrügen	betrügt	betrüg(e)!	betrog	betröge	betrogen	to deceive
bewegen	bewegt	beweg(e)!	bewog	bewöge	bewogen	to induce s.o. to do s.th.[1]
biegen	biegt	bieg(e)!	bog	böge	hat gebogen ist gebogen	to bend to turn (um die Ecke)
bieten	bietet	biet(e)!	bot	böte	geboten	to offer[2]
binden	bindet	bind(e)!	band	bände	gebunden	to bind, tie
bitten (um)	bittet	bitt(e)!	bat	bäte	gebeten	to ask (for), request
blasen	bläst	blas(e)!	blies	bliese	geblasen	to blow
bleiben	bleibt	bleib(e)!	blieb	bliebe	ist geblieben	to remain
braten	brät	brat(e)!	briet	briete	gebraten	to roast, fry
brechen	bricht	brich!	brach	bräche	hat gebrochen ist gebrochen	to break (tr.) to break (intr.)
brennen	brennt	brenn(e)!	brannte	brennte	gebrannt	to burn
bringen	bringt	bring(e)!	brachte	brächte	gebracht	to bring
denken	denkt	denk(e)!	dachte	dächte	gedacht	to think
dreschen	drischt	drisch!	drosch	drösche	gedroschen	to thresh
dringen	dringt	dring(e)!	drang	dränge	ist gedrungen	to penetrate, force one's way[3]
dünken	mich (or mir) deucht		deuchte	deuchte	gedeucht	to think o.s., to seem[4]
dürfen	darf		durfte	dürfte	gedurft, dürfen	to be allowed to
empfangen	empfängt	empfang(e)!	empfing	empfinge	empfangen	to receive (letters, presents, guests)
empfehlen	empfiehlt	empfiehl!	empfahl	empfähle	empfohlen	to recommend
empfinden	empfindet	empfind(e)!	empfand	empfände	empfunden	to feel
erkiesen	erkiest	erkies(e)!	erkor	erköre	erkoren	to choose (obs. and elev.)
erlöschen	erlischt	erlisch!	erlosch	erlösche	ist erloschen	to go out (of light, fire)[5]

INFINITIVE	3rd SING. PRES. INDIC.	2nd SING. IMPERATIVE	IMPERF. INDIC.	IMPERF. SUBJ.	PAST PART.	MEANING
erschallen	erschallt	erschall(e)!	erscholl	erschölle	ist erschollen	to resound[6]
erschrecken	erschrickt	erschrick!	erschrak	erschräke	ist erschrocken	to be startled[7]
erwägen	erwägt	erwäg(e)!	erwog	erwöge	erwogen	to weigh up, consider
essen	ißt	iß!	aß	äße	gegessen	to eat
fahren	fährt	fahr(e)!	fuhr	führe	hat gefahren / ist gefahren	to drive (tr.)[8] / to drive, travel (intr.)[8]
fallen	fällt	fall(e)!	fiel	fiele	ist gefallen	to fall
fangen	fängt	fang(e)!	fing	finge	gefangen	to catch
fechten	ficht	ficht!	focht	föchte	gefochten	to fight, fence
finden	findet	find(e)!	fand	fände	gefunden	to find
flechten	flicht	flicht!	flocht	flöchte	geflochten	to twine, plait
fliegen	fliegt	flieg(e)!	flog	flöge	hat geflogen / ist geflogen	to fly (tr.), to pilot (a plane) / to fly (intr.)
fliehen	flieht	flieh(e)!	floh	flöhe	hat geflohen / ist geflohen	to flee (tr.)[9] / to flee (intr.)
fließen	fließt	fließ(e)!	floß	flösse	ist geflossen	to flow
fressen	frißt	friß!	fraß	fräße	gefressen	to eat (of animals)
frieren	friert	frier(e)!	fror	fröre	hat gefroren / ist gefroren	to freeze, be cold[10] / to freeze (over)[10]
gären	gärt	gär(e)!	gor	göre	gegoren	to ferment (of wine)[11]

[1] meaning to move (physically) and to stir (emotionally), bewegen is weak.
[2] generally: an-bieten, BUT e.g. Er bot einen traurigen Anblick.
[3] (h) in a few specialized senses, e.g. Er hat darauf gedrungen *He insisted on it.*
[4] e.g. Er dünkt sich sehr wichtig; die Sache dünkt mir schwierig. Mainly archaic or facetious; commoner wk.
[5] löschen *to extinguish* is weak.
[6] also weak. Commonest current usage for (er-) (ver-) schallen: schallen *to resound*: weak; erschallen *to resound* erschallt, erschallte, ist erschollen; erschallen *to die away* (of sound): weak (ist verschallt), BUT: Er ist verschollen *He's never been heard of again* (fixed phrase).
[7] meaning to frighten, erschrecken is weak.
[8] see 350 ii.   [9] e.g. Ich habe seine Gegenwart geflohen; der Schlaf hat mich geflohen (Du. Stil.).
[10] see 350 iv.   [11] see 350 v; used fig, gären is weak, e.g. Es gärte in den Köpfen *There was a ferment in men's minds.*

INFINITIVE	3rd SING. PRES. INDIC.	2nd SING. IMPERATIVE	IMPERF. INDIC.	IMPERF. SUBJ.	PAST PART.	MEANING
gebären	gebärt	gebär(e)!	gebar	gebäre	geboren	*to give birth to*
geben	gibt	gib!	gab	gäbe	gegeben	*to give*
gedeihen	gedeiht	gedeih(e)!	gedieh	gediehe	ist gediehen	*to thrive*
gehen	geht	geh(e)!	ging	ginge	ist gegangen	*to go*
gelingen	gelingt	geling(e)!	gelang	gelänge	ist gelungen	*to succeed* (mainly impers.)
gelten	gilt	gilt!	galt	gälte	gegolten	*to be valid, carry weight, be considered* (as)
genesen	genest	genese!	genas	genäse	ist genesen	*to recover* (from illness)
genießen	genießt	genieß(e)!	genoß	genösse	genossen	*to enjoy*
geraten	gerät	gerat(e)!	geriet	geriete	ist geraten	*to turn out (well), to get (into some state)*[1]
geschehen	geschieht		geschah	geschähe	ist geschehen	*to happen*
gewinnen	gewinnt	gewinn(e)!	gewann	gewönne	gewonnen	*to win*
gießen	gießt	gieß(e)!	goß	gösse	gegossen	*to pour*
gleichen	gleicht	gleich(e)!	glich	gliche	geglichen	*to equal, resemble*
gleiten	gleitet	gleit(e)!	glitt	glitte	ist geglitten	*to glide, slide*
glimmen	glimmt	glimm(e)!	glomm	glömme	geglommen	*to glimmer*[2]
graben	gräbt	grab(e)!	grub	grübe	gegraben	*to dig*
greifen	greift	greif(e)!	griff	griffe	gegriffen	*to grip, seize*[3]
haben	hat	hab(e)!	hatte	hätte	gehabt	*to have*
halten	hält	halt(e)!	hielt	hielte	gehalten	*to hold; to stop* (intr.)
hängen	hängt	häng(e)!	hing	hinge	gehangen	*to hang* (intr.)[4]
hauen	haut	hau(e)!	hieb	hiebe	gehauen	*to hew, cut*[5]
heben	hebt	heb(e)!	hob	höbe	gehoben	*to lift*
heißen	heißt	heiß(e)!	hieß	hieße	geheißen, heißen	*to be called; to mean; to bid*
helfen	hilft	hilf!	half	hülfe	geholfen, helfen	*to help*
kennen	kennt	kenn(e)!	kannte	kennte	gekannt	*to know, to be acquainted with* (person, place, film etc.)
klimmen	klimmt	klimm(e)!	klomm	klömme	ist geklommen	*to climb*[6]
klingen	klingt	kling(e)!	klang	klänge	geklungen	*to sound*

INFINITIVE	3rd SING. PRES. INDIC.	2nd SING. IMPERATIVE	IMPERF. INDIC.	IMPERF. SUBJ.	PAST PART.	MEANING
kneifen	kneift	kneif(e)!	kniff	kniffe	gekniffen	to pinch
kommen	kommt	komm(e)!	kam	käme	ist gekommen	to come
können	kann		konnte	könnte	gekonnt, können	to be able to, can
kriechen	kriecht	kriech(e)!	kroch	kröche	ist gekrochen	to creep, crawl[7]
laden	lädt	lad(e)!	lud	lüde	geladen	to load; to invite[8]
lassen	läßt	lass(e)!	ließ	ließe	gelassen, lassen	to leave (alone); to let, cause to, allow
laufen	läuft	lauf(e)!	lief	liefe	hat gelaufen	to run, (walk) (tr. and refl.)[9]
					ist gelaufen	to run (walk) (intr.)
leiden	leidet	leid(e)!	litt	litte	gelitten	to suffer
leihen	leiht	leih(e)!	lieh	liehe	geliehen	to lend
lesen	liest	lies!	las	läse	gelesen	to read
liegen	liegt	lieg(e)!	lag	läge	gelegen	to lie
lügen	lügt	lüg(e)!	log	löge	gelogen	to (tell a) lie
mahlen	mahlt	mahl(e)!	mahlte	mahlte	gemahlen	to grind
meiden	meidet	meid(e)!	mied	miede	gemieden	to avoid[10]
melken	melkt	melk(e)!	molk	mölke	gemolken	to milk[11]
messen	mißt	miß!	maß	mäße	gemessen	to measure
mißlingen	mißlingt		mißlang	mißlänge	ist mißlungen	to fail (mainly impers.)
mögen	mag		mochte	möchte	gemocht, mögen	to like (to)
müssen	muß		mußte	müßte	gemußt, müssen	to have to, must

[1] e.g. Er ist in Gefahr (Schulden, Schwierigkeiten, Wut) geraten.
[2] also weak, especially in the imperf.
[3] e.g. Die Räder griffen nicht. Transitively, 'ergreifen' is more serviceable.
[4] archaic and dialectal: hangen, hangt, hing, gehangen. to hang (tr.) = hängen (wk.).
[5] The imperf. is generally weak and must be weak for hauen to thrash and sich hauen to fight.
[6] sometimes weak; elev.; commoner is the trans. verb erklimmen to climb, scale.
[7] kriechen vor + dat. to cringe before someone (h).
[8] in the sense of 'invite, summon', 3rd sing. pres. indic. is also ladet (archaic and regional); ein-laden is the normal verb 'to invite'.
[9] e.g. Er hat einen Weg für mich gelaufen He did an errand for me. See also 348(a) Exc. ii and (b).
[10] commoner: vermeiden.
[11] There is a weak alternative, and 'melkte' is commoner than 'molk'.

Infinitive	3rd Sing. Pres. Indic.	2nd Sing. Imperative	Imperf. Indic.	Imperf. Subj.	Past Part.	Meaning
nehmen	nimmt	nimm!	nahm	nähme	genommen	*to take*
nennen	nennt	nenn(e)!	nannte	nennte	genannt	*to name, call*
pfeifen	pfeift	pfeif(e)!	pfiff	pfiffe	gepfiffen	*to whistle*
preisen	preist	preis(e)!	pries	priese	gepriesen	*to praise*
quellen	quillt	quill!	quoll	quölle	ist gequollen	*to gush, swell up*
raten	rät	rat(e)!	riet	riete	geraten	*to advise ; to guess*
reiben	reibt	reib(e)!	rieb	riebe	gerieben	*to rub*
reißen	reißt	reiß(e)!	riß	risse	hat gerissen	*to tear* (tr.)
					ist gerissen	*to tear* (intr.)
reiten	reitet	reit(e)!	ritt	ritte	hat geritten	*to ride* (a horse) (tr.)
					ist geritten	*to ride* (on a horse) (intr.)
rennen	rennt	renn(e)!	rannte	rennte	hat gerannt	*to run, thrust* (tr.)[1]
					ist gerannt	*to run, race* (intr.)
riechen	riecht	riech(e)!	roch	röche	gerochen	*to smell*
ringen	ringt	ring(e)!	rang	ränge	gerungen	*to wrestle, struggle*
rinnen	rinnt	rinn(e)!	rann	ränne	ist geronnen	*to flow, trickle*
rufen	ruft	ruf(e)!	rief	riefe	gerufen	*to call*
salzen	salzt	salz(e)!	salzte	salzte	gesalzen	*to salt*
saufen	säuft	sauf(e)!	soff	söffe	gesoffen	*to drink* (of animals), *to booze*
saugen	saugt	saug(e)!	sog	söge	gesogen	*to suck*[2]
schaffen	schafft	schaff(e)!	schuf	schüfe	geschaffen	*to create*[3]
schallen: see erschallen						
scheiden	scheidet	scheid(e)!	schied	schiede	hat geschieden	*to separate* (tr.)
					ist geschieden	*to part (from), depart* (intr.)
scheinen	scheint	schein(e)!	schien	schiene	geschienen	*to shine; to seem*
schelten	schilt	schilt!	schalt	schölte	gescholten	*to scold*
scheren	schert	scher(e)!	schor	schöre	geschoren	*to shear*[4]
schieben	schiebt	schieb(e)!	schob	schöbe	geschoben	*to shove, push*
schießen	schießt	schieß(e)!	schoß	schösse	hat geschossen	*to shoot*
					ist geschossen	*to shoot, rush*[5]
schinden	schindet	schind(e)!	schund	schünde	geschunden	*to flay; to ill-treat, overwork*[6]

INFINITIVE	3rd. SING PRES. INDIC.	2nd SING. IMPERATIVE	IMPERF. INDIC.	IMPERF. SUBJ.	PAST PART.	MEANING
schlafen	schläft	schlaf(e)!	schlief	schliefe	geschlafen	to sleep
schlagen	schlägt	schlag(e)!	schlug	schlüge	geschlagen	to hit, beat
schleichen	schleicht	schleich(e)!	schlich	schliche	ist geschlichen	to creep
schleifen	schleift	schleif(e)!	schliff	schliffe	geschliffen	to grind, sharpen[7]
schließen	schließt	schließ(e)!	schloß	schlösse	geschlossen	to close
schlingen	schlingt	schling(e)!	schlang	schlänge	geschlungen	to wind, twine
schmeißen	schmeißt	schmeiß(e)!	schmiß	schmisse	geschmissen	to fling, chuck
schmelzen	schmilzt	schmilz!	schmolz	schmölze	hat geschmolzen ist geschmolzen	to melt (tr.) to melt (intr.)
schneiden	schneidet	schneid(e)!	schnitt	schnitte	geschnitten	to cut
schreiben	schreibt	schreib(e)!	schrieb	schriebe	geschrieben	to write
schreien	schreit	schrei(e)!	schrie	schriee	geschrie(e)n	to shout, scream
schreiten	schreitet	schreit(e)!	schritt	schritte	ist geschritten	to stride
schweigen	schweigt	schweig(e)!	schwieg	schwiege	geschwiegen	to be silent
schwellen	schwillt	schwill!	schwoll	schwölle	ist geschwollen	to swell (intr.)[8]
schwimmen	schwimmt	schwimm(e)!	schwamm	schwömme	ist geschwommen	to swim
schwinden	schwindet	schwind(e)!	schwand	schwände	ist geschwunden	to contract, disappear[9]
schwingen	schwingt	schwing(e)!	schwang	schwänge	geschwungen	to swing, brandish
schwören	schwört	schwör(e)!	schwor	schwüre	geschworen	to swear, vow[10]
sehen	sieht	sieh(e)!	sah	sähe	gesehen, sehen	to see
sein	ist	sei!	war	wäre	ist gewesen	to be

[1] e.g. Er hat ihm den Degen durch den Leib gerannt; er hat ihn zu Boden gerannt *he ran him down.*

[2] commoner weak.

[3] schaffen *to work, to be busy; to convey* is weak.

[4] scheren *to concern* and sich scheren (um) *to clear off, depart; to bother about* are weak, e.g. Was scherte das den Beamten? *What did that matter to the official?*

[5] e.g. Das Blut ist ihm ins Gesicht geschossen; er ist aus dem Zimmer geschossen.

[6] The imperfect is rarely used.

[7] schleifen *to drag; to raze to the ground* is weak.

[8] schwellen (tr.) is weak e.g. Der Wind schwellte die Segel.

[9] e.g. Holz schwindet beim Trocknen (Du. Stil.). For 'to disappear' verschwinden is commoner.

[10] regionally also weak; imperf. indic. also schwur (obsolescent).

INFINITIVE	3rd SING. PRES. INDIC.	2nd SING. IMPERATIVE	IMPERF. INDIC.	IMPERF. SUBJ.	PAST PART.	MEANING
senden	sendet	send(e)!	sandte / sendete	sendete	gesandt / gesendet	to send[1]
sieden	siedet	sied(e)!	sott	sötte	gesotten	to boil (tr.)[2]
singen	singt	sing(e)!	sang	sänge	gesungen	to sing
sinken	sinkt	sink(e)!	sank	sänke	ist gesunken	to sink (intr.)[3]
sinnen	sinnt	sinn(e)!	sann	sänne	gesonnen	to meditate[4]
sitzen	sitzt	sitz(e)!	saß	säße	gesessen	to sit
sollen	soll		sollte	sollte	gesollt, sollen	am to
spalten	spaltet	spalt(e)!	spaltete	spaltete	hat gespalten / ist gespalten	to split, cleave (tr.)[5] / to split, divide (intr.)
speien	speit	spei(e)!	spie	spie	gespie(e)n	to spit, spew[6]
spinnen	spinnt	spinn(e)!	spann	spönne	gesponnen	to spin
sprechen	spricht	sprich!	sprach	spräche	gesprochen	to speak
sprießen	sprießt	sprieß(e)!	sproß	sprösse	ist gesprossen	to sprout
springen	springt	spring(e)!	sprang	spränge	ist gesprungen	to jump
stechen	sticht	stich!	stach	stäche	gestochen	to prick, sting
stecken	steckt	steck(e)!	steckte	steckte / stäke	gesteckt	to be (fixed) in a place[7]
stehen	steht	steh(e)!	stand	(stände) / stünde	gestanden	to stand
stehlen	stiehlt	stiehl!	stahl	stähle	gestohlen	to steal[8]
steigen	steigt	steig(e)!	stieg	stiege	ist gestiegen	to climb (intr.), rise[9]
sterben	stirbt	stirb!	starb	stürbe	ist gestorben	to die
stieben	stiebt	stieb(e)!	stob	stöbe	ist gestoben	to fly up (like dust)[10]
stinken	stinkt	stink(e)!	stank	stänke	ist gestunken	to stink
stoßen	stößt	stoß(e)!	stieß	stieße	hat gestoßen / ist gestoßen (auf)	to knock, thrust / to encounter, come across[11]
streichen	streicht	streich(e)!	strich	striche	hat gestrichen / ist gestrichen	to run one's hand over; to spread (butter, bread)[12] / to roam, pass over[13]
(sich) streiten	streitet	streit(e)!	stritt	stritte	gestritten	to quarrel, contend

INFINITIVE	3rd SING. PRES. INDIC.	2nd SING. IMPERATIVE	IMPERF. INDIC.	IMPERF. SUBJ.	PAST PART.	MEANING
tragen	trägt	trag(e)!	trug	trüge	getragen	to carry; to wear
treffen	trifft	triff!	traf	träfe	getroffen	to meet; to hit (e.g. a target)
treiben	treibt	treib(e)!	trieb	triebe	hat getrieben	to drive (e.g. cattle); to pursue (an activity)
					ist getrieben	to drift (intr.)
treten	tritt	tritt!	trat	träte	hat getreten	e.g. to kick[14]
					ist getreten	to tread, step, come etc.[14]
trinken	trinkt	trink(e)!	trank	tränke	getrunken	to drink
tun	tut	tu(e)!	tat	täte	getan	to do
verderben	verdirbt	verdirb!	verdarb	verdürbe	hat verdorben	to spoil, ruin (tr.)[15]
					ist verdorben	to spoil, go bad (intr.)
verdrießen	verdrießt	verdrieß(e)!	verdroß	verdrösse	verdrossen	to vex
vergessen	vergißt	vergiß!	vergaß	vergäße	vergessen	to forget
verlieren	verliert	verlier(e)!	verlor	verlöre	verloren	to lose
verschallen: see 'erschallen'						

[1] The forms 'sandte, gesandt' are commoner, but 'sendete, gesendet' *must* be used in the sense of to broadcast by radio, e.g. Das heutige Konzert wird gesendet. 'schicken' is the commoner word for 'to send'.

[2] also weak; only weak when intr.; 'kochen' is commoner for both uses.

[3] There is one transitive use: Man *hat* im Bergwerk einen neuen Schacht gesunken *A new shaft has been sunk in the mine*. To sink (a ship) = versenken (wk.).

[4] elev.; nach-sinnen (über), also rather literary, is commoner.

[5] past part. also gespaltet, e.g. Die Partei hatte sich in zwei Teile gespaltet.

[6] The normal word is spucken (wk.).

[7] stak is literary; stecken *to put* is exclusively weak.

[8] to steal, creep=sich stehlen.

[9] to climb, ascend (tr.) = besteigen.

[10] e.g. Die Funken sind zum Himmel gestoben (Du. Haupt.)

[11] e.g. Wir sind auf den Feind/auf Schwierigkeiten gestoßen; also with 'sein' in the sense of 'to join up with': Unser Regiment ist zur Hauptarmee gestoßen.

[12] also: *to cross out, cancel, paint*; for constructions and further meanings, see dictionary.

[13] e.g. Die Vögel sind über das Land gestrichen.

[14] see 350 vi.

[15] verderbt (adj.) *corrupt, depraved*. To spoil, pamper=verwöhnen (wk.).

Infinitive	3rd. sing Pres. Indic.	2nd. sing. Imperative	Imperf. Indic.	Imperf. Subj.	Past Part.	Meaning
verziehen	verzeiht	verzeih(e)!	verzieh	verziehe	verziehen	to pardon
wachsen	wächst	wachs(e)!	wuchs	wüchse	ist gewachsen	to grow (intr.)[1]
wägen	wägt	wäg(e)!	wog	wöge	gewogen	to weigh (one's words)[2]
waschen	wäscht	wasch(e)!	wusch	wüsche	gewaschen	to wash (tr.)
weben	webt	web(e)!	wob	wöbe	gewoben	to weave[3]
weichen	weicht	weich(e)!	wich	wiche	ist gewichen	to yield, give way
weisen	weist	weis(e)!	wies	wiese	gewiesen	to point, show[4]
wenden	wendet	wend(e)!	{ wandte / wendete	wendete	gewandt / gewendet }	to turn[5]
werben	wirbt	wirb!	warb	würbe	geworben	to recruit; für: to canvass for; um: to woo
werden	wird	werde!	wurde[6]	würde	ist geworden	to become
werfen	wirft	wirf!	warf	würfe	geworfen	to throw
wiegen	wiegt	wieg(e)!	wog	wöge	gewogen	to weigh[7]
winden	windet	wind(e)!	wand	wände	gewunden	to wind, twist
wissen	weiß	wisse!	wußte	wüßte	gewußt	to know (facts, e.g. date, rule, name, answer, the way, that . . .)
wollen	will	wolle!	wollte	wollte	gewollt, wollen	to want (to)
ziehen	zieht	zieh(e)!	zog	zöge	hat gezogen / ist gezogen	to pull / to go, pass; to move[8]
zwingen	zwingt	zwing(e)!	zwang	zwänge	gezwungen	to force

[1] wachsen to smear with wax is weak; to grow is weak; to grow (tr.) = an-bauen (e.g. Kartoffeln), züchten (e.g. Rosen).
[2] sometimes weak; for 'to weigh up, consider', use 'erwägen', exc. Erst wägen, dann wagen Look before you leap.
[3] generally weak in current usage.
[4] for further meanings and constructions, see dictionary.
[5] The forms 'wandte, gewandt' are commoner, also with prefixes. Main exceptions: 1. Er wendete den Anzug, das Auto, den Braten, das Heu 2. Der Bus, das Schiff hat gewendet 3. Das Glück, die Lage, das Wetter, der Wind hat sich gewendet 4. entwenden to purloin, verwenden to use.
[6] The sing. forms ich ward, du wardst, er ward are archaic and poetic.
[7] wiegen (wk.) = to rock (e.g. a baby).
[8] e.g. Die Truppen zogen durch die Stadt; er ist nach Berlin gezogen.

E. THE USE OF THE TENSES

352. Scheme of the German tenses and their English equivalents
(This is modified and completed in the paragraphs that follow. It will be noted that there is no continuous form in German).

Active

PRESENT
ich schreibe — *I write / I am writing*

IMPERFECT
ich schrieb — *I wrote / I was writing*

PERFECT
ich habe geschrieben — *I wrote / I have written / I have been writing*

PLUPERFECT
ich hatte geschrieben — *I had written / I had been writing*

FUTURE
ich werde schreiben — *I shall write / I shall be writing*

FUTURE PERFECT
ich werde geschrieben haben — *I shall have written / I shall have been writing*

CONDITIONAL
ich würde schreiben — *I would write / I would be writing*

CONDITIONAL PERFECT
ich würde geschrieben haben — *I would have written / I would have been writing*

Passive

PRESENT
ich werde gestört — *I am disturbed / I am being disturbed*

IMPERFECT
ich wurde gestört — *I was disturbed / I was being disturbed*

PERFECT
ich bin gestört worden — *I was disturbed / I have been disturbed*

PLUPERFECT
ich war gestört worden — *I had been disturbed*

FUTURE
ich werde gestört werden — *I shall be disturbed*

(FUTURE PERFECT
ich werde gestört worden sein — *I shall have been disturbed*)

CONDITIONAL
ich würde gestört werden — *I would be disturbed*

CONDITIONAL PERFECT
   ich würde gestört worden sein   *I would have been disturbed*

353. The rendering of the English continuous form

(a) Frequently, no special device is required:

Was hast du heute morgen getan?	*What have you been doing this morning?*
Ich habe Briefe geschrieben	*I've been writing letters*
Ich werde heute fortwährend gestört	*I'm constantly being disturbed today*

(b) If it is desired to emphasize the continuous nature of an activity, various means are available:

  i the insertion of gerade or eben *just*:

Ich schreibe eben Briefe	*I'm writing letters*

  ii (gerade or eben) dabei sein zu + infin.:

Ich bin gerade dabei, ein bißchen aufzuräumen	*I'm tidying up a bit*

  iii beim (or am) + infinitive used as a noun; when the verb has an object, this construction is only occasionally possible, and never when it has an adverbial qualification:

Als ihr Mann zurückkam, war sie beim/am Kochen (Briefeschreiben)	*When her husband returned, she was cooking (writing letters)*
Es ist immer noch am Regnen[1]	*It's still raining*

  iv begriffen sein in + dat.:

Ich war gerade im Anziehen begriffen, als er anrief	*I was just dressing when he rang up*

  v Other insertions will suggest themselves to fit the context, e.g.

Ich habe ihn letzthin (*recently*) zweimal in der Woche getroffen	*I've been meeting him twice a week*

354. Four special uses of the Present

(a) In describing a state or activity beginning in the past and still continuing (e.g. Ich warte seit zwanzig Minuten *I've been waiting for twenty minutes*; ich kenne ihn schon lange); see 532(b), 554.

(b) The historic present, sometimes sustained over many pages, is commoner in German than in English:

Mit zuckenden Nerven marschieren sie näher, noch immer versuchen sie sich gegenseitig zu täuschen, so sehr sie alle schon die Wahrheit wissen: daß die Norweger, daß Amundsen ihnen zuvorgekommen ist. Bald zerbricht der letzte Zweifel ... (Stefan Zweig: *Der Kampf um den Südpol* in *Sternstunden der Menschheit*)

Compare its effective colloquial use: Ich ging gestern ins Café—auf einmal, da seh' ich meinen Vetter.

(c) As in English, the present is the accepted tense for summaries of plays or stories and for 'history notes'.

(d) The use of 'ich komme' for English 'I have come' in sentences such as the following deserves mention:[2]

Ich komme die Miete zu bezahlen	*I've come to pay the rent*

---

[1] beim is not used with Regnen, Schneien, Frieren etc.
[2] cf. Collinson, op. cit., p. 80.

355. Present and Future[1]

(a) The future tense is relatively little used in German; where a time phrase or the context shows that the future is referred to, the present tense is preferred; the future is, as it were, experienced as if it were the present:

Ich gehe nächstes Jahr nach Amerika	*I'm going to America next year*
Morgen um diese Zeit bin ich in Wien	*This time tomorrow I shall be in Vienna*
Ich bin gleich fertig	*I'll be ready in a moment*
Er findet uns nie	*He will never find us*
Ich weiß, was wir machen	*I know what we'll do*
Also, du holst mich um 7 Uhr ab	*Well then, you'll call for me at 7 o'clock*
(Es) wird gemacht	*It shall be done*

(b) Where the present is thus used in a sub. clause + a main clause or in a series of sentences, the effect can be particularly vivid:

Wenn Sie herauskommen (*when you come out of prison*), nimmt kein Hund ein Stück Brot von Ihnen, Ihre Kinder kennen Sie nicht mehr. Sie sind dann eine alte Frau (W. Schreyer).

(c) The future tense may be used to underline the contrast between present and future:

Nächstes Jahr wird alles besser sein	*Next year everything will be better*

(d) The future tense may be used to express the speaker's intention:[2]

Ich werde es ihm morgen bestimmt sagen	*I'll tell him tomorrow without fail*

(e) A series of future tenses has emphatic or prophetic force:

Ich werde nicht mehr wie ein Irrer durch die Welt laufen. Ich werde nicht mehr eifersüchtig sein (Ch. Wolf).

(f) For the use of the future tense to express probability and as an imperative equivalent, see 358 and 459(b) respectively.

356. Two special uses of the Imperfect

(a) In describing a state or activity beginning in the past and still continuing at a more recent point in the past (e.g. Ich wartete schon seit zwei Stunden *I had been waiting for two hours*); see 532(c) and 554 N.iv.

(b) It is occasionally used in the course of a narrative in the past to point into the future; the conditional is the more usual tense:

Die Felsennase raste auf mich zu. Sekunden noch, dann überrollte und begrub uns die Lawine (K. Mundstock)[3]	*The sharp crag was rushing towards me. A few more seconds and the avalanche would roll over us and bury us*

357. Imperfect and Perfect

(a) Apart from sentences with 'since' or its equivalent (see 354(a)), the

---

[1] This paragraph owes much to an article 'Präsens oder Futur' (*Deutsch als Fremdsprache* 2/1967) by W. A. Sherebkow, including the examples in (b) and (e).
[2] cf. Schulz-Griesbach, op. cit., B 564.
[3] from Pawel Petkov: Futurische Verhältnisse im präteritalen Zeitplan (*Deutsch als Fremdsprache* 3/1969).

English forms 'I have done, I have been doing, he has done, he has been doing etc.' are rendered by the German perfect.

But the simplest past form (he did, he wrote etc.) may be either imperfect or perfect, depending on the context and the distinctive character of the two tenses.

(b) **The imperfect is used to record events or scenes belonging definitively to the past and without reference to the present; it is the staple narrative tense of German fiction.** E.g.

Es klingelte. Sie öffnete ihm die Tür. Er stand da, der Knecht Persenning, und starrte sie an. Seine Kopfschmerzen schwanden augenblicklich. Sie nickte mit dem Kopf, trat zur Seite und sagte dann: 'Bitte sehr, mein Herr.' (W. Altendorf)

(c) **The perfect looks back from the present into the past** or, to put it differently, **it links up the past with the present.** From this stem its two main uses:

i **It is used to record past events whose influence extends into the present:**

Er [Lessing] hat der deutschen Dichtung nicht nur ihre ersten unsterblichen Dramen, sondern auch der deutschen Prosa Klarheit und Beweglichkeit, Stil geschenkt. (H. Röhl: *Wörterbuch zur deutschen Literatur*, 1931)

ii **It is the predominant past tense of German conversation and, to a lesser extent, of German letter-writing.** (It particularly preponderates in South Germany):

Mutter, es hat geklopft	*Mother, there was a knock at the door*
Ich habe neulich Ihren Bruder gesehen	*I saw your brother the other day*[1]
Wo haben Sie ihn gesehen?	*Where did you see him?*
Lieber Karl!	*Dear Karl,*
Wir sind gestern nachmittag hier angekommen und Peter hat sofort gebadet	*We arrived here yesterday afternoon and Peter immediately went for a bathe*

(d) This fundamental difference between the imperfect and the perfect is stated in different terms by H. T. Betteridge in two articles on 'The Preterite (=Imperfect) and the Perfect in Modern German',[2] in which he stresses 'the essentially subjective notion underlying the perfect tense', while 'The preterite is the more "objective" tense'.

To quote one of H. T. Betteridge's illustrations, it is the subjective element which explains the use of the perfect in the following: 'Für dasselbe haben meine Väter den Kopf auf den Henkerblock legen müssen' (G. von le Fort).

(e) The perfect may be used to record a habitual or repeated action in the past as well as a state or condition, though for the latter the imperfect is commoner and safer:

Wenn das Wetter schön war, habe ich früher nach dem Mittagessen einen Spaziergang gemacht	*When the weather was fine, I used to go for a walk after lunch*

---

[1] Significantly, a German speaking imperfect English will say: I have seen your brother the other day.

[2] *Modern Languages*, December 1958 and March 1959.

Ich habe ihn früher gekannt	*I used to know him*
Das Haus hat schrecklich ausgesehen	*The house looked awful*

(f) In North Germany, even in conversation, the imperfect is by no means unidiomatic, while its greater brevity is a merit. In practice, **German conversation (and letter-writing) is often an unthinking mixture of the two tenses, in which an instinctive sense of rhythm plays its part**: Als ich nach Hause kam, hab' ich zu Abend gegessen und hab' noch ein paar Briefe geschrieben; dann ging ich früh zu Bett, aber ich konnte nicht schlafen.

(g) In certain domains the imperfect is used where one would expect the perfect:

Sie sahen soeben . . .	*You have just seen . . .* (on TV)
Wilson selbst übernahm die Gesamtverantwortung für das Wirtschaftsministerium (from 'Informationen', a summary of the past week's news in *Die Zeit*)	*Wilson himself has assumed overall responsibility for the Department of Economic Affairs*

In headlines it has the obvious merit of brevity:

Zug raste in Arbeitskolonne: 5 Tote (*Bild-Zeitung*)	*Train hurtles into gang of workmen—5 dead*

358. A special use of the Future and Future Perfect: to express a supposition or probability:

Er ist nicht gekommen; er wird wieder zu viel zu tun haben	*He hasn't come; presumably he's again got too much to do*
Er wird den Zug verpaßt haben	*He's probably missed the train*

359. Apart from the use indicated in 358, the future perfect is relatively rare; in conversation it is frequently rendered by the perfect:

Bis morgen um diese Zeit habe ich alles geregelt	*By this time tomorrow I shall have settled everything*

Compare the use of the perfect in both languages in e.g.

Wenn ich von ihm gehört habe, werde ich dir schreiben	*When I've heard from him, I'll write to you*

360. For the use of **the conditional and conditional perfect**, see 462 f., 466, 473, 479 ff.

For the use of **the subjunctive tenses**, see 460 ff.

F. THE USE OF THE PASSIVE[1]

361. Paragraphs 354(a) and (b), 355(a) and 356(a) apply equally to the passive voice

Present (or imperf.) tense in a sentence with 'seit':

Diese Sache wird schon seit Wochen erörtert	*This matter has been under discussion for weeks*

[1] see also 381, 419, 432, 496.

Present tense with future meaning:

Ich werde nächsten Montag benachrichtigt	*I shall be informed next Monday*

The conversational preference for the perfect (357(c)ii) applies less to the passive, where the shorter imperfect (Ich wurde gestern von meinem Neffen besucht) is preferred.

362. The cumbersome **Future Perfect Passive** exists in theory, but is virtually never used, e.g.

Bis sieben Uhr wird man mich von dem Ergebnis benachrichtigen	*By seven o'clock I shall have been informed of the result*

363. The equally cumbersome **Conditional Perfect Passive** is used rather more, in conjunction with conditional clauses, though the alternative tense, the Pluperfect Subjunctive, will generally be preferred (see 462):

Ich wäre gestört worden *I would have been disturbed*, instead of: Ich würde gestört worden sein.

In a subordinate clause, these forms would run: obwohl ich gestört worden wäre, and: obwohl ich gestört worden sein würde.

364. While the passive is used less in German than in English, sentences like the following, which could obviously be turned into the active, are completely convincing in their passive form:

Dieses Haus wurde von Studenten gebaut	*This house was built by students*
Das Hotel ist anscheinend seit Jahren nicht angestrichen worden	*The hotel can't have been painted for years*

A preference for the active form, with or without 'man', is perhaps strongest in the future:

Natürlich wird man ihn kritisieren	*Of course he will be criticized*
Sogar seine Freunde werden ihn kritisieren	*He will be criticized even by his friends*

365. Constructions where the passive is used in English but cannot be used in German:

Ein Vorbeigehender sah ihn in das Haus einbrechen	*He was seen breaking into the house by a passer-by*
Man hörte ihn singen	*He was heard singing*
Man fand ihn auf dem Fußboden liegen	*He was found lying on the floor*
Er ist bekanntlich unzuverlässig	*He is known to be unreliable*
Man glaubt, er ist verreist	*He is thought to have gone away*
	It is thought that he has gone away

366. Some substitutes for the passive:

(a) man (one, someone, cf. Fr. 'on') + active:

Man hatte ihn davor gewarnt	*He had been warned about it*
Das macht man nicht	*It isn't done*

(b) verloren-gehen *to be lost, to get lost*:
Der Schlüssel ist verlorengegangen   *The key has been lost*

(c) Verbs used reflexively with an inanimate subject:
Das lernt sich rasch   *That is quickly learnt*
Das erklärt sich leicht   *That is easily explained*
Der Schlüssel hat sich gefunden   *The key has been found*
Mein Verdacht hat sich bestätigt   *My suspicion has been confirmed*

(d) bekommen or kriegen (coll.) + past part. is the German equivalent of
    an analogous English alternative for a direct passive:
Ich bekomme/kriege das Geld   *I have the money paid out to me*
  regelmäßig ausgezahlt   *regularly*
Wir haben viel gezeigt bekommen   *We had a lot shown to us, we were*
                                              shown a lot

(e) A noun with a verbal content introduced by a suitable verb:[1]
seine Vollendung finden (for 'vollendet werden') *to be completed.*
eine große Vereinfachung erfahren *to be greatly simplified* (for 'sehr vereinfacht
  werden')
eine Veränderung erleiden   *to be changed*
zur Erörterung gelangen   *to be discussed*

For some comments on Nominalstil (i.e. a current preference for nouns
as opposed to verbs and clauses), of which these phrases are examples,
see Du. Haupt., pp. 456 f. and Moeller, op. cit., pp. 53 ff., 65 ff. and
115 ff.; see also 404 in this book.

367. 'Das Zustandspassiv'[2]

(a) A distinction must be made between the true passive, with its stress
    on the action, and the resultant state, expressed by 'sein' (not
    'werden'); the past part. is here a complement:
Der Tisch wird gedeckt   *The table is being laid*
Der Tisch ist gedeckt   *The table is laid*
Die Stadt wurde allmählich von   *The town was gradually surrounded by*
  Truppen umringt   *troops*
Die Stadt war von Truppen umringt   *The town was surrounded with troops*
Dieser Bericht ist von einem   *This report is written by a friend of*
  Freund von mir geschrieben   *mine*
Früher waren die zwei Teiche   *Formerly the two ponds had been*
  verbunden gewesen   *connected*

(b) Sometimes the right choice is less clear:
Die zwei Dörfer werden (coll. sind)   *The two villages are separated by a wood*
  durch einen Wald getrennt
Dort werden Mechaniker gebraucht   *Mechanics are required there*
  (J. Ziem)
Ich war die ganze Zeit versucht,   *The whole time I was tempted to help him*
  ihm zu helfen
Das will überlegt sein   *That needs thinking about*
Der Schreiber war bald festgestellt   *The writer was soon identified*
  (A. Goes) (more incisive than
  imperf. or pluperf. passive)

---

[1] The first three examples are taken from an article by Herbert Kolb in *Sprache im tech-nischen Zeitalter*, 19/1966.
[2] Cf. *Modern Languages*, June 1983, pp. 110–13.

(c) **was born**: a serviceable rule is to use 'ist geboren' of the living and 'wurde (or: war) geboren' of the dead:

Wann sind Sie geboren?   *When were you born?*
Ich bin 1940 geboren   *I was born in 1940*
Goethe wurde/war 1749 geboren   *Goethe was born in 1749*

G. VERBS WITH PREFIXES:
INSEPARABLE, SEPARABLE, DOUBLE, VARIABLE

368. The 8 Inseparable Prefixes:

be- emp- ent- er- ge- miß-[1] ver- zer-

Characteristics:
(a) In contrast with the separable prefixes, none of these exists as an independent word.
(b) They are never separated from the stem of the verb.
(c) They never carry the stress.
(d) A verb with an insep. prefix has no ge- in the past part.: besuchen: besucht.

EXAMPLES:
beeinflussen *to influence*, entkommen *to escape*, erröten *to blush*, geleiten *to escort*, zerreißen *to tear to pieces*

The force of the insep. prefixes is treated in 677 ff.

369. Separable Prefixes:

All prefixes other than the 8 insep. prefixes are, or—in the case of the 9 variable prefixes—may be, separable.

Characteristics:

(a) In contrast with the insep. prefixes, these are words with a meaning, the majority being independent parts of speech as well as prefixes, e.g. prepositions (aus-gehen *to go out*), adverbs (dazwischen-treten *to intervene*), nouns (teil-nehmen *to take part*), adjectives (frei-lassen *to release*), infinitives (spazieren-gehen *to go for a walk*).
Only a few are meaningless except as prefixes: danieder-, ein-, einher-, hernieder-, herzu-, hintan-, hinzu-, inne-, umhin-.
For the 3 types of sep. prefix and for the individual prefixes, see 692 ff.

(b) A sep. prefix always carries the main stress. Nouns formed from these verbs are likewise accented on the prefix: der Abflug, die Voraùssage.

(c) Position of a sep. prefix, illustrated by 'aus-gehen':
 i It stands at the end of the sentence in the imperative, and in the present and imperfect tenses except in a subordinate clause; here the verb itself comes last, forming one word with the prefix:[2] Gehen Sie früh aus! Er geht (ging) früh aus. Obwohl er früh ausgeht (ausging), . . .

---

[1] miß- does not entirely qualify as an insep. prefix; it is fully treated in 691.
[2] Exc. Indirect Statements and other noun clauses without 'daß'; here normal order is used: Er sagte (ich glaubte), er gehe früh aus (cf. 484(b)).

ii It precedes the ge- of the past part., which is written as one word: Er ist früh ausgegangen.

iii Where the infinitive is used with 'zu', the latter comes between the sep. prefix and the simple verb, the whole being written as one word: um auszugehen.

iv Present part.: ausgehend.

370. Double Prefixes:

When a sep. prefix is attached to a verb with an insep. prefix, the verb is treated as separable, except that there is no ge- in the past part. Thus the principal parts of an-vertrauen *to entrust* are:

anvertrauen – vertraut an – vertraute an – anvertraut

Infin. with 'zu': um es mir anzuvertrauen.
Pres. tense in sub. clause: wenn er es mir anvertraut, . . .
Imperative: Vertraue es mir an!

Further common examples:
an-erkennen *to acknowledge*
aus-verkaufen *to sell out* (one's stock)
bei-behalten *to keep on, retain* (e.g. a high standard of living, an old custom)
vor-enthalten *to withhold*

Note:

i In modern German some verbs with double prefixes are sometimes treated as inseparable verbs (though not in the infinitive) with the effect of a certain incisiveness. This occurs particularly: 1. when the insep. prefix is er- or ent- 2. in written rather than spoken German 3. in Swiss and Austrian authors. (cf. Du. Haupt. Verb 2d).

e.g. Das anerkannte Tuzzi voll und ganz (R. Musil, quoted by Duden)
Er vorenthält ihnen den Lohn, BUT: statt ihnen den Lohn vorzuenthalten.

ii The opposite combination, i.e. an insep. prefix attached to a verb with a sep. prefix, does not occur. What at first sight appear to be instances of it in reality consist of an insep. prefix attached to a compound noun or adjective to form an inseparable verb; such verbs are always weak. E.g.

beauftragen *to commission, instruct* formed from 'der Auftrag'
benachteiligen *to treat disadvantageously* formed from 'nachteilig'
veranlassen *to occasion, cause* formed from 'der Anlaß'

iii Regarding 'wieder' when prefixed to a verb with a sep. prefix, see 689(b)ii.

371. The 9 Variable Prefixes:

über	durch	voll	hinter
unter	um	wider	miß
		wieder	

Characteristics:

(a) These are sometimes sep., sometimes insep., and are correspondingly stressed or unstressed.

(b) über, unter, durch, voll, wider and hinter show the following tendencies:

i When the prefix is separable:

1. verb and prefix each retain their original meaning.
2. where the simple verb is intransitive, the compound verb is intransitive.

ii When the prefix is inseparable:

1. a derived or figurative meaning arises from the combination of verb and prefix.
2. even where the simple verb is intransitive, the compound verb is transitive.

These tendencies may be illustrated by some instances where a prefix is used both separably and inseparably with the same simple verb:

Das Obergeschoß steht etwas über	*The upper storey overhangs a bit*
Er übersteht alle Schwierigkeiten	*He surmounts all difficulties*
Ich hatte ihm eine Decke übergelegt	*I had put a rug over him*
Ich hatte mir die Sache überlegt	*I had considered the matter*
Ich fand ein Loch im Zaun und schaute durch	*I found a hole in the fence and looked through*
Ich schaute die Papiere durch	*I glanced through the papers*
Ich durchschaute ihn/seine Absichten	*I saw through him/his intentions*

The force of the variable prefixes is treated in 683 ff.

H. IMPERSONAL VERBS AND EXPRESSIONS

372. Introductory

(a) Impersonal verbs and expressions are of two kinds:

i **genuinely impersonal verbs and expressions** in which the 'es' cannot be equated with, or replaced by, a specific noun, a phrase or a clause, e.g. Es regnet; es fehlt mir an Geld; es ist mir warm; es graut mir vor Schlangen; es wurde mir schlecht; wie geht es Ihnen?

ii **pseudo-impersonal expressions**, in which the 'es' anticipates, or stands for, the real subject. Thus the sentences 'Es freut mich sehr, Sie wiederzusehen' and 'Es freut mich sehr, daß Sie wieder gekommen sind' could be recast in more emphatic form to read: 'Sie wiederzusehen freut mich sehr' and 'Daß Sie wieder gekommen sind, freut mich sehr'. Compare the following:

A.: Kurt hat das Examen bestanden.

B.: So? Es freut mich sehr, in which 'es' stands for 'daß er das Examen bestanden hat', and could be replaced by 'sein Erfolg'.

The 'es' may similarly be regarded as introductory when the expression is followed by a 'wenn' clause: Es würde mich freuen, wenn Sie morgen kämen.

In what follows, debatable cases have been classified as genuinely impersonal verbs.

(b) The main practical difficulty in connection with impersonal expressions of both the types mentioned in (a) above is that of the retention or omission of 'es' in a main clause beginning with something other than the 'es' and in a subordinate clause.

373. Impersonal verbs and expressions which never drop the 'es'

(a) weather phrases, e.g. es ist warm (kalt, kühl etc.) *it is warm (cold, cool etc.*): warm ist es heute; heute ist es warm; da es warm ist, . . . es wird warm *it is getting warm*, es ist Winter, es wird Winter *winter is coming on*, es dämmert 1. *it is dawning, growing light* 2. *it is growing dusk*, es donnert, es friert, es gießt *it is pouring*, es schneit.

(b) onomatopoeic verbs used impersonally, e.g. es klingelt *there's a ring*, es klopft *there's a knock*, es knallt *there's a report, a shot*, es läutet 1. *there's a ring* 2. *the bells are pealing*.

(c) fire and draught: Es brennt! es brennt in der Stadt; es zieht.

(d) **(S)** miscellaneous:

es fehlt mir an + dat.	*I lack*
es fehlt mir an Geld[1]	*I'm short of money*
es fragt sich, ob	*the question is whether*
es fügte sich, daß	*it so happened that*
es gefällt mir in Heidelberg/bei ihm	*I like it (I like being) in Heidelberg/at his place*
es geschieht Ihnen recht	*it serves you right*
Jetzt gilt es zu handeln	*Now the thing is to act*
es handelt sich um + acc.	*it is a question of* (Fr.: il s'agit de)
es hängt davon ab, ob	*it depends on whether*
es heißt (daß) (see N.i below)	*it is said (that)*
es kommt darauf an,[2] (ob)	*it depends (on whether)*
es kommt auf seine Reaktion an	*it depends on his reaction*
es kommt zu + dat.	*'it comes to', there occurs*, e.g.
Am Abend kam es zu neuen Zusammenstößen	*In the evening there were fresh clashes*
es liegt an + dat.	*it is due to*
woran liegt es, daß . . .?	*why is it that . . .?*
es macht (or: tut) nichts	*it doesn't matter*
es steht Ihnen frei, zu gehen oder zu bleiben	*you are free to go or stay*
es verhält sich	*it is (the case)*, e.g.
Ähnlich verhält es sich im Baugewerbe	*Things are similar in the building-trade*

Note:

i es heißt (daß) *it is said (that)*
   e.g. Es heißt, er wäre angekommen. Er ist nach Wien geflogen, heißt es.
cf. In der Erklärung heißt es, die   *In the declaration it says that the Federal*
   Bundesregierung werde . . . (*FAZ*)   *Government will . . .*
   „Schade!" hieß es überall   '*A pity,' people were saying everywhere*

Two idiomatic uses:
Wie heißt es doch im „Faust"?   *What's that bit in 'Faust'?*
Hier heißt es handeln   *Now the thing is to act*

---

[1] Compare: es fehlt mir das (nötige) Geld, um diese Reise zu machen *I haven't the (necessary) money to go on this journey*; contrast: es fehlt mir Geld *some of my money is missing*.
[2] Many idiomatic uses include: es kommt darauf an zu handeln *the thing is to act*; auf ein paar Mark (mehr oder weniger) kommt es mir nicht an *I don't mind a few marks more or less*.

ii In literary German, a wide range of verbs are used impersonally, generally conveying the feeling of an impersonal force at work (cf. 143(f)):

Anna stand am Fenster und schaute	*Anna stood at the window and gazed out.*
hinaus. Es wirbelte, wogte, es schlug	*There was a whirling and surging.*
den Schnee gegen das Glas, als	*The snow was beaten against the glass,*
wollte er alles zuschütten	*as if it would block up everything*
(G. Kölwel)	

374. Pseudo-impersonal expressions which never drop the 'es'

Es ist mir unangenehm, das zu	*It's disagreeable for me to do that/*
tun/daß er kommt	*that he's coming*

Mir ist es unangenehm/Unangenehm ist es mir, . . . Natürlich ist es mir
unangenehm, . . . Obwohl es mir unangenehm ist, . . .

es ärgert mich	*it annoys me*
es fällt mir leicht/schwer	*it is easy/difficult for me*
es fehlt nur noch, daß er auch krank ist[1]	*if he's ill too, it's the last straw*
es gelingt (glückt) mir	*I succeed*
es hat keinen Sinn/Zweck, das zu tun	*there is no point in doing that*
es ist (nicht) der Mühe wert	*it's (not) worth while*
est ist mir eine Freude	*it's a pleasure for me*
es ist ein Glück	*it's fortunate*
es ist eine Schande	*it's a disgrace (or shameful)*
es ist (mir) gleich,[2] ob er kommt oder nicht[3]	*it's all the same (to me) whether he comes or not*
es ist leicht/schwer[3]	*it's easy/difficult*
es ist möglich[3]	*it's possible*
es ist nötig	*it's necessary*
es ist (mir) peinlich	*it's embarrassing (for me)*
es ist mir recht	*I agree to it, I'm agreeable*
es ist schade	*it's a pity*
es ist (mir) wichtig[3]	*it's important for me*
es ist zu bedauern, zu befürchten, zu hoffen (etc.), daß[4]	*it is to be regretted, to be feared, to be hoped that*
es kann passieren, daß[3]	*it may happen that*
es läßt sich nicht bestreiten, daß[4]	*it cannot be denied that (or: the fact remains that)*
es liegt mir fern, Schwierigkeiten zu machen	*the last thing I want to do is to make difficulties*
es liegt nahe, daraus zu schließen, daß	*the obvious thing is to conclude that*
es lohnt sich (nicht)	*it's (not) worth while*
es macht mir Freude, das zu tun	*it gives me pleasure to do that*
es macht nichts aus	*it doesn't matter*
es macht mir Spaß	*it amuses me (or: I enjoy)*
es mißlingt (mißglückt) mir	*I fail*
es spricht sich herum, daß	*the word is going round that*
es stellt sich heraus, daß[3]	*it turns out that*
es versteht sich von selbst, daß	*it goes without saying that*
es ziemt sich nicht	*it's not fitting*

---

[1] The 'es' may be omitted with inversion. [2] for variants of 'gleich', see 117: gleich. [3] The 'es' is sometimes omitted with inversion. [4] The 'es' may be omitted except in normal order.

375. **With the following impersonal and pseudo-impersonal expressions, if, in a main clause, the personal pronoun (other than 'sie' or 'Sie') is placed first, the 'es' is often omitted**; in most cases, its retention, especially in the form 's, is colloquially more usual, while its omission is more literary and sometimes old-fashioned; with a noun, the 'es' is usually retained.

Es ist mir warm	*I am feeling warm*
Mir ist/ist's warm	
Es ist meinem Vater warm	*My father is feeling warm*
Meinem Vater ist es/ist's warm	
Mich hat('s) gewundert/Meinen Bruder hat es/hat's gewundert, daß sie nichts gesagt hat	*I was surprised/My brother was surprised that she didn't say anything*

impersonal:

es graut mir vor + dat.	*I have a horror of* (e.g. snakes)
es ist mir, als ob	*I feel as if, it seems to me that*
es ist mir kalt, es friert mich	*I am feeling cold*[1]
es kommt mir vor, als ob	*it seems to me as if*
es schaudert mir[2] bei dem Gedanken/ wenn ich daran denke	*I shudder at the thought/ when I think of it*
es scheint mir, daß/als ob	*it seems to me that/as if*
es wird mir warm/kalt	*I am getting warm/cold*

pseudo-impersonal:

es enttäuscht mich, daß	*I am disappointed that*
es erstaunt mich, daß	*I am astonished that*
es fällt mir auf, daß	*it strikes me as strange that*
es freut mich, daß/zu + infin.	*I am glad that/to*
es interessiert mich, daß/zu + inf.	*I am interested that/to*
es ist mir lieb, daß	*I am glad* (lit.: *it is agreeable to me*) *that*
es tut/es ist mir leid, daß	*I am sorry that*

Note:

i With some of the above expressions the 'es' is not infrequently omitted in cases other than that mentioned in the rubric.

E.g. Wenn (es) dir zu warm ist, ziehe die Jacke aus.
  Natürlich graut (es) mir vor Schlangen.
  Obwohl (es) mich interessieren würde, ihn zu sehen, . . .
BUT: Obwohl es mich enttäuschen würde, ihn nicht zu sehen.
Some 'Sprachgefühl' is here desirable.

ii es hungert mich (mich hungert) and es dürstet mich (mich dürstet) belong here, but are obsolete, poetic and biblical; modern usage: ich bin hungrig/durstig or ich habe Hunger/Durst.

376. **The following impersonal expressions usually drop the 'es', except:** i in normal order.
  ii when applied to a noun in a direct question.
  iii when applied to a proper name.

---

[1] also: ich friere.
[2] slightly less common: es schaudert mich.

Es ist mir (nicht) wohl[1]	*I am (not) well*
Gestern war meinem Bruder nicht wohl	*Yesterday my brother wasn't well*
Gestern war es Karl nicht wohl	*Yesterday Karl wasn't well*
weil meinem Bruder nicht wohl ist	*because my brother isn't well*
War dir nicht wohl?	*Weren't you well?*
War es deinem Bruder nicht wohl?	*Wasn't your brother well?*

es ist mir besser	*I'm feeling better*
es ist (or wird) mir schlecht	*I feel sick*
es ist (or wird) mir übel	*I don't feel well*
es ist mir gut zumute[2]	*I'm in good spirits*
es träumt mir von + dat./daß[3]	*I dream about/that*

377. In the following expressions the 'es' is omitted except in normal order:

Es steht in der Zeitung, daß . . .	*It says in the paper that . . .*
Gestern stand in der Zeitung, daß . . .	*Yesterday it said in the paper that . . .*
Obwohl in der Zeitung steht, daß . . .	*Although it says in the paper that . . .*

es fällt mir ein, daß	*it occurs to me that*
es liegt mir viel/wenig/nichts daran (dies zu tun)	*I attach great/little/no importance to it (to doing this)*
es ist mir viel/wenig/nichts daran gelegen (dies zu tun)	

378. Impersonal expressions with 'gehen'; 'es' is always retained:

es geht	1. *it can be done*
	2. *so so; pretty well*
es geht nicht	*it can't be done*
es wird schon gehen	*it will be all right*
es wäre auch ohne ihn gegangen	*we could have managed without him*
so geht es im Leben	*such is life*
aber wie es so geht	*but as is so often the case*
Wie geht es Ihnen?[4]	*How are you?*
Es geht mir gut, danke[4]	*I'm all right, thank you*
Jetzt geht es wieder	*I'm better again now*
wie wird mir's gehen?	*how shall I fare?*
es ist mir geradeso gegangen	*the same thing happened in my case*
wenn es nach mir ginge	*if I had my way*
es geht um Leben und Tod	*it's a matter of life and death*
es geht um seine ganze Zukunft	*his whole future is at stake*
Mit dem Zug geht's freilich schneller	*Certainly it's quicker by train*
Wo geht's nach Osnabrück?	*Which is the way to Osnabrück?*
Heute geht's nach Freiburg	*Today I'm (we're) going to Freiburg*

---

[1] used more negatively than affirmatively; cf. the more colloquial: es ist mir nicht gut.
[2] 'gut' can be replaced by e.g. schlecht, sonderbar, traurig.
[3] elev.; normal usage: ich träumte von/daß.
[4] more colloquial: Wie geht's? Gut, danke.

Note: Other verbs with numerous impersonal uses are an-kommen, gelten, kommen, stehen; with few exceptions, the 'es' is always retained.

379. **In spoken German, the 'es' of a number of the impersonal expressions listed in the preceding paragraphs is often omitted or slurred in normal order.** Such are:

Es ist warm (kalt) heute, es geschieht dir recht, es macht (tut) nichts, es kommt darauf an, es hängt davon ab, es scheint mir, daß . . ., es kommt mir vor, als ob . . ., es freut mich, daß . . ., es ist mir lieb, es tut mir leid, es ist mir leid, es geht nicht, es geht mir gut (schlecht); and all those in 374 beginning with 'es ist'. E.g.

Is' warm heute	*It's warm today*
„Scheint so“, sagt Pinneberg. „Fragt sich nur wie lange.“ (H. Fallada)	*'It seems so', says Pinneberg. 'The question is only for how long'*
Freut mich sehr	*I'm very glad*

380. **A reflexive impersonal construction,** generalizing an activity; the 'es' always remains. E.g.

Es schreibt sich so leicht mit dieser Feder	*It's so easy writing with this pen*
Im eignen Bett schläft es sich noch einmal so gut	*One sleeps twice as well in one's own bed*

381. **The Impersonal Passive**

This is a much used construction, denoting a general activity not attributed to a particular agent. The 'es' drops out except in normal order:

Es wurde im Nebenzimmer geredet	*There was talking in the next room*

Wurde im Nebenzimmer geredet? Hin und wieder wurde im Nebenzimmer geredet. Da im Nebenzimmer geredet wurde, . . .

Vor Hunden wird gewarnt	*Beware of dogs*
Bei Müllers ist eingebrochen worden	*The Müllers have had burglars*
Von einem Nachfolger wird nicht gesprochen	*There is no talk of a successor*
Hier wird gelegen, gestöhnt, geliebt, gestorben (A. Goes)	*Here men lie, moan, love, die* (from a description of a military hospital)

See also 459(e) and 496(b)iii.

I. THERE IS

382. **There are two specific German equivalents of 'there is'** (for other renderings see 387).

(a) **es gibt + accusative**

The origin and explanation of this phrase, 'it gives', is: Nature (or Providence) gives (provides, produces). This is a clue to the uses of 'es gibt', e.g. Es hat letztes Jahr eine gute Ernte gegeben *There was a good harvest last year*. The 'es' is thus a real subject, which is retained whatever the word order, e.g. Letztes Jahr hat es eine gute Ernte gegeben.

(b) **es ist, es sind + nominative**

Here the 'es' is merely an introductory subject, which drops away in inversion or a subordinate clause, when it is no longer separated, by the verb, from the real subject; the number of the latter determines that of the verb (ist or sind). E.g. Es ist eine Maus in der Küche; oft ist eine Maus in der Küche; wenn eine Maus in der Küche ist, . . .; es sind zwei Hunde im Garten.

383. es gibt is used:

(a) **(S) to denote existence as such, without reference to a particular place:**

Wenn es uns nicht gegeben hätte, wäre er verloren gewesen	*But for us* (lit. *if we had not existed*), *he would have been lost*
Es gibt verschiedene Gründe dafür	*There are various reasons for it*
Urlaub gibt es jetzt sowieso nicht (G. Gaiser)	*In any case there is no leave at present*
Gleichmaß und Ruhe hat es da nur selten gegeben (*Zeit*: from a review of Zuckmayer's autobiography)	*There was rarely proportion and tranquillity in his life*

Typical of this use are broad, general statements:

Es gibt Tage, wo alles schiefgeht	*There are days when everything goes wrong*
So etwas gibt es nicht	*There's no such thing*
Es hat immer Kriege gegeben (Th. Valentin)	*There have always been wars*
O ja, Unglückliche gibt es in allen Häusern, in jedem Stand! (M. Walser)	*Oh yes, there are unhappy individuals in every kind of home, in every walk of life*

Occasional fluctuations are found, e.g. Es gab/es war/wir hatten keine Zeit, das zu tun. Warum sollte ein Unterschied sein, zwischen einem weißen und einem schwarzen Mann? (I. Wendt) (Also possible: Warum sollte es einen Unterschied geben, . . .)

(b) **to denote existence in a large area**, e.g. a town, a country (but see 384(b)):

Es gibt drei alte Kirchen in unserer Stadt	*There are three old churches in our town*
Es gibt in München so viel zu sehen	*There is so much to see in Munich*
Es gab Holme in dem Fjord (G. Gaiser)	*There were islets in the fjord*
Es dürfte in der Bundesrepublik wenige geben, die so gut wie er informiert sind (*Zeit*)	*There are probably few persons in the Federal Republic who are as well informed as he is*

(c) **in recording the consequences of some event:**

Wenn du das tust, gibt's ein Unglück (Du. Stil.)	*If you do that, there'll be a calamity*
Bei den Unruhen soll es bisher vier Tote gegeben haben (*FAZ*)	*So far there are said to have been four killed in the course of the disturbances*
Er mußte auswärts ein Konzert dirigieren . . . So gab es eine kleine Pause in ihrem gemeinsamen Glück (H. H. Jahnn)	*He had to conduct a concert away from home . . . Thus there was a break in their joint happiness*

384. es ist is used:

(a) **(S) to denote permanent or temporary presence in a definite and limited place** (e.g. a house, a room):

Es war eine kleine Gastwirtschaft im Keller (V. Baum). Schade, daß hier im Haushalt keine Nähmaschine ist (H. Fallada). Es ist irgend jemand an der Tür.

Note:

i When 'es ist' is used in this context and in that described in 384(b), the sentence must contain a word or phrase denoting place; if there is none, supply da, darin etc.:

Auf dem Kaminsims ist eine Uhr; es sind auch zwei Vasen da (or: da sind auch zwei Vasen)	*On the mantelpiece there is a clock; there are also two vases*
Es ist ein Brief für Sie da	*There's a letter for you*

ii Occasionally 'es gibt' is used in this context, particularly if it is desired to underline the distinctive character of the thing concerned. (With 'es gibt' the stress is on the thing, not on the place.)

In dieser Diele gab es gegenüber der Tür einen offenen Kamin (I. Wendt)	*In this lounge there was a fireplace opposite the door*

(b) **to denote temporary presence in a large area:**

Es waren noch viele Menschen auf den Straßen	*There were still a lot of people in the streets*
Es sind heute viele Auswärtige in der Stadt	*There are many strangers in town today*
Es waren Wolken am Himmel	*There were clouds in the sky*
Es war ein Frühlingsgefühl in der Luft	*There was a feeling of spring in the air*

N.B. See Note i in (a) above.

(c) **in recording events** (though here practice varies a good deal):

Letzte Woche war in Hamburg ein Streik. Gestern war das zweite Sinfoniekonzert. Im Fernsehn war eine Diskussion darüber (Th. Valentin). [es] war ein Gehen und Schieben hinter der Reling hin (G. Gaiser) *There was much moving about and pushing behind the ship's rail.* In Mainz war ein Aufenthalt (or: gab es einen Aufenthalt) von fünf Minuten.

When 'es gibt' is used in this context, it is especially in connection with events of a striking or exceptional character and with future events:

Es gab in der Fabrik eine Explosion	*There was an explosion in the factory*
Eine Verhandlung wie diese hat es in der Geschichte der deutschen Luftfahrt noch nie gegeben (*Zeit*)	*In the history of German aviation there has never been an investigation such as this one*
Es wird nächste Woche in Hamburg einen Streik geben	*Next week there will be a strike in Hamburg*

(d) **in speaking of weather conditions** (though 'es gibt' is also used, especially referring to the future and in speaking of events e.g. ein Sturm, ein Gewitter):

Am nächsten Morgen war dichter Nebel	*Next morning there was a thick fog*
Morgen wird schönes Wetter sein/ wird es schönes Wetter geben	*It will be fine to-morrow*

Gestern gab es ein Gewitter	*There was a thunderstorm yesterday*

385. (S) Some idiomatic uses of 'es gibt'

Was gibt's?	1. *What's the news?*
	2. *What's the matter?*
Was gibt's heute (zu Mittag)?	*What is there for lunch today?*
Gestern gab es Kalbsbraten	*Yesterday there was roast veal*
Was gibt es heute abend im Theater?[1]	*What's on at the theatre tonight?*
Es gibt nichts zu lachen	*There's nothing to laugh at*
Es gibt noch viel zu tun	*There's still a lot to do*
Nein, das gibt's nicht	*No, you're/we're not doing that*
Gleich gibt's was[1]	1. *In a minute you'll get a box on the ears*
	2. *There'll be a thunderstorm in a minute*
	3. *Lunch will soon be ready*

386. Two special uses of 'es ist'
i Once upon a time there was . . . Es war einmal . . .
ii in describing a picture:

Im Hintergrund ist ein Wald	*In the background there is a forest*

387. (S) Other renderings of 'there is' (important)

Where 'there is' is normal in English, German frequently uses neither 'es ist' nor 'es gibt', but some other, generally more definite, verb. E.g.

In der Diele steht ein Flügel	*There's a grand piano in the lounge*
Auf dem Tisch lagen Äpfel	*There were some apples on the table*
Es lagen Wolken um den Gipfel	*There were clouds round the summit*
Vor mir war der Hafen: zuerst sah ich die Dampfer, sodann . . .	*Before me was the harbour: first, there were the steamers, then . . .*
Es herrschte tiefe Stille	*There was deep silence*
An unseren Schulen herrschte Disziplin (Th. Valentin)	*In our schools there was discipline*
Letzte Woche wurde in Hamburg gestreikt	*Last week there was a strike in Hamburg*
Im Gebüsch knisterte es	*There was a crackling sound in the undergrowth*
Es ist eingebrochen worden	*There's been a burglary*
Es kamen letztes Jahr viele Ausländer nach England	*There were a lot of foreigners in England last year*
Es besteht kein Zweifel, daß . . .	*There is no doubt that . . .*

See also 143(e) and 373 N.ii.

J. THE MODAL VERBS

388. können[2] *to be able to, can*	müssen *to have to, must*
dürfen *to be allowed to, may*	sollen *am to*
mögen *to like, to like to*	wollen *to want, to want to, to be willing to*

---

[1] from Wahrig, op. cit.
[2] 'können' has been placed first as being the commonest of the six and therefore the most suitable as a model in the paragraphs that follow.

These 6 verbs are generally known as the Modal Verbs or Modal Auxiliaries because they are mainly used in conjunction with other verbs whose significance they *modify*. As may be seen from the above table, the modals respectively express ability, permission, inclination, necessity, obligation and volition to perform the action of the verb dependent on them (cf. Stopp, op. cit., 63).

389. The forms of the Modal Verbs

(a) The singular of the present indicative is irregular, being an extinct strong imperfect:

können: ich kann, du kannst, er kann, wir können, ihr könnt, sie können
dürfen: ich darf, du darfst, er darf, wir dürfen etc.
mögen: ich mag, du magst, er mag, wir mögen etc.
müssen: ich muß, du mußt, er muß, wir müssen etc.
sollen: ich soll, du sollst, er soll, wir sollen etc.
wollen: ich will, du willst, er will, wir wollen etc.

(b) The present subjunctive is regular:

ich könne	ich dürfe, du dürfest etc.
du könnest	ich möge, du mögest etc.
er könne	ich müsse, du müssest etc.
wir können	ich solle, du sollest etc.
ihr könnet	ich wolle, du wollest etc.
sie können	

(c) i The imperf. indic. and past part. are weak, but where the infinitive is modified this modification is dropped; mögen also has a consonant change.

ii The modals have two past participles; the second is identical with the infinitive and is used when, as is preponderantly the case, there is an infinitive dependent on the modal, e.g.: Er hat das Buch gewollt, BUT: Er hat das Buch lesen wollen.

(d) The principal parts are therefore as follows:

INFIN.	PRES. INDIC.	IMPERFECT.	PAST PARTICIPLE
können	kann	konnte	gekonnt, können
dürfen	darf	durfte	gedurft, dürfen
mögen	mag	mochte	gemocht, mögen
müssen	muß	mußte	gemußt, müssen
sollen	soll	sollte	gesollt, sollen
wollen	will	wollte	gewollt, wollen

(e) The imperf. subj. is the same as the imperf. indic., but where the infin. is modified, the modification is here restored:

ich könnte, dürfte, möchte, müßte, sollte, wollte

(f) The -e of the 1st and 3rd sing. imperf. indic. and subj. is often dropped in conversation, especially before a vowel, e.g. Er konnt' uns nicht finden; er möcht' mitgehen.

(g) Owing to their meanings, the modals are not found in the imperative, apart from some curios of 'wollen' not worth quoting.

390. Infinitives dependent on the modals are used without 'zu': Er will sein Haus verkaufen; er kann nichts als arbeiten.

391. Straightforward examples of the modals in their four commonest tenses

(a) **Present Indicative**:

Darf ich heute Tennis spielen?	*May I play tennis today?*
Ich soll ihm das Buch morgen zurückgeben	*I'm to return the book to him tomorrow*

(b) **Imperfect Indicative**:

Ich konnte gestern nicht kommen	*I couldn't come yesterday*
	I wasn't able to come yesterday
Ich mochte ihm nichts davon sagen	*I didn't like to tell him about it*
Ich mußte fleißig arbeiten	*I had to work hard*

(c) **Imperfect Subjunctive**:

Ich könnte morgen kommen	*I could come tomorrow*
	I would be able to come tomorrow
Ich dürfte morgen kommen	*I would be allowed to come tomorrow*
Ich möchte das Buch (gern) lesen	*I should like to read the book*
Wenn er darauf bestehen würde, müßte ich das Buch lesen	*If he insisted on it, I should have to read the book*
Ich sollte das Buch lesen	*I ought to read the book*
Ich wollte dir gern helfen	*I would be very willing to help you*

(d) **Pluperfect Subjunctive**:

Ich hätte das Buch lesen können	*I could have read the book*
Ich hätte das Buch lesen dürfen	*I would have been allowed to read the book*
Ich hätte das Buch lesen mögen[1]	*I would have liked to read the book*
Ich hätte das Buch lesen müssen	*I would have had to read the book*
	I ought to have read the book[2]
Ich hätte das Buch lesen sollen	*I ought to have read the book*[2]
(Ich hätte das Buch lesen wollen[3]	*I would have liked to read the book*)

392.

(a) **A special order rule**: when a modal is used concurrently 1. in a compound tense 2. in a subordinate clause 3. with a dependent infinitive, then the auxiliary of the compound tense precedes the dependent infinitive, instead of coming at the end.

(b) Examples:

Da er heute hat schwimmen dürfen, muß es ihm besser gehen	*As he has been allowed to swim today, he must be better*
Es war klar, daß er sich würde anstrengen müssen	*It was clear that he would have to exert himself*
Das Buch, das ich hätte kaufen sollen, kostet 30 Mark	*The book that I should have bought costs 30 marks*
daß die letzte Filmaufnahme . . . hat verschoben werden müssen (I. Wendt)	*that the final shooting of the film has had to be postponed*

(c) Where another word or phrase forms a unit with the dependent infinitive, the auxiliary generally precedes the complete unit:

---

[1] commoner: Ich hätte das Buch gern gelesen.
[2] 'sollen' expresses a stronger sense of duty than 'müssen'.
[3] 'wollen' is rarely used in this tense.

Obwohl er hat Fußball spielen dürfen, . . .	*Although he has been allowed to play football,* . . .
Obwohl er hat nach Hause gehen müssen, . . .	*Although he has had to go home,* . . .
Obwohl er sich hätte geschmeichelt fühlen sollen, . . .	*Although he ought to have felt flattered,* . . .

(d) In conversation, and even in letters, most Germans avoid the above construction by using a simple tense; thus the first two examples in (b) would normally become: Da er heute schwimmen durfte and Es war klar, daß er sich anstrengen müßte (imperf. subj.).

(e) A modal may have a second modal dependent on it, the second modal itself having a dependent infinitive:

| Er müßte einen raschen Erfolg erzielen können | *He ought to be able to achieve a rapid success* |

Where this occurs in a subordinate clause, there is an occasional tendency to place the first modal, though it is not in a compound tense, in front of the dependent infinitives. Of the following examples 1. is correct, while 2. illustrates the tendency just noted:

| 1 Sein Lehrer behauptete, daß er es eigentlich übersetzen können müßte | *His teacher maintained that really he should be able to translate it* |
| 2. Das war ein merkwürdiges Liebespaar, das da sich abmühte, damit eines das andere sollte behalten können (G. Gaiser) | *It was a strange pair of lovers who toiled and laboured in order that the one should be able to keep the other* |

393. The ellipsis of verbs of motion (gehen, fahren and others) **after the modals is very common**; the idea of movement is wholly conveyed by the adverb or adverb phrase indicating the destination.

(a) With mögen, this ellipsis occurs only after the imperf. subj.:

| Ich möchte jetzt nach Hause | *I'd like to go home now* |

With the other five, it occurs mainly after the present and imperfect (indic. or subj.):

Wo wollen Sie morgen hin?	*Where are you going tomorrow?*
Ich will nach Frankfurt	*I'm going to Frankfurt*
Ich sollte zu meinem Onkel	*I was to go to my uncle's*
	I ought to go to my uncle's
Ich könnte heute abend ins Theater	*I could go to the theatre this evening*

With können and müssen, and occasionally with dürfen, also after the pluperf. subj.:

| Er hätte gestern ins Kino gedurft[1] | *He would have been allowed to go to the cinema yesterday* |

With müssen occasionally also after the perf. and pluperf. indic.:

| Er hat ins Geschäft gemußt[1] | *He's had to go to the office* |

(b) This usage is preponderantly, but not exclusively, colloquial (as in the examples in (a) above). According to the context, the omitted verb

---

[1] In the perf. and pluperf. there is not pure ellipsis, in that, with the omission of gehen, the past part. is changed from können, dürfen, müssen to gekonnt, gedurft, gemußt (cf. 389 (c) ii).

may be fliegen, klettern, kommen, rudern, schwimmen, springen, ziehen or some other verb of motion:

Er wollte über die Mauer [klettern]	*He wanted to climb over the wall*
Die Strömung war so stark, daß er nicht bis ans Ufer [schwimmen] konnte	*The current was so strong, that he couldn't swim as far as the bank*
Er mußte in den Krieg [ziehen] (H. Böll)	*He had to go to the war*

(c) The modals may be similarly used (i.e. without 'gehen' or some analogous verb) with a large number of separable prefixes signifying motion, e.g.

Ich will ihm nach	*I'll go after him*
Er kletterte über die Mauer, aber er konnte nicht zurück	*He climbed over the wall, but he couldn't get back*
Ich möchte jetzt fort	*I'd like to leave now*
Ich hätte eigentlich hingemußt	*I really ought to have gone there*
Mich wundert, daß er um diese Zeit noch hinausdarf (Th. Valentin)	*I'm surprised that he's allowed out at this time of night*

The verbs in these sentences may be regarded as 'jemandem nachwollen' *to want to go after someone,* 'zurück-können' *to be able to go back* etc.

The tense-restrictions given in 393(a) again apply, except that 'können' and 'müssen' can here often be used in the future:

Ich glaub', ich werd' vorbeikönnen	*I think I'll be able to get past*
Wir werden bald zurückmüssen	*We shall have to go back soon*

The main prefixes in question are:

dahin	heraus	herunter	hinaus	nach
durch	herein	hierher	hinein	vorbei
fort	herüber	hin	hinüber	weg
herauf	herum	hinauf	hinunter	weiter
				zurück

394. Other ellipses with the modals

(a) As in English (though sometimes 'es' is added):

Ich wollte Tennis spielen, aber ich konnte/durfte nicht	*I wanted to play tennis, but I couldn't/ wasn't allowed to*
Soll ich?	*Shall I?*
Ich versuchte, ihn zu überzeugen, aber ich konnte (es) nicht (habe es nicht gekonnt)	*I tried to convince him, but I couldn't*
Mußt du diesen Brief lesen?	*Must you read this letter?*
—Natürlich muß ich ('s)	*—Of course I must*

(b) Idiomatic ellipsis of 'tun': Das kann ich nicht; das darfst/sollst du nicht; was soll ich damit? *What am I to do with it?*

(c) **(S)** Idiomatic ellipsis of other verbs:

Ich kann nichts dafür [machen]	*I can't help it*
Ich kann nicht mehr [weitermachen]	*I'm tired out*
Was soll dieser Brief eigentlich [bedeuten]?	*What is really the point of this letter?*

395. The following paragraphs deal with the various uses of the individual modals; in each case, section (a) covers the basic meaning of the verb, of which further examples are to be found in 391: Straightforward examples of the modals in their four commonest tenses.

396. können

(a) to be able to, to know how to, to be in a position to (cf. 391):

Kann er Auto fahren?	*Can he drive a car?*

(b) elliptical use with the above meanings (cf. 394(b)(c)):

Was andere können, kann ich auch	*What others can do, I can do too*
Ich kann nicht anders	*I cannot act otherwise*
Oh ja, er kann etwas	*Oh yes, he's quite able*

(c) to know things learnt,[1] e.g. languages, other school subjects, homework (Aufgaben, Vokabeln, ein Gedicht), one's craft (sein Handwerk), a skill. This is really an elliptical use, as indicated in the first example:

Er kann Französisch [sprechen]	*He knows French*
Er kann gut Physik (commoner: Er ist gut in Physik)	*He's good at physics*
Er wird nie eine richtige Stellung bekommen, weil er nichts kann	*He'll never get a proper job because he's not trained for anything*

(d) used colloquially for 'dürfen':

Kann ich herein?	*May I come in?*
Du kannst den Bleistift behalten	*You can keep the pencil*

(e) it denotes possibility:

Das kann sein	*That may be*
Ich kann mich irren	*I may be mistaken*
Er kann krank sein	*He may be ill*
Er kann krank gewesen sein	*He may have been ill*
Er könnte krank sein	*He might be ill*
Er könnte krank gewesen sein	*He might have been ill*

Note: To express a negative possibility, often some further word must be inserted in addition to 'nicht', or 'vielleicht' must be used, as the mere insertion of 'nicht' may exclude the possibility: Er kann nicht krank gewesen sein *He can't/couldn't have been ill.* Thus:

Er *kann* auch *nicht* krank gewesen sein	*He may (on the other hand) not have been ill*
Er ist vielleicht gar nicht krank gewesen	*He may/might not have been ill at all*

(f) miscellaneous:

Ich konnte nicht anders, ich mußte lachen	*I couldn't help laughing* 1. normal usage
Ich mußte einfach lachen	
Ich konnte nicht umhin zu lachen	2. old-fashioned
Ich lief, was ich nur konnte	*I ran for all I was worth*
So etwas kann mich ärgern[2]	*That kind of thing always annoys me*
Ich bezweifle nicht sein Können	*I'm not questioning his ability*

---

[1] cf. S. Latzel: 'wissen, kennen und können' in *Deutschunterricht für Ausländer*, Heft 3/4, 12. Jahrgang (1962), pp. 81–6 and Heft 1/2, 13. Jahrgang (1963), pp. 52–3.

[2] from Wahrig, op. cit.

397. dürfen

(a) to be allowed to, may: see 391.

(b) polite turns of phrase, based on the above meaning:

Hierher, wenn ich bitten darf | *This way, if you please*
Verkäufer: Was darf es sein, bitte? | *Shop-assistant: What can I get you?*
Dürfte ich Sie um das Salz bitten? | *Might I ask you for the salt?*
Ich darf Ihnen mitteilen, daß ... | *May I inform you that ...* (commercial)

(c) used with a negative, it denotes 'must not, may not':

Das darfst du nicht (tun) | *You mustn't do that*
Aber ich darf mich nicht loben | *But I mustn't praise myself*
(E. Langgässer)

Note: Logically, 'du mußt das nicht tun' means 'you are not obliged to do that', but it is quite commonly used in the sense of 'you musn't do that'; the situation and vocal inflexion will show which is meant; in the first sense 'mußt' will have a more drawn out emphasis.

(d) instead of 'sollen', in negative sentences:

Er hätte so etwas nicht tun dürfen | *He shouldn't have done that kind of thing*
Er durfte so etwas nicht tun | —a more incisive version

(e) instead of 'können':

Das darf als Vorzug betrachtet werden | *That can be regarded as an advantage*
Von der Mannschaft durfte er [Blücher] das Unmögliche verlangen, wenn sein 'Vorwärts' aus seinen Augen blitzte (Treitschke) | *He could demand the impossible of his troops, when 'Advance!' flashed from his eyes*

(f) it denotes probability; 'dürfte' implies greater probability than 'könnte', but is at the same time more tentative and polite (cf. Collinson, op. cit., pp. 87 f.):

Er dürfte krank gewesen sein | *He might well have been ill*
Wenn dies der Fall ist, dann dürfte dieser Anzug auch für Mondfahrer unbrauchbar sein (*Zeit*) | *If that is the case, then this space-suit would probably be of no use to lunar astronauts either*

398. mögen

(a) to like, to like to (cf. 391):

Mögen sie sich auch? (Du. Stil.) | *And are they fond of each other?*
Ich mag nicht | *I don't like to*
Ich möchte nicht, daß er heute kommt | *I would not like him to come today*

(b) instead of 'können':

Wer mag das (nur) sein? | *Who can that be?*
Wie mag das gekommen sein? | *How can that have come about?*
und da mit diesem [Toten] schon jemand sich abgab, mochte das genügen (G. Gaiser) | *and as someone was already seeing to this dead man, there was no need to do anything (lit. that could suffice)*

(c) it is used to express a wish or command: see 476(a): e.g. Möge er glücklich sein! *May he be happy!* In an **indirect command**, 'Ich sagte ihm, er möchte kommen' (*I told him to come*) is less peremptory than 'Ich sagte ihm, er sollte (or müßte) kommen'. 'Ich sagte ihm, daß er kommen sollte (müßte)' is possible, but not 'daß er kommen möchte'. Cf. Ich hoffte, er möchte kommen (only without 'daß').

(d) it is used in concessive clauses: see 471, 472, 474.

(e) it denotes possibility or probability:

Das mag sein	*That may be*
Er mag krank sein	*He may be ill*
Er mag sein Bestes getan haben, aber er hat nicht viel erreicht	*He may have done his best, but he hasn't achieved much*
Das Kind mochte vier Jahre alt sein	*The child was perhaps four years old*
ein korrektes, sehr britisches Englisch, das sie in irgendeinem Pensionat gelernt haben mochte (V. Baum)	*a correct, very British English, that she had probably learnt in some boarding-school*

(f) 'möchte' often conveys a hesitant or polite doubt:

Sie möchten zu rasch gehandelt haben	*Maybe you acted too quickly*
Man möchte meinen, daß . . .	*One would almost think that . . .*

399. müssen[1]

(a) to have to, must: compulsion, necessity, inevitability (cf. 391):

Wenn Sie studieren wollen, müssen Sie das Abitur gemacht haben	*If you want to go to a university you must have passed the Abitur (school leaving examination)*
Muß das sein?	*Is that really necessary?*
Es mußte so kommen	*It had to come like this*
Er hat es gut gemacht, das muß man sagen	*He certainly did it well* (idiomatic)
Das muß man gesehen haben	*It's worth seeing* (idiomatic)

Note: For the rendering of 'must not', see 397(c).

(b) instead of 'sollen', in the imperf. (or pluperf.) subj., if there is little or no emphasis on duty:

Deutschlands Kohle ist teurer, als sie sein müßte (*Zeit*)	*Germany's coal is dearer than it should be*
Sie ist hübsch, nur müßte sie schlanker sein (Du. Stil.: nur)	*She's pretty, only she ought to be slimmer*
Wo ist der Brief?—Er müßte (not 'sollte') in dieser Schublade sein	*Where's the letter?—It should be in this drawer*
Jeder müßte einmal auf einem Bauernhof gearbeitet haben	*Everyone ought to have worked on a farm some time*

(c) it denotes logical deduction:

Er spielt heute Tennis, also muß es ihm besser gehen	*He's playing tennis today, so he must be better*

Note:
i logical deduction in the context of a narrative in the past; note the tense:

Draußen stieg . . . jemand, der den gleichen Gang haben mußte wie Fräulein Gröschel, die Hintertreppe . . . hinauf (E. Fried)	*Outside, someone who must have had the same gait as Fräulein Gröschel was coming up the back stairs*

---

[1] Regarding the uses of müssen, sollen and wollen, I am indebted to an article by Gerhard Kaufmann in *Deutschunterricht für Ausländer* (1962 Heft 5/6 and 1963 Heft 1/2; also 1965 Heft 1/2); some of the examples are his.

ii müssen may question a logical deduction:

Er war nicht im Büro, aber deshalb muß er nicht krank sein (Commoner: aber deshalb braucht er nicht krank zu sein)	*He wasn't at the office, but that doesn't mean that he's ill*

iii a negative logical deduction is denoted by können + negative:

Er spielt heute Tennis, also kann er nicht krank sein	*He's playing tennis today, so he can't be ill*

400. sollen[1]

(a) am to, ought to, should: it conveys a moral obligation or an action that is fitting or advisable or that has been decided on beforehand (cf. 391):

Du sollst Vater und Mutter ehren	*Thou shalt honour thy father and thy mother*
Man soll (or sollte) immer geduldig sein	*One should always be patient*
Ich soll nicht so viel rauchen	*I'm not supposed to smoke so much*
Wir sollten uns gestern treffen	*We were to have met yesterday*
Du solltest doch deinem Freund helfen?	*Surely you were to have helped your friend?*
Du hattest doch deinem Freund helfen sollen?	
Wie weit sollen (or wollen) wir gehen?	*How far shall we go?*
Was soll ich in Hamburg (tun)?	*What am I to do in Hamburg?*
Warum sollte ich denn nicht ins Theater gehen?	*Why shouldn't I go to the theatre?*
Ich weiß nicht, was ich tun soll	*I don't know what to do*
Ich wußte nicht, an wen ich mich wenden sollte	*I didn't know whom to apply to*

Note on the last 2 examples: Attention is drawn to the clauses with sollen which render English infinitives. 'Ich weiß nicht, was zu tun' is not German. 'Ich weiß nicht was tun' is possible, but only with 'tun' or with 'anfangen' used colloquially for 'to do', e.g. Diese zwei Zimmer sind übriggeblieben, und kein Mensch hat gewußt, was damit anfangen (H. Fallada). NB: Was tun? *What is one to do?*

(b) it may express intention:

Eine zweite Fabrik soll bald gebaut werden	*A second factory is soon to be built*
Soll das ein Kompliment sein?	*Is that supposed to be a compliment?*
Was soll das (heißen)?	*What's the meaning of this?* (generally indignantly)
Es sollte eine Überraschung sein	*It was meant to be a surprise*

Note the ironical application of this use, conveying indignation:

Und in diesem Gebäude soll sich einer zurechtfinden!	*And you're supposed to find your way about this building!*

(c) it may express a promise or warning:

Ja, du sollst mitgehen	*Yes, you shall go too*
Es soll nicht wieder vorkommen	*It shan't happen again*
Du sollst das noch bereuen	*You'll live to regret this*

---

[1] see 399: footnote to 'müssen'.

(d) it may express what was, or was not, destined to happen:

Er sollte früh sterben	*He was (destined) to die young*
Er sollte niemals nach Deutschland zurückkehren	*He was never to return to Germany*
Es hat so sein sollen	*It was meant to be*

(e) it may express a rumour or report:

Er soll steinreich sein	*He is said to be enormously rich*
Bei den Unruhen soll es bisher vier Tote gegeben haben (*FAZ*)	*So far four are reported killed in the course of the disturbances*
Das soll *er* gewesen sein?	*Do you mean to say it was him?*
Der Geschäftsführer sollte schon nach Hause gegangen sein	*The manager was said to have gone home already*

(f) it may be used instead of 'können' in certain questions:

Wie sollte (konnte) ich das wissen?	*How could I have known that?*
Sollte (könnte) es doch ein Mißverständnis gewesen sein?	*Could it have been a misunderstanding after all?*
Warum sollte (könnte) er nicht einmal in London gewesen sein?	*Why shouldn't he have been to London some time?*

(g) it may be used in conditional clauses: see 462(e)(f).
E.g. Sollte es regnen, so komme ich nicht.
  cf. the use of sollte, with the sense of 'would, should', in the two following idiomatic expressions:

Man sollte meinen, er würde es gern tun	*One would think he'd be glad to do it*
Es sollte (or: Es würde) mich wundern, wenn ...	*I should be surprised if ...*

(h) it is used to express a command or wish:

Du *sollst* das tun[1]	*You're to do that*
Du sollst *fleißig* sein[1]	*I want you to work hard*
Er soll sich in acht nehmen	*Let him beware!*
Sie sollen sofort kommen	*Let them come at once*
	They/you are to come at once
Nein, soll[2] Groenewold mit ihnen über diesen Film sprechen—du nicht (Th. Valentin)	*No, let Groenewold talk with them about this film (if he wants to)—not you*

Note: It may voice a command which ironically conveys a threat or a challenge:

Der soll noch mal kommen und Geld pumpen wollen![3]	*Let him come again to borrow some money!*

The imperf. and pluperf. subj. may be used with similar effect:

Das sollte er mal mit unserem Chef versuchen![3]	*He should try that on with our boss*
So hätte der früher mal mit mir reden sollen![3]	*If he had spoken to me like that in the past!*

  Compare the phrase:

Das sollte mir mal passieren!	*If I were to do that, there'd be a fine row!*

---

[1] from Collinson, op. cit., p. 90; Collinson points out the effect of stress and tone on the meaning of sollen, the first remark expecting absolute obedience.
[2] in place of the optative subjunctive 'möge'; not to be imitated.
[3] G. Kaufmann's example (see 399: footnote to müssen)

(i) it is used in **indirect commands**:

Ich sagte ihm, er solle (or: sollte) es tun	*I told him to do it*
Ich will, daß er es tut	BUT: *I want him to do it*
Ich wollte, daß er es tat	*I wanted him to do it*

401. wollen[1]

(a) (**S**) to want, to want to, to wish (to) (cf. 391):

Ich will meine Ruh'	*I want peace and quiet*
Ich will nur dein Bestes	*I only want what is best for you*
Ich will ihm nichts (Böses)	*I wish him no harm*
Was wollen Sie von mir?	*What do you want of me?*
Nun denn, mach, was du willst (Du. Stil.)	*Well then, do what you like* (implying: I don't care)
Der Arzt will, daß ich mir mehr Bewegung mache	*The doctor wants me to take more exercise*
Ich wollte (imperf. subj.), ich wäre zu Hause	*I wish I were at home*
Ich wollt', ich könnt' es	*I wish I could do it*

(b) to be willing to (cf. 391 (c)):

Willst du mir helfen?	*Will you help me?*
—Ja, ich will dir helfen	*—Yes, I'll help you*
Er will es nicht zugeben	*He won't admit it*
Ich bat ihn es zu tun, aber er wollte nicht	*I asked him to do it, but he wouldn't*
Ich wäre Ihnen sehr dankbar, wenn Sie es tun wollten (=imperf. subj.)	*I'd be very grateful to you if you'd do it*

Note: In sentences such as the first two in (b), the ordinary future tense (Wirst du mir helfen? Ja, ich werde dir helfen) would sound cold and impersonal. Contrast: Wirst du bald bereit sein? *Will you soon be ready?*

(c) it may express intention:

Wir wollen uns bald einen neuen Fernseher anschaffen	*We intend getting a new TV soon*
Wie wollen Sie ihm das klarmachen?	*How do you intend explaining that to him?*
Ich will ihn jetzt anrufen	*I'm going to phone him up now*
Ich wollte Sie darüber fragen	*I was going to ask you about it*
Was wollen Sie damit sagen?	*What do you mean by that (remark)?*
Sie wollen doch nicht behaupten, daß ich es getan habe?	*Surely you're not trying to say that I did it?*
Wollen (or: Sollen) wir uns den Dom ansehen?	*Shall we have a look at the cathedral?*

Note: In the last example 'wollen' implies that the speaker is in favour; 'sollen' leaves the decision entirely to the other.

(d) to claim, maintain, pretend:

Er will eine Mosquito abgeschossen haben (G. Gaiser)	*He claims to have shot down a Mosquito (plane)*
Er wollte mich nicht erkennen	*He pretended not to recognize me*
Zur gleichen Zeit, da ich das Judenauto gesehen haben wollte, . . . (F. Fühmann)	*At the same time at which I said I had seen the car with the Jews, . . .*
cf. Keiner will es getan haben	*No one admits having done it*

[1] See 399: footnote to müssen.

(e) with inanimate subjects:
 i basic meaning generally 'to need, demand':

Tomaten wollen viel Sonne	*Tomatoes need a lot of sun*
Eine solche Arbeit will Zeit haben	*A piece of work of that sort demands time*
Solche Dolmetscherarbeit will gelernt sein, das darf man mir glauben (M. Walser)	*This kind of interpreter's work needs learning, believe me*

 ii with nicht: basic meaning 'to refuse to':

Der Koffer wollte nicht zugehen	*The suit-case refused to close*
Meine Beine wollen nicht mehr	*My legs won't carry me any further*
Das will mir nicht in den Kopf	*I can't grasp that*

(f) with impersonal subject:

Es will mir scheinen, daß er zuviel unternimmt	*I have the impression that he undertakes too much*
Es scheint regnen zu wollen	*It looks as if it were going to rain*

(g) as a substitute for the imperative: see 459(a).

(h) miscellaneous idiomatic uses:

Na, dann wollen wir mal (anfangen) (Du. Stil.)	*Well then, let's start*
Er will eben (or gerade) fort	*He's just going*
Er wollte eben (or gerade) fort, als ich ankam	*He was about to leave when I arrived*
Er hat allerhand versprochen, aber das will nicht viel sagen	*He has promised all sorts of things, but that doesn't mean much*
Das will ich gern glauben	*I quite believe it*
Ich will nur hoffen, daß er . . .	*I do hope he . . .*
Ich will nichts gehört/gesehen/ gemerkt haben	*I shall do as if I hadn't heard/seen/ noticed anything*
Also, ich will nichts gesagt haben	*Well then, act as if I hadn't said anything*
Da ist nichts/nicht viel zu wollen	*There's nothing/not much one can do about it*
Mit ihm ist nichts zu wollen	*There's nothing to be done with him*
Dagegen ist nichts zu wollen	*You can't prevent that*
eine gewollte Beleidigung[1]	*a deliberate insult*
Der Schluß des Romans ist zu gewollt[2]	*The end of the novel is forced*

402. Miscellaneous points relative to the modals

(a) Where possibility or logical deduction is to be expressed and können, dürfen, mögen and müssen might equally well have their literal meaning, adverbs such as 'vielleicht', 'wahrscheinlich' or 'sicher' should be used instead. (The context and vocal inflection make these ambiguities relatively rare). E.g.

Er wird mir vielleicht helfen	*He might help me*
('Er könnte' would mean: He could . . .)	
Er ist heute sicher in Frankfurt	*He must be in Frankfurt today*
('Er muß' might mean: He has to be . . .)	

(b) Distinguish:

Er muß es getan haben	*He must have done it*
Er hat es tun müssen	*He has had to do it*

[1] from Schulz-Griesbach, op. cit., B 833.
[2] from E. Agricola, op. cit., p. 751.

Er kann es getan haben	*He may have done it*
Er hat es tun können	*He has been able to do it*
Er könnte es getan haben	*He might have done it*
Er hätte es tun können, (wenn er gewollt hätte)	*He could have done it (if he had wanted to)*
Ich hätte ihn gern einmal gesehen	*I should have liked to see him some time*
Ich möchte die Sache vor meiner Abreise erledigt haben	*I should like to have settled the matter before my departure*
Er hätte heute ankommen müssen (or sollen)	*He should have arrived today* (implying: but he hasn't)
Er müßte schon längst angekommen sein	*He should have arrived long ago* (implying: and he probably has)

(c) **etwas zu tun haben** *to have to do something* is sometimes the equivalent of 'etwas tun sollen' (Type i below), sometimes of 'etwas tun müssen' (Type ii). Though not uncommon, it is used less than 'sollen' or 'müssen'.

Type i (=sollen) (See also 459(c))

Eva Dumont überlegte, was sie zu tun habe (G. Gaiser)	*Eva Dumont considered what she ought to do*

Type (ii) (=müssen)

Ein Schuß, zwei Schüsse? Die Verhandlung wird es zu klären haben (*Spiegel*)	*One shot or two shots? The question will have to be cleared up at the trial*

Note: The above use of 'etwas zu tun haben' should be distinguished from its use in sentences such as the following, in which the infinitive phrase qualifies the object and the element of necessity or obligation is far weaker:

Er hat ein Haus zu verkaufen	*He has a house to sell*
Ich habe mehrere Briefe zu schreiben	*I have several letters to write*
See also 434(a)ii.	

K. THE USES OF THE INFINITIVE WITHOUT 'ZU'

403. Survey of uses of the infinitive without 'zu':[1]
1. as a verbal noun 404
2. as the nominative complement of heißen 405
3. as the objectival complement of nennen and heißen 406
4. in elliptical exclamations 407
5. in place of an imperative 408
6. after the 6 modal verbs 409
7. after 11 other verbs (e.g. sehen, lassen, lehren) 410–21
8. in certain applications of bleiben, gehen, haben, legen, schicken, tun 422

404. The infinitive without 'zu' is used as a verbal noun, always neuter, often corresponding to an English form in -ing (see also 713):

Das Bekleben der Wände ist verboten (Erben, op. cit., 88)	*Stick no bills*

[1] for punctuation, see 743 (f) iii.

Ich hörte das laute Bellen eines Hundes	*I heard the loud barking of a dog*
Der Fuß tut mir beim Gehen weh	*My foot hurts me when walking*
Der Wagen kam ins Gleiten	*The car got into a skid*

Dann kam das Schiff, und ich beobachtete, wie so viele Male schon, das vorsichtige Längsfahren, Stoppen, Zurückweichen in dem Sprudeln und Rauschen und Räderklatschen (*the slapping sound of the paddle-wheels*), das Taueschleudern und Festbinden (Emil Strauß).

The extensive and often elaborate use of the infinitive as a noun is undoubtedly one of the hallmarks of modern German style. Two examples may illustrate the arresting possibilities (and temptations) of this usage:

Jede Nacht bedeutete für ihn ein Nichts, ein Grab, ein Ausgelöscht- werden (R. Musil)	*Every night meant for him a void, a grave, extinction*
In der Bundesrepublik beginnt sich diese Basis humanen Miteinander- lebens, Untereinanderaussprechens und Miteinanderwirkens aufzulösen (quoted in *FAZ*)	*In the Federal Republic this foundation of humane living together, freely exchanging ideas and co-operating, is beginning to dissolve*

405. It is used as the nominative complement of 'heißen' *to mean, to be (the equivalent of)*:

Das heißt lügen	*That amounts to lying*
Das hieße wieder von vorne anfangen	*That would mean starting again from the beginning*

406. It is used as the objectival complement of 'nennen' and 'heißen' *to call*. (In current usage nennen is by far the commoner.):

Das nennst du höflich sein!	*You call that being polite!*

407. In elliptical exclamations the infin. is generally used without 'zu', e.g. Einen Menschen danach bewerten, wieviel Hosen er verkaufen kann! (H. Fallada).

408. It is used in place of an imperative (cf. 459(g)):

Nicht rauchen! Bitte anschnallen!	*No smoking. Please fasten seat-belts*

This 'imperative infinitive' is sometimes effectively used in the course of a narrative to render a thought-stream, as in the second sentence of the following:
Es hatte ihm wohlgetan, bei der Rückkehr den exotischen Wagen umstanden zu sehen von Passanten, die sich über das kleinstädtische Nummernschild (*the provincial number-plate*) wunderten. Dann in aller Ruhe einsteigen, anlassen, über die Schulter blicken (*Then get in quite calmly, start the engine, glance over your shoulder*) (U. Johnson).

409. It is used after the 6 modal verbs: see 388 and 390.

410. The infinitive without 'zu' is used, with varying consistency (treated in the subsequent paragraphs), **after the following 11 verbs:**

5 verbs of perception:
sehen *to see*
hören *to hear*
fühlen *to feel*
spüren *to feel, perceive*
finden *to find*

3 causative verbs:
heißen *to bid*
lassen *to let* (causative and permissive)
machen *to make*

3 others:
helfen *to help*
lehren *to teach*
lernen *to learn*

Ich sah ihn ins Zimmer kommen	*I saw him come into the room*
Ich hörte das Kind weinen	*I heard the child crying*
Ich ließ ihn das Geld behalten	*I let him keep the money*
Er lehrt mich schwimmen	*He is teaching me to swim*

411. After sehen and hören, and even more after **fühlen and spüren,** a 'wie' or 'daß' clause is the commoner construction in colloquial German, especially if the sentence is of any length or complexity:

Ich sah, wie sich der Polizist nach dem alten Mann umsah	*I saw the policeman looking out for the old man*
Ich fühlte mein Herz klopfen	*I felt my heart beating*
Ich fühlte, wie er zitterte	*I felt him trembling*
Ich spürte seinen Einfluß wachsen	*I sensed how his influence was growing*
Ich spürte, wie er mir die Hand auf die Schulter legte	*I felt him lay his hand on my shoulder*

412. After finden the infin. construction is used for finding someone or something standing or lying somewhere:

Ich fand ihn am Fenster stehen	*I found him standing by the window*
Ich fand die Bücher auf dem Tisch liegen	*I found the books lying on the table*

In other contexts, either the pres. part. or some different construction is used:

Ich fand ihn in seinem Sessel (sitzend)	*I found him sitting in his armchair*
Ich fand ihn schlafend	*I found him sleeping*
Ich fand ihn lesend (commoner: beim Lesen)	*I found him reading*
Ich fand ihn bei einer Tasse Kaffee	*I found him having coffee*
Ich fand ihn dabei (or: damit beschäftigt), seine Papiere zu sortieren	*I found him sorting his papers*

413. heißen is used almost exclusively with a plain infinitive:

Er hieß mich über meine Zukunft entscheiden	*He bade me decide about my future*

Note: heißen, in the sense of 'to bid, order,' is little used in everyday German, where it sounds stilted and literary. Thus normal usage for the above sentence would be: Er sagte mir, ich müßte über meine Zukunft entscheiden.

414. lassen may mean 1. to let, allow 2. to cause to, make; it is generally clear from the context which of the two meanings applies; it is used exclusively with a plain infinitive.

    1. to let, allow:

Er ließ mich das Buch behalten	*He let me keep the book*

    2. to cause to, make:

Er ließ die Mannschaft halten	*He stopped his men*
Die Nachricht ließ ihn erblassen	*The news made him turn pale*

415. machen *to make, cause to* is used far less than lassen, being relatively rare apart from the idiomatic expression 'Er machte von sich reden' *He caused a stir.*

Er machte mich lachen (commoner: Er brachte mich zum Lachen). Du mußt Kurt glauben machen, daß ich bei dir bin (V. Baum).

416. After helfen, lehren and lernen, practice varies a good deal, but the following rule is the most serviceable: a mere infinitive, with no object, adverb etc., is used without 'zu'; where there is an object or adverbial limitation, 'zu' is used:

und jetzt hilf mir anpacken (E. M. Remarque)	*and now give me a hand*
Er . . . half Carla, die Weinflaschen zu öffnen (M. Horbach)	*He helped Carla open the wine-bottles*
Sie lehrte mich kochen	*She taught me to cook*
Sie lehrte mich, Suppe zu kochen	*She taught me to prepare soup*
Ich habe schwimmen gelernt	*I've learnt to swim*
Ich habe ja nie richtig kochen gelernt (H. Fallada)	*You know, I've never properly learnt to cook*
Ich habe schneller zu schwimmen gelernt	*I've learnt to swim more quickly*

Note: After lehren and lernen, a 'wie' clause is common usage:

Ich habe gelernt, wie man eine durchgebrannte Sicherung repariert	*I've learnt to repair a fuse*

417. After 'merken' and 'bemerken' *to notice* **and 'erblicken'** *to catch sight of, behold,* the infinitive is so rare that its use is best ruled out; it is never used after 'beobachten' or 'zusehen' *to watch.* After all these verbs, relative, 'daß' and 'wie' clauses are the accepted constructions:

Ich erblickte einen Bettler, der auf mich zukam	*I caught sight of a beggar coming towards me*
Ich merkte, daß er hinkte	*I noticed his limping*
Knudsen sah ihr zu, wie sie sich wieder auf die Bank setzte (A. Andersch)	*Knudsen watched her sitting down on the seat again*

418. After 'brauchen' *to need to do something* normal usage is zu + infin., but a plain infinitive is sometimes used colloquially; brauchen is used almost exclusively interrogatively or in conjunction with a negative word, with 'nur' or with 'bloß' *merely*:

Warum brauchst du in die Stadt zu gehen?	*Why need you go into town?*

Ich brauche nicht hinzugehen (or: hingehen)	*I needn't go there*
Du brauchst bloß anzurufen (or: anrufen), und ich komme	*You need only phone up and I'll come*
Er muß fleißiger arbeiten	BUT: *He needs to work harder*

Used in a compound tense or in a subordinate clause, brauchen always encloses the dependent infinitive: Du wirst dieses Fensterchen niemals aufzumachen brauchen; obwohl ich es nur dem Chef zu erwähnen brauche, . . .

Like the modals, it may be used elliptically:

Ich brauch' heute nicht mehr ins Büro	*I needn't go to the office again today*

See also 420 f.

419. After sehen, hören, heißen *to bid* **and lassen, the active infin. may have a passive meaning**; with lassen this is common; with the other three it is unusual:

Er läßt sich (dat.) ein Haus bauen	*He is having a house built*
Er ließ sich sehen	*He showed himself*
Er sah die Kisten auf den Laster laden (commoner: wie die Kisten auf den Laster geladen wurden)	*He saw the packing-cases being loaded onto the lorry*

The origin and explanation of these active infinitives with passive meanings is doubtless the omission of the accusative of an active accusative and infinitive construction.[1] Thus the above examples are contractions of: Er läßt einen Architekten für ihn ein Haus bauen; er ließ die Leute ihn sehen; er sah Männer die Kisten auf den Laster laden. This explanation is reinforced by the fact that the accusative is frequently omitted before a straightforward active infinitive: Auf der Straße sah ich [Leute] tanzen; in der Küche hörte ich [jemand] lachen. The following quotation, where 'tollen' can only have active force, is particularly revealing: Ich hörte drin tollen und Türen aufreißen (Max Mell) *Inside I heard people romping about and flinging doors open.*

Despite this explanation, the infinitive in sentences such as our three original examples is undoubtedly regarded as having passive force. This is shown by expanding the first example to 'Er läßt sich von dieser Firma ein Haus bauen', where there can no longer be any question of an omitted accusative.

Finally it should be mentioned that on no account can an orthodox passive infinitive be used after the four verbs in question. Thus 'I heard him being called' is 'Ich hörte, wie man ihn rief'; theoretically it could be 'Ich hörte ihn rufen', but this is obviously ambiguous; could *not* be: Ich hörte ihn gerufen werden.

Further examples of lassen + active infin. with passive meaning:

Er ließ sich um 7 Uhr wecken	*He had himself wakened at 7 o'clock*
Laß dich nicht beschwindeln!	*Don't let yourself be cheated*
Er ließ seine Überraschung nicht merken	*He concealed his surprise*

---

[1] cf. Eggeling, op. cit., accusative and infinitive.

Ich hätte mir doch ein Zimmer nach   *I ought after all to have asked for a front*
vorne 'raus geben lassen sollen   *room*
(A. Andersch)
Das läßt sich leicht ändern   *That can easily be changed*

420. Six of the 11 verbs used with a plain infinitive (cf. 410) **and one
other have a second past participle, identical with the infinitive,**
which is used, with varying consistency, when they have a dependent
infinitive preceding the past participle (cf. the Modal Verbs, 389(c)(ii),
e.g. Er hat das Buch lesen wollen).

These verbs are: sehen   heißen   and brauchen *to need,*
                 hören   lassen   though generally used
                 fühlen   helfen   with zu + infin. (cf. 418)

With **sehen and hören**, the infinitive form of the past part. predominates:
Ich habe ihn hereinkommen sehen/hören. In modern conversation the
1st past part. (Ich habe ihn hereinkommen gesehen) sounds slovenly,
though Eggeling (op. cit., p. 10) quotes numerous instances of its use
by authors from Storm to Werfel, both colloquial and narrative. A
more usual colloquial alternative would be: Ich habe gesehen, wie er
hereinkam.

With **fühlen**, a 'wie' clause is commoner: Ich habe gefühlt, wie das
Fieber kam, rather than: Ich habe das Fieber kommen fühlen.

heißen (little used in conversation, cf. 413): with a plain dependent infin.,
the 2nd past part. is used:
Er hat's mich tun heißen   *He bade me do it*
But with a more elaborate dependent infinitive phrase, 'geheißen' fol-
lowed by zu + infin. is preferred:
Er hatte seine Truppen geheißen, die Burg bis zum letzten Mann zu verteidigen.

With **lassen**, the infin. form predominates and *must* be used when it
means 'to cause to' (3rd example):
Ich hatte den Brief fallen lassen   *I had dropped the letter*
Ich habe meine Aktentasche irgendwo   *I've left my brief-case somewhere*
liegenlassen (more usual than
'liegengelassen')
Ich habe ihn zu mir kommen lassen   *I sent for him*

With **helfen**, the 2nd past part. is mainly literary (Er hat das Vater-
land verteidigen helfen) while colloquial usage is 'geholfen' followed
by zu + infin.: Sie hat mir geholfen, die Küche zu reinigen

With **brauchen**, the infin. form predominates:
Du hättest nicht zu kommen brauchen   *You needn't have come*
(occasionally: gebraucht)

Note: There are two cases in which the 1st past part. of the above seven
verbs (i.e. gesehen, gehört etc.) *must* be used:
  (a) in the passive:
Der Plan wurde fallengelassen   *The plan was dropped*

Except with fallen-lassen (see 710) and liegen-lassen, such passives
are rare. Thus: 'He was seen to enter' is 'Man sah ihn hereinkommen' (not: Er wurde hereinkommen gesehen) (cf. 365).

(b) in the perfect infin. (rarely used with a dependent infinitive) (cf. 433):

Ich glaubte ihn hereinkommen gesehen zu haben	*I thought to have seen him enter*

Normal usage: Ich glaubte, ich hätte ihn hereinkommen sehen, or, more coll., Ich glaubte, ich hätte gesehen, wie er hereinkam.

421. When the 2nd past part. of the 7 verbs treated in 420 is used in a subordinate clause, the auxiliary precedes the dependent infinitive instead of coming at the end. (Cf. the modals: Da er heute hat schwimmen dürfen, muß es ihm besser gehen (392)).

Da ich ihn habe spielen sehen, weiß ich, daß es ihm besser geht	*As I have seen him playing, I know that he's better*
obwohl du nicht hättest (zu) kommen brauchen	*although you needn't have come*
Ich hob den Brief auf, den er hatte fallen lassen	*I picked up the letter which he had dropped*

The man in the street will avoid this construction, saying e.g. (for the 1st example above) Ich sah ihn spielen, also weiß ich, daß es ihm besser geht.

The order of the future and conditional of these 7 verbs, used in a subordinate clause and with a dependent infinitive, is not affected, in contrast with the modals, e.g.

Ich wußte nicht, ob ich ihn kommen sehen würde	*I didn't know if I would see him come*
Ich wußte nicht, ob ich es würde tun können (normal usage: ob ich es tun könnte)	BUT: *I did not know if I should be able to do it*
	For good measure:
Ich wußte nicht, ob ich ihn würde kommen sehen können (normal usage: ob ich ihn kommen sehen könnte)	*I did not know if I should be able to see him come*

422. The infin. without 'zu' is used in certain applications of (a) bleiben (b) gehen (c) haben (d) legen (e) schicken (f) tun

(a) **bleiben** *to remain* is used with a number of plain infinitives denoting postures or situations (stehen bleiben, sitzen bleiben) with both literal and derived connotations: see 710; also: bestehen-bleiben *to continue*, e.g. of an old custom, and wohnen bleiben: Er will in Hamburg wohnen bleiben.

(b) After **gehen** it is used to denote purpose 'where the emphasis lies not so much on 'gehen' as on the idea expressed in the infinitive':[1]

Ich gehe heute (im Fluß) schwimmen	*I'm going swimming (in the river) today*
Ich gehe bald schlafen	*I'm soon going to bed*
Er ist einen neuen Anzug kaufen gegangen	*He's gone to buy a new suit*
Er ist in die Stadt gegangen, um einen neuen Anzug zu kaufen	BUT: *He's gone to town to buy a new suit*

---

[1] Eggeling, op. cit., p.159.

Note:
i Though it occurs less frequently, 'kommen' can be used like 'gehen' above, especially in the 2nd person: Kommst du heute schwimmen? Komm doch mit mir einkaufen!

ii Colloquially, the past tenses of 'sein' are used with a plain infinitive to convey 'I went swimming' etc.:

Ich war heute morgen schwimmen   *I went swimming this morning*
Ich bin einkaufen gewesen   *I went/I've been shopping*

iii In spazieren-gehen (spazieren-fahren etc.) the infin. spazieren is treated as a separable prefix (cf. 709).

(c) **haben** + plain infin.:
  i to have something in a certain position somewhere, e.g.:
Ich hatte ein paar Bücher auf dem Tisch liegen; ich habe drei Sack Kartoffeln im Keller stehen. Cf. fig.:

Wir haben eine Anfrage/mehrere   *We have an inquiry/several orders*
Aufträge vorliegen

  Applied to persons, this usage is virtually limited to 'wohnen', e.g. Wir haben eine alte Tante in Hamburg wohnen.

  ii Du hast gut reden/lachen   *It's easy enough (it's all very well) for you to talk/laugh*

(d) (**sich**) **schlafen legen**: Die Mutter legte das Kind schlafen (*put the child to bed*); ich legte mich schlafen (*I went to bed*)

(e) After **schicken** the plain infin. of a certain number of verbs may be used to denote purpose, e.g. Sie schickte das Kind schlafen (commoner: zu Bett); ich habe ihn einkaufen geschickt (BUT: Ich habe ihn geschickt, um eine Zeitung zu kaufen); meine Mutter schickt mich immer Blumen pflücken.

(f) **tun** + plain infin.:
  i a very colloquial, pleonastic use (bad German):
Ich tu jetzt ins Kino gehen   *I'm going to the cinema now*
Gern tät' ich ins Kino gehen   *I'd like to go to the cinema*
Tust du mich auch verstehen?   *Are you sure you understand me?*

  This use of 'tun' is, however, an accepted means of starting the sentence with an emphasized infinitive:

Bewundern tu ich ihn nicht, aber er   *I don't admire him, but he impresses me all*
imponiert mir doch   *the same*
Aber schmerzen tat es darum nicht   *But it was no less painful on that account*
weniger (G. Reuter)

  ii nichts tun als:
Er tut nichts als arbeiten   *He does nothing but work*

L. THE USES OF THE INFINITIVE WITH 'ZU'

423. In all cases other than those treated in 404–22, the infinitive is used with 'zu'; most of these offer no difficulty; for punctuation see 743(f).

424. It is the commonest usage where the infin. is the subject of a verb or the complement of 'sein', except in proverbs or comparable formulations:

Meiner Großmutter zu helfen macht mir immer Spaß	*I always enjoy helping my grandmother*
So etwas zu erlauben ist unerhört	*To allow that kind of thing is preposterous*
Sein Ziel ist, einen Roman zu schreiben	*His aim is to write a novel*

BUT:

Irren, ist menschlich	*To err is human*
Früh aufstehen ist etwas Schreckliches	*Getting up early is horrible*

'zu' is essential

i where the infin. is the real subject after an introductory 'es':

Es wird schwer sein, ihn zu überzeugen	*It will be difficult to convince him*

ii where the infin. has a relative pronoun as its object:

Wir erörterten die Frage, die zu erledigen so wünschenswert wäre	*We discussed the question to settle which would be so desirable*

425. After all verbs other than the 6 modals and those treated in **410 ff.**: Er begann zu singen; er verdient, belohnt zu werden.

426. After impersonal and pseudo-impersonal expressions: Es ist mir viel daran gelegen, dies zu tun; es ist unmöglich, alles zu wissen.

427. To complete the sense of adjectives and adjectival participles: Diese Frage ist schwer zu entscheiden; ich war erstaunt, ihn zu Hause zu finden, BUT:

Er war der erste (der letzte, der einzige, der beste Redner), der kam	*He was the first (the last, the only one, the best speaker) to come*

428. In comparative phrases: after als *than* practice varies, zu + infin. being commoner; after so *as*: zu + infin. E.g. Schwimmen ist besser als im Garten (zu) arbeiten; du kannst nichts Besseres tun, als zu Hause (zu) bleiben; ich bin nicht so dumm, das zu glauben (Du. Stil.).

429. To limit nouns:

Gibt es eine Möglichkeit, ihm zu helfen?	*Is there a possibility of helping him?*

430. After prepositional constructions with verbs, adjectives and nouns, provided there is no change of subject, e.g. Ich freue mich darauf, ihn wiederzusehen: see 504.

431. After 'um'; and after 'ohne' and '(an)statt', provided there is no change of subject:

Ich konnte nichts tun, (um) ihn zu beruhigen	*I could do nothing to reassure him*
Er verließ das Haus, ohne gesehen zu werden	*He left the house without being seen*

Er verließ das Haus, ohne daß ich ihn sah	BUT: *He left the house without my seeing him*
statt sich aufzuregen	*instead of getting excited*

Note:

i The 'um' of 'um . . . zu + infin.' *in order to* is sometimes omitted (cf. the first example above); it is safer to include it.

ii For 'in order that, so that' see 467.

iii Note the two following formulae, which do not express purpose:

Er ist zu alt, um das zu tun	*He is too old to do that*
Er ist alt genug, (um) das zu wissen	*He is old enough to know that*

With a change of subject, 'um . . . zu' becomes 'als daß' (cf. 469(a)) and 'daß' respectively, e.g. Er ist alt genug, daß man sich auf ihn verlassen kann.

iv Provided there is no glaring ambiguity, um . . . zu + infin. may be used without any implication of purpose as an effective substitute for a second main clause; it tends to suggest the idea of 'destined to' (cf. Du. Gram. 6080 and English usage):

Mit achtzehn Jahren verließ er Deutschland, um niemals wiederzukehren (= und sollte niemals wiederkehren)	*At eighteen he left Germany never to return*

432. Used after sein *to be*, **zu + active infin. has a passive meaning**, e.g. Er war nirgends zu sehen *He was nowhere to be seen*. This construction is the equivalent either of können + passive infin., as in the foregoing example, or of müssen or sollen + passive infin.

= können + passive infin.:

Dieses Buch ist nicht zu haben	*This book is unobtainable*
Ist der Direktor heute zu sprechen?	*Can I see the manager today?*
An Schachspielen war nicht zu denken (V. Baum)	*There could be no question of playing chess*

= müssen + passive infin.:

Das ist unbedingt zu vermeiden	*That must be avoided at all costs*
Es ist zu befürchten, daß . . .	*It is to be feared that . . .*

= sollen + passive infin.:

Dieses Haus ist zu verkaufen	*This house is for sale*

The attributive counterpart of this construction is present-participial in form; it is limited to transitive verbs taking an object in the accusative:

eine nicht zu vermeidende Schwierigkeit	*an unavoidable difficulty*
Er sprach mit einer nur zu bewundernden Sachlichkeit	*He spoke with an objectivity which was only to be admired*
Dies ist ein Versprechen, dem zu mißtrauen ist (commoner: dem man mißtrauen muß)	BUT: *This is a promise to be mistrusted*

433. After verbs indicating 'certain mental processes or actions associated with these',[1] an infinitive (most frequently a perfect

[1] Stopp, op. cit., 107(e)2.

infinitive) **with 'zu' is often used**, though a clause is commoner.
The subject of the infinitive phrase must be the same as that of the
introductory verb:

Er behauptete (erinnerte sich, glaubte, meinte, war überzeugt, gab zu), mich gesehen zu haben	*He maintained (remembered, thought, was convinced, admitted) that he had seen me*

N.B. Commoner e.g. Er glaubte, er hätte mich gesehen.

Further examples:

Sie . . . glaubte zu lesen, zu häkeln, tat aber nichts als warten (V. Baum)	*She thought she was reading, crocheting, but she was doing nothing but wait*
A. behauptet von B. bedroht worden zu sein (*Hbg. Abendblatt*)	*A asserts that he was threatened by B*

Note: The above must not be confused with an English accusative and
infinitive construction, which requires a clause in German, e.g. I
believed him to be ill = Ich glaubte, er sei krank (cf. 484(a)).

434. Three remaining uses of zu + infin. may be grouped together:

(a) **after 'haben':**
  i 'etwas zu tun haben' as the equivalent of 'etwas tun sollen or müssen':
     see 402(c).
  ii other uses after haben cause no difficulty, e.g.

Ich habe viel zu tun	*I have a lot to do*
Ich habe an seinem Vorschlag nichts auszusetzen	*I have no fault to find with his suggestion*
Sie haben hier nichts zu suchen	*You have no business here* (idiomatic)

(b) **after 'kommen', denoting chance or result:**

Wir kamen auf Rußland zu sprechen	*We got on to the subject of Russia*
Wir arrangierten es so, daß wir nebeneinander zu sitzen kamen	*We arranged things so that we came to sit next to each other*

(c) **after 'wissen', *to know how to, to be able to:***

Er weiß mit den Leuten umzugehen	*He knows how to deal with people*
Er wußte alles schnell zu finden	*He was able to find everything quickly*

Note: The English infinitives in 'He told me what to do', 'I didn't know
when to come' etc. require clauses in German; see 400 (a): last two
examples and Note.

M. PARTICIPLES

435. The adjectival and substantival use of participles is treated in
detail in 97 f. and 106 ff.; **their adverbial use** is illustrated in 261.

EXAMPLES: ein lachendes Kind; mein verlorener Schirm; er war sehr
aufgeregt; ein Angestellter; die Sterbenden; sie kocht überraschend
gut.
It will become clear in the course of the following pages that participles
are less widely used in German than in English.

436. The attributive participial phrase

(a) A distinctively German feature is that an attributive participle may be preceded by an object and/or by qualifying adverbs and adverb phrases. Where there are several items, they are arranged according to the guide-lines given in 652 ff.

Ihr gegenwärtig in München Chemie studierender Sohn hat sie kürzlich besucht	*Their son, at present studying chemistry in Munich, recently visited them*
Ich habe dieses von meinem Vetter warm empfohlene Buch sehr genossen	*I very much enjoyed this book which was strongly recommended by my cousin*
Wegen Überproduktion entlassene Arbeiter demonstrierten im Fabrikhof	*Workers who had been dismissed on account of overproduction demonstrated in the factory yard*

(b) This construction is not common in conversation, where the first two of the above examples would probably run:

Ihr Sohn, der gegenwärtig in München Chemie studiert, hat sie kürzlich besucht.
Mein Vetter hat mir dieses Buch warm empfohlen, und ich habe es sehr genossen.

But a letter recently received from Germany contained a typical example: Wir waren erlebnisreiche, im ganzen von gutem Wetter begünstigte drei Wochen unterwegs.

(c) The attributive participial phrase is much used, and abused, in literary and journalistic German. One example of each must suffice:

Meta Nackedey, ein ewig errötendes, jeden Augenblick in Scham vergehendes Geschöpf von einigen dreißig Jahren (Th. Mann)	*Meta Nackedey, some thirty years old, a perpetually blushing creature, who every moment almost died of bashfulness*
Zwar gilt der in den vergangenen vier Jahren auf der Basis einer deutsch-amerikanischen Regierungs-vereinbarung für bislang 552 Millionen Mark entwickelte Panzer als Spitzenmodell seiner Klasse (Spiegel)	*Admittedly the tank which has been developed during the past four years, so far at a cost of 552 million marks, on the basis of an agreement between the German and American governments is regarded as the outstanding one of its class*

(d) The same type of attributive phrase may be found with an adjective instead of a participle, e.g. Er hielt eine von rhetorischen Effekten völlig freie Rede.

437. Other types of participial phrase and the position of the participle

In the attributive participial phrase dealt with in 436 the participle must come last.

Other types of participial phrase are:

(a) absolute participial expressions.
(b) phrases with adjectival or adverbial force following the noun to which the participle refers.
(c) phrases with adverbial force standing at the beginning of the sentence.

Discounting rare literary effects, the position of the participle is as follows: in type (a) it comes last.

in types (b) and (c) the present part. comes last, while the past part. may come first or last, as determined by emphasis or rhythm; where the participial phrase is long and intricate, the past part. comes first.

EXAMPLES:

Type (a)

Ihre Zustimmung vorausgesetzt, möchte ich . . .	Assuming your consent, I should like to . . .
Die Geschäfte beendet und signiert, kam Isaak Landauer[1] . . . (L. Feuchtwanger)	The transactions completed and signed, Isaak Landauer came . . .

Type (b)

das Gehege, . . . zusammengebrochen, niedergelegt durch das Gewicht der auf ihm Lastenden (H. Mann)	the enclosure, collapsed, flattened by the weight of those who pressed upon it
Zwar hatte dieses Mal der Dolch, durch ein seidenes Unterkleid abgelenkt, das Opfer nicht sogleich tödlich getroffen (P. Heyse)	This time, indeed, deflected by a silken undergarment, the thrust of the dagger had not been immediately fatal

Type (c)

Ein altes Lied summend, wanderte er durch den Garten	Humming an old song, he strolled through the garden
Geblendet von dem Glanz einer Krone, bemerkte Wallenstein den Abgrund nicht, der zu seinen Füßen sich öffnete (Schiller)	Dazzled by the glitter of a crown, Wallenstein did not see the abyss that yawned at his feet
Von der Wucht seiner Rede hinge- rissen, brachen die Zuhörer immer wieder in Beifall aus	Carried away by the force of his speech, the audience continually broke out into applause

438. Absolute participial expressions

(a) A German passive past participle may form an absolute participial expression: see 437: Examples: Type (a).

(b) Those with an active past participle or a present participle in English are rendered in German by a subordinate clause, a main clause or a prepositional phrase:

Als der Vorsitzende angekommen war, (or: Nach Ankunft des Vorsitzenden) begann die Konferenz	The chairman having arrived, the conference began
Da der Fluß rasch stieg, wurden Notmaßnahmen getroffen (or: Der Fluß stieg rasch, und Notmaßnahmen wurden getroffen)	The river rising rapidly, emergency measures were taken
Er saß in seinem Sessel mit den Füßen auf einem Schemel	He sat in his armchair, his feet resting on a footstool

439. An English participial phrase which constitutes a separate statement and is thus the equivalent of a main clause is rendered as such in German, especially where the two actions are consecutive, as in the first of the following examples:

Er öffnete die Schublade und nahm das Testament heraus	Opening the drawer, he took out the will

[1] quoted by R. Kurth in *Muttersprache*, 1958, pp. 122 ff.

Er saß an seinem Pult und schrieb einen Brief (literary alternative: einen Brief schreibend)	*He sat at his desk writing a letter*

440. An English participial phrase conveying manner may be rendered in two ways: (a) by a German participial phrase (rather literary) (b) by an 'indem' clause (normal usage):

Nach jedem Satz pausierend, erzählte er seine Geschichte Er erzählte seine Geschichte, indem er nach jedem Satz eine Pause machte	*Pausing after every sentence, he told his story*

441. English participial phrases which are the equivalent of temporal, causal or concessive clauses are mostly rendered by these in German:

Nachdem ich die Briefe beantwortet hatte, ging ich spazieren	*Having answered the letters, I went for a walk*
Da ich wußte, daß er verreist war, habe ich ihn nicht angerufen	*Knowing that he was away, I didn't ring him up*
Obwohl ich wußte, daß er absagen würde, habe ich ihn trotzdem eingeladen	*Knowing that he would refuse, I nevertheless invited him*

In two cases a participial phrase may, however, be used:
i where a past part. has a passive meaning, being that of a transitive verb:

Vor Einbrechern gewarnt, brachte er das Geld auf die Bank	*Warned against burglars, he took the money to the bank*

ii where a past part. has an active meaning, being that of an intransitive verb conjugated with 'sein' and signifying a completed action:

Zu Hause angelangt, ging ich bald zu Bett	*Having reached home, I soon went to bed*

cf. An einer schmerzhaften Krankheit jung gestorben, hatte er doch ein halbes Dutzend Bücher geschrieben.

442. The English elliptical construction: While waiting for you, ... Though admiring his achievements, ... etc. is restricted in German to obwohl (obgleich etc.) followed by a passive past participle; otherwise a clause must be used:

Obwohl von seinen Kollegen geachtet, war er nicht sehr beliebt	*Though respected by his colleagues, he was not very popular*
BUT: Als ob er vor Einbrechern gewarnt war, brachte er das Geld auf die Bank	*As if warned against burglars, he took the money to the bank*

443. (S) wie+passive past participle is used in a number of contracted and parenthetical phrases:[1]

Also, wie ausgemacht: wir treffen uns um acht Uhr	*Well then, as arranged, we'll meet at eight o'clock*
wie gesagt	*as I said*

[1] cf. Eggeling, op. cit.: wie 2 (c).

9*

wie erwartet	*as expected*
wie vorausgesehen	*as foreseen*
Cf. the set phrase:	
Er blieb wie angewurzelt stehen	*He stopped as if rooted to the ground*

444. For **the past part. as an imperative equivalent**, see 459(f).

445. The past part. of a verb conjugated with 'sein' may be used with 'kommen' to describe the manner of coming, corresponding to a pres. part. in English:

Er kam ins Zimmer gelaufen	*He came running into the room*
Er kam herbeigeeilt	*He came hurrying along*
Ein Dachziegel kam auf den Bürgersteig heruntergefallen	*A tile came crashing onto the pavement*

446. Certain participles are used as prepositions or conjunctions or to form prepositional or conjunctional phrases, e.g. entsprechend *in accordance with*, vorausgesetzt, daß *assuming that, provided that*. These are not listed here, but are included with the appropriate prepositions and conjunctions.

ausgenommen *excepting* and **eingeschlossen** *including*, though prepositional in force, are better dealt with here. (Both words are somewhat stilted, normal usage being außer + dat. and auch respectively.)
The commonest usage is for the noun or pronoun to follow ausgenommen and to precede eingeschlossen, its case being determined by the main verb of the sentence; eingeschlossen is often strengthened with 'mit':
Alle waren da, ausgenommen mein Bruder.
Ich traue allen, ausgenommen dem neuen Sekretär.
Alle waren da, er mit eingeschlossen.
Er hat alle eingeladen, meinen Bruder eingeschlossen.
Versicherung eingeschlossen *including insurance*.

Note:
i Where the noun on which the exception depends is dat. after a preposition, ausgenommen is followed by the acc.: Ich hatte keine Zeit, mit den anderen zu sprechen, ausgenommen meinen Vetter.
ii eingeschlossen is not preceded by a dative: Ich traue allen, den neuen Sekretär mit eingeschlossen.

447. Some idiomatic uses of the past participle

ein (aus)gedienter Soldat	*one who has completed military service*
ein gelernter Glaser	*a trained (or skilled) glazier*
Das Bild ist sehr geschmeichelt	*The picture is very flattering*
Er sah seinen Verdacht bestätigt	*He saw his suspicions confirmed*
offen gesagt	*to be frank*
strenggenommen	*strictly speaking*
Verstanden?	*Understand?*

448. The German renderings of English participles in the following cases are dealt with in the paragraphs indicated:

1. the English continuous form: I am writing etc.: 353.
2. a participle as the objective complement of to see, to hear, to feel, to find, e.g. I saw him coming: 410–12.

3. He is having a house built: 419.
4. certain uses of the participles with to remain (he remained seated) and to have (I had a few books lying on the table): 422(a) and (c).
5. for the German construction 'eine nicht zu vermeidende Schwierigkeit' *an unavoidable difficulty*, see 432.

See also 455: Miscellaneous illustrations of the rendering of the verb form in -ing.

N. THE TRANSLATION OF THE ENGLISH GERUND

449. The English gerund (the verb form in -ing used as a noun) **has no fixed equivalent in German and is rendered in a variety of ways. One of these is to use an ordinary German noun** if a suitable one suggests itself, e.g. Der Anstrich des Hauses geht gut voran *The painting of the house is going ahead well*. This method is possible in any of the contexts treated in the following paragraphs; it will not be mentioned again as such, but is illustrated in some of the examples.

450. The English gerund may frequently be rendered by a German infinitive used as a noun (always neut.) (cf. 404) **or simply by the infinitive, generally with 'zu':**

(a) as subject:

Ihn zu überzeugen wird nicht leicht sein — *Convincing him won't be easy*

(b) as object:

Ich hörte das laute Bellen eines Hundes — *I heard the loud barking of a dog*

Er begann zu lachen — *He began laughing*

(c) as complement:

Sein Hobby ist Briefmarkensammeln — *His hobby is stamp-collecting*

Das nennst du höflich sein[1] — *You call that being polite*

(d) in prepositional phrases limiting a noun or completing the sense of an adjective:

Ich habe keine Zeit zum Üben — *I have no time for practising*

Ich habe keine Zeit, im Garten zu arbeiten — *I have no time for working in the garden*

die Freuden des Schilaufens — *the pleasures of skiing*

die Wichtigkeit einer baldigen Entscheidung — *the importance of deciding soon*

Er ist nicht fähig, so etwas zu tun (or: Er ist einer solchen Tat nicht fähig) — *He is not capable of doing that kind of thing*

451. 'without' and 'instead of' + gerund: see 431

452. by or through + gerund, expressing means: use a clause introduced by 'indem' or 'dadurch, daß'; 'indem' should only be used

[1] no 'zu'; see 406.

when the action of the 'indem' clause is simultaneous with that of the main clause:

Er rettete sich, indem er aus dem Fenster sprang	*He saved himself by jumping out of the window*
Er erreichte sein Ziel dadurch, daß wir ihm geholfen haben	*He attained his goal through our having helped him*

Note: Where there is a strong causal element, 'dadurch, weil' is also used (cf. Du. Haupt.: daß 3):

Seine Lage wird dadurch schwierig, weil sògar seine Freunde nicht mehr an ihn glauben	*His position is becoming difficult through even his friends' no longer believing in him*

453. Prepositions such as after, before, since, in spite of, followed by a gerund, are rendered by adverb clauses:

Trotzdem er mir geholfen hatte (or: Trotz seiner Hilfe), kam ich spät	*In spite of his having helped me, I was late*

454. For a gerund or a gerundial phrase following the preposition of a verbal, substantival or adjectival construction (e.g. I rely on finding him at home; his indignation at our not having told him) see 504 ff.

455. Miscellaneous illustrations of the rendering of the verb form in -ing. Since the use of participles is more restricted in German than in English and since German has no fixed equivalent of the English gerund, language sense is often required to produce an organic German equivalent of the English verb form in -ing. This may be illustrated by a number of examples:[1]

Es muß jedenfalls ein schreckliches Leben sein, dauernd erst um sieben Uhr abends nach Hause zu kommen	*It must be a dreadful existence anyhow, not getting home till seven in the evening*
Wenn er nur als ein unbestimmtes, graugrünes Gebilde erscheint, dessen Baumgruppen sich bloß als blasse Schatten zeigen, ...	*If it [Brensham Hill] appears only as a vague grey-green shape with the clumps of trees showing only as faint shadows ... (J. Moore)*
Er verbringt seine Zeit mit Lesen	*He spends his time reading*
Er verbringt seine Zeit damit, daß er über die Vergangenheit brütet	*He spends his time brooding about the past*
Er ging in Gedanken versunken dahin, während die Kinder weiter voran waren	*He walked along brooding, the children being farther ahead*
Wenn man seine Nervosität berücksichtigt, sprach er recht gut	*Allowing for his nervousness, he spoke very well*

---

[1] The first two are taken from A and S Level proses set by the Oxford and Cambridge Schools Examination Board in 1962 and 1963.

So weilten sie, bis die Stunde, wo man sich für die Nacht trennt, längst vorbei war	*Thus they lingered on till the hour of separating for the night was long past* (Ch. Dickens)
Haben Sie etwas dagegen, daß mein Bruder es erfährt?	*Have you any objection to my brother hearing about it?*
Ich schreibe sein Verbrechen der Tatsache zu, daß er als Kind nie geliebt worden ist	*I ascribe his crime to his never having been loved as a child*

See also 497 and 502.

O. THE IMPERATIVE AND ITS EQUIVALENTS[1]

456. Straightforward examples of the imperative: Hans, sei nicht so dumm! Kinder, bringt ein paar Stühle in den Garten! Kommen Sie bald wieder! Bitte, setzen Sie sich!

Note the following difference between English and German usage:

Seien Sie so gut und schließen Sie die Tür!	*Be so good as to shut the door*

457. (a) **Occasionally a stressed 'du' and 'ihr' are used after the familiar forms for the sake of emphasis**; see 342(b)vii and (c)ii.

(b) For **the intensification of the imperative by a particle,** see 286(h), 290(c), 294(c), 297(f), 302(c), 303(f).

458. The function of the imperative proper is a direct command in the 2nd person; **for the rendering of a wish or exhortation in all persons and of a command in the 3rd pers., see 476.**

459. Imperative equivalents (cf. Du. Gram. 1040, 1045)

(a) Modal verbs: müssen, sollen (400(h)), dürfen (397(c)) and one use of wollen: Willst du gleich still sein! *Will you be quiet now!*

(b) 2nd sing. or plur. of pres. or future indic.: either a question or a statement, to which the intonation gives their imperative force:

Hörst du jetzt zu?	*Are you going to listen now?*
Wirst du jetzt zuhören?	
Ihr hört jetzt zu!	*You're going to listen now*
Ihr werdet jetzt zuhören!	
„Du hebst das [ein Bonbon] auf bis nach dem Abendessen", erklärte das Fräulein (V. Baum)	*'You're keeping that [a sweet] till after supper', declared the governess*

(c) haben zu + infin.:

Du hast dir jetzt die Hände zu waschen	*You're to wash your hands now* (a sharp injunction)

(d) a 'daß' clause, generally containing a stressed 'ja':

Daß du *ja* zum Mittagessen pünktlich bist!	*Be sure you're punctual for lunch*

---

[1] For the forms of the imperative, see 342.

(e) the impersonal passive (cf. 381):

| Jetzt wird gearbeitet! | *You're going to work now* |
| Jetzt wird nicht gelacht! | *No laughing now!* |

(f) a past participle:[1]

Stillgestanden!   *Attention!* (military command)

(g) an infinitive:[2]

Antreten! Wegtreten!	*Fall in! Dismiss!*
Einsteigen und Türen schließen!	*Take your seats! Close the doors!*
4 Eiweiß zu sehr steifem Schnee schlagen	*Beat 4 whites of egg stiffly*

(h) a noun, an adjective, an adverb, a phrase, all used elliptically:
Achtung! *Look out!* Ruhig! *Be quiet!* Vorwärts! *Forward!* Tür zu!
Shut the door!

Es erscholl das Einsatzkommando   *The order to act rang out: Truncheons*
„Knüppel frei! Räumen!" (*Spiegel*)   *ready! Clear the street!*

P. THE SUBJUNCTIVE AND ITS USES

460. Survey of the uses of the subjunctive[3]

1. Introductory 461
2. Conditional Clauses 462–5
3. 'as if' clauses 466
4. Final Clauses 467
5. Other clauses with a final element 468
6. Negative contexts 469
7. Concessive Clauses 470–74
8. The Subjunctive of Modest Assertion 475
9. The Optative Subjunctive 476
10. Indirect Speech 477–85

461. Introductory

(a) The fundamental difference between the indicative and subjunctive
moods is that the indicative expresses fact, certainty and agreement,
while the subjunctive expresses the hypothetical, the unreal, supposition, doubt and disagreement. The imperf. subj. is not a past tense.

(b) In spoken German there is a strong tendency to replace the subjunctive by the indicative, a tendency which is strongest among, but not
confined to, the less educated.

(c) In subordinate clauses, the imperf. subj. is more used by North
Germans, the pres. subj. by South Germans, especially in the Ale-
mannic area: Baden-Württemberg, Switzerland and parts of Bavaria
and Austria (cf. Du. Gram. 6750). In general, the imperf. subj. is
gaining ground at the expense of the pres. subj., which, in conversation, is felt to be stilted and affected. (Perhaps for that very reason the
pres. subj. continues to flourish in journalistic and literary German:

---

[1] Duden's explanation (Gram. 1045): the command is regarded as fulfilled.
[2] used elliptically, 'Sie sollen', or something similar, being omitted.
[3] For the forms of the Subjunctive, see 334 ff., 340(c)(g), 345 f., 389(b)(e)(f).

Du. Gram. 6750). More specifically, the 2nd sing. and 2nd plur. of the pres. subj. (e.g. du kommest, ihr kommet) are the forms that sound most affected and are most regularly avoided. The singular of the pres. subj. of 'sein' is freely used, 'er sei' perhaps more frequently than any other pres. subj. form in the language.

(d) Per contra, many imperfect subjunctives with the root vowels ä, ü and particularly ö (e.g. er läse, er grübe, er löge, from lesen, graben and lügen) sound stilted and are likewise avoided; these include all the irregular imperfect subjunctives given in 345(c).

(e) The method of avoiding the forms of the subjunctive that sound stilted (e.g. by an interchange of present and imperfect subjunctive or by the use of the conditional or a modal verb) varies according to the grammatical context and is treated under the separate uses of the subjunctive.

(f) A glance at the conjugational paradigms in 334 ff. and 389 will show that, except for 'sein' and the modal verbs, the 1st sing., 1st plur. and 3rd plur. of the pres. indic. and the pres. subj. are identical; that the imperf. subj. of all weak verbs is the same as the imperf. indic.; and that strong verbs with a vowel that cannot modify have identical forms in the 1st and 3rd plur. of the imperf. indic. and subj. The extent to which, and the methods by which, German usage takes account of this factor is referred to under the separate uses of the subjunctive. It may be said that the identity of subjunctive and indicative is felt to matter less in the imperfect than in the present.

462. Conditional Clauses

(a) Basic types

i **Open Condition** (**no** *would* **or** *would have*): indic. in both parts.
Wenn ich ihm heute schreibe, bekommt er den Brief morgen
If I write to him today, he'll get the letter tomorrow

ii **Improbable Condition** (*would*)
    'wenn' clause: imperf. subj.
    main clause: imperf. subj. or condit.
Wenn ich ihm heute schriebe,
   { bekäme er den Brief morgen
   { würde er den Brief morgen bekommen
If I wrote to him today, he would get the letter tomorrow

iii **Rejected Condition** (*would have*)
    'wenn' clause: pluperf. subj.
    main clause: pluperf. subj. or condit. perf.
Wenn ich ihm heute geschrieben hätte,
   { hätte er den Brief morgen bekommen
   { würde er den Brief morgen bekommen haben
If I had written to him today, he would have got the letter tomorrow

Note:
i In the main clause of type ii, the conditional is commoner in conversation than the imperf. subj.

ii **A warning**: 'would' expressing habit or meaning 'was willing to' is not rendered by 'würde'.

After lunch he would go for a walk:
> Nach dem Mittagessen pflegte er einen Spaziergang zu machen (slightly stilted)/machte er immer (or: gewöhnlich) einen Spaziergang (normal usage).

I asked several of my friends but none would go with me:
> Ich forderte mehrere meiner Freunde auf, aber keiner wollte mitgehen.

(b) **An Open Condition, with the indic. in both parts, may occur in the past**:

Wenn man Schwierigkeiten hatte, konnte man sich an den Werkmeister wenden	*If one was in difficulties, one could apply to the foreman*

(c) Where, as in all the examples in (a) above, the condit. cl. precedes the main cl., the latter often begins with 'so' or 'dann' (Engl. then) (See also 463(a)N.i):
> Wenn ich ihm heute schreibe, so (or: dann) bekommt er den Brief morgen.

(d) It is not unusual to use normal order in the main clause following a conditional clause, the effect being to give additional emphasis to the main clause:

Wenn ich es nicht mit eignen Augen gesehen hätte, ich hätte es nie geglaubt	*If I hadn't seen it with my own eyes, I should never have believed it*

(e) **Stilted, awkward or ambiguous forms of the imperf. subj.** (cf. 461(d)(e)(f)) **may be avoided** by using either the conditional or 'sollte' or 'wollte'. The conditional should preferably not be used in both the condit. clause and the main clause.

Wenn du schneller arbeiten würdest (better: wolltest) (in place of 'arbeitetest'), könntest du mehr verdienen.
Wenn das Konzert früher beginnen sollte (in place of 'begönne'), . . .
Wenn er mich fragte (or: fragen sollte), würde ich ihm alles sagen.[1]
Wie wäre es, wenn wir ihm helfen wollten? (in place of 'hülfen').

Colloquially, the imperf. indic. is sometimes used:

Wenn er die Notleine zog (in place of 'zöge'), würde der Zug sofort stehenbleiben (E. Kästner)	*If he pulled the communication cord, the train would stop at once*

Finally, the imperf. subj. of 'tun' is sometimes enlisted (bad German):
> Wenn ich ihm schreiben täte, würde er den Brief morgen bekommen.

(f) In addition to the function noted in (e), 'sollte' may be used to increase the improbability, the remoteness, of an Improbable Condition:

Wenn ich einmal in diese Lage kommen sollte,[2] . . .	*If ever I were to find myself in that situation, . . .*

---

[1] If the weak imperf. subj. were used in both parts (Wenn er mich fragte, sagte ich ihm alles), this would be more likely to mean: When he asked me, I used to tell him everything.
[2] from Erben, op. cit., 68.

463. Alternatives for 'wenn'

(a) In place of 'wenn' with the verb at the end, inversion of verb and subject, without 'wenn', may be used.

Note:

i Following a conditional clause of this type, the main clause usually begins with 'dann' or 'so', 'so' being a shade literary.

ii Used in Open or Improbable Conditions (types i and ii in 462(a)), the inversion construction is slightly more literary (cf. Du. Gram. 6375).

iii In contrast with English, there is in German no restriction on this usage, except that it is uncommon where the condit. clause follows the main clause.

Thus the examples in 462(a) could run:
Schreibe ich ihm heute, dann bekommt er den Brief morgen.
Schriebe ich ihm heute, ... Hätte ich ihm heute geschrieben, ...
and, from 462(e): Sollte er mich fragen, so würde ich ihm alles sagen.

(b) The following words and phrases are used with the same tenses as 'wenn'; in practice, they mainly introduce Open Conditions (462(a): type i) (for punctuation see 743 (e) ii):

vorausgesetzt, daß	*assuming that, provided that*
angenommen, (daß)	
falls; sofern; im Falle, daß	*in case*
für den Fall, daß	
unter der Bedingung, daß	*on condition that*
unter der Voraussetzung, daß	*on the assumption that*
sofern; wofern (relatively rare)	*provided that*
gesetzt, (daß)	*supposing that*
gesetzt den Fall, daß	

Note:

i vorausgesetzt, (daß), angenommen, (daß) and gesetzt, (daß): without 'daß' these are followed by normal order; with 'daß' the verb goes to the end: Angenommen, er hat dein Telegramm erhalten/ Angenommen, daß er dein Telegramm erhalten hat, wird er bald hier sein.

ii für den Fall, daß is used in a context with an element of purpose, such as: Er gab mir seine Telefonnummer für den Fall, daß ich ihn erreichen wollte.

iii for 'even if', see 473.

464. Conditional Clause equivalents

(a) An imperative, or a sentence with 'sollen ... nur' or 'brauchen ... nur', may be the equivalent of a conditional clause if followed by so (or dann) + a second sentence:[1]

Gib mir das Geld, so kann ich die Plätze besorgen	*Give me the money, then I can get the seats*
Er soll nur anrufen/Er braucht nur anzurufen, so sage ich ihm Bescheid	*Let him ring up/He need only ring up and I'll give him the information*

---

[1] cf. Schulz-Griesbach, op. cit., G 418.

(b) A noun clause or a relative clause may be the equivalent of a conditional clause; thence the tenses in the following:

Wer (or: Jemand, der) diese Entwicklung vorausgesehen hätte, hätte viel Geld verdienen können	*Anyone foreseeing this development could have made a lot of money*

(c) An adverb or a prepositional phrase may take the place of a conditional clause; thence the tenses in the following simple sentences:

Sonst würde ich es nicht tun	*Otherwise I would not do it*
Unter anderen Umständen wäre ich erfolgreicher gewesen (from Du. Gram. 6465)	*Under other circumstances I should have been more successful*

(d) A conditional clause may be implied; thence the tenses in the following simple sentences:

Lieber bliebe ich zu Hause [wenn ich die Wahl hätte]	*I would rather stay at home [if I had the choice]*
Ich hätte dasselbe getan [wenn ich an deiner Stelle gewesen wäre]	*I would have done the same thing [if I had been in your place]*

465. unless

i wenn . . . nicht: tenses as for 'wenn'.

ii außer wenn;[1] ausgenommen, wenn[1] *except if*: used mainly in Open Conditions (462(a): type (i)).

iii es sei denn, daß:[1] used mainly in Open Conditions; see 289(h).

iv denn (with imperf. subj. of 'müssen'): archaic and literary; see 289(h).

Wenn er nicht bald kommt, wird es zu spät sein	*Unless he comes soon, it will be too late*
Er kommt immer pünktlich nach Hause, außer wenn Sitzung ist	*He always comes home punctually except if there's a meeting*

Note: The 'nicht' of 'wenn . . . nicht' must follow a pronoun object, generally follows def. art., demonstrative or possessive + noun, must precede words like jemand, etwas, alles, einiges, and generally precedes other types of object:

Wenn du ihn nicht fragst, . . .
Wenn du meinem Bruder nicht hilfst, . . .
Wenn du ihr nicht alles sagst, . . .
Wenn er nicht (deutsche) Zeitungen liest, . . .

466. 'as if' clauses (Comparative-cum-Conditional): als ob, als wenn

(a) **Basic types** (Both alternatives, als ob and als + inversion, are widely used; the latter is slightly more literary.)

i **Appearances are accepted as probably true**

Er sieht (sah) aus, {als ob er krank sei / als sei er krank}　　　pres. subj.

He looks (looked) as if he were ill

{als ob er krank gewesen sei / als sei er krank gewesen}　　　perf. subj.

as if he had been ill

---

[1] for punctuation see 743(e).

$\begin{cases} \text{als ob er zuverlässig sein werde} \\ \text{als werde er zuverlässig sein} \end{cases}$ fut. subj.
   as if he would be reliable

Note: Colloquial usage prefers the conditional (sein würde) to the future subj.

ii Appearances are regarded as misleading

Er tut (tat), $\begin{cases} \text{als ob er krank wäre} \\ \text{als wäre er krank} \end{cases}$ imperf. subj.
He acts (acted) as if he were ill

$\begin{cases} \text{als ob er krank gewesen wäre} \\ \text{als wäre er krank gewesen} \end{cases}$ pluperf. subj.
   as if he had been ill

$\begin{cases} \text{als ob er in zwei Jahren ein reicher Mann sein würde} \\ \text{als würde er in zwei Jahren ein reicher Mann sein} \end{cases}$ condi-
                                                      tional
   as if he would be a rich man in two years' time

or appearances are regarded as purely imaginary

Er arbeitete mit der Zahnbürste, als wenn viel davon abhinge (V. Baum)	*He plied his toothbrush, as if much depended on it*
Das wird ganz laut und ist fast fort, als hätte es der Wind geschluckt (H. Fallada)	*It [the distant roar of a big city] grows quite loud and almost vanishes, as if the wind had swallowed it*

Note: In the English of all the examples, 'as though' would, of course, be an alternative for 'as if'.

(b) The distinction between these two basic types, made in Du. Gram. 6705, is borne out by the preponderant practice of a considerable range of authors and by the reaction of Germans tested on the above examples.

Nevertheless, this distinction is one of which the average German, and many German authors, are not consciously aware and it is frequently infringed. Moreover it is often overridden by the instinctive aversion for subjunctive forms that sound affected or awkward (cf. 461(c) and (d)); these may be avoided by using the 'wrong' tense, by a modal or by some other means, e.g. instead of: Er tat, als ob er hervorragend schwömme, say: als ob er hervorragend schwimme/schwimmen könnte, or: als ob er ein hervorragender Schwimmer wäre.

(c) **Colloquially, 'als ob' is frequently used with the indic.**
Note:
i this is common when the main verb is in the present, relatively rare when it is in the past.
ii als + inversion cannot be used with the indic.

E.g. Er sieht aus, als ob er krank ist; er tut, als ob er oft an seine Eltern schreibt; mir war, als ob er mich nicht verstand.

(d) To introduce an illustrative parallel, 'as if' may be rendered by 'wie wenn': Das wäre, wie wenn (or: als wenn) ein Kommunist zum Katholizismus bekehrt würde.

(e) **'als wenn'** can also mean **'than if, than when'**; the context will
make this clear:

Man kann ihn nicht besser ärgern, als
wenn man ihm fortwährend Rat
gibt

*One cannot annoy him more effectively
than if one constantly gives him advice*

467. Final Clauses

(a) **In spoken German,** they generally have the indicative and often
use können:[1]

Ich helfe ihm, damit[2] er rechtzeitig
abfährt/abfahren kann

I'm helping him so that he leaves on time

Ich half ihm, damit er rechtzeitig
abfahren konnte/damit alles gut
ging

*I helped him so that he should leave on
time/so that everything should be all
right*

(b) **In literary German,** the pres. or imperf. subj. is often used,[1]
especially when the main verb is in a past tense, as in the first example, but also when it is in the present, as in the second:

Er half ihnen, damit sie rechtzeitig abführen.

Und damit diese Autorität intakt bleibe, wird ihm [dem Bundespräsidenten]
angeraten, sich möglichst wenig in aktuelle Streitfragen einzumischen
(*to interfere as little as possible in current controversies*) (*Zeit*)

(c) **Alternatives for damit** *in order that, so that*

i (so) daß: Arbeite fleißig, (so) daß du das Examen bestehst.

ii auf daß is a specifically literary alternative. Thus, in a passage too
long to quote, Thomas Mann tells of the building of the pyramids
in long years of agonizing forced labour 'auf daß Gottkönig Chufu
tief innen darunter ruhe'.

iii When the subject of the main clause is also that of the final clause, it
is neater and more usual to use um zu + infin.:

Ich gehe nach Hause, um ihm zu
helfen

I'm going home so that I may help him

(d) **lest** = damit . . . nicht or daß . . . nicht.

Ich helfe ihm, damit er nicht zu spät
abfährt

*I am helping him lest he should leave too
late*

Note: I fear lest . . . = Ich fürchte, daß . . .

468. The imperf. or pluperf. subjunctive may be used in a relative clause or in a temporal clause introduced by 'bis', 'ehe' or 'bevor', which has a final sense:

Er suchte . . . nach jemandem, der ihn
anspräche (G. Gaiser)

*He was looking for someone who might
address him*

Sie beschlossen zu warten, bis er käme
(or: kam, or: kommen würde)

They decided to wait for him to come

Er weigerte sich, den Vertrag zu
unterzeichnen, bevor wir ihm
weitere Zugeständnisse gemacht
hätten (or: machten)

*He refused to sign the agreement before
we had made further concessions*

---

[1] cf. Collinson, op. cit., p. 133.
[2] accented on the second syllable.

469. Use of the subjunctive in negative contexts

(a) Because of their negative character, their concern with what did *not* happen or was *not* the case, **nicht daß, ohne daß, (an)statt daß and zu (alt), als daß are frequently followed by the imperf. or pluperf. subj.** The effect is less brusque than that of a straightforward indicative tense, which is always a possible alternative (cf. Du. Gram. 6485, 6680):

Nicht, daß er faul wäre (or: ist), aber er kommt in seinem Beruf nicht vorwärts	*Not that he's lazy, but he's not getting on in his profession*
nicht daß ich wüßte (set phrase; indic. not possible)	*not that I know*
und er [Zuckmayer] hat, ohne daß es ihm geglückt wäre, immer wieder . . . versucht, seine Herkunft vom wohlanständigen Bürgertum abzustreifen (*Zeit*)	*and, without succeeding, he tried again and again to divest himself of his respectable middle-class origin*
Statt daß er mir geholfen hätte (statt daß er mir half, statt mir zu helfen), las er die Zeitung	*Instead of helping me, he read the paper*
Er ist zu vernünftig, als daß ich dies von ihm erwartet hätte	*He is too sensible for me to have expected this of him*

(b) Similarly, the imperf. or pluperf. subj. may on occasion be used **in other subordinate clauses** where the main clause or the subordinate clause or both are negative. Again, the indic. is perfectly possible, but more brusque (cf. Du. Gram. 6485, 6690, 6720):

Dies bedeutet keineswegs, daß ich mit allem zufrieden wäre (or: bin)	*This by no means signifies that I'm satisfied with everything*
Nicht eine einzige Großstadt, keine Mittel- oder Kleinstadt, kein Dorf, die nicht ihr Gesicht in zwei Jahrzehnten gründlich . . . gewandelt hätten[1]	*Not a single large, medium-sized or small town, not a village, that has not radically changed its appearance in the course of two decades*

(c) Similarly, the pluperf. subj. is often used **in sentences containing 'fast' or 'beinah'** (with their negative implications), with or without nicht:[2]

Ich wäre fast nicht gekommen	*I almost didn't come*
Wir hätten das Spiel beinah gewonnen	*We almost won the game*

470. Concessive Clauses beginning with although or its equivalent

(a) The relevant conjunctions are:
i obgleich *although*; its variants: obwohl, obschon; and the rarer obzwar and wiewohl.
ii trotzdem (stressed on 'dem') *despite the fact that.*
iii ungeachtet (daß) *notwithstanding that.*
iv zugegeben, daß *granted that.*
Of these, obwohl is the commonest in current usage.

(b) The mood is normally the indicative.

[1] from an article on 'Das Bergische Land', south of the Ruhr, in *Die Zeit* (11.11.1966).
[2] cf. Schulz-Griesbach, op. cit., B 739.

(c) Where the concessive clause precedes the main clause, the contrast between them may be emphasized by the use of so ... doch,[1] or occasionally of normal order, in the main clause:

Obwohl sie sehr bescheiden leben, so scheinen sie doch ganz glücklich zu sein	*Although they live very modestly, they seem to be quite happy*
Obwohl er mein Vetter ist, ich kann nichts für ihn tun	*Although he's my cousin, I can do nothing for him*

471. Concessive Clauses beginning with whoever, however, whenever etc.

(a) Here there is an immense range and complexity of variations and no attempt will be made to include them all.

(b) **The following four types represent normal usage and cover most requirements**; they start respectively with 1. an indefinite pronoun 2. an indefinite adverb 3. however + adjective 4. however + adverb.

Wer er auch ist/sein mag, ich kann nichts für ihn tun	1. *Whoever he may be, I can do nothing for him*
Wann er auch ankommt/ ankommen mag, ich will ihn sofort sprechen	2. *Whenever he may arrive, I want to speak to him at once*
Wie (or: So) teuer das Bild auch ist/sein mag, ich will es doch kaufen	3. *However expensive the picture may be, I'll buy it all the same*
Wie (or: So) schnell er auch lief/ laufen mochte, der Polizist holte ihn ein	4. *However quickly he ran, the policeman caught him up*

(c) **Comments on the above types**

  i Following these concessive clauses, the main clause has normal order; this emphasizes the contrast between the two clauses, the magnitude of the concession: e.g. sentence 2 conveys: No matter at what hour he may arrive, I want to speak to him at once. Occasionally, where this element of contrast is weaker, the main clause may have inversion, e.g. Wo er sich auch zeigte, wurde er mit Beifall begrüßt *Wherever he showed himself, he was cheered.*

  ii If these clauses are in the present, the verb may be either indicative or subjunctive. Normal usage is the indicative (as above); the subjunctive may make the concession a shade more sweeping and is stylistically more *recherché*, e.g. Wer er auch sei/sein möge, ich kann nichts für ihn tun. In the past (illustrated in type 4), the verb can only be in the indicative.

  iii Alternatives for 'auch' (though 'auch' is commonest and safest): nur, auch nur, immer, auch immer, nur immer; 'immer' generally

comes immediately after the pronoun or adverb and is not used
in types 3 and 4:

Sie verstehen sich ohne Worte, was immer sich begibt (*whatever occurs*) (W. Dieß).
Wo immer er sich zeigte/Wo er sich auch nur (auch immer) zeigte, wurde er mit
Beifall begrüßt.

iv   In types 3 and 4, 'wie' is slightly commoner than 'so', but for
'however much', expressing degree, 'sosehr' is commoner than
'wie sehr'; these, like 'sowenig', may be used alone or followed by
'auch':

Sosehr ich es (auch) bedauere, ich kann unmöglich mitgehen	*However much I regret it, I can't possibly go with you*
Sowenig er mir gefällt, ich muß ihn doch bewundern	*Little as I like him, I can't help admiring him*

(d) 'whatever' used as an indefinite adjective is rendered by 'was für (ein)' or 'welcher':

Was für Schwierigkeiten du auch hast, es ist der Mühe wert	*Whatever difficulties you may have, it's worth the bother*
... diese Vorgänge, von welcher Seite man sie auch betrachtet (*SZ*)	*these events, from whatever side one considers them*

Note: 'welcher' may be used elliptically:

aus welchem Land auch immer	*from whatever country*
mit welchen Mitteln auch immer (*SZ*)	*with whatever resources*

472. 'noch so' is the equivalent of '(n)ever so' with concessive force:[1]

Er mag noch so gescheit sein, (er) paßt aber für diese Stellung nicht	*He may be ever so intelligent, but he's not suitable for this post*
Nein, er war kein guter Ehemann, so dachte Xanthippe, mochte er ein noch so großer Philosoph sein (S. Andres)	*No, he was not a good husband, thought Xanthippe, though he might be never so great a philosopher*

According to the context, 'noch so' may require other English renderings:

jede noch so nebensächliche Bemerkung	*every remark, however trivial,*
Es mögen sich (auch) noch so viele Leute beschweren, es wird nichts geschehen	*No matter how many people complain, nothing will happen*

473. Concessive Clauses of the Conditional type: even if, even though:

German renderings are of four kinds, (a) being the commonest; the same
tenses are used as in conditional clauses (see 462(a)).

(a) selbst wenn, auch wenn, sogar wenn; a following main clause generally
has inversion:

Selbst wenn ich ihm heute schriebe, würde er den Brief morgen nicht bekommen.

(b) wenn ... auch; also, relatively rare: ob ... auch, wenngleich
(divisible), wennschon (divisible); in a following main clause, normal
order is more emphatic and more usual:

Wenn ich ihm auch heute geschrieben hätte, er hätte den Brief morgen (doch)
nicht bekommen.

Note:

i The 'auch' of 'wenn ... auch' must follow a pronoun object, generally

---

[1] contrast its colloquial use: He was ever so nice: Er war wirklich furchtbar nett.

follows def. art., demonstrative or possessive + noun, but must precede all other types of object:

Wenn du ihr auch alles gesagt hättest, ...
Wenn du das/dieses/dein Haus auch verkauft hättest, ...
Wenn du auch kein Buch von ihm gelesen hast, ...
Wenn er auch (deutsche) Bücher liest, ...

ii 'wenn auch', 'wenngleich' and 'wennschon' may be used elliptically:
Das Buch ist, wenn auch nicht hervorragend, (so) doch interessant.
Er hatte viel zu berichten, wennschon nichts sehr Wichtiges.

(c) Inversion with auch or with gleich, the latter being old-fashioned; in a following main clause, normal order is more emphatic and more usual:
Ist er auch (or gleich) ein alter Freund, ich kann ihm nicht helfen. Hätte ich ihm auch heute geschrieben, er hätte den Brief morgen nicht bekommen.

Note: After any of the 'even if' clauses mentioned in (a) (b) and (c), a following main clause frequently begins with so (+ inversion) and/or contains doch *nevertheless*:
Wenn ich ihm auch heute geschrieben hätte, so hätte er den Brief morgen doch nicht bekommen.[1]

(d) An 'even if' clause which is closely linked to a preceding noun or pronoun may be rendered by 'und' + conditional clause:

Keiner von den Arbeitern, und wenn man ihm die dreifache Bezahlung verspricht, wird diese Aufgabe übernehmen
Not one of the workers, even if he is promised treble pay, will take on this job

Gervaise, und wäre sie eine Göttin, ist eine klägliche Partie (A. Kolb)
Gervaise, even if she were a goddess, is a poor match

474. (S) Miscellaneous types of clause with concessive force

Ich mag tun, was ich will, es hilft doch nichts
Whatever I do, it doesn't help

koste es, was es wolle
whatever the cost

Gleichviel, wer es getan hat, er soll bestraft werden
No matter who has done it, he shall be punished

(Einerlei) ob er Erfahrung hat oder nicht, ich werde ihn anstellen
Whether he has experience or not, I shall engage him

Ich habe ihn eingeladen; nicht, daß ich seine Gesellschaft besonders schätze[2]
I have invited him, not that I particularly value his company

wie dem auch sei (set phrase)
be that as it may

das mochte sein, wie es wollte,
however that might be

wie auch immer (*Zeit*) (elliptical)
however that may be

475. The Subjunctive of Modest Assertion, a hallowed and admirable phrase, which, in conjunction with the following examples, requires no explanation. Its main tense is the imperfect, though it may occur in the pluperfect. In every case a blunt indicative would be possible, e.g. (first example) Ich weiß, was zu tun ist.

---

[1] cf. Schulz-Griesbach, op. cit., G 553. [2] for nicht daß, see also 469(a).

Ich wüßte wohl, was zu tun wäre (Du. Gram. 6470)	*I think I know what ought to be done*
Eine Frage hätte ich *doch* noch (Th. Valentin)	*There's one more thing I* would *like to ask*
Da wäre er nun aufgewacht (F. Dürrenmatt)	*He seems to have woken up*[1]

This subjunctive is frequently used in registering the completion of a task or the reaching of one's destination:

Diese Sache hätten wir also geregelt	*That would appear to be completed*
Da wären wir also endlich	*So here we are at last*

A question may likewise be made less blunt by the use of the subjunctive:

Wäre das alles?	*Will that be all?*
Wären Sie also jetzt zufrieden?	*Well, are you satisfied now?*

476. The Optative Subjunctive is used to express a wish, exhortation or command in a main clause (as in (a) below) or in a conditional clause, the main clause being suppressed (as in (b) below).

(a) **Present Subjunctive**
1st pers. sing. (relatively rare)

Möge ich's nicht bereuen!	*May I not regret it!*

(Somewhat stilted; normal usage: Hoffentlich werd' ich's nicht bereuen).

Sage ich's lieber ganz offen	*I'd better say so quite frankly*

2nd pers. sing. and plur.: A direct command in the 2nd person being the function of the imperative, the optative subjunctive is limited to the expression of a wish or exhortation by means of 'mögen':

Mögest (or: Möchtest) du immer so denken!	*May you always think thus!*

(Somewhat stilted; normal usage: Hoffentlich wirst du immer so denken.)

3rd pers. sing.
i it is used in a number of set phrases expressing a wish:

Gott segne dich!	*God bless you!*
Gott behüte dich!	*May God protect you!*
Gott behüte!*[2]*	*God forbid! Certainly not!*
Gott (dat.) sei Dank!	*Thank heavens!*
Es lebe die Freiheit!	*Long live freedom!*
Er lebe hoch! (or: Er soll leben!)	*Long may he live! Here's to his health!*

ii the pres. subj. of 'mögen' may be used to express a wish:
Möge er glücklich sein! Möge es ihm gelingen! (Somewhat stilted; normal usage: Hoffentlich wird er glücklich sein. Hoffentlich gelingt es ihm.)

iii with 'man' as subject, it is fairly common as the equivalent of an imperative addressed to whom it may concern:

Im Notfall wende man sich an den Hausmeister!	*In case of need apply to the caretaker*
Man bedenke, was die Folgen sein könnten	*Consider what the consequences might be*

[1] thus translated by L. Forster in his edition of Dürrenmatt: Der Verdacht (Harrap).
[2] short for: Gott behüte mich davor!

iv it may express an exhortation or command, but only in literary
language:

Bezähme jeder die gerechte Wut	*Let each man curb his righteous anger and*
Und spare für das Ganze seine Rache	*save his vengeance for the common*
(Schiller: *Wilhelm Tell*)	*cause*
Er komme sofort!	*Let him come at once*
Er möge sofort kommen!	—less peremptory
Er soll sofort kommen	—normal usage

1st pers. plur.

Na also, gehen wir ganz langsam.	*Well then, let's walk quite slowly. Take*
Faß mich unter (H. Fallada)	*my arm*
Seien wir dankbar, daß nichts passiert ist!	*Let's be thankful that nothing happened*
Gehen wir in den Garten!	*Let's go into the garden*
Also, spielen wir jetzt Karten!	*Well, let's play cards now*

Note:

i Laß uns/Laßt uns + infin. is here frequently used instead of the pres. subj.,
but would not be idiomatic in the last example above. 'Laßt uns' may
be used in talking to someone one addresses as 'Sie', e.g. Laßt uns in
den Garten gehen!

ii Let's see the letter (coll.) = Laß mich mal den Brief sehen!

3rd pers. plur.

A wish may be expressed by means of 'mögen'; a command is expressed
by means of 'sollen':

Mögen sie es nicht bereuen!	*May they not regret it!*
(Normal usage: Hoffentlich werden sie es nicht bereuen.)	
Sie sollen sofort kommen!	*Let them come at once*

(b) **Imperfect Subjunctive, Pluperfect Subjunctive and Conditional**: to express a wish (If only . . .)

Note:

i Instead of 'wenn' with the verb at the end, inversion of verb and subject
may be used with the pluperf. subj. and, in the case of strong verbs,
but less commonly, with the imperf. subj.

ii The inclusion of doch, nur, bloß, doch nur or doch bloß is virtually
essential to convey that it is a wish.

Wenn er doch nur käme!	*If only he would come!*
(Käme er doch nur!)	
Wenn er bloß besser arbeitete!	*If only he worked better!*
Hätte mein Vater doch dieses Haus nie gekauft!	*If only my father had never bought this house!*
Wenn er Ihnen das Geld doch bloß geben würde!	*If only he would give you the money!*

Q. INDIRECT SPEECH

477. Survey of the treatment of Indirect Speech

6. Notes on 479–83: 484, e.g. 484(b): the use of 'daß', 484(d): subordinate clauses in reported speech
7. Deviations from the rules given in 479–83: 485

478. Introductory

German practice varies immensely in the handling of indirect speech. It has been thought best to start by giving and illustrating a set of definite rules (for Indirect Statement, Indirect Question and Noun Clauses depending on verbs other than those of saying and asking) which represent preponderant usage and which will rarely produce impossible German. Thereafter deviations from those rules will be considered. The user is recommended to read 484(b) (on the use of 'daß') before proceeding.

479. Indirect Statement

The main verb will here be 'sagen' or one of its equivalents, e.g. antworten *to answer*, behaupten *to maintain*, erklären *to declare; to explain*, erwähnen *to mention*, erzählen *to relate*, leugnen *to deny*, meinen *to say*,[1] versichern *to assure*, zugeben *to admit*.

Rules

(a) If sagen, or its equivalent, is present, future or imperative, it is generally followed by the indicative: Er sagt, er ist krank. Er wird sagen, daß er nichts davon weiß. Sagen Sie ihm, er soll sofort kommen!

(b) If sagen is past, it is normally followed by the subjunctive or conditional, with the following scheme of tenses:

Tense of Original Direct Statement	Tense of Indirect Statement	
	Conversational	Literary
Present	Imperf. Subj.	Pres. Subj.
Past { Imperfect / Perfect / Pluperfect }	Pluperf. Subj.	Perf. Subj.
Future	Conditional (but Fut. Subj. in 3rd sing.)[2]	Fut. Subj.

Examples

„Ich schreibe einen Brief"	Er sagte, er schriebe (schreibe) einen Brief
„Ich schrieb einen Brief" „Ich habe einen Brief geschrieben" „Ich hatte einen Brief geschrieben"	Er sagte, er hätte (habe) einen Brief geschrieben
„Ich werde einen Brief schreiben"	Er sagte, er werde einen Brief schreiben

[1] The basic meaning of meinen, 'to be of the opinion', is frequently extended to 'to express an opinion' or 'to say', e.g. „Das geht aber nicht", meinte sie.
[2] This applies to Indirect Statement only; not to Indir. Questions (481) or after indefinite verbs (482).

(c) The above scheme of tenses is modified by the principle that distinctive subjunctive forms should be used whenever possible. Therefore:

CONVERSATIONAL TENSES: Weak Verbs: as their imperf. subj. is the same as their imperf. indic., use the pres. subj., where it is different from the pres. indic.: Er sagte, Hans spiele Tennis (not: spielte)

LITERARY TENSES: where these have the same form as the indicative, use the corresponding conversational tense:
Er sagte, sie sängen alte Volkslieder (not: singen)
Er sagte, sie hätten nichts vergessen (not: haben)
Sie sagten, sie würden nie heimkehren (not: werden)

In the case of the pres. subj. this rule should be followed even where the imperf. subj. is likewise identical with the indicative. Thus:
„Wir arbeiten fleißig" Sie sagten, sie arbeiteten fleißig (not: arbeiten)

480. When sagen (or its equivalent), fragen (cf. 481), hören etc. (cf. 482) are in the perfect, they are often followed by the indicative

(a) This will generally be the case when the perfect refers to the recent past and thus approximates to the present:
Was hat er gesagt? Er hat gesagt, daß er krank ist/Er hat erwähnt, daß er dich gesehen hat. Er hat eben gefragt, ob wir zufrieden sind. Ich habe gerade gehört, daß er angekommen ist.

(b) Where the occasion of 'Er hat gesagt', 'Er hat gefragt' etc. lies further back, the subjunctive is more usual, especially where the matter referred to in the statement or question may have changed in the meantime (2nd and 3rd examples):
Letzte Woche hat er mir gesagt, er hätte sein Haus verkauft (or: daß er sein Haus verkauft hat) (cf. 484(b)).
Letzte Woche hat er mir gesagt, er wäre krank.
Er ist letzte Woche hier gewesen und hat gefragt, ob du zu Hause wärst.

481. Indirect Question

(a) If 'fragen' is present, future or imperative, it is normally followed by the indicative: Er fragt, ob Sie zu Hause sind. Frage ihn, wer ihm geholfen hat.

(b) If 'fragen' is past, it is normally followed by the subjunctive or conditional, with the same scheme of tenses as in 479 (see also 480):
„Ist Herr A. zu Hause?"—Er fragte, ob Sie zu Hause wären (seien).
„Was hast du verloren?"—Ich fragte ihn, was er verloren hätte (habe).
„Wann werden Sie Ihren Bruder sehen?"—Er fragte mich, wann ich meinen Bruder sehen würde.

482. Noun Clauses depending on indefinite verbs. Such are:

ahnen *to have a presentiment, to suspect*
annehmen *to assume*
denken *to think*

sich einbilden *to imagine* (generally erroneously)
erwarten* *to expect*

fühlen *to feel*
fürchten* *to fear*
glauben *to believe, think*
hoffen* *to hope*
hören *to hear*
meinen *to be of the opinion*
schreiben *to write*

träumen *to dream*
vermuten *to presume*
voraussetzen *to presuppose*
sich vorstellen *to imagine* (deliberately)
wünschen* *to wish*
zweifeln* *to doubt*

(a) If these verbs are present, future or imperative, the indicative is normally used in the noun clause: Er schreibt, daß er krank ist. Er wird glauben, daß ich krank bin.

(b) If these verbs are past, the subjunctive or conditional is normally used in the noun clause, with the same scheme of tenses as in 479 (see also 480):

Er glaubte, ich wäre (sei) krank   *He thought I was ill*
       (Original thought: A. is ill)

Ich hörte, er hätte (habe) die Schlange   *I heard he killed the snake*
getötet

Note: After the five verbs marked with an asterisk, only the Conversational Tense will always be correct, e.g.

Ich fürchtete, er würde zu spät   *I feared he would come too late*
kommen

483. Noun Clauses depending on verbs denoting certainty. Such are:

bedauern *to regret*[1]
beweisen *to prove*
entdecken *to discover*
erfahren *to hear, learn* (as a fact)
sich erinnern *to remember*
es tut mir leid *I am sorry*[1]
feststellen *to ascertain, establish*

gewiß sein *to be certain*
herausfinden *to find out*
merken *to notice*
sehen *to see*
sicher sein *to be sure*
überzeugen *to convince*
wissen *to know*

After these verbs, the indicative is normally used in the noun clause:
Ich wußte, daß er es getan hat *I knew that he had done it*; ich weiß nicht, ob er krank ist; ich wußte nicht, daß er krank war; wenn ich nur wüßte, wo er geblieben ist! Ich entdeckte, daß er Frankfurt verlassen hatte; es tat ihm leid, daß er dich nicht gesehen hat.

Note:

i Where the context requires the conditional, the imperf. subj. is a common alternative (as in conditional clauses): Ich wußte nicht, ob er kommen würde/käme; cf. ich wollte wissen, wann er nach Hause käme (*when he was coming* (=*would come*) *home*).

ii Other deviations from wissen + indic. are not infrequent and are generally to be explained by sometimes subtle contextual factors. A straightforward instance may be cited:
Ich wußte nicht, ob er krank wäre/sei   *I didn't know if he were ill*
(introductory verb in the past + complete uncertainty)

iii Note the elliptical use of ob:
[Ich möchte wissen] Ob er mich   *Can he have misunderstood me after all?*
doch mißverstanden hat?

[1] denotes certainty in the sense that one regrets something that one regards as a fact.

484. Notes on 479–83

(a) **After many of the verbs listed in 482 and 483, an accusative and infinitive construction is frequently used in English,** e.g. I believed (presumed, expected, knew, discovered) him to be ill. **This is impossible in German,** where a clause must be used: Ich glaubte, er sei krank; ich wußte, daß er krank war. Compare:

Dies ist ein Buch, von dem ich weiß,   *This is a book that I know to be reliable*
daß es zuverlässig ist

(b) **The use of 'daß'**

   i In indirect statements and after the indefinite verbs,[1] the use of 'daß' is optional, except that it *must* be used after the indefinite verbs when they are negative and is more usual after 'sagen' or its equivalent when negative. Apart from this exception, the form without 'daß' is preferred before a subjunctive, especially in conversation.

Er sagte, er wäre krank/daß er krank wäre.
Er glaubte, ich wäre krank/daß ich krank wäre.
Er sagte nicht, daß er krank wäre.
Er glaubte nicht, daß ich krank wäre.

   ii Before an indicative practice varies, but it is in general commoner (and safer) to use 'daß', which, in the absence of a subjunctive, makes it clearer that here is a subordinate clause. After bedauern, beweisen, sich erinnern, es tut mir leid, feststellen, herausfinden and überzeugen, 'daß' is essential.

Ich wußte, daß er krank war (or: er war krank)
Ich habe herausgefunden, daß er jetzt in Berlin lebt.

   iii From ii it follows that not infrequently daß + indic. is an alternative to the subjunctive without 'daß': Er hat mir gesagt, er hätte sein Haus verkauft/daß er sein Haus verkauft hat.

(c) **The subjunctive may be required in a noun clause depending on a noun** (usually with 'daß' or some other introductory word) e.g. das Gerücht, daß . . ., meine Frage, ob . . .

(d) In reported speech in the subjunctive, all **subordinate clauses** that were part of the original direct statement or question go into the subjunctive, e.g.

Er sagte, er werde das Buch kaufen,   *He said he would buy the book, as his*
da sein Onkel, dessen Urteil er hoch   *uncle, whose judgement he greatly*
achte, es ihm empfohlen hätte   *respected, had recommended it to him*

But the reporter may independently add some information in a subordinate clause and this will go into the indicative:

Er sagte, er bewerbe sich um diese   *He said he was applying for this job, for*
Stelle, für die er gar nicht geeignet   *which he is not at all suitable*
ist

(e) **After 'hoffen' and 'wünschen', modals are sometimes used:**

Er hoffte, daß ich seinem Sohn helfen   *He hoped that I might help his son*
möge
Er wünschte, ich sollte ihm alles   *He wanted me to explain everything to him*
erklären

---

[1] zweifeln *to doubt*, used affirmatively, is followed by ob *whether*.

(f) **The subjunctive can neatly show that a statement is a reported one without the insertion or repetition of a verb of saying**:

Bei seiner Vernehmung berief sich	*In the course of his cross-examination H.*
H. auf Notwehr. Er sei mit S. in	*pleaded self-defence. He said he had*
Streit geraten und habe sich von	*become involved in a quarrel with S. and*
diesem bedroht gefühlt (*SZ*)	*had felt himself to be threatened by him*
Papa möchte auch gern selbst lenken,	*Daddy would also like to drive, but*
Mama will es aber nicht, weil es	*Mummy doesn't want him to, because,*
die Nerven angreife (R. Huch)	*she says, it's a strain on the nerves*

(g) In **hybrids of direct and indirect speech** such as the following, the subjunctive is used:

Der Laden, sagte er, sei erst seit	*The shop, he said, has only been going for*
kurzem eröffnet, mache aber schon	*a short time, but is already doing quite*
ganz gute Geschäfte	*good business*

(h) According to German grammarians,[1] the domain of the present subjunctive is reported speech, while the domain of the imperfect subjunctive is the hypothetical (Wenn ich ihm heute schriebe, . . .), the imagined (Ich träumte, ich wäre zu Hause), the erroneous (Ich dachte, der Zug führe eine Stunde später). While Erben and Duden are able to muster plentiful illustrations supporting this differentiation, they admit, and show, that it is by no means consistently adhered to. According to Duden the imperf. subj. may be used in indirect speech to imply a greater degree of scepticism towards the statement reported than would the pres. subj. (Gram. 6440 and 6668).

To the present writer all this seems too doctrinaire to be advocated as a basic guide-line. The following figures for the use of tenses in indirect speech resulted from an examination of Ricarda Huch's *Der letzte Sommer, eine Erzählung in Briefen* (1910), the correspondents being cultured people; cases where the choice was determined by the desirability of using a distinctive subjunctive form were ignored:

Literary Tenses (Pres., Perf., Fut. Subj.): 75
Conversational Tenses (Imperf., Pluperf. Subj., Condit.): 301

It is significant 1. that the most sustained use of the literary tenses occurs in an account of a serious political discussion (in the letter dated 28. Mai) and 2. that the imperf. subj. of weak verbs is frequently used even where the pres. subj. would supply a distinctive subjunctive form.

485. Deviations from the rules for the use of the Subjunctive in Indirect Speech given in 479-83

Introductory

As indicated in 478, the above rules for the use of the subjunctive in indirect speech and in other noun clauses are subject to variations and these must now be considered in some detail.

Basic to these deviations are the general considerations regarding the functions and use of indicative and subjunctive stated in 461(a)(b), which the user should re-read at this point. It should, however, be

---

[1] e.g. J. Erben: Zur Frage des Konjunktivs (*Zeitschrift für deutsche Sprache*, Band 22, Heft 3), with confirmatory references to W. Flämig, O. Behaghel and others; also Duden: Grammatik 6580 ff.

added that the subjunctive is the normal medium of reported speech and does not necessarily imply disbelief in, or disagreement with, the statement reported.

(a) **Examples of the conversational tendency to replace the subjunctive by the indicative**:

Er sagte, er schwimmt gern	*He said he likes swimming*
Ich sah nach, ob mein Vater noch schlief	*I had a good look whether my father was still asleep*
Er glaubte, ich war krank	*He thought I was ill*

We may repeat the well-tailored sentence given in 484(d) to illustrate the use of the subjunctive in the subordinate clauses of reported speech, followed by what it would probably become in workaday conversation:

Er sagte, er werde das Buch kaufen, da sein Onkel, dessen Urteil er hoch achte, es ihm empfohlen hätte.

Er sagte, er werde das Buch kaufen; sein Onkel hat es ihm nämlich empfohlen und anscheinend gibt er viel auf sein Urteil.

(b) **Choice of indicative explained by its fundamental function**:

Ich sagte ihm, von wo wir gekommen sind	*I told him where we've come from*

('where we've come from' represents a definite fact.)

Ich habe schon gehört, daß er angekommen ist	*I've already heard that he's arrived*

(the speaker has accepted his arrival as a fact.)

Ich fühlte, daß ich ihn beleidigt hatte	*I felt [pretty sure] that I had offended him*
Er ahnte nicht, was sich indessen ereignet hatte	*He did not suspect what had meanwhile occurred*

(the speaker is thinking of what actually did take place.)

(c) **When the main verb is pres. tense but 3rd person, a subjunctive often follows, especially without 'daß'**:

i Miscellaneous instances:

Er sagt, er müsse (muß) nach Hause (BUT: Er sagt, daß er nach Hause muß)	*He says he's got to go home*
Man sagt, er sei gestorben (strong element of uncertainty)	*They say he's died*
Er glaubt, ich wär' (bin) krank	*He thinks I'm ill*
Er meint, es sei besser mit dem Auto zu fahren	*He thinks it's better to go by car*

('meinen' strongly indicates a personal opinion.)

Er schreibt, er sei krank	*He writes that he's ill*

(the sense of 'er schreibt' is past, not present.)

ii Where, in a narrative, sagen is used in a vivid historic present, which is thus the equivalent of 'sagte':

Und er sagt zu ihr, daß es besser sei, man verschwinde, ehe der Kerl zurückkomme (W. Heinrich).

iii In newspaper reporting; here the subjunctive (always the literary tenses) is used whatever the tense of the introductory verb:

Die Opposition behauptet, diese Politik sei verkehrt. Man müsse die Frage ganz anders anpacken.

(d) **Further illustrations of the use of indicative and subjunctive**:

Du sagst, du bist müde	*You say you're tired*
Sagst du, du wärst müde?	*Do you say you're tired?*

Er fragte mich, ob ich krank bin	*He asked me if I were ill*
(Indic.: 1. indic. tends to replace subj. 2. the answer is known.)	
Ich fragte ihn, ob er krank sei	*I asked him if he were ill*
(Subj.: the answer is not known.)	

Ich möchte wissen, ob er kommt	*I wonder if he's coming*
Ich fragte mich, ob er käme	*I wondered if he were coming*

Der Angeklagte konnte beweisen, daß er unschuldig war	*The accused was able to prove that he was innocent*
Der Angeklagte versuchte zu beweisen, daß er unschuldig sei	*The accused tried to prove that he was innocent*

Er erzählte mir, was er in Wiesbaden getan hat	*He told me what he did in Wiesbaden*
(Indic.: the emphasis is on what he actually did.)	

Glauben Sie, ich hätte nichts davon gewußt? (from Du. Gram.)	*Do you think I knew nothing about it?*
(Subj., implying: but I did.)	

i A. gab zu, daß Peter intelligent ist
ii A. gab zu, daß Peter intelligent wäre (sei)
   For the first reporter of A's admission, Peter's being intelligent is an
   accepted fact; the second reporter is subconsciously giving greater
   weight to the fact that he is reporting what A admitted.

R. VERBS FOLLOWED BY THE DATIVE

486. Introductory

As the name indicates, the dative case is the case of the recipient. As such,
it is occupied preponderantly by persons rather than things, persons to
whom something is given (shown, told, allowed etc.) or to whom
something pleasant or unpleasant, beneficial or injurious, is done. The
old concepts 'Dative of Advantage' and 'Dative of Disadvantage' are
helpful for getting the feel of the dative and its use; in some instances
the more neutral 'Dative of the Person Concerned' is more apt. In
many instances, the indirect (dative) object depends on the presence of a
direct (accusative) object; the latter may be a noun or pronoun, an infinitive-phrase or a subordinate clause (cf. examples in 488).

Note: The following are not included here:
i Verbs concerned with parts of the body and articles of clothing, where
   a pronoun in the dative is generally used instead of a possess. adj.:
   see 82(b)–(f).
ii Impersonal verbs and expressions taking the dative: see 372 ff.

487. Verbs of the basic type: to give something to someone, e.g. Er
gab dem Lehrer den Bleistift.

10+

Here may be included: an-bieten *to offer*, beweisen *to prove*, bringen *to bring*, empfehlen *to recommend*, leihen *to lend*, opfern *to sacrifice*, reichen *to hand, pass*, schenken *to present*, schicken *to send*, schulden *to owe*, vererben *to bequeath*, verkaufen *to sell*, zeigen *to show*, zu-flüstern *to whisper*, zu-teilen *to allot*.

jemandem ein Rätsel, eine Hausarbeit auf-geben	*to set s.o. a riddle, homework*
jemandem Mut, Vertrauen ein-flößen	*to inspire s.o. with e.g. courage, confidence*
jemandem etwas verschaffen	*to procure s.th. for s.o.*
and many analogous instances	

Note:

i **beweisen**:

Er bewies mir, daß ...	*He proved to me that ...*
Nichts konnte ihm bewiesen werden	*Nothing could be proved against him*

ii **bringen**: used in the sense of to take, it is followed by 'zu', e.g. Er hat seinen Sohn zum Arzt gebracht.

iii **schicken**: also used with an+acc., the effect being less personal, e.g. Schicken Sie ein Telegramm an den Minister (cf. Erben, op. cit., 122).

iv **vererben**: also used with an+acc., which gives greater emphasis to the legatee.

v **verkaufen**: also used with an+acc., which gives greater emphasis to the purchaser, e.g. Er hat sein Haus an einen Fabrikanten verkauft.

488. The personal object of verbs meaning **to say, to tell, to answer, to advise, to command, to allow, to forbid, to obey, to forgive is in the dative**; here, as generally in 487, there is frequently an indirect and a direct object, the latter being another noun or pronoun, an infinitive-phrase or a clause, e.g.

Der Arzt hat meinem Bruder Ruhe angeraten.
Das kann ich ihm nicht verzeihen.
Er riet mir, mein Haus zu verkaufen.
Er versicherte mir, daß er alles erledigt hätte.

Note:

i Most of these verbs may also be used only with a direct object, e.g. Wer hat das befohlen? Die Polizei hat die Versammlung erlaubt (more official: genehmigt)/verboten.

ii **antworten**: Er hat mir geantwortet; er hat auf meinen Brief/auf meine Frage geantwortet (or: Er hat meinen Brief/meine Frage beantwortet.)

iii Before the beginning of a quotation, 'sagen zu' is more usual: Dann sagte er zu mir: ,,Du bist schuld daran."

489. Examples of the dative of advantage (cf. 486 and 83)

jemandem seine Arbeit, ein Paket ab-nehmen	*to relieve s.o. of their work, of a parcel*
jemandem zur Verfügung stehen	*to be at s.o.'s disposal*
Das werde ich dir nie vergessen	*I shall never forget that you did that for me*

jemandem etwas vor-machen[1]	*to demonstrate s.th. to s.o.*
jemandem zugute kommen (s)	*to stand s.o. in good stead*
Seine lange Erfahrung kommt ihm nun zugute (Du. Stil.)	*His long experience now stands him in good stead*

490. Examples of the dative of disadvantage (cf. 486 and 83)

jemandem etwas auf-drängen	*to force s.th. on s.o.*
jemandem etwas rauben	*to rob s.o. of s.th.*
jemandem etwas verheimlichen (or verschweigen)	*to keep s.o. in ignorance of s.th.*
jemandem etwas zu-muten	*to demand or expect s.th. of s.o.*
Das kann man ihm nicht zumuten	*One cannot expect that of him*
jemandem zur Last fallen (s)	*to be a burden or charge on s.o.*

491. Examples of the dative of the person concerned (cf. 486)

jemandem etwas an-hören[2]	*to tell s.th. by s.o.'s speech*
Man kann ihm den Franzosen anhören	*You can tell by his accent that he's French*
jemandem etwas verdanken	*to be indebted to s.o. for s.th.*
jemandem etwas zu-schreiben	*to ascribe s.th. to s.o.*
jemandem etwas zu-trauen	*to credit s.o. with s.th.*
Ich hätte ihm mehr Vernunft zugetraut	*I should have credited him with more sense*

492. to escape (from): ent- + various verbs of motion + dat. (All are conjugated with sein.) E.g.

Der Name ist mir entfallen	*The name has escaped my memory*
Er ist der Gefahr/der Strafe entgangen	*He escaped the danger/the punishment*
Es ist mir nicht entgangen, daß . . . (Du. Stil.)	*It did not escape my notice that . . .*
Er ist den Wärtern entschlüpft	*He escaped from the warders*

Note:

i to escape from prison: aus dem Gefängnis aus-brechen, entfliehen, entwischen.

ii to escape from a cage: aus einem Käfig aus-brechen (for large, fierce animals), entwischen (for any animals).

iii For 'to escape' without either a noun in the dat. or a prepositional phr., entkommen and entweichen are most used, e.g. Die Polizei war sofort zur Stelle, aber die Diebe entkamen.

493. The following verbs, outside the preceding groups, also take the dative:

jemandem ab-sagen	*to refuse s.o.'s invitation*
jemandem ab-schreiben	1. *to refuse s.o.'s invitation*
	2. *to put s.o. off, to ask them not to come*
ähneln	*to resemble*
auf-fallen (s)	*to strike, astonish*
Sein merkwürdiges Benehmen ist mir aufgefallen	*I was struck by his strange behaviour*
aus-weichen (s)	*to evade*

[1] cf. 693, vor-: 2nd example [2] cf. start of 515.

jemandem/einer Sache aus dem Wege gehen (s)	*to evade*
begegnen (s)	*to meet* (by chance) [1]
bei-stehen	*to stand by, help*
bei-stimmen	*to agree with* (e.g. a suggestion)
bei-wohnen	*to attend* (e.g. a ceremony)
bekommen (s)	*to agree with one* (of food)
danken	*to thank*
dienen	*to serve* (e.g. one's master, the state, the truth)
Sie servierte das Mittagessen	BUT: *She served the lunch*
Sie bediente die Gäste (mit Bier)	*She served the customers* (*with beer*)
drohen	*to threaten*
ein-fallen (s)	*to occur to* (one's mind), e.g.
Plötzlich fiel mir der Name ein	*Suddenly I remembered the name*
entgegen-gehen (s)	*to go to meet; to face* (e.g. difficulties)
entsagen	*to renounce*
entsprechen	*to correspond to*
fehlen	**to be lacking, missing**
Ihm fehlt der nötige Mut	*He lacks the necessary courage*
Er fehlt mir sehr	*I miss him a lot*
Was fehlt dir?	*What's wrong with you?*
Mir fehlt nichts	*There's nothing wrong with me*
folgen (s)	*to follow*[2]
frönen	*to be a slave to* (e.g. fashion, a vice), *to be addicted to*
gefallen	*to please* (see 278 iii)
gegenüber-stehen	*to stand opposite, face*
gehören	**to belong to** (possession)
Diese Uhr gehört mir	*This watch belongs to me*
Er gehört zu unserm Klub	BUT: *He belongs to our club*
Er gehört unserm Klub an	
Dieses Feld gehört zu unserm Garten	*This field belongs to our garden*
genügen	*to suffice*
geraten (s)	*to succeed*, e.g.
Der Kuchen ist ihr gut geraten	*Her cake turned out well*
glauben	**to believe** (a person)
Ich glaube ihm	*I believe him*
Das glaube ich ihm nicht	*I don't believe him* (*I don't believe that statement of his*)
Ich glaube diese Nachricht nicht	BUT: *I don't believe this news*
Ich glaube an ihn	*I believe* (*have faith*) *in him*
Er glaubt an Gespenster, an den Kommunismus, an sein Glück	*He believes in ghosts, in Communism, in his luck*
gleichen	*to be equal to; to resemble*
gleich-sehen	*to resemble*
jemandem etwas gönnen	*not to begrudge s.o. s.th.*, e.g.
Ich gönne ihm seinen langen Urlaub	*I'm pleased for him that he's got a long holiday*

---

[1] treffen (h) + Acc. = to meet by chance or by arrangement.

[2] to follow, succeed = folgen (s) auf + acc., e.g. Auf die Egmont-Ouvertüre folgte die siebte Sinfonie.

gratulieren	*to congratulate*
helfen	*to help*
imponieren	*to impress*
kondolieren	*to express one's sympathy with*
jemandem kündigen	*to give s.o. notice*
mißtrauen	*to distrust*
munden	*to taste good,* e.g.
Die Suppe hat mir gemundet	*I enjoyed the soup*
nach-jagen (s)[1]	*to pursue s.o.* (also fig. e.g. wealth, success)
nahe-gehen (s)	*to grieve, affect,* e.g.
Sein Tod ist mir (sehr) nahegegangen	*I felt his death keenly*
sich nahen, sich nähern	*to approach*
nutzen, nützen	*to benefit, be of use to,* e.g.
Das nützt mir nichts	*That's of no use to me*
passen	*to suit; to fit*
schaden	*to harm*
schmecken	*to taste good:* see 'munden'
schmeicheln	*to flatter*
schreiben[2]	*to write to*
sein	*to belong to* (regionally coll.) e.g.
Ist dieser Schirm dir?	*Is this umbrella yours?*
Was ist dir?	*What's the matter with you?*
Ihm ist etwas	*There's something the matter with him*
trauen	*to trust*
trotzen	*to defy*
voran-gehen (s)	*to go ahead of*
vor-beugen	*to forestall* (e.g. difficulties)
(sich) weh tun	*to hurt (o.s.),* e.g.
Du hast deinem Bruder weh getan	*You've hurt your brother*
Sein Bein tut ihm weh	*His leg hurts him*
Ich habe mir weh getan	*I've hurt myself*
sich widersetzen	*to oppose* (e.g. an order)
widersprechen	*to contradict*
widerstehen	*to resist*
winken	*to beckon, wave to*
jemandem zu-jubeln	*to cheer s.o.*
zu-reden[3]	*to urge, encourage s.o.* (*to do s.th.*)
zu-sehen	*to watch*
zuvor-kommen (s)	*to anticipate, forestall*

494. Reflexive Verbs with the reflexive pronoun in the dative

(a) A large number of verbs and expressions in the preceding paragraphs may also be used reflexively, e.g.

Ich erlaubte mir, ihm zu widersprechen	*I allowed myself to contradict him*
Ich muß mir Arbeit verschaffen	*I must find work*
Ich habe mir zuviel zugemutet	*I've taken on too much*

[1] see also 693, nach-.
[2] Ich habe meinem Bruder (einen Brief) geschrieben; rather less personal: Ich habe (einen Brief) an den Betriebsleiter geschrieben (cf. Erben, op. cit., 122).
[3] see also 693: zu-.

(b) The following is a selection of commonly used refl. verbs (with refl. pronoun in dat.) which are not merely reflexive adaptations of verbs already given; the first four are exclusively reflexive:

sich etwas an-eignen	*to appropriate, acquire s.th.*
Er hat sich meinen Schirm angeeignet	*He's appropriated my umbrella*
sich ein-bilden	*to imagine* (generally erroneously)
sich gleich-bleiben (s)	*to remain unchanged*
sich etwas verbitten	*to refuse to tolerate s.th.*
Solche Bemerkungen verbitte ich mir	*I won't tolerate such remarks*
sich vor-nehmen, etwas zu tun	*to make up one's mind to do s.th.*
sich vor-stellen	*to imagine, visualize*

See also 679(a).

495. Accusative or Dative?

(a) **Ich klopfte ihm/ihn auf die Schulter**
Either is possible and Duden's distinction (Du. Haupt. p. 600) seems sound: ihm (which is commoner) gives greater emphasis to 'on the shoulder'; ihn gives greater emphasis to 'him'. Cf. Der Hund biß ihm/ihn ins Bein. Er schoß mir/mich ins Bein.

(b) **to imitate**
nach-ahmen in current usage takes the accusative not only meaning 'to mimic s.o.', but also meaning 'to follow s.o.'s example', e.g. Er versucht, seinen Bruder nachzuahmen.
nach-machen + acc. = to imitate, mimic, e.g. Er machte den Lehrer nach. It can, however, be used with a direct and an indirect object, e.g. Mein Söhnchen macht mir alles nach. Das soll mir einer nachmachen! *I defy anyone to do the same.*

(c) **Verbs with a double accusative**
i A double accusative is the normal construction with kosten and lehren, e.g.
Die Reise hat mich 900 Mark gekostet; es kostet meinen Vater viel Zeit; er lehrt mich Deutsch.

ii A dative of the person is, however, also to be found and heard, in the case of 'kosten' especially in figurative contexts, e.g.
Das kann ihm/ihn den Hals kosten; es hat ihm/ihn das Leben gekostet; es kostete ihm/ihn große Überwindung (*a great effort*)

iii A double accusative also occurs with fragen, e.g.
Er fragte mich etwas; er fragte mich allerlei Schwieriges.

496. The dative object of the active voice cannot be the subject of the passive; it is thus impossible to say: Er wurde von seinen Freunden geholfen.

(a) There are two exceptions:
i 'folgen' and particularly the participial phrase 'gefolgt von': Zwei Männer trugen die Bahre, gefolgt von Lene (G. Hauptmann).
ii the phrase 'Ich fühlte mich geschmeichelt' *I felt flattered.*

(b) In English, this prohibition generally does not apply (e.g. He had been promised a new bike); moreover, what is in German a dative object is often a direct object in English (e.g. His friends helped him). The resultant English passive sentences may be rendered in German in one of three ways:

i With verbs taking a direct and an indirect object, the direct object of the active version can be made the subject of the passive:

Ein neues Fahrrad war ihm von seinen
Eltern versprochen worden
(or, with introductory es: Es war
ihm von seinen Eltern ein neues Fahrrad versprochen
worden)

He had been promised a new bike by his parents

ii The sentence can be turned into the active, with or without 'man':

Seine Freunde halfen ihm
Man half ihm

He was helped by his friends
He was helped

iii Most verbs taking the dative that are conjugated with 'haben' can be used impersonally in the passive (cf. 381)

Es wurde ihm (von seinen Freunden)
geholfen (or: Ihm wurde (von seinen
Freunden) geholfen)
Es ist mir empfohlen worden,
Baden-Baden zu besuchen[1]
Es wird ihm nie widersprochen

He was helped (by his friends)

I have been recommended to visit Baden-Baden
He is never contradicted

The following verbs + dat., conjugated with 'sein', may be found in the impersonal passive, generally without the 'es': ausweichen, nachgehen, nachjagen, nachlaufen, nachsetzen, e.g.

Dem Feind wurde geschickt
ausgewichen
Dem Problem ist nachgegangen
worden

The enemy was skilfully evaded

The problem has been investigated

N.B. Reflexive Verbs cannot be used in the passive.

497. When the dative object is, in English, a gerundial phrase, in German a suitable noun must be supplied, followed by a 'daß' clause or an infin. phr. in apposition; often a free translation is a less cumbersome alternative or, as in the last two examples, the only satisfactory solution:

zu-schreiben *to ascribe*: see 455, last example.
vor-beugen *to forestall, guard against*
I guarded against his finding out
Ich beugte der Möglichkeit vor (or: Ich verhütete), daß er es herausfinden könnte.
sich widersetzen *to oppose*
I opposed his being entrusted with the task
Ich widersetzte mich dem Versuch, ihm diese Aufgabe anzuvertrauen.
Ich war dagegen, daß man ihm diese Aufgabe anvertraute.
That is equal to ruining his life
Das heißt sein Leben ruinieren.

---

[1] Strictly speaking, the 'es' is here not impersonal, but an introductory subject, the infinitive phrase being the real subject.

He escaped being interrogated
Er entging einem Verhör.
Er konnte es vermeiden, verhört zu werden.

S. VERBS FOLLOWED BY THE GENITIVE

498. Introductory

A verb used with the genitive tends to sound stilted, and alternative constructions or verbs are normally preferred in spoken German. (This applies least to reflexive verbs.) In literary and official German these verbs are by no means eschewed; it will be noted that a number of them are of a judicial character (cf. Du. Gram. 5320).

The following lists are confined to verbs which are still used in current German; wherever an alternative construction exists, it is given.

499. Non-reflexive Verbs used with the genitive

jemanden (wegen) eines Verbrechens an-klagen	*to accuse s.o. of a crime*
Er wurde wegen Diebstahl(s) angeklagt	*He was accused of theft*
bedürfen (conjug. like dürfen)	*to need, require*[1]
jemanden seines Geldes berauben jemandem sein Geld rauben	*to rob s.o. of their money*
jemanden eines Verbrechens beschuldigen or bezichtigen	*to accuse s.o. of a crime* (two official verbs)
entbehren	*to lack* (elev.)
Es entbehrte . . . der Folgerichtigkeit (H. Risse)	*It lacked consistency*[2]
gedenken	*to remember, recall* e.g.
Wir haben deiner gedacht	*We gave you a thought*
jemanden eines Verbrechens überführen	*to convict s.o. of a crime*
jemanden einer Sache versichern	*to assure s.o. of s.th.*
Ich versichere Sie meines Interesses	*I assure you of my interest*
jemanden einer Sache würdigen	*to deem s.o. worthy of s.th.* e.g.
Er würdigte mich seiner Freundschaft (from Betteridge op. cit.)	*He honoured me with his friendship*

500. Reflexive Verbs used with the genitive

sich jemandes/einer Sache an-nehmen	*to show interest in, assist, befriend s.o.; to take an interest in, look after a matter*
sich einer Sache bedienen[3]	*to use, make use of s.th.*
sich jemandes /einer Sache bemächtigen	*to gain possession of s.o. or s.th.*
sich einer Sache enthalten	*to abstain, refrain from s.th.* (e.g. laughter, criticism)

---

[1] normal conversational equivalents: brauchen or nötig haben + Acc.

[2] BUT: Ich kann das Buch gegenwärtig nicht entbehren *I can't do without the book at present*; ich entbehre ihn sehr *I miss him very much.*

[3] commoner: benutzen + acc.

sich jemandes/einer Sache (less common: an jemanden etc.) entsinnen	*to recollect s.o. or s.th.*
sich jemandes erbarmen	*to take pity, have mercy on s.o.*
sich jemandes/einer Sache (or: an jemanden etc.) erinnern[1]	*to remember s.o. or s.th.*
sich einer Sache erwehren	*to refrain from* (e.g. laughter), *to resist* (e.g. an urge)
sich einer Sache rühmen	*to boast of, pride o.s. on s.th.*
sich jemandes (für jemanden)/ (wegen) einer Sache schämen	*to be ashamed of s.o. or s.th.*
sich einer Sache vergewissern (less common : über eine Sache)	*to make sure of s.th.* (e.g. the time of departure)
sich jemandes versichern	*to make sure of, gain control of s.o.*
sich einer Sache versichern	*to make sure of, secure s.th.* (e.g. s.o.'s consent)

501. Idiomatic uses of certain verbs with the genitive

sich bester Gesundheit erfreuen	*to enjoy the best of health*
sich eines guten Rufes erfreuen	*to enjoy a good reputation*
der Ruhe pflegen	*to take a rest*
Es spottet jeder Beschreibung	*It beggars description*
ehe ich mich dessen (or: mich's) versah	*before I was aware of it, all of a sudden*
seines Amtes walten	*to discharge the duties of one's office;* sometimes facetious, e.g.
Also, walte deines Amtes!	*Now then, do your job*
sich seines Lebens (or: seiner Haut) wehren	*to fight for one's life*
Er würdigte mich keines Blickes	*He didn't deign to look at me*

502. How to deal with verbs followed by the genitive when the 'genitive object' is, in English, a gerundial phrase or a noun clause. The following are the main relevant verbs:

(a) After an-klagen, beschuldigen, sich entsinnen, sich erinnern, sich rühmen, sich schämen, überführen, use zu + infin. or a 'daß' clause:

Er wurde beschuldigt, das Geld gestohlen zu haben	*He was accused of stealing the money*
Ich schämte mich, daß mein Bruder es getan hatte	*I was ashamed at my brother's having done it*

(b) sich enthalten: use sich davon zurückhalten + zu + infin.:

Ich hielt mich davon zurück, mich in seine Angelegenheiten einzumischen	*I abstained from interfering in his affairs*

(c) würdigen: use the corresponding noun:

Man würdigte ihn einer öffentlichen Ehrung	*He was deemed worthy of being publicly honoured*

(d) With the phrase 'sich (dat.) einer Sache bewußt sein', use dessen + 'daß' clause:

Ich bin mir dessen bewußt, daß . . .	*I am conscious (of the fact) that . . .*

---

[1] 'eine Sache erinnern' is regional; 'sich (dat.) eine Sache erinnern' is obsolete.

10*

T. VERBS, ADJECTIVES AND NOUNS WITH PREPOSITIONAL CONSTRUCTIONS[1]

503. Examples

Ich verlasse mich auf deine Hilfe	*I am relying on your help*
Ich bin von diesem Geld abhängig	*I am dependent on this money*
Seine Empörung über den Zeitungsartikel war begreiflich	*His indignation at the newspaper article was understandable*

504. Where verbs with prepositional constructions are directed not at a noun or pronoun, but at something happening or being done (frequently a gerund in English), normal usage is to prefix da (or dar, before a vowel) to the preposition, followed by an infinitive phrase, with 'zu', where the subject of the infinitive is the same as the subject of the introductory verb and by a 'daß' clause where the subject changes.

The same applies, mutatis mutandis, in the case of adjectives and nouns with prepositional constructions.

Ich verlasse mich darauf, ihn zu Hause zu finden	*I rely on finding him at home*
Ich verlasse mich darauf, daß er alles arrangiert	*I rely on his arranging everything*
Ich bin davon abhängig, dieses Geld zu bekommen	*I am dependent on receiving this money*
Ich bin davon abhängig, daß mir mein Bruder hilft	*I am dependent on my brother helping me*
Seine Empörung darüber, niemand zu Hause zu finden, war begreiflich	*His indignation at finding no one at home was understandable*
Seine Empörung darüber, daß wir ihm nichts davon gesagt hatten, war begreiflich	*His indignation at our not having told him anything about it was understandable*

Note:

i It would not be wrong to have a 'daß' clause in the first, third and fifth of the above examples, e.g. Ich verlasse mich darauf, daß ich ihn zu Hause finde.

ii An infinitive phrase may also be used where its subject is the same as the object of the introductory verb:

Er hinderte mich daran, den Brief zu schreiben	*He hindered me from writing the letter*
Ich werde meinen Freund davor warnen, es zu tun	*I shall warn my friend against doing it*

iii da + prep. is enclosed in a compound tense, a subordinate clause or an infinitive phrase:

Ich hatte mich darauf verlassen, daß er kommen würde.
Obwohl ich mich darauf verlasse, ihn zu Hause zu finden, ...
Anstatt mich darauf zu verlassen, daß er es tun wird, ...

---

[1] This section owes much to Gunnar Bech, op. cit. Regarding the position of the prepositional phrase, see 653 N.ii and 658(c).

505. Deviations from the rule and examples given in 504

i with a large number of verbs, adjectives and nouns the inclusion of da + prep. is optional.

ii with a small number da + prep. is omitted.

Examples of i

Ich ärgerte mich (darüber), daß er so wenig getan hatte	*I was annoyed that he had done so little*
Ich bin (davon) überzeugt, daß er sein Bestes tut	*I'm convinced that he's doing his best*
Er hat eine Abneigung (dagegen), Einkäufe zu machen	*He has an aversion to doing shopping*

(See 509, List A).

Note: The inclusion or omission of da + prep. is purely a matter of personal choice; its inclusion tends to produce a more intensive effect, while its omission is a shade more colloquial.

Examples of ii

Ich hoffe auf seine Unterstützung; ich hoffe, ihn heute zu sprechen; ich hoffe, daß du kommen wirst.

Ich war überrascht über seinen Sinn für Humor; ich war überrascht, ihn zu sehen; ich war überrascht, daß er da war.

meine Bitte um Geld; meine Bitte, ihn zu sprechen, wurde mir gewährt.

(See 510, List B).

506. Where the preposition is 'wegen', a 'weil' clause is used, sometimes heralded by 'deswegen':

Er machte mir Vorwürfe (*reproached me*) wegen meiner Faulheit.

Er machte mir (deswegen) Vorwürfe, weil ich alles vergessen hatte.

Where 'für' is an alternative to 'wegen', 'dafür, daß' is preferable:

Ich lobte ihn wegen seines Fleißes/für seinen Fleiß.

Ich lobte ihn dafür, daß er alles erledigt hatte.

507. After some verbs, adjectives and nouns, the clause is introduced not by daß, but by some interrogative word, e.g. ob *whether*, wie, wann, wer, was. This arises naturally from the sense, e.g.

Ich dachte darüber nach, ob ich es unternehmen könnte/wie ich ihm helfen könnte/was er wohl dazu sagen würde.

508. The lists that follow cannot aim at completeness, but at the inclusion of most relevant words in common use. Verbs predominate as it is with them that prepositional constructions are most frequently used. **After most verbs, adjectives and nouns not included in Lists A and B, the inclusion of da + prep. is essential.**

509. List A: i Verbs ii Adjectives and Participles iii Nouns after which the inclusion of da + prep. is optional

i ab-halten (davon) zu *to deter*, jemandem ab-raten (davon) zu *to advise against*, acht-geben (darauf) zu/daß *to take care*, sich amüsieren (darüber) zu/daß/wie *to be amused*, sich ärgern (darüber) zu/daß *to be annoyed*, auf-fordern (dazu) zu *to invite s.o.* (e.g. to accompany one), auf-passen (darauf), daß *to take care,* autorisieren (dazu) zu *to authorize s.o. to do s.th.*

sich beklagen (darüber), daß *to make a complaint about,* benutzen/gebrauchen (dazu) (um) zu *to use in order to,* betteln (darum) zu/daß *to beg* (e.g. to be allowed to do s.th. or that s.o. should help one), (dazu) da-sein, um . . . zu *to be there in order to,* sich einigen (darüber), daß *to reach agreement,* ein-laden (dazu) zu *to invite,* es ekelt mich (davor) zu *it fills me with abhorrence,* sich entscheiden (dafür) zu *to decide to,* sich entschließen (dazu) zu *to make up one's mind,* erinnern (daran) zu/daß *to remind,* sich erinnern (daran), daß *to remember that,* BUT: sich erinnern daran zu ('daran' is essential) *to remember to*

sich freuen (darüber) zu/daß *to be glad,* sich fürchten (davor) zu *to be afraid,* sich (dazu) herab-lassen zu *to condescend,* hindern (daran) zu *to hinder, prevent,* sich hüten (davor) zu *to take care not to,* jammern (darüber), daß *to lament that,* klagen (darüber), daß *to complain*

sich schämen (darüber) zu/daß *to be ashamed,* sich scheuen (davor) zu *to shrink from* (doing s.th. unpleasant), sich sehnen (danach) zu *to long to,* sich sträuben (dagegen) zu/dagegen, daß *to oppose, boggle at,* sich streiten (darüber), wer, wieviel etc. *to quarrel about who, how much etc.,* mit jemandem (darin) überein-stimmen, daß *to agree with s.o. that,* überzeugen (davon), daß *to convince,* urteilen (darüber), ob, wie gut etc. *to judge whether, how good etc.,* sich wundern (darüber) zu/daß *to be surprised*

ii ärgerlich (darüber) zu/daß *annoyed,* empört (darüber) zu/daß *indignant,* entsetzt (darüber) zu/daß *shocked,* enttäuscht (darüber) zu/daß[1] *disappointed,* entzückt (darüber) zu/daß[1] *delighted,* erfreut (darüber) zu/daß *pleased,* erstaunt (darüber) zu/daß[1] *astonished,* froh (darüber) zu/daß[1] *glad,* (dazu, dafür) geeignet sein zu *to be fitted to,* (darauf) gespannt sein zu *to be (expectantly) eager to,* (darauf) gespannt sein, ob *to wonder whether,* stolz (darauf) zu/daß *proud,* traurig (darüber) zu/daß[1] *sad,* überzeugt (davon), daß *convinced,* unentschieden (darüber), ob, wer, wann etc. *undecided,* vorbereitet (darauf) zu/daß *prepared*

iii ein Abkommen (darüber) zu/daß *an (official) agreement,* eine Abneigung (dagegen) zu *aversion,* Angst haben (davor) zu/daß *to be afraid,* Aussicht haben (darauf) zu *to have prospects of,* eine Beschwerde (darüber), daß *complaint,* die Empörung (darüber), daß *indignation,* das Erstaunen (darüber) zu/daß *astonishment,* die Freude (darüber) zu/daß *joy, pleasure,* aus Furcht (davor), daß *for fear that,* der Gedanke (daran) zu/daß *thought,* der Grund (dafür), daß *reason,* die Sehnsucht (danach) zu *longing,* sich Sorgen machen (darum), daß, ob etc. *to worry,* die Überraschung (darüber) zu/daß *surprise,* das Verlangen (danach) zu *desire, craving,* im Zweifel sein (darüber), ob *to be in doubt*

510. List B: i Verbs ii Adjectives and Participles iii Nouns after which da + prep. is omitted

i an-klagen wegen (Er wurde angeklagt, das Geld gestohlen zu haben) jemanden um etwas bemühen (Dürfte ich Sie bemühen, ihm dies zu geben?) bitten um (Ich bat ihn, mir zu helfen) erzählen von/über (Er erzählte uns, daß . . .) hoffen auf (Ich hoffe, es zu tun; ich hoffe, daß . . .)

ii begeistert von *in raptures about* (Er war begeistert, sie zu sehen)

---

[1] generally without darüber in both constructions.

begierig nach (Ich bin begierig, ihn zu sehen; ich bin begierig (zu erfahren),
ob . . . *anxious to hear*)
bereit zu (Ich bin bereit, es zu tun)
böse über (Ich war böse, daß er nicht gekommen war)
enttäuscht über/von (Ich war enttäuscht, ihn nicht zu sehen/daß er nicht
da war)
neugierig auf *curious as to, anxious to know* (Ich bin neugierig, ob er kommen
wird; ich bin neugierig (zu hören), was er dazu sagt)
überrascht über (Ich war überrascht, ihn zu sehen/daß . . .)

iii Angst haben um *to be anxious about* (Ich hatte Angst, daß er sich erkälten
könnte *I was afraid lest* . . .)
die Anklage wegen (die Anklage, Geld gestohlen zu haben)
der Anlaß, die Veranlassung zu *occasion, cause for* (Ich habe keine Veranlassung, ihm Geld zu geben)
die Bitte um (Er ignorierte meine Bitte, pünktlich zu sein)
die Furcht vor (seine Furcht, beschwindelt zu werden)
eine Gelegenheit zu *an opportunity for* (Ich hatte keine Gelegenheit, mit ihm
zu sprechen)
die Hoffnung auf (meine Hoffnung, ihn zu sehen/daß er kommen würde)
eine Neigung zum Pessimismus *inclination, proneness to* (seine Neigung,
alles zu kritisieren)
das Recht auf (das Recht zu streiken)

511. Some special cases

i the idiomatic use of 'dazu' with the following verbs:[1]
Er hat mich dazu gebracht *induced me*, (dazu) erzogen *brought me up*, dazu
getrieben *driven me*, (dazu) überredet *persuaded me*, dazu verführt *en-
ticed me*, dazu verleitet *led me astray*, (dazu) gezwungen *forced me*
es zu tun.

Er ist (dazu) geboren, Künstler zu sein	*He is born to be an artist*
Wie kommt er nur dazu, so was zu tun?	*However did he come to do such a thing?*
Ich bin dazu verurteilt, seine Launen hinzunehmen	*I am condemned to put up with his whims*

ii streben nach to strive after
Er strebte (danach), anerkannt zu werden	*He strove to win recognition* (recognition = a desired goal)
Er strebte, seinen Mitmenschen zu helfen	*He strove to help his fellow-men* (continuous endeavour)

iii träumen von to dream of
Er träumte davon, einmal Italien zu sehen	*He dreamt of seeing Italy some day* (= hoped to)
Er träumte, daß man ihm gekündigt hätte	*He dreamt that he had been given notice* (= an actual dream)

iv warnen vor + dat. to warn about or against
Er warnte mich davor, allein in die Stadt zu gehen	*He warned me against going into the town alone*

[1] cf. Gunnar Bech, op. cit., 289, and 613(f) in this book.

Er warnte mich, nicht allein in die Stadt zu gehen	*He warned me not to go into the town alone*
Er warnte mich (davor), daß der Chef es übelnehmen könnte	*He warned me that the director might take it badly*

N.B. similarly after 'seine Warnung'.

v zweifeln an + dat. *to doubt*

Ich zweifle (nicht) an seiner Ehrlichkeit	*I doubt (do not doubt) his honesty*
Ich zweifle nicht (daran), daß er kommen wird	*I don't doubt that he will come*
Ich zweifle, ob er kommen wird	BUT: *I doubt if he will come*

U. THE USE OF THE ANTICIPATORY 'ES'[1]

512. The use of 'es' to anticipate zu + infin. or a 'daß' clause

(a) The following are typical examples of verbs having zu + infin. or a 'daß' clause as their object:

Er begann zu singen; er versprach zu kommen; er erlaubte mir, nach Hause zu gehen.

Ich wußte, daß er krank war; er versprach, daß ich alles sehen sollte; er wollte, daß mein Bruder kommen sollte.

(b) After some such verbs, the infinitive phrase or the 'daß' clause is regularly or usually anticipated by an accusative 'es', to which the infinitive phrase or the 'daß' clause is in apposition:

Ich konnte es kaum ertragen, ihn so leiden zu sehen	*I could hardly endure to see him suffer so*
Evelyn hatte es abgelehnt zu essen (V. Baum)	*Evelyn had declined to have lunch*
Ich konnte es nicht ertragen, daß er so litt	*I could not endure that he should suffer so*
Ich habe es erlebt, daß Riemann die beste Rede gehalten hat	*I've known Riemann to give the best speech*

(c) After others, the anticipatory 'es' is optional:

Er hat (es) unternommen, einen neuen Plan zu entwerfen	*He has undertaken to draw up a new plan*
Er will (es) verhindern, daß die Kundgebung stattfindet	*He wants to prevent the demonstration from taking place*

(d) There is no 'es':

i if, for the sake of emphasis, the infinitive phrase or the 'daß' clause is placed at the beginning of the sentence, but 'das', in apposition to the inf. phr. or the 'daß' clause, is possible: Ihn so leiden zu sehen, (das) konnte ich kaum ertragen.

ii if the infin. phrase is enclosed in a main sentence or in a subordinate clause: Ich habe ihn zu warnen unternommen; ich fragte ihn, ob er zu singen abgelehnt hätte.

513. Notes on the lists that follow:

i They cannot aim at completeness, but at including a high proportion of relevant verbs in common use.

---

[1] This section owes much to Gunnar Bech, op. cit.

ii Verbs of which the English equivalent has 'it' corresponding to the German 'es' are not included, e.g.

es jemandem ermöglichen zu	*to make it possible for s.o. to do s.th.*
es für ratsam halten zu	*to consider it advisable to*
es zustande/zuwege bringen, daß	*to bring it about that*

iii With a few verbs 'wie' is substituted for 'daß', as required by the sense, e.g. erklären *to explain.*

514. List A: Verbs after which the anticipatory 'es' is essential or usual

es ab-lehnen zu	*to decline to do s.th.*
es jemandem hoch an-rechnen, daß	*to think highly of s.o. for doing s.th.*, e.g.
Ich rechne es ihm hoch an, daß er dieses Opfer gebracht hat	*I think highly of him for making this sacrifice*
es aus-halten zu/daß	*to endure doing s.th./that . . .*
es über sich bringen zu	*to bring o.s. to do s.th.*
es durch-setzen zu/daß	*to succeed (in the face of opposition) in doing s.th. or in arranging that*
es eilig haben zu	*to be in a hurry to do s.th.*
es erleben, daß	*to have known s.th. to happen, to live to see s.th. happen*
es erreichen zu/daß	*to manage to do s.th.*
es jemandem ersparen zu	*to save s.o.'s having to do s.th.*
es ertragen zu/daß	*to endure doing s.th./that . . .*
es fertig-bringen zu	*to manage to do s.th.*
es genießen zu	*to enjoy doing s.th.*
es lassen zu	*to refrain from doing s.th.*, e.g.
Ich konnte es nicht lassen, dies zu tun	*I couldn't refrain from doing this*
es leicht haben, zu	*to be easy for s.o. to do s.th.*, e.g.
Ich hatte es leicht, ihn zu überzeugen	*It was easy for me to convince him*
es leid sein zu	*to be tired of doing s.th.*
es sich leisten können zu	*to be able to afford to do s.th.*
es lieben zu	*to love doing s.th.*
es jemandem nach-tragen, daß	*to bear s.o. a grudge for having done s.th.*
es (nicht) nötig haben zu	*(not) to need to do s.th.*
es satt haben zu	*to be sick of doing s.th.*
es unterlassen zu	*to omit doing s.th.*
es jemandem nicht verdenken, wenn	*not to blame s.o. for doing s.th.* e.g.
Man kann es ihm nicht verdenken, wenn er protestiert	*He can't be blamed for protesting*
es verlernen zu	*to forget how to do s.th.*
es verschmähen zu	*to disdain to do s.th.*
es verstehen zu	*to know how to do s.th.*
Ich habe es ihm zugute gehalten, daß er alles offen zugab	*I took into favourable consideration the fact that he frankly admitted everything*
es jemandem zu-muten zu	*to expect s.o. to do s.th.*, e.g.
Man kann es diesem alten Mann nicht zumuten, Überstunden zu machen.	*One cannot expect this old man to work overtime*

515. List B: Verbs after which the anticipatory 'es' is optional

(es) sich ab-gewöhnen zu	*to break o.s. of doing s.th.*
(es) sich an-gewöhnen zu	*to become accustomed to doing s.th.*
(es) jemandem an-hören, daß	*to tell by s.o.'s speech that*, e.g.

Man kann (es) ihm anhören, daß er Franzose ist	*You can tell by his accent that he's French*
(es) jemandem an-merken, daß	*to notice that* (e.g. s.o. is tired)
(es) jemandem an-sehen, daß	*to tell from s.o.'s appearance that* (e.g. they have been ill)
(es) auf-geben zu	*to give up doing s.th.*
(es) auf-schieben zu	*to put off doing s.th.*
(es) begreifen, daß/warum	*to grasp (comprehend) that/why*
(es) bereuen zu/daß	*to repent, regret having done s.th./that . . .*
(es) erfassen, daß	*to grasp (comprehend) that . . .*
(es) gewohnt sein zu/daß	*to be used to doing s.th/that . . .*
(es) jemandem gönnen, daß	*to be glad for s.o. that, e.g.*
Ich gönne (es) ihm, daß er wieder ausgehen kann	*I'm glad for him that he can go out again*
(es) lernen zu/wie	*to learn (how) to do s.th., e.g.*
Ich habe (es) gelernt, ihn taktvoll zu behandeln	*I've learnt to treat him tactfully*
(es) leugnen, daß	*to deny that . . .*
(es) unternehmen zu	*to undertake to do s.th.*
(es) jemandem verbieten zu	*to forbid s.o. to do s.th.*
(es) jemandem vergeben, daß	*to forgive s.o. for doing s.th.*
(es) jemandem verheimlichen, daß	*to conceal from s.o. that . . .*
(es) verhindern, daß	*to prevent s.th. happening*
(es) vermeiden zu/daß	*to avoid doing s.th. or s.th. happening*
(es) vermögen zu	*to be able to do s.th.*
(es) versäumen zu	*to omit or miss doing s.th.*
(es) jemandem verschweigen, daß	*not to tell s.o. that . . .*
(es) jemandem verzeihen, daß	*to pardon s.o. for doing s.th.*
(es) vor-ziehen zu	*to prefer to do s.th.*
(es) wagen zu	*to dare or venture to do s.th.*
(es) jemandem zu-trauen zu	*to believe s.o. capable of doing s.th.*

XII CONJUNCTIONS

A. INTRODUCTORY NOTE

516. Note: Some textbooks include in their chapter on Conjunctions a class known as **Adverbial Conjunctions**, e.g. jedoch *however*, *nevertheless*, dagegen *on the other hand*, deshalb *therefore*, sonst *else*. When they stand at the beginning of a sentence, these are normally followed by inversion. In this book they are regarded as adverbs. Where they require comment or illustration, they are dealt with elsewhere; the Index should be consulted.

B. THE SIX SIMPLE CO-ORDINATING CONJUNCTIONS

517. The simple co-ordinating conjunctions are:

und[1] *and*	aber *but*	sondern *but* (*on the contrary*)
oder[1,2] *or*	allein *but*	denn *for* (*because*)

Where they introduce a clause, they take normal order unless they are followed by something other than the subject (cf. 642(d)).

518. 'aber' may also stand inside a sentence with the sense of 'however':

Alle verloren den Kopf; er aber blieb ganz ruhig	*Everyone lost their head, but he* (or: *he, however,) remained quite calm*

Where two verbs have the same subject, 'aber' is frequently used in this way, being placed after the second verb:

Er runzelte die Stirn, sagte aber nichts (more idiomatic than: aber sagte nichts)[3]	*He frowned but said nothing*

N.B. For 'aber' as a particle, see 284.

519. aber and sondern[4]

sondern is only used after a negative and then only when a wrong idea is

---

[1] for punctuation, see 743(a).   [2] for agreement rules, see 524(c).
[3] cf. Erben, op. cit., 186.   [4] for punctuation, see 743(b).

replaced by a correct one;[1] in other words, nicht . . ., sondern . . . presents two ideas which are incompatible:

Er ist nicht reich, sondern arm	*He is not rich, but poor*
Wir gingen nicht ins Kino, sondern arbeiteten im Garten	*We didn't go to the cinema, but worked in the garden*

aber, too, may be used after a negative, but nicht . . ., aber . . . presents two ideas which are compatible, which may co-exist (cf. 657(d)iiN):

Er ist nicht reich, aber ehrlich	*He is not rich but honest*
Wir gingen nicht ins Kino, aber wir wollten doch nicht zu Hause bleiben	*We didn't go to the cinema, but yet we didn't want to stay at home*

Note: 'nicht nur' is always followed by 'sondern auch' (see 523 ff.).

520. allein is rather literary; its characteristic use is to introduce, or explain, the non-fulfilment of a hope or expectation;[2] it is lightly stressed, in contrast with allein *alone, only*. For punctuation, see 743(b).

Ich hatte gehofft, ihn nach der Sitzung zu sprechen, allein er war nicht zugegen	*I had hoped to speak to him after the meeting, but he was not present*

521. denn,[3] as a co-ordinating conjunction, is the exact equivalent of English 'for'. Thus a 'denn' clause can never precede the clause with which it is co-ordinate, nor can it be used alone: Er kann nicht kommen, denn er hat Grippe. Warum ist er nicht gekommen? Weil er Grippe hat.

522. und and sondern are sometimes omitted between two sentences, as a stylistic device, e.g. Julika holt Aschenbecher in der Art einer Gastgeberin, [und] bittet mit Geste, Platz zu nehmen (M. Frisch).

C. CO-ORDINATING CONJUNCTIONAL PHRASES[4]

523. Co-ordinating conjunctional phrases

sowohl . . . als (auch)	*as well as, both . . . and*
sowohl . . . wie (auch)	
sowie (auch)	
nicht nur . . ., sondern auch	*not only . . ., but also*
entweder . . . oder	*either . . . or*
weder . . . noch	*neither . . . nor*
sei es, daß/weil . . ., sei es, daß/ weil[5]	*whether . . . or whether*

---

[1] cf. W. J. Hearn and G. Seidmann, *Graded German Composition* (Macmillan, 1966) 97, Note 3.
[2] cf. Du. Synonymwörterbuch: aber etc.
[3] for denn as a particle see 289.
[4] for punctuation see 743(b)(c) (d) Exc..
[5] somewhat literary.

(gleichviel,) ob . . . oder (ob)   *whether . . . or (whether)*
teils . . ., teils   *partly . . ., partly*

524. Agreement of verb with singular and plural subjects

(a) After sowohl . . . als (auch), sowohl . . . wie (auch) and sowie (auch), the verb is generally plural, even when they connect two singular subjects:

Sowohl mein Bruder als auch meine Schwester sind dagegen; A. sowie (auch) B. sind dagegen

(b) After weder . . . noch and teils . . ., teils the verb is generally singular if both subjects are singular, otherwise plural:

Weder mein Bruder noch meine Schwester ist dagegen; weder meine Brüder noch meine Schwester sind dagegen

(c) Where nicht nur . . ., sondern auch, entweder . . . oder or oder alone connect two singular subjects, the verb is singular: Entweder Hans oder Karl wird mir helfen; where they connect one singular and one plural subject, the verb agrees with the nearer subject: Entweder Hans oder seine Brüder werden mir helfen; where both subjects are plural, the verb is, of course, plural. (In the case of (entweder . . .) oder there is no deviation from this practice.)

525. (S) Agreement of verb where the subjects differ in person

The following examples should cover most contingencies:
Sowohl mein Bruder wie auch ich sind dagegen.
Nicht nur meine Brüder, sondern auch ich bin dagegen.
Entweder du hast recht oder ich.
Weder mein Bruder noch ich sind dagegen.
Ob du es tust oder ich, ist einerlei.

526. Word order in two sentences joined by the co-ordinating conjunctional phrases

(a) sowie (auch): normal order in main clause, verb to end in the 'sowie' clause:

Ich bewundere ihn, sowie ich ihn auch fürchte	*I admire as well as fear him*

(b) nicht nur . . ., sondern auch: inversion in the first, normal order in the second:

Ich bleibe zu Hause: nicht nur regnet es, sondern ich habe auch viel zu tun	*I'm staying at home: not only is it raining, but also I've got a lot to do*

(c) entweder . . . oder: inversion in the first, normal order in the second:

Entweder leihst du mir das Geld, oder ich gebe den Plan auf	*Either you lend me the money or I shall give up the plan*

Note: Normal order is possible in the first, giving the whole a more menacing note.

(d) weder . . . noch: inversion in both:

Weder habe ich seinen Brief bekommen, noch habe ich sonst von ihm gehört	*Neither did I receive his letter, nor did I hear from him in any other way*

(e) (gleichviel) ob . . . oder (ob): verb to the end in both; a following main clause has normal order:

Ob er nun krank ist oder nicht kommen will, er hat jedenfalls abgesagt	*Whether he's ill or doesn't want to come, in any case he's refused the invitation*

(f) teils . . ., teils: inversion in both.

527. nor (without a preceding neither) may generally be rendered by 'noch'; 'auch nicht' or 'auch kein' are common alternatives:

Ich kenne nicht ihn noch seinen Bruder (or: Ich kenne ihn nicht und auch seinen Bruder nicht)	*I don't know him nor (or) his brother*[1]
Sie ist nicht sehr hübsch, noch hat sie Geld (or: und hat auch kein Geld)	*She's not very pretty nor has she any money*

Only 'auch nicht' is possible in the following:

Ich mag ihn nicht sehr.—Ich auch nicht	*I don't like him much.—Nor I (either)*

N.B.

Ich sagte, ich hätte es nicht getan, und das stimmte auch	*I said I hadn't done it, nor had I*

D. SUBORDINATING CONJUNCTIONS

528. Introductory notes on the subordinating conjunctions

i Survey of types

1. Conjunctions of Time 529–35
2. Conjunctions of Place 536 f.
3. Conjunctions of Manner and Degree 538–42
4. Causal Conjunctions 543 f.
5. Consecutive Conjunctions 545 f.
6. Final Conjunctions 467
7. Conditional Conjunctions 462–5
8. Concessive Conjunctions 470–74

Within each type, the conjunctions are arranged in the alphabetical order of the English equivalents, except for types 2 and 8.

ii All these introduce subordinate clauses, with the verb at the end.

iii Unless indicated, they are normally followed by the indicative. The main exception occurs when they form part of reported speech: see 484(d).

iv For ob *whether* and daß *that* introducing noun clauses, see the section on Indirect Speech, especially 481 and 484(a)–(c).

---

[1] while 'or' would here be more usual in English, 'oder' could not be used in German.

E. CONJUNCTIONS OF TIME

529. Conjunctions of time

nachdem *after*	seitdem, seit *since*
wie, indem, als *as (while, when)*	bis *till, until*; *by the time*
solang(e) *as long as*	wann, als, wenn, *when*
sooft *as often as, whenever*	da, wo
sobald, sowie *as soon as, (when) once*	während *while*
bevor, ehe *before*	(indes, indessen) *while*
kaum (daß) *hardly . . . when,*	
no sooner . . . than	

530. Notes on conjunctions of time

(a) **as (while, when)**

i 'wie' is commonly used in this sense, but is mildly colloquial.

ii 'indem' can only be used, and 'wie' should only be used, when the action of the time clause is simultaneous with that of the main clause: Indem/Wie ich mir die Sache überlegte, kamen mir mancherlei Zweifel.

(b) **as long as**

i stylistically, 'solange' is preferable to 'solange als' or 'solange wie'.

ii 'solang(e)' may have a purely temporal sense (1st example) or a temporal-cum-conditional sense (2nd example), but not a purely conditional sense (3rd example):

Solange ich zu Hause war, hat niemand angerufen	*As long as I was at home, no one rang up*
Solange er sein Bestes tut, bin ich zufrieden	*As long as he does his best, I shall be satisfied*
Wenn er nur heute pünktlich kommt, wird alles klappen	*As long as he's punctual today, everything will be all right*

iii see 532(d)

(c) **as often as, whenever**

Sooft er kam, brachte er uns Geschenke	*Whenever he came, he brought us presents*

This purely temporal sense of 'whenever' must be distinguished from its concessive use, treated in 471, e.g. Whenever he may arrive, I want to speak to him at once.

(d) **as soon as**

i stylistically, 'sobald' is preferable to 'sobald als' or 'sobald wie'.

ii 'sowie' is common in conversation.

(e) **before and till** (see also 468)

When the main clause is negative, a pleonastic 'nicht' is frequently inserted in the subordinate clause:

Ehe (or Bis) du das nicht getan hast, brauchst du nicht nach Hause zu kommen	*You needn't come home before (or until) you've done that*

531. hardly . . . when, no sooner . . . than

(a) the conjunctional phrase 'kaum daß':

Kaum daß wir das Wirtshaus erreicht hatten, begann es zu regnen (or: als es zu regnen begann)	*No sooner had we reached the inn than it began to rain*

(b) Commoner than (a) are the following alternative versions in which kaum is an adverb:

Kaum hatten wir das Wirtshaus erreicht, (so) begann es zu regnen.
Wir hatten das Wirtshaus kaum erreicht, als (*when*) es zu regnen begann.

(c) With any of these constructions, the swift sequence of events may be emphasized by inserting 'auch schon': Wir hatten das Wirtshaus kaum erreicht, als es auch schon zu regnen begann.[1]

(d) 'kaum daß' (in (a) above) must be distinguished from the restrictive phrase 'kaum, daß' (cf. Du. Haupt. p. 337):

Ich kann dir kein Geld leihen; kaum, daß ich für mich selber genug habe (commoner: ich habe kaum für mich selber genug)	*I can't lend you any money—I've hardly got enough for myself*

532. since

(a) 'seitdem' is used rather more than 'seit'.

(b) When the since clause refers to a state or activity beginning in the past and still continuing, the present tense is used in German. The same applies to the main clause with the following qualifications:

   i When a series of actions or states is referred to, the perfect is used (3rd example) unless it is desired to indicate a continuing habit (4th example).

   ii When the main clause is negative, the perfect is used (5th example) except in cases of clear continuity (6th example).

1. Seitdem ich die Tabletten (nicht mehr) nehme, fühle ich mich wohler	*Since I've (no longer) been taking the tablets, I've been feeling better*
2. Seitdem er sein Haus verkauft hat,[2] wohnt er in einem Hotel	*Since he sold his house, he's been living in a hotel*
3. Seitdem ich ihn kenne, ist er mehrmals krank gewesen	*Since I've known him, he has been ill several times*
4. Seitdem ich ihn kenne, besuche ich ihn jeden Sonntag	*Since I've known him, I've been visiting him every Sunday*
5. Seitdem ich ihn kenne, haben wir uns nie gestritten	*Since I've known him, we have never quarrelled*
6. Seitdem ich im Dorf wohne, bin ich nie einsam	*Since I've been living in the village, I'm never lonely*

(c) When the since clause refers to a state or activity which, beginning in the past, still continued at a more recent point in the past, the imperfect tense is used in German, with the same qualifications as in (b) above, substituting the pluperf. for the perf.:

Seitdem ich ihn kannte, besuchte ich ihn jeden Sonntag	*Since I had known him, I had been visiting him every Sunday*

---

[1] cf. Schulz-Griesbach, op. cit., G 351 ff.

[2] The sale of his house was a self-contained action, completed in the past; therefore not present tense.

| Seitdem ich ihn kannte, hatten wir uns nie gestritten | *Since I had known him, we had never quarrelled* |
| Seitdem ich im Dorf wohnte, war ich nie einsam | *Since I had been living in the village, I was never lonely* (neg., but a continuous state) |

(d): (b) and (c) apply equally to solange *as long as,* which could be substituted for seitdem in all the above examples except 2. and 3. in (b). In Example 1. in (b), solange could be used, but with a different sense: As long as I take . . .

(e) **ever since**: the German rendering depends on the context:

Von der Zeit an, wo er das Vermögen seines Onkels erbte, . . .	*Ever since he inherited his uncle's fortune,* . . .
Solang ich ihn kenne, . . .	*Ever since I've known him,* . . .
Soweit ich zurückdenken kann, . . .	*Ever since I can remember,* . . .

533. till, until

(a) See 530(e).

(b) **not until**:
   i 'erst als' or 'erst wenn' *only when* (cf. 321).
   ii less common: nicht eher . . . als bis ('not sooner . . . than till').

Erst als mein Bruder zurück war, ging ich aus	*Not until my brother was back did I go out*
Ich werde erst ausgehen, wenn mein Bruder zurück ist	*I shan't go out till my brother is back*
Ich werde nicht eher ausgehen, als bis mein Bruder zurück ist	

(c) 'bis' may also render **by the time**, as in: Bis du zurückkommst, habe ich alles erledigt. Cf. the use of the preposition: Ich bin bis Montag zurück.

534. when

(a) **wann**, used as an interrog. adv. to introduce direct questions, is used conjunctionally in noun clauses, i.e. in reported speech and the like:
Wann kommt er nach Hause? Ich fragte ihn, wann er nach Hause käme. Ich weiß nicht, wann ich nach Hause komme.

(b) **als** introduces adverb clauses referring to a single occurrence or state in the past:
Als ich ihn sah, bekam ich einen Schreck. Als ich jung war, las ich seine Bücher gern.

Note: als is used with the present tense in two cases:
   i the historic present: Gerard wird heftiger, als er sein [Grouchys] Zögern sieht (St. Zweig: *Die Weltminute von Waterloo* in *Sternstunden der Menschheit*) ('wie', cf. 530(a), is also frequently used thus).
   ii in summaries of plays or stories: Als Othello die Wahrheit erfährt, nimmt er sich das Leben.

(c) **wenn** introduces adverb clauses in the present[1] or future or referring to a repeated occurrence in the past:

Wenn er kommt, werde ich ihm alles sagen. Wenn ich zum Zahnarzt mußte, weinte ich immer.

Note the following case:

| Ich wollte zu Hause sein, wenn Karl ankam | I wanted to be at home when Karl arrived |

(wenn is used because, as viewed by the speaker, Karl's arrival lay in the future)

(d) **da** is an archaic alternative for 'als' in its main use: Die Sonne schien an einem wolkenlosen Himmel, da er seinen Heimatort verließ (F. Dürrenmatt). See also 534(f).

(e) Following an 'als' clause, the main clause often begins with 'da' *then*; following a 'wenn' clause, it often begins with 'da' or 'dann':[2]

Als ich in Hamburg ausstieg, da sah ich ihn sofort.
Wenn du mit der Arbeit fertig bist, dann wollen wir alles besprechen.

(f) **'when' introducing relative clauses**

i Stylistically, the best rendering is prep. + rel. pron.:

Ich werde den Tag, an dem er ankam, nie vergessen	I shall never forget the day when he arrived
in einer Zeit, in der die Jugend immer unabhängiger wird	at a time when youth is becoming ever more independent
Es war eine Gelegenheit, bei der Sie ihn hätten sprechen können	It was an occasion when you could have spoken to him

ii Other common renderings are wo, da, als and wenn:

Es vergeht kaum ein Tag, wo er mich nicht anruft	Hardly a day passes when he doesn't give me a ring
Ach, wo sind die Zeiten, da Pinneberg sich für einen guten Verkäufer hielt? (H. Fallada)	Oh, where are the times when Pinneberg considered himself a good salesman?
aber in dem Augenblick, als der Hund aufsprang, schrie er: . . . (Th. Valentin)	but at the moment when the dog jumped up he shouted
an seinem nächsten Geburtstag, wenn er volljährig wird (from Erben, op. cit., 257)	on his next birthday when he comes of age

In place of prep. + rel. pron. in i above, 'wo' could be used in any of the examples, 'als' in the first, 'da' in the second.

N.B. | Es war das erste Mal, daß ich ihn gesehen hatte | It was the first time that I had seen him |

iii Where the relative 'when' is not restrictive but continuative, it is generally rendered in German by a second main clause:

| Es war jetzt drei Uhr. Zu dieser Zeit ging er immer spazieren | It was now three o'clock, when he always went for a walk |
| Letztes Jahr ist er nach München gezogen und seitdem habe ich ihn nicht gesehen | Last year he moved to Munich since when I haven't seen him |

---

[1] with the two exceptions noted in 534(b)N.
[2] cf. Schulz-Griesbach, op. cit., G 057 and G 538.

(g) **when clauses with concessive force**

Wie konntest du das tun, obwohl du wußtest (or: wo du doch wußtest), daß es unrecht war?	*How could you do that, when you knew it was wrong?*

(h) **than when**: see 131(d)i

535. while

(a) 'während' is the normal equivalent, 'indessen' and 'indes' being archaic ('indessen', less commonly 'indes', is quite a usual equivalent of 1. meanwhile 2. nevertheless).

Du kannst mich füttern, indes ich die Ente rupfe (E. Langgässer)	*You can feed me while I'm plucking the duck*

(b) All three conjunctions, as well as 'wogegen', may also denote contrast (while, whereas), 'während' again being the normal choice:

Ich lese gern Romane, während mein Bruder sich mehr für Politik interessiert.

F. CONJUNCTIONS OF PLACE

536. Conjunctions of place

wo *where*	worin *wherein, in which, in what*[1]
wohin *whither, where to, to which*	worauf (*whereon*), *on which, on*
woher *whence, from where, from which*	*what*[1]
	etc.

537. Notes on conjunctions of place

(a) **wo, wohin and woher** may introduce relative and noun clauses:

Der Ort, wohin wir jetzt fahren, . . .	*The place to which we are now driving . . .*
Er wohnt (dort), wo wir früher wohnten	*He lives where we used to live*
Ich fragte ihn, woher er käme	*I asked him where he came from*

Note:

i For the meanings of wo other than 'where' see (b) below.

ii For the use of wohin and woher, see also 266–7.

(b) **Further uses of 'wo'**

i as a rendering of 'when': see 534(f)(g).

ii as a colloquial rendering of 'seeing that' (causal); generally **wo doch**: Wir können morgen später aufstehen, wo es doch Sonntag ist.

iii **wo nicht** is a colloquial alternative for 'wenn nicht' *if not*: Wo du es nicht brauchst, kannst du es mir geben (bad German). Es wird schwierig sein, wo nicht unmöglich.

iv **wo möglich** *if possible* (coll.); **womöglich** *possibly, perhaps*.

v as a colloquial alternative for 'irgendwo' *somewhere*:

Die hab' ich doch schon wo gesehen (I. Wendt)	*Surely I've seen her somewhere*

[1] see 171, 183.

vi as a dialectal and illiterate substitute for the rel. pron.:

diese Bilder, wo Sie hier sehen   *these pictures that you see here*
(heard on a conducted tour)

vii in the exclamations I wo! Ach wo (denn)! *Nonsense! Whatever makes you think that?*

G. CONJUNCTIONS OF MANNER AND DEGREE

538. Conjunctions of manner and degree

je nachdem (ob) *according as, according to whether etc.*
abgesehen davon, daß *apart from the fact that*[1]
wie, so wie, gleichwie *as, like*
soviel, soweit *as far as*
als ob, als wenn *as if, as though*[2]
indem; dadurch, daß *by* + gerund, *expressing means*[3]
außer daß; ausgenommen, daß *except that*[1]
inwiefern, (in)wieweit *how far, to what extent*
in dem (im) Maße, wie (or: in dem) (*in proportion*) *as . . ., so*
(in)sofern als, (in)soweit als *inasmuch as, in so far as*
(an)statt daß *instead of* + gerund[4]
(genauso) wie . . ., so *just as*
nur daß *only that*
als *than*
je . . ., um so; je . . ., desto; je . . ., je *the more . . ., the more*[5]
so . . ., so; so sehr . . ., so sehr *to the same extent that; as . . ., so*
zu (alt), als daß *too (old) for*[6]
ohne daß *without* + gerund[4]
indem: participial phrase conveying manner[7]

539. according as, according to whether etc.

(a) Je nachdem du dich anstrengst,   *According as you exert yourself, you will*
bringst du mehr oder weniger   *get more work done or less*
fertig

(b) Commoner than 'je nachdem' alone (as in (a) above) is 'je nachdem' followed by 'ob' *whether* or by an interrogative pronoun (wer, was), adjective (welcher) or adverb (wie, wann, wo, warum). E.g.

Je nachdem ob es ihm besser geht   *According to whether he is better, he is*
oder nicht, wird er morgen   *going away tomorrow*
verreisen

Je nachdem wen du sprichst, kannst   *According to whom you see, you can*
du mehr oder weniger Auskunft   *obtain more or less information*
erhalten

Je nachdem wie mir sein Gemälde   *According to how I like his painting, I*
gefällt, werde ich es kaufen oder   *shall buy it or not buy it*
nicht

---

[1] for punctuation see 743(e).
[2] see 466.   [3] see 452.   [4] see 431, 469(a).
[5] see 134.   [6] see 469(a).   [7] see 440.

(c) 'je nachdem' is sometimes used without a clause, the latter being implied by the context:

Kommst du morgen mit?—Je nachdem [e.g. wie ich mich fühle]	*Are you coming with us tomorrow?—It depends*

540. as, like (see also 130 and 142)

(a) 'wie' clause truncated:

Er kämpfte wie ein Löwe (= wie ein Löwe kämpft)	*He fought like a lion (= as a lion fights)*
Wie gesagt, ich kann mit diesem Buch nicht fertig werden	*As I said, I can't get on with this book*

Note: In the first of the above examples 'so wie' or 'gleichwie' could be used; both are rather more emphatic than 'wie'; 'gleichwie' is also rather literary.

(b) 'wie' clause complete:

Faul, wie er ist, wird er es nie zu etwas bringen	*Lazy as he is, he'll never get on in the world*
Wie ich erwartet hatte, kam er spät	*As I had expected, he was late*
Wie Sie sehen, die Lage ist kritisch (or: ist die Lage kritisch)	*As you see, the situation is critical*

Note: After 'Wie Sie sehen', the main clause may have either normal order or inversion, the former being more emphatic.

541. as far as

(a) 'soviel' is used before 'wissen' and 'sich erinnern':

Soviel er wußte, ging es ihr besser	*As far as he knew, she was better*
soviel (or: soweit) ich mich erinnere	*as far as I remember*

(b) 'soweit' is used in most other contexts:

Soweit man sehen konnte, war nichts als Wald und Wiesen	*As far as one could see, there was nothing but forest and meadows*
soweit ich urteilen kann	*as far as I can judge*
soweit dies möglich war	*as far as this was possible*
soweit bisher bekannt	*as far as is known up to now*
N.B. was mich betrifft	*as far as I'm concerned* (See also 582(b), 586(d))

542. Examples of further conjunctions of manner and degree

(a) **how far, to what extent**

Ich weiß nicht, inwieweit Sie davon informiert sind	*I don't know to what extent you have been informed about this*

(b) **(in proportion) as . . ., so**

Aber in dem Maße, wie seine Gesundheit geschwächt ward, verschärfte sich seine Künstlerschaft (Th. Mann)	*But (in proportion) as his health suffered, so his artistry was sharpened*

(c) inasmuch as, in so far as

Er ist insofern ein angenehmer Mensch, als er nie klagt	*He is an agreeable person inasmuch as he never complains*
einer Partei . . ., die er selbst nur insoweit schätzt, als sie seine Politik unterstützt (*Christ und Welt*)	*of a party, which he himself values only in so far as it supports his policy*

(d) just as

Genauso wie er selber kocht, so stopft er auch seine Socken	*Just as he does his own cooking, he darns his own socks*

(e) than

i 'als' clause truncated:

Er läuft schneller als ich [laufe]	*He runs quicker than I*

ii 'als' clause complete:

Er diktiert schneller, als ich stenographieren kann	*He dictates faster than I can take down in shorthand*

(f) to the same extent that; as . . ., so

So international der Sport ist, so national begrenzt ist oft das Interesse seines Publikums (*FAZ*)	*To the same extent that sport is international, the interest of its devotees is often narrowly national*
So sehr sie ihn liebt, so sehr haßt sie uns[1]	*As she loves him, so she hates us*

H. CAUSAL CONJUNCTIONS

543. Causal conjunctions

da *as, since*	nun (da) *now that, seeing that*
weil *because*	da nun mal (coll.) *seeing that*
zumal (da) *especially as*	wo doch (coll.) *seeing that*

544. Notes on causal conjunctions

(a) The lighter 'da' and the heavier 'weil' exactly correspond to 'as' or 'since' and 'because' respectively; so, too, a 'da' clause tends to precede, and a 'weil' clause to follow, the main clause.

After a preceding 'da' clause, the main clause sometimes opens with 'so': Da er nicht gekommen ist, (so) wird er wohl anrufen.

(b) The causal clause may be given prominence by inserting 'darum', 'deshalb' or 'deswegen' in the main clause before a following 'weil' clause:[2] Ich muß deshalb heute zu Hause bleiben, weil ich Besuch erwarte.

(c) **all the more because** = um so mehr, als (or da):

Ich freute mich über seinen Erfolg, um so mehr, als/da er völlig unerwartet kam	*I was glad about his success, all the more because it was totally unexpected*

(d) For 'denn' *for, because*, see 521.

---

[1] taken from Muret-Sanders, op. cit.
[2] cf. Schulz-Griesbach, op. cit., G 531.

(e) Examples of the remaining causal conjunctions:

Er wird uns sicher helfen, zumal er dich so gern hat	*He's sure to help us, especially as he's so fond of you*
Nun alles geschehen ist, bleibt nur zu wünschen, daß . . . (*FAZ*, quoted in Du. Gram. 3590)	*Now that everything has been done, one can only wish that . . .*
Ich muß es tun, da ich es nun mal (or: wo ich es doch) versprochen habe	*I've got to do it seeing that I've promised to*

I. CONSECUTIVE CONJUNCTIONS

545. Consecutive conjunctions

so daß *so that, such that*	derart . . ., daß *so . . . that*
so . . ., daß	dermaßen, daß *to such an extent that*

546. Notes on consecutive conjunctions

(a) Examples:

Das Wetter war schlecht, so daß wir wenig wandern konnten.

Das Wetter war so schlecht, daß wir wenig wandern konnten.

Er hat sich derart aufgeregt, daß wir den Plan fallenlassen mußten.

(b) Occasionally 'daß' alone is used for 'so that':

Kleines Volk setzte sich lustig in Trab, daß der Eisbrei umherspritzte (Th. Mann)	*Youngsters trotted off gaily so that the slush splashed in all directions*

(c) As a stylistic variant, consequence may be conveyed by two main clauses: Wir konnten wenig wandern, so schlecht war das Wetter.

(d) For consecutive clauses of the type 'zu (alt), als daß' see 469(a).

XIII PREPOSITIONS

Note:

i With few exceptions, **time phrases with prepositions** are not included here; **see Chap. X.**

ii **An asterisk denotes that the preposition is further dealt with in 597 ff.: Main figurative uses of German prepositions.**

A. PREPOSITIONS TAKING THE DATIVE

547. Nine common prepositions taking the dative[1]

*aus *out of, from*
außer (a) *outside, out of*
    (b) *except, besides*
*bei (a) *near, by*
    (b) *at the house of, with*
*gegenüber (a) *opposite*
    (b) *compared with*

mit *with*
*nach (a) *after* (b) *to* (especially before place-names)
seit *since*
*von (a) *from* (b) *by* (with passive)
    (c) *of*
*zu *to*

548. *aus

(a) *out of*: Er kam aus dem Haus; ich sah aus dem Fenster; er trank aus einer Tasse; er ging mir aus dem Weg; aus der Mode kommen/sein.

(b) *from*: where 'from' basically means 'out of', aus is used in German: Er stammt aus (*comes from*) Hamburg; er ist gerade aus der Schule gekommen; ein Zitat aus 'Faust'; dieser Schrank ist aus dem achtzehnten Jahrhundert; aus dieser Richtung *from this direction.*

549. (S) außer

(a) *outside, out of*: it is mainly used in a large number of fixed phrases, e.g.

Wir essen heute außer Hause	*We are eating out today*
Die Fabrik ist außer Betrieb	*The factory is not working*
außer Dienst (a. D.)	*retired (Retd.)*
außer der Zeit	*out of season; not at the official time*

---

[1] for 17 less common ones, see 557.

außer der Reihe	*out of turn*
außer Kontrolle geraten	*to get out of control* (e.g. car)
Aber dies war etwas, das ganz außer seiner Macht lag (R. Musil)	*But this was something that lay quite outside his power*

cf. außer Atem, außer Form, außer Gefahr, außer Hörweite *out of earshot*, außer Mode, außer Sicht, außer Übung, außer Zweifel *beyond doubt*

(b) *except, besides*: Niemand hat ihn gesehen außer dem Nachtwächter; außer dienstags.

Note: außer *except* is sometimes treated as a conjunction and is then followed by the same case as the word to which it refers back: Ich konnte nichts außer Lichter sehen.

550. *bei[1]

(a) (**S**) *near, by*

| Er stand (nahe) bei mir (or: in meiner Nähe)[2] | *He stood near me* |

cf. bei dem Rathaus/in der Nähe vom Rathaus; er saß beim Feuer; Bad Homburg ist (nahe) bei Frankfurt

(b) *at the house of, with*

Er wohnt bei seinem Onkel	*He lives at his uncle's (with his uncle)*
Ich habe dieses Fleisch beim neuen Metzger gekauft	*I bought this meat at the new butcher's*
Ich habe ihn bei Müllers getroffen	*I met him at the Müllers'*
bei uns	*at our house*
bei uns in der Fabrik	*in our factory* (idiomatic)

Note: bei cannot be used with verbs of motion; it is thus not synonymous with French 'chez'. E.g.

Er geht zu seinem Onkel	*He is going to his uncle's*
Er kam dicht an mich heran (or: in meine Nähe)	*He came near me*
Er kam dem Tode nahe	*He came near to death*

(c) *nearer, nearest (to)*

Er stand näher am Fenster als ich	*He stood nearer the window than I*
Mainz ist näher bei Frankfurt als Mannheim	*Mainz is nearer to Frankfurt than is Mannheim*
Er stand dem Fenster am nächsten	*He stood nearest the window*

551. *gegenüber, in both the senses treated here, follows a pronoun, but may precede or follow a noun, the latter position being the commoner.

(a) (**S**) *opposite*: Ich saß ihr gegenüber, wir wohnen dem Krankenhaus gengenüber/gegenüber dem Krankenhaus.

| N.B. schräg gegenüber | *almost* (lit. obliquely) *opposite* |
| am gegenüberliegenden (or anderen) Ufer | *on the opposite bank* |

(b) *compared with*: Seinem Bruder gegenüber ist er ein Faulenzer; gegenüber dem Vorjahr *compared with last year*

---

[1] see also 590(b)N.ii and (c)ii iii.
[2] cf. Er stand in der Nähe *He stood near*

552. mit covers all straightforward meanings of *with*, e.g. Er kam mit ihr; Frankfurter Würstchen mit Kartoffelsalat; ich spiele oft mit ihm Tennis; er schreibt mit einem Füller. See also 560(c) and 631.

N.B. mit der Arbeit anfangen/aufhören *to start/stop work*

553. *nach

(a) *after*: nach drei Wochen; nach dem Konzert; nach Tisch; bitte, nach Ihnen!

Ich las ein Buch nach dem andern	*I read book after book*
Nach dem Chef hat der Betriebs-leiter am meisten zu sagen	*After the boss, the manager has the biggest say*

(b) *to*: see 593.

554. seit *since*: seit dem Krieg, seit drei Wochen *for the last three weeks*, seit einiger Zeit *for some time past*.

Note on tenses used with 'since' phrases

i When the 'since' phrase applies to a state or activity which, beginning in the past, still continues, the present tense is used in German:

Ich arbeite seit acht Uhr	*I've been working since eight o'clock*
Seit Oktober liegt sie im Krankenhaus	*Since October she's been in hospital*
Seit wann wohnen Sie hier?	*Since when have you been living here?*
Seit meiner frühsten Kindheit habe ich eine Abneigung gegen Katzen	*Since my earliest childhood I've had an aversion to cats*[1]
Ich habe ihn seit dem Tod seines Vaters nur einmal gesehen	BUT: *I have only seen him once since his father's death*

ii When a series of actions or states is referred to, the perfect is used, unless it is desired to indicate a continuing habit (3rd example):

Er ist seit Weihnachten mehrmals krank gewesen	*He has been ill several times since Christmas*
Ich habe ihn seit Weihnachten jeden Sonntag besucht	*I have visited him every Sunday since Christmas*
Seit Weihnachten besuche ich ihn jeden Sonntag	*Since Christmas I've taken to visiting him every Sunday*

iii In negative statements, the perfect is used, except in cases of clear continuity, as in the 2nd example:

Ich habe ihn seit langem nicht gesehen	*I haven't seen him for a long time*
Seit Anfang des Jahres arbeitet er nicht mehr	*He has not been working since the beginning of the year*

iv When the 'since' phrase, or its equivalent, applies to a state or activity which, beginning in the past, still continued at a more recent point in the past, the imperfect tense is used in German, with the same qualifications as above, substituting the pluperf. for the perf.:

Ich wartete schon seit zwei Stunden (or: schon zwei Stunden), als er endlich ankam	*I had been waiting for two hours when at last he arrived*

---

[1] BUT (less usual): Seit meiner frühsten Kindheit habe ich immer eine Abneigung gegen Katzen gehabt. While the sentence still implies that the aversion continues, 'immer' gives greater weight to its existence throughout the past.

Ich hatte ihm seit Jahren (or: jahrelang) zugeredet, sein Haus zu verkaufen	*For years I had been urging him* (i.e. on a series of occasions) *to sell his house*
Als ich ihn besuchte, arbeitete er schon zwei Jahre nicht mehr	*When I visited him, he hadn't been working for two years*

555. *von

(a) *from*

von covers all straightforward uses of 'from' (but see 548(b)), e.g. Ich fuhr von Frankfurt nach München; ich habe einen Brief von meinem Vetter bekommen; ich wohne zwanzig Minuten vom Bahnhof (entfernt); ich war vom ersten bis zum zehnten Oktober in Berlin; von außen *from outside*; von zu Hause weg *away from home*; von da an *from there/from then onwards*.

Note:

i To denote a point of vantage or departure, von is frequently strengthened by another preposition, mainly 'aus', used adverbially:

Von diesem Fenster (aus) hat man eine gute Aussicht auf den See; von heute an *from today*.

from a German letter: Sie sind . . . vom Libanon aus mit dem Schiff nach Zypern gefahren. Wir sind gespannt (*we're wondering*), wie es nun von dort aus weitergehen wird.

ii Idiomatic:

Er war von Haus aus Lehrer, ist aber jetzt Schauspieler	*He was originally a teacher, but he's now an actor*
von Grund aus falsch	*completely wrong*
von mir aus	*as far as I'm concerned, if you like*

(b) *by* (with passive) (See also 560(c)):
Dieses Haus wurde von Studenten gebaut; cf. eine Sinfonie von Mozart.

(c) *of*: **'von' is used instead of the genitive case in the following instances:**

i **partitively**:

Wir aßen von dem Kuchen	*We ate some of the cake*
einer/der intelligenteste/viele von meinen Freunden (or: meiner Freunde)	*one/the most intelligent/many of my friends*
viel von seinem Leben	*much of his life*
ein Teil von dem, was er sagte	*part of what he said*

Similarly: einer von ihnen, einer von denen *one of whom*, jeder von uns, etwas von ihrem Charme, nichts von der Wirkung *none of the effect*, welches von diesen Büchern?

ii **in phrases which in some way characterize a preceding noun**:

ein Mann von Geschmack	*a man of taste*
eine Frau von deutscher Abstammung	*a woman of German descent*
Er war von bezaubernder Höflichkeit	*He was enchantingly courteous*
ein kräftiger Kerl, ein Klotz von einem Türken (*Zeit*)	*a strong fellow, a great lout of a Turk*

. . . einen völlig neuen Typ von Viermächte-Konferenz (*Spiegel*)	*a completely new type of Four-Power Conference*
ein Junge von fünfzehn (Jahren)	*a boy of fifteen (years)*

iii **to denote possession, or to render an objective genitive**[1] (last two examples), **where the genitive case is not shown**:

der Geschmack von Schokolade	*the taste of chocolate*
die Redakteure von Berliner Zeitungen	*the editors of Berlin newspapers*
die Herstellung von Knöpfen	*the manufacture of buttons*

iv **when the person or thing following a Saxon genitive**[1] **is itself in the genitive** (especially common after proper names):

die Ziele von Bismarcks Politik[2]	*the objectives of Bismarck's policy*

v **before proper names**

    1. before geographical names forming part of a title or ending in a sibilant and which are not used with the def. art.:

der König von Schweden; die Straßen von Paris BUT: die Königin der Niederlande; die Dörfer des Elsaß.

Note: Up to 1918, 'von' was accorded for use before a surname as a title of nobility, e.g. Generalfeldmarschall Paul von Hindenburg; cf. French 'de', e.g. Alfred de Vigny.

    2. frequently before geographical names in preference to a possible genitive, especially in conversation: die Kirchen von Nürnberg, im Süden von England (rather than Nürnbergs, Englands).

    3. frequently to render the gen. sing. of proper names ending in a sibilant, e.g. die Operetten von Johann Strauß: see 51(g).

vi **in conversation**

    1. von is much used instead of the genitive because the latter is felt to be somewhat affected, e.g. ein Teil von dem Kuchen, die Kinder von meinem Bruder.

    This is particularly so in the case of a gen. plur. without a def. art., possessive or demonstrative:

die Gehälter von einigen neuen Angestellten (rather than: einiger neuer Angestellter); die Bilder von anderen italienischen Malern.

    2. von generally replaces the first of two successive genitives, especially if they are masc. and/or neut., here avoiding a succession of sibilants:

Er klopfte an die Tür von dem Schlafzimmer des Generals (not: des Schlafzimmers des Generals)

Das ist die Schwester (von) der Frau meines Freundes.

556. *zu *to*, e.g. Er ging zum Bahnhof, zur Bank, and always for going to a person: Er ging zu seinem Onkel. See 594.

---

[1] cf. 60.

[2] A common error is 'die Ziele Bismarcks Politik', in which only one of the two genitives (Bismarck's) is rendered.

557. Seventeen less common prepositions taking the dative

ab (*starting*) *from, as from*
abgesehen von *apart from*
binnen *within* (a period of time)
dank *thanks to*
entgegen *contrary to, against*
entsprechend *in accordance with*
fern *far from*
gemäß *in accordance with*
gleich *like*
mitsamt *together with*

nächst *next after; next to*
nebst *together with, in addition to*
samt *together with*
zufolge i *in accordance with* ii *as the result of*
zuliebe *to please* (*s.o.*), *for the sake of*
zunächst *next to, close to*
zuwider *contrary to, against*

(a) **ab** (*starting*) *from, as from* is commercialese and officialese, but is fairly widely used in a time sense, where it takes the accusative.

Examples: i Place: ab (unserer) Fabrik *ex works*; ab Jericho folgten wir einer langen Kolonne israelischer Touristenbusse (*Zeit*) ii Time: ab neun Uhr, ab heute, ab ersten Mai, ab nächste Woche.

Note: The 1st example is a fixed phrase; otherwise, the normal equivalents are 'von . . . ab' for places (von Jericho ab) and 'von . . . an' in a time sense (vom ersten Mai an).

(b) **abgesehen von** *apart from*
abgesehen von allem andern   *apart from everything else*

(c) **binnen** *within* (a period of time). With a singular noun it may also take the genitive. E.g. binnen sechs Tagen, binnen eines Monats, binnen kurzem *before long, shortly*.
Commoner equivalents: in + dat. or innerhalb + gen.

(d) **dank** *thanks to*
dank seinen Bemühungen   *thanks to his efforts*

It is also used with the genitive:
dank seiner Sprachkenntnisse   *thanks to his knowledge of languages*
  (A. Goes)

(e) **entgegen** *contrary to, against* may precede or follow its noun:
entgegen den Erfahrungen früherer   *contrary to the experience of former years*
  Jahre (*FAZ*)
seiner Gewohnheit entgegen   *contrary to his habit*

(f) **entsprechend** *in accordance with* may precede or follow its noun; it is largely commercialese:
Ihren Anordnungen entsprechend   *in accordance with your instructions*

(g) **fern** *far from* is elevated style, normal usage being fern von or weit von; only these can be used with pronouns:
Wir wollen ein paar schöne Stunden fern (von) der Stadt verbringen; er wohnt fern/weit von uns.

(h) **gemäß** *in accordance with* may precede or, more frequently, follow its noun: seiner Gewohnheit gemäß, ihren Wünschen gemäß. –

(i) **gleich** like
Meine Frau grüßt Sie gleich mir   *My wife sends you her kindest regards as*
  herzlich   *I do*

(j) **mitsamt** and **samt** *together with* are somewhat stilted; they may be used slightly ironically, as in the 2nd example:

Er hat sein Haus samt allen Habseligkeiten verloren	*He has lost his house together with all his possessions*
Das große Krögersche Haus stand mitsamt seiner würdigen Geschichte zum Verkaufe (Th. Mann.)	*The great Kröger house, together with its stately history, came up for sale*

Normal equivalents: mit or zusammen mit.

(k) **nächst** *next after*; *next to* (rare)

Nächst Gott verdanke ich vor allem dir meine Rettung (from Du. Stil.; normal usage: nach)	*After God, I owe my being saved above all to you*
nächst dem Schrank (normal usage: neben)	*next to the cupboard*

(l) **nebst** *together with, in addition to* is mainly formal or officialese; sometimes used facetiously.

Herr Direktor Karl Müller ist nebst Gemahlin und Kindern eingetroffen	*Herr Direktor Karl Müller has arrived together with his wife and children*
nebst den Reisespesen	*in addition to travelling expenses*

Normal equivalents: (zusammen) mit, außer.

(m) **samt** *together with*: see (j) above.

(n) **zufolge**: meaning *in accordance with*, it is generally used with a preceding dative, e.g. seinem Befehl zufolge (normal equivalent: gemäß; see (h) above); meaning *as the result of*, it is used with a following genitive (normal equivalent: infolge + gen.).

(o) **zuliebe** *to please* (*s.o.*), *for the sake of* is much used; it follows its noun or pronoun: Ich habe es meiner Mutter zuliebe getan; dir zuliebe gibt es Spargel (*asparagus*).

(p) **zunächst** *next to, close to* may precede or follow a noun but must follow a pronoun:
Zunächst dem Fenster stand ein Tischchen; mir zunächst stand ein Italiener.
Normal equivalents: neben, dicht bei or dicht an (all + dat.).

(q) **zuwider** *contrary to, against* follows its noun, e.g. seinem Befehl zuwider.
Normal equivalent: gegen.

B. PREPOSITIONS TAKING THE ACCUSATIVE

558. Six common prepositions taking the accusative[1]

bis (a) *till, until* (b) *as far as*	*gegen (a) *against* (b) *contrary to*
durch (a) *through* (direction)	(c) *compared with* (d) *in return*
(b) *through, throughout*	*for* (e) *towards* (f) *about,*
(c) *through, by, by means of*	*approximately*
für *for*	ohne *without*
	*um *round, around, round about*

---

[1] for 10 less common ones, see 565.

559. bis[1]

(a) *till, until*: bis nächsten Sommer, bis letzte Woche, bis Sonnenuntergang, bis heute abend, bis jetzt, bis Ende 1967.

(b) *as far as*

Ich fahre nur bis Frankfurt	*I am only going as far as Frankfurt*
Bis dahin gehe ich mit	*I'll go with you as far as there*
bis hierher und nicht weiter	*thus far and no further*

Note:

i **not until = erst**, e.g. Er kommt erst am Montag (see 321).

ii **Used before an article or a demonstr., possess. or interrog. adj., 'bis' is followed by another preposition which determines the case.**

(α) **When it means 'till'** (or 'to', 'up to' with the sense of 'till'), this preposition is 'zu': bis zum vierten Mai, bis zu einer Krise, bis zu diesem Augenblick, bis zu seinem Tode, bis zu welchem Tag?

EXCEPTIONS:

    (a) 'bis zu' with no article etc.: bis zu Beginn des Weltkrieges; von Anfang bis (zu) Ende; Kinder bis zu zwölf Jahren; von Alexander bis zu Napoleon.

    (b) 'bis' before a demonstrative: bis diesen Montag (Dienstag) etc.

(β) **When it means 'as far as'**, the second preposition is the appropriate equivalent of 'to' (see 589 ff.):

Wir gingen bis zum Wald, bis zu seinem Haus.
Er ging bis zur Tür/bis an die Tür.
bis an den Rhein, bis an die Grenze *as far as the frontier*.
. . . standen sie im Wasser bis an die Knöchel (*up to their ankles*) (H. Mann).

Before the name of a country or town, 'as far as' is 'bis' or 'bis nach'; 'bis' is commoner, 'bis nach' is more intensive; whichever is used, a phrase in apposition is in the dative (cf. Du. Gram. 3385):

Ich fahre bis (nach) Lübeck, der alten Hansastadt	*I'm going as far as Lübeck, the old Hanseatic city*
Alexander der Große drang bis nach Indien vor	*Alexander the Great advanced as far as India*

N.B. Der Feind drang bis auf zwei Kilometer von der Stadt vor.
    The enemy advanced to within two kilometres of the town.

bis über die Ohren verschuldet	*up to one's ears in debt*
bis zu vierzig Mark pro Tag	*up to 40 marks a day*

iii **bis auf + acc.** may mean *down to* (*and including*) or *all but, except*:

Die Kabinen waren mit 447 Passagieren bis auf das letzte Klappbett belegt (*Zeit*)	*With 447 passengers, the cabins were full down to the last camp-bed*
Die Passagiere kamen alle um bis auf drei	*All but three of the passengers were killed*

Ambiguity can be avoided by using einschließlich + gen. and außer + dat. respectively.

---

[1] see also 248 N.iii and 330: 'by' and 'till'.

560. durch

(a) *through* (direction): Ich ging durch das Dorf; er atmet durch den Mund.

(b) *throughout*

durch viele Generationen hindurch	*throughout many generations*
die ganze Nacht (hindurch)	N.B. *throughout the night*
im ganzen Land	*throughout the country*

(c) **through, by,**[1] **by means of, with: durch, mit, von**

durch indicates the animate or inanimate agent or means through whom or which an action is performed:

Mein Onkel hatte mich durch seinen Sohn/durch ein Telegramm gewarnt	*My uncle had warned me through his son/ by a telegram*
Durch harte Arbeit hat er sein Ziel erreicht	*By hard work he attained his aim*

mit indicates the instrument used in performing an action:

Er hat ihn mit einem Messer getötet	*He killed him with a knife*

Compare: Er kam mit der Bahn, mit dem Schiff, mit dem Flugzeug, mit seinem Wagen, mit einem Taxi, mit dem Rad; cf. mit der Post, mit Luftpost.

Note: All these phrases except 'mit seinem Wagen' and 'mit dem Rad' could also be turned, colloquially and commercially, with 'per': per Bahn, per Schiff etc.

In passive sentences:

i **von** is used to indicate the author or doer of a deed:

Ich war von meinem Onkel durch seinen Sohn gewarnt worden	*I had been warned by my uncle through his son*
Er wurde von zwei Polizeibeamten verhaftet	*He was arrested by two police-officers*

ii the inanimate cause of an occurrence is normally indicated by **durch**:

Die Ernte wurde durch Hagel vernichtet	*The crop was destroyed by hail*
Ich wurde durch den starken Verkehr aufgehalten	*I was delayed by the heavy traffic*
Er wurde von einem Auto überfahren	BUT: *He was run over by a car*

(The accident was caused by car and driver)

Das Haus war von Bäumen umgeben (fixed usage)	N.B. *The house was surrounded with trees*

Where an action is conveyed, not by a passive verb, but by a noun with verbal force, the doer is indicated by 'durch':

die Annahme des Kaisertitels durch den König (Bismarck)	*the assumption of the imperial title by the King*
der Ersatz der Muskelkraft durch die Maschine	*the replacement of muscular strength by the machine*

561. für is the equivalent of *for* in a wide range of senses, e.g. Er hat viel für mich getan; das ist kein Buch für Kinder; es war sehr unangenehm

[1] see also 621.

für mich; genug für heute; für einen Ausländer spricht er recht gut Englisch; ein gutes Mittel für (or: gegen) Kopfweh; ich habe die Bücher für vierzig Mark bekommen/verkauft.

See also 117 N.ii and 175.

562. *gegen

(a) *against*

Er warf den Ball gegen die Mauer; er schwamm gegen den Strom (lit. and fig.); er verteidigte sich gegen seine Verleumder (*slanderers*); ich bin gegen diesen Plan; haben Sie etwas dagegen?

(b) *contrary to*

Ich handelte gegen seinen Befehl; das geschah gegen seinen Wunsch; gegen die Natur; gegen alle Erwartungen; gegen alle Vernunft *contrary to reason*.

(c) *compared with*

Gegen ihn bin ich nur ein Stümper gegen früher	*Compared with him I'm a mere bungler compared with formerly*

(d) *in return for*

Er gab mir das Geld gegen eine Quittung	*He gave me the money in return for a receipt*
Ich tauschte meinen Füller gegen seinen Kugelschreiber	*I exchanged my fountain-pen for his ball-point pen*

(e) *towards* (see also 311 N.i)

Wir fahren jetzt gegen Süden (elev.) (normal usage: nach Süden)	*We are now driving in a southerly direction*
Er kam gegen Abend an	*He arrived towards evening*
Es war schon gegen Ende März	*It was already near the end of March*

(f) *about, approximately* (see also 311 N.i)

Es waren gegen 400 Personen im Saal

563. ohne *without*[1]

The indef. art. is generally omitted after ohne, e.g. Er geht gern ohne Hut (from Du. Stil.); er kam ohne Bleistift in die Stunde; bitte, ein Frühstück ohne Ei; ein Zimmer ohne Tisch (BUT: Ohne ein Wort verließ er das Zimmer).

Where there is no ambiguity, the possess. adj. is sometimes omitted: Sie kam heute ohne Brille, ohne Fahrrad, ohne Kinder. See also 74(a).

One elliptical use may be noted, its meaning varying according to the context: Sein Vorschlag ist nicht so ohne *His suggestion is not at all bad/ not without its difficulties* (or *risks*)

564. *um[2] *round, around, round about* is frequently strengthened with one of the adverbs 'rings' and 'herum':

Rings um den Garten lief eine Mauer; wir standen rings um den Teich.

Um das Haus (herum) liegt ein Garten; um mich herum (or: her) war alles still; er kam um die Ecke (herum); er kommt gewöhnlich um diese Zeit (herum), um Ostern (herum); ich habe um hundert Mark herum.

---

[1] see also 632.
[2] see also 311, second group of examples.

Idiomatic use of 'um' in conjunction with 'bringen' and 'kommen':

jemanden um eine Sache bringen	*to deprive s.o. of s.th.*
Die Aufregung hat mich um den Schlaf gebracht	*The excitement deprived me of my sleep*
Sie haben ihn ums Leben gebracht	*They killed him*
Er hat sich ums Leben gebracht	*He has killed himself*
um eine Sache kommen	*to lose something*
Er ist um sein ganzes Geld gekommen	*He has lost all his money*
Er ist bei dem Unfall ums Leben gekommen	*He lost his life in the accident*

565. Ten less common prepositions taking the accusative

ab (*starting*) *from, as from*[1]	hindurch *throughout*[3]
betreffend *with regard to*	per *per, by* etc.
eingerechnet *including* (in the account)	pro *per* (meaning 'for each')
entlang *along, alongside*[2]	sonder *without*
gen *towards*	wider *against, contrary to*

(a) **betreffend** *with regard to* (commercialese) generally follows its noun:
Ihr Schreiben vom 1. Oktober betreffend, . . .

(b) **eingerechnet** *including* (in the account) (commercialese) follows its noun:

meine Unkosten eingerechnet   *including my expenses*

(c) **gen** *towards* is a contraction of 'gegen' and is only used in poetic style (e.g. Er wanderte gen Norden) and in a few set phrases (e.g. Schreit es nicht gen Himmel? *Isn't it revolting?*)

(d) **per** *per, by* etc. is mainly officialese and commercialese, e.g. viermal per Jahr, per Post, per Schiff, 500 DM per (or pro) Tonne. (See also 560(c)N.)

per Luftfracht	*by air* (for goods)
per Einschreiben	*by recorded delivery*[4]
per LKW (Lastkraftwagen)	*by road*
per Adresse (p.A.)	*care of (c/o)*
Die Waren sind per 1. Januar bestellt	*The goods are ordered for 1 January*
per Anhalter fahren	*to hitchhike*
per Autostopp reisen	

(e) **(S) pro** *per* (meaning 'for each') is commercialese and colloquial, e.g. Die Pfirsiche kosten 30 Pf. pro Stück. Was ist der Preis pro Tag? Wir fuhren 100 Kilometer pro Stunde (or: die Stunde) (100 km/st). Fünf Prozent (5%)

Unsere Reisekosten betragen im Schnitt pro/je Vertreter pro/je Monat 920 DM	*Our travelling expenses average 920 marks per traveller per month*

(f) **sonder** *without*: archaic; limited to a few rare phrases, e.g. sonder Zweifel, sonder Zahl *countless*.

---

[1] see 557(a).   [2] see 618.   [3] see 560(b).
[4] by registered letter = als Wertbrief.

Commoner is the indeclinable adjective sondergleichen *unequalled, unparalleled*, which follows its noun, e.g. Es war ein Erfolg sondergleichen.

(g) **wider** *against, contrary to* is biblical, poetic and used in certain stock phrases:

Wer nicht mit mir ist, der ist wider mich	*He who is not with me, is against me*
wider Erwarten	*contrary to expectation*
wider Willen	*reluctantly*
Das geht mir wider den Strich	*That goes against the grain*

(S) See 565 (h) via

C. NINE PREPOSITIONS TAKING DATIVE OR ACCUSATIVE

566. (S) Nine prepositions take:

> **the dative** when they denote 1. rest 2. movement within a place or area;
> **the accusative** when they denote movement towards or to a new position.

Grouped mnemonically they are:

in *in; into*
*an *at, on (up against);*
    to, on (to) (up against)
*auf *on; (down) on (to)*

*über *above, over, across*
*unter i *under, below, beneath*
    ii *among*

*vor *before, in front of*
hinter *behind*

neben *beside, next to*
zwischen *between*

EXAMPLES:

in

Er wohnt in diesem Haus	*He lives in this house*
Wir gingen im Wald spazieren	*We went for a walk in the forest*
Ich ging ins Eßzimmer	*I went into the dining-room*

an

Das Bild hing an dieser Wand	*The picture hung on this wall*
Ich hängte das Bild an die Wand	*I hung the picture on the wall*

über

Ein Flugzeug kreiste über der Stadt	*A plane was circling over the town*
Ich ging über die Brücke	*I went across the bridge*

unter

Der Fluß floß träge unter der Brücke[1]	*The river flowed sluggishly under the bridge*
Ich fand das Rezept unter meinen Papieren	*I found the recipe among my papers*
Er tauchte den Kopf unters Wasser	*He dipped his head under the water*

---

[1] dative, as the prep. does not denote movement to a new position.

11*

neben

Neben mir ging ein junger Kerl[1]	*A young fellow was walking beside me*
Sie stellte die eine Vase neben die andere	*She stood the one vase next to the other*

zwischen

Sein Laden ist zwischen dem Kino und der Post	*His shop is between the cinema and the post-office*
Der Junge ging zwischen seinen Eltern[1]	*The boy was walking along between his parents*
Der Junge drängte sich zwischen seine Eltern	*The boy pushed himself between his parents*

567. Note:

i 'an' and 'auf'

At an earlier stage of the language 'an' was used in the sense of 'down on' and this use has survived in the phrases 'am Boden, an der Erde' (beside: auf dem Boden, auf der Erde) meaning 'on the floor, on the ground'.

Note the following:

Am Flußufer lag Seetang	*Seaweed lay on the river bank*
Am Strande lagen Boote	*Boats lay on the beach*
am Berg	*on the mountain-side*
auf dem Berg	*on the mountain-top*
Ich drückte auf den Knopf	*I pressed the button*
Ich klopfte ihm auf die Schulter	*I patted him on the shoulder*
auf diesem Bild	*in this picture*

ii unter: *under* and *among*: where the meaning might be ambiguous, 'among' is best rendered by 'zwischen' or by a free translation, e.g.

Das Häuschen stand unter Bäumen	*The cottage stood under some trees*
Das Häuschen stand zwischen Bäumen (or: war von Bäumen umgeben)	*The cottage stood among trees*

iii For the use of in, an and auf in the translation of to, into, at and in, see 589 ff.

568. In temporal senses: dative or accusative?

(a) in, an and vor take the dat. (exc. 'in' meaning *into*): im Sommer, am Montag, vor dem Krieg, BUT: Er arbeitete bis tief in die Nacht hinein.

(b) auf takes the acc.:
Ich reise auf (or: für) vierzehn Tage nach Deutschland.

569. In verbal constructions: dative or accusative?

(a) *auf and *über take the acc., e.g. sich verlassen auf *to rely on*, sich freuen über *to be glad about*.

SIX EXCEPTIONS:

basieren auf + dat.	*to be based on*
beharren auf + dat.	*to insist on, persist in* (elev.)

---

[1] dative, as the prep. does not denote movement to a new position.

beruhen auf+dat.	to rest, be based on (e.g. a misunderstanding)
bestehen auf+dat. (occasionally + acc.)	to insist on
fußen auf+dat.	to be based on
brüten über +dat. (also +acc.)	to brood, meditate on

N.B. In a sentence such as 'Er ruhte auf der Couch', 'auf' is clearly not an essential part of the verbal construction.

(b) *vor takes the dat., e.g. sich fürchten vor *to be afraid of.*

(c) *an varies, e.g. erkennen an+dat. *to recognize by*; denken an+acc. *to think of.*

570. In other contexts: dative or accusative?

Elsewhere, if the concepts of rest and movement cannot be even figuratively applied:

(a) in, an, unter, vor, zwischen preponderantly take the dat.:[1]

im ganzen	*on the whole*
der Bedarf an Arbeitskräften	*the demand for labour*
unter dieser Bedingung	*on this condition*
vor allem	*above all*
Was ist der Unterschied zwischen diesen zwei Wörtern?	*What is the difference between these two words?*

(b) auf and über preponderantly take the acc.:[1]

auf diese Weise *in this way*	über alle Maßen *beyond measure*

571. Dative or Accusative? Some special cases

(a) **There are certain instances of an action being denoted either by means of a simple verb or, more explicitly, by a verb with a separable prefix.** Used in conjunction with the simple verb, these prepositions take the acc.; used in conjunction with the compound verb, they are used with the dat.; they are then felt to denote an action occurring in a place.

EXAMPLES:
(an-)binden *to tie, fasten*
Das Pferd war an einen Baum gebunden (an einem Baum angebunden, festgebunden, festgemacht).
(auf-)hängen (wk.) *to hang (up)* (tr.)
Er hängte das Bild an die Wand (an der Wand auf).
(auf-)schreiben *to write (down)*
Ich schrieb seine Adresse in mein Notizbuch (in meinem Notizbuch auf).

(b) In the case of **the prefix hin-** *down*, there is much fluctuation of usage, but the dative is probably commoner: Er stellte die Lampe neben mir hin; er legte das Buch vor mir hin.

(c) **In conjunction with the prefix ein-, 'in' generally takes the accusative,** e.g.
Er stieg in den Zug ein; er wickelte/schlug das Buch in ein Stück Papier

[1] cf. Du. Gram. 3360 and in this book 597 ff.

ein; sie hüllte sich in eine Reisedecke ein *she wrapped herself up in a travelling rug*; ich trug seinen Namen in meine Liste ein; wir haben ihn in das Geheimnis eingeweiht *we have initiated him into the secret*. Cf. unser Einzug in unsre neue Wohnung *our move into our new flat*.

Note:

i 'in' here generally takes the acc. even when the sentence denotes not action but the resultant state, though in the latter case the dat. may also be found, as in the last two examples:

Sie war in eine Reisedecke eingehüllt	*She was wrapped up in a travelling-rug*
Ich bin in das Geheimnis eingeweiht	*I have been initiated into the secret*
Das Buch war in ein/einem Stück Papier eingewickelt	*The book was wrapped up in a piece of paper*
Ich fand seinen Namen in die/der Liste eingetragen	*I found his name entered in the list*[1]

ii (sich) ein-schließen in + acc. or dat.: Sie schloß sich in ihr/ihrem Zimmer ein *She locked herself up in her room.*

iii in einem Wirtshaus ein-kehren *to turn in at an inn*: this unexpected dative is a fixed usage.

iv The dative is used in conjunction with ein-treffen (as with all verbs meaning *to arrive*) and with sich ein-finden *to appear*, e.g. (journalese):

Am Bahnhof hatten sich eingefunden . . .	*The following were present at the station . . .*

v for ein-bringen and ein-führen, see 573.

572. Miscellaneous cases that may cause doubt or difficulty. (In a few instances, either case is possible without a substantial difference in meaning; only the commoner usage is given below.)

(a) **The dative is used in conjunction with the following:**

an-bringen *to fix*: An dieser Wand könnten wir ein Bücherbrett anbringen.
an-kommen, an-langen *to arrive*, e.g. in der Stadt (cf. zu Hause)
befestigen an *to fasten to*
drucken *to print*, e.g. auf schlechtem Papier gedruckt.
empor-ragen über *to tower above*
fest-halten an *to stick to* (e.g. one's opinions)
sich fest-halten an *to cling to, hold on to*
gipfeln in *to culminate in*
hervor-gucken/hervor-treten hinter *to peep out/step forth from behind*: Er trat hinter dem Baum hervor.
hervor-kriechen unter *to creep out from under*
landen e.g. am Ziel *at one's destination*; Menschen auf dem Mond (tr. and intr.)
notieren *to note down* e.g. auf einem Zettel *on a slip of paper*
die Richtung *direction*:
 Ich schlenderte in der Richtung der Stadt.
 Wir müssen in dieser Richtung weitergehen.

---

[1] cf. Eggeling, op. cit.: ein-

BUT: Wir müssen jetzt in diese Richtung gehen.

(N.B. Wir fuhren in Richtung Rom.)

der Unterschied zwischen *the difference between*

(sich) verbergen, (sich) verstecken *to hide*, e.g. hinter dem Schrank.

verschwinden *to disappear*: Er verschwand in dem Haus.

verstauen in *to stow away in*

(b) The accusative is used in conjunction with the following:

an-bauen an *to build on to*: Wir haben eine Garage an das Haus angebaut.

sich an-schließen an *to adjoin*: An unseren Garten schließt sich ein Wäldchen an.

beugen: gebeugt über *bent over*: Sie saß über ihre Arbeit gebeugt.

grenzen an *to border on*

hinaus-ragen über *to jut out over*

sich klammern an *to cling to, hold on to*

schauen, sehen *to look*: Er schaute/sah über die Mauer.

sich setzen: Ich setzte mich ans Fenster. Ich setzte mich nahe am Bahnhof in ein Kino (H. Böll).

der Sieg (*victory*) der Athener über die Perser.

(sich) stützen auf *to support* (*o.s.*) *on* e.g. den Tisch; cf. das Kinn in die Faust gestützt (M. Frisch).

verteilen unter or an *to distribute* (e.g. money) *among, to*

vertieft/versunken in *buried/engrossed in*: Er war in die Zeitung vertieft.

verwickelt in *involved in*: in eine Sache verwickelt sein.

573. Verbs with which dative and accusative are used in different contexts or with different meanings

auf-nehmen in + acc.

Er ist in den Chor/in das Krankenhaus aufgenommen worden	*He has been admitted to the choir/to the hospital*

auf-nehmen in + dat.[1]

Ich wurde in seiner Familie sehr freundlich aufgenommen	*I was very amiably received in his family*

ein-bringen in + acc.

Getreide in eine Scheune einbringen	*to bring grain into a barn*

ein-bringen in + dat.

ein Gesetz im Parlament einbringen	*to introduce a law in parliament*

ein-führen in + acc.

jemanden in eine Familie, in eine Gesellschaft einführen	1. *to introduce s.o. into a family, a society etc.*
Waren in ein Land einführen	2. *to import goods into a country*

einführen in + dat.

Er will dieses Buch/diese Sitte in unserer Schule einführen	*in other figurative senses, e.g.* *He intends to introduce this book/this custom in our school*

[1] cf. Du. Haupt.

halten with dat.

Er hielt den Hut vor dem Gesicht	*He held his hat in front of his face* (emphasis on posture)

halten with acc.

Er hielt den Hut einen Augenblick vors Gesicht	*For a moment he held his hat in front of his face* (emphasis on gesture)

kleben an + dat.

to stick to (intr.)

Die Haare klebten an seiner Stirn	*His hair stuck to his forehead*
nie am Manuskript klebend (*Zeit*)	*never sticking to his manuscript*

etwas kleben an, auf + acc.

to stick s.th. to, on (tr.)

Ich klebte die Marke auf den Brief	*I stuck the stamp on the letter*

klopfen an, auf + acc.

Ich klopfte an die Tür/auf den Tisch	*I knocked at the door/on the table*

klopfen an + dat.

Es klopfte an der Tür	*There was a knock at the door*
ein Klopfen an der Tür	*a knock at the door*

cf. Der Regen prasselte (*pattered*) an die Fensterscheiben, BUT: das Prasseln des Regens an den Fensterscheiben.

lehnen an + dat.

Das Brett lehnte an der Mauer	*The board was leaning against the wall*

(sich) lehnen an + acc. (or gegen)

Er lehnte sein Rad an (or gegen) die Mauer	*He leant his bike against the wall*
Er lehnte sich an (or gegen) die Wand[1]	*He leant against the wall* (action)
Er stand (saß) an (or gegen) die Wand gelehnt	*He was leaning against the wall* (position)

(sich) an-lehnen an + acc.

Er lehnte das Bild an die Wand an	*He leant the picture against the wall*
Er lehnte sich an die Wand an	*He leant against the wall*

D. PREPOSITIONS TAKING THE GENITIVE

574. Thirteen common prepositions taking the genitive, grouped mnemonically:

während *during*	innerhalb *inside, within*
wegen *because of, an account of*	außerhalb *outside*
statt, anstatt *instead of*	oberhalb *above*
trotz *in spite of*	unterhalb *below*
diesseits *on this side of*	um . . . willen *for the sake of*
jenseits *on the other side of, beyond*	. . . halber *for the sake of, because of*
beiderseits *on both sides of*	

---

[1] cf. Er lehnte sich über die Brüstung der Brücke *He leant over the parapet of the bridge.*

575. Forty-seven less common prepositions taking the genitive

abseits *away from*
abzüglich *deducting, less*
angesichts *in view of, in the face of*
an Hand (anhand) *with the aid of*
anläßlich *on the occasion of*
an Stelle (anstelle) *in place of*
auf Grund (aufgrund) *on the strength of*
auf seiten *on the side of*
ausschließlich *exclusive of, excluding*
behufs *for the purpose of*
betreffs (betr.) *with regard to*
bezüglich (bez.) *with regard to*
eingangs *at the beginning of*
einschließlich *inclusive of, including*
exklusive (exkl.) *excluding*
gelegentlich *on the occasion of*
hinsichtlich *with regard to*
in betreff *with regard to*
infolge *in consequence of*
inklusive (inkl.) *including*
inmitten *in the midst of*
kraft *by virtue of, by dint of*
längs *along, alongside*
längsseits *alongside* (nautical)
laut *according to, in accordance with*
mangels *for want of*

mittels(t) *by means of*
namens *in the name of*
ob *on account of*
(in) punkto *with regard to*
rücksichtlich *with regard to*
seitens *on the part of, from*
unbeschadet 1. *without prejudice to*
2. *in spite of*
unerachtet *notwithstanding, in spite of*
unfern *not far from*
ungeachtet *notwithstanding, in spite of*
unweit *not far from*
vermittels(t) *by means of*
vermöge *by dint of*
von seiten *on the part of, from*
vorbehaltlich *subject to*
zeit seines Lebens *during his lifetime*
zufolge *as the result of*
zugunsten *for the benefit of, in favour of*
zuungunsten *to the detriment of, to the disadvantage of*
zuzüglich *in addition to, plus*
zwecks *for the purpose of*

576. (a) The following are also used with the dative; but see 578.

während	anläßlich	hinsichtlich	ob
wegen	ausschließlich	inklusive	unbeschadet
statt, anstatt	betreffs	längs	ungeachtet
trotz	bezüglich	laut	vermittels(t)
	einschließlich	mangels	vermöge
angesichts	exklusive	mittels(t)	zugunsten[1]
			zuungunsten[1]

(b) **The following are often used with von + dative.** (They are then technically adverbs.)

diesseits	außerhalb	abseits	infolge
jenseits	oberhalb	an Hand	unfern
beiderseits	unterhalb	an Stelle	unweit
innerhalb		auf Grund	

577. The prepositions listed in 576 are generally used with the dat. and with von + dat. respectively in the following three contexts:

(a) If they are followed by a plural noun, not preceded by an article or adjective with a distinctive gen. plur. ending:

während fünf Jahren   *during five years*

[1] used with preceding dative.

wegen ein paar Hindernissen	*because of a few obstacles*
ungeachtet allerhand Protesten	*notwithstanding various protests*
innerhalb von vier Jahren	*within four years*
anstelle von Briefen	*in place of letters*
infolge von allerhand Protesten	*as a consequence of various protests*
	BUT:
wegen dieser Hindernisse	*because of these obstacles*
ungeachtet scharfer Proteste	*notwithstanding sharp protests*

(b) If the noun they govern is preceded by a noun in the genitive denoting possession (the Saxon genitive):

während Vaters (kurzem) Urlaub	*during father's short holiday*
hinsichtlich des Kanzlers (langem) Schweigen	*with regard to the Chancellor's (long) silence*
anstelle von Beethovens letztem Streichquartett	*in place of Beethoven's last string quartet*

(c) If they govern an adjective or participle used substantivally in the neut. sing. and not preceded by a qualifying word with a distinctive gen. sing. ending:

wegen verschiedenem	*because of various things*
Mangels etwas Neuem hat er nur das Alte wiederholt	*For want of something new, he only repeated the old stuff*
anstelle von jemand Intelligentem[1]	*in place of someone intelligent*
	BUT:
trotz des Schönen in diesem Gedicht	*in spite of the beautiful things in this poem*
einschließlich alles Neuen	*including everything new*

(S) See 577(d)

578. Apart from the three cases treated in 577:

(a) **während, wegen, statt and trotz** are often used with the dative, either colloquially or for the sake of euphony, as in the fourth example: während dem Mittagessen; wegen dem schlechten Wetter; ach, wegen so 'nem Quatsch (H. Fallada); trotz dem Rollen des Zuges (Th. Mann).

(b) In the case of **längs, laut, ob, zugunsten and zuungunsten,** the dative is a recognized alternative (with the last two, a preceding dative): Wir wanderten längs dem Flusse (normal usage: am Fluß entlang); laut neuem Vertrag *in accordance with the new agreement.*

(c) **The remaining prepositions listed in 576(a)** are only used with the genitive.

(d) **The prepositions listed in 576(b)** are often used with von + dative, either colloquially or for the sake of euphony, as in the third example: außerhalb von London; oberhalb von der Straße; infolge von dem plötzlichen Tod des Pfarrers.

579. The genitives of the personal pronouns (meiner, deiner etc.) sound stilted and **are usually avoided in conversation,** e.g.:

wegen mir	*because of me*
Ich bin an seiner Stelle (or: für ihn) gekommen	*I have come instead of him*

[1] The genitive of 'jemand Intelligentes' is avoided (cf. 212(b)).

Note:

i It should be stated that not all Germans would eschew 'statt seiner' in the
   second example above.

ii See also 153(a).

580. **The following of the 47 less common prepositions taking the
     genitive are stilted officialese and/or commercialese:**

abzüglich	einschließlich	mangels	vermittels(t)
ausschließlich	exklusive	mittels(t)	vermöge
behufs	inklusive	rücksichtlich	vorbehaltlich
betreffs	kraft	unbeschadet	zuzüglich
bezüglich	laut	ungeachtet	zwecks

These are preferably replaced by simpler prepositions or by other constructions. The following illustrations of this are based on the examples given
in 587, which should be referred to:

ausschließlich: ohne Heizungskosten.

mangels: da es keine anderen Verwertungsmöglichkeiten gab.

unbeschadet: ohne seine Ansprüche zu gefährden.

vorbehaltlich: vorausgesetzt, daß er zustimmt.

zuzüglich: wozu noch die Versandkosten kommen (or: plus Versandkosten).

zwecks: um die Lage gründlich zu erörtern.

581. **The following prepositions**, most of them listed in 580, **are fre-
     quently used with an unqualified and uninflected noun**, especially
     in commercial and official phrases:

ausschließlich	in betreff	mangels	wegen
behufs	infolge	mittels(t)	zuzüglich
einschließlich	inklusive	(in) punkto	zwecks
exklusive	laut	trotz	

die Kosten ausschließlich Porto	*the expenses excluding postage*
(in) betreff Marktsituation in Belgien	*regarding the state of the market in Belgium*
infolge Kurzschluß	*owing to a short circuit*
laut Faktura	*as per invoice*
trotz Schnee	*in spite of snow*
Wegen Umbau geschlossen!	*closed for alterations*
wegen Diebstahl(s)[1]	*because of theft*

Junge Dame ... möchte netten, gebildeten Herrn zwecks Heirat kennenlernen
(from a personal column in the *FAZ*)

See also 51(c).

E. ILLUSTRATIONS AND PECULIARITIES OF INDIVIDUAL
PREPOSITIONS TAKING THE GENITIVE:
582–7 (order as in 574 f.)

582. **wegen** *because of, on account of*

(a) While it normally precedes its noun, it also frequently follows it,
    particularly, though not exclusively, in elevated style:

[1] BUT: wegen fortgesetzten schweren Diebstahls (*SZ*).

wegen des Wetters	*because of the weather*
des Wetters wegen (*Zeit*)	
dieser schweren Opfer wegen	*because of these great sacrifices*

(b) **Used with personal pronouns, wegen has the following forms**: meinetwegen *for my sake*, deinetwegen, seinetwegen, ihretwegen, unsertwegen, euertwegen, ihretwegen, Ihretwegen; cf. the demonstrative and relative forms dessentwegen and derentwegen (see 165 N.iv, 176(a)N.ii).

Alongside these, there are the colloquial wegen mir (dir) etc. *because of me (you)* and the rare and regional wegen meiner (deiner) etc. (cf. Du. Gram. 3450).

Note the idiomatic meaning:

Meinetwegen/unsertwegen kannst du ins Kino gehen	*As far as I'm/we're concerned, you can go to the cinema*

(c) The formula '**von + noun in gen. + wegen**' is mainly used in a number of set phrases, e.g. von Amts wegen *ex officio*, von Berufs wegen *in virtue of/on account of one's profession*, von Rechts wegen *by rights*.

(d) **von wegen + dat.** (generally 'because of') is very colloquial:

Jetzt hört mir nur auf von wegen Idealismus! (Th. Valentin)	*For heaven's sake stop talking about idealism*

It is also used by itself to challenge the statement of another speaker:

Also, du bezahlst heute abend alles.— Von wegen!	*Well now, you're paying for everything tonight.—That's what you think!*

(e) Where 'for' means 'because of', it generally either is, or can be, rendered by 'wegen':

Er bat um Entschuldigung wegen seiner Verspätung	*He apologised for being late*
Ich lobte ihn wegen seines Fleißes (or: für seinen Fleiß)	*I praised him for his industry*

583. statt, anstatt *instead of*

Statt eines Grammophons habe ich mir ein Radio gekauft	*Instead of a gramophone I've bought myself a radio*

statt is frequently used not as a preposition, but as a conjunction, the equivalent of 'und nicht' (which may indeed be preferred); the case of the following noun or pronoun is then determined by the part it plays in the sentence.

This use may avoid ambiguity:

Ich besuchte meinen Vetter anstatt (or: und nicht) meinen Bruder	*I visited my cousin instead of (visiting) my brother*

or it may avoid using the genitive of the personal pronoun:

Sein Haus hat er mir anstatt ihm (preferably: und nicht ihm) vermacht	*He bequeathed his house to me instead of to him*

Further example:

Ich schreibe jetzt mit einer Füllfeder statt mit einem Kugelschreiber	*I now write with a fountain-pen instead of a ball-point pen*

See also 729(a) ii.

584. trotz *in spite of, notwithstanding*

trotz seines letzten Briefes	*in spite of his last letter*

trotz is much used with the dat., and not only colloquially, e.g. trotz schlechtem Wetter. The dative is fixed in 'trotz allem' *despite everything* and 'trotz alledem' *for all that*; cf. the adverb and conjunction 'trotzdem' *nevertheless*; *in spite of the fact that, although*.

585.

diesseits des Waldes	*on this side of the forest*
jenseits der Grenze	*beyond the frontier*
beiderseits der Straße	*on both sides of the road*
innerhalb des Lagers	*inside the camp*
innerhalb dieser Grenzen	*within these limits*
innerhalb eines Monats	*within a month*
Ich war nicht mehr als eine Stunde/eine Meile von zu Hause, als das Unglück sich ereignete	BUT: *I was within an hour/a mile of home when the accident happened*
Er wohnt in Reichweite von London	N.B. *He lives within easy reach of London*
außerhalb der Arbeitszeit	*outside working hours*
Oberhalb der Straße war ein Felsenvorsprung	*Above the road there was a rocky ledge*
Der Loreleifelsen liegt oberhalb der Stadt St. Goar	*The Lorelei Rock lies above (upstream from) the town of St. Goar*

Note:
i Colloquially, 'hinter' is used more than 'jenseits': Das Dorf liegt hinter der Grenze, hinter dem Wald, hinter Hannover.
ii 'innerhalb' and 'außerhalb' only denote rest, or movement within or outside a place. BUT: We went inside/outside the hut = Wir gingen in die Hütte hinein/aus der Hütte hinaus.
iii All the prepositions dealt with in this paragraph may also be used adverbially.

586. for the sake of (see also 582(b))

(a) **um + gen. + willen** *for the sake of*

Ich tat es um meiner Mutter willen	*I did it for my mother's sake*
um Mutters willen (cf. 51(f))	*for mother's sake*
um ihrer Ruhe willen	*for the sake of her peace of mind*
um Himmels (or Gottes) willen	*for heaven's sake*
Um Gottes willen! Was ist denn das?	*Heavens! Whatever's that?*
um seiner selbst willen	*for his own sake*

(b) (**um**) **meinetwillen** *for my sake*; cf. (um) ihretwillen, (um) unsertwillen etc., um wessentwillen? Demonstrative and relative: (um) dessentwillen, (um) derentwillen.

(c) **gen.+halber** *because of, for the sake of*

der Umstände halber	*because of the circumstances*
der Wahrheit halber	*for the sake of the truth*
nur der Form halber	*only for the sake of form*

Note the compounds formed with some feminine nouns:
krankheitshalber *because of illness*
sicherheitshalber *for safety's sake*
vorsichtshalber *as a precaution, to be on the safe side*
also: anstandshalber (from *der* Anstand) *for propriety's sake*

(d) **meinethalben** *for my sake*; cf. ihrethalben, unserthalben etc.; dessenthalben, derenthalben (demonstr. and rel.)

IDIOMATIC: Meinethalben/ Unserthalben kann er tun, was er will	*As far as I'm/we're concerned, he can do what he likes*

587. Illustrations of the 47 less common prepositions+gen.

Unser Haus liegt **abseits** der Hauptstraße	*Our house is situated away from the main street*
abzüglich der Unkosten	*less charges*
angesichts der ernsten Lage	*in view of the serious situation*
angesichts des Zahlenverhältnisses der Rassengruppen (*FAZ*)	*in view of the numerical relationship of the racial groups*
Ich will die Regel **an Hand** einiger Beispiele erklären	*I will explain the rule with the aid of a few examples*
Anläßlich seines 70. Geburtstags wurde er zum Ehrenbürger ernannt	*On the occasion of his 70th birthday he was made a freeman of the city*
anstelle einer Antwort	*in place of an answer*
auf Grund seiner juristischen Ausbildung (*FAZ*)	*on the strength of his legal training*
Er steht **auf seiten** der Regierung	*He is on the side of the government*
die Miete **ausschließlich** der Heizungskosten (from Du. Haupt.)	*the rent exclusive of the charge for heating*
behufs einer Verhandlung	*for the purpose of a discussion*
betreffs (**bezüglich**) Ihres Angebots	*with regard to your offer*

Note on 'with regard to': betreffs, bezüglich and in betreff are officialese; the commonest German equivalents are: in bezug auf+acc., hinsichtlich+gen. and, especially, the clause 'was—object—betrifft (or: anbelangt)': Was seinen Bruder betrifft, bin ich nicht so sicher *With regard to his brother, I'm not so sure.*

eingangs der Zielgeraden	*at the beginning of the straight* (racecourse)
einschließlich der Angehörigen (*SZ*, referring to immigrants)	*including their dependants*
exklusive: see 'ausschließlich'	
gelegentlich seines Besuchs	*on the occasion of his visit*
hinsichtlich (or: in Hinsicht auf+acc.): see 'betreffs' and Note	
in betreff: see 'betreffs' and Note	

infolge der neuen Steuer | *in consequence of the new tax*
inklusive Bedienung/Heizung[1] | *including service/heating*

inmitten *in the midst of*: also used with the dative.
inmitten üppiger Blütenpracht | *in the midst of a riot of blossom*
(*Hbg. Abendblatt*)

kraft seines Amtes | *in virtue of his office*
das Spiel, kraft der Intelligenz | *the game of exerting power*
unauffällig Macht auszuüben | *unostentatiously by dint of intelligence*
(Th. Valentin)

längs *along, alongside*: also used with the dative:
längs des Flusses/dem Flusse | *along the river bank*

längsseits des Schiffes | *alongside the ship*

laut *according to, in accordance with*: also used with the dative:
laut einer Rundfunkmeldung | *according to a wireless report*
laut dem Plan der OECD | *in accordance with the plan of the*
(*Spiegel*) | *OECD*[2]

ich fand dieses Haus vor, das | *I found this house awaiting me, which,*
mangels anderer Verwertungs- | *for want of other possible uses, had*
möglichkeiten . . . zur Arztwohnung | *been earmarked as the doctor's house*
bestimmt worden war (H. Broch)
mittels(t) eines gefälschten Passes | *by means of a forged passport*
namens[3] der Opposition | *in the name of the Opposition*

ob *on account of* (archaic, poetic or ironical): also found with the dat.
Lax, glücklich ob des Tumultes, | *Lax, glad of the commotion, goes on*
schürt weiter (H. Broch) | *stirring it up*

Note: 'ob' here means 'über', in the sense of 'about, concerning'; its main original meaning 'over, above' survives in Rothenburg ob der Tauber (=Rothenburg on the River Tauber); cf. words like das Obdach *shelter*, die Obhut *care, protection*. It has no connection with the conjunction ob *if, whether*.

(in) punkto *with regard to* (from Latin); used colloquially:
(in) punkto seines Einwands | *with regard to his objection*
(in) punkto Geld (cf. 581) | *as regards the question of money*

rücksichtlich dieses Beschlusses (rare) | *with regard to this decision*
Die neuesten Vorschläge **seitens** der | *The latest proposals on the part of the*
Russen müssen sorgfältig erwogen | *Russians must be carefully con-*
werden[4] | *sidered*

unbeschadet 1. *without prejudice to* 2. *in spite of*: it may precede or, less commonly, follow its noun.
unbeschadet seiner Ansprüche | *without prejudice to his claims*
Heute ist London das kulturelle | *Today London is the cultural centre of the*
Zentrum der Welt, unbeschadet | *world despite the foreign trade deficit*
des Außenhandelsdefizits und des | *and the ailing state of sterling*
kränklichen Pfund Sterling
(*Zeit*, 26.8.66)

---

[1] cf. 581.
[2] = Organization for European Co-operation and Development.
[3] In the sense of 'by the name of, named', namens is followed by the nom., e.g. ein Kollege namens Hessenberg.
[4] Used with personal pronouns, seitens has the forms meinerseits *for/on my part*, deinerseits etc. (unsererseits and euerseits are rare).

unerachtet: obsolescent: see 'ungeachtet'

unfern *not far from*: colloquially it is also used with the dat.
unfern des Bahnhofs   *not far from the station*

ungeachtet *notwithstanding, in spite of*: it may precede or, less commonly, follow its noun.
ungeachtet dieser Lage auf dem   *notwithstanding this situation in the*
  Arbeitsmarkt (*Die Welt*)   *labour market*

unweit des Dorfes   *not far from the village*
vermittels, vermittelst: see 'mittels', which is commoner.
vermöge seines unermüdlichen   *by dint of his indefatigable industry*
  Fleißes
von seiten: see 'seitens'
vorbehaltlich seiner Zustimmung   *subject to his consent*
zeit seines Lebens (set phrase)   *during his lifetime*
zufolge: see 557(n)

zugunsten *for the benefit of, in favour of*: can also be used with a preceding dative and must be so used with a personal pronoun:
eine Sammlung . . . zugunsten der   *a collection for the benefit of the State and*
  Niedersächsischen Staats- und   *University Library of Lower Saxony*
  Universitätsbibliothek (*Die Welt*)
Ich bin ihm zugunsten (von meinem   *I have resigned (my office) in his favour*
  Amt) zurückgetreten

zuungunsten *to the detriment of, to the disadvantage of*: can also be used with a preceding dative and must be so used with a personal pronoun.
zuungunsten des Angeklagten   *to the detriment of the defendant*

Das bestellte Gerät kostet 200 Mark   *The instrument ordered costs 200 marks*
  zuzüglich der Versandkosten   *plus forwarding costs*
  (from Du. Haupt.)
Er besucht mich heute **zwecks**   *He is visiting me today for the purpose of a*
  einer gründlichen Erörterung der   *thorough discussion of the situation*
  Lage

588. north of the town

After the points of the compass, the genitive may be used, though 'von' is commoner, especially with place-names; these are also found uninflected, without 'von':
nördlich (von) der Stadt   *to the north of the town*
östlich von Köln   *to the east of Cologne*
nordwestlich Saigon (*Zeit*)   *to the north-west of Saigon*

F. THE TRANSLATION OF 'INTO, TO' and 'IN, AT' IN LITERAL CONTEXTS

Note:
i In what follows, some alternatives have deliberately been omitted.
ii For the translation of **as far as**, see 559(b) and N.ii(β).

589. in + acc. is used for going into a place, and generally for 'to' implying 'into', and **in + dat.** for being in or at that same place:

Er ging ins Büro, ins Dorf, ins Kino, in die Kirche *to church*, in ein Museum, in ein (neues) Restaurant, in die Stadt *to (the) town*, ins Tal, ins Theater, in den Wald, in sein Zimmer, in den Zoo.

Correspondingly: Er ist im Büro, im Haus, in der Kirche *at church* etc.

Note:

i By extension of 'Er ging ins Kino' etc.: Er ging in einen Film, in ein Konzert, in die Oper, in ein Schauspiel.

ii 'zu' is used with the nouns listed above:
  (a) where 'to' specifically means 'as far as, up to' and not 'into': Ich ging zum neuen Kino und wartete auf ihn; dieser Pfad führt zum Wald; die Straßenbahn fährt zum Zoo (from Du. Haupt.)
  (b) where the sentence concerns the journey rather than the reaching of an objective: Wir machten einen Ausflug zum Dorf; ich war auf dem Weg zu einem einsamen Tal; er wanderte zum Wald.

iii With some nouns, 'zu' is also found with the same connotation as in + acc.; this applies to four of those listed above: Er ging zum Dorf, zur Kirche, zur Stadt, zum Zoo.

iv **He went to his room**: if he went upstairs to his room, 'Er ging auf sein Zimmer' and 'Er ist auf seinem Zimmer' are often used, especially in hotels.

590. auf + acc. is used for *to (into)* and **auf + dat.** for *in* or *at*:

(a) **in a number of fixed phrases**, e.g.
Er ging auf den (Bauern)hof,[1] auf seine Bude *to his (student's) digs*, aufs Feld, auf den Flur *into the entrance-hall, passage*, auf den Gang, auf sein Gut *to his estate*, auf den Hof *into the courtyard*, aufs Land *into the country* (as opp. to town), auf die Straße,[2] auf die Toilette, auf die Wiese;[3] er stieg auf die Kanzel (*pulpit*).

Correspondingly: Er arbeitet auf dem Feld; er stand auf dem Flur, auf der Kanzel; er wohnt auf seinen Gütern etc.

Note:

i When 'Feld' denotes 'field' in the military sense (battlefield, front), auf is not used: ins Feld (or: zu Feld) ziehen *to take the field*; im Felde stehen *to be at the front*.

ii With 'Hof', 'in' is used to denote an enclosed courtyard, surrounded by buildings, e.g. Die Kinder können nur in sonnenlosen Höfen spielen (from Du. Stil.)

iii Er wohnt auf dem Lande, BUT: Er ist wieder im Lande *He is back in this country*; im ganzen Lande.

(b) **with public buildings and places** (obsolescent)
Er ging auf den Bahnhof, auf den Markt.
Er ist auf dem Bahnhof, auf dem Markt.
This use of auf was formerly more widespread; current usage fluctuates

---

[1] or zum Bauernhof, but only: Er ist auf dem Bauernhof.
[2] see also 595.
[3] 'in' is also used.

a good deal, with a preference for 'zu' for *to*, 'an+dat' for *at* and 'in+dat.' for *in*. In all the following cases auf would be possible; where it is used in the right-hand column, this signifies that auf is essential in the case in question.

Er ging/fuhr	Ich sah ihn
zum Bahnhof	am (im) Bahnhof
zur Bank	in der Bank
zur Bibliothek	in der Bibliothek
zur Börse (*Stock Exchange*)	an der Börse
zum Markt	auf dem Markt
zur Post	auf der Post
zum Rathaus	im Rathaus

Note:

i **To denote actual entry, use in+acc.:** Als ich ihn sah, ging er gerade in den Bahnhof, in die Post.

ii Note the following:
Er ging zur Bahn; ich sah ihn an der Bahn (colloquial alternative for 'Bahnhof').
Er ist Kassierer bei einer Bank.
Er ist auf dem Rathaus (BUT: in der Bibliothek) beschäftigt *He works at the town-hall* (*in the library*).
Der Zug hält nicht auf allen Stationen.

iii With **die Burg** *castle, stronghold* and **das Schloß** *castle, palace*, 'to' is denoted by auf+acc. if they are situated high up; otherwise by zu or in.

iv For **Schule** and **Universität**, see 595.

(c) **with formal occasions, e.g. a dance, wedding, conference**

i To denote going to these occasions, auf+acc. is obsolescent, normal colloquial usage being zu:
Er ging zu einem (auf einen) Empfang, Kongreß, Tanz; zu einer (auf eine) Hochzeit, Konferenz, wichtige(n) Sitzung.

ii To denote presence or occurrences at these occasions, auf is more widely used, e.g. (from *Die Zeit*): auf einem abendlichen Empfang, auf Parties, auf einer Pressekonferenz; it may be an alternative to 'bei': sie haben sich auf/bei einer Hochzeit kennengelernt.

iii Note the following:
  1. die Ausstellung *exhibition*
     Er ging zur (or: in die) Ausstellung.
     Ich sah ihn in (or: auf) der Ausstellung.
  2. with das Fußballspiel, das Pferderennen, die Regatta, only 'zu' and 'bei' are used.
  3. auf die Jagd gehen *to go hunting*; auf der Jagd sein.
  4. Ich habe in (or: bei) dieser Sitzung mehrmals gesprochen.
  5. die Stunde *lesson*
     Ich gehe jetzt zur (or: in die) Musikstunde.
     Der Lehrer hat in der Geschichtsstunde über Luther gesprochen.

591. **an + acc.** denotes *to, up to*, generally implying greater closeness of approach than the rather vaguer 'zu'; correspondingly, **an + dat.** denotes *at, by, near, on* (e.g. on the coast).

an + acc. is mainly used:

(a) **with limited and precise objectives**
Er ging an den Tisch, an die Tür, an die Tafel, ans Mikrofon, an seinen Platz.
Er kam an die Bushaltestelle, an die Straßenkreuzung; an die Stelle, wo der Mann ermordet wurde; an eine Brücke.
Er brachte mein Gepäck ans Auto.

Correspondingly an + dat.: Er stand am Tisch; er zeigte sich am Fenster; er saß an seinem Platz; wir warteten an der Haltestelle; an jedem Zeitungskiosk erhältlich; an der Ecke der Straße.

Where an + acc. is used, the sentence often indicates the purpose of the action:
Er eilte ans Fenster und sah hinaus; er ging an die Schublade und nahm etwas heraus; er ging an die Kasse, um zu zahlen.

Note:
i In all the above examples of an + acc., zu could also be used with the slight difference in connotation explained above.
ii The same difference between an and zu applies when they are used after bis *as far as*, e.g.

Ich begleitete ihn	*I accompanied him*
bis zur Fabrik	*as far as the factory*
bis an die Fabrik	*to the factory gates*
bis an den Wald	*to the edge of the forest*

(b) **with objectives which extend lengthwise**
Er ging an den Fluß, an den Rhein, ans Flußufer, an den Strand, an die See *to the seaside*, an den Zaun *to the fence*, an die Theke *to the bar (counter)*, bis an den Fuß des Berges.
Er trat an den Rand der Brücke.
Wir kamen an die Front (milit.), an die Grenze *to the frontier*.

Correspondingly an + dat.: Rüdesheim liegt am Rhein; das Dorf liegt an der Küste.
Er wohnt an der Riviera, an der See *by the seaside*, am See *by the lake*, am Waldrand, am Marktplatz.
Er stand am Fuß des Berges, des Bettes.

592. **A special use of an + dat.: before academic and similar institutions at which someone is employed**, e.g.

Er ist Professor an der Universität Göttingen.
Er lehrt an dieser Schule, an einem Gymnasium (*grammar school*).
Er ist Pfarrer an der Peterskirche.
Er ist Intendant (*director*) am Staatstheater (cf. Das Stück wurde an vielen Theatern/an vielen Bühnen aufgeführt).
Er ist am Städtischen Krankenhaus tätig.

Correspondingly an + acc.:

Er erhielt einen Ruf an die Universität Kiel *He was offered a chair at the University of Kiel.*

Er wurde an eine andere Schule versetzt (*transferred*).

Er kam als Regisseur (*producer*) an die Frankfurter Oper.

593. nach is used for 'to':

(a) **before the names of continents, countries and towns:**
Er reiste nach Amerika, nach Deutschland, nach München.[1]
Er schlenderte nach Bacharach hinunter *He strolled down into Bacharach.*
BUT: Ich bin in Deutschland gewesen *I've been to Germany.*

Note:

i Before the names of countries and regions used with the def. art. (see 84(a)(b) and 6(b)) in + acc. is generally used: Ich reise in den Jemen, in die Schweiz (also: nach der Schweiz), in die USA (also: nach der USA), in das Elsaß.

ii With other geographical place-names, various prepositions are used, e.g. Wir fuhren in die Alpen, in den Harz, nach dem/auf den Feldberg, nach dem/an den Bodensee, nach der/an die Riviera; nach Korsika (N.B. Wir waren im Sommer auf Korsika; auf dem Balkan).

(b) **before points of the compass not limited by an adjective**: Wir fuhren nach Süden, BUT: Wir fuhren in den sonnigen Süden.

(c) **before adverbs of place**: Sie müssen nach rechts gehen; er kam nach vorne; er ging nach oben.

Note:

iii In addition to the above fixed uses, there is a tendency to use 'nach' for 'to' in the sense of 'towards, in the direction of': Er bewegte sich langsam nach der Tür; ich sah nach der Tür; er richtete seine Schritte (*turned his steps*) nach der alten Brücke; als ich nach dem Dorf eilte, begegnete ich dem Pfarrer.

iv See also 594(d).

594. zu

(a) **It *must* be used for going to a person**, both in the sense of going up to someone and of going to their house or shop: Er ging zu seinem Onkel, zu Müllers, zum Frisör.
Correspondingly: Er stand/wohnte bei seinem Onkel.

(b) **It is the commonest preposition for going to a place or to an occasion**; as such, it has already figured frequently in 589, 590 and 591 as an alternative for in, auf and an. There follow some further examples of its use; the right-hand column gives the preposition required to denote presence in the place in question.

Er ging	Er ist
zum Denkmal	am (beim) Denkmal
zur Fabrik	in der Fabrik[2]

---

[1] cf. Er fuhr nach einer süddeutschen Stadt.

[2] BUT: Der Arbeiter ist noch auf der Fabrik (still at work, not home yet).

zum Hafen	im Hafen
zur Höhle	vor (bei, in) der Höhle
zur Straßenbahn *tram*	in der Straßenbahn
zur Treppe	auf der Treppe
Sie kehrte zu ihrer Arbeit zurück	Sie ist wieder bei der Arbeit
Der Rauch stieg zur Decke	An der Decke war Rauch
Er fuhr zur Insel	Er ist auf der Insel
eine Expedition zum Mond	ihr Aufenthalt auf dem Mond

Note:

i Before 'Denkmal' and 'Treppe', an + acc. could be used to convey 'up to' with greater proximity.

ii **To denote actual entry**, use in + acc., e.g. Als ich ihn sah, ging er gerade in die Fabrik.

iii **The prefix hin- is often used in conjunction with the preposition 'zu'**; the effect is to strengthen the idea that the objective was, is or will be reached. E.g. Er ging zur Post/zum Fenster hin; dieser Pfad führt zum Wald hin; ich werde morgen zu ihm hingehen.

(c) **A special use of 'zu'**: it means in (or: at), linking a prominent building with the town in which it is situated or indicating a birthplace; the alternative is generally in + dat. (Occasionally zu is found before the name of a town, instead of in + dat., outside these contexts.)

der Dom zu Köln (generally: der Kölner Dom)	*Cologne Cathedral*
im Wehrmachtheim zu Proskurov (A. Goes)	*in the transit-camp at Proskurov*
J. S. Bach wurde zu Eisenach geboren	*J. S. Bach was born in Eisenach*

(d) **North Germans have a marked tendency to use nach instead of zu**, e.g. Er ging nach dem Bahnhof, nach dem Hafen, nach der Tür; er fuhr nach der Insel.[1]

595. Some special cases

Schule etc.[2] (S)

Er geht noch nicht in die Schule (or: zur Schule)	*He doesn't go to* (attend) *school yet*
Er ging um halb acht in die Schule (or: zur Schule)	*He went to school at half past seven*
Er ist noch auf der Schule (or: in der Schule)	*He is still at school* (= still attends school)
Er ist noch in der Schule	*He is still at school* (= not home yet)
Sie schicken ihr Kind in die Schule (or: zur Schule)	*They are sending their child to school*
Er geht aufs Gymnasium/in ein Internat	*He goes to a grammar-school/a boarding-school*
Er studiert an einer Technischen Hochschule	*He's studying at a technical college*

[1] cf. M. Tamsen in *Deutschunterricht für Ausländer*, Jan./Febr. 1957, pp. 6 ff.: Die Präpositionen nach und zu bei Verben der Bewegung.

[2] see also 592.

Straße

(a) **Where Straße means an open road** without contiguous houses—or preponderantly this—**'auf' is used**: Das Unglück ereignete sich auf dieser Straße (cf. auf der B-6 (Bundesstraße 6), auf der A-1 (Autobahn 1)); ich ging auf der gleichen Straße zurück, auf der ich gekommen war (Du. Stil.); in einer Zeit, in der noch Raum genug war auf unseren Straßen (*Zeit*).

(b) **Where Straße means a street** between contiguous houses (or 'road' used in this sense), **'auf' is used in 3 phrases**:

i auf der Straße *in the street*: Die Kinder spielen auf der Straße; ich begegnete ihm/hörte ein Geräusch auf der Straße; der Mann auf der Straße.

ii auf die Straße *into the street*: Ich ging auf die Straße; die Studenten gingen auf die Straße *the students took to the streets* (to demonstrate).

iii auf den Straßen *in the streets*; 'in' is also possible: Es waren große Menschenmengen auf/in den Straßen.

Otherwise 'in' is used: Das Unglück ereignete sich in dieser Straße, in der Goethestraße; er spielt/wohnt in unserer Straße; das Auto hielt in einer engen Straße; er kam in die Straße, wo er früher gewohnt hatte; in den Geschäftsstraßen hastete die Menge wie in London (*Zeit*).

Note: Der Gasthof liegt an der Göttinger Straße (open road).
Der Gasthof liegt in der Bahnhofstraße (city street).

Universität

Im Oktober geht er auf die Universität; er ist auf der Universität (or simply: Er studiert).

Er geht an die Universität H.; er studiert (Jura) an der Universität H.; er ist Professor an der Universität H.[1]; an unseren Universitäten.

Ich gehe heute nachmittag zur Universität.

Karl ist noch nicht zu Hause; er arbeitet noch in der Universität.

596. Miscellaneous cases

bei Hofe	*at court*
am Hof Ludwigs XIV.	*at the court of Louis XIV*
Der Hund legte sich/lag mir zu Füßen	*The dog lay down/lay at my feet*
Ein Apfel fiel zur Erde/zu Boden	*An apple fell to the ground*
Der Junge fiel auf den Boden/auf die Erde	*The boy fell on the ground*[2]
Der Junge sprang auf den Boden/zur Erde	*The boy jumped to the ground*[2]
Wir gehen heute in die Heide	*We're going on to the heath today*
ein winziges Häuschen in der Heide (Arno Schmidt)	*a tiny cottage on the heath*
Es waren Wolken am Himmel	*There were clouds in the sky*

---

[1] cf. 592.

[2] Here Erde may refer to the ground outside or the floor inside; Boden only to the latter.

Ich sah eine Lerche/ein Flugzeug in der Luft	*I saw a lark/an aeroplane in the sky*
Das Flugzeug stieg in die Luft	*The aeroplane rose into the sky*
im Himmel	*in heaven*
Der Hund sprang an ihm hoch	*The dog jumped up at him*
Er kam/trat zu mir	*He came up to me*
Er trat an mich heran	
mein Besuch bei meinem Onkel	*my visit to my uncle*
ein Besuch des Zoos (or: ein Zoobesuch)	*a visit to the zoo*
eine Besichtigung des Doms	*a visit to the cathedral*
Ein Besuch in München (or: der Besuch von München) ist sehr lohnend[1]	*A visit to Munich is well worthwhile*

G. MAIN FIGURATIVE USES OF GERMAN PREPOSITIONS

597. an + dat.

(a) **in respect of, in the way of**: the 'an' phrase generally depends on, and qualifies, a word which denotes or implies amount:

ein großer Aufwand an Energie	*a great expenditure of energy*
Der Bedarf an Arbeitskräften verringert sich	*The demand for labour is decreasing*
Es fehlt ihm an Takt	*He is lacking in tact*
Wir haben 2 Mill. DM an Aufträgen vorliegen	*We have 2 m. marks worth of orders on the books*
Er ist seinem Bruder an Urteilskraft überlegen/gleich/unterlegen	*He is superior/equal/inferior to his brother in power of judgement*
Sein Brief läßt an Klarheit nichts zu wünschen übrig	*His letter leaves nothing to be desired in the way of clarity*
Ich wage nicht, hier darzustellen, was alles an Komplikationen hier eintreten könnte (*SZ*)	*I do not dare describe here all that might arise in the way of complications*

cf. brauchen an *to need in the way of*, knapp sein an *to be short of*, aus Mangel an *for lack of*, reich an, ein großer Unterschied an (e.g. Begabung), an Boden verlieren *to lose ground*, an Höhe verlieren, ein großer Vorrat an *a large stock of*, an Wichtigkeit zu-nehmen *to increase in importance*

(b) **in connection with, about, in**

Er hat etwas Eigenartiges an sich	*He has something peculiar about him*
was mir an ihm auffiel	*what struck me about him*
Was gefällt dir an ihm?	*What do you like about him?*
Das hasse ich an den Schulmeistern am meisten (Th. Valentin)	*That's what I hate most about schoolmasters*
Das Schönste an der Sache ist, daß . . .	*The best of it is that . . .*

cf. Was ist komisch an meinem Hut? Es ist nichts an dem Gerücht; es ist was dran *there's something (some truth) in it*.

---

[1] commoner: Es lohnt sich sehr, sich München anzuschauen.

(c) with verbs and nouns denoting being interested, participating or taking pleasure in something

Er hat Anteil am Geschäft, am Gewinn	*He has an interest in the business, participates in the earnings*
Ich nehme Anteil an seinem Wohl	*I take an interest in his welfare*
Er hat viel Freude an seinen Kindern	*His children give him a lot of pleasure*

cf. sich beteiligen an, teil-nehmen an, die Augen/sich weiden an *to feast one's gaze on/to delight in, gloat over*. See also 634.

(d) with verbs denoting falling ill with, suffering or dying from an illness: erkranken an, leiden an, sterben an (cf. sein Tod an einem Herzschlag); cf. zugrunde gehen an *to be ruined by* (e.g. alcohol):

Er leidet an Schwindelanfällen	*He suffers from attacks of dizziness*
Er leidet unter der Einsamkeit/ unter der Hitze	BUT: *He suffers from loneliness/ from the heat*

598. an + acc.

(a) introduces the objective of certain mental processes[1]

Du erinnerst mich an ihn	*You remind me of him*
Ich erinnere mich an ihn	*I remember him*
die Erinnerung an	*the memory of*
zum Andenken an	*in memory of*

cf. denken an, der Gedanke an, sich gewöhnen an, glauben an *to believe in* (e.g. ghosts, Communism), der Glaube an.

(b) is used to complete the sense of a number of nouns often corresponding to verbs taking the dative, e.g.

Die Anpassung an die neuen Verhältnisse ist nicht leicht	*Adapting oneself to the new circumstances is not easy*
(sich an-passen + dat.	*to adapt o.s. to)*
Er hat keinen Anschluß an Deutsche	*He has made no contact with Germans*
(sich jemandem an-schließen	*to join s.o. e.g. for a walk)*

cf. seine Antwort an mich, sein Befehl an die Truppen, sein Bericht an die Direktion, viele Grüße (*love*) an Onkel Fritz, die Kriegserklärung an Japan, der Verkauf des Hauses an seinen Vetter, sein Vermächtnis (*legacy*) an seinen Neffen, der Verrat von Geheimnissen an den Feind.

599. Summary of two uses of 'an' that recur in their various contexts in Section H below:

i **an + dat.** is used before the feature *by* which one recognizes someone or notices a state of affairs and before an example *by* which one shows something or the phenomena *in* which one studies something. E.g. Ich bemerkte an seinem Benehmen, daß . . .; man kann diesen Instinkt an Tieren studieren; Experimente an Tieren.

ii **an + acc.** is used before the person *to* whom one addresses (richten) a request, one's words etc.; to whom one appeals; directs, addresses or writes a letter; passes s.th. on (weitergeben); or turns for advice: Ich werde mich an ihn um Rat wenden.

[1]cf. Collinson, op. cit., p. 107.

600. auf + acc.

(a) is used to denote the objective of a large number of actions and mental attitudes[1] (S)

Note:
i This use of auf is the figurative parallel of zielen auf *to aim at*, schießen auf, feuern auf.
ii Whereas 'um' in its analogous use (cf. 609(a)) almost exclusively introduces something that it is sought to gain or obtain, 'auf' is wider in its application.

an-wenden auf	*to apply to*
Man könnte dieses Wort kaum auf ihn anwenden	*One could hardly apply this word to him*
Ich bin gespannt auf seine Antwort	*I'm curious as to what his answer will be*
Wir tranken auf sein Wohl	*We drank to his health*
	to refer to:
Seine Bemerkung bezog sich auf dich	*His remark referred to you*
Er wies auf die Schwierigkeiten hin	*He referred (pointed) to the difficulties*
Er wies mich auf die Vorschriften hin	*He referred me to the regulations*[2]
Du kannst dich auf mich berufen	*You can refer to me* (as a reference or witness)

cf. after verbs and nouns:
achten, acht-geben auf *to pay heed to, to keep an eye on*, an-spielen auf *to allude to, hint at*, eine Anspielung auf, Anspruch erheben/haben auf *to lay/have a claim to*, jemanden auf etwas aufmerksam machen *to draw s.o.'s attention to s.th.*, auf-passen auf *to keep an eye on*, Aussicht haben auf *to have prospects of*, sich beschränken auf *to confine o.s. to, to be limited to*, sich besinnen auf *to try to remember*, dringen auf *to demand urgently* (e.g. an interview, new measures), ein-gehen auf *to go into a matter; to agree to a suggestion*, sich erstrecken auf *to extend to, include*.
sich freuen auf *to look forward to*, hoffen auf, die Hoffnung auf, sich konzentrieren auf, lauern auf *to lie in wait for*, coll.: *to await s.o. impatiently*, reagieren auf, ein Recht haben auf, schimpfen auf *to swear at, grumble at*, sich stürzen auf *to rush at*, (sich) vorbereiten auf *to prepare for*,[3] warten auf.

after adjectives and participles:
eifersüchtig auf, aufs Schlimmste gefaßt *prepared for the worst*, neidisch auf, neugierig auf *curious about* (e.g. the result),[4] stolz auf, versessen (or erpicht) auf *bent on having, mad about* (e.g. money).

(b) to rely on, to be based on and similar verbs
sich verlassen auf *to rely on, count on*, cf. bauen auf, rechnen auf, zählen auf; spekulieren auf *to speculate, gamble on* (e.g. a quick success); vertrauen auf *to put one's trust in*.
sich gründen auf, sich stützen auf; basieren auf + dat., beruhen auf + dat. *to be based on*; cf. ich gründe meine Meinung auf diese Tatsache.

(c) denoting 'in response to, as the result of'; the relevant expressions are sometimes strengthened through the addition of 'hin':

Auf meine Bitte (hin) hat er die Sache für sich behalten	*At my request he kept the matter to himself*

---

[1] cf. Collinson, op. cit., p. 108.
[2] BUT: Er wies mich an seinen Kollegen *He referred me to his colleague.*
[3] BUT: (sich) bereit-machen für, (sich) fertig-machen für; see also 622 i.
[4] neugierig auf is only applied to something that lies in the future; otherwise a paraphrase is used e.g. Ich möchte mehr über seine Vergangenheit wissen.

Auf meinen Brief hin hat er sofort gehandelt	*As the result of my letter he immediately took action*

cf. auf Anfrage *on application,* auf Anraten meines Onkels *on my uncle's advice;* antworten/die Antwort auf einen Brief, eine Frage; auf seine Empfehlung (hin) *on the strength of his recommendation,* auf seine Initiative, auf seinen Rat (hin); auf Verabredung *by arrangement, by appointment;* auf meine Verantwortung (hin) *on my responsibility,* auf einen Verdacht hin *on the strength of a suspicion,* auf ein Wort von ihm, auf Wunsch *by request,* auf meinen Wunsch (hin) *at my wish.*

601. aus

(a) **to denote origin, reason, motive: from, out of**

Er tat es aus Dankbarkeit	*He did it out of gratitude*
Ich weiß es aus Erfahrung	*I know it from experience*
Ich frage nur aus Interesse	*I'm just asking from interest*

cf. aus Furcht vor seinem Vater, aus Gewohnheit *from habit,* aus diesem Grund, aus Langerweile *out of boredom,* aus Liebe zu seiner Mutter, aus Neid, aus reiner Neugierde *out of sheer curiosity,* aus Spaß *for fun,* aus Überzeugung *out of conviction,* aus freiem Willen *of one's own free will.*

(b) **to denote 'made of'**

Die Kaffeekanne war aus Silber (gemacht); sie trug ein Kleid aus blauer Seide (commoner: ein blaues Seidenkleid) BUT: Er hat ein Herz von Stein.

Compare:

Er hat viel aus dem Geschäft gemacht	*He has developed the business very successfully*
aus der Not eine Tugend machen	*to make a virtue of necessity*
bestehen aus	*to consist of*
zusammengesetzt aus	*composed of*

602. bei

(a) **on the occasion of, in the course of, at**

bei dieser Gelegenheit	*on this occasion*
bei Gelegenheit	*when an opportunity occurs*
Ich half ihr beim Abwasch	*I helped her with the washing up*
bei dem bloßen Gedanken	*at the very thought*
Er erblaßte bei der Nachricht	*He turned pale at the news*
Bei *dem* Radau kann ich nicht arbeiten	*I can't work with that row going on*
Acht Menschen kamen bei diesem . . . Verkehrsunfall ums Leben (*FAZ*)	*Eight people were killed in this road accident*
bei Vollbeschäftigung	*in the case of full employment*

cf. bei diesem Anblick, bei seiner Ankunft, bei der Arbeit sein, er hinderte mich bei der Arbeit, bei der Erwähnung des 'Faust', beim Essen, beim Fußball, bei einem Glas Wein *over a glass of wine,* bei Straßenkämpfen, bei Tageslicht, bei Tisch, bei seinem Tod, bei näherer Überlegung (or: bei Licht besehen) *on further consideration,* bei schönem Wetter, bei jeder Wiederholung *at every repetition,* bei Wind, bei Wind und Wetter *in all weathers,* bei diesen Worten, bei unserer letzten Zusammenkunft.

(b) **in view of, with**

Bei seinem unzuverlässigen Charakter muß man vorsichtig sein	*In view of his unreliable character you have to be careful*
bei den immer steigenden Preisen	*in view of the constantly rising prices*
Bei diesem Gehalt kann ich mir kein Auto leisten	*With this salary I can't afford a car*

(c) despite

Bei all seinen Verlusten bleibt er ein Optimist	*Despite all his losses he remains an optimist*

cf. bei allen Vorteilen *for all the advantages*, bei alledem *for all that*, beim besten Willen *with the best will in the world*.

(d) Various applications derived from its literal sense 'at the house of, with' (see 550(b))

Bei ihm kann man nie sicher sein	*With him you can never be certain*
bei Hunden	*in the case of dogs*
Das hat ihm bei den Amerikanern sehr geschadet	*That did him a lot of harm in the eyes of the Americans*
beliebt bei	*popular with*
sich bei jemandem entschuldigen/ beklagen	*to apologize/to complain to s.o.*
sich bei jemandem erkundigen	*to inquire of s.o.*
Ich dachte bei mir	*I thought to myself*

cf. Er hat großen Einfluß bei dem Premierminister; wir haben Mathematik bei Dr. Schulze; dieses Wort kommt bei Goethe oft vor (*often occurs in Goethe*); bei uns tut man das nicht; er arbeitet bei dieser Firma; er hat bei der Infanterie/bei der Luftwaffe gedient.

(e) 4 common but somewhat unexpected uses

Er war bei guter/schlechter Laune	*He was in a good/bad mood*
Er nennt mich beim Vornamen	*He calls me by my Christian name*
Er nahm mich beim Wort	*He took me at my word*
Er nahm mich bei der Hand	*He took me by the hand*

603. gegen, gegenüber and **zu** are all used to denote conduct towards, a mental attitude towards, or relations with, someone or something (cf. Fr. envers). Often two or all of them may be used in the same context, though each has its distinctive features.

(a) zu

i It mainly, but not exclusively, denotes friendly attitudes and is mostly used with adjectives:

Er war sehr freundlich zu mir	*He was very kind to me*

cf. frech zu *impudent to*, gerecht zu/gegen *just towards*, grausam zu/gegen *cruel to*, gut zu *good, kind to*, hart zu/mit/gegen *hard towards*, (un)höflich zu (*im*)*polite to*, nett zu *nice to*, respektvoll zu *respectful to*, unfreundlich zu *unkind to*.
BUT: seine Frechheit, Gerechtigkeit, Grausamkeit, Härte, (Un)höflichkeit gegen mich; sein Respekt vor mir.

ii It is used with a certain number of nouns, e.g.

Wir haben freundliche Beziehungen zu Müllers	*We are on friendly terms with the Müllers*
die Einstellung Rulls zur Schule (Th. Valentin)	*Rull's attitude to school*
aus Freundschaft zu ihm	*out of friendship for him*
seine Liebe zu seiner Mutter/zur Musik	*his love for his mother/of music*
seine Neigung zu dem Mädchen	*his liking for the girl*
Stellung zu etwas nehmen	*to define one's attitude to s.th.*
das Verhältnis des Einzelnen zum Staat	*the relation of the individual to the state*

iii It is rarely used with adverbs; thus: Er benahm sich sehr höflich gegen mich.

(b) gegen mainly, but not exclusively, **denotes hostile attitudes:**
Er war mißtrauisch gegen mich   *He was distrustful towards me*

cf. with adjectives and participles:
abgehärtet gegen *hardened to*, abweisend gegen *unfriendly towards*, argwöhnisch gegen *suspicious of*, empfindlich gegen *sensitive to*, gesichert gegen *secure against*, gleichgültig gegen *indifferent to*, rücksichtslos, rücksichtsvoll gegen *(in)considerate towards*, taub gegen alle Warnungen *deaf to all warnings*, treulos gegen *disloyal to*.

with nouns:
die Abneigung gegen *aversion for*, der Haß gegen/auf + acc. *hatred of*, das Mißtrauen gegen *distrust of*, seine Pflicht gegen seine Eltern *his duty to his parents*, sein Verhalten gegen seinen Chef *his attitude to his employer*.

See also (a) above: i and iii.

(c) gegenüber
i It follows a pronoun; it may precede, but generally follows, a noun.

ii **It can generally be used as an alternative to 'zu' and 'gegen';** in the examples in (a) and (b) above, gegenüber could *not* be used in the following: gut zu, nett zu, Beziehungen zu, seine Liebe zu, seine Neigung zu, das Verhältnis zu, abgehärtet gegen, empfindlich gegen.

iii It is frequently the preferred preposition, e.g.: Er handelte durchaus gerecht mir gegenüber (gegen mich); seine Güte mir gegenüber (zu mir) war rührend (*touching*).

iv **It is flexibly used to denote 'towards, in relation to' in a variety of other and less straightforward contexts,** e.g.

die Politik der USA gegenüber Rußland	*the policy of the USA towards Russia*
Erhards Hilflosigkeit gegenüber Positionskämpfen und taktischen Finten (*Zeit*)	*Erhard's helplessness in the face of jockeying for position and tactical feints*
Doch auch Herr Lautenschlag verfügte über allerlei Schachzüge den Seinen gegenüber (A. Kolb)	*But, like a chess-player, Herr Lautenschlag too had at his disposal various moves in his dealings with his family*
Er konnte seiner Frau gegenüber ein Gefühl von unbezahlten Schulden nicht loswerden (V. Baum)	*He could not get rid of a feeling of unpaid debt towards his wife*

(d) 3 common adjectives have 'mit': böse mit *angry with*, sanft mit *gentle with*, streng mit *strict with*.

604. nach

(a) denotes the object of a desire, striving and numerous purposeful actions

Er sehnt sich nach Ruhe	*He is longing for peace*
Er forscht nach der Wahrheit	*He is seeking after the truth*
Die Kinder schrien nach Brot	*The children cried for bread*

Ich telefonierte nach dem Arzt/nach einem Taxi	*I phoned for the doctor/for a taxi*
Ich sah mich nach ihm um	*I looked out for him*
die Forderung nach einer Lohnerhöhung	*the demand for a wage-increase*

cf. after verbs:

angeln nach *to fish for*, aus-schauen nach, dürsten nach *to thirst for*, crave for (e.g. fame) (intr. and impers.; elev.), nach Komplimenten fischen, graben nach, greifen/langen nach *to reach for*, jagen nach *to pursue* (e.g. fame, pleasure), schicken nach *to send for*, schlagen nach *to hit out at*, schmachten nach *to thirst for, pine for* (lit. and fig.; elev.), streben nach, suchen nach, tasten nach *to grope for*, verlangen nach *to crave for*; *to ask to see* (e.g. a doctor).

after adjectives:

begierig nach *eager, impatient, ambitious for*, gierig nach *greedy for*.

after nouns:

das Heimweh nach der Schweiz, die Jagd nach Glück, die Nachfrage nach diesen Waren *the demand for these goods*, die Sehnsucht nach, auf der Suche nach, die Sucht nach Genuß *the mania for pleasure*, das Verlangen nach *the craving for*, der Wunsch nach.

(b) according to, in accordance with

Note: In this sense, 'nach' sometimes precedes and sometimes follows its noun; an asterisk after the phrase indicates that both positions are possible; it always precedes a proper name or a personal pronoun, but is rarely used with the latter.

nach diesem Gesetz (more official: diesem Gesetz gemäß)	*according to this law*
nach dem Testament ihres Vaters	*under her father's will*
nach Art der Betrunkenen (H. Böll)	*after the manner of drunkards*
nach der Häufigkeit seiner Besuche zu urteilen	*to judge by the frequency of his visits*
Das ist ein Mann so recht nach meinem Herzen	*He's a man just after my own heart*
Ich kenne ihn nur dem Namen nach	*I only know him by name*
Es sieht nach (or wie) Regen aus	*It **looks like** rain*
Es sieht nach reiner Verschwendung aus	*It looks like sheer wastefulness*
Er trinkt zuviel.—Er sieht auch danach aus	*He drinks too much.—He looks like it too*
Er sah wie ein Landstreicher aus	BUT: *He looked like a tramp*

cf. with 'nach' preceding its noun:

nach allem, was ich höre; Namen nach dem Alphabet ordnen;* nach Ansicht meines Bruders *according to my brother*;[1] nach Ansicht Lessings/nach Lessing; nach diesem Bericht;* nach Geschmack *according to taste*; nach meinem Geschmack; nach Herzenslust *to one's heart's content*; nach der Karte essen *to eat à la carte*; nach (besten) Kräften *to the best of one's ability*; nach deutschen Maßstäben *by German standards*; nach dieser Methode; nach der Natur malen *to paint from nature*; nach der Regel;* riechen nach *to smell of*; schmecken nach *to taste of*; nach dem Sommerfahrplan; nach meiner Überzeugung* *I am convinced that . . .*; nach meiner Uhr ist es halb zwei; nach Wunsch *as desired*.

---

[1] In conversation, a paraphrase is more usual: Mein Bruder meint/ist der Ansicht/ behauptet, daß man diesem Mann nicht trauen kann.

cf. with 'nach' following its noun:

allem Anschein nach *to all appearances*, meiner Ansicht nach,* seinem Aussehen nach *to judge by his appearance*, meiner Meinung nach,* der Reihe nach *in turn*, aller Wahrscheinlichkeit nach, seinem Wesen nach *by its very nature*.

N.B. je nach *according to, depending on*

Je nach dem Preis kannst du ein oder zwei Pfund kaufen	*According to the price you can buy one or two pounds*
je nachdem	*all according, it depends*

605. über + acc: about, concerning. E.g.

sich ärgern über	*to be annoyed about*
Er hat mich über seine Pläne beruhigt	*He has reassured me about his plans*
Ich war über seinen Vorschlag empört	*I was indignant at his suggestion*
ein Aufsatz über 'Faust'	*an essay on 'Faust'*

cf. after verbs:

sich amüsieren über, sich beklagen/sich beschweren über *to make a complaint about*, erröten über *to blush at*, sich freuen über, klagen über *to complain of* or *about*, *to grumble about*, sich lustig machen über *to make fun of*, nach-denken über, sich wundern über *to be surprised at*, **and many others.**

after adjectives:

bekümmert über *worried about*, entsetzt über *shocked at*, enttäuscht über/von *disappointed at*, entzückt über/von *delighted about*, froh über, unentschieden über **and many others.**

after nouns:

die Ansicht über, ein Buch über Schmetterlinge, die Freude über, die Klage über *the complaint* or *lament about*, in Verzweiflung über *in despair about*,[1] im Zweifel sein über[2] **and many others.**

606. about, concerning: some common instances in which prepositions other than 'über' are used:

die wachsenden Zweifel an seiner Fähigkeit (*Zeit*)	*The growing doubts about his capability*
neugierig auf + acc.	*curious about* (see 600(a))
sich irren in + dat.	*to be mistaken about s.th., in one's judgement of s.o.*
begeistert von	*in raptures about*
Das kann ich nicht von ihm glauben	*I can't believe that of him*
Was halten Sie von ihm?	*What do you think of him?*
Es ist von einer Gehaltserhöhung die Rede	*There's talk of a pay-increase*
schwärmen von	*to rave, go into raptures about*
träumen von	*to dream about*
nervös wegen	*nervous about*

See 609(b) for the use of 'um' to denote 'about, concerning'.

---

[1] BUT: verzweifeln an + dat. *to despair of.*
[2] But see 606.

607. about, concerning: verbs with alternative prepositions

(a) **denken, hören, lesen, sagen, schreiben, sprechen** and **wissen** may be used with über or von: 'über' generally implies length and thoroughness, 'von' brevity and cursoriness:

Wie denken Sie darüber?	*What is your view of the matter?*
Was denken Sie von ihm?	*What do you think of him?*
Wir haben darüber gesprochen	*We talked about it*
Er hat davon gesprochen	*He mentioned it*
Er weiß viel über Flugzeuge	*He knows a lot about aeroplanes*
Ich wußte schon von seinem Tod	*I already knew of his death*

Note:
i lesen über may mean to give a course of lectures on:
   Professor Schulze liest über Schillers Dramen.
ii sagen zu: to say to, to give as one's opinion about:

Was sagt die Regierung zu Ungarn?	*What does the government say to (events in)*
(M. Horbach)	*Hungary?*

iii for wissen um, see 609(b).
iv **erzählen** *to relate* is used with von or über, with no difference in meaning: Er hat viel von seinen Ferien/über seine Ferien erzählt.

(b) **sich erkundigen** and **fragen** may be used with i nach ii über.
i

Ich erkundigte mich nach ihm	*I inquired after his health*
Ich fragte nach ihm	1. *I asked about his health*
	2. *I asked to see him*
Ich erkundigte mich/fragte nach	*I inquired after/asked for his name,*
seinem Namen, nach dem	*the shortest way*
kürzesten Weg	

ii

Ich erkundigte mich über den neuen Film	*I inquired about the new film*
Ich fragte ihn über seine Arbeit	*I asked him about his work*

Note: fragen is also used with 'um':

Ich fragte ihn um Rat	*I asked him for advice*

(c) **reden** über:

Die Leute reden bereits über ihn	*People are beginning to talk (disparagingly) about him*
Darüber läßt sich reden	*That's a sensible idea (worth discussing)*

reden von:

Er redete von seinen Erlebnissen, von seiner Familie	*He spoke of his experiences, his family*
Reden wir von etwas anderem!	*Let us talk about something else*
(viel) von sich reden machen	*to cause a (great) stir*
nicht zu reden davon, daß . . .	*not to mention the fact that . . .*

(d) **schimpfen** über + acc.   *to grumble about*
   schimpfen auf + acc.   *to swear at*

(e) **sich streiten, sich zanken** *to quarrel* um/über: see 609(a).

(f) **sich täuschen** über + acc.   *to be mistaken about* (e.g. the probable difficulties)

sich täuschen in + dat.   *to be mistaken in* (e.g. one's expectations of s.o.)

608. über + acc.: other figurative uses

(a) it may denote superiority or control over

Kaiser Karl V. herrschte über viele Länder   *The Emperor Charles V ruled over many lands*

Er war nicht mehr Herr über seine Gefühle/über sich selbst[1]   *He was no longer master of his feelings/of himself*

cf. es über sich bringen, etwas zu tun *to bring o.s. to do s.th.*, über jeden Verdacht erhaben *above suspicion*, siegen über, der Sieg über, verfügen über *to have at one's disposal.*

Compare über + dat.: Im Geschäft habe ich nur den Chef über mir; er steht über der Sache *he has complete command of* (i.e. conversance with) *the matter.*

(b) it may denote 'over, (going) beyond'

Er lebt über seine Verhältnisse   *He lives beyond his means*

Ich bin über die Neugierde hinaus   *I am past curiosity*

Es geht nichts über ein Glas Rheinwein[2]   *There's nothing like a glass of hock*

cf. über alle Maßen *beyond measure*; er liebt die Ruhe über alles; über Erwarten *beyond expectation*; das geht über meine Kräfte, über meinen Verstand *that is beyond me*; über die Stränge schlagen *to kick over the traces.*

N.B. For über before a cardinal (e.g. über hundert Bücher), see 248 N.iii.

609. um

(a) it introduces the objective of some action (see 600(a)N.ii)

der Kampf ums Dasein   *the struggle for existence*

Er tat es nur um das Geld   *He only did it for the money*

Sie stritten sich (zankten sich) um das Geld   *They quarrelled over the money* (i.e. as to who should have it)

Sie stritten sich über den Preis   BUT: *They quarrelled about the price*

um Geld schreiben   *to write for money* (asking for it)

für Geld schreiben   BUT: *to write for money* (to earn it)

Wir liefen um die Wette   *We raced each other* (lit.: we ran for a wager)

Sie logen um die Wette   cf. *They vied with each other in telling lies*

Er wandte sich an mich um Rat   *He turned to me for advice*

cf. jemanden um etwas bemühen *to trouble s.o. for s.th.*, sich um eine Stelle bemühen (or bewerben) *to apply for a post*, zu Gott um etwas beten, betteln um, bitten um, die Bitte um, um etwas flehen, *to plead, beg for s.th.* kämpfen um *to fight for* (a strategic position, victory), konkurrieren um *to compete for*, losen um *to draw lots for*, um Hilfe schreien, um Geld spielen, streiken um *to strike for* (e.g. a wage increase), werben um *to woo.*

---

[1] more literary: Herr seiner Gefühle/seiner selbst.

[2] from Betteridge, op. cit., über.

(b) **it denotes 'about, concerning, regarding' in a limited number of cases**, e.g.

Ich beneide ihn um seine Schlagfertigkeit	*I envy him his quickness of repartee*
es handelt sich um	*it is a question of* (Fr.: il s'agit de)
Es ist schade um den Verlust	*It's a pity about the loss*
Es steht schlecht um meinen Bruder	*My brother is in a bad way*
Ich war um eine Entschuldigung verlegen (from Du. Stil.)	*I was at a loss for an excuse*

cf. die Angst ums Leben *fear for one's life*; sich ängstigen um *to be anxious about*; sich Sorgen machen um *to worry about*; die Sorge um ihren Sohn; trauern um *to mourn for*.

It frequently has a literary flavour:

der heilige Schmerz . . . um die Gegenwart des Vaterlandes (Treitschke on H. von Kleist)	*the sacred sorrow for the present state of his fatherland*
Es war etwas Besonderes um diese Landerziehungsheime (K. Mann)	*There was something special about these boarding-schools*
Ich wußte nicht um seinen Tod (normal usage: von seinem Tod)[1]	*I didn't know of his death*

(c) **it denotes degree of difference**

Er ist (um) einen Kopf größer als ich	*He is a head taller than I am*
Ich werde meinen Aufenthalt um zwei Tage verlängern	*I shall extend my stay by two days*
Er hat sich um zwei Mark verrechnet	*He was two marks out in his calculation* (or *accounts*)
um die Hälfte mehr	*half as much again*
Die Mehrheit der CDU hatte um 15 Sitze abgenommen	*The CDU (Party's) majority had decreased by 15 seats*
eine Erweiterung der EWG um England und andere EFTA-Länder (*SZ*)	*an expansion of the EEC by the inclusion of England and other EFTA countries*

610. unter + dat.

(a) **it is used to introduce the accompanying circumstances of an action or occurrence:**

unter diesen Umständen[2]	*under these circumstances*
unter dieser Bedingung	*on this condition*
unter diesem Vorwand	*on this pretext*
unter Tränen	*amid tears*
und unter wachsendem Hallo wurde auch dies bestätigt (Th. Mann)	*and amid the growing uproar this too was confirmed*

(b) **it is used in a number of straightforward figurative contexts** (English: *under, beneath, below*):

Ich habe zehn Arbeiter unter mir; ich kann es nicht unter 60 Mark verkaufen; es geschah unter meinen Augen; unter dem Schutz der Dunkelheit; unter Zwang handeln *to act under compulsion*; unter den Waffen *under arms*; dieser Film ist unter aller Kritik (sl. unter aller Kanone).

---

[1] Möller (op. cit., p. 88) calls 'um' a 'Modepräposition', especially when used with 'wissen'.

[2] cf. unter allen Umständen *in any case, without question*; unter Umständen *under certain circumstances, if need be, possibly*.

(c) it denotes 'by' in the phrases:

Was verstehst du unter einer Präposition/ unter „Idealismus"?	*What do you understand (mean) by a preposition/ by 'idealism'?*
Er ist unter diesem Namen bekannt	*He is known by this name*

611. von

(a) of, on the part of

Es war sehr liebenswürdig/nett/ vernünftig von Ihnen	*It was very kind/nice/sensible of you*
Es war dumm von mir	*It was silly of me*
Es ist nicht recht von ihm	*It's not right of him*

(b) about, concerning: see 606, 607(a)(c).

(c) it is used figuratively in a wide range of contexts, most of which are included in Section H below; its appropriateness is in most cases not difficult to feel, e.g.

Das kommt vom vielen Trinken	*That comes of drinking so much*
Er tat es von selbst	*He did it of his own accord*
Er lebt von seinen Aktien	*He lives on his investments*

612. vor + dat.

(a) it denotes the emotional or physical cause of some state or action

Ich war außer mir vor Entzücken	*I was beside myself with delight*
Mir war vor Kälte elend	*I was miserable with cold*
fallend und sterbend . . . im Wüstenbrand vor übernatürlicher Anstrengung (Th. Mann)	*falling and dying in the burning heat of the desert from superhuman exertion*

cf. Ich konnte vor Aufregung nicht einschlafen; ich schwitzte vor Hitze; ich brüllte vor Lachen; er gähnte vor Müdigkeit; er war gelb vor Neid (*green with envy*); er stöhnte vor Schmerz; er strahlte vor Zufriedenheit *he beamed with satisfaction.*

N.B. Er starb vor Hunger; ich starb fast vor Langerweile BUT: Er starb an einer Lungenentzündung (*pneumonia*), an Altersschwäche.

(b) it introduces a source of danger or aversion, which is feared, loathed or guarded against

Ich fürchtete mich (hatte Angst) vor dem Hund	*I was afraid of the dog*
Ich erschrak vor dem Hund	*I was scared by the dog*
Ich erschrak über sein schlechtes Aussehen (Du. Stil.)	BUT: *I got a fright at his unhealthy appearance*
Alles war in heiligem Respekt vor ihm	*Everyone was in unholy awe of him*
Es ekelt mich vor ihm	*He fills me with abhorrence*
Er warnte mich vor dem Hund	*He warned me about the dog*
Gott bewahre mich vor meinen Freunden!	*Heaven protect me from my friends!*
Er drückt sich immer vor dem Abwasch	*He always gets out of washing up*

cf. after verbs:

sich in acht nehmen (sich hüten, auf der Hut sein) vor *to be on one's guard against, to beware of*; fliehen vor; sich vor jemandem schämen *to feel ashamed in s.o.'s presence*; sich scheuen vor *to shrink from* (e.g. a formidable task, a lie); (sich) schützen vor; (sich) verbergen/verstecken vor *to hide from*

after nouns and adjectives:
der Abscheu/der Ekel vor *abhorrence of*; die Angst/Furcht vor; auf der Flucht vor *fleeing from*; der Schutz vor; sicher vor *safe from*; eine Warnung vor.

Note: **to rescue from**: Er rettete mich aus dem brennenden Haus; er befreite mich von den Banditen; er rettete mich vor dem Tod.

613. zu

(a) it denotes purpose

Wozu gebrauchst du dieses Messer?	*What do you use this knife for?*
Ich gebrauche es zum Kartoffel-schälen	*I use it for peeling potatoes*
Mach dich zum Ausgehen fertig!	*Get ready for going out*
Er ist zum Nachprüfen des Fernsehers da	*He's come to check the television*
Ich sage dir dies zu deiner Beruhigung	*I'm telling you this to reassure you*
Ich tue es zu deinem Besten	*I'm doing it for your own good*
Hier gibt es Möglichkeiten zum Schilaufen	*There are possibilities for skiing here*
der Mut zu einer Entscheidung	*the courage for a decision*

cf. Ich habe ihn zum Abendessen (BUT: ins Theater) eingeladen; zur Ansicht *on approval*; Stoff zu einem neuen Anzug; zum Besten der Armen *for the benefit of the poor*; zur Erholung verreisen *to go away to recuperate.*
Er war zum Wissenschaftler geboren (*born to be*); er hat mir zum Geburtstag diese Uhr geschenkt; er ist (nicht) zum Lehrer geeignet ((*not*) *fitted to be*); wir hatten keine Gelegenheit zu einem Gespräch; er paßt nicht zum Pfarrer *he is not made to be a parson*; ein Plan zur Lösung dieser Probleme; dieses Wasser ist nicht zum Trinken; ich hänge das Tuch hierhin zum Trocknen; ein Verein zur Ver-breitung der Bibel *a society for the propagation of the Bible*; zu diesem Zweck; ein Mittel zum Zweck *a means to an end*; wozu machst du das?

Note:
dienen zu = to serve a purpose

Wozu dient dieser Apparat?	*What is this appliance used for?*
Er dient zur Entsaftung von Obst und Gemüse	*It is used as a liquidizer for fruit and vegetables*
Er dient dazu, Obst und Gemüse zu entsaften	*It is used to liquidize fruit and vegetables*

dienen als = to serve as, in the capacity of

Ich diene ihm als Sekretär	*I serve him as secretary*
Das frühere Schloß dient jetzt als Museum (Du. Stil.)	*The former palace now serves as a museum*
Dieser Satz könnte als Beispiel dienen	*This sentence might serve as an example*

Sometimes either can be used: Dieses Erlebnis diente mir zur/als Warnung.

(b) it denotes 'by way of, for, as'

Er murmelte etwas zur Antwort	*He muttered something by way of a reply*
Seine Rede hatte eine politische Krise zur Folge	*His speech resulted in a political crisis*
Er tat es mir zu Gefallen	*He did it to oblige me* (lit. *as a favour*)

12*

Du solltest dir deinen Bruder zum   *You should take your brother as a model*
  Muster nehmen

cf. zur Abwechslung *for a change*; zum Andenken an+ acc. *in memory of*; zum
  Beispiel; zum (or als) Dank für; ihm zu Ehren *in his honour*; er hat eine Deutsche
  zur Frau; zum (or als) Lohn für *as a reward for*; zum Scherz *by way of a joke*;
  zur Strafe; zum Überfluß *needlessly*; zum Vergnügen *for pleasure*.

(c) **it denotes result or effect**

Zu meinem Erstaunen hat er das   *To my astonishment he has passed the*
  Examen bestanden   *examination*
Diese Maßnahmen werden zum   *These measures will be to the advantage/*
  Vorteil/zum Schaden der Stadt sein   *to the detriment of the town*

cf. zu meinem Ärger, zu meiner Befriedigung *to my satisfaction*, zu meiner Be-
  ruhigung *to my relief*, zu meiner großen Freude; es ist zum Lachen *it's laughable*;
  es ist zum Verrücktwerden *it's enough to drive you mad.*

(d) **Sie wählten ihn zum Präsidenten** *They elected him president:* 'zu' is
  similarly used with the following analogous verbs: befördern *to
  promote*, bestimmen *to destine to be*, degradieren *to demote*, ernennen *to
  appoint*, krönen *to crown* (s.o. king), machen *to make*, weihen *to ordain*.

Er wurde zum Major befördert   *He was promoted major*
Ich habe ihn mir zum Feind   *I've made an enemy of him*
  gemacht
Ich mache es mir zur Regel, dies zu   *I make it a rule to do this*
  tun

With nouns: seine Beförderung, Ernennung, Wahl zum Direktor.

See also 636(b).

(e) **it denotes conduct towards, a mental attitude towards, or
  relations with**: see 603.

(f) Apart from the specific cases dealt with above, **'zu' is used in a
  variety of abstract or figurative contexts, where English has
  'to' or 'into'**:

Ich kam zu dem Schluß, daß . . .   *I came to the conclusion that . . .*
zur Sache kommen   *to come to the point*
Er trieb mich zur Verzweiflung   *He drove me to despair*
Er zwang mich zu einer Entscheidung   *He forced me into a decision*
Ich kam nicht zum Briefeschreiben   *I didn't get round to letter-writing*
Er ist zum katholischen Glauben   *He has gone over to the Catholic faith*
  übergegangen
der Schlüssel zur Wahrheit   *the key to the truth*
Er wurde zu allerlei Dummheiten   *He was misled into various foolish acts*
  verleitet
Er überredete mich zu einem Glas   *He talked me into having a glass of wine*
  Wein

H. THE RENDERING OF ENGLISH PREPOSITIONS
IN FURTHER CONTEXTS

614. Turning English idiomatic phrases

Not infrequently, one realizes instinctively that a particular English
phrase, involving a preposition, is highly unlikely to have an analogous

German equivalent; in such cases the basic meaning of the English idiom must be determined and a straightforward but convincing German rendering of it must be aimed at. E.g.

Lesen Sie es, wenn Sie einmal Zeit haben (or: gelegentlich)	*Read it at your leisure*
Ich wußte wirklich nicht (or: Ich war ratlos), wie ich ihm helfen könnte	*I was at a loss to know how I could help him*
Wir haben zusammen nur einen Schirm	*We've only got one umbrella between us*
Wenn ich mich nur ausruhen könnte!	*Oh, for a rest!*
Du kannst es mir glauben	*You can take it from me*
Das ist gerade was für mich	*That is just in my line*
Er lebt von meinem Geld	*He lives on me*
Es ist nun einmal mein sehnlichster Wunsch, Italien zu sehen	*I've set my heart on seeing Italy*

615. Note on the lists that follow

In a great many cases the German is far closer to the English than in the instances dealt with in 614. Phrases were selected for inclusion by a combination of three criteria: 1. that they seem essential or useful to know; 2. that the German preposition either differs from the English one or, in some cases, rather surprisingly tallies with it; 3. that they are not, at least in some cases, easily accessible in a dictionary.

The more advanced student may like to use the lists to test his knowledge and 'Sprachgefühl'.

The lists are in general arranged in alphabetical order of the English.

616. about

	What about it?
Wie wär's damit?	1. = *Shall we do it?*
Na und?	2. = *So what?*
Wie wär's mit noch einem Stück Kuchen?	*What about another piece of cake?*
Wie ist es mit dir?	*What about you?*
Was ist da zu machen?	*What can you do about it?*
Wir müssen (da) irgendwas machen	*We must do something about it*
Da ist nichts zu machen	*There's nothing you can do about it*
Er wanderte durch die Straßen	*He walked about the streets*
Er ging im Garten umher (or herum)	*He walked about the garden*

Note on 'herum' and 'umher' (cf. the last example):
The distinction between herum (circling round: Er lief um den Baum herum) and umher (criss-crossing) is no longer adhered to in current and particularly not in colloquial German, herum being frequently used for umher. Moreover, in a context such as the following, only herum is used: Er kramte in der Schublade herum *He rummaged about in the drawer* (cf. Du. Haupt: herum/umher).

617. against

Er hat mir davon abgeraten	*He advised me against it*
gegen meine bessere Einsicht	*against my better judgement*
Ich bin an das Pult angestoßen	*I knocked against the desk*
Ich habe mit dem Knie an das Pult gestoßen	*I knocked my knee against the desk*
Ich bin in der Klemme	*I'm up against it*

618. along (here treated both as adverb and as preposition)

Ich ging langsam dahin	*I was walking slowly along*
Als er so dahinging, . . .	*As he walked along (cf. 304(f))*
Er schritt einher	*He strode along (implying stateliness)* [1]
Er ging vor/neben/hinter mir her	*He was walking along in front of/beside/ behind me*
Ich ging den Weg entlang	*I walked along the path*
Ich ging am Fluß (less common: den Fluß) entlang	*I walked along the river*
Am Fluß entlang wuchsen Weiden	*Willows grew along the river*
entlang der Grenze (dat.)	*along the frontier*
Packe dich! Mach dich fort!	*Get along with you! (lit.)*
Unsinn! Sei nicht so blöde!	*Get along with you! (fig.)*
Er kommt gut vorwärts	*He is getting along well*
Er macht gute Fortschritte	

See also 699, 700(b)(d), 706: daher.

619. among

in den Bergen	*among the hills*
unter anderem	*among other things*
unter manchem anderen	*among many other things*
Wir waren unter uns	*We were among ourselves*
Ich rechne/zähle ihn zu meinen Freunden	*I count him among my friends*
Er trat aus der Schar seiner Kollegen heraus	*He stepped forward from among his colleagues*

620. (S) at

	i with verbs
von vorn an-fangen	*to begin at the beginning*
Er warf mir einen wütenden Blick zu	*He cast a furious glance at me*
Ich schätze sein Einkommen auf 3000 DM[2] (acc.)	*I estimate his income at 3,000 marks (a month)*
hinter die Wahrheit kommen	*to get at the truth*
Was wollen Sie damit sagen?	*What are you getting at?*
Worauf wollen Sie (mit Ihren Bemerkungen) hinaus?	
Machst du dich über mich lustig?	*Are you getting at me?*
Gilt diese Bemerkung mir?	
Ich sah auf die Uhr	*I looked at my watch*
Er sah nach mir herüber	*He looked across at me*
Er nörgelt an mir herum	*He nags at me*
hinter den Büchern sitzen	*to sit at one's books*
Er warf einen Stein nach mir	*He threw a stone at me*
Er versuchte sich im Malen	*He tried his hand at painting*

---

[1] cf. Betteridge, op. cit., einher.   [2] often pronounced 'D-Mark'.

Er versuchte sich daran, Gedichte zu schreiben

He tried his hand at writing verse

an einer Sache arbeiten

to work at something

ii with adjectives

Er ist gut in Physik

He is good at physics (at school)

Er schreinert gut

He is good at carpentry

Stück Draht, ganz einfach. Ich bin gut mit Schlössern (E. M. Remarque) (coll.)

Bit of wire—quite simple. I'm good at locks

iii phrases

bei einem flüchtigen Blick

at a casual glance

in 200 Meter Höhe

at a height of 200 metres

mit 70 Stundenkilometer Geschwindigkeit

at a speed of 70 kilometres an hour

um jeden Preis

at any price

im Grunde (genommen), eigentlich

at bottom, fundamentally, actually

im Grunde meines (seines) Herzens, eigentlich

at heart

ein Paar Handschuhe zu 20 Mark

a pair of gloves at 20 marks

auf meine Kosten

at my expense (lit. and fig.)

auf eigne Kosten

at my (his, our, etc.) own expense

Das Hotel war gut und noch dazu billig

The hotel was good and cheap at that

auf Kosten + gen.

at the expense of

die Männer an der Spitze

the men at the top (of an organization)

zu diesem Preis

at this price

Auf diese Art werden wir nichts erreichen

At this rate (in this way) we shall achieve nothing

Er ist eifrig dran

He is hard at it

um keinen Preis

not at any price

Er lief hinauf und nahm dabei zwei Stufen auf einmal

He ran upstairs two at a time

621. by

i with verbs

Der Antrag wurde mit 90 gegen 31 Stimmen bei 17 Enthaltungen angenommen

The motion was approved by 90 votes to 31 with 17 abstentions

Wir fuhren diese Straße

We came by this road

zum Fenster hinaus-klettern

to climb out by the window

Ich kenne ihn nur vom Ansehen

I only know him by sight

jemanden an der Hand führen

to lead s.o. by the hand

Er faßte mich am Arm

He seized me by the arm

etwas an einem Beispiel zeigen

to show s.th. by an example

Er schwört auf diese Tabletten

He swears by these tablets

Ich konnte an seinem Gesichtsausdruck erkennen, was er sich dachte

I could tell by his expression what he was thinking

ii phrases

bei Tageslicht

by daylight

beim Feuerschein

by fire-light

Er ist von Natur (aus) schüchtern (Du. Stil.)

By nature he is shy

auf dem nächsten Wege

by the nearest way

Wir fahren über Stuttgart

We are going by way of (via) Stuttgart

622. for

	i with verbs
bewundern wegen	*to admire for*
Nach Baden-Baden umsteigen!	*Change for Baden-Baden*
ein Examen machen	*to go in for an examination*
Sein Hobby ist Fotografieren	*He goes in for photography*
Ich habe sie für[1] Dienstagabend (für[1] halb acht) eingeladen	*I have invited them for Tuesday evening (for half past seven)*
Er ist nach Hamburg abgereist	*He has left for Hamburg*
jemanden/sich auf etwas Unangenehmes ein-lassen	*to let s.o./o.s. in for s.th. unpleasant*
Er ging auf die Tür zu	*He made for the door*
Ich habe ihn auf deinen Besuch vorbereitet	*I've prepared him for your visit (=warned him about it)*
Ich habe alles für deinen Besuch vorbereitet	*I've prepared everything for your visit*
Um drei Uhr	*At three o'clock*
gingen wir ins Dorf/machten wir uns auf den Weg zum Dorf	*we set out for the village (on foot)*
fuhren wir ins Dorf	*(by car)*
gingen/fuhren wir nach Hause[2]	*we set out for home*
Man sieht das Fernsehen als etwas Selbstverständliches an	*One takes television for granted*
Ich setze voraus, daß . . .	*I take it for granted that . . .*
Ich nahm ihn mit zu einem Spaziergang	*I took him for a walk*
Ich führte das Kind/den Hund spazieren	*I took the child/the dog for a walk*
Das Mehl wird auf seine Reinheit (hin) geprüft	*The flour is tested for purity[3]*

	ii with adjectives
Wir waren für den Angriff bereit/ zum Angriff bereit	*We were ready for the attack (to meet it/ to make it)*
bekannt wegen (or für)[4]	*well known for*

	iii with nouns
ein Hilferuf	*a cry for help*
seine Abreise nach Hamburg	*his departure for Hamburg*
Es besteht kein Grund zur Beunruhigung	*There are no grounds for alarm*
der Grund für (or + gen.)	*the reason for*

	iv phrases
für alle Fälle	*for all eventualities*
meinetwegen	*for all I care*
Es ist sehr gut möglich, daß er krank ist	*For all I know, he's ill*
Ich riskiere einmal, an ihn zu schreiben (or: Was auch dabei herauskommt, ich will einmal an ihn schreiben)	*For better or for worse, I'm going to write to him*
Er ist zunächst einmal zu alt	*For one thing, he's too old*
ich für meinen Teil (or: was mich betrifft)	*I for my part*
ich zum Beispiel	*I for one*

[1] less usual: auf.
[2] a rather literary alternative: traten wir den Heimweg/die Rückfahrt an.
[3] cf. Ich habe den Brief auf Fehler (hin) durchgesehen.
[4] Only für is idiomatic when a 'daß'-clause follows: Er ist dafür bekannt, daß er immer auf sich warten läßt *He is well known for being late.*

Er ist hinter dem Geld her	*He is out for money*
Er ist auf Geld aus	
Es hat etwas für sich	*There is something to be said for it*

623. (S) from

i with verbs

Ich habe ihn davon abgebracht, dies zu tun	*I dissuaded him from doing this*
Die Wäsche hing an der Leine	*The washing hung from the line*
Ich habe die Bücher bei Rothmann bestellt	*I have ordered the books from Rothmanns*
Er hinderte mich daran, den Brief zu schreiben	*He prevented (i.e. hindered) me from writing the letter*
Er hat verhindert, daß ich den Brief schrieb	*He prevented (i.e. stopped, barred) me from writing the letter*
Ich war verhindert, in die Kirche zu gehen	*I was prevented from going to church*
etwas aus der Nähe/aus der Ferne sehen	*to see s.th. from close up/from far away*

ii with adjectives and nouns

Ich bin müde von der vielen Arbeit	*I'm tired from so much work*
Ich habe keine Geheimnisse vor dir	*I have no secrets from you*

iii phrases

von Kopf bis Fuß	*from head to foot*
Er liest alles, von der Philosophie bis zum Krimi	*He reads everything, from philosophy to thrillers*
Bonn ist 35 Kilometer von Köln entfernt (coll.: Von Bonn nach Köln sind's 35 Kilometer)	*Bonn is 35 kilometres from Cologne*

624. (S) in, into

i with verbs

vor Gericht erscheinen	*to appear in court*
zusammen-stoßen (s) mit	*to bump into (s.o.)*
sich stoßen an+dat.	*to bump into (s.th.)*
Er änderte etwas an dem Bild, an seinem Plan	*He changed s.th. in the picture, in his plan*
sich jemandem an-vertrauen	*to confide in s.o.*
Sein Leben gliedert sich in drei Abschnitte	*His life falls into three parts*
zum Film gehen	*to go into films*
Eins hatten wir alle gemeinsam	*One thing we all had in common*
Diesen Zug haben wir mit den Amerikanern gemein	*This trait we have in common with the Americans*
zu jemandem/zu einer Sache Vertrauen haben	*to have confidence in s.o./in s.th.*
An ihm hast du einen treuen Freund	*In him you have a faithful friend*
einer Sache nach-gehen (s)	*to look into a matter*
Er läßt sich nicht davon abbringen, es zu tun	*He persists in doing it*
einen Schnitzer machen	*to put one's foot in it*
einen Satelliten in eine Umlaufbahn bringen	*to put a satellite into orbit*
Wir fuhren gegen einen Baum	*We ran into a tree*
Ich bin ihm gestern zufällig begegnet	*I ran into him yesterday*
Wie sagt man das auf deutsch?	*How do you say that in German?*
Er sagte es in gebrochenem Deutsch	*He said it in broken German*

Wie sagt man das in Ihrer Sprache?	*How do you say that in your language?*
Ich sah es im Geiste vor mir	*I saw it in my mind's eye*
Ich konnte mir sein Erstaunen vorstellen	*In my mind's eye I could see his astonishment*
mit fester Stimme sprechen	*to speak in a firm voice*
Er hat dem Kuchen tüchtig zugesprochen/Er hat tüchtig zugelangt	*He tucked into the cake*
Er wurde am Bein verwundet	*He was wounded in the leg*

ii phrases

nach allen Seiten	*in all directions*
am hellen Tage	*in broad daylight*
in guten Verhältnissen sein	*to be in good circumstances*
(sehr) gefragt sein (sometimes: werden)	*to be in (great) demand*
in meiner Angst, in meiner Verlegenheit etc. (wandte ich mich an ihn)	*in my anxiety, in my dilemma etc. (I turned to him)*
Seine Bemerkung war sehr am Platz/sehr angebracht	*His remark was very much in place*
In der Praxis ist es nicht ganz so	*In practice it's not quite like that*
für jemanden voreingenommen sein	*to be prejudiced in s.o.'s favour*
die betreffende Zeitung	*the newspaper in question*
klein von Gestalt	*small in stature*
in diesem Fall/wenn das der Fall ist	*in that event*
Er war im Begriff, es zu tun	*He was in the act of doing it*
auf dem Gebiet der Politik	*in the domain of politics*
Schlagzeilen machen	*to be in the headlines*
(tief) in den roten Zahlen stecken	*to be in the red*
nichts auf der Welt	*nothing in the world*
an Ihrer Stelle würde ich . . .	*in your place I should . . .*

625. (S) of   i with verbs

Note: Numerous verbs with 'of' will be found in 499 f. among verbs followed by the genitive.

Er wurde freigesprochen	*He was acquitted of the crime*
jemandem gegenüber mit etwas prahlen/protzen[1]	*to boast to s.o. of s.th.*
Er ist von deutschen Eltern (geboren)	*He was born of German parents*
Er stammt aus einer alten Bremer Familie	*He comes of an old Bremen family*
Das kommt davon	*That's what comes of it*
Es ist nichts daraus geworden	*Nothing has come of it*
Ich werd' aus seinem Brief nicht klug	*I can make nothing of his letter*
Was meinst du zu seinem Brief?	*What do you make of his letter?*
etwas in Besitz nehmen	*to take possession of s.th.*
Wie finden Sie dieses Buch?	*What do you think of this book?*
Was halten Sie von diesem Buch?	*What do you think of this book?*
—Ich finde es sehr langweilig	*—I think it very boring*
—Ich halte nicht viel davon	*—I don't think much of it*

---

[1] also = to show off, cf. an-geben mit: Er gibt mit seinem Mercedes an *He boasts of/shows off with his Mercedes.*

Ich traue ihm nicht/Ich habe ihn in Verdacht	*I'm suspicious of him*

ii with adjectives

Ich habe diesen Prozeß satt	*I'm tired/sick of this lawsuit*
Ich bin diesen Prozeß leid	
Dieser Prozeß steht mir bis oben hin (sl.)	
Ich habe es satt, von ihm belästigt zu werden	*I'm tired of his pestering me*
Das gilt nicht von ihm	*That is not true of him*

iii with nouns

die Kritik an der Regierung	*criticism of the government*
der erste Blick auf Heidelberg	*the first glimpse of Heidelberg*
der Einfall in Polen (acc.)	*the invasion of Poland*
der Mord an + dat. (or: die Ermordung + gen.)	*the murder of*
die Beschäftigung mit einem Steckenpferd	*the pursuit of a hobby*
ein Sinn für Naturschönheit	*a sense of natural beauty*
mein Anteil an dem Geld	*my share of the money*

iv phrases

Er war mir weit voraus	*He was far ahead of me* (lit. and fig.)
gar nicht zu reden von	*not to speak of*
ein eignes Haus	*a house of one's own*
von selbst, aus eignem Antrieb	*of one's own accord*
die Schlacht bei Leipzig	*the Battle of Leipzig* (see also 64(a))

626. (S) on, upon

i with verbs

Wir haben uns über den Preis/auf den Preis von 1000 Mark geeinigt	*We've agreed on the price/on the price of 1000 marks*
Ich habe mich für diesen Hut entschieden	*I've decided on this hat*
zur Bühne/zum Theater gehen	*to go on the stage* (*become an actor*)
Ich hatte den Hund an der Leine	*I had the dog on the lead*
Ich habe kein Geld bei mir	*I have no money on me*
auf einen Gedanken kommen	*to hit upon an idea*
Er lebt von seinen Aktien	*He lives on his investments*
Er schaute eben bei seinem Freund herein	*He looked in on his friend*
Mein Fenster geht auf den Garten (hinaus)	*My window looks out on to the garden*
operieren + acc.	*to operate on s.o.*
Er nahm den Hund an die Leine	*He put the dog on the lead*
eine neue Stellung an-treten	*to start on a new job*
sein Geld für etwas verschwenden	*to waste one's money on s.th.*
seine Zeit mit etwas verschwenden	*to waste one's time on s.th.*
seine Zeit an jemanden verschwenden	*to waste one's time on s.o.*
Er trägt einen Ring (am Finger)	*He wears a ring*

ii phrases

Er ist darauf versessen/erpicht, es zu tun	*He is bent on doing it*
ein Wagen nach dem andern	*car upon car*
Reihe auf Reihe	*row upon row*

Er schwärmt für moderne Kunst	*He's mad on modern art*
Die Ausstellung war von großem/ kleinem Umfang	*The exhibition was on a large/small scale*
Dies wird per Saldo die beste Lösung sein	*On balance this will be the best solution*
an Bord (des Dampfers)	*on board (the steamer)* (with 'to be' and 'to go')
Er ist auf/an Deck	*He is on deck*
Er ging auf Deck spazieren	*He went for a walk on deck*
Ich ging an Deck	*I went on deck*
Ich habe heute abend Dienst	*I'm on duty this evening*
aus zuverlässiger Quelle	*on good authority*
Der Direktor ist in Urlaub gefahren	*The manager has gone on holiday*
Der Direktor ist im Urlaub	*The manager is on holiday*
am Horizont	*on the horizon*
Der Soldat kommt/ist auf Urlaub	*The soldier is coming/is on leave*
im Fernsehen	*on television*
im Erdgeschoß, im Parterre, zu ebener Erde	*on the ground floor*
im zweiten Stock	*on the second floor*
auf gut Glück, aufs Geratewohl	*on the off-chance*
obwohl es unwahrscheinlich ist, daß er zu Hause ist	*on the off-chance of his being at home*
Ich wollte es gerade tun	*I was on the point of doing it*
Ich war drauf und dran, es zu tun	
im stillen	*on the quiet*
auf der Stelle	*on the spot, immediately*
Die Feuerwehr war bald zur Stelle	BUT: *The fire-brigade was soon on the spot*
unterwegs	*on the way*
auf dem Weg zum Bahnhof[1]	*on the way to the station*
auf meinem Weg ins Dorf	*on my way to the village*
im Rundfunk, im Radio	*on the wireless*
auf/zu beiden Seiten	*on both sides, on either **side***
Ich legte meine Papiere beiseite	*I put my papers on one side (aside)*
Er trat zur Seite	*He stepped on one side (aside)*
Er stand auf einer Seite des Präsidenten	*He stood on one side of the President*
Ich nahm ihn beiseite/auf die Seite	*I took him on one side*
Er war immer auf unserer Seite	*He was always on our side*
Er ist eher ruhig	*He's on the quiet side*
Ich muß mich gut (or: auf guten Fuß) mit ihm stellen	*I must get on the right side of him*
Ich muß ihn richtig anpacken	—the same, meaning to cajole on some particular occasion
Ich darf mir sein Wohlwollen nicht verscherzen	*I must keep on the right side of him*
auf dieser Seite (des Hauses)	*on this side (of the house)*

627. out of

34 von hundert Patienten	*34 out of 100 patients*
Ich fühle mich ausgeschlossen (or: nicht zugehörig)	*I feel out of it*
Ich habe zehn Mark zu wenig	*I'm ten marks out of pocket*

[1] commoner than: unterwegs zum Bahnhof.

Mir fehlen zehn Mark	*I'm ten marks out of pocket*
Ich habe zehn Mark dabei verloren	
Er kommt nie aus sich heraus	*He never comes out of his shell*
See also 549(a)	

628. over

Mein Plan hat gewisse Vorteile vor Ihrem	*My plan has certain advantages over yours*
über der Arbeit ein-schlafen	*to fall asleep over one's work*
Was er sagt, ist uns zu hoch	*He talks over our heads*

629. to   i with verbs

eine Frage/eine Bitte/seine Worte an jemanden richten	*to address a question/a request/one's words to s.o.*
sich an die Vorschriften halten	*to adhere to the regulations*
Der Film hält sich eng an den Roman	*The film adheres closely to the novel*
sich mit jemandem versöhnen	*to become reconciled to s.o.*
sich mit etwas ab-finden	*to become reconciled to s.th.*
Wieviel macht das?	*What does it come to (cost)?*
Die Sache kommt zur Krise	*The matter has come to a head*
Er wurde zu fünf Jahren Gefängnis verurteilt	*He was sentenced to five years' imprisonment*
bei-tragen zu	*to contribute to*
für eine Zeitung schreiben	*to contribute to a paper*
jemandem Gerechtigkeit widerfahren lassen	*to do (mete out) justice to s.o.*
Um ihm gerecht zu werden, muß man zugeben, daß . . .	BUT: *To do him justice, one must admit that . . .*
Er hat sich den Kalbsbraten schmecken lassen (or, slightly precious: Er hat dem K. tüchtig zugesprochen)	*He did full justice to the roast veal*
zu Ende gehen	*to draw to a close*
Ich habe ohne Schwierigkeiten zu ihm gefunden	*I found my way to him without any difficulty*
Diese Tradition geht auf Bismarck zurück	*This tradition goes back to Bismarck*
Seine neue Stellung ist ihm zu Kopfe gestiegen	*His new post has gone to his head*
Der Preis ist von 10 auf 12 Mark gestiegen	*The price has gone up from 10 to 12 marks*
Ich hörte meinem Onkel/der Rede/der Musik zu	*I **listened to** my uncle/the speech/the music*
Ich höre gern klassische Musik/Mozart/Radio	*I like listening to classical music/Mozart/the radio*
Er wollte auf meinen Rat nicht hören	*He wouldn't listen to my advice*
Vernunft an-nehmen[1]	*to listen to reason*
Er murmelte etwas vor sich (acc.) hin	*He muttered s.th. to himself*
reduzieren auf + acc.	*to reduce to*
sich an die Arbeit machen	*to set to work*
sich dran machen	

---

[1] from Betteridge, op. cit.

zu jemandem sprechen	*to speak* (*talk*) *to s.o.* (without the idea of a conversation)[1]
Der Lehrer sprach zu der Klasse über dieses Thema (Du. Stil.)	*The teacher spoke to the form about this subject*
jemanden sprechen	*to speak to, to see s.o.* (generally on an official matter)
mit jemandem sprechen	*to speak* (*talk*) *to* or *with s.o.* (*to converse with*)
jemandem/seinen Grundsätzen treu bleiben	*to stick to s.o./to one's principles*
bei der Sache/bei der Wahrheit bleiben	*to stick to the point/to the truth*
Ich bleibe bei meinen Pferdebüchern (Th. Mann)	*I'll stick to my books about horses*
Er schlug ihn zu Boden	*He struck him to the ground*
sich jemandem zu-wenden	*to turn to* (*towards*) *s.o.*
sich an jemanden wenden	*to turn* (*apply*) *to s.o.*
Er wandte sich an mich um Rat	*He turned to me for advice*
(streng) nach Vorschrift arbeiten	*to work to rule*

ii with adjectives and participles

Diesen Charakterzug haben alle Engländer gemeinsam	*This trait is common to all Englishmen*
Dieses Unternehmen liegt ihm am Herzen	*This enterprise is dear to him*
Er hängt an seiner Mutter	*He is devoted to his mother*
angepaßt (with preceding dat.)	*geared* (*adapted*) *to*
Er neigt zu(m) Rheumatismus, zur Verschwendung	*He is prone to rheumatism, to extravagance*
bis auf die Haut durchnäßt	*soaked to the skin*
Er ist empfänglich für Schmeichelei/ für weibliche Schönheit	*He is susceptible to flattery/to female beauty*

iii with nouns

der Zugang zu	*access to*
ein Beitrag zu dem Fonds/zum menschlichen Wissen	*a contribution to the fund/to human knowledge*
am Eingang zum Bahnhof	*at the entrance to the station*
die Reaktion der Regierung auf diese Ereignisse	*the reaction of the government to these events*
Die Neuromantik war eine Reaktion gegen den Naturalismus	*Neo-Romanticism was a reaction to Naturalism*
Sie waren damit gemeint	*It was a reference to you*

iv phrases

Sie saßen sich gegenüber (or: Aug' in Auge)	*They sat face to face*
Der Saal war zum Bersten voll	*The hall was full to overflowing*
bis ans Ende der Welt	*to the ends of the earth*
Diese Entwicklung ist günstig	*This development is to the good*
rechts vom Haus	*to the right of the house*
in gleichem Maße	*to the same extent*
bis zu welchem Grade?	*to what extent?*

---

[1] cf. Corbett, op. cit., p. 215.

800 bis 900 Mark	*800 to 900 marks*
Wir haben zwei zu eins (2:1) über Österreich gesiegt	*We had a 2 to 1 win over Austria*

630. towards

Er kam auf mich zu	*He came towards me*
Er schaute nach mir herüber	*He gazed over towards me*
Ich sah nach der Tür	*I looked towards the door*
sich um-drehen nach	*to turn round towards* (or *after*)

631. (S) with

i with verbs

Ich kaufe nicht bei diesem Bäcker ein	*I don't **deal with** this baker*
Er weiß mit den Leuten umzugehen	*He knows how to deal with people*
Ich werde die Sache erledigen	*I'll deal with the matter*
Dieses Buch handelt von der Französischen Revolution (or: behandelt die Fr.R.)	*This book deals with the French Revolution*
Er hat an allem etwas auszusetzen	*He finds fault with everything*
Glück haben; Schwein haben (sl.)	*to get away with it*
Er ist mit einem Armbruch davongekommen	*He got off with a fractured arm*
Er hat eine gewisse Art	*He has a way with him*
Schritt halten mit	*to keep up with* (lit. and fig.)
Mit meinem Rheumatismus muß ich mich abfinden	*I've got to live with my rheumatism*
sich behelfen mit	*to make do with*
sich trennen von	*to part with*
Leg dieses Buch zu den andern	*Put this book with the others*
Mit dem Lärm mußt du dich abfinden	*You'll have to put up with the noise*
Ich kann ihn nicht mehr aushalten	*I can't put up with him any longer*
Er ist bei einem Freund zu Besuch	*He's staying with a friend*
wimmeln von	*to swarm with*
Ich nehme Zucker zum Tee	*I take sugar with my tea*

ii with adjectives and participles

Ich bin vom Tennisspielen müde	*I'm exhausted with playing tennis*
Ich stehe vor einer schwierigen Entscheidung	*I'm faced with a difficult decision*
Ich habe das Tennisspielen satt	*I'm fed up with playing tennis*
Er ist sehr von ihr eingenommen	*He is very much taken with her*

iii phrases

Es geht mir genauso	*It's the same with me*
mit jemandem in Verbindung stehen	*to be in touch with s.o.*

632. without

entbehren + acc.	*to do without*
fertig werden ohne (coll.)	
Ich mußte auf das Mittagessen verzichten	*I had to go without lunch*
Ich mußte ohne Mittagessen gehen (coll.)	

I. SELECTED WORDS USED WITH PREPOSITIONS

633. to be accustomed (used) to[1]

Distinguish:

i eine Sache/jemanden gewohnt sein

to be used to s.th. or s.o. through long habit or experience:

Ich bin diesen Kaffee/diesen Lehrer gewohnt.

Ich bin eine solche Behandlung nicht gewohnt.

Ich bin gewohnt, nach dem Mittagessen spazierenzugehen.

ii an eine Sache/an jemanden gewöhnt sein

to be (to have become) accustomed to s.th. or s.o. through conscious habituation:

Ich bin jetzt an diesen Kaffee/an diesen Lehrer gewöhnt.

Ich bin jetzt daran gewöhnt, weniger zu rauchen.

634. to interest/be interested in etc.

Er versucht, mich für moderne Musik zu interessieren.

Ich interessiere mich für Musik/für diesen Kühlschrank.

Sie ist auch an Musik interessiert.

Ich habe kein Interesse für Musik/an diesem Angebot.

Interesse nehmen an + dat.; Interesse zeigen für

Hat das Interesse an der Politik nachgelassen? (*FAZ*)

Hätten Sie Interesse (daran), dies zu kaufen?

Er ist an diesem Unternehmen beteiligt.

He has a (financial) interest in this enterprise.

635. to see to, look after

nach jemandem sehen	*to see to, attend to s.o.*
sich um eine Sache bekümmern	*to see to, attend to a matter* (often intermittently)
sorgen für (or: versorgen)	*to see to* (e.g. the household), *to look after* (e.g. children, old people)
Ich werde dafür sorgen, daß er kommt	*I'll see (to it) that he comes*
besorgen	1. *to see to* (e.g. the household, a task) 2. *to procure s.th. for s.o.* 3. *to buy* (coll.)
Ich habe alles besorgt	*I've seen to* (or *bought*) *everything*
erledigen	*to see to, deal with* (e.g. one's correspondence), *to settle* (a question)

636. 'werden' and 'werden zu'

(a) **werden + nom.** is used:

i before the names of professions and other types: Er wird Lehrer; er ist Katholik/Kommunist geworden; was will er werden?

---

[1] based on Du Haupt.: gewohnt/gewöhnt.

ii in two phrases: Sie wird Mutter *She is having a child*; sie wurden Freunde.

(b) **werden zu + dat.** denotes 'to change, turn, develop into':

Die Felder waren zu Seen geworden	*The fields had turned into lakes*
Es wurde zur Mode	*It became a fashion*
Das ist mir zur Gewohnheit geworden	*That's become a habit of mine*
Dieser Prozeß wurde zu einer Qual für ihn (V. Baum)	*This case became a torment for him*
Er wurde zum Verbrecher	*He became a criminal*

J. MISCELLANEOUS NOTES ON THE USE OF PREPOSITIONS

637. Miscellaneous points

i **Where two prepositions taking different cases are joined by 'und' or 'oder'**, the commonest usage is to put the noun or pronoun into the case required by the nearer preposition:

Kommen Sie nur, mit oder ohne Kinder! Menschen strömten in und aus dem Bahnhof.

ii **With co-ordinating conjunctional phrases, the preposition is generally repeated**:

Dieser Brief ist entweder für dich oder für deinen Vater

iii **As in English, a preposition may precede a prepositional phrase:**

außer am Donnerstag	*except on Thursday*
Diese Unterlagen sind für unter die Schüsseln	*These mats are for under the dishes*

iv **Where the force of a preposition is strengthened by a separable prefix**, it is important to remember that the preposition is the essential word:

Er kam in das Zimmer (herein)	*He came into the room*
Er ging über die Straße (hinüber)	*He crossed the road*
Er kam um die Ecke (herum)	*He came round the corner*

K. CONTRACTION OF PREPOSITION + DEFINITE ARTICLE

638. The following contractions of prep. + def. art. are usual unless the article is emphasized:

with 'den': hintern, übern, untern.
with 'das': ans, aufs, durchs, fürs, hinters, ins, übers, ums, unters, vors.
with 'dem': am, außerm, beim, hinterm, im, überm, unterm, vom, vorm, zum.
with 'der' (fem. dat.): zur.

Note:
i In some figurative and idiomatic uses of 'zu', 'zum' and 'zur' may be contractions of 'zu einem' and 'zu einer':
Er ist zum Lehrer geeignet; ich nehme mir ihn zum Muster; zur Abwechslung; zum Beispiel; zur Strafe; er wurde zum Verbrecher.

ii In time phrases and in most other prepositional formulae only the contracted form is used, e.g.

am Dienstag, am 10. Mai, im Frühling, zur Zeit.

Er läuft am schnellsten; ich nahm ihn beim Wort; sie war beim Kochen; im Freien; ins Freie; im Vertrauen; ein Jahrmarkt war im Gang *a fair was in progress*; zum Frühstück.

iii Where the noun is particularized, the uncontracted form is more usual:

an dem Nachmittag, an dem Sie anriefen	*on the afternoon when you rang up*
Er geht zu der Schule, wo sein Vater früher war	*He goes to the school where his father used to be*

iv Outside set phrases 1. the uncontracted form is more literary 2. the rhythm of the sentence will often determine the choice, e.g. Die Truppen marschierten durch das Tor. Dann ging ich durchs Tor.

In examining the first 200 pages of E. M. Remarque's novel *Drei Kameraden* and of Thomas Mann's *Doktor Faustus*, Witold Manczak found that before commonly used nouns the contracted form was by far the more frequently used; in Remarque the contracted form occurred in 83% of such cases, in Thomas Mann in 67%.[1]

v Where the article is strongly emphasized and is used as a demonstrative, the uncontracted form is essential:

Gerade an *dem* Nachmittag kann ich nicht kommen	*That's the one afternoon when I can't come*
Bei *dem* Radau kann ich nicht arbeiten	*I can't work with this row going on*

vi **Further contractions of prep. + def. art.** are purely colloquial (cf. Du. Gram. 1580), but many of them are very common in rapid speech:

an'n	for	an den	für'n	for	für den
auf'n	,,	auf den	gegen's	,,	gegen das
auf'm	,,	auf dem	in'n	,,	in den
aus'm	,,	aus dem	nach'm	,,	nach dem
bei'n	,,	bei den	vor'n	,,	vor den
durch'n	,,	durch den	zu'n	,,	zu den (dat. plur.)

Ich hab' das Buch auf'n Tisch gelegt. Nach'm Essen geh' ich in'n Garten.

vii **The indef. art. is similarly frequently slurred after prepositions in rapid speech,** e.g. Was hast du da für'n Bleistift? Wir kamen an'n Tor. Wir gingen zu'nem Fest.

---

[1] *Muttersprache* 1966: 5/6, pp. 144–8.

XIV INTERJECTIONS AND EXCLAMATIONS

639. A selection of interjections and exclamations expressing specific feelings and reactions

Au! Aua! Autsch!	*Ow! Ouch!* (pain)
Hu!	1. coldness 2. horror
Pfui! Pfui Teufel!	*Ugh!* (nausea, disgust)
Sch! Pss! Pst!	*Hush!*
Bràvo!	*Bravo! Well done!*
Verflucht (noch mal)!	*Confound it!*
Verflixt! Zum Kuckuck!	
Denk mal an! Ach! Ach was!	*Fancy! Would you believe it!*
Ach nein! Na, *so* was! Aber *so* was!	*Well I never!*
So? (drawn out, rising intonation)	*Really?*
Donnerwetter!	*By Jove!*
Sieh mal an!	*Well I never* (surprise + pleasure)
Ach, du lieber Himmel!	*Heavens above!* (dismay)
Oh, du liebe Zeit!	
(O) Jemine![1] Herr Jemine! Oje!	*Good gracious!*
Wie lästig!	*What a nuisance!*
(Es ist) *zu* dumm!	*It really is a nuisance*
Na ja!	*Ah well* (resignation)
Unsinn! Blödsinn! Quatsch!	*Nonsense! Rubbish!*
Ach was! (gruff intonation)	(see also 537(b)vii)
Aber natürlich! (Na,) freilich!	*Rather! I should think so!*
Gehst du gern auf Reisen?	*Do you like travelling?*
—(Na,) und ob![2]	*—Rather!*

640. Notes on occasional exclamations

(a) hailing, greeting and leave-taking

Hallo! He! Heda! *Hi!* Hör mal! Du! *I say!* Guten Tag! *Good day + Good afternoon* ('Guten' is frequently omitted or slurred: Tag! Morgen! N'Abend! Gun'—amd (*Zeit*))

(Auf) Wiedersehen! (Auf) Wiederschauen! On the phone: (Auf) Wiederhören!

---

[1] a distortion of Latin Jesu domine! (Du. Rechtschreibung).

[2] = Und du fragst, ob ich das gern tue! i.e. no need to ask.

(b) **at meals**

Nehmen Sie noch etwas?	*Will you have some more?*
—Ja, danke!	—*Thank you* (helping oneself)
—Ja, bitte! Bitte!	—*Thank you* (when being helped)
—Nein, danke! Danke! Danke, nein!	—*No thank you*

(c) **seasonable greetings**: Frohe Weihnachten und ein glückliches Neues Jahr! Prost Neujahr! Fröhliche Ostern/Pfingsten!

(d) **miscellaneous good wishes** (in which German is very prolific)

Herzlichste Glückwünsche zum Geburtstag!	*Best wishes for your birthday* (*Many happy returns*)
Zum Wohl! Zum Wohlsein! Prost! Prosit!	*Your good health! Cheers!* (raising one's glass)
(Gesegnete) Mahlzeit!	*I hope you enjoy/have enjoyed your meal*
Angenehme Ruh'!	*I hope you sleep well*
Gute Besserung!	*I hope you'll soon be better*
Viel Vergnügen!	*Have a good time*
Schönen Sonntag!	*Have a nice Sunday*
Meinen herzlichsten Glückwunsch!	*Congratulations!*
(Ich) gratuliere!	

641. Miscellaneous interjections and exclamations (arranged in alphabetical order of the English) (see also 297(a))

Schon! Is' gut (coll.)	*All right. Right you are*
Na gut!	*All right then* (*if that's what you think*)
Lassen Sie nur!	*Don't bother*
Bitte sehr! Gern geschehen!	*Don't mention it*
Gott behüte/bewahre! (I) bewahre!	*Heaven forbid! Certainly not! Nothing of the kind*
Na bitte!	*I beg your pardon* (protest)
Hast *du* 'ne Ahnung!	*If you knew!*
Laß mich in Ruh!	*Leave me alone*
Achtung!	*Look out!*
Klar!	*Obviously. Of course*
(Also) los!	*Off we go* (or: *Fire away*)
Ach *so*! Ahà!	*Oh, I see*
Basta![1] Und damit basta!	*Settled. Finished*
(O) Verzeihung!	*Sorry. I beg your pardon*
Es war beim Zahnarzt gar nicht so schlimm.—Na also!	*It wasn't so bad at the dentist's.—There you are.* (*What did I tell you?*)
Na also!	*What more do you want?* (as a rejoinder)
Tja! (from 'ja')	*Yes* (implying: *But what can one do about it?*)
Was Sie sagen!	*You don't say!*

[1] Italian: it is enough

XV WORD ORDER

A. THE THREE ORDER-TYPES OF GERMAN SENTENCES AND CLAUSES

I Normal Order

642. Normal order = subject + verb + (if any) complement, objects, adverbial limitations. It is used in the following cases:

(a) **in a main clause beginning with the subject:**
Mein Vater liest die Zeitung im Eßzimmer. Wer arbeitet im Garten?

(b) **in a series of main clauses, each beginning with the subject, expressed or understood:**
Mein Vater liest die Zeitung, meine Mutter strickt, (und) mein Bruder schreibt einen Brief. Er kam ins Zimmer, machte das Licht an und nahm ein Buch aus dem Schrank.

(c) **in a main clause beginning with one of the following** (These are followed by a comma or exclamation mark, are regarded as standing outside the sentence and therefore do not cause inversion; contrast 643(b)):

i interjections and exclamations:
Ach, es regnet schon wieder! Um Gottes willen! Ich hab' den Schlüssel vergessen. Auf Wiedersehen! Ich muß jetzt gehen.

ii ja and nein: Ja, du hast recht.

iii the name or other designation of the person addressed:
Karl, ich habe dein Buch gefunden. Lieber Freund, ich kann nichts dafür.

iv a number of parenthetical words and phrases:

also *well now, well then*	siehst du *d'you see*
das heißt (d.h.) *that is (i.e.)*	so *well now, well then*
im Gegenteil *on the contrary*	um es anders auszudrücken *to put it differently*
kurz, kurzum, kurz gesagt, kurz und gut *in short*	unter uns (gesagt) *between ourselves*
mit andern Worten *in other words*	weiß Gott *Heaven knows*
mit einem Wort *in a word*	wie gesagt *as I said*
nun, na *well*	wissen Sie *d'you know*

Also, wir wollen jetzt zu Mittag essen. Kurz und gut, die Lage ist kritisch. Wissen Sie, ich habe ihn noch nie getroffen.

v. a 'was' clause, limiting the main clause as a whole, but placed parenthetically in front of it:

Was so wichtig ist, das Buch verkauft sich gut	*What is so important, the book is selling well*

vi A few introductory words and phrases may be followed either by a comma and normal order, or by inversion without a comma; inversion is more usual; normal order gives greater edge to the statement. (Ultimately, the ear must help to decide whether an introductory word or phrase belongs here or to (c)iv above.) E.g.

allerdings *admittedly, to be sure*	jedoch *however*
erstens *firstly*	natürlich *of course*
(zweitens etc.) *(secondly etc.)*	offen gesagt *to be frank*
freilich *admittedly, to be sure*	übrigens *incidentally*
immerhin *nevertheless, for all that*	zum Beispiel *for example*

Er ist unzuverlässig; zum Beispiel kommt er immer spät zum Beispiel, er kommt immer spät	*He's unreliable; for example, he's always late*

Note:
1. When they take normal order, erstens, zweitens etc. are usually followed by a colon.
2. No comma after jedoch with either order.
3. doch *yet, nevertheless* may be followed by normal order (without a comma) or by inversion; see 290(a).

(d) **after one of the 6 simple co-ordinating conjunctions: und, oder, aber, allein, sondern, denn** (see 517). E.g. Er kann nicht kommen, denn er hat Grippe. But if the conjunction is followed by something other than the subject, this causes inversion of verb and subject: Er kann nicht kommen, denn seit gestern hat er Grippe.

(e) **in indirect statements and other noun clauses, if 'daß' is not used**; see 484(b). E.g. Er sagte, er sei krank. Ich glaubte, ich hätte ihn schon einmal gesehen.

(f) See 645(e) and (f)ii.

(g) For word order in two sentences joined by the co-ordinating conjunctional phrases (e.g. nicht nur . . ., sondern auch . . .) see 526.

II Inversion

643. Inversion of verb and subject is used in the following cases (see also 646):

(a) **in direct questions**, unless the subject is an interrog. pron. (wer, was) or begins with an interrog. adj. (welcher, was für ein), as in the last two examples:
Arbeitet er im Garten? Wann kommt er gewöhnlich nach Hause? BUT: Wer arbeitet im Garten? Was für ein Kleid steht ihr am besten?

Note: Colloquially, a plain sentence in normal order may be given an interrogative twist by suitable emphasis and intonation, e.g. Du glaubst es nicht? (cf. Erben op. cit., 272 N.3).

(b) **in a main clause beginning with something other than the subject or preceded by a sub. cl.** A wide range of items may in German stand at the beginning of the sentence, causing inversion:

1. an adverb: Gestern war ich im Theater.
2. a prep. phr.: Im Garten war er nicht zu finden.
3. the object: Seinen Bruder sehe ich selten.
4, 5. the complement: Ein guter Kerl ist er trotz alledem. Merkwürdig ist (es) nur, daß er es nie erwähnt hat.
6. a phrase referring to the subject: Optimistisch wie immer, kaufte er ein paar hundert Aktien.
7. an infin.: Anzeigen wird sie ihn (H. Fallada) *Report him to the police, that's what she'll do.*
8. an infin. phr.: Ihm Geld zu leihen, habe ich nie versprochen.
9, 10. past part. of a compound tense:
   Gesehen hab' ich ihn noch nie, nur von ihm gehört.
   Zurückgeblieben war überall ein zäher Schlick aus Schlamm und ausgelaufenem Heizöl (*a thick slime composed of mud and escaped fuel oil*) (*Zeit*, 18.11.1966: Florence after the floods).
11. part of an idiomatic phrase: Sehr leid hat es mir getan, daß . . .
12. an adv. cl.: Als er mich rief, übte ich Klavier.
13. an objectival noun cl.: Nur, daß er sich selbst nicht sehen konnte, bedauerte er (G. Hauptmann).

Note: A preceding sub. cl. may be the subject of the main verb, in which case the sentence, regarded as a whole, has normal order:

Daß er das Examen nicht bestanden   *That he hasn't passed the exam doesn't*
hat, erstaunt mich nicht   *surprise me*

644. Inversion has several functions (The numbers below refer to the examples in 643(b)):

It may be a completely normal and neutral way of beginning a sentence, as in 1 and 12.

It may give emphasis to the part of the sentence placed at the beginning (its commonest function), as in 5, 6, 7, 8, 9, 10, 11 and 13. (In English this emphasis will generally be achieved merely vocally.)

It may give emphasis to another part of the sentence, as in 4: trotz alledem.

It may be determined by contextual factors:
   i by what precedes, including the remark of another speaker (as in the 4th example below):
Wir suchten im Garten, aber im Garten . . . (see 2)
Ich sehe *ihn* oft; seinen Bruder sehe ich selten. (see 3)
Reinhard hatte hier . . . ein Haus aus Rasenstücken (*pieces of turf*) aufgeführt; darin wollten sie die Sommerabende wohnen (Th. Storm).[1]
Ich war drei Wochen auf Sylt.—Darum siehst du auch so gut aus.

   ii by what is to follow:
Das Geld gab er seinem Bruder, der dann die Rechnung bezahlte.

[1] quoted in an article on Word Order by N. P. Fomina in *Deutsch als Fremdsprache*, 6/1968.

645. Special points relevant to inversion

(a) **(S) If something other than the subject stands at the beginning of two or more main clauses**, normal usage is to have inversion only in the first clause (examples 1 and 2), unless the sense makes it essential (examples 3 and 4), or the speaker or writer desires (5), to emphasize the applicability of the opening word or phrase to all the main clauses:

1. Zu Hause schrieb Mutter Briefe, und Vater arbeitete im Garten.
2. Am Abend blieb ich zu Hause, (ich) spielte Klavier und ging früh zu Bett.
3. In diesem Hause bin ich aufgewachsen, haben wir die Kriegsjahre durchgemacht und ist meine Mutter gestorben.
4. Innerhalb von drei Tagen wurde sein Bruder überfahren und starb sein Onkel an einem Schlaganfall.
5. Bereitwillig . . . interpretierte er . . . die einzelnen Stellen seines Films, gab er Auskunft . . . und wich er allen Fragen aus (*Hbg. Abendblatt*).

(b) **When something other than the subject stands at the beginning of the second of two main clauses joined by und, oder, aber or sondern**, the second clause must have its own subject-word, to show the inversion. (Failure to observe this rule is a common error, due, no doubt, to its irrelevance in English.)

Ich schrieb ein paar Briefe, und dann ging ich zu Bett	*I wrote a few letters and then went to bed*

(c) **Mainly colloquially, the foregoing word that causes the inversion is sometimes omitted**, as in the following:

Du solltest früh zu Bett gehen	*You ought to go to bed early*
—[Das] Tu ich auch	*—But I do*
—[Das] Werd' ich auch	*—Yes, I shall*
[Da] Sagt mein Verteidiger: 'Kommen wir zur Sache!' (M. Frisch)	*Says my counsel: 'Let's come to the point'*

This frequently occurs in exclamations:

Ach, [wie] bin ich ungeschickt! (H. Fallada)	*Oh, how clumsy I am!*
[So] Hatte ich also doch recht!	*So I was right after all*
[Was] Ist *das* [für] ein Vergnügen![1]	*What a pleasure it is!* (e.g. to see you again)

(d) **A sentence does not normally start with two consecutive items other than the subject**, e.g. adverb, adverb phrase, adverb clause; the first item is immediately followed by the inversion of verb and subject:

Dann stand er plötzlich auf	*Then suddenly he got up*

Grubačić (op. cit. pp. 55 ff.) adduces numerous examples of exceptions to this, e.g. und gleich darauf, mit erregten Schwüngen, kam ein Reiher (*heron*) geflogen (H. Carossa). Recognized exceptions are: 1. two closely connected items (Um halb drei, kurz nach dem Mittagessen, hatte er einen Schlaganfall) and 2. the desire to produce exceptional emphasis (Dann, ganz plötzlich, stand er auf).

---

[1] 'was für ein' is divisible: cf. 175(e).

(e) **When words or phrases such as auch, nur, sogar** *even,* **wenigstens, allein** *only,* **nicht allein** *not only,* **nicht einmal** *not even* **stand at the beginning of the sentence and limit the subject, normal order is used:**

Auch der Bürgermeister war dagegen	*The Mayor too was against it*
Nicht einmal der Lehrer wußte die Antwort	*Not even the teacher knew the answer*

(f) **No inversion in the following cases:**
   i after one of the six simple co-ordinating conjunctions: see 642(d).
   ii after some types of concessive clause: see 470–74, especially 471(c)i.
   iii see 642(c), e.g. Ja,/Kurz und gut, die Lage ist kritisch.

646. Other instances of inversion

(a) with a verb of saying or asking placed after or within a quotation:
,,Mein Bruder", sagte er, ,,kann Ihnen helfen."
cf. Eine schöne Entschuldigung! dachte ich bei mir.

(b) the polite form of the imperative: Kommen Sie in den Garten!

(c) many forms of the optative subjunctive (see 476), e.g. Mögest du immer so denken! Hoffen wir das Beste! Hätte mein Vater doch dieses Haus nie gekauft!

(d) see also 298(e), 642(g), 647 N.vi 2.

III Verb to the end of Subordinate Clauses

647. The finite verb goes to the end in all subordinate clauses, apart from the exceptions listed in Note vi below.

Ich weiß, daß er krank ist (noun cl.)
Der Junge, der krank ist, ist mein Freund (rel. cl.)
Er bleibt zu Hause, weil er krank ist (adv. cl.)

Note:

i **Two subordinate clauses joined by und, oder, aber or sondern: verb to the end in both:**

Obwohl er fast nie ausgeht, sondern die ganze Zeit arbeitet, scheint es ihm gut zu bekommen	*Although he hardly ever goes out but works all the time, it seems to agree with him*

If the two clauses have compound tenses with the same auxiliary, the latter appears only once, at the end of the second clause:

Nachdem ich Tee getrunken und eine Weile gelesen hatte, machte ich einen Spaziergang	*After I had had tea and read for a while, I went for a walk*

If the second clause has its own subject, it is more usual to repeat the conjunction:

Wenn deine Familie dagegen ist oder wenn du keine Zeit hast, dann wollen wir den Plan fallenlassen	*If your family is against it or you have no time, we'll drop the plan*

ii One subordinate clause enclosed in another:[1] **verb to the end in both clauses.** (This is, of course, to be expected, but is often a source of error.)

Ich weiß, daß mein Vetter, der nach Kanada ausgewandert ist, viel Geld verdient	*I know that my cousin, who has emigrated to Canada, is making a lot of money*

iii The introductory conjunction of a subordinate clause is normally followed by the subject. (But see 655(b), 656(b) and 664 (c).)

Da ich morgen zu Hause sein werde, . . .	*As tomorrow I shall be at home, . . .*

The same applies to a relative pronoun which is not itself the subject:

Der Minister, den Sie so oft kritisiert haben, . . .	*The minister, whom so often you have criticized, . . .*

If the conjunction is followed by an adverb or adverb phrase, this does not cause inversion; the verb still goes to the end:

Wir hoffen, daß nächstes Jahr wieder viele Ausländer nach England kommen.

iv In exclamations, the finite verb usually goes to the end, though inversion is also common:

Wie *kalt* es heute ist!	*How cold it is today!*
Was für *komische* Bemerkungen er immer macht!	*What funny remarks he's always making!*
Wie der Chef darüber *geschimpft* hat!	*How the boss swore about it!*
Wie (coll.: Was) *hat* der Chef darüber geschimpft!	
Was *haben* wir dieses Jahr für Birnen!	*What lovely* (or: *awful*) *pears we've got this year!*

Inversion *must* be used when the exclamation is in the form of a rhetorical question (Wie konntest du nur so etwas tun!) and in the elliptical type: Ach, [wie] bin ich ungeschickt! (see 645(c)).

v See 642(g).

vi Exceptions (i.e. subordinate clauses with the verb not at the end):
1. indirect statements etc. without 'daß': normal order is used (see 642(e)).
2. alternative versions of conditional, 'as if' and 'even if' clauses (see 463, 466(a), 473(c)), e.g. Schreibe ich ihm heute, dann bekommt er den Brief morgen.
3. see 649 N.ii.
4. see 666 ff.: The Freer Word Order.

vii For **the use of the comma with subordinate clauses,** see 743(d).

B. POSITION OF SEPARABLE PREFIXES

648. For **the position of separable prefixes** see 369(c), and 666 ff.: The Freer Word Order.

---

[1] A noun clause is never enclosed in another subordinate clause: see 651(e).

One point may be added: a separable prefix may enclose or exclude a short infinitive phrase, but does not enclose a longer one:
Er fing an zu singen or Er fing zu singen an. Er fing an, mit Gefühl ein altes Volkslied zu singen.

C. POSITION OF PARTICIPLES AND INFINITIVES

649. **The past participles and infinitives of compound tenses go to the end, except in subordinate clauses, where the auxiliary, being the finite verb, comes last.** (See also 666 ff.: The Freer Word Order.)

Ich bin heute morgen in der Stadt gewesen	*I've been in town this morning*
Obwohl ich heute morgen in der Stadt gewesen bin, . . .	*Although I've been in town this morning, . . .*
Vielleicht wird er uns das Geld leihen	*Perhaps he will lend us the money*
Da er uns das Geld leihen wird, . . .	*As he will lend us the money, . . .*

Note:
i Where a sentence ends with both an infinitive and a past participle or with two infinitives, the item on which the other depends comes last:

Er hat mich schwimmen gelehrt	*He has taught me to swim*
Ich werde es ihm sagen müssen	*I shall have to tell him*

This obviously does not apply where a phrase with zu + infin. is not enclosed by the compound tense on which it depends (cf. 650(d) ii):

Ich habe meinem Sohn versprochen, mich darüber zu erkundigen	*I've promised my son to inquire about it*

ii There is one case in which the auxiliary does not go to the end of a subordinate clause, e.g.
Da er heute hat schwimmen dürfen, muß es ihm besser gehen (see 392).
Ich hob den Brief auf, den er hatte fallen lassen (see 421).

N.B. For the position of the participle in participial phrases, see 437.

650. **The position of dependent infinitives and infinitive phrases**[1]

(a) **An infinitive always stands at the end of its own phrase:**

Um den Vertrag zu unterzeichnen, mußte er nach Neuyork fliegen	*In order to sign the contract he had to fly to New York*
Seine Aufgabe, den Etat ins Gleichgewicht zu bringen, ist keine leichte	*His task of balancing the budget is not an easy one*

(b) **Where it depends on a verb in a simple tense and not in a subordinate clause, the infinitive goes to the end of the sentence:**
Ich muß das Buch so bald wie möglich finden.
Gestern versuchte ich, ihm bei seiner Arbeit zu helfen.

[1] See also 666 ff.: The Freer Word Order.

13+

(c) **A verb that takes a plain infinitive without 'zu'** encloses the
dependent infinitive phrase in the following cases:[1]
i where the verb is used in a compound tense:

Natürlich wirst du Tennis spielen dürfen	*Of course you'll be allowed to play tennis*
Ich hatte ihn gegen elf Uhr ins Haus kommen sehen	*I had seen him come into the house about eleven o'clock*

ii where the verb is used as a dependent infinitive:

Er schien die Sache nicht erwähnen zu wollen	*He seemed not to want to mention the matter*

iii where the verb is used in a subordinate clause:

Da er plötzlich nach Frankfurt fliegen mußte, ...	*As he suddenly had to fly to Frankfurt, ...*

(d) **A verb that takes zu + infinitive**
i when the verb is in a simple tense in a subordinate clause, it generally
encloses the dependent infinitive phrase, provided it is not too long:
Ich weiß, daß mein Bruder sein Geschäft zu verkaufen versucht.

Note: Where an infinitive has a relative pronoun as its object, it is generally enclosed in the rel. cl.: das Spiel, das wir kaum zu gewinnen
hofften (or gehofft hatten); das Liebesversprechen, das zurückzunehmen
er sich nicht traute (U. Johnson).

ii when the verb is used 1. in a compound tense or 2. as a dependent
infinitive, whether in a main clause or in a subordinate clause, it
generally excludes the dependent infinitive phrase:

1. Er hat versucht, sein Geschäft zu verkaufen	*He has tried to sell his business*
Ich weiß, daß er versucht hat, sein Geschäft zu verkaufen	*I know that he has tried to sell his business*
2. Er muß versuchen, sein Geschäft zu verkaufen	*He must try to sell his business*

Note:
1. A pseudo-impersonal expression (cf. 372(a)ii, 374, 375) used in a compound tense never encloses a dependent infinitive phrase:
Es wäre nötig gewesen, das zu tun; es wird mir gelingen, ihn zu finden; es hat
mir leid getan, das zu hören.

2. An infinitive phrase with a clause dependent on it is never enclosed:

Ich habe versucht zu erfahren, was geschehen ist	*I have tried to learn what happened*

(e) **um ... zu + infin., ohne ... zu + infin. and (an)statt ... zu +
infin. are not usually enclosed in a sentence or clause:**
Er hat große Opfer gebracht, um dir zu helfen. Da ich Zeitung gelesen habe,
anstatt zu arbeiten, ...

(f) See 648.

---

[1] The same applies to brauchen *to need*, even when used with zu + inf. (cf. 418).

D. FURTHER CASES OF ENCLOSING AND EXCLUDING PHRASES AND CLAUSES

651. The following further cases of enclosing and excluding should be noted:

(a) **Comparative phrases**

i The second element in a comparison ('than' or 'as') is not usually enclosed in a sentence or clause:

Gestern haben wir einen besseren Wein getrunken als diesen	*Yesterday we drank a better wine than this one*
Ich wußte, daß er ebenso ärgerlich war wie ich	*I knew that he was just as annoyed as I*

ii Comparative phrases beginning with 'wie', meaning 'like' or 'as': brief ones are enclosed, especially in sentences or clauses of any length:

da ... die Orangen und Zitronen von den Kindern wie Schneebälle über die Gartenmauern geworfen wurden (S. Andres).[1]

Otherwise, practice varies:

ein Mann, der aussah wie ein Italiener (or: der wie ein Italiener aussah); er hat mit mir gesprochen wie mit einem alten Freund.

(b) **A phrase beginning with 'als' meaning 'in the capacity of, by way of, as being'** is generally enclosed unless it is of some length:

Er hatte die Sache als Franzose beurteilt.

(c) **sondern and oder + object or phrase** may be enclosed or excluded, the latter being commoner; **oder nicht** is always excluded:

Ich habe nicht die „Frankfurter Allgemeine" bekommen, sondern die „Süddeutsche Zeitung".

Da wir uns nicht in Köln, sondern in Hamburg treffen, ...

Die Proben (*rehearsals*) fanden durchweg nachts statt oder an späten Nachmittagen (C. Zuckmayer).

Ich weiß nicht, ob es wichtig ist oder nicht.

(d) **außer** *except* **+ noun or pronoun** is generally excluded:

Ich habe alles gefunden außer dem Wörterbuch.

(e) **A noun clause** is never enclosed in:

a main cl.: Ich hatte vergessen, daß er hier wohnt.
    Er gab zu, daß er sich irrte.

a sub. cl.: Da ich wußte, daß er hier wohnt, ...

um/ohne/anstatt ... zu + infin.

Er hat angerufen, um mir zu sagen, wo er wohnt.

The same applies to the introductory word of a truncated noun clause, e.g. Er ist heute nach Hamburg gefahren; er hat mir nicht gesagt, warum [er nach Hamburg gefahren ist].

Exc. A noun cl. in apposition, e.g. Ich konnte den Gedanken, daß wir ihn hintergangen hatten (*that we had deceived him*), nicht loswerden.

[1] from Grubačić, op. cit., p. 78.

(f) **A relative clause** is frequently excluded if its antecedent comes near the end of its sentence or clause, e.g.

Und wie dürfte man eine Zeitung verbieten, die sich wiederholt so nachhaltig (*effectively*) für die Wahl der staatstragenden Partei (*the party in office*) eingesetzt hat? (*Spiegel*)
(Exclusions with early antecedents are also found, cf. Grubačić, op. cit., pp. 67 ff.)

(g) **Adverb clauses** may be enclosed if not too long, e.g.

. . . in dem . . . Sälchen, welches, sobald man die Fenster schloß, seinen Eigengeruch verströmte (*exuded its distinctive odour*) (E. Langgässer)

(h) See 504 N.iii.

E. THE POSITION AND ORDER OF COMPLEMENTS, OBJECTS AND ADVERBS

652. The position of complements, objects and adverbs: three introductory points:

(a) The items following the finite verb are normally arranged in order of increasing importance, passing from the known to the unknown, with the end of the sentence, as the climax, carrying the greatest emphasis.[1] Two instances of this pattern, which will be frequently referred to, may be given here:

i The complement, something essential, as its name implies, goes to the end: Er war zehn Jahre in Berlin Zeitungskorrespondent.

ii Pronouns, since they refer to persons or things already named, occupy an unemphatic position,[2] preceding adverbs, noun objects and even noun subjects:
Er hatte es mir sofort gegeben.
Er hat es seinem Vater gezeigt.
Gestern hat ihn mein Bruder gesehen.

(b) In the paragraphs that follow, frequent reference is made to changing the position of some element in the sentence in order to give it emphasis. It should be noted that in the spoken language emphasis through word order is strengthened, or rendered superfluous, by vocal stress, e.g. Ich habe den Pfirsich *ihr* versprochen, or: Ich habe *ihr* den Pfirsich versprochen.

(c) Wherever there is a reference to one of the above items (complements, objects and adverbs) coming at the end of the sentence, this implies 'or immediately before a closing past participle, infinitive, separable prefix or finite verb (in a subordinate clause)'.

653. The complement generally comes at the end of the sentence:

Er ist trotz all seiner Eigen- tümlichkeiten ein guter Kerl	*He's a good chap despite all his peculiarities*

[1] cf. Schulz-Griesbach, op. cit., H 702 f. and Du. Gram. 7065; but also see 666 ff. below: The Freer Word Order.
[2] cf. Du. Gram. 7065.

Er hat mich gestern abend im Beisein meiner Eltern einen Faulenzer genannt	*Yesterday evening he called me an idler in the presence of my parents*

Note: Two points relevant to this order rule:

i The majority of adjectives used with the dative normally follow the dative noun or pronoun dependent on them; for exceptions see 117 N.i; all adjectives used with the genitive except bar (see 118) follow the dependent noun.

Seine Entscheidung ist seinen Freunden unbegreiflich	*His decision is incomprehensible to his friends*
Er ist einer solchen Tat nicht fähig	*He is not capable of such a deed*

ii Most adjectives and adjectival participles used with prepositions can precede or follow the prepositional phrase when the preposition is followed by a noun, but precede the phrase when the preposition is followed by a personal pronoun, e.g.

Er ist ärgerlich über den neuen Lehrling.
Er ist über den neuen Lehrling ärgerlich.
Er ist ärgerlich über ihn.
Sei immer höflich zu deinen Vorgesetzten!
Sei zu deinen Vorgesetzten immer höflich!
Sei immer höflich zu ihnen!

The following almost always precede the prepositional phrase: arm an, böse auf/mit/über, dumm von, frech zu, gut zu, hart zu/mit/gegen, nett von/zu, (nicht) recht von, reich an, stolz auf, voll von/mit, e.g.

Das war sehr dumm von dir/von deinem Bruder
Er ist stolz auf dich/auf deinen Erfolg

654. The direct object (acc.) and the indirect object (dat.)

Note: The following rules apply to all verbs used with an accusative object and a dative object in German; in some of the examples it will be found that the English equivalent is differently compounded. See also 655(d).

(a) **something to someone** (the commonest type)

i Normal usage: the indirect object precedes the direct object unless the direct object is a personal pronoun:

Er gab seinem Vater den Brief	*He gave the letter to his father*
Er gab ihm den Brief	*He gave him the letter*
Er gab ihn seinem Vater	*He gave it to his father*
Er gab ihn ihm	*He gave it to him*
Ich habe meinem Freund das Haus abgekauft	*I have bought the house from my friend*
Ich habe es ihm abgekauft	*I have bought it from him*
Ich kann seinen Eltern ihre Enttäuschung nachfühlen	*I can feel for his parents in their disappointment*

ii Variants:

1. If the indirect object is to be emphasized, it can follow the direct object even if this is a noun:

Er hat sein ganzes Vermögen seinem Neffen vermacht	*He left his whole fortune to his nephew*

Ich habe diesen Pfirsich ihr versprochen	*I have promised this peach to her*

2. Colloquially, the dir. obj. 'es' may follow the pronominal indir. objects 'mir' and 'dir' in the truncated form 's:

Er hat mir's/dir's gezeigt	*He showed it to me/to you*

(b) someone to something

Here the dir. obj. precedes the indir. (except when the dir. obj. is a noun and the indir. obj. is a pronoun, which is in practice rare):

Sie überantworteten den Verbrecher der Justiz	*They delivered up the criminal to justice*

(c) someone to someone

If both are nouns, either order is possible, the more emphasized item coming last:

Er stellte seinen Neffen dem Pfarrer vor	*He introduced his nephew to the parson*
Er stellte dem Pfarrer seinen Neffen vor	*He introduced his nephew (not his son) to the parson*

If one of the two is a pronoun, it comes first:

Er stellte ihn dem Pfarrer vor	*He introduced him to the parson*
Er stellte ihm seinen Neffen vor	*He introduced his nephew to him*

If both are pronouns, the dir. obj. precedes the indir., unless the dir. obj. is to be emphasized (3rd example):

Er stellte ihn ihr vor	*He introduced him to her*
„Damit ich dich mir vorstellen kann— später—, wenn du fort bist" (V. Baum)	*'So that I can picture you (to myself)— later on—when you've gone'*
Ich nahm mir *ihn* zum Muster	*I took him as a model*

(d) (S) something to something

If both are nouns, the one that carries the natural emphasis comes last:

Er hat dem Experiment viel Zeit gewidmet	*He devoted much time to the experiment*
Er hat sein Glück seiner Karriere geopfert	*He has sacrificed his happiness to his career*
Er hat seiner Karriere sein ganzes Glück geopfert	BUT: *He has sacrificed his whole happiness to his career*

If one of the two is a pronoun, it comes first; if both are pronouns, the dir. obj. precedes the indirect.

655. Position of the object when it is a personal pronoun

(a) In normal order it usually follows the finite verb:

Mein Bruder hat ihn gestern in der Stadt gesehen	*My brother saw him in town yesterday*
Er hat mir oft davon erzählt	*He often told me about it*

(b) With inversion and in a subordinate clause, it usually precedes a noun subject (including jeder, jedermann, jemand, niemand), but must follow a pronoun subject:

Gestern hat ihn mein Bruder in der Stadt gesehen	*Yesterday my brother saw him in town*
Gestern hat er ihn in der Stadt gesehen	*Yesterday he saw him in town*

Da ihn jemand in der Stadt gesehen hatte, ...	*As someone had seen him in town,* ...
Er fragte, ob mir der Wein geschmeckt hätte	*He asked if I had enjoyed the wine*

Note: While the above is normal usage, it is neither wrong nor uncommon for a pronoun object to follow a noun subject with inversion or in a subordinate clause: Gestern hat mein Bruder ihn in der Stadt gesehen. Da mein Bruder ihn in der Stadt gesehen hatte, ... This order is usual if the pronoun object is 'sie' and the noun subject is fem., neut., or plur., as there could otherwise be uncertainty as to which is the subject and which is the object:

Gestern hat meine Mutter sie in der Stadt gesehen	*Yesterday my mother saw her in town*
Da das Mädchen sie in der Stadt gesehen hatte, ...	*As the girl had seen her in town,* ...
Da meine Brüder sie in der Stadt gesehen hatten, ...	*As my brothers had seen them in town,* ...

(c) **If the subject is etwas, nichts or a neuter collective such as alles, mehreres, viel, vieles,** with inversion and in a subordinate clause the pronoun object almost always precedes the subject, especially when the verb is in a simple tense. In the first three examples, the reverse order would be impossible:

Eben ist mir etwas eingefallen	*Something has just occurred to me*
Gewöhnlich stört mich nichts bei der Arbeit	*Usually nothing disturbs me at my work*
Er wußte, daß ihm nicht viel fehlte	*He knew that there wasn't much wrong with him*
Obwohl mich mehreres ohne Grund beunruhigt hatte, ...	*Although several things had worried me for no reason,* ...

(d) **With verbs taking a direct and an indirect object the following is the commonest usage:**

with inversion

dir. obj.: a pronoun; indir. obj.: a noun

Dann hat mein Bruder ihn (sie, es) meinem Vater gegeben	*Then my brother gave it to my father*

indir. obj.: a pronoun; dir. obj.: a noun

Dann hat ihm (mir, uns etc.) mein Bruder den Brief gegeben	*Then my brother gave him (me, us etc.) the letter*

both objects pronouns: both pronouns follow the noun subject:

Dann hat mein Bruder ihn (sie, es) mir (dir, uns etc.) gegeben	*Then my brother gave it to me (you, us etc.)*

Exc. i in a simple tense:

Schließlich gab sie mir mein Bruder	*Finally my brother gave them to me*

ii for phonetic reasons, 'ihn' is usually separated from 'ihm' or 'ihnen':

Dann hat ihn mein Bruder ihm/ihnen gegeben	*Then my brother gave it* (masc.) *to him/ to them*

in a subordinate clause: the pronoun object or objects generally follow the noun subject, though in a simple tense an indirect pronoun object tends to precede it (4th example):

Nachdem mein Bruder ihn [den Brief] meinem Vater gegeben hatte, ...
Nachdem mein Bruder ihm den Brief gegeben hatte, ...
Nachdem mein Bruder ihn ihm gegeben hatte, ...
Als ihm mein Bruder den Brief gab, ...

656. Position of the reflexive pronoun

(a) **In normal order it follows the finite verb**:

Der Deutsche beschwerte sich mit Recht über das Essen
The German rightly complained about the food

(b) **With inversion and in a subordinate clause it usually precedes a noun subject, but must follow a pronoun subject, incl. 'man':**

Gestern beschwerte sich der Deutsche über das Essen. Gestern beschwerte er sich über das Essen.

Obwohl sich der Deutsche über das Essen beschwert hatte, ... (less usual: Obwohl der Deutsche sich ... beschwert hatte).

Obwohl er sich über das Essen beschwert hatte, ...

Note: Where the refl. pron. follows the subject, it should follow it immediately, as in the above examples and e.g. Mein Vetter, der sich erst vor kurzem von einer schweren Krankheit erholt hatte, ...

(c) **If the subject is einer, etwas, jeder, jedermann, jemand, nichts, niemand or a neuter collective such as alles, mehreres, vieles,** with inversion and in a subordinate clause the reflexive pronoun almost always precedes the subject, especially when the verb is in a simple tense. In the first two examples the reverse order would be impossible:

Plötzlich bewegte sich etwas
Suddenly something moved

In seiner Lebensweise ändert sich nichts
Nothing changes in his mode of life

Oder vielleicht hatte sich einer geduckt (F. Fühmann)
or perhaps one of them had ducked down

Da sich alles verbessert, ...
As everything is improving, ...

Nachdem sich jemand beschwert hatte, ...
After someone had complained, ...

(d) **Note the order in the following sentences (reflexive verb + dative pronoun object):**

Inversion:

Jetzt näherte sich mir das Auto/ etwas/jemand
Now the car/something/someone was approaching me

Inzwischen hatte sich das Auto/etwas/jemand mir genähert.

Subordinate clause:

Ich beobachtete, wie sich das Auto mir näherte.
Ich merkte, daß sich das Auto mir genähert hatte.
Ich merkte, daß sich jemand mir näherte.
BUT: Ich merkte, daß sich mir etwas näherte.

(e) **In an infinitive phrase, the reflex. pron. comes first:**

Ich habe vor, mich bei dem Ober über das Essen zu beschweren
I intend complaining to the head waiter about the food

Ich versuche, mir deine Lage   *I am trying to imagine your situation*
  vorzustellen

657. nicht/nie and the object

(a) **Where it is merely the action denoted by the verb that is negatived, 'nicht' follows the object or objects:**

Er erwähnte seinen Zweck nicht   *He did not mention his purpose*
Er hat mir das Buch nicht gegeben   *He didn't give me the book*
Verkaufe die Bücher nicht!   *Don't sell the books*

(b) **Where two persons or things are explicitly contrasted** (not A but B), **'nicht' precedes the first of these**; if indirect objects are contrasted, they generally follow the direct object, as in the second example:

Er hat mir nicht das *Buch* gegeben,   *He did not give me the book but the*
  sondern die *Zeitschrift*   *periodical*
Er hat das Buch nicht *mir* gegeben,   *He did not give the book to me but to my*
  sondern meinem *Bruder*   *brother*

Alternatively, the element negatived may be placed at the beginning of the sentence, with 'nicht' preceding it (rhetorical) or coming later:

Nicht das *Buch* hat er mir gegeben, sondern die *Zeitschrift*.
Mir hat er das Buch *nicht* gegeben, sondern meinem *Bruder*

Where the contrast is implicit, the element negatived is generally placed at the beginning of the sentence:

Mir hat er das Buch *nicht* gegeben [sondern wahrscheinlich jemand anderem].

(c) **'not a' is rendered by 'kein'**, though 'nicht ein' is sometimes used before 'sondern':

Ich besitze keinen Atlas   *I don't possess an atlas*
Er hat nicht einen Roman   *He has not written a novel but a biography*
  geschrieben, sondern eine
  Biographie

(d) **nie *never* and the object**

i Where it negatives the action denoted by the verb, 'nie' follows a pronoun object, but may precede or follow a noun object, the former position being slightly more emphatic:

Ich habe ihn nie getroffen. Ich habe nie seinen Bruder getroffen, or: ich habe seinen Bruder nie getroffen.

ii The contrasting of two persons or things through 'nie' is illustrated by the following examples:

Er hat mir nie *Geld* geschenkt,   *He has never given me* money *but* books
  sondern *Bücher*
Geld hat er mir nie geschenkt, sondern
  Bücher
Mir hat er nie Geld geschenkt, aber   *He has never given money to* me *but to my*
  meinem *Bruder*   brother

Note: Regarding the use of 'sondern' and 'aber' in the above examples, see 519. The last example implies 'aber meinem Bruder hat er oft Geld geschenkt'; his stinginess towards one brother does not exclude generosity towards the other.

13*

    iii If 'nie' itself is to be emphasized, it is placed at the beginning of the sentence.

(e) **Where 'nicht' is used not in its negative sense, but in seeking confirmation or to make a question sound more polite and tentative:**[1]
    it precedes a noun object:

Hast du nicht die Königin gesehen?	*Didn't you see the Queen?*

    it may precede or follow a noun subject:[2]

War nicht dein Vater eigentlich etwas enttäuscht? (or: War dein Vater nicht . . .)	*Wasn't your father really a bit disappointed?*

    it follows a pronoun subject or object:

Sah er nicht ein bißchen blaß aus?	*Didn't he look a bit pale?*

    'not a' is here better rendered by 'nicht ein' than by 'kein':

Könnte ich nicht ein Zimmer für mich haben?	*Couldn't I have a room to myself?*

(f) for **'nicht' and the object in 'unless' clauses** (wenn . . . nicht), see 465 N.

658. The order of adverbs and adverbial phrases

(a) The traditional rule is that adverbial items are arranged in the order: time, reason, manner, place, as in the sentences:
1. Sie sind gestern wegen des schlechten Wetters zu Hause geblieben.
2. Er ist am 1. Mai hoffnungsvoll nach Bonn gefahren.

But what of the following perfectly normal sentences?
3. Der junge Tenor hat in Berlin gut gesungen.
                     (place before manner)
4. Ich arbeite im Büro bis um 18 Uhr.
                (place before time)

(b) To understand the apparent discrepancy between the two pairs of sentences it is essential to distinguish between two functionally different types of adverb and adverb phrase, which we may call adverbial complements and adverbial limitations respectively.[3]

    Adverbial complements are adverbs and adverb phrases which are essential to complete the sense of the verb, with which they form a unit. They therefore come last in the sentence or immediately before a closing past participle, infinitive, separable prefix or finite verb (in a subordinate clause) and are always stressed.

    Adverbial limitations, on the other hand, while they may be important to convey precisely what the speaker or writer has to say, do not have that same close link with the verb, that same essential character.

---

[1] cf. Collinson, op. cit., pp. 114 f.
[2] cf. Erben, op. cit., 162.
[3] I owe this important distinction, usefully high-lighted by Colin H. Good in *Deutschunterricht für Ausländer* 6/1967, pp. 161 ff., to Schulz-Griesbach, op. cit., H 415, K 050 and p. 409, and to Du. Gram. 5255 ff. and 5650. 'Adverbial complements' corresponds to Schulz-Griesbach's 'Prädikatsergänzungen' and Duden's 'Umstandsergänzungen'; 'adverbial limitations' to the former's 'freie Angaben' and the latter's 'freie Umstandsangaben'.

In the first two of our initial examples, 'Sie sind ... geblieben' and 'Er ist ... gefahren' are meaningless without 'zu Hause' and 'nach Bonn'; the verbs have meaning only when we know where they stayed and whither he journeyed. (It would, of course, be possible for the context to have made clear that Bonn was his objective, in which case 'Er ist am 1. Mai hoffnungsvoll gefahren' would mean 'On 1 May he hopefully set out'.)

But the 3rd and 4th of the initial examples convey something even without any of the adverbs and adverb phrases: Der junge Tenor hat gesungen. Ich arbeite. Two adverbial limitations give precision to each statement. In the third, the important thing is to know how the young tenor acquitted himself and so, without acquiring exceptional emphasis, 'gut' comes last. In the fourth, the person addressed probably already knows that the speaker works in an office, so that 'im Büro' is unimportant, almost superfluous; what the speaker wishes to impart is the length of his working day and so 'bis um 18 Uhr' comes last.

As indicated, the order in the 3rd and 4th examples is determined by the context. This is frequently the case, as for instance in the following quotation from Storm's *Immensee*, where 'hier' is brought closer to 'Wiese': und dann liefen beide Kinder ... hinaus auf die Wiese ... Reinhard hatte hier mit Elisabeths Hilfe ein Haus aus Rasenstücken aufgeführt.

(c) **Further examples of adverbial complements**:

Causal: Der Brand entstand neulich in der Fabrik durch Unvorsichtigkeit.[1]

Temporal: Die Konferenz dauerte leider ganze fünf Stunden.

Set Phrase: So etwas würde in England nicht in Frage kommen.

Verbal Construction: Ich werde mich in Frankreich auf deine Sprach-kenntnisse verlassen. Ich habe ihn gestern im Büro an sein Versprechen erinnert.

N.B. In practice, 'time, reason, manner, place' remains a serviceable guide, especially for adverbial limitations and as regards the end-position of place. But, as has now been shown, it is not 'a rule', deviations from which are 'exceptions'.

(d) Of **two or more time adverbs or phrases**, the more general precedes the more specific, unless the former is to be emphasized: Ich reise jedes Jahr im Juli in die Schweiz. Er kommt morgen um sieben Uhr an.

(e) For **the position of gern, lieber, am liebsten**, see 281.

659. The position of 'nicht' among adverbs

Its neutral position, where it applies to the statement as a whole, is before an adverb of manner or, failing this, of place:

Ich bin gestern nicht mit meinem Bruder in die Stadt gegangen.

[1] from Schulz-Griesbach, op. cit., H 729.

Other possible positions:

i If 'gestern' is to be negatived, 'nicht' will immediately precede it.

ii If 'mit meinem Bruder' is to be negatived, there are three possibilities:

   1. commonest: 'nicht mit meinem Bruder' can be placed before 'gestern'.

   2. rhetorical: 'nicht mit meinem Bruder' can be placed at the beginning of the sentence, followed by inversion.

   3. 'mit meinem Bruder' can be placed at the beginning, 'nicht' being left where it is and stressed.

iii If 'in die Stadt' is to be negatived, it should be placed at the beginning, with 'nicht' (stressed) either remaining where it is or placed before 'gegangen'.

If, however, the sentence were followed by 'sondern ins Gebirge', it would run: Ich bin gestern mit meinem Bruder nicht in die Stadt gegangen, sondern ins Gebirge.

Note: 'nicht' never precedes the adverbs hoffentlich, glücklicherweise, unglücklicherweise and leider.

660. The position of 'nie' among adverbs

i Its neutral position is the same as that of nicht (see 659), e.g.

Ich bin diesen Sommer wegen des Wetters nie mit meinem Bruder ins Gebirge gegangen	*I've never been into the mountains with my brother this summer because of the weather*

ii If 'nie' is to be emphasized, it is placed at the beginning of the sentence.

iii If some other element in the sentence is to be particularly negatived, it should be placed at the beginning and stressed, 'nie' being left where it is and also stressed, e.g.

Ins Gebirge bin ich diesen Sommer *nie* mit meinem Bruder gegangen.

661. Emphasizing particular adverbs or adverb phrases: where something other than the natural emphasis is desired, this may be achieved in two ways:

1. By placing the adverb to be emphasized at the beginning of the sentence, followed by inversion (cf. 643(b)):

Hoffnungsvoll ist er am ersten Mai nach Bonn gefahren.
In Berlin hat der junge Tenor gut gesungen, aber nicht in Hamburg.
Durch Unvorsichtigkeit entstand der Brand neulich in der Fabrik.

2. By a change in the natural word order:

Er ist hoffnungsvoll am ersten Mai nach Bonn gefahren.
Der junge Tenor hat gut in Berlin gesungen, aber nicht in Hamburg.
Er hatte oft über seine Zukunft konzentriert nachgedacht.

662. In normal order, an adverb, adverbial phrase or adverb clause cannot in general come between subject and verb

Er kommt oft	*He often comes*

EXCEPTIONS:

i aber, jedoch, indessen (all in the sense of 'however') and dagegen *on the other hand,* used unstressed to emphasize the subject: Die Kinder aber gingen zu Bett.

ii occasionally, an adverb clause that is closely bound up with the subject. (This should not be lightly imitated.)

Mein Freund, obwohl er nicht faul ist, arbeitet nie abends	*My friend, though he isn't lazy, never works in the evenings*

663. The order of objects and adverbs

(a) **Pronoun objects normally precede all adverbs and adverb phrases**: Ich habe ihn gestern im Theater gesehen. Er hatte es mir heimlich gegeben.

Pronouns other than 'es' can be emphasized by placing them at the beginning of the sentence, followed by inversion; 'es' must be changed to 'das' if used thus.

(b) **Adverbs and noun objects**

i Where the adverb or adverb phrase is an adverbial complement, it comes last (cf. 658(b)):

Er hat die Maschine in Gang gebracht	*He got the machine going*
Er lernt viele Gedichte auswendig	*He learns many poems by heart*

ii Where the object is analogous to an adverbial complement, being essential to complete the sense of the verb, it comes last:

Ich spiele oft mit meinem Vetter im Club Tennis.
Er hat gestern in Berlin eine Rede gehalten.
um im nächsten Dorf Hilfe zu suchen.

Such objects may be felt as the equivalent of a separable prefix. They are always stressed and are not difficult to determine. Further instances are:

Deutsch sprechen, Wurzel fassen *to take root*, (keine) Zeit haben, Briefe schreiben, den Führerschein machen *to pass one's driving test*, die Macht ergreifen *to seize power*, die Stirn runzeln *to frown*, jemandem einen Stoß geben *to give s.o. a push*

iii Apart from the cases dealt with in i and ii, the item which has the natural emphasis follows the other:

Er fand unerwartet in einer der Schubladen ein Testament	*Unexpectedly he found a will in one of the drawers*
Er hat schnell ein Pfund Äpfel gekauft	*He quickly bought a pound of apples*
Er fand das Testament unerwartet in einer der Schubladen	*He found the will unexpectedly in one of the drawers*
Er hat den Film warm empfohlen	*He warmly recommended the film*

iv A time adverb precedes a noun object without causing the latter to be emphasized:

Ich habe gestern die ganze Sache erledigt	*I settled the whole matter yesterday*

Where the noun object is to be emphasized it is placed at the start.

F. THE POSTPONED SUBJECT

664. The subject, other than a personal pronoun, is sometimes postponed with inversion and in subordinate clauses

(a) Where there is inversion of verb and subject, the latter may be emphasized by being given the end position:

Nun begrüßte den Dirigenten (*conductor*) und den Virtuosen lautes Händeklatschen (G. Kapp).

Zwei Tage, darauf wurde gegen die Streikenden Militär eingesetzt (B. Brecht).[1]

Sometimes the postponement of the subject gives an easier rhythm to the sentence: Gestern hat mich den ganzen Tag niemand gestört.

In the following sentence from a letter from a German teacher 'die Klassenhefte' is slightly emphasized and is brought immediately before its relative clause:

Außerdem stapeln sich (*are piling up*) einmal wieder die Klassenhefte, die alle noch korrigiert werden müssen.

(b) In the case of verbs denoting to happen, this postponement of the subject is almost the norm; the colourlessness of the verb gives the subject an added importance:[2]

Gestern ereignete sich um 5.30 Uhr am Stadtrand ein Verkehrsunfall.

(c) Though less frequently,[3] the subject is sometimes similarly postponed in a subordinate clause for reasons of rhythm and/or emphasis:

Wir hoffen, daß nächstes Jahr wieder viele Ausländer nach England kommen.

Er erwähnte, daß morgen zugunsten der Armen in der Stadthalle ein Konzert stattfindet.

G. THE ORDER AND POSITION OF ADJECTIVES

665. The following points should be noted regarding the order and position of adjectives:

(a) Several adjectives are normally arranged in the same order as in English:

eine arme, heimatlose alte Frau	*a poor homeless old woman*
ein großes, braunes Paket	*a large brown parcel*

(b) Attributive adjectives normally precede their noun, but if there is more than one they may follow it, as in English, with a somewhat literary effect; see 86, second example.

(c) Adjectives are sometimes separated from their noun, the effect being to emphasize both the noun and the adjective; this construction, which

---

[1] from Grubačić, op. cit., p. 59.

[2] This is well noted by Schulz-Griesbach (op. cit. H 475), two of whose examples I have used in (b) and (c).

[3] Grubačić, op. cit., p. 61, came upon 274 instances of the postponed subject after inversion and 24 in subordinate clauses.

is not particularly to be recommended, is commonest with adjectives indicating number or quantity:

Menschen sind um diese Zeit *wenige* unterwegs (G. Gaiser)	*There are few people about at this time*
Fehler habe ich in seiner Arbeit *mehrere/keine* gefunden	*I found several/no mistakes in his work*
Beweise hat er äußerst *triftige* vorgebracht (from Du. Gram.)	*The evidence that he produced was extremely cogent*
cf. Er hat Geld/Bücher die Menge (coll.)	*He's got lots of money/books*

(d) See also 173(c) and 653 N. i and ii.

H. THE FREER WORD ORDER

666. The phrase **'the freer word order'** is from *Modern German Usage* (1937) by W. Witte, who there notes and illustrates (pp. 12 ff.) the declining authority, in modern German prose, of the rule by which the past participles of compound tenses, infinitives and separable prefixes stand at the end of the sentence and subordinate clauses end with the verb. The same phenomenon is the subject of E. Grubačić's 'Untersuchungen' (see Bibliography) and, concerning separable prefixes only, of an article by Rainer Rath: Trennbare Verben und Ausklammerung (*Wirkendes Wort*, 1/1965).

667. We may first illustrate each of the **four types of freer word order** named above:

Part of sentence placed after a past participle

1. Vieles hatte Glum schon gesehen auf seinem Weg von seiner Heimat bis über den Rhein hinweg (H. Böll).
2. B. hätte das [=his taxi-driver's interest] merken können an den gelegentlichen Rückblicken und dem Arm, der entspannt auf der freien Vorderlehne lag (U. Johnson).

Part of sentence placed after an infinitive

3. Seitdem Rodrigue seine Chronik begonnen hatte, freute er sich darauf, sie zu beschließen mit der Darstellung der Regierung dieses seines lieben Schülers und Beichtkindes (*confessant*) (L. Feuchtwanger).[1]

Part of sentence placed after a separable prefix

4. Die Kunst des herrschenden Geschmacks im vergangenen Jahrhundert ist zwar verschwunden, ihr Einfluß dauert jedoch fort in der Gefühlsstruktur (*the emotional make-up*) des Publikums, der großen und der kleinen Diktatoren, der demokratischen Politiker und Regierungsleute.[2]
5. „Du hebst das [ein Bonbon] auf bis nach dem Abendessen", erklärte das Fräulein. (V. Baum). '*You will keep that (sweet) till after supper*', *declared the governess.*

---

[1] from Grubačić, op. cit., p. 15.
[2] from Rath, loc. cit., p. 223.

Part of sentence placed outside a subordinate clause

6. . . . und ihm bewies, daß Ulla doch recht zu haben <u>schien</u> mit ihrem
   Pessimismus (I. Wendt).

668. It will be noted that in all the above examples what is excluded from
the framework of the sentence is one or more **prepositional phrases**,
and these **constitute by far the commonest type of 'Ausklammerung' or exclusion.**

In the first four examples the exclusion is explained by the length of what
is excluded: in 1, three interdependent phrases; in 2, two linked prepositional phrases, the second extended by a relative clause; in 3 and 4, a
single prepositional phrase elaborated by genitives, which, in the case
of 4, would threaten to split the seams of the sentence if the light-weight
prefix 'fort' were placed last.[1]

If in these four examples the function of the exclusion is to give the sentence a more relaxed rhythm and to ease comprehension, in 5 the effect
is to give emphasis to the part excluded (bis nach dem Abendessen), in
6 to emphasize what precedes the exclusion (recht zu haben schien).

669. Two sentences from letters received from Germany may serve to show
that **'Ausklammerung' is not a purely literary phenomenon**:
1. Am 28.10.68 ist X. gestorben an einem Schlaganfall. 2. Ich freue
mich, daß alles gut klappte auf Deiner Reise (*that your journey went off all
right*).

670. Some statistics and conclusions

In the 52 works by 26 authors which he examined, Grubačić noted 1587
instances of exclusion, of which 1401 were prepositional phrases, while
Rath found exclusions after a quarter of 552 sentences with separable
prefixes—the longer the sentences, the more frequent were the exclusions.

In an examination of 25 consecutive pages by each of seven modern writers,
the author came upon 54 instances of freer word order; of these 25
occurred in narrative and description, 29 in dialogue and thought-
stream; over half the exclusions were from subordinate clauses; in 14
cases the placing was due to the length of the prepositional phrase
excluded or to the fact that there were two phrases.

Both Grubačić and Rath conclude that exclusions can no longer be regarded as exceptions, but rather as an alternative type of syntactical
structure.

Grubačić sees a tendency for the emphatic position in the German sentence to move, with the help of exclusions, from the end to the middle,
giving 'die neue Satzmelodie' a relaxed and natural quality: 'Man
schreibt gesprochenes Deutsch.' This he illustrates from Thomas Mann,
who, instead of writing 'Raoul Überbein war in der Residenz nicht
beliebt', wrote: 'Raoul Überbein war nicht <u>beliebt</u> in der Residenz.'

---

[1] cf. Rath, loc. cit., pp. 222f.

To put the matter in perspective: the frequent occurrence of the freer word order means that a number of 'rules' given earlier, while they retain their general validity, are by no means absolute. The paragraphs to which this modification specifically applies are 369(c) (on the position of separable prefixes), 647 (on the position of the finite verb in subordinate clauses), 649 f. (on the position of participles and infinitives) and 652.

XVI AGREEMENT

A. AGREEMENT IN NUMBER AND PERSON

671. (a) Where the complement precedes and the subject follows the verb, the verb still agrees in number with the subject:

Mein Lieblingsobst sind Kirschen   *My favourite fruit is cherries*

(b) When das, dies, es (as a demonstrative) and welches (as an interrog. pron.) are used with the verb sein, the latter agrees with the real subject: Das sind meine Brüder. Sind es deine Bücher? Welches sind deine Bücher?

(c) After a subject consisting of different grammatical persons, the verb form is determined as in English:

Du und ich (= wir) gehen heute aus   *You and I (= we) are going out today*
Du und deine Brüder (= ihr) habt   *You and your brothers (= you) have*
mich enttäuscht   *disappointed me*

(d) For the agreement of the verb, in number and person, after sowohl . . . als auch, nicht nur . . . , sondern auch, entweder . . . oder, weder . . noch, ob . . . oder (ob) etc., see 524 f.

(e) Where the finite verb precedes two or more singular subjects, it is often used in the singular, e.g. Links war der Fluß, die Brücke und die Burg.

(f) Where the writer feels two singular subjects as forming a unity, the verb may be in the singular:

Diese Haltung und Miene war ihm   *This posture and look were peculiar to him*
eigentümlich (Th. Mann)

(g) When a singular word of quantity, e.g. eine Anzahl, ein Dutzend, die Hälfte, ein Haufen, eine Herde, die Mehrheit, eine Menge, ein Paar *a pair*, eine Schar, is followed by a plural noun, German usage prefers a singular verb, though a plural verb is sometimes found:

Eine Gruppe von Studenten sprach aufgeregt; die Hälfte der Äpfel war schlecht; eine Schar Kinder kam um die Ecke; es war/waren eine Menge Leute da.

Note: In contrast with occasional English practice, die Familie, die

Polizei, die Regierung and similar collectives always take a singular verb:

Seine Familie weiß davon   *His family knows/know about it*

B. AGREEMENT IN GENDER[1]

672. (a) Doktor and Professor used of women

Sie ist Doktor der Philosophie; Frau (Professor) Doktor Meyer.
BUT: Sie ist Doktòrin (=Ärztin); sie ist Professòrin (or Professor) (an der Universität Köln).

(b) Neuter diminutives referring to persons

i das Fräulein *young lady*, das Mädchen, das Töchterchen, das Söhnchen etc. are often referred to as 'sie' (possess. 'ihr') and 'er', especially when 1. das Mädchen is not a little girl 2. the personal pron. is some way from the neut. diminutive 3. a fresh speaker replies to a question.

E.g. Das junge Mädchen da ist gestern abend angekommen; sie ist sehr liebenswürdig.

BUT: Dann wurde das kleine Mädchen geboren und füllte die stillen Wände mit seinem Geschrei (P. Ernst).

Was tut Ihr Söhnchen?—Er (or Es) spielt im Garten.

Note:
1. The relative pron. referring to these words must be 'das' or 'welches'.
2. 'das Kind' is referred to as 'es'.

ii Fräulein Müller (=Miss Müller) is treated as feminine except when preceded by an article and at the beginning of a letter. Thus: Fräulein Müller, die schon fort ist, hat ihren Schirm vergessen. Das junge Fräulein Müller, das schon fort ist, hat seinen Schirm vergessen. Liebes Fräulein Müller! (BUT: Grüßen Sie Ihre Fräulein Schwester!)

Note: Many unmarried women, especially professional women no longer young, officially call themselves 'Frau' and not 'Fräulein'.

iii **Proper names**: Before those in -el, def. art. and adj. are masc. or fem.: Lieber Hansel! die fleißige Liesel; before other endings they are neut.: Liebes Peterle! das fleißige Mariechen (cf. Du. Gram. 6945).

All are referred to as 'er' and 'sie' (with fem. possessive 'ihr'), except where the name has been preceded by 'das' (cf. 84(e)iii): Mariechen konnte nicht schlafen; sie dachte an ihre kranke Mutter, BUT: Das Mariechen konnte nicht schlafen; es dachte an seine kranke Mutter.

[1] see also 141.

C. MISCELLANEOUS AGREEMENT POINTS

673. Zwanzig Mark ist zu viel — *Twenty marks is too much*

Zwei Kilo Fleisch werden nicht genug sein — *Two kilograms of meat won't be enough*

vier und fünf ist neun — *four and five are nine*

Alle drehten den Kopf — *They all turned their heads*

Wir nahmen den Hut ab — *We took off our hats*

Viele haben ihr Leben dabei verloren — *Many lost their lives through it*

das Haus und der Garten — *the house and garden*

mein Onkel und meine Tante — *my uncle and aunt*

Lieber Herr Müller! Liebe Frau Müller! — *Dear Mr. and Mrs. Müller (letter)*

Warst du es, der es getan hat? — *Was it you who did it?*
(see 184 N.)

XVII WORD FORMATION[1]

A. INTRODUCTORY:
FOUR METHODS OF WORD FORMATION

674. German words are formed from simple root-words in four different ways:

(a) by means of Ablaut (vowel changes)[2] or Umlaut (modification): werfen–warf–geworfen *to throw*: der Wurf *the throw*. scharf: schärfen *to sharpen*.

(b) by means of prefixes: siegen, besiegen; der Busch, das Gebüsch.

(c) by means of suffixes (sometimes with Umlaut): bunt, die Buntheit; der Tod, tödlich.

(d) by forming compound words, with or without a linking letter or syllable: der Bauernhof, hellblau.

Note:

i The word **productive** is used to indicate that new words are still being produced by the type of word-formation in question.

ii Considerations of space have necessitated restricting examples in most parts of this chapter to a bare minimum.

B. THE FORMATION OF VERBS OTHERWISE THAN BY A PREFIX

675. The most fruitful type of verb-formation is by means of a prefix (treated in 676–712); **three other types may be usefully mentioned:**

(a) **Factitive or causative verbs**

i The main type is a weak verb formed from the imperfect of an intr. strong verb by means of Umlaut, with ä often appearing as e: ertrinken *to drown* (intr.), ertrank: ertränken *to drown* (tr.); springen *to jump*, sprang: sprengen *to blow up, burst open*.

---

[1] At various points of this chapter I am indebted to articles by Wolfgang Fleischer in *Deutsch als Fremdsprache* 3, 4/1965 and 1/1967 and to his *Wortbildung der deutschen Gegenwartssprache* (see Bibliography), from which some of my examples are taken; a few others come from Wahrig, op. cit.

[2] More precisely, Ablaut is a vowel change, showing certain regularities, in the root syllable (Stammsilbe) of etymologically related words (Du. Gram. p. 759).

ii Deviations from the main type include fallen *to fall*, fiel: fällen *to fell*; hängen *to hang*, hing: hängen (wk.) *to hang up*.

(b) **A number of verbs in -eln**, with Umlaut, denote a weakened form of an action: husten, hüsteln; lachen, lächeln; others are mildly pejorative (productive): frömmeln *to affect piety*.

(c) **Foreign verbs naturalized with the suffix -ieren** (productive)
   i These exist in vast quantities; stylistically, their excessive use is to be frowned upon. E.g. arrangieren, eskalieren, produzieren, trainieren.
   ii Many verbs with the suffix -isieren are factitives, e.g. amerikanisieren, motorisieren, standardisieren.
   iii Verbs in -ifizieren include exemplifizieren, identifizieren, klassi-fizieren.
   iv A few verbs with German stems are also formed with -ieren, e.g. buchstabieren *to spell*, halbieren *to halve*, stolzieren *to strut*.
   v A warning: some verbs in -ieren do not, or do not only, mean what they might appear to mean, e.g. absolvieren, sich blamieren, kombinieren, kontrollieren, phantasieren, raffinieren, referieren (über), reflektieren auf, sich rentieren, sich revanchieren, spendieren, taxieren. E.g.

kontrollieren 1. *to check, inspect* (e.g. brakes, passport) 2. *to control*
raffiniert 1. *refined* (e.g. sugar, oil) 2. *exaggerated* (luxury)
      3. *sly, subtle* (e.g. swindler, question)

C. VERBS FORMED BY MEANS OF AN INSEPARABLE PREFIX[1]

676. Verbs are formed from nouns, adjectives and verbs by means of an insep. prefix; some knowledge of the main effects and functions of these prefixes is particularly useful for comprehension.

677. be-

Note: with few exceptions, verbs with be- are transitive.
(a) it makes intransitive verbs transitive: steigen *to go up, rise*: besteigen *to climb* (a mountain).
(b) it directs an action to a different object (productive): eine Mahlzeit kochen: eine Wandergruppe bekochen (*to feed*).
(c) it forms verbs from nouns, generally denoting 'to furnish with' (productive): der Reifen *tyre*: ein Auto bereifen.
(d) it forms mainly factitive verbs from adjectives: befreien.

678. ent-

(a) it denotes origin or beginning: entstehen (s) *to come into being, begin, arise* (of e.g. a law, a political party, a dispute), entwerfen *to draw up* (a plan), *to draft* (a letter).
(b) it forms opposites: entehren *to dishonour*, (sich) entspannen *to relax*.
(c) it denotes 'to deprive of' or 'to free from' (productive): enteisen *to de-ice* (a plane), enterben *to disinherit*.

---

[1] For the general characteristics of insep. prefixes, see 368.

(d) it denotes removal and separation: entgleisen (s) *to leave the rails*, jemandem etwas entreißen *to snatch s.th. away from s.o.*

(e) it gives the meaning 'to escape' to various verbs of motion: see 492.

Note: Through assimilation, ent- appears as **emp-** in empfangen *to receive*, empfehlen *to recommend*, empfinden *to feel*.

679. er-

(a) it denotes achievement (einen Erfolg, eine Wirkung erzielen) and, as a distinctive and productive application of this, it denotes 'to acquire s.th. by means of the action expressed by the simple verb': Er hat sich (dat.) eine bessere Stellung erarbeitet/erschlichen *He has obtained a better job by hard work/surreptitiously.*

(b) it denotes the beginning of an action or state: erklingen *to ring out*; und plötzlich erstrahlt ihr Gesicht (H. Fallada) *and suddenly she looks radiant.*

(c) it forms verbs from adjectives 1. denoting getting into the state described by the adjective: erröten *to blush* 2. factitive verbs: erfrischen *to refresh*, erleichtern *to make easier* (from compar.).

(d) it is prefixed to a number of verbs when they are used in a figurative or derived sense: Er öffnete das Fenster. Er eröffnete die Sitzung, die neue Bibliothek, ein Konto.

N.B. schließen *to close*: erschließen *to open up* (e.g. a new region).

680. miß-: see 691.

681. ver- (productive)

(a) it forms transitive verbs:
  i with the explicit or implicit sense of 'away': verbrauchen *to use up, consume*, die Zeit verträumen.
  ii with a broadly negative or unfavourable sense: destruction (vernichten), spoiling (der Ausflug war verregnet), error (verkennen *to fail to recognize, misjudge*). Cf. the opposites achten: verachten; lernen: verlernen *to unlearn, forget.*

(b) it forms intr. verbs with the sense of 'away', deterioration, out of existence (all (s)): verhallen *to die away* (of sound), verhungern *to starve to death.*

(c) it forms refl. verbs meaning to make a mistake in doing s.th.: sich verfahren *to take the wrong road*, sich versprechen *to make a slip of the tongue.*

(d) it makes a number of intr. verbs tr.: verfolgen *to pursue.*

(e) it forms verbs from nouns: verchromen *to plate with chromium*, verkörpern *to embody*; also some factitives e.g. ein Buch verfilmen.

(f) from adjectives it forms 1. factitives: vereinfachen *to simplify*, verbessern *to improve* 2. verbs denoting getting into the corresponding state: verstummen (s) *to become silent*, verwildern (s) *to become a wilderness/depraved.*

682. zer- denotes apart, to pieces; mainly prefixed to verbs (productive): ein Problem zerreden *to discuss a problem ad nauseam*, zerreißen (h & s) *to tear (to pieces)* (tr. and intr.).

D. VERBS FORMED, MAINLY FROM VERBS, BY MEANS OF A VARIABLE PREFIX[1]

683. über

(a) Sep.

   i across: Wir setzten über *We ferried across*.[2]

   ii over: Er legte mir eine Decke über *He put a rug over me*.

(b) Insep.

   i over: überreden *to persuade* ('to talk over'), überschwemmen *to inundate* (also fig.), übersehen *to survey*; *to overlook*.

   ii over-, implying excess: übermüden *to overtire*.

(c) Sep. and Insep. with the same simple verb, e.g.

über-ragen *to project* (intr.); überragen *to tower above, surpass* (tr.)

über-setzen (h & s) *to ferry across* (tr. and intr.)

übersetzen *to translate*.

684. unter[3]

(a) Sep.: under: unter-bringen *to house, find a place for*, unter-gehen (s) *to go down* (sun, ship), *to go under* (drowning).

(b) Insep.

   i under (including insufficiency): unterdrücken *to suppress*, unterschätzen *to underrate*, unterschreiben *to sign* (a letter).

   ii corresponds to Latin 'inter' (between): unterbrechen *to interrupt*, unterscheiden *to distinguish*.

685. durch

(a) Sep.: through: durch-arbeiten *to work through* (1. a book 2. without a break), durch-fallen (s) 1. *to fall through* 2. *to fail* (e.g. in an exam), durch-lassen *to let through* (s.o. or water).

(b) Insep.: through: durchnässen *to soak*, durchsuchen *to search* (e.g. luggage).

(c) Sep. and Insep. with the same simple verb, e.g.

durch-reisen (s) (intr.) *to travel through* (*a country*) (generally = without a stay): Ich bin (durch Frankreich) durchgereist.

durchreisen (tr.) *to travel all over a country*: Letztes Jahr habe ich Frankreich durchreist.

Note: With a number of verbs denoting change of place, durch may be sep. or insep. with only a slight difference in sense: the sep. form, with the stress on 'durch', generally conveys the completed action; the insep. form, with the stress on the verb, emphasizes the action as such or in progress:

Er eilte durch die Vorhalle durch   *He hurried through the vestibule*

---

[1] For the general characteristics of variable prefixes, see 371.

[2] With some verbs denoting change of place, where the prefix über is possible, hinüber (or: herüber) is more usual, e.g. Wir fuhren hinüber *We crossed over* (*the river*); see also 704.

[3] see also 704.

Er durcheilte die Vorhalle   *He hurried through the vestibule*
cf. durch-schleichen, durch-schreiten, durch-ziehen *to pass through, march through.*
durch-kommen can only be sep.
durchgehen (insep.) *to traverse* is very rare.

686. um[1]

(a) Sep.
   i turning: um-graben *to dig over* (e.g. a flower-bed), sich um-sehen *to look round, back, about one.*
   ii falling and upsetting: um-fallen (s) *to fall over,* um-kippen (h & s) *to tip over, overturn* (tr. and intr.).
   iii change: um-arbeiten *to recast* (e.g. a book), um-steigen (s) *to change (trains).*
(b) Insep.: surrounding: umarmen *to embrace,* umgeben *to surround.*
(c) Sep. and Insep. with the same simple verb, e.g.
um-ziehen 1. (s) *to move (to another house)* 2. (h) ein Kind um-ziehen *to change a child's clothes;* sich um-ziehen *to change (one's clothes).*
umziehen *to surround, encircle* (elev.); sich umziehen *to cloud over:* Der Himmel umzieht sich.

687. voll

(a) Sep.: full: voll-gießen, voll-stopfen (mit) *to cram (with)*
(b) Insep.: completion, carrying out: vollbringen *to accomplish* (e.g. a deed, a task), vollenden 1. *to complete*[2] 2. *to die* (elev.).

688. wider

Note: 'wider' and 'wieder' were originally the same word (OHG widar, MHG wider), not separating till the 17th century. Accordingly, as a prefix, wider may mean:
i against, e.g. widerstehen + dat. *to resist.*
ii back, e.g. wider-hallen *to echo, resound* (intr.) (cf. wieder in wiederkommen).

(a) Sep.: Two verbs only: wider-hallen and (sich) wider-spiegeln; both are occasionally used inseparably in the pres. and imperf.
(b) Insep.: widerlegen *to refute,* widersprechen + dat. *to contradict.*

689. wieder

Sep.: always, except in wiederholen *to repeat.*
(a) back: wieder-bekommen *to recover, get back,* wieder-kehren (s) 1. *to come back* 2. *to recur.*
(b) again
   i Here wieder should be treated as a prefix provided that a new, distinctive meaning arises from its combination with the verb (the

---

[1] see also 704.
[2] somewhat stilted; normal usage e.g. er erledigte seine Arbeit; er war mit seiner Arbeit fertig; ich habe den Brief fertig.

English equivalent will generally begin with re-). Otherwise it is to be regarded as an adverb (Du. Haupt. p. 690). E.g.

Er hat sein Studium wieder-aufgenommen	*He has resumed his studies*
Er hat das Paket wieder auf-genommen	*He took up the parcel again*
Du sollst dies nicht wiedererzählen	*You're not to repeat this, you're not to pass this on*
Willst du den Witz, bitte, wieder erzählen?	*Will you please tell us the joke again?*

ii When prefixed to a verb which itself has a sep. prefix, wieder is written as a separate word in the imperative, and in a simple tense, exc. in a sub. cl.: Nimm deine Studien wieder auf! Er nimmt seine Studien wieder auf. Wenn er seine Studien wieder-aufnimmt, . . .

iii Further examples: wieder-auf-leben (s) *to revive* (intr.) fig. (e.g. of trade), wieder-ein-führen *to re-introduce* (e.g. a custom), wieder-her-stellen *to restore* (a building, picture, law and order), *to cure* (s.o. ill), wieder-wählen *to re-elect*.

690. hinter

(a) Sep.: to the back or down, confined to a number of inorganic and unlovely regional colloquialisms, e.g. hinter-schlucken *to gulp down* (water), *to swallow* (a tablet).

(b) Insep.
i behind (after): hinterlegen *to deposit* (money as a security).
ii acting stealthily: Steuern hinterziehen *to evade full payment of taxes*.

(c) Sep. and Insep. with the same simple verb, e.g.
hinter-gehen (s) *to go to the back.*
hintergehen *to deceive.*

691. miß

Insep. (see N.i below)
(a) opposite: mißachten *to disdain, despise*, mißtrauen + dat. *to distrust.*
(b) badly or wrongly: mißdeuten *to misinterpret*, mißhandeln *to ill-treat*, mißverstehen *to misunderstand.*

Note:
i Correctly and normally, miß is insep., but in some verbs alternative variations occur, e.g. ohne ihn mißzuachten, ich hatte ihn mißgeach-tet/gemißachtet. These variations being less common than the norm, they may be ignored, exc. in the case of **mißverstehen**: 1. the stress is here always on miß 2. it is insep. except in the infin. used with 'zu': um ihn nicht mißzuverstehen; cf. in nicht mißzuverstehender Weise *in an unmistakable manner* (cf. 432).

ii The following are the only infinitives of verbs with miß which are commonly used as nouns:
das Mißglücken, Mißlingen, Mißraten *failure*, das Mißbehagen *un-comfortable feeling*, das Mißfallen *displeasure, dissatisfaction*, das Miß-trauen *distrust.*

E. VERBS FORMED, MAINLY FROM VERBS, BY MEANS OF A SEPARABLE PREFIX[1]

692. Separable prefixes may be divided into three types:

(a) simple, e.g. ab-, an-: 693–9.
(b) compound, e.g. herein-, voraus-: 700–706.
(c) special, e.g. teil-nehmen, offen-lassen, spazieren-gehen: 709–12.

693. The simple separable prefixes. Considerations of space preclude a semantic analysis of these prefixes, nor do the assimilation and comprehension of verbs formed with them offer particular difficulty; there follow two or three characteristic examples of each prefix, which include illustrations of the productive character of some of them.

ab-[2] (productive): ab-fliegen *to take off*, jemandem etwas ab-gaunern *to obtain s.th. from s.o. by fraudulent means* (der Gauner *swindler*), ab-reißen *to pull down* (a house), ab-lehnen *to reject*.

an-[2] (productive): an-probieren *to try on* (clothes), eine Stadt an-fliegen *to approach a town by plane* (or, of an airline, *to serve a town*), an-springen (s) *to start* (an engine) (intr.).

auf-[2]: auf-bleiben *to stay up*, auf-räumen *to tidy up*, auf-setzen *to put on* (hat, water to boil), auf-schließen *to unlock*.

aus-[2] (productive): aus-arbeiten *to work out* (a plan), aus-fräsen *to mill out* (a hole), aus-schlafen *to have a good long sleep*.

bei-: bei-treten + dat. *to join* (e.g. a club), bei-tragen zu *to contribute to*, einen Streit bei-legen *to settle a dispute*.

da-: da-bleiben, da-sein, da-stehen; see 710, 712(e).

dar- means 'there' and so 'before s.o.'; one common product: dar-stellen 1. *to represent, portray* 2. *to perform* (a part) 3. *to constitute, be* (Die Sache stellt ein Problem dar).

ein-[2] replaces 'in' as a prefix (productive): ein-dosen *to tin* (fruit, etc.), ein-fahren (h) *to run in* (a new car); see also 571(c).

fehl- denotes error or failure: fehl-gehen (s) *to miss one's way*, fehl-greifen 1. *to miss one's hold* 2. *to make a blunder*.

fort- and **weg-** meaning 'away' are synonymous, though weg- is used more: weg-bleiben/fort-bleiben, weg-nehmen/fort-nehmen 1. *to take away* 2. *to take up* (space) etc. BUT: weg-sehen (not: fort-sehen) *to look away*.

fort- (but not weg-) also denotes continuation: fort-setzen (tr.).

her- and **hin-**: see 695–9.

inne- within; limited to 5 verbs, e.g. inne-haben *to occupy* (a position).

los-: los-gehen 1. *to come off* (e.g. a button) 2. *to go off* (e.g. a gun) 3. *to commence* (coll.), los-stürzen auf *to rush at*.

mit-, a flexible and pregnant prefix, denotes one of two things:
(a) with some specific person(s), determined by the context:
Gehst du mit? *Are you going with me/us/them etc.?*
Er brachte das Buch mit. Ich hab' ihr das Buch mitgegeben.

(b) more vaguely, 'with the rest', conveying joining in, co-operating or a joint experience: Du mußt mitsingen; unsre Arbeiter bestimmen über den Urlaub mit (*have a say in fixing holidays*); du hast diese Jahre nicht mitgemacht *you didn't go through those years.*

Note: 'mit' may also have independent adverbial force: together with others or with other things, also, partly: Er ist mit der Beste seiner Klasse (*one of the best*); er war mit verantwortlich (*partly responsible*).

nach-: nach-gehen + dat. *to follow* (s.o.), *to investigate* (a problem), *to pursue* (pleasure), nach-datieren *to post-date*, nach-geben *to give way.*

nieder-: nieder-brennen *to burn down*, nieder-lassen *to lower.*

ob-: sometimes insep.; elev. or facetious; 3 verbs: see dictionary.

vor-: vor-gehen *to go forward* or *ahead; to be fast* (clock), vor-spielen *to play a piece of music to s.o.*, viel vor-haben *to have a lot on* (engagements).

weg-: see fort-

zu-: zu-fahren + dat. or, more incisive, auf + acc. *to drive towards*, zu-drehen *to turn off* (tap), Geld zu-schießen *to give additional money.*

694. A number of sep. and variable prefixes are used elliptically, e.g.

Ich fühle mich etwas ab (coll.) [abgespannt]	*I feel a bit low*
Ich habe das Buch aus [ausgelesen]	*I've finished the book*

cf. Ist er schon auf? Die Tür war auf; das Licht war noch an; er ist schon fort; sie ist schon hinauf; zurück!

F. HIN- AND HER- AND THEIR COMPOUNDS[1]

695. The orthodox distinction between 'hin' and 'her' is that 'hin' denotes motion away from the speaker or his original situation, whereas 'her' denotes motion towards the speaker or his present situation (For 'the speaker' it may be necessary to substitute 'the person concerned'):

Heute ist die Wahlversammlung, und ich gehe hin	*Today is the election meeting and I'm going (there)*
Ich hielt ihm die Zeitung hin	*I held out the newspaper to him*
Ich hörte einen Ruf und sah hin	*I heard a shout and looked in the direction from which it came*
Komm mal her!	*Just come here*
Er hat mich mit dem Auto hergebracht	*He brought me here by car*
Halt den Teller her!	*Hold out your plate*
Setz dich her zu mir!	*Come and sit down next to me*

696. Where verbs formed with 'hin' or 'her' have a derived, abstract or figurative meaning, the basic directional force of 'hin' may still generally be felt, while the use of 'her' is generally purely idiomatic:

sein Leben für etwas hingeben	*to sacrifice one's life for s.th.*
Die Zeit ging rasch hin	*Time passed quickly*

[1] see also 266–70.

Sie fielen über ihn her	*They assailed him*
Ich will mich nicht dazu hergeben	*I won't lend myself (be a party) to that*
Es geht lustig her	*Things are going on merrily*

697. In nouns formed with 'hin' or 'her', their basic directional force generally holds:

die Hinreise, die Hinfahrt	*the outward journey*
auf der Herreise, Herfahrt	*on the journey here*
auf dem Hinweg[1]	*on the way there*

Purely idiomatic: der Hergang *course of events, occurrence*

698. A particular meaning of hin-: down, as in: Er legte das Buch hin; er legte sich hin; er fiel hin; setz dich hierhin! *Sit down here.*

699. A particular meaning of her-: along, i.e. movement along in relation to some other person or thing:

Er ging neben mir her	*He walked along beside me*
Ein ausländischer Wagen fuhr vor uns her	*A foreign car was going along in front of us*

cf. the compound prefixes: Er lief nebenher, hinterher; 'vorher' is not used thus.

700. Compound separable prefixes formed with hin- and her-

(a) **Six much used pairs**:

hinein, herein *in*	hinunter, herunter *down*
hinaus, heraus *out*	hinab, herab *down*
hinauf, herauf *up*	hinüber, herüber *over, across*

Note: hinunter, herunter and hinab, herab are synonymous; the former are commoner in conversation.

Er kam (aus dem Haus) heraus	*He came out (of the house)*
Er starrte (in die Dunkelheit) hinaus	*He stared out (into the darkness)*
Darf ich Sie herüberbitten?	*May I ask you to come across?*

(b) hinan *upward* (elev.)
    heran *along* (approaching),
        up (to); *upward*

hinzu *as an addition*
herzu *along* (approaching), *up*
    (rare)

Er trat an mich heran	*He came up to me*
Geh nicht zu nah heran!	*Don't go too near* (idiomatic)
Sie fügte etwas Zucker hinzu	*She added some sugar*

(c) **with 'hin' only**:

hindurch *through*	hinweg *away* (but often idiomatic)
Er drang (durch die Menschen-menge) hindurch	*He made his way through (the crowd)*
Die Rollbahn sauste unter uns hinweg	*The runway sped away beneath us*

---

[1] 'auf dem Herweg' is not much used.

(d) **with 'her' only:**

herbei *along* (approaching), *up*	herum[1] *round*; also static, as in
hernieder *down* (elev.; rare)	3rd example
	hervor *forth, out*

Polizisten kamen herbei	*Some policemen came along*
Er kam um die Ecke herum	*He came round the corner*
Meine Bücher lagen auf dem Tisch herum	*My books lay around on the table*
Plötzlich trat er (aus dem Gebüsch) hervoṙ	*Suddenly he stepped forth (from the shrubbery)*

701. **to go/come up and to go/come down** sometimes cause difficulty; the following plain examples may be helpful:

Er ging den Berg hinauf	*He went up the hill*
Er ging zum Gipfel hinauf	*He went up to the summit*
Er kam die Treppe herunter	*He came down the stairs*
Er ging ins Tal hinunter	*He went down into the valley*
Ich ging zu ihm	*I went up to him*
Ich trat an ihn heran	
Mein Bruder kam heran (or: herbei)	*My brother came up*

Note: In the 1st and 3rd examples, den Berg and die Treppe are adverbial accusatives, not direct objects, the perfect being 'Er ist den Berg hin-aufgegangen' and 'Er i̱st die Treppe heruntergekommen'.

702. Colloquially these compound prefixes are often abbreviated, if the second element begins with a vowel

North German favours the abbreviation of her (e.g. 'reinkommen, 'rauf-kommen, 'runterkommen) and adheres to this, irrespective of direction, e.g. Gehen Sie 'rüber! Er nahm die Bücher 'rauf. Warten Sie, ich gehe gleich hier rein (H. Fallada).

South German favours the abbreviation of hin (e.g. 'neingehen, 'nauf-gehen, 'nuntergehen), but in general uses the correct abbreviation in respect of direction. E.g. Er ging 'naus, BUT: Er kam 'raus.[2]

An illustration from *Die Zeit*: Ob er nicht 'rausmöchte aus dem Loch, in eine anständige Wohnung? . . . „Hier kriegt mich keiner 'raus."

703. Where the verb has a figurative meaning, the prefix is more frequently the form with her- than the form with hin- and the two forms are then rarely interchangeable. E.g.

with her-

herab-sehen auf + acc.	*to look down on, despise*
heraus-geben	1. *to edit, publish*
	2. *to give money as change*
Es stellte sich heraus, daß . . .	*It turned out that . . .*
herunter-leiern	*to reel off* (e.g. a prayer)

with hin-

sich hinaus-ziehen	*to drag on* (e.g. of negotiations)

---

[1] see also 616: last example and Note.
[2] Du. Gram. 3240 and 3275.

with her- or hin-

die Preise herauf-/hinauf-setzen	*to put up prices*
Es kommt auf dasselbe heraus/hinaus	*It comes to the same thing*

704. An important distinction and warning

Although, as was shown in 703, verbs formed with the compound prefixes may have a figurative sense, they preponderantly have a literal and concrete meaning, denoting movement in the direction in question (cf. the examples in 700).

On the other hand, verbs formed with the simple prefixes ab-, an-, auf-, aus-, ein-, über-, um- and unter-, while they may have a literal and concrete meaning (cf. 693), often have a derived or figurative sense. (For the literal and derived meanings of the variable prefixes über, unter and um, see also 683, 684, 686.)

EXAMPLES

hinein-, herein-, ein-

Er ist hineingegangen	*He has gone in*
Die Zeitung ist eingegangen	*The paper has ceased publication*
herein-bringen	*to bring (carry) in*
ein-bringen	*to bring in* e.g. crops, money, a parliamentary bill

hinaus-, heraus-, aus-

Er stand auf und ging (aus dem Zimmer) hinaus	*He got up and went out (of the room)*
Ich gehe heute nachmittag aus	*I'm going out this afternoon*
Wer weiß, wie es ausgeht!	*Who knows how it will end*
Er kam heraus	*He came out*
Er kommt mit den andern Jungen gut aus	*He gets on well with the other boys*
Ich kann mit 20 Mark nicht auskommen	*I can't make do with 20 marks*
N.B. Er streckte die Hand aus	*He stretched out his hand*

hinüber-, über-

Ich ging zu ihm hinüber	*I went across to him*
Er ist zur SPD übergegangen	*He's gone over to the Social Democrats*

705. The 6 pairs of prefixes in 700(a) and also 'herum' may be compounded with 'da', 'dort' and 'hier', these carrying the stress. E.g.

Er ging dahinein	*He went in there*
Er kam hierheraus	*He came out of here*
Wir gehen jetzt dorthinauf	*We're going up there now*
Du kannst daherum gehen	*You can go round there*

G. OTHER COMPOUND SEPARABLE PREFIXES

706. Note: The following are used as prefixes with only one or two verbs and are not illustrated below: bevor, dahinter, daneben, danieder, darüber, darum, drauf, hintan, umhin, vorweg, zuvor.

dabei: presence, proximity: dabei-sein, dabei-stehen.

daheim: at home: daheim-bleiben.

daher: along (approaching): Er schlenderte daher.

dahin: away, past (and idiomatic): Eine Staffel Düsenjäger pfiff über Köln dahin (*Zeit*); die Zeit flog dahin.

daran, dran: 'to it': sich daran-machen *to set to work*

darein, drein: 'into it': sich darein-finden *to adapt o.s., resign o.s.*

davon: away: davon-brausen *to set off with a roar* (motor-bike).

dazu: addition (and idiomatic): Später kam er auch noch dazu.

dazwischen: 'in between': dazwischen-reden *to interrupt* (a conversation).

einher: along (implying stateliness):[1] Er schritt einher.

empor: upward (mainly elev.): sich empor-arbeiten, empor-blicken.

entgegen: 1. meeting: Er kam mir entgegen 2. opposition: in entgegengesetzter Richtung.

hierher: hither: see 266.

überein: agreement: Ich stimme mit ihm in dieser Sache überein.

umher: around, about:[2] umher-blicken, umher-wandern.

voran: ahead, forward: Er ist schon vorangegangen; die Arbeit geht gut voran.

voraus: in advance, ahead: voraus-bezahlen, voraus-sagen *to foretell*.

vorbei, vorüber: past, by; vorbei is commoner in conversation except in a time sense: Er ging (an unserem Haus) vorbei; der Winter ging vorüber.

vorher: before, in advance; commonest use: vorhergehend *preceding*.

vorüber: see vorbei.

zurecht: right, in order: zurecht-machen *to prepare*.

zurück: 1. back, backward, behind: zurück-gehen *to recede, go down* (e.g. of floods, earnings), zurück-lassen *to leave behind*. 2. back, returning: zurück-bekommen *to get back, recover*, zurück-gehen *to return*.

zusammen: together: zusammen-bringen, zusammen-rücken (h & s) *to move closer together* (in order to make room) (tr. and intr.). By a fig. extension of 'closer together': zusammen-fallen (s) *to collapse*, zusammen-fahren (s) *to start* (with surprise).

707. A certain number of **prepositional formations, analogous to some of the above compound separable prefixes**, are, in normal practice, not compounded with the verb (cf. Du. Gram. 5940), but their position in the sentence is that of a separable prefix, e.g.

außer acht lassen	*to leave out of account*
beiseite legen	*to lay aside*
instand setzen	*to repair, make ready*
zugrunde gehen	*to perish, be ruined*
zugrunde liegen (+dat.)	*to form the basis (of), to be at the bottom (of)*
zustande bringen	*to bring about, achieve*
jemandem zuteil werden	*to fall to s.o.'s share*

N.B. The corresponding adjectival participles, verbal nouns and derived nouns are, however, written as one word: die instandgesetzte Maschine, der zugrundeliegende Gedanke, das Zugrundegehen, die Instandsetzung.

---

[1] Betteridge, op. cit.

[2] see also 616: last example and Note.

708. Preposition + einander (*one another*) in relation to the verb[1]

(a) **prep. + einander is *not* joined to the verb:**
　　i if the sentence expresses genuine reciprocity:

Wir haben aneinander gedacht	*We thought of each other*
Wir werden aufeinander warten	*We shall wait for each other*
Sie passen zueinander	*They suit each other*

　　ii if prep. + einander is the equivalent of an adverb:

Wir haben nacheinander mit ihm gesprochen	*We spoke to him in turn (successively)*

(b) **prep. + einander is joined to the verb**, like a separable prefix, if together they form a single concept:

Ich habe die Bücher aufeinander-gelegt	*I have put the books on top of one another (stacked the books)*
aneinandergrenzende Grundstücke	*adjacent pieces of land*
Es hat sich gezeigt, daß die Meinungen hierüber aus-einandergehen	*It has become evident that opinions differ about this*

This does not apply if the verb already has a prefix:

Sie haben aneinander vorbeigeredet	*They were at cross purposes*

H. SPECIAL SEPARABLE PREFIXES

709. The special separable prefixes are nouns, adjectives, participles, adverbs and infinitives which are used as separable prefixes (productive)

EXAMPLE: teil-nehmen an + dat. *to take part in*
Er nimmt an dem Konzert teil.
Da er an dem Konzert teilnimmt, . . .
Er hat an dem Konzert teilgenommen.
Er hat versprochen, an dem Konzert teilzunehmen.

FURTHER EXAMPLES (**S**):
Nouns: acht-geben (auf + acc.) *to pay heed* (*to*), haus-halten *to keep house*, statt-finden[2] *to take place*
Adjectives: lieb-gewinnen *to grow fond of*, offen-lassen *to leave open*, sauber-halten *to keep clean*, eine Sache tot-schweigen *to hush a matter up*
Participles: gefangen-nehmen *to take prisoner*, verloren-gehen *to get lost, go astray* (of things)
Adverbs: blind-fliegen *to fly blind*, fest-halten *to hold fast*, irre-leiten *to lead astray*, schwarz-arbeiten[3] *to be a blackleg*
Infinitives:
kennen-lernen *to make the acquaintance of*
liegen-bleiben 1. *to stay in bed* 2. *to be left behind, to be forgotten* (of things) 3. *to remain unsold*
sitzen-lassen *to leave in the lurch, to jilt*
spazieren-gehen *to go for a walk*
　　BUT N.B. (sich) schlafen legen (see 422(d))

---

[1] cf. Du. Haupt. pp. 718 f.
[2] for the noun die Statt, see 729(a)ii.
[3] BUT: schwarz färben *to dye black*.

14

710. Limitation of the use of adjectives, adverbs and infinitives as separable prefixes: some are treated as separable prefixes when their combination with the verb produces a new meaning, but not when both components retain their literal meaning.

EXAMPLES:
Adverbs/Adjectives

Du sollst dableiben	*You're to stay (on)*
Du sollst *da* bleiben	*You're to stay there* (where you are)
Wir können weiterspielen	*We can go on playing*
Er hat mir weitergeholfen	*He has helped me on*
Ich werde dir weiter helfen	*I shall continue to help you* (as in the past)
Er hat es mir leichtgemacht, die Stellung zu bekommen	*He made it easy for me to get the job*
N.B. Er hat es mir sehr leicht gemacht, . . . (adj. written separately when qualified)	*He made it very easy for me . . .*

Infinitives (the position of the infin. in the sentence is not affected)
fallen-lassen *to drop* (fig.), e.g. a plan, a member of a team, a remark, one's mask.
fallen lassen *to drop* (lit.), e.g. a book.

stehen-bleiben 1. *to stop, stand still* 2. *to stop* (of a clock) 3. idiomatic: Wo sind wir in der letzten Stunde stehengeblieben? *Where did we get to in the last lesson?*
stehen bleiben *to remain standing*

711. (a) **Verbs like the following are formed from compound nouns and are conjugated like simple weak verbs:**

frühstücken *to have breakfast*: um zu frühstücken, ich frühstücke, ich habe gefrühstückt.
làngweilen *to bore* (from die Làngweile *boredom*)
wètteifern (mit) *to compete, vie (with)* (from der Wètteifer *rivalry, competition*).

(b) A number of verbs, not formed from compound nouns, are nevertheless conjugated like simple weak verbs (cf. (a) above) E.g.
hàndhaben *to handle, manipulate*, lièbäugeln mit 1. *to give s.o. the glad eye* 2. *to toy with* (an idea), lièbkosen *to caress*, schlàfwandeln *to walk in one's sleep*.

712. Separable prefixes: some anomalies and miscellaneous points[1]

(a) **rad-fahren** *to cycle*: Ich fahre gern Rad; da ich gern radfahre, . . . Ich bin viel radgefahren. N.B. Auto fahren.

(b) **maschine-schreiben** *to type* is only used intransitively: Ich schreibe nicht Maschine; ich habe früher nicht maschinegeschrieben, BUT: Ich habe den Brief mit der Maschine geschrieben. One exception: the passive past part.: ein maschinegeschriebener Brief.

(c) **not-landen** *to make a forced landing*: wir sind notgelandet; um notzulanden; BUT: wir notlandeten.

---

[1] Du. Haupt. pp. 715 ff.

(d) **Some compounds exist only in the infinitive,** e.g. brustschwimmen, kettenrauchen, kopfrechnen *to do mental arithmetic,* kugelstoßen *to put the weight,* segelfliegen *to glide,* wettlaufen *to race;* **others, only in the infin. and past part.,** e.g. seiltanzen *to walk the tightrope,* uraufführen: Das Stück wurde in Frankfurt uraufgeführt *The play was first performed in Frankfurt.*

(e) **Compounds of sein and werden** are written as one word only in their non-finite forms:
Er ist dagewesen, BUT: wenn er da ist.
Es ist bald bekanntgeworden, BUT: wenn es bekannt wird.
um das Bild loszuwerden, BUT: wenn ich es los werde.

(f) **auf und ab, hin und her**: ich bin auf und ab gegangen; während die Kinder hin und her liefen, BUT: mein langes Aufundabgehen.

(g) **Separable prefixes placed emphatically at the beginning of the sentence** are written as a separate word:
Fest steht, daß ...   *It is certain that ...*
Hinzu kommt, daß ...   *Add to this the fact that ...*

(h) **Some cases where a separable prefix might be expected but where it has not yet developed**:
auswendig lernen *to learn by heart,* jemandem Bescheid sagen *to inform s.o.,* Bescheid wissen *to be informed, to know,* Klavier spielen, Posten stehen *to be on guard duty,* sich satt essen *to eat one's fill,* Schach spielen, Schi laufen, Schlitten fahren, Schlittschuh laufen.
BUT: das Auswendiglernen *learning by heart,* das Schilaufen *skiing* etc.

I. THE FORMATION OF NOUNS

713. **All infinitives may be used as verbal nouns,** always neut., often corresponding to an English form in -ing (cf. 404): das Aufstehen *getting up,* das Reiten *riding.*
In many cases, such nouns are felt as ordinary nouns, e.g. das Einkommen *income,* das Essen *meal, lunch, food,* das Leben *life,* das Unternehmen *enterprise, venture; concern, business,* das Versprechen *promise.* Though such nouns may be used in the plur., there is a tendency, because of their verbal origin, to avoid it or to use another noun, e.g. Wir verglichen unser Einkommen *We compared our incomes;* verpfuschte Existenzen *wasted lives;* all seine Versprechungen.

714. **Some nouns** (preponderantly masc.) **are formed from verb-stems without a suffix**: der Lauf, der Stoß, der Rückfall *relapse,* das Lob; also with Ablaut: der Schluß, der Stich *stab, sting,* der Ersatz (ersetzen) *substitute, replacement.*

715. **Nouns are formed from verbs and/or adjectives and/or nouns by means of a suffix**

(a)
-e: from verbs: die Grube *pit,* and adjectives (largely qualities): die Größe.

-ei, -erei: from verbs (productive); often pejorative; -ei with verbs in -eln, -ern: die Prügelei *fight, scrap*; otherwise -erei: die Rekordhascherei *record hunting* (haschen *to snatch*); from nouns denoting professions: die Gärtnerei *gardening; nursery*.

-el: from verbs: der Hebel *lever*, der Stachel *thorn, prickle*.

-er (-ler, -ner) (productive): 1. professions and some other personal designations: der Bäcker, der Bühnenbildner *set designer*, der Witwer *widower*; -ler is sometimes pejorative: der Ausflügler *tripper*; name of a town + er forms the name of its inhabitants: der Frankfurter, mit den Kölnern (deviations include der Bremer, der Göttinger, der Hannoveràner, der Münchner) 2. instruments (see 2(c)) and some other inanimates: der Seufzer *sigh*.

-heit (-keit, -igkeit) (numerous and productive), mainly from adjectives: nouns denoting qualities and states: die Laxheit, die Gleichheit; -keit is used instead of -heit with adjectives in -bar, -ig, -lich, -sam (e.g. die Sparsamkeit) and with some in -el and -er (e.g. die Eitelkeit *vanity*, BUT: die Dunkelheit); -igkeit, originating in nouns such as Schwierigkeit, has become an independent ending, e.g. die Schwerelosigkeit *weightlessness*.

-ling (productive): personal designations; generally with Umlaut; often pejorative: der Flüchtling *fugitive, refugee*, der Schwächling.

-nis: largely from verbs 1. with prefixes 2. denoting the result of an action: die Ersparnis *saving*, das Vermächtnis *legacy*.

-schaft (productive): 1. collectives: die Gewerkschaft *trade union* 2. nouns denoting states: die Bereitschaft *readiness*, die Gefangenschaft.

-sel: from verbs: das Rätsel *puzzle* (raten *to guess*); sometimes acts as a diminutive (productive): das Einschiebsel *insertion*.

-tum (productive): mainly from nouns and denoting institutions and typical conduct or outlook: das Papsttum, das Gangstertum, das Deutschtum *German ethos*.

-ung: very common; productive, especially in denoting processes: die Frischhaltung *keeping fresh*, die Wasserung der Kapsel *splash-down*.

(b) **-chen and -lein form diminutives**, which are always neut.; both generally cause Umlaut. North Germans use -chen (productive); the South German -lein sounds stilted, and dialectal forms are preferred, e.g. das Häusle (in Baden), das Hunderl (in Bavaria), das Blättli (in Switzerland).

Note:

i Declension: Diminutives in -chen and -lein are Group 1 nouns (cf. 18). The dialectal forms (with local variations) are left uninflected, von + dat. replacing the gen. sing. E.g. (dat. plur.): Die Kinder spielten mit den Hundle/mit die [sic] Hunderl (also: mit den Hunderln)/mit den Blättli.

ii -chen is not used with nouns in -ch and generally not with nouns in -ng; here North German usually has a double diminutive: das Büchelchen, das Ringelchen.

iii The ending -e disappears before the diminutive endings: das Pflänzchen; likewise -en (das Kästchen), though it is sometimes changed to -el (das Wägelchen).

iv All the diminutive endings may also convey affection (Weibchen *wifie*, das Hundle), unless used ironically: Also, Freundchen . . ., ein nettes Sümmchen![1] Diebe mit Köpfchen *clever thieves.*

v The diminutive endings are virtually never used after the suffixes -ei, -erei, -heit, -in, -keit, -ling, -nis, -schaft, -ung; therefore: die kleine Lehrerin (not: das Lehrerinchen) (see (c) below).

(c) **(S) -in forms nouns denoting the female of most persons and many animals**, often with Umlaut: die Ärztin, die Beamtin, die Hündin, die Landsmännin *fellow-countryman.* The following have no fem. form: der (Film)Star, der Gast, der Lehrling, der Liebling, e.g. Sie ist der Liebling der Familie. For Doktor and Professor, see 672(a).

(d) 4 noun suffixes which are themselves nouns:[2] **-gut** (possession, goods) and **-werk** (work) form collectives: das Ideengut *stock of ideas*, das Steingut *stoneware*, das Balkenwerk *woodwork, beams*; **-wesen** (being, nature etc.) mainly denotes spheres of administration and of human activity (productive): das Schulwesen *educational system*, das Flugwesen *aviation*; **-zeug** (stuff, cloth etc.) forms collectives (das Schreibzeug) and instruments (das Werkzeug *tool*, das Fahrzeug *vehicle*).

716. Nouns are formed from verbs and/or nouns by means of a prefix. (These prefixes always carry the main stress, exc. Erz- as in 2nd example, Ge- and Miß-)

(a)
Erz-: der Erzbischof *archbishop*; der Erzgauner *thorough scoundrel.*

Ge-,[3] sometimes in conjunction with the suffix -e: 1. from verbs: nouns denoting a protracted activity; often pejorative (productive): das Gelaufe *running about, bustle*, das Geschwätz(e) *idle talk, gossiping* 2. from nouns: collectives, with Umlaut where possible: das Geäst *branches*, das Gebirge 3. many nouns outside 1. and 2.; cf. 27.

Miß- 1. opposite: der Mißerfolg 2. pejorative: der Mißbrauch *misuse, abuse.* (Main stress on Miß- exc. die Mißártung and die Mißhàndlung; but see also 691 N.ii).

Mit- 1. being together: der Mitreisende 2. co-operation: der Mitarbeiter 3. contemporariness: die Mitwelt.

Rück- is the prefix normally used with nouns corresponding to the verbal prefix zurück-: die Rückfahrt, der Rückstoßantrieb *jet-propulsion* (zurückstoßen). Note: 1. some nouns have the prefix Zurück-, e.g. die Zurückhaltung *restraint* 2. with some nouns Rück- is a contraction of 'der Rücken', e.g. die Rückwand *back wall.*

Un-, from nouns only: 1. opposite: die Unruhe 2. an undesirable deviation: der Unmensch *hard-hearted wretch* 3. with nouns denoting quantity, it has a magnifying and/or pejorative effect: eine Unsumme *a vast sum.*

Ur-, from nouns only, denotes origin and beginnings (in OHG ur=aus

[1] cf. Fleischer, op. cit., pp. 166 f.
[2] cf. Fleischer, op. cit., pp. 64, 161 ff.
[3] For the gender and plural of Ge- nouns, see 27.

out of, from) (productive): die Uraufführung *first performance,* der
Ur(ur)großvater, Urtierchen *protozoa.*

Wohl- denotes the good or agreeable: der Wohltäter, der Wohlklang
pleasing sound, euphony.

(b) 3 noun prefixes which are themselves nouns (productive):[1] **Grund-**
foundation, basis: der Grundgedanke; **Haupt-** head: der Haupt-
angeklagte; **Spitzen-** (die Spitze *peak*): die Spitzenbelastung *peak-load*
(electr.).

(c) Many of the separable and all the variable prefixes treated under the
formation of verbs also appear attached to nouns; these are mainly
nouns formed from the corresponding verb, e.g. der Abflug, die
Darstellung, die Voraussage, but in many cases these prefixes are
attached to nouns with no verbal counterpart, e.g. der Abgott *idol,*
der Ausweg, die Nachsilbe, Überstunden, die Umgegend.

717. Compound nouns are formed by joining together two or more
words, the last being a noun; this process, not limited to nouns, is an
extremely common, productive and distinctive feature of the German
language. The first word of a compound noun or adjective carries the
main stress and in most cases defines the sense of the second.

The first word of a compound noun may be:

a noun (the commonest type)	die Haarbürste *hair-brush*	
an adjective	der Edelstein	*gem*
a superlative	der Kleinstbildfilm	*sub-miniature film*
a participle	der Gebrauchtwagen	*second-hand car*
a numeral[2]	der Dreifuß	*tripod*
a verbal stem	der Hörsaal	*lecture theatre*
a preposition	die Untertasse	*saucer*
an adverb	die Jetztzeit	*the present day*

**718. Where the first word is a noun, some compounds are formed
with, and others without, a linking letter or syllable.** The following are the only serviceable rules for these links:[3]

-s is regularly attached to the following:
  i the masc. or neut. endings -ing (der Heringssalat), -ling (meine
    Lieblingsfarbe), -tum (die Altertumskunde).
  ii infinitives used as neut. nouns: die Lebensversicherung.
  iii the fem. endings -heit (Sicherheitsmaßnahmen), -keit (Müdig-
    keitserscheinungen), -schaft (die Gesellschaftslehre), -ung (die
    Meinungsumfrage *opinion poll*), -ion (die Präzisionsarbeit), -tät (die
    Universitätsbibliothek).
  iv in most compounds of the fem. words Geschichte, Hilfe, Liebe: das
    Geschichtsbuch, das Hilfsmittel *remedy,* der Liebesbrief.

Group 7 nouns and substantival adjectives have the link -n or -en: die
Heldentat, das Fremdenzimmer.

---

[1] cf. Fleischer, op. cit., pp. 201 f.
[2] Zwei- has the form Zwie- in certain compounds; see 728(d).
[3] cf. Du. Gram. 3790, 3805.

-n is the commonest link for fem. nouns in -e: der Scheibenwischer, die Straßenecke; Schule is a common exception: das Schulbuch.

719. Further miscellaneous examples of compound nouns

der Bergfrühling *spring in the mountains* (taken from a letter)
der Feinschmecker *gourmet*
Madames Goldplombenlächeln (V. Baum) *Madame's smile with its gleam of gold fillings*
das Kernwaffenversuchsverbot *nuclear test ban*
der Schwarzhörer *owner of an unlicensed wireless set*
das Spritzschweißen *spray welding*
die Tiefkühltruhe *deep freeze*
die Vorfreude *pleasure of anticipation*

J. THE FORMATION OF ADJECTIVES AND ADVERBS

720. Adjectives are formed from verbs, nouns, adjectives and adverbs by means of a suffix

(a)
-artig (productive): resembling, of the type indicated: bösartig *ill-natured*; *malignant* (disease), vogelartig *bird-like*.
-bar: common and productive, particularly with verbs; = Engl. -able: erreichbar *attainable*, zusammenklappbar *collapsible*. See also -lich i below.
-haft: mainly from nouns: greisenhaft *senile*, tierhaft *animal-like*.
-ig: common and productive; often causes Umlaut; mainly denotes qualities: günstig *favourable*, holperig *bumpy*, dortig *of that place, there*: das dortige Museum. See also -lich N.3.

-isch (productive):
i it forms adjectives from proper names (homerisch: see also 734) and from geographical names (europäisch, französisch; frankfurterisch: see 116(d)N.v).
ii it forms numerous other adjectives, preponderantly from nouns and applicable to persons, often pejorative and often with Umlaut: bäuerisch *boorish* (contrast bäuerlich *rustic*), modisch, närrisch, wählerisch *fastidious*.
iii it is the commonest suffix for adjectives based on foreign words: buddhistisch, klimatologisch, musikalisch.

-lich (often with Umlaut):
i from verbs: here -lich frequently = -able (like -bar), especially negatively: unbeschreiblich, unvermeidlich (or: unvermeidbar); there may be a difference in meaning, e.g. sträflich *criminal, unpardonable*; strafbar *punishable* (by law).
ii from nouns (productive): schiedsrichterlich *by arbitration*, tödlich.
iii from adjectives: generally a weakened or derived sense of the attribute in question: rötlich *reddish*, kleinlich *petty*.
Note:
1. After en, t (or d) is inserted before -lich: öffentlich *public*, morgendlich *matutinal*.

2. From e.g. ärgerlich, there developed the extended suffix -erlich: leserlich *legible*, weinerlich *lachrymose*.

3. Distinguish 'mein dreiwöchiger Urlaub, ein dreiwöchiges Kind' from 'unsere dreiwöchentliche Konferenz' *our (regular) three-weekly conference*; cf. -stündig/-stündlich etc.

-los (productive) = Engl. -less: funktionslos, rauchlos.

-mäßig (productive):
i in accordance with, as demanded by: gewohnheitsmäßig *habitual*, planmäßig. (Here **-gemäß** is sometimes an alternative for -mäßig, e.g. ordnungsgemäß, plangemäß; normal usage generally makes no semantic distinction and prefers -mäßig.)
ii with regard to: die verkehrsmäßige Wichtigkeit der Stadt.
iii resembling the type indicated: der lehrbuchmäßige Stil.

-n, -en, -ern: adjectives denoting materials: golden, hölzern, seiden. In general, compound nouns are preferred: eine Holzbrücke, ein Seidenkleid, though not with gold and silver: eine goldene Uhr.

-sam: furchtsam *timid*, gemeinsam *(in) common*, sparsam *thrifty*.

(b) 9 adjectival suffixes which are themselves adjectives (productive):
-arm poor in: ein getreidearmes Land *a country growing little grain*.
-fähig capable of: konkurrenzfähig *competitive*.
-fertig ready for: reisefertig *ready to set out*.
-frei free from: eine atomwaffenfreie Zone *a nuclear free zone*.
-gerecht: lit. just; here: in accordance with: altersgerechte Wohnungen *dwellings suitable for old people*.
-reich rich in: ein fischreicher Teich, einflußreich.
-voll full of: geheimnisvoll *mysterious*.
-wert worth: lesenswert, sehenswert.
-würdig worthy of: abbauwürdig *ready for demolition*, sehenswürdig.

721. Adjectives are formed, mainly from adjectives, by means of a prefix. (These prefixes always carry the main stress.)

erz-: intensifying; limited in use: erzdumm *extremely stupid*, erzkatholisch.
grund-: intensifying; limited in use: grundfalsch *radically wrong*.
miß-: mißmutig *ill-humoured*, mißtönend *out of tune, discordant*, mißtrauisch, mißverständlich *misleading, ambiguous*.
un-: normally it negates a meaning and produces the opposite: unartig *naughty*; where the adj. has an independent opposite (e.g. klug: dumm, schön: häßlich), the form with un- is less radical or less literal in meaning: unklug *unwise*, unschön *dubious, reprehensible* (action).
N.B. unheimlich *uncanny*, unmutig (elev.) *annoyed*, unscheinbar *plain-looking*, unwillig (elev.) 1. *angry* 2. *unwilling*.
ur- 1. origin and beginnings: urgermanisch *from oldest Germanic times* 2. intensification: urgemütlich *extremely cosy*, urkomisch.
wohl-: mainly with participles: wohlschmeckend, wohlverdient.

722. Compound adjectives are formed by joining together two or more words, the last being an adj. (cf. beginning of 717). In some cases the second word does not exist as an independent adjective, e.g. blauäugig, eintönig, gegenseitig.

The first word of a compound adjective may be:

a noun	pflichttreu	*dutiful*
an adjective	kleinlaut	*meek, subdued*
a numeral[1]	dreijährig	*lasting 3 years; 3 years old*
a verbal stem	kauflustig	*keen to buy*
a preposition	unterirdisch	*subterranean*
an adverb	frühreif	*precocious*

723. Where the first word is a noun, the compound is frequently formed with a linking letter or syllable, e.g. geisteskrank, menschenähnlich. The only worthwhile rules are that, as in the case of compound nouns, where the first word is a noun ending in -heit, -keit, -schaft, -ung, -ion, -tät, an s is added (e.g. gesundheitsschädlich) and where the first word is a fem. noun in -e, -n is the commonest link: krisenfest, sonnengereift, BUT e.g. hilfsbereit, sprachempfindlich.

724. Further examples of compound adjectives (The second word is often a participle, as in the 2nd and 5th examples.)

gebrauchstüchtige Anzüge *hard-wearing suits* (from Du. Gram. 3955)
hochglanzpoliert *with high-gloss finish*
scheinheilig *sanctimonious*
todunglücklich *desperately unhappy*
zweckentsprechend *appropriate, expedient*
diebesselige Kirschensommer (H. Hesse) *blissful summers of cherry stealing*
ein greisenbrüchiges ,,Grüß Gott, Herr Doktor" (H. Broch) *'Good day, doctor', in a croaky senile voice*

725. Hyphenating two adjectives, whose association is not current enough to justify a single compound word, e.g. eine schaurig-schöne Erzählung (from Du. Gram. 2195) *a gruesome and beautiful tale* (contrast: ein naßkalter Herbsttag); this effective type of compound adjective is difficult to render adequately in English.[2] Cf. end of 119: 3rd literary example.

726. Adverbs may be formed by means of suffixes: erstens, meistens, hoffentlich, blindlings, rechts, vorwärts. There are also **many compound adverbs:** bergauf, diesmal, geradeaus, *straight ahead*, unterwegs, vorgestern, wortwörtlich *word for word*.

---

[1] zwei- has the form zwie- in certain compounds; see 728(d).
[2] cf. D. V. White: Words and Notions in German (*Modern Languages* Sept. 1964).

XVIII ORTHOGRAPHY

A. MISCELLANEOUS ORTHOGRAPHICAL POINTS

727. (a) **Points treated elsewhere**: plur. in -n or -en? 17 iv; masc. and neut. gen. sing.: -es or -s? 45; masc. and neut. dat. sing.: add e? 47; adjectives ending in -el, -en, -er when inflected: 92(b), 103, 190(c), and possess. pron. unserer, euerer: 161(a)N.iii; verbs in -eln and -ern: 340(g).

(b) **The e of el in nouns with the suffix -ung formed from verbs in -eln is dropped in many words**, in both speech and writing, e.g. die Sammlung, die Wandlung, die Entwick(e)lung.

The corresponding e of er is more frequently retained: die Neuerung, die Wanderung, die Verbess(e)rung.

For analogous adjectives (e.g. neb(e)lig) and possess. pronouns (e.g. der uns(e)rige) see 103(d)N.iii, 161(b)N.ii and (c)N.ii.

(c) **Nouns in -ee and -ie** do not add an e in forming the plur., even where the plur. is pronounced as an additional syllable, e.g.

der See *lake*, die Seen (pron. See-en)

die Industrie, die Industrien (pron. Industrie-en)

das Knie, die Knie (pron. Knie-e or Knie) (cf. the verb knien (pron. knie-en or knien), kniend, sie knien, knie!)

(d) **Nouns containing a double vowel** drop one vowel where their plural form or a derivative has Umlaut: der Saal, die Säle; das Paar, das Pärchen; das Boot, das Bötchen.

(e) One of **a potential sequence of 3 identical consonants** in a compound word is dropped before a vowel: das Bettuch, stillegen *to close down* e.g. a factory, BUT: der Fetttropfen.

(f) **An optional e occurs at the end of**: **14 adjectives**: 104; **16 adverbs**: 104 N.i and ii, 277, and, colloquially, fest(e), sacht(e), vorn(e); **some nouns,** the e or its absence being here often dialectal or archaic, e.g. der Bursch(e), das Geklirr(e), das Geschwätz(e) (and others in Ge-), der Hirt(e), der Ochs(e), der Schütz(e), die Stirn(e), die Tür(e).

728. (a) **f or ph?** ph is yielding, or has yielded, to f in the following words and their derivatives (and in a number of less common analogous words):

das Autograf (autografieren etc.), das Foto (der Fotograf etc.), die Grafik *graphic arts*, das Mikrofon, die Sinfonie, der Stenograf, das Telefon, der Telegraf.
Distinguish: die Fantasie *fantasia*, die Phantasie *imagination*.

(b) **-eur or -ör?** French loan-words in -eur retain that spelling (e.g. der Chauffeur, der Ingenieur) exc. der Likör and der Frisör (commoner than the older Friseur).

(c) **ss or ß?** (It is the predominant usage, in both writing and printing, to make this distinction; if a typewriter lacks the ß symbol, ss may be used instead.)
RULE: ss is only used to denote the voiceless 's' sound between vowels if the preceding one is short; all diphthongs count as long vowels.
EXAMPLES: der Fluß, die Flüsse; der Fuß, die Füße; die Masse *mass*, die Maße *measurements*; wir lassen, ihr laßt, ich lass' ihn kommen, laß ihn kommen! wässerig, wäßrig; beißen, gebissen; die Schlußsitzung, russisch.
EXCEPTIONS:
i compound words, e.g. das Meßamt *celebration of mass*, mißachten *to disdain, despise*, flußabwärts *downstream*, weissagen *to foretell*.
ii a few proper names end in -ss: Günter Grass, Theodor Heuss, Richard Strauss (BUT: Johann Strauß), Carl Zeiss (whence: das Zeissglas *binoculars*).

(d) **Zwei- or Zwie-?**
Zwie-, an old variant of zwei, occurs at the beginning of the following, and of a few less common words:
der Zwieback *rusk*, das Zwiegespräch *dialogue, colloquy*, das Zwielicht *twilight*, der Zwiespalt, die Zwietracht *discord, dissension*, zwiespältig *discordant, conflicting*
Contrast: der Zweisitzer, die Zweiteilung, zweideutig, zweimotorig etc. etc.

729. (a) **die Stadt, die Statt, die Stätte**

i die Stadt (ÿe) *town, city*: die Hauptstadt, die Stadtmitte, der Städter *townsman*.

ii die Statt *place, stead*: only used in set phrases, e.g.
an Vaters Statt, an Kindes Statt annehmen *to adopt (a child)*, an Eides Statt *in lieu of oath*.
cf. (an)statt + gen., stattfinden, Statthalter *representative, governor*, die Freistatt *refuge*, die Werkstatt (plur. Werkstätten) *workshop*.

iii die Stätte *place, abode* (elev.) e.g. eine bleibende/heilige/liebgewordene Stätte.
cf. die Brandstätte *scene of a fire*, die Freistätte *refuge*, die Gaststätte *restaurant*, die Werkstätte (-n) *place of work, workshop*.

(b) **der Tod** *death*: **tot** *dead*. **Compounds**:
der Todfeind, todblaß, todmüde, todsicher, tödlich.
sich tot-arbeiten, sich tot-lachen, tot-schießen, totgeboren *stillborn*, die Totgeburt.

B. CAPITALS AND SMALL LETTERS

730. **Basic rule**: all nouns are written with a capital (der Sack, beim Lesen, das Für und Wider, eine Drei, ein Drittel), while all other parts of speech are written with a small letter, unless they open a new sentence.

731. **Miscellaneous exceptions and special cases**

(a) **Nouns used as separable prefixes** have a small letter, e.g. acht-geben, teil-nehmen; but see 712(a)(b).

(b) **Personal pronouns and possess. adjectives and pronouns**:
i the polite you (your): Sie (Ihr).
ii in a letter, Du (Dein), Ihr (Euer), Deinetwegen etc. are written with a capital.
iii Er, Dein, Sein may have a capital when referring to the Deity, but this is less regular than in English usage.

(c) **Indeclinable adjectives in -er** formed from the names of towns have a capital: die Berliner Straßen.

(d) **Adjectives forming part of geographical or established names** have a capital: das Schwarze Meer, das Neue Testament, das Auswärtige Amt *Foreign Office*, die Ewige Stadt (Rome), die Französische Revolution.
Note:
der Eiserne Vorhang, BUT: der kalte Krieg
das Goldene Kalb, BUT: die goldene Hochzeit
das Schwarze Brett *notice-board*, BUT: der schwarze Markt

(e) For the **titles of books, poems etc.**, see 55.

(f) **Note the use of small letters in the following miscellaneous items**:
außer acht lassen *to leave out of account*; sich in acht nehmen *to take care*; in bezug auf *with regard to*; ein bißchen; es tut mir leid; ein paar *a few* (BUT: ein Paar *a pair*); er hatte recht/unrecht; es ist schade; er ist schuld daran (BUT: es ist seine Schuld); ich lerne schwimmen (or: (das) Schwimmen); im voraus *in advance*.

732. **Adjectives and participles used as nouns normally have a capital**: see 106 ff. and cf. die Seinen *his people*; du mußt das Deinige tun *you must do your share*. The neut. adj. has a capital in nichts Neues, alles Neue and analogous phrases (see 111).

EXCEPTIONS:
(a) Substantival adjectives are written with a small letter in many set phrases: see 110.
(b) Distinguish: Es ist das richtige (=richtig), ihm alles zu sagen; tue das Richtige!   Es ist das beste (=am besten), wenn wir ihm alles sagen; es ist das Beste, was ich je gegessen habe (and analogous instances).
(c) The indefinite adjectives (listed in 112(b)) have a small letter, even when used substantivally, e.g. nichts anderes, ich habe noch einiges zu tun, alles übrige, viele sind dagegen, die meisten sind dafür.

Main deviations:

    i The following have a capital after nichts etc. and alles etc. (see 111):
ähnlich, bestimmt, derartig, gewiß, weiter, e.g. nichts Ähnliches,
alles Weitere.

    ii die Folgenden *those who followed*

    iii Weiteres (das Weitere) *further details*

(d) All the miscellaneous adjectives and pronouns treated in 187–239
always have a small letter, with the exceptions given before 187.

733. deutsch or Deutsch?[1]

with a small letter:

    i when used adjectivally (das deutsche Volk, eine deutsche Stadt)
except in official names ((die) Deutsche Bundesbahn (DB)).

    ii when it is the equivalent of an adverb phrase:

Der Botschafter hat mit dem Außenminister deutsch gesprochen.

Das Buch ist auch deutsch (or: in Deutsch) erschienen.

Er denkt sehr deutsch.

Wenn ich deutsch reden soll, . . . *If I'm to speak plainly,* . . .

    iii after auf: Wie sagt man das auf deutsch? auf gut deutsch *to put it
plainly.*

with a capital, when used substantivally:

Wir haben Deutsch in der Schule.

Er spricht (kann, lehrt, lernt, liest, versteht) (kein, gut) Deutsch.

Er kann kein Wort Deutsch; sein Deutsch ist schlecht; das ist gutes
Deutsch; im heutigen Deutsch.

ein Deutscher, eine Deutsche, die/wir Deutschen.

Er hat das Buch aus dem Deutschen ins Französische übersetzt.

734. Adjectives formed from proper names (by means of the suffix -isch (-sch)):

    i they have a capital when they denote the creator or possessor, a small
letter when they denote 'in the manner of'.

    ii they frequently have the suffix -sch when used attributively and -isch
when used predicatively or adverbially.

die Shakespearischen[2] Lustspiele, eine Wagnersche Oper, die Bismarcksche
Politik, das Müllersche Grundstück.

Der Humor in dieser Szene ist fast shakespearisch; er versuchte, wagner-
isch zu komponieren; die platonische Liebe.

735. Numerals

    i For hundert and tausend, see 245.

    ii **Ordinals** are written with a small letter with the following main
exceptions:

Er ist der Erste in der Klasse; der Erste unter Gleichen; Wilhelm der
Erste; die Erste Hilfe; der Erste Weltkrieg; er kommt am Ersten (des
Monats) zurück; ein Dritter *a third party, outsider.*

---

[1] mutatis mutandis, this paragraph applies to all national adjectives: französisch, nor-
wegisch etc.

[2] Names in -e generally drop the e and add -isch.

iii **Fractions** are written with a capital: zwei Drittel: see 250. Two exceptions: dreiviertel is almost always written as one word with a small letter; halb almost always has a small letter: see 251.

736. **Time phrases**, being the equivalents of adverbs, are in general written with small letters unless a preposition, article, adjective or numeral stresses the fact that a noun is involved.

Thus: sonntags, gestern abend, monatelang.
BUT: am Sonntag, eines Abends, drei Monate lang, letzten Mittwoch.

Main exceptions: i Er arbeitete Tag und Nacht.
ii Er kommt Mittwoch zurück; er kommt Weihnachten.
iii Er kommt Anfang/Mitte/Ende Mai zurück.
iv seit langem, seit/vor kurzem.

C. ONE WORD OR TWO?[1]

737. Miscellaneous cases

(a) **Cases treated elsewhere**: irgend 207(h); soviel, zu wenig etc. 235; Mal 254 f.; ebenso¹ *S 291(b); sep. prefix or independent adv. (or infin. or noun)? 689(b), 693 (mit-), 707 f., 710, 712(e)–(h).

(b) **noun object + pres. part.**: grauenerregend *horrifying*. Some further instances where this combination has established itself as a unit and is generally written as one word:
aufsehenerregend *sensational*, bahnbrechend *pioneering*, *epoch-making*, herzerquickend *heart-warming*, vertrauenerweckend or vielversprechend *promising*, zeitraubend.

Generic compounds of this type are always written as one word: blutstillende Watte *styptic cotton-wool*.

(c) **noun + pres. or past part. with suppressed prepositional link**: this combination is always written as one word, e.g. staubbedeckt (= mit Staub bedeckt), freudestrahlend *beaming with joy*.

(d) **Distinguish**:

sobald *as soon as* (conj.)	so bald *so soon*
solange *as long as* (conj.)	so lange *for such a long time*
sooft *as often as, whenever* (conj.)	so oft *so often*
wieweit *how far, to what extent*	wie weit *how far, what distance*
woanders *elsewhere*	wo anders? *where else?*
womöglich *possibly, perhaps*	wo möglich *if possible* (coll.)

Note: 'so daß' is always written as two words.

738. **Adverb + Adjective or Participle**: many short and common adverbs (unless they are limited by an adverb of degree) are compounded with adjectives and participles used attributively, but not when they are used predicatively:
eine leichtverdauliche Speise *an easily digestible dish*

---

[1] based on *Duden-Taschenbücher 3*, pp. 130 ff.; the examples in 737(b)(c)(d) and 738 are mainly selected from the lists there given.

BUT: eine sehr leicht verdauliche Speise.
Diese Speise ist leicht verdaulich.

Compare:

blankpoliert, blaugestreift, engbefreundet, ernstgemeint, fettgedruckt *in bold type*, gleichgesinnt *like-minded*, gutbezahlt, halboffen, hochbegabt, neugeboren, obenerwähnt, schwerbeschädigt[1] *badly damaged*.

Note:

i Adverbs which are **not** compounded include eben and soeben *just (now)*, fast, gerade, kaum: das soeben erschienene Buch.

ii Generic and figurative compounds of this type are always written as one word:

Der Mann ist schwerbeschädigt;[1] cf. minderbegabt *backward, handicapped*, reinwollen *pure wool*.

Seine Reden sind oft etwas hochtrabend (*pompous*); cf. weitblickend *far-sighted*.

iii 'nicht' is compounded in generic compounds used attributively: nichtamtlich *unofficial*, nichtrostend, nichtübertragbar *non-transferable*, BUT: Diese Karte ist nicht übertragbar.

D. THE USE OF THE HYPHEN

739. Miscellaneous uses[2]

(a) occasionally, to break up unwieldy compound words, e.g. der Provinzial-Marktregulierungskommission gegenüber (G. Grass).

(b) in ad hoc combinations, e.g. Schließlich taten sich die Protest-Demonstranten mit den Ostermarschierern zusammen (*Zeit*).

(c) to link the words of an elaborated substantival infinitive, e.g. die unaufdringliche Eleganz des Immer-aus-dem-Ei-gepellt-Seins (*Zeit*) *the unobtrusive elegance of being perpetually spick and span*.

(d) Where two or more compound nouns, adjectives, adverbs or verbs, generally joined by 'und' or 'oder', have their final component in common, the repetition of the latter is often avoided by means of a hyphen:

Funk-, Fernseh- und Filmautoren (E. Kreuder)	*writers of radio, television and film scripts*
genuß- und ergebnisreiche Tage	*enjoyable and fruitful days*
ein- und aussteigen	*to get in and out*
Compare:	
Geld- und andere Sorgen	*financial and other worries*
nicht alle Fach- und praktischen Ärzte	*not all specialists and general practitioners*

(e) to avoid a sequence of 3 identical vowels in a substantival compound: die Tee-Ernte *tea-harvest*, BUT: schneeerhellt *lit up by the snow* (participial compound).

---

[1] applied to a car, schwerbeschädigt is purely descriptive; applied to a person, it is generic and officialese: *seriously disabled*.

[2] see also 725.

740. Hyphenation at the end of a line

(a) Compound words are divided up into their component parts: Apfel-baum, ent-erben, nach-geben.

(b) For all other words a serviceable rule is to divide them according to the syllables that result from saying them slowly: Glä-ser, Ka-tho-lik, Näch-te, Trans-port.

(c) Some special points:

i a single vowel is never divided off, e.g. Ahorn, Klaue.

ii double consonants should be hyphenated after the first consonant: Bet-ten, rol-len, flüs-sig; ß is regarded as a single consonant: Fü-ße, sto-ßen, BUT: if ss is written in place of ß: Füs-se, stos-sen.

iii where one of a potential sequence of 3 identical consonants is dropped in forming a compound (see 727(e)), it reappears when hyphenated: Bett-tuch, still-legen.

iv st is not divided in simple words, e.g. Fen-ster, Gä-ste, BUT: aus-teilen, Donners-tag.

v ck is hyphenated as k-k: drucken: druk-ken; lecker: lek-ker; Stockung: Stok-kung.

741. (S) The chief remaining uses (and non-uses) of the hyphen are shown by the following examples, almost all taken from Duden-Taschenbücher 3, pp. 158 ff.:

die H-Bombe, die U-Bahn, der I-Punkt, der K.-o.-Schlag, C-Dur *C major*, O-beinig *bandy-legged*

die 1000-Jahr-Feier (BUT: die Tausendjahrfeier), eine 10-Pfennig-Briefmarke, die 4 × 400-Meter-Staffel (*relay*)

die römisch-katholische Kirche, deutsch-amerikanische Beziehungen (*relations*)

Ost-West-Gespräche, Hals-Nasen-Ohren-Arzt, Erste-Hilfe-Ausrüstung *first-aid equipment*

das Schiller-Museum, ein Bach-Konzert, die Nixon-Mannschaft *President Nixon's team*, die Dresdner-Bank-Aktien (*shares*), BUT: der Dieselmotor, Röntgenstrahlen *X-rays*, das Schillertheater

die Bahnhofstraße, die Goethestraße, die Münchener Straße, die Richard-Wagner-Straße; Sankt Peter (St. Peter), die Sankt-Peter-Kirche (die St.-Peter-Kirche), Karl-Heinz Müller.

der Rheinwein, das Nildelta, Großbritannien, Kleinasien *Asia Minor*, Westdeutschland (BUT: West-Berlin), der Dortmund-Ems-Kanal, Nordrhein-Westfalen (one of the 11 West German 'Länder'), Hamburg-Altona (a part of Hamburg), Dresden-Nord, Bad Ems.

E. THE USE OF THE APOSTROPHE[1]

742. The apostrophe is used to indicate the omission of letters and words in colloquial or dialectal pronunciation and sometimes in poetic style (e.g. ird'sche Güter).

---

[1] see also 51(g).

Ihm geht's gut. Siehst du's? Ja, ich seh's. Ich hab's gesehen.
Hast du's Paket? Ich hab' meinem Bruder's Geld gegeben. Ich hab'm
Lehrer geholfen. So'n Blödsinn! 'n richtiger Grabstein? Wie auf'm
Friedhof? (Th. Valentin) (cf. 638 N.vi)
Seine Freud' war groß (BUT: (in) Freud und Leid: fixed phrase). Nach
wen'gen Wochen; die Leut'; der Käs'.
Ich kauf' noch was. Ich möcht' dir helfen. Hätt' ich das gewußt, . . .
'n Abend! (=Guten Abend!) Was 'ne Frau! (H. Fallada) (=Was für
eine Frau!) Was schreibst'n da? (J. Rehn) (=Was schreibst du denn
da?) Is' gut (=es ist gut *right you are*).

Note: Omissions of the following three types are accepted as constituting
alternative forms and no apostrophe is needed:
i the e of -en after a verbal stem ending in a vowel or a vowel+h: sie
schrein, wir haben gesehn.
ii the e of the imperative sing.: Komm her! Schlaf gut!
iii the e of el, en, er occurring in the middle of a word: ich segle, neblig;
seltner; unsre, der Wandrer.

XIX PUNCTUATION RULES

Note:
i Most cases in which German and English practice is the same
   have been omitted.
ii For the punctuation of a postal address, see 260.

A. THE COMMA

743. (a) **Two sentences joined by 'und' or 'oder'**: comma before 'und' or
'oder' if the second sentence has its own subject-word: Mein Vater
arbeitet im Garten, oder er macht einen Spaziergang.
   Exc. if something other than the subject, standing at the beginning of
   the first sentence, causes inversion in both: see 645(a), examples 3–5.

(b) **Always put a comma before aber, sondern, allein** *but*, **doch** *yet*,
nevertheless, **jedoch** *yet*, *however*, **vielmehr** *rather*, *on the contrary*: Er
ist nicht sehr intelligent, aber fleißig.
   Exc. when aber (meaning 'however') and jedoch occur in the middle
   of the sentence: Er aber/jedoch ist ein Deutscher.

(c) **No comma with entweder ... oder, weder ... noch, sowohl ...**
als auch, sowie (auch) (unless they connect clauses):
   Weder er noch sie hat mich gesehen.
   Schmidt sowie auch Müller fehlten heute.

Note: 'und/oder' is used, though less than English 'and/or'.

(d) **Divide off all subordinate clauses with commas**, including noun
   clauses without 'daß': Er sagte, er käme bald zurück.[1]
   Exc. No comma after the first of two sub. cl. joined by und or oder.

(e) **Compound conjunctions and conjunctional phrases**
   i Where they are felt to form a single unit, they have a comma in front,
   e.g. Er war hinausgegangen, ohne daß ich es merkte. Cf. als daß
   (see 469(a)), anstatt daß, außer daß, außer wenn, besonders wenn,
   gerade als, insofern als, je nachdem ob/wie/wann etc., kaum daß
   (but see 531(d)), selbst wenn, BUT: dadurch, daß (cf. 452).

---

[1] Note position of comma in e.g. Er starb, zwei Jahre nachdem er Deutschland verlassen
hatte.

ii The remainder are of two kinds:
    1. prep.+def. art.+noun+daß: these have a comma before daß.
Ich will nach Bonn fahren in der Hoffnung, daß ich ihn sprechen kann.
Cf. im Falle, daß; unter der Bedingung, daß; unter der Voraussetzung,
daß *on the assumption that.*
    2. participle or miscellaneous phrase+conjunction: these have a
    comma in front and also before the conjunction.
Ich bin um sechs Uhr zurück, vorausgesetzt, daß alles gut geht. Ich freue
mich über seinen Erfolg, um so mehr, als er völlig unerwartet kam.
Cf. abgesehen davon, daß; angenommen, daß; ausgenommen, wenn
except if; es sei denn, daß *unless*; gesetzt, daß *supposing that.*

(f) **Infinitive phrases**
  i **zu+infin., with nothing else**, is not divided off:
    Ich hoffte zu gewinnen.
Except:
    1. when there is more than one such phrase: Ich hoffte, zu reiten und
    zu schwimmen.
    2. when it forms the complement: Mein Ziel war, zu gewinnen.
    3. when it is a perf. or passive infin.: Sie glaubten, gesiegt zu haben. Er
    verlangte (*demanded*), bezahlt zu werden.

  ii **zu+infin. with at least one other word** is divided off:
    Ich bat ihn, mir zu helfen. Er kam, um zu arbeiten.
Except:
    1. when the infin. phr. stands alone as the subject:
    So etwas zu erlauben ist unerhört.
    (BUT: So etwas zu erlauben, das ist unerhört.)
    2. when the infin. phr. is enclosed by a compound tense or a sub. cl.:
    Ich habe ihm zu helfen versprochen.
    Ich weiß, daß er sein Geschäft zu verkaufen versucht.
    3. when the infin. phr. is not self-contained:
    Das will ich dir zu erklären versuchen.
    (BUT: Ich will versuchen, dir das zu erklären.)
    4. after brauchen, haben, pflegen *to be accustomed to*, scheinen, sein,
    vermögen *to be able to*, wissen *to know how to* (cf. 434 (c)):
    Ich brauche heute nicht ins Geschäft zu gehen.
    Du hast dir jetzt die Hände zu waschen.
    So ein Transistor ist in London (leicht) zu bekommen.

  iii **an infin. phrase without 'zu'** is not divided off:
    Ich muß spätestens um acht Uhr im Büro sein.

(g) **Divide off participial, adjectival and absolute phrases with
    commas:**
Später wanderte er, ein altes Lied summend, durch den Garten.
Bald darauf verließ er, blaß vor Wut, das Zimmer.
Die Hände in den Taschen, kam er auf mich zu.

(h) **Adverb phrases and qualifying words and expressions are not
    normally divided off** (But see 642(c)):
An diesem schönen Nachmittag ging er wie gewöhnlich spazieren.
Bitte bringen Sie mir wenn möglich eine Zeitung.
Erstaunlicherweise war er im großen und ganzen zufrieden.

(i) **Two or more adjectives** are divided off by commas if they are of equal status (put differently: if they could be joined by 'und'): gute, billige Äpfel, BUT: gute englische Äpfel; 'englische Äpfel' forms one concept. Some German authors eschew commas in any list of adjectives.

(j) **Comma and semi-colon**: Germans (including German authors) frequently put a comma between two main clauses, where English usage would put a semi-colon. In many instances this is not officially correct, but in some it is due to Germans' regarding as a conjunction what in English is classified as an adverb or adverbial phrase, e.g. insofern *to that extent*, stattdessen *instead*, trotzdem *in spite of this*, unterdessen *meanwhile*. E.g. Gehe in die Stadt und kaufe Mehl, unterdessen heize ich schon den Backofen an (Schulz-Griesbach, op. cit., G 510).

B. PUNCTUATION MARKS OTHER THAN THE COMMA

744. (a) **The semi-colon**: see 743(j).

(b) **The colon**: when direct speech is introduced by a preceding verb of saying, a colon is used: Dann sagte er: ,,Ich kann es nicht.``

(c) **Inverted commas:** ,,...`` or "..." or (in print only) »...«. Single inverted commas are used for a quotation, or a title, within a quotation: ,,Hast du Goethes ‚Faust' gelesen?`` fragte er.

(d) **The exclamation mark** is used in the following cases:
  i after interjections and exclamations: see 639 ff.
  ii after imperatives: Seid vorsichtig, Kinder! BUT: after completely unemphatic imperatives, a full stop or comma may be used: ,,Geben Sie mir bitte die Zeitung``, sagte er. (cf. 456–8)
  iii after most substitutes for the imperative: see 459.
  iv after the optative subjunctive: see 476.
  v after the words of address at the beginning of a letter: Lieber Hans! Sehr geehrter Herr Dr. Müller![1] (cf. 673) (Some Germans prefer a comma.)
  vi more frequently than in English in public notices (Kein Zutritt!) and in letters (Ich bin gespannt auf seine Reaktion! Von meinem Fenster aus sehe ich schon den ersten Schnee auf den Bergen!)

(e) **The use of the full stop in abbreviations**
  i If an abbreviation is pronounced in the form of actual words, the letters forming it are followed by a full stop: d.h. (das heißt) ev. (evangelisch) s.o. (siehe oben!) z.B. (zum Beispiel). N.B. usw. (und so weiter)
  ii If an abbreviation is pronounced (a) as individual letters or (β) as a new word constituted by those letters, no full stops:
  (a) DGB (Deutscher Gewerkschaftsbund *German Trades Union Federation*), LKW (Lastkraftwagen *motor-lorry*), USA

---

[1] These two letters might respectively end: Herzliche Grüße, auch an Deine Schwester, Dein Karl. Mit vorzüglicher Hochachtung (verbleibe ich) Ihr (sehr) ergebener Karl Kramer.

(β) NATO, Degussa (Deutsche Gold- und Silberscheideanstalt *German Gold and Silver Refinery*)

iii No full stop after A (Ampere) C (Celsius) cm (Zentimeter) DM (Deutsche Mark) ff (fortissimo) g (Gramm) l (Liter) s (Sekunde) SW (Südwesten) and analogous abbreviations.

C. PUNCTUATION IN NUMERALS

745. (a) Millions and thousands are indicated by a gap, not by a comma:
3 835 500   10 000 (BUT: 9000)
(b) Ordinals are indicated by a full stop: am 3. Mai; Heinrich III.; am Hofe Ludwigs XIV. von Frankreich.
(c) A decimal point is indicated by a comma: 8,5 Kilometer
(d) See also 257, 313(b)(c).

SUPPLEMENT

I NOUNS

14 (b) v exc. die Bouillon *beef-tea*

22 cf. Erlaß *decree* (Pl. Erlasse)
Trakt *tract* (of land); *wing* (of building)

57 (a) i The same applies to 'das Herz' (see 50): der Zustand von Peters Herz.

60 **Saxon Genitive:** see also 51 (f)

II SOME SPECIAL USES AND OMISSIONS OF THE ARTICLES

84 (e) iii cf. (Der) Vater ist nicht zu Hause.

III ADJECTIVES

99 NOUN OF MEASUREMENT+ADJECTIVE+NOUN: A not very common variation is: **Adj.+noun of measurement+ noun denoting the thing measured:** 20 englische Pfund Äpfel.
First group of examples: cf.
Tausende Tonnen glühendes   *thousands of tons of glowing metal*
Metall (Th. Plievier)

100 (a) NB: Where Dutzend and Paar are preceded by the def. art., German practice is inconsistent, e.g. die zwei Dutzend frische Eier, BUT: die zwei Paar braunen Schuhe.

107 (d) eine Unbekannte *an unknown quantity* (Maths)

116 (d) This -er ending may include the force of the str. decl. gen. plur., e.g. der Absatz West-Berliner Erzeugnisse (*Zeit*) *the sale of West Berlin Products*

IV COMPARISON OF ADJECTIVES AND ADVERBS

136 (d) cf. Gemessen an indischen   *Compared with Indian conditions, my*
Verhältnissen ist mein Haus   *house is now most luxuriously*
nun üppigst ausgestattet   *furnished*
(Gabriele Venzky in *Zeit-*
Magazin)

V THE PERSONAL PRONOUN

143 (a) cf. Bis zum Bahnhof sind es   *It's about* 10 *minutes walk to the*
          ungefähr zehn Minuten zu   *station*
          gehen

143 (g) cf. es halten mit   *to side with*
          es genau nehmen mit   *to be particular about*
          Sie hat es ihm angetan   *She has captivated him*
          es in sich haben   *to be tough, to have substance or*
                              difficulties

          Verbote gibt es [in Skandinavien]   *There are fewer prohibitions* [in
          weniger als bei uns—aber sie   Scandinavia] *than with us—but*
          haben es in sich (*Zeit*)   *they are tough*
          ein Begriff, der es in sich hat   *a concept which has something to it*

VI MISCELLANEOUS ADJECTIVES AND PRONOUNS: SECTION A

157 Note: Current usage is for phrases with 'als' which form the
      objective complement of refl. verbs to go into the nominative:
      Er erwies sich als der Mörder   *He proved to be the murderer*
      Er sah sich als unser Freund an   *He looked upon himself as our friend*
      cf. Er betrachtete, fühlte, zeigte
          sich als unser Freund

                                   BUT:
      Er betrachtet mich als seinen   *He regards me as his friend*
      Freund

173 (e) **Whoever? Whatever? (emphatic)**
          Wer kann es denn (nur) getan   *Whoever can have done it?*
          haben?
          Was hat er denn (nur) dagegen?   *Whatever has he got against it?*

175 (c) Referring to a substance, 'was für welcher' is used in the singular:
          Ich habe auch Käse gekauft.   *I've also bought some cheese.*
          —Was für welchen?   *–What kind?*

176 (a) Note:
      iii In the gen. fem. and plur. there is a strong tendency, even on
          the part of educated Germans and reputable authors (cf.
          Eggeling op. cit. deren 2 (b)), to use 'derer' instead of
          'deren'; while this should not be imitated, one hesitates to
          call it wrong.

VI MISCELLANEOUS ADJECTIVES AND PRONOUNS: SECTION B

194 (f) und was sonst noch   *and what have you*
197   Beide haben sie recht   *They're both right*
199 (b) Den einen oder anderen Film   *I quite like seeing the occasional film*
          seh' ich ganz gern

VII NUMERALS

244   ein Mittsechziger   *a man in his middle sixties*
      eine Endfünfzigerin   *a woman in her late fifties*
      ein Dreitausender   *a mountain of* 3000 *metres*

245 (b) N. ii cf. einige Hundert (*a few hundred*) der 10 000 Zuschauer

248 E.g. . . . ein Buch von gut dreihundert Seiten. Mein Onkel hat mir ganze fünf Mark gegeben (*no less than* 5 *Marks*) (ironical); ganze fünf Stunden (*for fully five hours*)

Note iv: **zig** is an indeterminate cardinal: umpteen. E.g. Ich habe in zig Läden versucht; zigmal, zighundert, Zigtausende von Eltern.

255 erstmals *for the first time*

IX PARTICLES

286 (a) Auch das noch!   *The last straw!*

286 A   **da**

(a) **place: there, here**

von da (aus)	*from there*
Es war kein Minister da	*No minister was present*
Ist er schon da?	*Is he here yet?*
Montag bin ich nicht da	*I shan't be here on Monday*
War jemand da?	*Has anyone called?*

(b) **time: then**

Da fiel mir alles wieder ein	*Then I remembered everything*
Am Montag? Da bin ich nicht mehr da	*On Monday? I shan't be here then*
Da gab es noch kein Fernsehen	*There was no television then*
Da war es zu spät	*By that time it was too late*

(c) **It is used in relative clauses**, sometimes expletively, as in the first example, sometimes implying contempt, indignation or pity:

der Spaß, der da kommen sollte	*the fun that was to come*
diejenigen, die da meinen, man könne die Frage von heute auf morgen lösen	*those who fondly believe that the problem can be solved overnight*

Mit keinem Wort war dieser Kriegsrichter auf den Menschen zu sprechen gekommen, der da morgen früh erschossen werden soll, den Menschen aus Fleisch und Blut, aus Hoffnung und Angst, aus Sorge und Qual (A. Goes) (implication: the poor chap who is to be shot to-morrow morning)

(d) **Miscellaneous**

Ich weiß nicht, ob ich da helfen kann	*I don't know if I can help in this matter*
Was tut man da?	*What does one do in such a situation?*
und da wagt man (noch) zu sagen, . . .[1]	*and yet people venture to say . . .*
Er war verreist, da konnte ich nichts machen	*He was away, so I couldn't do anything*
Da können Sie sicher sein	*You can be sure of that*
Da sehen Sie![1]	*Now you see!*
Ist das sein Haus? Da ist unsers ja ein Palast!	*Is that his house? Why then, ours is a palace!*

291 (a) i Eben sind Äpfel knapp   *Apples are scarce just now*

[1] from Muret-Sanders, op. cit.: da

291 (b) i Wahrig (op. cit.) effectively illustrates the 'reminding function' of 'eben' by paraphrasing 'Das ist es ja eben!' with 'Davon rede ich ja die ganze Zeit!'

291 (b) end of i: Du hättest es ihm ebensogut sagen können (*You might just as well have told him*) BUT: Er spielt ebenso gut wie ich; er ist ein ebenso guter Spieler wie ich.

294 (h)	mal durch Schnee, mal durch Matsch (*Zeit*)	*now through snow, now through slush*
303 (d)	Wer ihn sprechen wollte, mußte sich schon anstrengen	*Anyone wanting to see him certainly had to exert himself*
	Wenn es ein Opernhaus . . . bei uns . . . gäbe, dann würde ich schon gern gelegentlich . . . dort hingehen (*Zeit*)	*If there were an opera-house here, I would certainly like to go occasionally*
	Wenn es schon wahr ist, so behalte es lieber für dich	*Even if it's true, you'd better keep it to yourself*
	Hatte ich schon nicht mit der Veröffentlichung meines Briefes gerechnet, so doch am allerwenigsten mit dieser Wirkung (Letter in *Die Zeit*)	*If I hadn't even reckoned on the publication of my letter, then least of all had I counted on this effect*
303 (g)	Und wenn schon Dirigismus, genügt es dann, den Preis zu regulieren? (*Zeit*) (elliptical)	*And if you are going to have a controlled economy, is it sufficient to regulate prices?*
304 (f)	Wenn ich mehr Zeit hätte, ich ginge mal schlendern, einfach so, gucken was es so gibt (*Zeit*)	*If I had more time, I'd go for a stroll some time, just like that, to have a look at what's in the shops*
	Wo sind Sie denn so geboren? (U. Johnson)	*Where for instance were you born?*
307 (c)	Eigentlich schlimm, nicht?	*Awful really, isn't it?*

X TIME PHRASES

Most of the additions to this chapter have been arranged in a single list, in alphabetical order of the English equivalents:

noch ein paar Tage	*a few more days*
immer wieder	*again and again*
um die Jahrhundertwende	*at the turn of the century*
am Wochenende	*at the weekend*
zuzeiten	*at times*
in nicht allzulanger Zeit	*before too long*
früher in diesem Jahr	*earlier this year*
am frühen Morgen	*early in the morning*
in aller Frühe	*first thing in the morning*
zuerst (einmal)	*first of all*
zunächst (einmal)	
von jetzt an	*from now on*
ab sofort	*from now on, with immediate effect* (officialese)
zeitlebens	*in all my (his etc.) life*
im April vorigen Jahres	*in April of last year*
zu unseren Lebzeiten	*in our lifetime*

im nachhinein	in retrospect
in der Nacht vom 1. zum 2. September	in the night from the 1st to the 2nd of September
In der Nacht von Dienstag auf Mittwoch	in the night from Tuesday to Wednesday
unter der Regierung von	in the reign of
zu Goethes Lebzeiten	in Goethe's time
Freitag vergangener Woche	on Friday of last week
auf Dauer	permanently
fortwährend	perpetually
alle naselang (sl.)	
voll arbeiten	to work full time
teilzeit-arbeiten	to work part time

321 ii   Und meine Oma, die will das Buch gar nicht erst lesen!   *And my granny, she won't even read the book!*

XI VERBS

349 (a)   cf. starten *to start (off)*; *to take off* (plane)

373 (d)   Hier läßt sich's leben   *It's very pleasant living here*

383 (a)   It may be said that 'es gibt' is used when the thing whose existence is being stated is abstract. E.g.
In unserm Block gibt es fortwährend Schwierigkeiten, weil die neuen Mieter laute Parties geben
Noch gibt es Hoffnung (*Zeit*)
damit es keine Mißverständnisse zwischen uns gibt
BUT: Es war plötzlich nur Wut und Haß und Protest in mir (Horst Krüger) (Here the existence is too circumscribed for 'es gibt'; see 384 (a))

384 (a)   Note ii: cf. Eine Schlange steht vorm Schuhgeschäft, in dem es zum Beispiel Salamanderschuhe gibt (*Zeit*)

385   Was gibt's Neues bei euch?   *Any news in your part of the world?*

387   Seine Stimme hatte etwas Schroffes   *There was abruptness in his voice (Arnold Bennett)*

394 (c)   Er kann mit den Leuten [umgehen]
Da kann ich nicht mit [machen]   *He knows how to get on with people*
That is beyond me

401 (a)   Ich will, daß er es tut
Ich wollte, daß er es tat   *I want him to do it*
I wanted him to do it

443   wie gehabt (coll.)   *as usual* (often pejorative)

474   aus welchem Grunde auch immer (elliptical)   *for whatever reason*

XII CONJUNCTIONS

525   Falls du, oder ein Bekannter, das Buch brauchen kannst, . . .
BUT: Falls du oder ein Bekannter euch für das Buch interessiert, . . .

XIII PREPOSITIONS

549 Note: While außer predominantly takes the dative, there are two exceptions:
  i The set phrase 'außer Landes gehen' (commoner: ins Ausland gehen or auswandern)
  ii It takes the accusative with verbs indicating motion, e.g. etwas außer allen Zweifel setzen, eine Maschine außer Betrieb setzen.

550 (a) cf. Ihr Durchschnittsalter liegt bei siebzehn Jahren (*Zeit*) *Their average age is about seventeen*

551 (a) Colloquially also 'gegenüber von dem Krankenhaus'

565 (e) (100 km/st) *or* (100 km/h): h=hora *hour*; further alternative: 100 Stundenkilometer

565 (h) **via:** Wir fuhren via (or: über) den Haag.

566 EXAMPLES: **über**
  Das Seil hing über der Mauer   *The rope hung above the wall*
  Das Seil hing über die Mauer   *The rope hung over the wall*

577 (d) After 'während' and 'laut' a relative pronoun is used in the dative:
  Die Reise, während der wir so viel Schönes sahen, . . .
  Der Bericht, laut dem keine Unruhen stattfanden, . . .
  Of the prepositions listed in 576 (b), abseits, unfern, and unweit are used with von+dat. before a rel. pron., e.g. Die Stadt, unweit von der wir wohnen, . . .
  After innerhalb, außerhalb, oberhalb and unterhalb, which are normally followed by the gen. or by von+dat., a rel. pron. may be used in the dat., e.g.
  Die Zone, innerhalb der Autos verboten sind, . . .
  Die Brücke, oberhalb der die Fabrik gebaut werden soll, . . .

595 **Schule**
  An einigen Schulen wird   *Italian is taught at some schools*
  Italienisch unterrichtet

600 (a) cf. die Jagd auf Füchse, auf den Verbrecher (BUT: nach Füchsen jagen)

620 **across**
  allgemein   *across the board*
  at
  an dieser Stelle   *at this spot*

623 von der Hand in den Mund leben   *to live from hand to mouth*

624 sich spezialisieren auf+acc.   *to specialize in*

625 seine Liebe zu seiner Mutter   *his love of his mother*
  seine Liebe zu Volksliedern   *his love of folk-songs*

626 sich konzentrieren auf+acc.   *to concentrate on*
  auf etwas zu sprechen kommen   *to get onto a subject*
  auf unserer Reise   *on our journey*
  auf einem Spaziergang   *on a walk*

631 „in" sein   *to be with it*
Verstehen Sie?   *Are you with me?*

XV WORD ORDER

645 (a) 6. Trotz vieler Jahre harter Arbeit und eines unglaublichen Stroms von Geld und Produkten sind die Wohnverhältnisse noch immer schlecht, sind die Japaner noch unzureichend mit den Annehmlichkeiten (*amenities*) des Lebens versorgt, steht zu wenig Geld für das Bildungs- und Gesundheitswesen sowie für die soziale Sicherheit zur Verfügung, gibt es kaum Reserven für schlechtere Zeiten (Jon Woronoff, quoted in *Die Zeit*)

654 (d) Er setzte seinen Plan dem   *He set his plan against mine*
meinigen entgegen
('seinen Plan' must come first to show what 'dem meinigen' stands for)

XVII WORD FORMATION

709 FURTHER EXAMPLES: Adverbs: cf. fern-sehen *to watch television* (e.g. Wir sehen viel fern)

715 (c) der Fachmann (*expert*) has no fem. form.

XVIII ORTHOGRAPHY

741 der Zwiespalt zwischen dem Sittlich-Guten und dem Sinnlich-Schönen (Karl Hoppe)

XV WORD ORDER

XVII WORD FORMATION

XVIII ORTHOGRAPHY

INDEX

Note:

1. A hyphen denotes a prefix or suffix.
2. Numbers refer to paragraphs, not pages.
3. In the case of some words and phrases (e.g. some misc. adjectives, adverbs, verbs) either the English or the German form is given, but not both; where both are given, fuller references follow the German form.